# Ford Escort & Orion
## Service and Repair Manual

## John S Mead

### Models covered

(1737-344-2AE6)

Ford Escort Hatchback, Saloon, Estate, Van and Cabriolet, and Ford Orion models, including special/limited editions
1297 cc, 1392 cc, 1596 cc, 1597 cc and 1796 cc petrol engines

*Does not cover RS2000 or Cosworth models, or Diesel engines*

ABCD

3

© Haynes Publishing 2001

A book in the **Haynes Service and Repair Manual Series**

ISBN **1 85960 763 2**

**British Library Cataloguing in Publication Data**
A catalogue record for this book is available from the British Library.

Printed in the USA

**Haynes Publishing**
Sparkford, Yeovil, Somerset BA22 7JJ, England

**Haynes North America, Inc**
861 Lawrence Drive, Newbury Park, California 91320, USA

**Editions Haynes**
4, Rue de l'Abreuvoir
92415 COURBEVOIE CEDEX, France

**Haynes Publishing Nordiska AB**
Box 1504, 751 45 UPPSALA, Sweden

# Contents

## LIVING WITH YOUR FORD ESCORT/ORION

## Roadside repairs

## Weekly checks

## Lubricants, fluids and tyre pressures

## MAINTENANCE

### Routine maintenance and servicing

# Contents

## REPAIRS & OVERHAUL

### Engine and associated systems

### Transmission

### Brakes and suspension

### Body equipment

### Wiring diagrams

## REFERENCE

### Index

The latest versions of the Ford Escort and Orion model range were introduced in September 1990. As with their predecessors, the line-up was extensive, including Escort three- and five-door Hatchback, five-door Estate, soft top Cabriolet, and Van versions, with the traditional four-door Saloon Orion featuring a conventional rear boot.

For the 1994 model year, in keeping with Ford's policy of enhanced product identity, the Orion badge was deleted and the Escort name was applied to all models in the range.

The power unit fitted is dependent on model. The options initially were revised versions of the engines fitted to the earlier Escort and Orion range, these being the 1.3 litre HCS overhead valve engine and the 1.4 or 1.6 litre CVH overhead camshaft engines. For the 1992 model year, the new 1.8 litre DOHC 16-valve Zetec (originally known as Zeta) engine was introduced, followed a year later by a 1.6 litre version. For the 1995 model year a revised version of the CVH engine was introduced, known as the PTE engine. Similarly, for 1996 the HCS engine was re-worked and renamed Endura-E, whilst the Zetec became Zetec-E. Essentially, these later engine revisions are mainly concerned with refinements to meet stricter emission regulations. All engines have electronic engine management control to the ignition and fuel systems to provide greater efficiency and performance, with later models featuring extensive emissions control systems to ensure compliance with the most stringent of the emissions control standards currently in force. The fuel system fitted is dependent on model, and will be either carburettor, CFi (central fuel injection), EFi (electronic fuel injection) or SEFi (sequential electronic fuel injection).

A four or five-speed manual transmission, or a CTX automatic transmission, is fitted, depending on model. All transmission types incorporate an integral differential unit to transfer drive directly to the front roadwheels.

Both the front and rear suspension assemblies have been redesigned to provide a high standard of road holding and ride comfort. Disc front brakes and drum rear brakes are fitted to most models covered by this manual, with rear disc brakes and/or an anti-lock braking system (ABS) being fitted on some models.

As with earlier variants of the range, all models are designed with the emphasis on economical motoring, ease of maintenance and good performance.

**Escort 1.4 LX Hatchback - 1993 model**

**Orion 1,8 Ghia Si 16V - 1993 model**

# The Escort/Orion Team

Haynes manuals are produced by dedicated and enthusiastic people working in close co-operation. The team responsible for the creation of this book included:

| | |
|---|---|
| **Author** | John Mead |
| **Sub-editors** | Carole Turk |
| | Sophie Yar |
| **Editor & Page Make-up** | Bob Jex |
| **Workshop manager** | Paul Buckland |
| **Photo Scans** | John Martin |
| | Paul Tanswell |
| **Cover illustration & Line Art** | Roger Healing |
| **Wiring diagrams** | Matthew Marke |

We hope the book will help you to get the maximum enjoyment from your car. By carrying out routine maintenance as described you will ensure your car's reliability and preserve its resale value.

*Acknowledgements*

Thanks are due to Champion Spark Plug, who supplied the illustrations showing spark plug conditions and to Duckhams Oils, who provided lubrication data. Certain other illustrations are the copyright of the Ford Motor Company, and are used with their permission. Thanks are also due to Draper Tools Limited, who provided some of the workshop tools, and to all those people at Sparkford who helped in the production of this manual.

*Your Escort and Orion Manual*

The aim of this manual is to help you get the best value from your vehicle. It can do so in several ways. It can help you decide what work must be done (even should you choose to get it done by a garage), provide information on routine maintenance and servicing, and give a logical course of action and diagnosis when random faults occur. However, it is hoped that you will use the manual by tackling the work yourself. On simpler jobs it may even be quicker than booking the car into a garage and going there twice, to leave and collect it. Perhaps most important, a lot of money can be saved by avoiding the costs a garage must charge to cover its labour and overheads.

The manual has drawings and descriptions to show the function of the various components so that their layout can be understood. Then the tasks are described and photographed in a clear step-by-step sequence.

References to the 'left' or 'right' are in the sense of a person in the driver's seat, facing forward.

**We take great pride in the accuracy of information given in this manual, but vehicle manufacturers make alterations and design changes during the production run of a particular vehicle of which they do not inform us. No liability can be accepted by the authors or publishers for loss, damage or injury caused by any errors in, or omissions from, the information given.**

Working on your car can be dangerous. This page shows just some of the potential risks and hazards, with the aim of creating a safety-conscious attitude.

# General hazards

### Scalding

• Don't remove the radiator or expansion tank cap while the engine is hot.
• Engine oil, automatic transmission fluid or power steering fluid may also be dangerously hot if the engine has recently been running.

### Burning

• Beware of burns from the exhaust system and from any part of the engine. Brake discs and drums can also be extremely hot immediately after use.

### Crushing

• When working under or near a raised vehicle, always supplement the jack with axle stands, or use drive-on ramps.
*Never venture under a car which is only supported by a jack.*
• Take care if loosening or tightening high-torque nuts when the vehicle is on stands. Initial loosening and final tightening should be done with the wheels on the ground.

### Fire

• Fuel is highly flammable; fuel vapour is explosive.
• Don't let fuel spill onto a hot engine.
• Do not smoke or allow naked lights (including pilot lights) anywhere near a vehicle being worked on. Also beware of creating sparks (electrically or by use of tools).
• Fuel vapour is heavier than air, so don't work on the fuel system with the vehicle over an inspection pit.
• Another cause of fire is an electrical overload or short-circuit. Take care when repairing or modifying the vehicle wiring.
• Keep a fire extinguisher handy, of a type suitable for use on fuel and electrical fires.

### Electric shock

• Ignition HT voltage can be dangerous, especially to people with heart problems or a pacemaker. Don't work on or near the ignition system with the engine running or the ignition switched on.

• Mains voltage is also dangerous. Make sure that any mains-operated equipment is correctly earthed. Mains power points should be protected by a residual current device (RCD) circuit breaker.

### Fume or gas intoxication

• Exhaust fumes are poisonous; they often contain carbon monoxide, which is rapidly fatal if inhaled. Never run the engine in a confined space such as a garage with the doors shut.
• Fuel vapour is also poisonous, as are the vapours from some cleaning solvents and paint thinners.

### Poisonous or irritant substances

• Avoid skin contact with battery acid and with any fuel, fluid or lubricant, especially antifreeze, brake hydraulic fluid and Diesel fuel. Don't syphon them by mouth. If such a substance is swallowed or gets into the eyes, seek medical advice.
• Prolonged contact with used engine oil can cause skin cancer. Wear gloves or use a barrier cream if necessary. Change out of oil-soaked clothes and do not keep oily rags in your pocket.
• Air conditioning refrigerant forms a poisonous gas if exposed to a naked flame (including a cigarette). It can also cause skin burns on contact.

### Asbestos

• Asbestos dust can cause cancer if inhaled or swallowed. Asbestos may be found in gaskets and in brake and clutch linings. When dealing with such components it is safest to assume that they contain asbestos.

# Special hazards

### Hydrofluoric acid

• This extremely corrosive acid is formed when certain types of synthetic rubber, found in some O-rings, oil seals, fuel hoses etc, are exposed to temperatures above 400°C. The rubber changes into a charred or sticky substance containing the acid. *Once formed, the acid remains dangerous for years. If it gets onto the skin, it may be necessary to amputate the limb concerned.*
• When dealing with a vehicle which has suffered a fire, or with components salvaged from such a vehicle, wear protective gloves and discard them after use.

### The battery

• Batteries contain sulphuric acid, which attacks clothing, eyes and skin. Take care when topping-up or carrying the battery.
• The hydrogen gas given off by the battery is highly explosive. Never cause a spark or allow a naked light nearby. Be careful when connecting and disconnecting battery chargers or jump leads.

### Air bags

• Air bags can cause injury if they go off accidentally. Take care when removing the steering wheel and/or facia. Special storage instructions may apply.

### Diesel injection equipment

• Diesel injection pumps supply fuel at very high pressure. Take care when working on the fuel injectors and fuel pipes.

⚠️ *Warning: Never expose the hands, face or any other part of the body to injector spray; the fuel can penetrate the skin with potentially fatal results.*

# Remember...

### DO

• Do use eye protection when using power tools, and when working under the vehicle.
• Do wear gloves or use barrier cream to protect your hands when necessary.
• Do get someone to check periodically that all is well when working alone on the vehicle.
• Do keep loose clothing and long hair well out of the way of moving mechanical parts.
• Do remove rings, wristwatch etc, before working on the vehicle – especially the electrical system.
• Do ensure that any lifting or jacking equipment has a safe working load rating adequate for the job.

### DON'T

• Don't attempt to lift a heavy component which may be beyond your capability – get assistance.
• Don't rush to finish a job, or take unverified short cuts.
• Don't use ill-fitting tools which may slip and cause injury.
• Don't leave tools or parts lying around where someone can trip over them. Mop up oil and fuel spills at once.
• Don't allow children or pets to play in or near a vehicle being worked on.

The following pages are intended to help in dealing with common roadside emergencies and breakdowns. You will find more detailed fault finding information at the back of the manual, and repair information in the main chapters.

## If your car won't start and the starter motor doesn't turn

- ☐ If it's a model with automatic transmission, make sure the selector is in 'P' or 'N'.
- ☐ Open the bonnet and make sure that the battery terminals are clean and tight.
- ☐ Switch on the headlights and try to start the engine. If the headlights go very dim when you're trying to start, the battery is probably flat. Get out of trouble by jump starting (see next page) using a friend's car.

## If your car won't start even though the starter motor turns as normal

- ☐ Is there fuel in the tank?
- ☐ Is there moisture on electrical components under the bonnet? Switch off the ignition, then wipe off any obvious dampness with a dry cloth. Spray a water-repellent aerosol product (WD-40 or equivalent) on ignition and fuel system electrical connectors like those shown in the photos. Pay special attention to the ignition coil wiring connector and HT leads.

A Check that the spark plug HT leads are securely connected to the spark plugs.

B Also check that the leads are secure in the DIS ignition coil.

C Check that all wiring connectors such as this at the mass air flow sensor are securely connected.

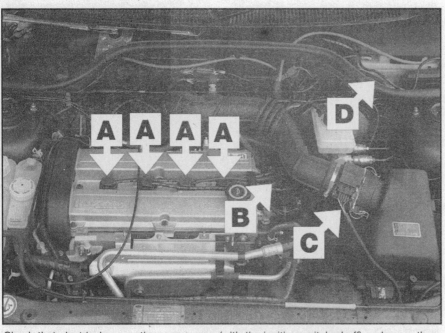

Check that electrical connections are secure (with the ignition switched off) and spray them with a water dispersant spray like WD40 if you suspect a problem due to damp

D Check the security and condition of the battery terminals.

# Jump starting

**HAYNES HINT**
Jump starting will get you out of trouble, but you must correct whatever made the battery go flat in the first place. There are three possibilities:

**1** The battery has been drained by repeated attempts to start, or by leaving the lights on.

**2** The charging system is not working properly (alternator drivebelt slack or broken, alternator wiring fault or alternator itself faulty).

**3** The battery itself is at fault (electrolyte low, or battery worn out).

When jump-starting a car using a booster battery, observe the following precautions:

✔ Before connecting the booster battery, make sure that the ignition is switched off.

✔ Ensure that all electrical equipment (lights, heater, wipers, etc) is switched off.

✔ Take note of any special precautions printed on the battery case.

✔ Make sure that the booster battery is the same voltage as the discharged one in the vehicle.

✔ If the battery is being jump-started from the battery in another vehicle, the two vehicles MUST NOT TOUCH each other.

✔ Make sure that the transmission is in neutral (or PARK, in the case of automatic transmission).

**1** Connect one end of the red jump lead to the positive (+) terminal of the flat battery

**2** Connect the other end of the red lead to the positive (+) terminal of the booster battery.

**3** Connect one end of the black jump lead to the negative (-) terminal of the booster battery

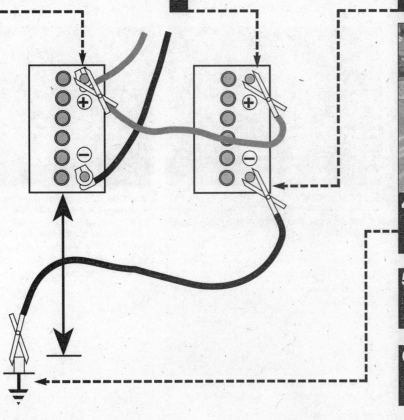

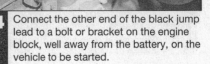

**4** Connect the other end of the black jump lead to a bolt or bracket on the engine block, well away from the battery, on the vehicle to be started.

**5** Make sure that the jump leads will not come into contact with the fan, drive-belts or other moving parts of the engine.

**6** Start the engine using the booster battery and run it at idle speed. Switch on the lights, rear window demister and heater blower motor, then disconnect the jump leads in the reverse order of connection. Turn off the lights etc.

# Wheel changing

Some of the details shown here will vary according to model. For instance, the location of the spare wheel and jack is not the same on all cars. However, the basic principles apply to all vehicles.

 **Warning: Do not change a wheel in a situation where you risk being hit by other traffic. On busy roads, try to stop in a lay-by or a gateway. Be wary of passing traffic while changing the wheel – it is easy to become distracted by the job in hand.**

## Preparation

☐ When a puncture occurs, stop as soon as it is safe to do so.
☐ Park on firm level ground, if possible, and well out of the way of other traffic.
☐ Use hazard warning lights if necessary.

☐ If you have one, use a warning triangle to alert other drivers of your presence.
☐ Apply the handbrake and engage first or reverse gear (or Park on models with automatic transmission.

☐ Chock the wheel diagonally opposite the one being removed – a couple of large stones will do for this.
☐ If the ground is soft, use a flat piece of wood to spread the load under the jack.

## Changing the wheel

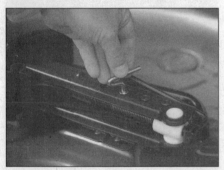

**1** Lift up the luggage compartment trim (where necessary) and remove the spare wheel, tools and jack from their location.

**2** Remove the wheel centre trim, either by pulling it straight off (plastic trim) or by prising off the centre trim.

**3** Slacken each wheel nut by half a turn using the wheel brace in the tool kit.

**4** Position the jack head under the reinforced jacking point on the sill nearest the wheel to be removed. With the base of the jack on firm ground, turn the jack handle clockwise until the wheel is raised clear of the ground. Unscrew the wheel nuts and remove the wheel.

**5** Fit the spare wheel, and screw in the nuts. Lightly tighten the nuts with the wheelbrace then lower the vehicle to the ground.

**6** Securely tighten the wheel nuts in the sequence shown then refit the wheel trim. Stow the punctured wheel and tools back in the luggage compartment and secure them in position. The wheel nuts should be slackened and then retightened to the specified torque at the earliest opportunity.

## Finally...

☐ Remove the wheel chocks.

☐ Check the tyre pressure on the wheel just fitted. If it is low, or if you don't have a pressure gauge with you, drive slowly to the nearest garage and inflate the tyre to the right pressure.

☐ Have the damaged tyre or wheel repaired as soon as possible.

## Identifying leaks

Puddles on the garage floor or drive, or obvious wetness under the bonnet or underneath the car, suggest a leak that needs investigating. It can sometimes be difficult to decide where the leak is coming from, especially if the engine bay is very dirty already. Leaking oil or fluid can also be blown rearwards by the passage of air under the car, giving a false impression of where the problem lies.

 Warning: Most automotive oils and fluids are poisonous. Wash them off skin, and change out of contaminated clothing, without delay.

 The smell of a fluid leaking from the car may provide a clue to what's leaking. Some fluids are distinctively coloured. It may help to clean the car carefully and to park it over some clean paper overnight as an aid to locating the source of the leak.
Remember that some leaks may only occur while the engine is running.

### Sump oil

Engine oil may leak from the drain plug...

### Oil from filter

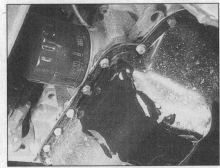

...or from the base of the oil filter.

### Gearbox oil

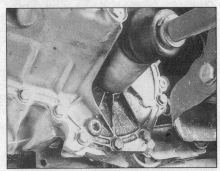

Gearbox oil can leak from the seals at the inboard ends of the driveshafts.

### Antifreeze

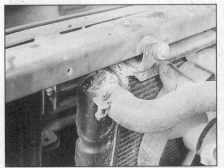

Leaking antifreeze often leaves a crystalline deposit like this.

### Brake fluid

A leak occurring at a wheel is almost certainly brake fluid.

### Power steering fluid

Power steering fluid may leak from the pipe connectors on the steering rack.

## Towing

When all else fails, you may find yourself having to get a tow home – or of course you may be helping somebody else. Long-distance recovery should only be done by a garage or breakdown service. For shorter distances, DIY towing using another car is easy enough, but observe the following points:
□ Use a proper tow-rope – they are not expensive. The vehicle being towed must display an 'ON TOW' sign in its rear window.
□ Always turn the ignition key to the 'on' position when the vehicle is being towed, so

that the steering lock is released, and that the direction indicator and brake lights will work.
□ Only attach the tow-rope to the towing eyes provided.
□ Before being towed, release the handbrake and select neutral on the transmission.
□ Note that greater-than-usual pedal pressure will be required to operate the brakes, since the vacuum servo unit is only operational with the engine running.
□ On models with power steering, greater-than-usual steering effort will also be required.

□ The driver of the car being towed must keep the tow-rope taut at all times to avoid snatching.
□ Make sure that both drivers know the route before setting off.
□ Only drive at moderate speeds and keep the distance towed to a minimum. Drive smoothly and allow plenty of time for slowing down at junctions.
□ On models with automatic transmission, special precautions apply. If in doubt, do not tow, or transmission damage may result.

# Introduction

There are some very simple checks which need only take a few minutes to carry out, but which could save you a lot of inconvenience and expense.

These "Weekly checks" require no great skill or special tools, and the small amount of time they take to perform could prove to be very well spent, for example;

☐ Keeping an eye on tyre condition and pressures, will not only help to stop them wearing out prematurely, but could also save your life.

☐ Many breakdowns are caused by electrical problems. Battery-related faults are particularly common, and a quick check on a regular basis will often prevent the majority of these.

☐ If your car develops a brake fluid leak, the first time you might know about it is when your brakes don't work properly. Checking the level regularly will give advance warning of this kind of problem.

☐ If the oil or coolant levels run low, the cost of repairing any engine damage will be far greater than fixing the leak, for example.

# Underbonnet check points

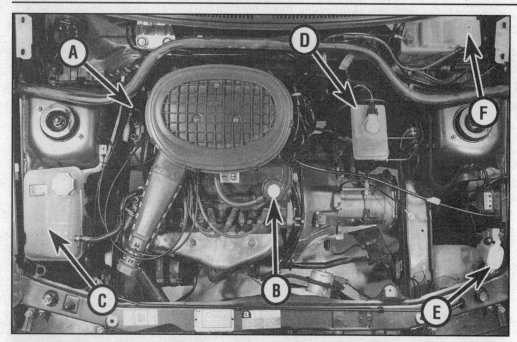

◀ **1.3 litre HCS & Endura-E**

**A** *Engine oil level dipstick*
**B** *Engine oil filler cap*
**C** *Coolant expansion tank*
**D** *Brake fluid reservoir*
**E** *Screen washer filler neck*
**F** *Battery*

◀ **1.4 & 1.6 litre CVH (carburettor)**

**A** *Engine oil level dipstick*
**B** *Engine oil filler cap*
**C** *Coolant expansion tank*
**D** *Brake fluid reservoir*
**E** *Screen washer filler neck*
**F** *Battery*

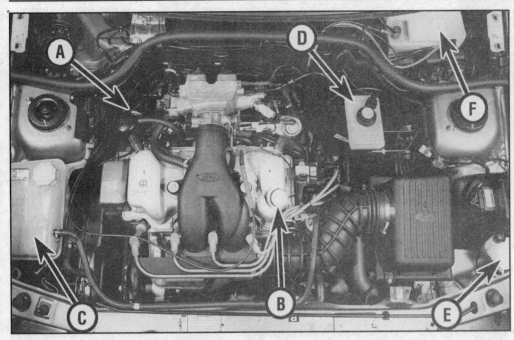

### ◀ 1.6 litre CVH (fuel injection)

A Engine oil level dipstick
B Engine oil filler cap
C Coolant expansion tank
D Brake fluid reservoir
E Screen washer filler neck
F Battery

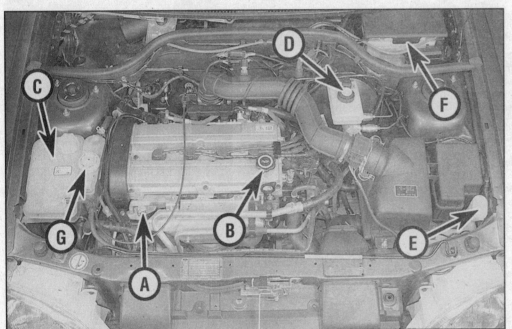

### ◀ 1.6 & 1.8 litre Zetec & Zetec-E

A Engine oil level dipstick
B Engine oil filler cap
C Coolant expansion tank
D Brake fluid reservoir
E Screen washer filler neck
F Battery
G Power steering fluid reservoir

# Engine oil level

## Before you start

✔ Make sure that your car is on level ground.
✔ Check the oil level before the car is driven, or at least 5 minutes after the engine has been switched off.

 **HAYNES HINT** *If the oil is checked immediately after driving the vehicle, some of the oil will remain in the upper engine components, resulting in an inaccurate reading on the dipstick!*

## The correct oil

*Modern engines place great demands on their oil. It is very important that the correct oil for your car is used (See "Lubricants, fluids and tyre pressures").*

## Car care

● If you have to add oil frequently, you should check whether you have any oil leaks. Place some clean paper under the car overnight, and check for stains in the morning. If there are no leaks, the engine may be burning oil *(see "Fault Finding")*.

● Always maintain the level between the upper and lower dipstick marks (see photo 3). If the level is too low severe engine damage may occur. Oil seal failure may result if the engine is overfilled by adding too much oil.

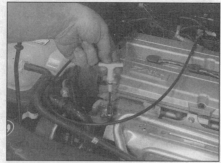

**1** The dipstick is brightly coloured for identification *(see "Underbonnet check points"* on pages 0•10 and 0•11 for exact location). Withdraw the dipstick.

**2** Using a clean rag or paper towel remove all oil from the dipstick. Insert the clean dipstick back into the engine as far as it will go, then withdraw it again.

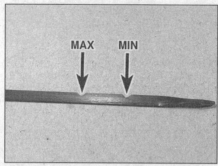

**3** Note the oil level on the end of the dipstick which should be between the upper ("MAX") mark and lower ("MIN") mark. Approximately 0.5 to 1.0 litre of oil will raise the level from the lower to the upper marks.

**4** Oil is added through the filler on the cylinder head cover. Unscrew or pull off the filler cap and top-up the level; a funnel may help to reduce spillage. Add the oil slowly, checking the level on the dipstick frequently. Avoid overfilling (see *"Car Care"*).

# Coolant level

⚠️ *Warning: DO NOT attempt to remove the expansion tank pressure cap when the engine is hot, as there is a very great risk of scalding. Do not leave open containers of coolant about, as it is poisonous.*

## Car care

● Adding coolant should not be necessary on a regular basis. If frequent topping-up is required, it is likely there is a leak. Check the radiator, all hoses and joint faces for signs of staining or wetness, and rectify as necessary.

● It is important that antifreeze is used in the cooling system all year round, not just during the winter months. Don't top-up with water alone, as the antifreeze will become too diluted.

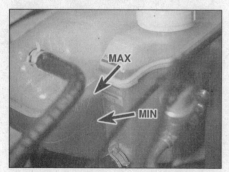

**1** The coolant level varies with the temperature of the engine. When the engine is cold, the coolant level should be up to the "MAX" mark on the side of the tank. When the engine is hot, the level may rise to above the "MAX" mark.

**2** If topping-up is necessary, **wait until the engine is cold.** Slowly unscrew the expansion tank cap, to release any pressure present in the cooling system, and remove it.

**3** Add a mixture of water and antifreeze through the expansion tank filler neck until the level is up to the "MAX" mark. Refit the cap and tighten it securely.

# Brake fluid level

**Warning:**
● Brake fluid can harm your eyes and damage painted surfaces, so use extreme caution when handling and pouring it.
● Do not use fluid that has been standing open for some time, as it absorbs moisture from the air, which can cause a dangerous loss of braking effectiveness.

● Make sure that your car is on level ground.
● The fluid level in the reservoir will drop slightly as the brake pads wear down, but the fluid level must never be allowed to drop below the "MIN" mark.

## Safety first!

● If the reservoir requires repeated topping-up this is an indication of a fluid leak somewhere in the system, which should be investigated immediately.

● If a leak is suspected, the car should not be driven until the braking system has been checked. Never take any risks where brakes are concerned.

**1** The "MAX" and "MIN" marks are indicated on the side of the reservoir. The fluid level must be kept between the marks at all times.

**3** Unscrew the reservoir cap and carefully lift it out of position, taking care not to damage the level sender float. Inspect the reservoir, if the fluid is dirty, the hydraulic system should be drained and refilled (see Chapter 1).

**2** If topping-up is necessary, first wipe the area around the filler cap with a clean rag before removing the cap. This will prevent dirt entering the system.

**4** Carefully add fluid, taking care not to spill it on surrounding components. Use only the specified fluid; mixing different types of fluid can cause damage to the system. After topping-up to the correct level, refit the cap securely and wipe off any spilt fluid.

# Power steering fluid level

## Before you start:
✔ Park the vehicle on level ground.
✔ Set the steering wheel straight-ahead.
✔ The engine should be turned off.

 For the check to be accurate, the steering must not be turned once the engine has been stopped.

## Safety first!
● The need for frequent topping-up indicates a leak, which should be investigated immediately.

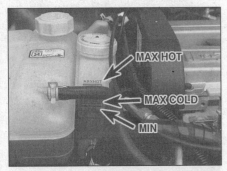

**1** The fluid reservoir is located next to the cooling system expansion tank on the right-hand side of the engine compartment. When the engine is cold, the fluid level should be up to the "MAX COLD" mark on the reservoir; when hot it should be up to the "MAX HOT" mark. The fluid should never be allowed to fall below the "MIN" mark.

**2** If topping-up is necessary, wipe clean the area around the reservoir filler neck and unscrew the filler cap from the reservoir.

**3** Use the specified type of fluid and do not overfill the reservoir. When the level is correct, securely refit the cap.

# Tyre condition and pressure

It is very important that tyres are in good condition, and at the correct pressure - having a tyre failure at any speed is highly dangerous. Tyre wear is influenced by driving style - harsh braking and acceleration, or fast cornering, will all produce more rapid tyre wear. As a general rule, the front tyres wear out faster than the rears. Interchanging the tyres from front to rear ("rotating" the tyres) may result in more even wear. However, if this is completely effective, you may have the expense of replacing all four tyres at once! Remove any nails or stones embedded in the tread before they penetrate the tyre to cause deflation. If removal of a nail does reveal that the tyre has been punctured, refit the nail so that its point of penetration is marked. Then immediately change the wheel, and have the tyre repaired by a tyre dealer.

Regularly check the tyres for damage in the form of cuts or bulges, especially in the sidewalls. Periodically remove the wheels, and clean any dirt or mud from the inside and outside surfaces. Examine the wheel rims for signs of rusting, corrosion or other damage. Light alloy wheels are easily damaged by "kerbing" whilst parking; steel wheels may also become dented or buckled. A new wheel is very often the only way to overcome severe damage.

New tyres should be balanced when they are fitted, but it may become necessary to re-balance them as they wear, or if the balance weights fitted to the wheel rim should fall off. Unbalanced tyres will wear more quickly, as will the steering and suspension components. Wheel imbalance is normally signified by vibration, particularly at a certain speed (typically around 50 mph). If this vibration is felt only through the steering, then it is likely that just the front wheels need balancing. If, however, the vibration is felt through the whole car, the rear wheels could be out of balance. Wheel balancing should be carried out by a tyre dealer or garage.

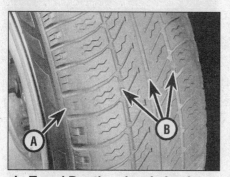

### 1 Tread Depth - visual check
The original tyres have tread wear safety bands (B), which will appear when the tread depth reaches approximately 1.6 mm. The band positions are indicated by a triangular mark on the tyre sidewall (A).

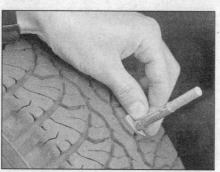

### 2 Tread Depth - manual check
Alternatively, tread wear can be monitored with a simple, inexpensive device known as a tread depth indicator gauge.

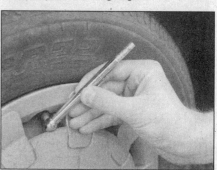

### 3 Tyre Pressure Check
Check the tyre pressures regularly with the tyres cold. Do not adjust the tyre pressures immediately after the vehicle has been used, or an inaccurate setting will result.

# Tyre tread wear patterns

### Shoulder Wear

**Underinflation (wear on both sides)**
Under-inflation will cause overheating of the tyre, because the tyre will flex too much, and the tread will not sit correctly on the road surface. This will cause a loss of grip and excessive wear, not to mention the danger of sudden tyre failure due to heat build-up.
*Check and adjust pressures*
**Incorrect wheel camber (wear on one side)**
*Repair or renew suspension parts*
**Hard cornering**
*Reduce speed!*

### Centre Wear

**Overinflation**
Over-inflation will cause rapid wear of the centre part of the tyre tread, coupled with reduced grip, harsher ride, and the danger of shock damage occurring in the tyre casing.
*Check and adjust pressures*

*If you sometimes have to inflate your car's tyres to the higher pressures specified for maximum load or sustained high-speed, don't forget to reduce the pressures to normal afterwards.*

### Uneven Wear

Front tyres may wear unevenly as a result of wheel misalignment. Most tyre dealers and garages can check and adjust the wheel alignment (or "tracking") for a modest charge.
**Incorrect camber or castor**
*Repair or renew suspension parts*
**Malfunctioning suspension**
*Repair or renew suspension parts*
**Unbalanced wheel**
*Balance tyres*
**Incorrect toe setting**
*Adjust front wheel alignment*
**Note:** *The feathered edge of the tread which typifies toe wear is best checked by feel.*

# Screen washer fluid level*

*On models so equipped, the screen washer fluid is also used to clean the headlights and the tailgate rear window.*

Screenwash additives not only keep the winscreen clean during foul weather, they also prevent the washer system freezing in cold weather - which is when you are likely to need it most. Don't top up using plain water as the screenwash will become too diluted, and will freeze during cold weather. **On no account use coolant antifreeze in the washer system - this could discolour or damage paintwork.**

1 The washer fluid reservoir is located at the front left-hand side of the engine compartment. Check the level by covering the hole on the filler cap with your finger and removing the cap and dipstick/tube.

2 View the fluid level in the tube which will indicate the fluid quantity in the reservoir.

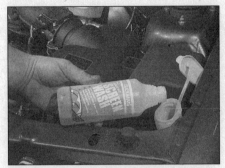

3 When topping-up the reservoir, a screenwash additive should be added in the quantities recommended on the bottle.

# Battery

**Caution:** *Before carrying out any work on the vehicle battery, read the precautions given in "Safety first" at the start of this manual.*

✔ Make sure that the battery clamp is in good condition and tight. Corrosion on the clamp and the battery itself can be removed with a solution of water and baking soda. Thoroughly rinse all cleaned areas with plain water. Any metal parts damaged by corrosion should be covered with a zinc-based primer, then painted.

✔ Periodically (approximately every three months), check the charge condition of the battery as described in Chapter 5A.

✔ If the battery is flat, and you need to jump start your vehicle, see **Roadside Repairs**.

1 The battery is located at the left-hand rear of the engine compartment. The exterior of the battery should be inspected periodically for damage such as a cracked case or cover.

2 Check the tightness of the battery cable clamps to ensure good electrical connections. You should not be able to move them. Also check each cable for cracks and frayed conductors.

*Battery corrosion can be kept to a minimum by applying a layer of petroleum jelly to the clamps and terminals after they are reconnected.*

3 If corrosion (white, fluffy deposits) is evident, remove the cables from the battery terminals, clean them with a small wire brush, then refit them. Automotive stores sell a tool for cleaning the battery post . . .

4 . . . as well as the battery cable clamps

# Bulbs and fuses

✔ Check all external lights and the horn. Refer to the appropriate Sections of Chapter 12 for details if any of the circuits are found to be inoperative.

✔ Visually check all accessible wiring connectors, harnesses and retaining clips for security, and for signs of chafing or damage.

 *If you need to check your brake lights and indicators unaided, back up to a wall or garage door and operate the lights. The reflected light should show if they are working properly.*

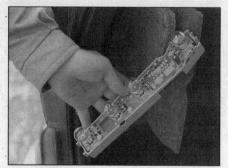

**1** If a single indicator light, stop light or headlight has failed it is likely that a bulb has blown and will need to be replaced. Refer to Chapter 12 for details. If both stop lights have failed, it is possible that the stop light switch is faulty or needs adjusting (see Chapter 12).

**2** If more than one indicator light or headlight has failed it is likely that either a fuse has blown or that there is a fault in the circuit (see Chapter 12). The fuses are located in the fuse box below the facia on the driver's side. Lift off the cover to inspect the fuses.

**3** To replace a blown fuse, simply pull it out from its contacts in the fuse block. Fit a new fuse of the same rating (refer to Chapter 12). If the fuse blows again, it is important that you find out why - a complete checking procedure is given in Chapter 12.

# Wiper blades

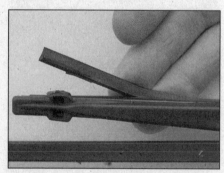

**1** Check the condition of the wiper blades; if they are cracked or show any signs of deterioration, or if the glass swept area is smeared, renew them. Wiper blades should be renewed annually.

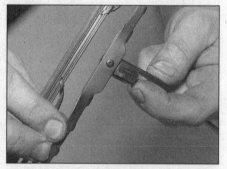

**2** To remove a wiper blade, pull the arm fully away from the glass until it locks. Swivel the blade through 90°, press the locking tab with your finger and slide the blade out of the arm's hooked end.

# Lubricants and fluids

**Engine**
Pre-July 1998 models:

  Recommended oil . . . . . . . . . . . . . . . . . . . . . . . . . . . . . . . . . . . .   Multigrade engine oil, viscosity SAE 5W/30, to Ford specification WSS-M2C913-A or WSS-M2C912-A1
*(Duckhams Fully Synthetic Engine Oil)*

  Alternative oil . . . . . . . . . . . . . . . . . . . . . . . . . . . . . . . . . . . . . . . .   Multigrade engine oil, viscosity SAE 5W/40 to 10W/40, to ACEA-A3 or A1
*(Duckhams QXR Premium Petrol Engine Oil)*

July 1998 models onwards* . . . . . . . . . . . . . . . . . . . . . . . . . . . . . .   Multigrade engine oil, viscosity SAE 5W/30, to Ford specification WSS-M2C913-A or WSS-M2C912-A1
*(Duckhams Fully Synthetic Engine Oil)*

**Cooling system**
Pre-September 1998 models (blue/green coolant)** . . . . . . . . . . . . .   Ethylene glycol-based antifreeze to Ford specification ESD-M97B49-A
*(Duckhams Antifreeze and Summer Coolant)*

September 1998 models onward (orange coolant)** . . . . . . . . . . . . .   Monoethylene glycol-based antifreeze to Ford specification WSS-M97B44-D

**Manual transmission**
B5 type manual transmission . . . . . . . . . . . . . . . . . . . . . . . . . . . . .   SAE 80 high-pressure gear oil to Ford specification SQM2C-9008-A
*(Duckhams Hypoid Gear Oil 80W GL-4)*

IB5 type manual transmission . . . . . . . . . . . . . . . . . . . . . . . . . . . .   SAE 75W/90 synthetic gear oil, to Ford specification WSD-M2C200-B
*(Duckhams Hypoid Gear Oil 75W-90 GL-4)*

MTX-75 type manual transmission . . . . . . . . . . . . . . . . . . . . . . . .   Transmission fluid to Ford specification ESD-M2C186-A
*(Duckhams ATF Autotrans III)*

**Automatic transmission** . . . . . . . . . . . . . . . . . . . . . . . . . . . . . . .   Transmission fluid to Ford specification ESP-M2C166-H or Tutela WSD-M2C199-A

**Braking system** . . . . . . . . . . . . . . . . . . . . . . . . . . . . . . . . . . . . . .   Hydraulic fluid to Ford specification ESD-M6C57-A, Super DOT 4 or equivalent
*(Duckhams Universal Brake and Clutch Fluid)*

**Power steering** . . . . . . . . . . . . . . . . . . . . . . . . . . . . . . . . . . . . . .   Transmission fluid to Ford specification ESD-M2C186-A
*(Duckhams ATF Autotrans III)*

**Wheel bearing grease** . . . . . . . . . . . . . . . . . . . . . . . . . . . . . . . . .   Grease to Ford specification SAM-1C9111-A
*(Duckhams LB 10)*

*Multigrade engine oil, viscosity SAE 5W/40 to 10W/40, to ACEA-A3 or A1 *(Duckhams QXR Premium Petrol Engine Oil)* may be used for topping-up only.
**Do not mix the two coolant types.

# Choosing your engine oil

Engines need oil, not only to lubricate moving parts and minimise wear, but also to maximise power output and to improve fuel economy. By introducing a simplified and improved range of engine oils, Duckhams has taken away the confusion and made it easier for you to choose the right oil for your engine.

## HOW ENGINE OIL WORKS

### • *Beating friction*

Without oil, the moving surfaces inside your engine will rub together, heat up and melt, quickly causing the engine to seize. Engine oil creates a film which separates these moving parts, preventing wear and heat build-up.

### • *Cooling hot-spots*

Temperatures inside the engine can exceed 1000° C. The engine oil circulates and acts as a coolant, transferring heat from the hot-spots to the sump.

### • *Cleaning the engine internally*

Good quality engine oils clean the inside of your engine, collecting and dispersing combustion deposits and controlling them until they are trapped by the oil filter or flushed out at oil change.

## OIL CARE - FOLLOW THE CODE

To handle and dispose of used engine oil safely, always:

**0800 66 33 66**
www.oilbankline.org.uk

• *Avoid skin contact with used engine oil. Repeated or prolonged contact can be harmful.*
• *Dispose of used oil and empty packs in a responsible manner in an authorised disposal site. Call 0800 663366 to find the one nearest to you. Never tip oil down drains or onto the ground.*

# Tyre pressures

| Saloon, Hatchback and Estate models: | Front | Rear |
|---|---|---|
| Normally-laden* . . . . . . . . . . . . . . . . . . . . . . . . . . . . . . . . . . . . | 2.0 bars (29 psi) | 1.8 bars (26 psi) |
| Fully-laden* . . . . . . . . . . . . . . . . . . . . . . . . . . . . . . . . . . . . . | 2.5 bars (37 psi) | 2.8 bars (41 psi) |
| Van "55" models: | | |
| Normally-laden* . . . . . . . . . . . . . . . . . . . . . . . . . . . . . . . . . . . . | 2.0 bars (29 psi) | 1.8 bars (26 psi) |
| Fully-laden* . . . . . . . . . . . . . . . . . . . . . . . . . . . . . . . . . . . . . | 2.4 bars (35 psi) | 3.0 bars (44 psi) |
| Van "75" models: | | |
| Normally-laden* . . . . . . . . . . . . . . . . . . . . . . . . . . . . . . . . . . . . | 2.4 bars (35 psi) | 2.6 bars (38 psi) |
| Fully-laden* . . . . . . . . . . . . . . . . . . . . . . . . . . . . . . . . . . . . . | 2.6 bars (38 psi) | 3.5 bars (51 psi) |

**Note:** *Normally-laden means up to 3 persons. For sustained high speeds above 100 mph (160 km/h), increased pressures are necessary. Consult the driver's handbook supplied with the vehicle. Pressures apply only to original-equipment tyres, and may vary if other makes or type is fitted; check with the tyre manufacturer or supplier for correct pressures if necessary.*

# Chapter 1
# Routine maintenance and servicing

## Contents

## Degrees of difficulty

 **Easy,** suitable for novice with little experience

 **Fairly easy,** suitable for beginner with some experience

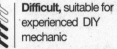 **Fairly difficult,** suitable for competent DIY mechanic

**Difficult,** suitable for experienced DIY mechanic

 **Very difficult,** suitable for expert DIY or professional

**Lubricants and fluids** .................................  Refer to end of *"Weekly Checks"*

## Capacities

### Engine oil

At oil and filter change:
| | |
|---|---|
| HCS and Endura-E engines ............................. | 3.25 litres |
| CVH and PTE engines ............................. | 3.50 litres |
| Zetec and Zetec-E engines ............................. | 4.25 litres |
| Difference between dipstick minimum and maximum level notches ... | 0.5 to 1.0 litre |

### Cooling system

| | |
|---|---|
| 1.3 litre HCS and Endura-E engines ............................. | 7.1 litres |
| 1.4 litre CVH engine ............................. | 7.6 litres |
| 1.6 litre CVH engine ............................. | 7.8 litres |
| 1.4 litre PTE engine ............................. | 7.6 litres |
| 1.6 and 1.8 Zetec engine ............................. | 7.0 litres |
| 1.6 and 1.8 Zetec-E engines ............................. | 7.0 litres |

**Note:** *These specifications refer to the use of Ford antifreeze only*

### Fuel tank ............................. 55.0 litres

### Manual transmission

| | |
|---|---|
| B5 type (four-speed) ............................. | 2.8 litres |
| B5 type (five-speed) ............................. | 3.1 litres |
| iB5 type (five-speed) ............................. | 2.8 litres |
| MTX-75 type ............................. | 2.6 litres |

### Automatic transmission

| | |
|---|---|
| Without fluid cooler ............................. | 3.5 litres |
| With fluid cooler ............................. | 3.6 litres |
| Zetec '96-on with cooler ............................. | 4.7 litres |

### Engine

| | |
|---|---|
| Direction of crankshaft rotation ............................. | Clockwise (seen from right-hand side of vehicle) |

Oil filter:*
| | |
|---|---|
| HCS, Endura-E, CVH and PTE engines ............................. | Champion C104 |
| Zetec and Zetec-E engines ............................. | Champion C148 |

*Champion product references correct at time of writing. If in doubt, please contact Champion on 01274 848283 for latest information.*

### Cooling system

Coolant protection at standard 40% antifreeze/water mixture ratio:
| | |
|---|---|
| Slush point ............................. | -25°C (-13°F) |
| Solidifying point ............................. | -30°C (-22°F) |
| Coolant specific gravity at standard 40% antifreeze/water mixture ratio and 15°C/59°F - with no other additives in coolant ............. | 1.061 |

### Fuel system

Idle speed*:
| | |
|---|---|
| 1.3 litre HCS (carburettor) engine ............................. | 750 ± 50 rpm (cooling fan running) |
| 1.4 litre CVH (carburettor) engine ............................. | 800 ± 50 rpm (cooling fan running) |
| 1.6 litre CVH (carburettor) engine ............................. | 800 ± 50 rpm (cooling fan running) |

1.6 litre CVH (fuel injection) engine:
| | |
|---|---|
| Idle speed ............................. | 900 ± 50 rpm |
| Base idle speed ............................. | 750 ± 50 rpm |

Idle mixture CO content*:
| | |
|---|---|
| 1.3 litre HCS (carburettor) engine ............................. | 1.0 ± 0.5% |
| 1.4 litre CVH (carburettor) engine ............................. | 1.0 ± 0.5% |
| 1.6 litre CVH (carburettor) engine ............................. | 1.5 ± 0.5% |
| 1.6 litre CVH (fuel injection) engine ............................. | 0.8 ± 0.25% |

*Note:* *The idle speed and mixture CO content is only adjustable on the engines shown above. On all other engines, it is controlled by the engine management system, and cannot be checked or adjusted without specialised test equipment.*

Air filter element:*
| | |
|---|---|
| 1.3 litre HCS engine ............................. | Champion W225 |
| 1.3 litre Endura-E engine ............................. | Champion W225 |
| 1.4 litre PTE engine ............................. | Champion U612 |
| 1.4 litre CVH engine ............................. | Champion W226 |
| 1.6 litre CVH (carburettor) engine ............................. | Champion W226 |
| 1.6 litre CVH (fuel injection) engine ............................. | Champion U612 |
| 1.6 and 1.8 litre Zetec engines ............................. | Champion U612 |
| 1.6 and 1.8 litre Zetec-E engines ............................. | Champion U612 |

*Champion product references correct at time of writing. If in doubt, please contact Champion on 01274 848283 for latest information.*

Fuel filter:*
   1.3 litre HCS (CFi fuel injection) engine . . . . . . . . . . . . . . . . . . . . . Champion type not available
   1.3 litre Endura-E engine . . . . . . . . . . . . . . . . . . . . . . . . . . . . . . . . Champion type not available
   1.4 litre PTE engine . . . . . . . . . . . . . . . . . . . . . . . . . . . . . . . . . . . . Champion L218
   1.4 litre CVH (CFi fuel injection) engine . . . . . . . . . . . . . . . . . . . . . Champion type not available
   1.6 litre CVH (EFi fuel injection) engine . . . . . . . . . . . . . . . . . . . . . Champion L204
   1.6 and 1.8 litre Zetec and Zetec-E engines . . . . . . . . . . . . . . . . . . Champion L218
*Champion product references correct at time of writing. If in doubt, please contact Champion on 01274 848283 for latest information.

## Ignition system

Firing order:
   HCS and Endura-E engines . . . . . . . . . . . . . . . . . . . . . . . . . . . . . . 1-2-4-3 (No 1 cylinder at timing chain end of engine)
   All other engines . . . . . . . . . . . . . . . . . . . . . . . . . . . . . . . . . . . . . . 1-3-4-2 (No 1 cylinder at timing belt end of engine)
Spark plugs*:
   1.3 litre HCS and Endura-E engines . . . . . . . . . . . . . . . . . . . . . . . Champion RS9YCC
   1.4 litre CVH and PTE engine . . . . . . . . . . . . . . . . . . . . . . . . . . . . Champion RC9YCC4
   1.6 litre CVH (carburettor) engine . . . . . . . . . . . . . . . . . . . . . . . . . Champion RC9YCC
   1.6 litre CVH (EFi fuel injection) engine . . . . . . . . . . . . . . . . . . . . . Champion RC9YCC4
   1.6 and 1.8 litre Zetec and Zetec-E engines . . . . . . . . . . . . . . . . . . Champion RE7PYC5
Electrode gap*:
   All 1.3 litre engines . . . . . . . . . . . . . . . . . . . . . . . . . . . . . . . . . . . . 0.9 mm
   1.4 litre CVH and PTE engine . . . . . . . . . . . . . . . . . . . . . . . . . . . . 1.0 mm
   1.6 litre CVH (carburettor) engine . . . . . . . . . . . . . . . . . . . . . . . . . 0.8 mm
   1.6 litre CVH (EFi fuel injection) engine . . . . . . . . . . . . . . . . . . . . . 1.0 mm
   1.6 and 1.8 litre Zetec and Zetec-E engines . . . . . . . . . . . . . . . . . . 1.3 mm
Maximum resistance per lead . . . . . . . . . . . . . . . . . . . . . . . . . . . . . 30 000 ohms
*Champion product references correct at time of writing. If in doubt, please contact Champion on 01274 848283 for latest information.
Information on spark plug types and electrode gaps is as recommended by Champion Spark Plug. Where alternative types are used, refer to their manufacturer's recommendations.

## Clutch

Pedal free-play '96 models on . . . . . . . . . . . . . . . . . . . . . . . . . . . . . 150 ± 5 mm (RHD)          145 ± 5 mm (LHD)

## Braking system

Minimum front or rear brake pad lining thickness . . . . . . . . . . . . . . . 1.5 mm
Minimum rear brake shoe lining thickness . . . . . . . . . . . . . . . . . . . . 1.0 mm
Minimum disc thickness . . . . . . . . . . . . . . . . . . . . . . . . . . . . . . . . . See Chapter 9

## Tyres

Tyre pressures . . . . . . . . . . . . . . . . . . . . . . . . . . . . . . . . . . . . . . . . See "Weekly Checks"

## Torque wrench settings

| | Nm | lbf ft |
| --- | --- | --- |
| Auxiliary drivebelt cover fasteners | 8 | 6 |
| Auxiliary drivebelt adjustment: | | |
|   Adjusting bolt (sliding arm) | 22 | 16 |
|   Central (locking) bolt | 22 | 16 |
|   Pinion (adjuster) nut | 12 | 9 |
|   Alternator mounting bolts | 25 | 18 |
| Engine oil drain plug | 25 | 18 |
| Handbrake cable adjuster nut (1996-on models) | 4 | 3 |
| Manual transmission filler/level plug: | | |
|   B5 and iB5 transmission | 20 | 15 |
|   MTX-75 transmission | 45 | 33 |
| Spark plugs: | | |
|   HCS and Endura-E engines | 17 | 13 |
|   CVH and PTE engines | 25 | 18 |
|   Zetec and Zetec-E engines | 15 | 11 |
| Roadwheel nuts | 85 | 63 |
| Seat belt mounting bolts | 38 | 28 |

**1**

# Maintenance schedule

The manufacturer's recommended maintenance schedule for these vehicles is as described below - note that the schedule starts from the vehicle's date of registration. These are the minimum maintenance intervals recommended by the factory for Escorts and Orions driven daily, but subjected only to "normal" use. If you wish to keep your vehicle in peak condition at all times, you may wish to perform some of these procedures even more often. Because frequent maintenance enhances the efficiency, performance and resale value of your vehicle, we encourage you to do so. If your usage is not "normal", shorter intervals are also recommended - the most important examples of these are noted in the schedule. The shorter intervals apply particularly if you drive in dusty areas, tow a caravan or trailer, sit with the engine idling or drive at low speeds for extended periods (ie, in heavy traffic), or drive for short distances in below-freezing temperatures.

When your vehicle is new, it should be serviced by a Ford dealer service department to protect the factory warranty. In many cases, the initial maintenance check is done at no cost to the owner. Note that this first free service (carried out by the selling dealer 1500 miles or 3 months after delivery), although an important check for a new vehicle, is not part of the regular maintenance schedule, and is therefore not mentioned here.

It should be noted that for the 1992 model year, the service time/mileage intervals were extended by the manufacturer to the periods shown in this schedule. Although these intervals can be applied retrospectively, owners of earlier vehicles may notice a discrepancy between this schedule and the one shown in the Service Guide supplied with the vehicle.

## Every 250 miles (400 km) or weekly
☐ Refer to "Weekly Checks".

## Every 10 000 miles (16 000 km) or 12 months, whichever occurs first
☐ Check the auxiliary drivebelt (Section 3).
☐ Check under the bonnet for fluid leaks and hose condition (Section 4).
☐ Check the condition of all engine compartment wiring (Section 5).
☐ Check the condition of all air conditioning system components (Section 6).
☐ Check the valve clearance adjustment - HCS and Endura-E engines only (Section 7).
☐ Renew the engine oil and filter (Section 8).
☐ Check and if necessary adjust the clutch pedal free play - 1996 models onward (Section 9).
☐ Check the manual transmission oil level (Section 10).
☐ Check the engine idle speed and mixture - HCS and CVH engines only, where possible (Section 11).
☐ Check the steering, suspension and roadwheels (Section 12).
☐ Check the driveshaft rubber gaiters and CV joints (Section 13).
☐ Check the exhaust system (Section 14).
☐ Check the underbody, and all fuel/brake lines (Section 15).
☐ Check the brake system (Section 16).
☐ Check the security of all roadwheel nuts (Section 17).
☐ Check the doors, boot, tailgate and bonnet, and lubricate their hinges and locks (Section 18).
☐ Check the seat belts (Section 19).
☐ Check the condition of the bodywork, paint and exterior trim (Section 20).
☐ Road test (Section 21).
☐ Automatic transmission fluid level check (Section 22).

**Note:** *If the vehicle is used regularly for very short (less than 10 miles), stop/go journeys, the oil and filter should be renewed between services (ie, every 5000 miles/6 months). Seek the advice of a Ford dealer if in doubt on this point.*

## Every 20 000 miles (32 000 km) or 2 years, whichever occurs first
*Carry out all operations listed above, plus the following:*
☐ Renew the spark plugs - all engines except Zetec and Zetec-E (Section 23).

## Every 30 000 miles (48 000 km) or three years, whichever occurs first
*Carry out all operations listed above, plus the following:*
☐ Renew the spark plugs - Zetec and Zetec-E engines only (Section 23).
☐ Renew the coolant (Section 24).
☐ Renew the air cleaner filter element (Section 25).
☐ Check the emission control system (Section 26).
☐ Renew the automatic transmission fluid (Section 27).
☐ Check the handbrake adjustment (Section 28).

**Note:** *If the vehicle is used regularly in dusty or polluted conditions, the air cleaner filter element should be renewed at more frequent intervals.*

## Every 40 000 miles
☐ Renew the timing belt - CVH and PTE engines (Section 29)

## Every 60 000 miles
*Carry out all operations listed above, plus the following:*
☐ Renew the timing belt - Zetec and Zetec-E engines (Section 29).
☐ Renew the fuel filter (Section 30).

## Every 3 years (regardless of mileage)
☐ Renew the brake fluid (Section 31).

## Engine compartment - 1.3 litre HCS carburettor engine

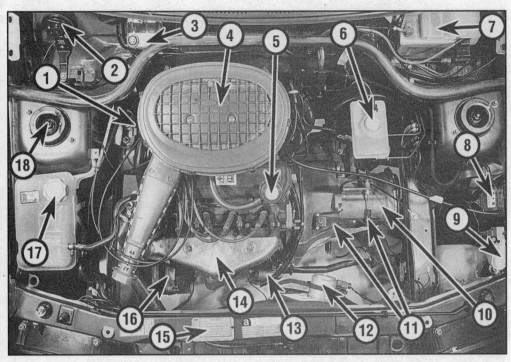

1 Oil level dipstick location
2 Anti-theft alarm horn
3 Windscreen wiper motor
4 Air cleaner
5 Engine oil filler cap
6 Brake master cylinder reservoir
7 Battery
8 Ignition module
9 Washer fluid reservoir
10 Transmission
11 Clutch operating lever and cable
12 Cooling fan
13 Starter motor
14 Exhaust heat shield/air deflector
15 Vehicle identification plate (VIN)
16 Alternator
17 Coolant expansion tank
18 Suspension upper mounting

## Engine compartment - 1.4 litre PTE SEFi fuel injection engine

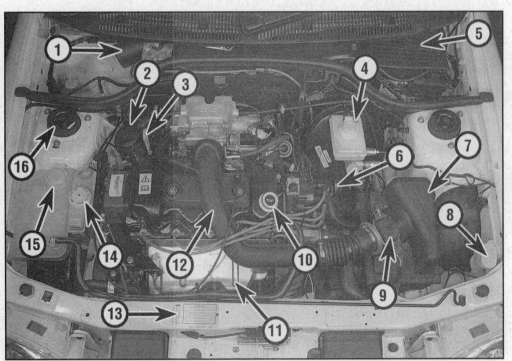

1 Windscreen wiper motor
2 Crankcase ventilation system filter
3 Oil level dipstick location
4 Brake master cylinder reservoir
5 Battery
6 EDIS ignition coil
7 Air cleaner housing
8 Washer fluid reservoir
9 Mass air flow sensor
10 Engine oil filler cap
11 Exhaust heat shield
12 Air inlet duct
13 Vehicle identification plate (VIN)
14 Power steering fluid reservoir
15 Coolant expansion tank
16 Suspension upper mounting.

1

## Engine compartment - 1.6 litre CVH carburettor engine

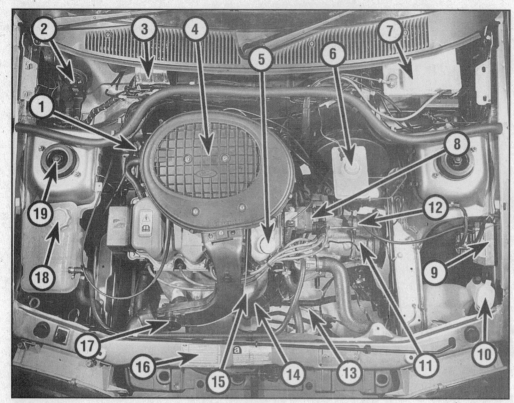

1 Oil level dipstick location
2 Anti-theft alarm horn
3 Windscreen wiper motor
4 Air cleaner
5 Engine oil filler cap
6 Brake master cylinder reservoir
7 Battery
8 DIS Ignition coil
9 Ignition module
10 Washer fluid reservoir
11 Transmission
12 Clutch cable
13 Cooling fan
14 Starter motor
15 Exhaust heat shield/air deflector
16 Vehicle identification plate (VIN)
17 Inlet air temperature control valve
18 Coolant expansion tank
19 Suspension upper mounting

## Engine compartment - 1.6 litre CVH EFi fuel injection engine

1 Oil level dipstick location
2 Anti-theft alarm horn
3 Windscreen wiper motor
4 Throttle housing
5 Inlet air temperature sensor
6 Fuel pressure regulator
7 EDIS ignition coil
8 Brake master cylinder reservoir
9 Battery
10 Ignition module
11 Air cleaner housing
12 Washer fluid reservoir
13 Engine oil filler cap
14 Cooling fan
15 Vehicle identification plate (VIN)
16 Starter motor
17 Auxiliary drivebelt
18 Coolant expansion tank
19 Suspension upper mounting
20 MAP sensor

## Engine compartment - 1.6 litre Zetec SEFi fuel injection engine

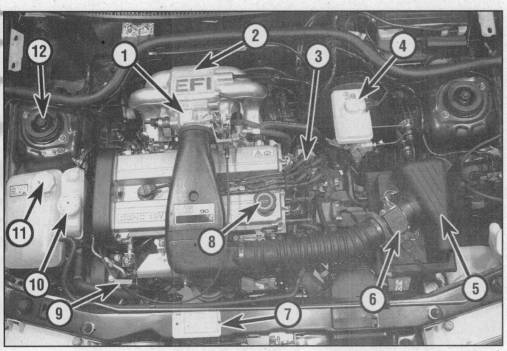

1  Throttle housing
2  Inlet manifold
3  EDIS ignition coil
4  Brake master cylinder reservoir
5  Air cleaner housing
6  Mass air flow sensor
7  Vehicle identification plate (VIN)
8  Engine oil filler cap
9  Oil level dipstick location
10 Power steering fluid reservoir
11 Coolant expansion tank
12 Suspension upper mounting

## Engine compartment - 1.6 litre Zetec-E SEFi fuel injection engine

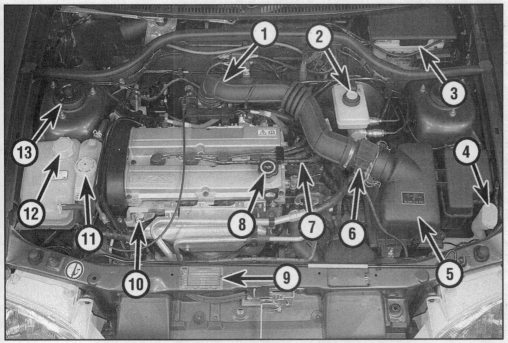

1  Air inlet duct
2  Brake master cylinder reservoir
3  Battery
4  Washer fluid reservoir
5  Air cleaner housing
6  Mass air flow sensor
7  EDIS ignition coil
8  Engine oil filler cap
9  Vehicle identification plate (VIN)
10 Oil level dipstick location
11 Power steering fluid reservoir
12 Coolant expansion tank
13 Suspension upper mounting

1

## Front underbody view of the 1.6 litre CVH EFi engine model

1  Driveshaft
2  Engine oil drain plug
3  Horn
4  Alternator
5  Exhaust downpipe
6  Oxygen sensor
7  Transmission
8  Brake caliper
9  Lower suspension arm
10 Track rod
11 Gearshift rod
12 Heatshield
13 Stabiliser rod (transmission)
14 Catalytic converter

## Front underbody view of the 1.6 litre Zetec SEFi engine model

1  Driveshaft
2  Horn
3  Alternator
4  Exhaust downpipe
5  Transmission
6  Brake caliper
7  Lower suspension arm
8  Track rod
9  Gearshift rod
10 Stabiliser rod (transmission)
11 Catalytic converter
12 Engine oil drain plug

## Rear underbody view of a 1.3 litre Hatchback model

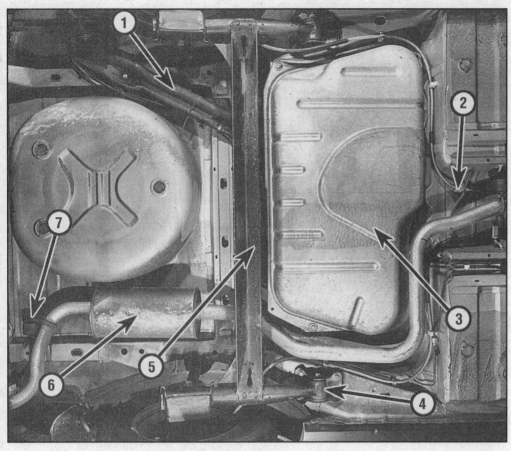

1 Fuel filler pipe
2 Handbrake cable adjuster
3 Fuel tank
4 Suspension mounting
5 Rear axle beam
6 Exhaust rear silencer
7 Exhaust system
  support/insulator

# Maintenance procedures

## 1 Introduction

This Chapter is designed to help the home mechanic maintain his/her vehicle for safety, economy, long life and peak performance.

This Chapter contains a master maintenance schedule, followed by Sections dealing specifically with each task in the schedule. Visual checks, adjustments, component renewal and other helpful items are included. Refer to the accompanying illustrations of the engine compartment and the underside of the vehicle for the locations of the various components.

Servicing your vehicle in accordance with the mileage/time maintenance schedule and the following Sections will provide a planned maintenance programme, which should result in a long and reliable service life. This is a comprehensive plan, so maintaining some items but not others at the specified service intervals will not produce the same results.

As you service your vehicle, you will discover that many of the procedures can - and should - be grouped together, because of the particular procedure being performed, or because of the close proximity of two otherwise-unrelated components to one another. For example, if the vehicle is raised for any reason, the exhaust should be inspected at the same time as the suspension and steering components.

The first step of this maintenance programme is to prepare yourself before the actual work begins. Read through all the Sections relevant to the work to be carried out, then make a list and gather together all the parts and tools required. If a problem is encountered, seek advice from a parts specialist or a dealer service department.

## 2 Intensive maintenance

**1** If, from the time the vehicle is new, the routine maintenance schedule is followed

closely, and frequent checks are made of fluid levels and high-wear items, as suggested throughout this manual, the engine will be kept in relatively good running condition, and the need for additional work will be minimised.
**2** It is possible that there will be some times when the engine is running poorly due to the lack of regular maintenance. This is even more likely if a used vehicle, which has not received regular and frequent maintenance checks, is purchased. In such cases, additional work may need to be carried out, outside of the regular maintenance intervals.
**3** If engine wear is suspected, a compression test (refer to Part A, B or C of Chapter 2) will provide valuable information regarding the overall performance of the main internal components. Such a test can be used as a basis to decide on the extent of the work to be carried out. If, for example, a compression test indicates serious internal engine wear, conventional maintenance as described in this Chapter will not greatly improve the performance of the engine, and may prove a waste of time and money, unless extensive overhaul work (Chapter 2D) is carried out first.

**1**

**4** The following series of operations are those often required to improve the performance of a generally poor-running engine:

### Primary operations

a) Clean, inspect and test the battery (See "Weekly Checks").
b) Check all the engine-related fluids (See "Weekly Checks").
c) Check the condition of the auxiliary drivebelt (Section 3).
d) Check and if necessary adjust the valve clearances on HCS and Endura-E engines (Section 7).
e) Renew the spark plugs and clean and inspect the HT leads (Section 23).
f) Check the condition of the air cleaner filter element and renew if necessary (Section 25).
g) Check and if necessary adjust the carburettor idle speed and mixture settings - where applicable (Section 11).
h) Renew the fuel filter - fuel injection models (Section 30).
i) Check the condition of all hoses, and check for fluid leaks (Section 4).

**5** If the above operations do not prove fully effective, carry out the following operations:

### Secondary operations

All the items under "Primary operations", plus the following:

a) Check the charging system (Chapter 5A).
b) Check the ignition system (Chapter 5B).
c) Check the fuel system (Chapter 4).
d) Renew the ignition HT leads (Section 23).

# Every 10 000 miles or 12 months

## 3  Auxiliary drivebelt check and renewal

### General

**1** The auxiliary drivebelt type depends on the engine fitted, and on whether the vehicle is equipped with power-assisted steering or air conditioning. The belt will be either a V-belt or a flat, multi-ribbed (or "polyvee") type. The drivebelt is located on the right-hand end of the engine, and drives the alternator, water pump (and, when fitted, the power steering pump and the air conditioning compressor) from the engine's crankshaft pulley.

**2** The good condition and proper tension of the auxiliary drivebelt is critical to the operation of the engine. Because of their composition and the high stresses to which they are subjected, drivebelts stretch and deteriorate as they get older. They must, therefore, be regularly inspected.

### Check

**3** With the engine switched off, open and support the bonnet, then locate the auxiliary drivebelt on the right-hand end of the engine (Be very careful, and wear protective gloves to minimise the risk of burning your hands on hot components, if the engine has recently been running). For improved access, jack up the front right-hand side of the vehicle, support it securely on an axle stand, remove the

roadwheel, then remove the auxiliary drivebelt lower cover from inside the wheel arch **(see illustration)**.

**4** Using an inspection light or a small electric torch, and rotating the engine when necessary with a spanner applied to the crankshaft pulley bolt, check the whole length of the drivebelt for cracks, separation of the rubber, and torn or worn ribs. Also check for fraying and glazing, which gives the drivebelt a shiny appearance. Both sides of the drivebelt should be inspected, which means you will have to twist the drivebelt to check the underside. Use your fingers to feel the drivebelt where you can't see it. If you are in any doubt as to the condition of the drivebelt, renew it (go to paragraph 19).

> **HAYNES HINT** *Turning the engine will be much easier if the spark plugs are removed first (Section 23).*

### Drivebelt tension

**5** It is only necessary to adjust the tension if the drivebelt is of the V-belt type. The flat, "polyvee" type drivebelts are fitted with an automatic tensioner to maintain the correct belt adjustment.

**6** On the V-belt type, Ford technicians use a special tension gauge for checking drivebelt adjustment, but for DIY purposes, checking the belt tension using firm finger pressure gives a good indication of correct adjustment. This is

done midway between the pulleys, on the longest run of the belt.

**7** If adjustment is necessary, proceed as follows according to belt type.

### V-belt with sliding arm type adjuster

**8** Open the bonnet. Jack up the front right-hand side of the vehicle, and support it securely on an axle stand. Remove the roadwheel, then remove the auxiliary drivebelt lower cover from inside the wheel arch.

**9** Apply firm finger pressure midway between the pulleys on the longest run of the belt, and look for a deflection of 2.0 mm (i.e. a total drivebelt "swing" of 4.0 mm). If adjustment is required, loosen off the alternator mounting and drivebelt adjustment bolts, pivot the alternator as required to provide the correct drivebelt tension, then retighten the bolts to the specified torque setting **(see illustrations)**.

**10** Refit the auxiliary drivebelt cover and roadwheel, then lower the vehicle to the ground.

**11** Run the engine for about five minutes, then recheck the tension.

### V-belt with rack-and-pinion type adjuster

**12** Open the bonnet. Jack up the front right-hand side of the vehicle, and support it securely on an axle stand. Remove the roadwheel, then remove the auxiliary drivebelt lower cover from inside the wheel arch.

**13** Check the adjustment as described in paragraph 9. If adjustment is required, loosen

**3.3** Removing the auxiliary drivebelt lower cover (arrowed) from inside the wheel arch

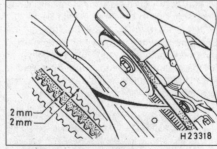

**3.9a  Checking drivebelt adjustment - V-belt types**
*The 4 mm dimension is the total belt swing and is equal to 2 mm of deflection*

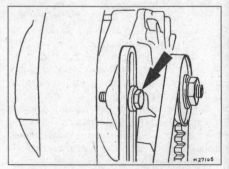

**3.9b** Alternator upper mounting/sliding arm adjuster bolt (arrowed) - V-belt with sliding arm type adjuster

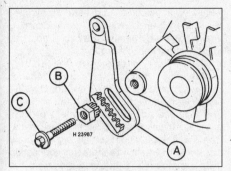

**3.13 Rack-and-pinion type auxiliary drivebelt adjuster**

A   *Adjuster arm*
B   *Pinion (adjuster) nut*
C   *Central (locking) bolt*

**3.23 Automatic drivebelt tensioner - "polyvee" type drivebelt**
*Turn tensioner clockwise to release tension*

## 4 Underbonnet check for fluid leaks and hose condition

*Caution: Renewal of air conditioning hoses must be left to a dealer service department or air conditioning specialist who has the equipment to depressurise the system safely. Never remove air conditioning components or hoses until the system has been depressurised.*

### General

1 High temperatures in the engine compartment can cause the deterioration of the rubber and plastic hoses used for engine, accessory and emissions systems operation. Periodic inspection should be made for cracks, loose clamps, material hardening and leaks.

2 Carefully check the large top and bottom radiator hoses, along with the other smaller-diameter cooling system hoses and metal pipes; do not forget the heater hoses/pipes which run from the engine to the bulkhead. Inspect each hose along its entire length, replacing any that is cracked, swollen or shows signs of deterioration. Cracks may become more apparent if the hose is squeezed. If you are using non-Ford specification antifreeze, and so have to renew the coolant every two years or so, it's a good idea to renew the hoses at that time, regardless of their apparent condition.

3 Make sure that all hose connections are tight. A leak in the cooling system will usually show up as white- or rust-coloured deposits on the areas adjoining the leak; if the spring clamps that are used to secure the hoses in this system appear to be slackening, they should be renewed to prevent the possibility of leaks.

4 Some other hoses are secured to their fittings with clamps. Where clamps are used, check to be sure they haven't lost their tension, allowing the hose to leak. If clamps aren't used, make sure the hose has not expanded and/or hardened where it slips over the fitting, allowing it to leak.

5 Check all fluid reservoirs, filler caps, drain plugs and fittings etc, looking for any signs of leakage of oil, transmission and/or brake hydraulic fluid, coolant and power steering fluid. If the vehicle is regularly parked in the same place, close inspection of the ground underneath it will soon show any leaks; ignore the puddle of water which will be left if the air conditioning system is in use. As soon as a leak is detected, its source must be traced and rectified. Where oil has been leaking for some time, it is usually necessary to use a steam cleaner, pressure washer or similar, to clean away the accumulated dirt, so that (when the engine is run again) the exact source of the leak can be identified.

off the alternator mounting bolts and the adjusting arm mounting bolt. Slacken the pinion central locking bolt, and turn the pinion nut as required to take up the tension of the drivebelt **(see illustration)**. Hold it at the required setting, and tighten the central bolt securely to lock the adjuster arm and set the tension.

14 Tighten the alternator mounting and adjusting arm bolts securely.

15 Refit the auxiliary drivebelt cover and roadwheel, then lower the vehicle to the ground.

16 Run the engine for about five minutes, then recheck the tension.

### Flat "polyvee" type drivebelt

17 As mentioned above, this type of drivebelt is tensioned by an automatic tensioner; regular checks are not required, and manual "adjustment" is not possible.

18 If you suspect that the drivebelt is slipping and/or running slack, or that the tensioner is otherwise faulty, it must be renewed. To do this, remove the drivebelt as described below, then unbolt and remove the tensioner. On fitting the new tensioner, ensure that it is aligned correctly on its mountings, and tightened to the specified torque wrench setting.

### Renewal

19 Open the bonnet. Jack up the front right-hand side of the vehicle, and support it securely on an axle stand. Remove the roadwheel, then remove the auxiliary drivebelt lower cover from inside the wheel arch.

20 The routing of the drivebelt around the pulleys is dependent on the drivebelt type, and on whether power steering and/or air conditioning is fitted. Before removing the drivebelt, it's a good idea to sketch the belt run around the pulleys; this will save a lot of frustration when it comes to refitting.

21 If the existing drivebelt is to be refitted, mark it, or note the maker's markings on its flat surface, so that it can be installed the same way round.

22 To renew the V-belt type of drivebelt, slacken the belt tension fully as described above, according to type. Slip the belt off the pulleys, then fit the new belt, ensuring that it is routed correctly. With the belt in position, adjust the tension as previously described.

23 To renew the flat, "polyvee" type drivebelt, reach up between the body and the engine (above the crankshaft pulley), and apply a spanner to the hexagon in the centre of the automatic tensioner's pulley. Rotate the tensioner pulley clockwise to release its pressure on the drivebelt, then slip the drivebelt off the crankshaft pulley, and release the tensioner again **(see illustration)**. Note that on certain models, a self-cocking tensioner is fitted, and that this will remain in the released position. Working from the wheel arch or engine compartment as necessary, and noting its routing, slip the drivebelt off the remaining pulleys and withdraw it.

24 Check all the pulleys, ensuring that their grooves are clean, and removing all traces of oil and grease. Check that the tensioner works properly, with strong spring pressure being felt when its pulley is rotated clockwise, and a smooth return to the limit of its travel when released.

25 If the original drivebelt is being refitted, use the marks or notes made on removal, to ensure that it is installed to run in the same direction as it was previously. To fit the drivebelt, arrange it on the grooved pulleys so that it is centred in their grooves, and not overlapping their raised sides, and is routed correctly. Start at the top, and work down to finish at the crankshaft pulley; rotate the tensioner pulley clockwise, slip the drivebelt onto the crankshaft pulley, then release the tensioner again.

26 Using a spanner applied to the crankshaft pulley bolt, rotate the crankshaft through at least two full turns clockwise to settle the drivebelt on the pulleys, then check that the drivebelt is properly installed.

27 Refit the auxiliary drivebelt cover and roadwheel, then lower the vehicle to the ground.

**1**

## Vacuum hoses

**6** It's quite common for vacuum hoses, especially those in the emissions system, to be colour-coded, or to be identified by coloured stripes moulded into them. Various systems require hoses with different wall thicknesses, collapse resistance and temperature resistance. When renewing hoses, be sure the new ones are made of the same material.

**7** Often the only effective way to check a hose is to remove it completely from the vehicle. If more than one hose is removed, be sure to label the hoses and fittings to ensure correct installation.

**8** When checking vacuum hoses, be sure to include any plastic T-fittings in the check. Inspect the fittings for cracks, and check the hose where it fits over the fitting for distortion, which could cause leakage.

**9** A small piece of vacuum hose (quarter-inch inside diameter) can be used as a stethoscope to detect vacuum leaks. Hold one end of the hose to your ear, and probe around vacuum hoses and fittings, listening for the "hissing" sound characteristic of a vacuum leak.

 *Warning: When probing with the vacuum-hose stethoscope, be very careful not to come into contact with moving engine components such as the auxiliary drivebelt, radiator electric cooling fan, etc.*

## Fuel hoses

 *Warning: There are certain precautions which must be taken when inspecting or servicing fuel system components. Work in a well-ventilated area, and don't allow open flames (cigarettes, appliance pilot lights, etc.) or bare light bulbs near the work area. Mop up spills immediately, and don't store fuel-soaked rags where they could ignite.*

**10** Check all fuel hoses for deterioration and chafing. Check especially for cracks in areas where the hose bends, and also just before fittings, such as where a hose attaches to the fuel filter.

**11** High-quality fuel line, usually identified by the word "Fluoroelastomer" printed on the hose, should be used for fuel line renewal. Never, under any circumstances, use unreinforced vacuum line, clear plastic tubing or water hose for fuel lines.

**12** Spring-type clamps are commonly used on fuel lines. These clamps often lose their tension over a period of time, and can be "sprung" during removal. Replace all spring-type clamps with screw clamps whenever a hose is replaced.

## Metal lines

**13** Sections of metal piping are often used for fuel line between the fuel filter and the engine. Check carefully to be sure the piping has not been bent or crimped, and that cracks have not started in the line.

**14** If a section of metal fuel line must be renewed, only seamless steel piping should be used, since copper and aluminium piping don't have the strength necessary to withstand normal engine vibration.

**15** Check the metal brake lines where they enter the master cylinder and ABS hydraulic unit (if used) for cracks in the lines or loose fittings. Any sign of brake fluid leakage calls for an immediate and thorough inspection of the brake system.

## 5 Engine compartment wiring check

**1** With the vehicle parked on level ground, apply the handbrake firmly and open the bonnet. Using an inspection light or a small electric torch, check all visible wiring within and beneath the engine compartment.

**2** What you are looking for is wiring that is obviously damaged by chafing against sharp edges, or against moving suspension/transmission components and/or the auxiliary drivebelt, by being trapped or crushed between carelessly-refitted components, or melted by being forced into contact with the hot engine castings, coolant pipes, etc. In almost all cases, damage of this sort is caused in the first instance by incorrect routing on reassembly, after previous work has been carried out.

**3** Depending on the extent of the problem, damaged wiring may be repaired by rejoining the break or splicing-in a new length of wire, using solder to ensure a good connection, and remaking the insulation with adhesive insulating tape or heat-shrink tubing, as appropriate. If the damage is extensive, given the implications for the vehicle's future reliability, the best long-term answer may well be to renew that entire section of the loom, however expensive this may appear.

**4** When the actual damage has been repaired, ensure that the wiring loom is re-routed correctly, so that it is clear of other components, and not stretched or kinked, and is secured out of harm's way using the plastic clips, guides and ties provided.

**5** Check all electrical connectors, ensuring that they are clean, securely fastened, and that each is locked by its plastic tabs or wire clip, as appropriate. If any connector shows external signs of corrosion (accumulations of white or green deposits, or streaks of "rust"), or if any is thought to be dirty, it must be unplugged and cleaned using electrical contact cleaner. If the connector pins are severely corroded, the connector must be renewed; note that this may mean the renewal of that entire section of the loom - see your local Ford dealer for details.

**6** If the cleaner completely removes the corrosion to leave the connector in a satisfactory condition, it would be wise to pack the connector with a suitable material which will exclude dirt and moisture, preventing the corrosion from occurring again; a Ford dealer may be able to recommend a suitable product.

**7** Check the condition of the battery connections - remake the connections or renew the leads if a fault is found. Use the same techniques to ensure that all earth points in the engine compartment provide good electrical contact through clean, metal-to-metal joints, and that all are securely fastened. (In addition to the earth connection at the engine lifting eye, and that from the transmission to the body/battery, there are others in various places, so check carefully).

**8** Refer to Section 23 for details of spark plug (HT) lead checks.

## 6 Air conditioning system check

 *Warning: The air conditioning system is under high pressure. Do not loosen any fittings or remove any components until after the system has been discharged. Air conditioning refrigerant must be properly discharged into an approved container, at a dealer service department or an automotive air conditioning repair facility capable of handling the refrigerant safely. Always wear eye protection when disconnecting air conditioning system fittings.*

**1** The following maintenance checks should be performed on a regular basis, to ensure that the air conditioner continues to operate at peak efficiency:

a) *Check the auxiliary drivebelt. If it is worn or deteriorated, renew it (see Section 3).*

b) *Check the system hoses. Look for cracks, bubbles, hard spots and deterioration. Inspect the hoses and all fittings for oil bubbles and seepage. If there's any evidence of wear, damage or leaks, renew the hose(s).*

c) *Inspect the condenser fins for leaves, insects and other debris. Use a "fin comb" or compressed air to clean the condenser.*

d) *Check that the drain tube from the front of the evaporator is clear - note that it is normal to have clear fluid (water) dripping from this while the system is in operation, to the extent that quite a large puddle can be left under the vehicle when it is parked.*

 *Warning: Wear eye protection when using compressed air!*

**2** It's a good idea to operate the system for about 30 minutes at least once a month, particularly during the Winter. Long term non-use can cause hardening, and subsequent failure, of the seals.

**3** Because of the complexity of the air conditioning system and the special equipment necessary to service it, in-depth fault diagnosis and repairs are not included in

**8.2 These tools are required when changing the engine oil and filter**

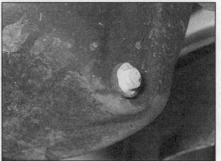

**8.7a Engine oil drain plug location in the sump on HCS and CVH engines**

**8.7b Removing the engine oil drain plug on the Zetec engine**

**8.9 Removing the oil filter on the CVH engine using a strap wrench**

**8.10 Lubricate the filter's sealing ring with clean engine oil before installing the filter**

this manual. For more complete information on the air conditioning system, refer to the Haynes *"Automotive Heating and Air Conditioning Manual"*.

4 The most common cause of poor cooling is simply a low system refrigerant charge. If a noticeable drop in cool-air output occurs, the following quick check will help you determine if the refrigerant level is low.

5 Warm up the engine to operating temperature.

6 Place the air conditioning temperature selector at the coldest setting, and put the blower at the highest setting. Open the doors - to make sure the air conditioning system doesn't cycle off as soon as it cools the passenger compartment.

7 With the compressor engaged - the clutch will make an audible click, and the centre of the clutch will rotate - feel the inlet and outlet pipes at the compressor. One side should be cold, and one hot. If there's no perceptible difference between the two pipes, there's something wrong with the compressor or the system. It might be a low charge - it might be something else. Take the vehicle to a dealer service department or an automotive air conditioning specialist.

## 7 Valve clearance adjustment (HCS and Endura-E engines)

Refer to Chapter 2A.

## 8 Engine oil and filter renewal

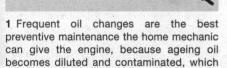

1 Frequent oil changes are the best preventive maintenance the home mechanic can give the engine, because ageing oil becomes diluted and contaminated, which leads to premature engine wear.

2 Make sure that you have all the necessary tools before you begin this procedure **(see illustration)**. You should also have plenty of rags or newspapers handy, for mopping up any spills. To avoid any possibility of scalding, and to protect yourself from possible skin irritants and other harmful contaminants in

used engine oils, it is advisable to wear gloves when carrying out this work.

3 Access to the underside of the vehicle is greatly improved if the vehicle can be lifted on a hoist, driven onto ramps, or supported by axle stands (see *"Jacking and Vehicle Support"*).

⚠️ **Warning: Do not work under a vehicle which is supported only by a jack, or by bricks, blocks of wood, etc.**

4 If this is your first oil change, get under the vehicle and familiarise yourself with the position of the engine oil drain plug location in the sump. The engine and exhaust components will be warm during the actual work, so try to anticipate any potential problems while the engine and accessories are cool.

5 The oil should preferably be changed when the engine is still fully warmed-up to normal operating temperature, just after a run (the needle on the temperature gauge should be in the "Normal" sector of the gauge); warm oil and sludge will flow out more easily. Park the vehicle on firm, level ground, apply the handbrake firmly, then select 1st or reverse gear (manual transmission) or the "P" position (automatic transmission). Open the bonnet and remove the engine oil filler cap from the cylinder head cover, then remove the oil level dipstick from its tube (see *"Weekly Checks"*).

6 Raise the front of the vehicle, and support it securely on axle stands (see *"Jacking and Vehicle Support"*). Remove the front right-hand roadwheel to provide access to the oil filter; if the additional working clearance is required, remove also the auxiliary drivebelt cover.

7 Being careful not to touch the hot exhaust components, place the drain pan under the drain plug, and unscrew the plug **(see illustrations)**. If possible, try to keep the plug pressed into the sump while unscrewing it by hand the last couple of turns.

**As the drain plug releases from the threads, move it away sharply, so the stream of oil issuing from the sump runs into the pan, not up your sleeve!**

8 Allow some time for the old oil to drain, noting that it may be necessary to reposition the pan as the oil flow slows to a trickle. Check the condition of the plug's sealing washer and renew it if worn or damaged. When the oil has completely drained, wipe clean the drain plug and its threads in the sump and refit the plug, tightening it to the specified torque wrench setting.

9 Reposition the drain pan under the oil filter then, using a suitable filter removal tool, unscrew the oil filter from the cylinder block; be prepared for some oil spillage **(see illustration)**. Check the old filter to make sure that the rubber sealing ring hasn't stuck to the engine; if it has, carefully remove it. Withdraw the filter through the wheel arch, taking care to spill as little oil as possible.

10 Using a clean, lint-free rag, wipe clean the cylinder block around the filter mounting. If there are no specific instructions supplied with it, fit a new oil filter as follows. Apply a light coating of clean engine oil to the filter's sealing ring **(see illustration)**. Screw the filter

1

into position on the engine until it seats, then tighten it through a further half- to three-quarters of a turn *only*. Tighten the filter by hand only - do not use any tools.

**11** Remove the old oil and all tools from under the vehicle, refit the roadwheel, and lower the vehicle to the ground.

**12** Refill the engine with oil, using the correct grade and type of oil, as given in *"Lubricants, fluids and tyre pressures"*. Pour in half the specified quantity of oil first, then wait a few minutes for the oil to fall to the sump. Continue adding oil a small quantity at a time, until the level is up to the lower notch on the dipstick. Adding approximately 0.5 to 1.0 litre will raise the level to the dipstick's upper notch.

**13** Start the engine. The oil pressure warning light will take a few seconds to go out while the new filter fills with oil; do not race the engine while the light is on. Run the engine for a few minutes, while checking for leaks around the oil filter seal and the drain plug.

**14** Switch off the engine, and wait a few minutes for the oil to settle in the sump once more. With the new oil circulated and the filter now completely full, recheck the level on the dipstick, and add more oil as necessary.

**15** Dispose of the used engine oil safely, with reference to *"General repair procedures"*.

*Note: It is antisocial and illegal to dump oil down the drain. To find the location of your local oil recycling bank, call this number free.*

OIL BANK LINE
**0800 66 33 66**

## 9 Clutch pedal free play adjustment (1996 models onward)

**Note:** *This adjustment is only applicable to 1996 models onwards with manual clutch adjustment, and earlier models which have been converted from automatic to manual adjustment retrospectively.*

**1** The clutch pedal free play is checked by measuring the clutch pedal travel. Before doing this, settle the cable by depressing and releasing the pedal a few times (at least ten times if new clutch components or cable have been fitted).

**2** Ensure that there are no obstructions beneath the clutch pedal then measure the distance from the third groove of the clutch pedal rubber to the floor with the pedal in the at-rest position. Depress the clutch pedal fully, and again measure the distance from the third groove of the pedal rubber to the floor.

**3** Subtract the second measurement from the first to obtain the clutch pedal travel. If this is

**10.1 Unscrewing the manual transmission oil filler/level plug**

not within the range given in the Specifications, adjust the clutch as follows.

**4** Locate the cable adjuster which is a bolt which protrudes through an opening near the top of the clutch pedal.

**5** To increase the pedal travel, turn the adjuster clockwise; to decrease the travel, turn the adjuster anti-clockwise.

**6** Recheck the pedal travel and make any further adjustments as necessary until the correct setting is obtained.

## 10 Manual transmission oil level check

**1** The manual transmission does not have a dipstick. To check the oil level, raise the vehicle and support it securely on axle stands, making sure that the vehicle is level (see *"Jacking and Vehicle Support"*). On the lower front side of the transmission housing, you will see the filler/level plug. Unscrew and remove it - an Allen key or bit will probably be required **(see illustration)**. If the lubricant level is correct, the oil should be up to the lower edge of the hole.

**2** If the transmission needs more lubricant (if the oil level is not up to the hole), use a syringe, or a plastic bottle and tube, to add more **(see illustration)**. Stop filling the transmission when the lubricant begins to run out of the hole.

**3** Refit the filler/level plug, and tighten it to the specified torque wrench setting. Drive the vehicle a short distance, then check for leaks.

**4** The need for regular topping-up can only be due to a leak, which should be found and rectified without delay.

## 11 Idle speed and mixture check and adjustment (HCS and CVH engines)

### General

**1** Many of the engines fitted to Escort and Orion models are equipped with fuel injection systems of one sort or another which are entirely controlled by the engine management

**10.2 Topping-up the oil level in the B5 type transmission**

system. On most of these vehicles, it isn't possible to make any adjustments to the idle speed or the mixture settings without specialist test equipment of a type usually only found at a Ford dealer or fuel injection specialist. However, the very nature of these highly-sophisticated systems means they don't go out of tune very often (if ever), so that it's one less maintenance operation to worry about.

**2** On carburettor engines and 1.6 litre EFi fuel injection engines, certain checks and adjustments are necessary as part of the service requirements, and these are described below.

### Idle speed and mixture check and adjustment - carburettor engines

**3** Before carrying out the following checks and adjustments, ensure that the spark plugs are in good condition and correctly gapped (Section 23). To carry out the checks/adjustments, an accurate tachometer and an exhaust gas analyser (CO meter) will be required.

**4** Make sure that all electrical components are switched off during the following procedures.

**5** Connect a tachometer to the engine in accordance with its manufacturer's instructions, and insert the probe of an exhaust gas analyser (CO meter) into the exhaust tailpipe. As previously mentioned, these items are essential in obtaining an accurate setting. If they are not available, an approximate check/adjustment can be made as a temporary measure, providing they are further checked out as soon as is possible using a tachometer and a CO meter (or by a Ford dealer).

**6** Run the engine at a fast idle speed until it reaches its normal operating temperature and the radiator cooling fan cuts in. Turn the engine off, then disconnect the radiator cooling fan lead at the thermostatic switch connector. Now connect a temporary wire to the fan switch multi-plug, as shown **(see illustration)** to enable the fan to operate continuously during the following checks and adjustments (if this is specified). Take care to keep clear of the fan during the following

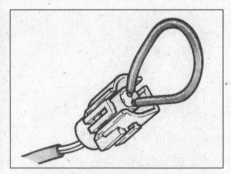

**11.6 Cooling fan thermostatic switch multi-plug with temporary bridging wire**

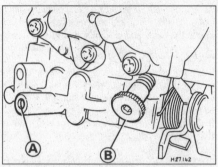

**11.11 Carburettor idle mixture adjustment screw (A) and idle speed screw (B)**

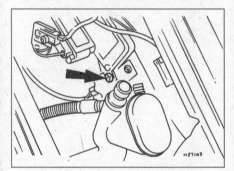

**11.16 Mixture CO adjusting screw (arrowed) on the 1.6 litre EFi engine**

**11.18 Base idle speed screw (arrowed) in throttle housing on the 1.6 litre EFi engine**

operations when working in the engine compartment.

**7** Where fitted, disconnect the throttle kicker vacuum pipe, and plug the end. To identify the throttle kicker unit, refer to Chapter 4A.

**8** Check that the vehicle lighting and other electrical loadings (apart from the radiator cooling fan) are switched off, then restart the engine. Increase the engine speed to 3000 rpm for 30 seconds, and repeat this at three-minute intervals during the check/adjustment procedures. This will ensure that any excess fuel is cleared from the inlet manifold.

**9** Ensure that the throttle is fully released, allow the meters to stabilise for a period of 3 to 5 seconds, then check the idle speed against that specified. If adjustment is necessary, turn the idle speed screw until the engine is idling at the specified speed. Any checks and adjustments must be completed within 30 seconds of the meters stabilising.

**10** If adjustment to the mixture is required, the tamperproof cap will need to be removed from the carburettor to gain access to the mixture screw. To do this, first unclip the fuel trap from the side of the air cleaner unit, then remove the air cleaner unit, ensuring that the crankcase ventilation hose remains connected. Prise free the tamperproof cap (with the aid of a thin-bladed screwdriver), reconnect the vacuum and emission control pipes, and temporarily refit the air cleaner unit into position.

**11** Turn the mixture adjustment screw clockwise to weaken the mixture, or anti-clockwise to richen it, until the CO reading is as given in the Specifications **(see illustration)**. If

a CO meter is not being used, weaken the mixture as described, then enrich the mixture until the maximum engine speed is obtained, consistent with even running.

**12** If necessary, re-adjust the idle speed then check the CO reading again. Repeat as necessary until both the idle speed and CO reading are correct.

**13** Where required by law (as in some European countries), fit a new tamperproof cap to the mixture adjustment screw.

**14** Disconnect the tachometer and the CO meter, refit the air cleaner unit, and reconnect the fan switch lead to complete.

### Base idle speed and mixture check and adjustment - 1.6 litre EFi engines

**15** Proceed as described above in paragraphs 4 to 6 inclusive, then continue as follows.

**16** Run the engine at a fast idle speed until it reaches its normal operating temperature and the cooling fan cuts in. Check the CO content of the exhaust, and compare it against the specified reading. If the CO content reading is incorrect, it can be adjusted by prising free the tamperproof cap for access to the CO adjustment screw **(see illustration)**, and turning the screw in the required direction to suit.

**17** Check the base idle speed by first disconnecting the multi-plug from the idle speed control valve. Increase the engine speed to 2000 rpm, hold that speed for 30 seconds, then fully release the throttle and check if the base idle speed registered is as specified.

**18** If adjustment is necessary, prise free the tamperproof plug using a suitable small screwdriver to gain access to the base idle adjustment screw in the throttle body. Turn the screw in the required direction to adjust the base idle speed to the specified amount. Turning the screw anti-clockwise increases the idle speed **(see illustration)**.

**19** Repeat the procedure outlined in paragraph 17 to recheck and further adjust the base idle speed if required, then fit a new tamperproof plug into position.

**20** Reconnect the idle speed control valve multi-plug, and check that the engine speed briefly rises to about 900 rpm, then drops down to the specified normal idle speed.

**21** On completion, disconnect the tachometer and the CO meter, but run the engine at idle speed for another five minutes, to enable the engine management module to relearn its values before switching it off.

**1**

## 12 Steering, suspension and roadwheel check

### Front suspension and steering check

**1** Chock the rear wheels then jack up the front of the car and support it on axle stands (see *"Jacking and Vehicle Support"*).

**2** Visually inspect the balljoint dust covers and the steering gear gaiters for splits, chafing or deterioration **(see illustrations)**. Any wear

**12.2a Check the condition of the track rod end balljoint dust cover (arrowed)**

**12.2b Check the condition of the lower arm balljoint dust cover (arrowed) . . .**

**12.2c . . . and check the condition of the steering rack gaiters**

of these components will cause loss of lubricant, together with dirt and water entry, resulting in rapid deterioration of the balljoints or steering gear.

**3** Check the power-assisted steering fluid hoses (where fitted) for chafing or deterioration, and the pipe and hose unions for fluid leaks. Also check for signs of fluid leakage under pressure from the steering gear rubber gaiters, which would indicate failed fluid seals within the steering gear.

**4** Grasp the roadwheel at the 12 o'clock and 6 o'clock positions, and try to rock it. Very slight free play may be felt, but if the movement is appreciable, further investigation is necessary to determine the source. Continue rocking the wheel while an assistant depresses the footbrake. If the movement is now eliminated or significantly reduced, it is likely that the hub bearings are at fault. If the free play is still evident with the footbrake depressed, then there is wear in the suspension joints or mountings.

**5** Now grasp the wheel at the 9 o'clock and 3 o'clock positions, and try to rock it as before. Any movement felt now may again be caused by wear in the hub bearings or the steering track rod balljoints. If the outer track rod end balljoint is worn, the visual movement will be obvious. If the inner joint is suspect, it can be felt by placing a hand over the rack-and-pinion rubber gaiter, and gripping the track rod. If the wheel is now rocked, movement will be felt at the inner joint if wear has taken place.

**6** Using a large screwdriver or flat bar, check for wear in the suspension mounting bushes by levering between the relevant suspension component and its attachment point. Some movement is to be expected, as the mountings are made of rubber, but excessive wear should be obvious. Also check the condition of any visible rubber bushes, looking for splits, cracks or contamination of the rubber.

**7** With the vehicle standing on its wheels, have an assistant turn the steering wheel back-and-forth, about an eighth of a turn each way. There should be very little, if any, lost movement between the steering wheel and roadwheels. If this is not the case, closely observe the joints and mountings previously described, but in addition, check the steering column universal joints for wear, and also check the rack-and-pinion steering gear itself.

### Rear suspension check

**8** Chock the front wheels then jack up the rear of the car and support it on axle stands (see "Jacking and Vehicle Support"). Remove the rear roadwheels.

**9** Check the rear hub bearings for wear, using the method described for the front hub bearings (paragraph 4).

**10** Using a large screwdriver or flat bar, check for wear in the suspension mounting bushes by levering between the relevant suspension component and its attachment point. Some movement is to be expected, as the mountings are made of rubber, but excessive wear should be obvious. Check the condition of the shock absorbers and their bushes/mountings. On Van models, check the leaves of the leaf springs for signs of cracking, distortion, or other damage.

### Roadwheel check and balancing

**11** Periodically remove the roadwheels, and clean any dirt or mud from the inside and outside surfaces. Examine the wheel rims for signs of rusting, corrosion or other damage. Light alloy wheels are easily damaged by "kerbing" whilst parking, and similarly, steel wheels may become dented or buckled. Renewal of the wheel is very often the only course of remedial action possible.

**12** The balance of each wheel and tyre assembly should be maintained, not only to avoid excessive tyre wear, but also to avoid wear in the steering and suspension components. Wheel imbalance is normally signified by vibration through the vehicle's bodyshell, although in many cases it is particularly noticeable through the steering wheel. Conversely, it should be noted that wear or damage in suspension or steering components may cause excessive tyre wear. Out-of-round or out-of-true tyres, damaged wheels and wheel bearing wear/maladjustment also fall into this category. Balancing will not usually cure vibration caused by such wear.

**13** Wheel balancing may be carried out with the wheel either on or off the vehicle. If balanced on the vehicle, ensure that the wheel-to-hub relationship is marked in some way prior to subsequent wheel removal, so that it may be refitted in its original position.

## 13 Driveshaft rubber gaiters and CV joints check

**1** The driveshaft rubber gaiters are very important, because they prevent dirt, water and foreign material from entering and damaging the constant velocity (CV) joints. External contamination can cause the gaiter material to deteriorate prematurely, so it's a

**13.2 Check the driveshaft gaiters by hand for cracks and/or leaking grease**

good idea to wash the gaiters with soap and water occasionally.

**2** With the vehicle raised and securely supported on axle stands (see "Jacking and Vehicle Support"), turn the steering onto full-lock, then slowly rotate each front wheel in turn. Inspect the condition of the outer constant velocity (CV) joint rubber gaiters, squeezing the gaiters to open out the folds. Check for signs of cracking, splits, or deterioration of the rubber, which may allow the escape of grease, and lead to the ingress of water and grit into the joint **(see illustration)**. Also check the security and condition of the retaining clips. Repeat these checks on the inner CV joints. If any damage or deterioration is found, the gaiters should be renewed as described in Chapter 8.

**3** At the same time, check the general condition of the outer CV joints themselves, by first holding the driveshaft and attempting to rotate the wheels. Any appreciable movement in the CV joint indicates wear in the joint, wear in the driveshaft splines, or a loose driveshaft retaining nut. Repeat this check on the inner joints, by holding the inner joint yoke and attempting to rotate the driveshaft.

## 14 Exhaust system check

**1** With the engine cold (at least three hours after the vehicle has been driven), check the complete exhaust system, from its starting point at the engine to the end of the tailpipe. Ideally, this should be done on a hoist, where unrestricted access is available; if a hoist is not available, raise and support the vehicle on axle stands (see "Jacking and Vehicle Support").

**2** Check the pipes and connections for evidence of leaks, severe corrosion, or damage. Make sure that all brackets and rubber mountings are in good condition, and tight; if any of the mountings are to be renewed, ensure that the replacements are of the correct type (see illustration). Leakage at any of the joints or in other parts of the system will usually show up as a black sooty stain in the vicinity of the leak. **Note:** Exhaust sealants

**14.2 If any of the exhaust system rubber mountings are to be renewed, ensure that the replacements are of the correct type - their colour is a good guide. Those nearest to the catalytic converter are more heat-resistant than the others**

*should not be used on any part of the exhaust system upstream of the catalytic converter - even if the sealant does not contain additives harmful to the converter, pieces of it may break off and foul the element, causing local overheating.*

3 At the same time, inspect the underside of the body for holes, corrosion, open seams, etc, which may allow exhaust gases to enter the passenger compartment. Seal all body openings with silicone or body putty.

4 Rattles and other noises can often be traced to the exhaust system, especially the rubber mountings. Try to move the system, silencer(s) and catalytic converter. If any components can touch the body or suspension parts, secure the exhaust system with new mountings.

5 Check the running condition of the engine by inspecting inside the end of the tailpipe; the exhaust deposits here are an indication of the engine's state of tune. The inside of the tailpipe should be dry, and should vary in colour from dark grey to light grey/brown; if it is black and sooty, or coated with white deposits, the engine is in need of a thorough fuel system inspection.

## 15 Underbody and fuel/brake line check

1 With the vehicle raised and supported on axle stands or over an inspection pit, thoroughly inspect the underbody and wheel arches for signs of damage and corrosion. In particular, examine the bottom of the side sills, and any concealed areas where mud can collect. Where corrosion and rust is evident, press and tap firmly on the panel with a screwdriver, and check for any serious corrosion which would necessitate repairs. If the panel is not seriously corroded, clean away the rust, and apply a new coating of underseal. Refer to Chapter 11 for more details of body repairs.

2 At the same time, inspect the PVC-coated lower body panels for stone damage and general condition.

3 Inspect all of the fuel and brake lines on the underbody for damage, rust, corrosion and leakage. Also make sure that they are correctly supported in their clips. Where applicable, check the PVC coating on the lines for damage.

## 16 Brake system check

**Note:** *For detailed photographs of the brake system, refer to Chapter 9.*

1 The work described in this Section should be carried out at the specified intervals, or whenever a defect is suspected in the braking system. Any of the following symptoms could indicate a potential brake system defect:

a) *The vehicle pulls to one side when the brake pedal is depressed.*
b) *The brakes make scraping or dragging noises when applied.*
c) *Brake pedal travel is excessive.*
d) *The brake fluid requires repeated topping-up.*

2 A thorough inspection should be made to confirm the thickness of the linings, as follows:

### Disc brakes

3 Jack up the front or rear of the vehicle, as applicable, and support it on axle stands (see *"Jacking and Vehicle Support"*). Where rear brake pads are fitted, also jack up the rear of the vehicle and support on axle stands.

4 For better access to the brake calipers, remove the wheels.

5 Look through the inspection window in the caliper, and check that the thickness of the friction lining material on each of the pads is not less than the recommended minimum thickness given in the Specifications. **Note:** *Bear in mind that the lining material is normally bonded to a metal backing plate.*

6 If it is difficult to determine the exact thickness of the pad linings, or if you are at all concerned about the condition of the pads, then remove them from the calipers for further inspection (refer to Chapter 9).

7 Check the remaining brake caliper(s) in the same way.

8 If any one of the brake pads has worn down to, or below, the specified limit, *all four* pads at that end of the car must be renewed as a set (ie all the front pads or all the rear pads).

9 Measure the thickness of the discs with a micrometer, if available, to make sure that they still have service life remaining. If any disc is thinner than the specified minimum thickness, renew it (refer to Chapter 9). In any case, check the general condition of the discs. Look for excessive scoring and discolouration caused by overheating. If these conditions exist, remove the relevant disc and have it resurfaced or renewed (refer to Chapter 9).

10 Before refitting the wheels, check all brake lines and hoses (refer to Chapter 9). In particular, check the flexible hoses in the vicinity of the calipers, where they are subjected to most movement. Bend them between the fingers (but do not actually bend them double, or the casing may be damaged) and check that this does not reveal previously-hidden cracks, cuts or splits.

### Rear drum brakes

11 Chock the front wheels, then jack up the rear of the vehicle and support on axle stands (see *"Jacking and Vehicle Support"*).

12 For better access, remove the rear wheels.

13 To check the brake shoe lining thickness without removing the brake drums, prise the rubber plugs from the backplates, and use an electric torch and mirror to inspect the linings of the leading brake shoes. Check that the thickness of the lining material on the brake shoes is not less than the recommendation given in the Specifications.

14 If it is difficult to determine the exact thickness of the brake shoe linings, or if you are at all concerned about the condition of the shoes, then remove the rear drums for a more comprehensive inspection (refer to Chapter 9).

15 With the drum removed, check the shoe return and hold-down springs for correct installation, and check the wheel cylinders for leakage of brake fluid. Check the friction surface of the brake drums for scoring and discoloration. If excessive, the drum should be resurfaced or renewed.

16 Before refitting the wheels, check all brake lines and hoses (refer to Chapter 9). On completion, apply the handbrake and check that the rear wheels are locked. The handbrake also requires periodic adjustment, and if its travel seems excessive, refer to Section 28.

## 17 Roadwheel nut tightness check

1 Apply the handbrake.

2 Remove the wheel covers, using the flat end of the wheelbrace supplied in the tool kit (on some models it will be necessary to unscrew the retaining bolts with a special key).

3 Using the wheelbrace, slacken each of the roadwheel nuts one quarter turn. If a nut is jammed, rusted or damaged making it difficult to undo, the wheel must be taken off and any dirt and mud on its interior and exterior surfaces, and on the disc/drum support surfaces, removed (see also Section 12). Using a wire brush, clean the thread of the bolts to eliminate rust, corrosion or any other matter. Grease the thread of each bolt with a thin layer of copper grease or anti-sieze compound and refit the wheel. Repeat as necessary on the other wheels.

4 Working diagonally, tighten the roadwheel nuts to the specified torque wrench setting.

5 Refit the wheel covers.

**1**

## 18 Door, boot, tailgate and bonnet check and lubrication

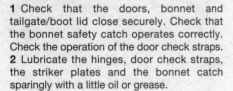

1 Check that the doors, bonnet and tailgate/boot lid close securely. Check that the bonnet safety catch operates correctly. Check the operation of the door check straps.
2 Lubricate the hinges, door check straps, the striker plates and the bonnet catch sparingly with a little oil or grease.

## 19 Seat belt check

1 Check the seat belts for satisfactory operation and condition. Inspect the webbing for fraying and cuts. Check that they retract smoothly and without binding into their reels.
2 Check that the seat belt mounting bolts are tight, and if necessary tighten them to the specified torque wrench setting.

## 20 Bodywork, paint and exterior trim check

1 The best time to carry out this check is after the car has been washed so that any surface blemish or scratch will be clearly evident and not hidden by a film of dirt.
2 Starting at one front corner check the paintwork all around the car, looking for minor scratches or more serious dents. Check all the trim and make sure that it is securely attached over its entire length.
3 Check the security of all door locks, door mirrors, badges, bumpers, front grille and wheel trim. Anything found loose, or in need of further attention should be done with reference to the relevant Chapters of this manual.
4 Rectify any problems noticed with the paintwork or body panels as described in Chapter 11.

## 21 Road test

### *Braking system*

1 Make sure that the vehicle does not pull to one side when braking, and that the wheels do not lock prematurely when braking hard.
2 Check that there is no vibration through the steering when braking.
3 Check that the handbrake operates correctly, without excessive movement of the lever, and that it holds the vehicle stationary on a slope.
4 Test the operation of the brake servo unit as follows. With the engine switched off, depress the footbrake four or five times to exhaust the vacuum, then hold the pedal depressed. Start the engine, and there should be a noticeable "give" in the brake pedal as vacuum builds up. Allow the engine to run for at least two minutes, and then switch it off. If the brake pedal is depressed again, it should be possible to detect a hiss from the servo as the pedal is depressed. After about four or five applications, no further hissing should be heard, and the pedal should feel considerably firmer.

### *Steering and suspension*

5 Check for any abnormalities in the steering, suspension, handling or road "feel".
6 Drive the vehicle, and check that there are no unusual vibrations or noises.
7 Check that the steering feels positive, with no excessive sloppiness or roughness, and check for any suspension noises when cornering and driving over bumps.

### *Drivetrain*

8 Check the performance of the engine, transmission and driveshafts.
9 Check that the engine starts correctly, both when cold and when hot.
10 Listen for any unusual noises from the engine and transmission.
11 Make sure that the engine runs smoothly when idling, and that there is no hesitation when accelerating.
12 On manual transmission models, check that all gears can be engaged smoothly without noise, and that the gear lever action is not abnormally vague or "notchy".
13 On automatic transmission models, make sure that the drive seems smooth without jerks or engine speed "flare-ups". Check that all the gear positions can be selected with the vehicle at rest. If any problems are found, they should be referred to a Ford dealer.
14 Listen for a metallic clicking sound from the front of the vehicle, as the vehicle is driven slowly in a circle with the steering on full-lock. Carry out this check in both directions. If a clicking noise is heard, this indicates wear in a driveshaft joint, in which case renew the joint if necessary.

### *Clutch*

15 Check that the clutch pedal moves smoothly and easily through its full travel, and that the clutch itself functions correctly, with no trace of slip or drag. If the movement is uneven or stiff in places, check that the cable is routed correctly, with no sharp turns.
16 Inspect both ends of the clutch inner cable, both at the transmission end and inside the car, for signs of wear and fraying.
17 Check the pedal self-adjusting mechanism as described in Chapter 6, if necessary.

### *Instruments and electrical equipment*

18 Check the operation of all instruments and electrical equipment.
19 Make sure all instruments read correctly, and switch on all electrical equipment in turn, to check that it functions properly.

## 22 Automatic transmission fluid level check

1 The level of the automatic transmission fluid should be carefully maintained. Low fluid level can lead to slipping or loss of drive, while overfilling can cause foaming, loss of fluid and transmission damage.
2 The transmission fluid level should only be checked when the transmission is hot (at its normal operating temperature). If the vehicle has just been driven over 10 miles (15 miles in a cold climate), and the fluid temperature is 160 to 175°F, the transmission is hot.
*Caution: If the vehicle has just been driven for a long time at high speed or in city traffic in hot weather, or if it has been pulling a trailer, an accurate fluid level reading cannot be obtained. In these circumstances, allow the fluid to cool down for about 30 minutes.*
3 Park on level ground, apply the handbrake, and start the engine. With the engine idling, depress the brake pedal and move the selector lever through all the gear positions three times, beginning and ending in "P".
4 Allow the engine to idle for one minute, then (with the engine still idling) remove the dipstick from its tube. Note the condition and colour of the fluid on the dipstick.
5 Wipe the fluid from the dipstick with a clean rag, and re-insert it into the filler tube until the cap seats.
6 Pull the dipstick out again, and note the fluid level. The level should be between the "MIN" and "MAX" marks. If the level is on the "MIN" mark, stop the engine, and add the specified automatic transmission fluid (see *"Lubricants and fluids"* on page 0•17) through the dipstick tube, using a clean funnel if necessary. It is important not to introduce dirt into the transmission when topping-up.
7 Add the fluid a little at a time, and keep checking the level as previously described until it is correct.
8 The need for regular topping-up of the transmission fluid indicates a leak, which should be found and rectified without delay.
9 The condition of the fluid should also be checked along with the level. If the fluid on the dipstick is black or a dark reddish-brown colour, or if it has a burned smell, the fluid should be changed. If you are in doubt about the condition of the fluid, buy some new fluid, and compare the two for colour and smell.

# Every 20 000 miles or 2 years

## 23 Spark plug renewal

**Note:** *Spark plug renewal at this service interval is only necessary on the HCS, Endura-E, CVH and PTE engines. On the Zetec and Zetec-E engines, the recommended interval for spark plug renewal is every 30 000 miles or three years.*

### Spark plug check and renewal

1 It is vital for the correct running, full performance and proper economy of the engine that the spark plugs perform with maximum efficiency. The most important factor in ensuring this is that the plugs fitted are appropriate for the engine. The suitable type is given in the Specifications Section at the beginning of this Chapter, on the Vehicle Emissions Control Information (VECI) label located on the underside of the bonnet (only on models sold in some areas) or in the vehicle's Owner's Handbook. If the correct type is used and the engine is in good condition, the spark plugs should not need attention between scheduled renewal intervals. Spark plug cleaning is rarely necessary, and should not be attempted unless specialised equipment is available, as damage can easily be caused to the firing ends.

2 Spark plug removal and refitting requires a spark plug socket, with an extension which can be turned by a ratchet handle or similar. This socket is lined with a rubber sleeve, to protect the porcelain insulator of the spark plug, and to hold the plug while you insert it into the spark plug hole. You will also need a set of feeler gauges, to check the spark plug electrode gap, and a torque wrench to tighten the new plugs to the specified torque **(see illustration)**.

3 To remove the spark plugs, first open the bonnet; the plugs are easily reached at the top of the engine. Note how the spark plug (HT) leads are routed and secured by clips, and on some engines, how they're positioned along the channel in the cylinder head cover. To prevent the possibility of mixing up spark plug (HT) leads, it is a good idea to try to work on one spark plug at a time.

4 If the marks on the original-equipment spark plug (HT) leads cannot be seen, mark the leads 1 to 4, to correspond to the cylinder the lead serves (No 1 cylinder is at the timing belt/chain end of the engine). Pull the leads from the plugs by gripping the rubber boot sealing the cylinder head cover opening, not the lead, otherwise the lead connection may be fractured.

5 It is advisable to soak up any water in the spark plug recesses with a rag, and to remove any dirt from them using a clean brush, vacuum cleaner or compressed air before removing the plugs, to prevent any dirt or water from dropping into the cylinders.

⚠ *Warning: Wear eye protection when using compressed air!*

6 Unscrew the spark plugs, ensuring that the socket is kept in alignment with each plug - if the socket is forcibly moved to either side, the porcelain top of the plug may be broken off. If any undue difficulty is encountered when unscrewing any of the spark plugs, carefully check the cylinder head threads and tapered sealing surfaces for signs of wear, excessive corrosion or damage; if any of these conditions is found, seek the advice of a Ford dealer as to the best method of repair.

7 As each plug is removed, examine it as follows - this will give a good indication of the condition of the engine. If the insulator nose is covered with light tan to greyish-brown deposits, then the mixture is correct, and it is likely that the engine is in good condition.

8 If the tip and insulator nose are covered with hard black-looking deposits, then this is indicative that the mixture is too rich. Should the plug be black and oily, then it is likely that the engine is fairly worn, as well as the mixture being too rich.

9 If the insulator nose of the spark plug is clean and white, with no deposits, this is indicative of a weak mixture.

10 If you are renewing the spark plugs, purchase the new plugs, then check each of them first for faults such as cracked insulators or damaged threads. Note also that, whenever the spark plugs are renewed as a routine service operation, the spark plug (HT) leads should be checked as described below.

11 The spark plug electrode gap is of considerable importance as, if it is too large or too small, the size of the spark and its efficiency will be seriously impaired. The gap should be set to the value given in the Specifications Section of this Chapter. New plugs will not necessarily be set to the correct gap, so they should always be checked before fitting.

12 The spark plug gap is correct when the correct-size feeler blade or wire gauge is a firm sliding fit between the electrodes **(see illustrations)**.

13 To adjust the electrode gap, bend open, or close up, the outer plug electrode until the correct gap is achieved **(see illustration)**. The centre electrode should never be bent, as this may crack the insulation and cause plug failure, if nothing worse. If the outer electrode is not exactly over the centre electrode, bend it gently to align them. Special spark plug gap adjusting tools are available from motor accessory shops, or from certain spark plug manufacturers.

14 Before fitting the spark plugs, check that the threaded connector sleeves at the top of the plugs are tight, and that the plug exterior surfaces and threads are clean. Brown staining on the porcelain, immediately above

**1**

**23.2 Tools required for changing spark plugs**

**23.12a Measuring a spark plug gap with a feeler blade**

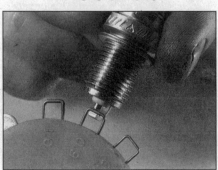

**23.12b Using a wire-type gauge when checking the gap**

**23.13 To change the gap, bend the outer electrode only**

the metal body, is quite normal, and does not necessarily indicate a "leak" between the body and insulator.

**15** Apply a smear of copper-based grease or anti-seize compound to the threads of each plug, and screw them in by hand where possible. Take extra care to enter the plug threads correctly, as the cylinder head is of aluminium alloy.

**HAYNES HINT** *It's difficult to insert spark plugs into their holes without cross-threading them. To avoid this possibility, fit a short piece of rubber hose over the end of the spark plug. The flexible hose acts as a universal joint, to help align the plug with the plug hole. Should the plug begin to cross-thread, the hose will slip on the spark plug, preventing thread damage.*

**16** When each spark plug is started correctly on its threads, screw it down until it just seats lightly, then tighten it to the specified torque wrench setting. If a torque wrench is not available - and this is one case where the use of a torque wrench is strongly recommended - tighten each spark plug through *no more than* 1/4 of a turn (CVH and PTE engines) or 1/16 of a turn (HCS and Endura-E engines) after it seats. HCS and Endura-E engines are fitted with taper-seat spark plugs, identifiable by not having a sealing washer, and these in particular should *NEVER* be overtightened -

their tapered seats mean they are almost impossible to remove if abused.

**17** Reconnect the spark plug (HT) leads in their correct order, using a twisting motion on the boot until it is firmly seated on the end of the spark plug and on the cylinder head cover.

### Spark plug (HT) lead check

**18** The spark plug (HT) leads should be checked whenever the plugs themselves are renewed. Start by making a visual check of the leads while the engine is running. In a darkened garage (make sure there is ventilation) start the engine and observe each lead. Be careful not to come into contact with any moving engine parts. If there is a break in the lead, you will see arcing or a small spark at the damaged area.

**19** The spark plug (HT) leads should be inspected one at a time, to prevent mixing up the firing order, which is essential for proper engine operation. Each original lead should be numbered to identify its cylinder. If the number is illegible, a piece of tape can be marked with the correct number, and wrapped around the lead (the leads should be numbered 1 to 4, with No 1 lead nearest the timing belt end of the engine). The lead can then be disconnected.

**20** Check inside the boot for corrosion, which will look like a white crusty powder. Clean this off as much as possible; if it is excessive, or if cleaning leaves the metal connector too badly eroded to be fit for further use, the lead must be renewed. Push the lead and boot back onto the end of the spark plug. The boot

should fit tightly onto the end of the plug - if it doesn't, remove the lead and use pliers carefully to crimp the metal connector inside the boot until the fit is snug.

**21** Using a clean rag, wipe the entire length of the lead to remove built-up dirt and grease. Once the lead is clean, check for burns, cracks and other damage. Do not bend the lead sharply, because the conductor might break.

**22** Disconnect the lead from the ignition coil by pressing together the plastic retaining catches and pulling the end fitting off the coil terminal. Check for corrosion and for a tight fit. If a meter with the correct measuring range is available, measure the resistance of the disconnected lead from its coil connector to its spark plug connector. If the resistance recorded for any of the leads exceeds the value specified, all the leads should be renewed as a set. Refit the lead to the coil, noting that each coil terminal is marked with its respective cylinder number, so that there is no risk of mixing up the leads and upsetting the firing order.

**23** Inspect the remaining spark plug (HT) leads, ensuring that each is securely fastened at the ignition coil and spark plug when the check is complete. If any sign of arcing, severe connector corrosion, burns, cracks or other damage is noticed, obtain new spark plug (HT) leads, renewing them as a set. If new spark plug leads are to be fitted, remove and refit them one at a time, to avoid mix-ups in the firing order.

# Every 30 000 miles or 3 years

### 24 Coolant renewal

**Note:** *If the antifreeze used is Ford's own brand, or of similar quality, the coolant renewal interval may be extended. If the vehicle's history is unknown, if antifreeze of lesser quality is known to be in the system, or simply if you prefer to follow conventional servicing intervals, the coolant should be changed periodically (typically, every 3 years) as described here. Refer also to "Antifreeze - notes on renewal" in this Section.*

⚠ *Warning: Do not allow antifreeze to come in contact with your skin or painted surfaces of the vehicle. Flush contaminated areas immediately with plenty of water. Don't store new coolant, or leave old coolant lying around, where it's accessible to children or pets - they're attracted by its sweet smell. Ingestion of even a small amount of coolant can be fatal! Wipe up garage-floor and drip-pan spills immediately. Keep antifreeze*

containers covered, and repair cooling system leaks as soon as they're noticed. *Warning: Never remove the expansion tank filler cap when the engine is running, or has just been switched off, as the cooling system will be hot, and the consequent escaping steam and scalding coolant could cause serious injury.*

### Coolant draining

⚠ *Warning: Wait until the engine is cold before starting this procedure.*

**1** To drain the system, first remove the expansion tank filler cap (see *"Weekly Checks"*).
**2** If the additional working clearance is required, raise the front of the vehicle and support it securely on axle stands (see *"Jacking and Vehicle Support"*).
**3** Where fitted, remove the radiator undershield (eight or nine screws), then place a large drain tray underneath, and unscrew the radiator drain plug - you can use a small coin to do this, as the plug's slotted for this purpose (see **illustration**). Direct as much of the escaping coolant as possible into the tray.

### System flushing

**4** With time, the cooling system may gradually lose its efficiency, as the radiator core becomes choked with rust, scale deposits from the water, and other sediment (refer also to *"Antifreeze - notes on renewal"* later in this Section). To minimise this, as well as using only good-quality antifreeze and clean soft water, the system should be flushed as follows whenever any part of it is disturbed, and/or when the coolant is renewed.

**24.3 Use a small coin to unscrew the radiator drain plug**

5 With the coolant drained, refit the drain plug, and refill the system with fresh water. Refit the expansion tank filler cap, start the engine and warm it up to normal operating temperature, then stop it and (after allowing it to cool down completely) drain the system again. Repeat as necessary until only clean water can be seen to emerge, then refill finally with the specified coolant mixture as described below.

6 If only clean, soft water and good-quality antifreeze (even if not to Ford's specification) has been used, and the coolant has been renewed at the suggested intervals, the above procedure will be sufficient to keep clean the system for a considerable length of time. If, however, the system has been neglected, a more thorough operation will be required, as follows.

7 First drain the coolant, then disconnect the radiator top and bottom hoses. Insert a garden hose into the top hose, and allow water to circulate through the radiator until it runs clean from the bottom outlet.

8 To flush the engine, insert the garden hose into the thermostat water outlet, and allow water to circulate until it runs clear from the bottom hose. If, after a reasonable period, the water still does not run clear, the radiator should be flushed with a good proprietary cleaning agent.

9 In severe cases of contamination, reverse-flushing of the radiator may be necessary. To do this, remove the radiator (Chapter 3), invert it, and insert the garden hose into the bottom outlet. Continue flushing until clear water runs from the top hose outlet. A similar procedure can be used to flush the heater matrix.

10 The use of chemical cleaners should be necessary only as a last resort. Normally, regular renewal of the coolant will prevent excessive contamination of the system.

## Coolant filling

11 With the cooling system drained and flushed, ensure that all disturbed hose unions are correctly secured, and that the radiator drain plug is securely tightened. Refit the radiator undershield, noting that it is located by three clips at its front edge; tighten the retaining screws securely. If it was raised, lower the vehicle to the ground.

12 Prepare a sufficient quantity of the specified coolant mixture (see below); allow for a surplus, so as to have a reserve supply for topping-up.

13 Slowly fill the system through the expansion tank; since the tank is the highest point in the system, all the air in the system should be displaced into the tank by the rising liquid. Slow pouring reduces the possibility of air being trapped and forming airlocks.

14 Continue filling until the coolant level reaches the expansion tank "MAX" level line, then cover the filler opening to prevent coolant splashing out.

15 Start the engine and run it at idle speed, until it has warmed-up to normal operating temperature and the radiator cooling fan has cut in; watch the temperature gauge to check for signs of overheating. If the level in the expansion tank drops significantly, top-up to the "MAX" level line, to minimise the amount of air circulating in the system.

16 Stop the engine, allow it to cool down *completely* (overnight, if possible), then uncover the expansion tank filler opening and top-up the tank to the "MAX" level line. Refit the filler cap, tightening it securely, and wash off any spilt coolant from the engine compartment and bodywork.

17 After refilling, always check carefully all components of the system (but especially any unions disturbed during draining and flushing) for signs of coolant leaks. Fresh antifreeze has a searching action, which will rapidly expose any weak points in the system.

18 If, after draining and refilling the system, symptoms of overheating are found which did not occur previously, then the fault is almost certainly due to trapped air at some point in the system, causing an airlock and restricting the flow of coolant; usually, the air is trapped because the system was refilled too quickly. In some cases, airlocks can be released by tapping or squeezing the various hoses. If the problem persists, stop the engine and allow it to cool down completely, before unscrewing the expansion tank filler cap or disconnecting hoses to bleed out the trapped air.

## Antifreeze mixture

19 If the antifreeze used is not to Ford's specification, it should always be renewed at the suggested intervals (typically, every 3 years). This is necessary not only to maintain the antifreeze properties, but also to prevent the corrosion which would otherwise occur as the corrosion inhibitors become progressively less effective. Always use an ethylene glycol-based antifreeze which is suitable for use in mixed-metal cooling systems.

20 If the antifreeze used is to Ford's specification, the levels of protection it affords are indicated in the Specifications Section of this Chapter. To give the recommended *standard* mixture ratio for this antifreeze, 40% (by volume) of antifreeze must be mixed with 60% of clean, soft water; if you are using any other type of antifreeze, follow its manufacturer's instructions to achieve the correct ratio. It is best to make up slightly more than the system's specified capacity, so that a supply is available for subsequent topping-up.

21 Before adding antifreeze, the cooling system should be completely drained, preferably flushed, and all hoses checked for condition and security. As noted earlier, fresh antifreeze will rapidly find any weaknesses in the system.

22 After filling with antifreeze, a label should be attached to the expansion tank, stating the type and concentration of antifreeze used, and the date installed. Any subsequent topping-up should be made with the same type and concentration of antifreeze. If topping-up using antifreeze to Ford's specification, note that a 50/50 mixture is permissible, purely for convenience.

23 Do not use engine antifreeze in the windscreen/tailgate washer system, as it will damage the vehicle's paintwork. A screenwash additive should be added to the washer system in its maker's recommended quantities.

## Antifreeze - notes on renewal

24 From approximately September 1998 onwards, all new Escort models were factory filled with an entirely new antifreeze type. This new antifreeze (which is orange in colour) is a concentration of monoethylene glycol and organic additives and is claimed to be greatly superior in comparison with the traditional ethylene glycol type antifreeze (blue/green in colour). Because of the different properties of the two types, they *must not* be mixed together in the same cooling system. If it is wished to change from one type to the other, the cooling system must be drained and thoroughly reverse-flushed before refilling with fresh coolant mixture.

25 Ford state that, where ethylene glycol antifreeze (blue/green) to Ford specification ESD-M97B-49-A is used, it will last approximately six years, whereas the monoethylene glycol type (orange) to Ford specification WSS-M97B44-D will last approximately ten years. Both these recommendations are subject to the antifreeze being used in the recommended concentration, unmixed with any other type of antifreeze or additive, and topped-up when necessary using only that antifreeze mixed 50/50 with clean water.

26 If the vehicle's history (and therefore the type and quality of the antifreeze in it) is unknown, owners who wish to follow Ford's recommendations are advised to drain and thoroughly reverse-flush the system before refilling with fresh coolant mixture. If the appropriate quality of antifreeze is used, the stated renewal intervals will apply.

27 If any antifreeze other than Ford's is to be used, the coolant must be renewed at regular intervals to provide an equivalent degree of protection; the conventional recommendation is to renew the coolant every two to three years.

## General cooling system checks

28 The engine should be cold for the cooling system checks, so perform the following procedure before driving the vehicle, or after it has been shut off for at least three hours.

29 Remove the expansion tank filler cap (see *"Weekly Checks"*), and clean it thoroughly inside and out with a rag. Also clean the filler neck on the expansion tank. The presence of rust or corrosion in the filler neck indicates that the coolant should be changed. The coolant inside the expansion tank should be relatively clean and transparent. If it is rust-coloured, drain and flush the system, and refill with a fresh coolant mixture.

30 Carefully check the radiator hoses and heater hoses along their entire length; renew any hose which is cracked, swollen or deteriorated (see Section 4).

1

25.1a On carburettor and CFi engines, undo the air cleaner cover screws . . .

25.1b . . . and release the clips . . .

25.1c . . . then lift off the cover and withdraw the element

**31** Inspect all other cooling system components (joint faces, etc.) for leaks. A leak in the cooling system will usually show up as white- or rust-coloured deposits on the area adjoining the leak. Where any problems of this nature are found on system components, renew the component or gasket with reference to Chapter 3.

**32** Clean the front of the radiator with a soft brush to remove all insects, leaves, etc, embedded in the radiator fins. Be careful not to damage the radiator fins, or cut your fingers on them.

25.1d On EFi and SEFi engines, undo the air cleaner cover retaining screws . . .

25.1e . . . and release the clips . . .

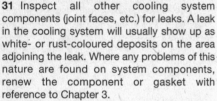

## 25 Air cleaner filter element renewal

**1** The air cleaner filter element is located in the air cleaner assembly mounted either on top of the carburettor or CFi unit, or on the left-hand side of the engine compartment. Undo the retaining screws and/or release the clips, and lift the air cleaner cover **(see illustrations)**.

**2** Lift out the element, and wipe out the housing. Check that no foreign matter is visible, either in the air inlet or in the air mass meter, as applicable.

**3** If carrying out a routine service, the element must be renewed regardless of its apparent condition. Note that on models so equipped, the small foam PCV filter in the rear right-hand corner of the air cleaner housing must be cleaned whenever the air filter element is renewed (see Section 26).

**4** If you are checking the element for any other reason, inspect its lower surface; if it is oily or very dirty, renew the element. If it is only moderately dusty, it can be re-used after blowing it clean from the upper to the lower surface with compressed air.

 **Warning: Wear eye protection when using compressed air! Because it is a pleated-paper type filter, it cannot be washed or re-oiled. If it cannot be cleaned satisfactorily with compressed air, discard and renew it.**
**Caution: Never drive the vehicle with the air cleaner filter element removed. Excessive**

25.1f . . . then lift off the cover and withdraw the element

*engine wear could result, and backfiring could even cause a fire under the bonnet.*
**5** Refitting is the reverse of the removal procedure. Ensure that the element and cover are securely seated, so that unfiltered air cannot enter the engine.

### *Air cleaner temperature control system check (carburettor fuel system)*

**6** In order for the engine to operate efficiently, the temperature of the air entering the inlet system must be controlled within certain limits.

**7** The air cleaner has two sources of air, one direct from the outside of the engine compartment, and the other from a shroud on the exhaust manifold. On HCS engines, a wax-controlled thermostatic valve controls a flap inside the air cleaner inlet. When the

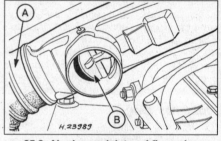

25.8 Air cleaner inlet and flap valve on the HCS engine
A Main air cleaner inlet (cool air)
B Warm air duct (flap open)

ambient air temperature is below a predetermined level, the flap admits air heated from the exhaust manifold shroud; as the ambient temperature rises, the flap opens to admit more cool air from the engine compartment until eventually it is fully open. A similar system is used on CVH engines, except that a vacuum actuator modifies any opening or closing action of the temperature sensor on the flap valve, according to the level of the inlet manifold vacuum under running conditions.

### HCS engines

**8** This check must be made when the engine is cold. Detach and remove the air cleaner inlet trunking. Examine the position of the check valve within the duct. When the underbonnet air temperature is below 28°C, the valve must be open to allow hot air to enter the filter **(see illustration)**.

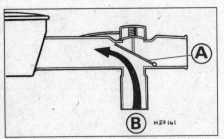

**25.12 Air cleaner inlet and flap valve on the CVH engine**

A  Flap open (cool air inlet closed)
B  Warm air inlet

**9** Refit the inlet trunking. Start the engine and run it until it reaches its normal operating temperature, then stop the engine, remove the inlet trunking and check that the valve has closed off the air passage from the exhaust and opened the main (cool) air inlet.
**10** If the flap does not operate correctly, check that it is not seized. Apart from this there is no adjustment possible, and the unit should be renewed if faulty. Refit the air inlet trunking on completion.

## CVH engines

**11** This check must be made when the engine is cold. Disconnect the main air inlet duct, and visibly check that the flap to the hot-air inlet is closed (i.e. open to the passage of cold air).
**12** Start the engine, and check that with the engine idling, the hot-air inlet is open to allow warm air from the exhaust manifold area to enter the air cleaner. If the flap operates as described, it is functioning correctly **(see illustration)**.
**13** If the flap fails to operate as described, check the condition of the vacuum pipe and its connections, and check that the flap valve has not seized. If these are in order, either the temperature sensor or vacuum actuator is faulty, and a new air cleaner assembly must be obtained. Refit the main air duct on completion.

## 26 Emission control system check

### General

**1** Of the emission control systems that may be fitted, only the crankcase ventilation system and the evaporative emission control systems require regular checking, and even then, the components of these systems require minimal attention.
**2** Should it be felt that the other systems are not functioning correctly, the advice of a dealer should be sought.

### Crankcase ventilation system

**3** The function of the crankcase ventilation system is to reduce the emission of unburned hydrocarbons from the crankcase, and to minimise the formation of oil sludge. By ensuring that a depression is created in the crankcase under most operating conditions, particularly at idle, and by positively inducing fresh air into the system, the oil vapours and "blow-by" gases collected in the crankcase are drawn from the crankcase, through the air cleaner or oil separator, into the inlet tract, to be burned by the engine during normal combustion.
**4** On HCS engines, the system consists of a vented oil filler cap (with an integral mesh filter) and a hose connecting it to the oil separator/engine breather valve connector on the underside of the air cleaner housing. A further hose leads from the adapter/filter to the inlet manifold.
**5** On CVH engines, a closed-circuit type crankcase ventilation system is used, the function of which is basically the same as that described for the HCS engine types, but the breather hose connects directly to the rocker cover. A separate filter is fitted in the hose to the rocker cover in certain applications.
**6** The systems fitted to the Endura-E and PTE engines are similar to those used on the earlier (HCS and CVH) engines on which these two engines are based, but with revisions to the hose arrangement to suit the remotely sited air cleaner and fuel injection system layout.
**7** On Zetec and Zetec-E engines, the crankcase ventilation system main components are the oil separator mounted on the front (radiator) side of the cylinder block/ crankcase, and the Positive Crankcase Ventilation (PCV) valve set in a rubber grommet in the separator's left-hand upper end. The associated pipework consists of a crankcase breather pipe and two flexible hoses connecting the PCV valve to a union on the left-hand end of the inlet manifold, and a crankcase breather hose connecting the cylinder head cover to the air cleaner assembly. A small foam filter in the air cleaner prevents dirt from being drawn directly into the engine.
**8** Check that all components of the system are securely fastened, correctly routed (with no kinks or sharp bends to restrict flow) and in sound condition; renew any worn or damaged components.
**9** On HCS engines, remove and inspect the oil filler cap to ensure that it is in good condition, and not blocked up with sludge.
**10** Disconnect the hoses at the cap, and clean the cap if necessary by brushing the inner mesh filter with petrol, and blowing through with light pressure from an air line. Renew the cap if it is badly congested.
**11** If oil leakage is noted, disconnect the various hoses and pipes, and check that all are clear and unblocked. Remove the air cleaner assembly cover, and check that the hose from the cylinder head cover to the air cleaner housing is clear and undamaged.
**12** Where fitted, the PCV valve is designed to allow gases to flow out of the crankcase only,

**26.13 The PCV system foam filter is located in the rear right-hand corner of the air cleaner housing on Zetec engines**

so that a depression is created in the crankcase under most operating conditions, particularly at idle. Therefore, if either the oil separator or the PCV valve are thought to be blocked, they must be renewed (Chapter 4E). In such a case, however, there is nothing to be lost by attempting to flush out the blockage using a suitable solvent. The PCV valve should rattle when shaken.
**13** While the air filter element is removed (see Section 25), wipe out the housing, and on Zetec engines, withdraw the small foam filter from its location in the rear right-hand corner of the housing **(see illustration)**. If the foam is badly clogged with dirt or oil, it must be cleaned by soaking it in a suitable solvent, and allowed to dry before being refitted.

### Evaporative emission control systems

**14** Refer to the checks in Chapter 4E.

## 27 Automatic transmission fluid renewal

**1** The transmission fluid should only be changed when the transmission is cold.
**2** Position the vehicle over an inspection pit, on vehicle ramps, or jack it up, but make sure that it is level.
**3** Place a suitable container beneath the drain plug on the transmission sump pan. Remove the transmission fluid dipstick to speed up the draining operation.
**4** Thoroughly clean the area around the drain plug in the transmission sump pan, then unscrew the plug and allow the fluid to drain into the container.
**5** When all the fluid has drained (this may take some time) clean the drain plug, then refit it together with a new seal and tighten securely.
**6** Place a funnel with a fine mesh screen in the dipstick tube, and fill the transmission with the specified type of fluid. It is essential that no dirt is introduced into the transmission during this operation.
**7** Depending on the extent to which the fluid was allowed to drain, it is possible that the amount of fluid required when filling the transmission may be more than the specified

**1**

amount (see *"Servicing specifications"* on page 1•2). However, due to fluid remaining in the system, it is more likely that less than the specified amount will be required. Add about half the specified amount, then run the engine up to its normal operating temperature and check the level on the dipstick. When the level approaches the maximum mark, proceed as detailed in Section 22 to check the level and complete the final topping-up as described.

## 28 Handbrake adjustment

### Pre-1996 drum brake models

**1** Chock the front wheels then jack up the rear of the car and support it on axle stands (see *"Jacking and Vehicle Support"*). Fully release the handbrake.
**2** Check that the handbrake cables are correctly routed and secured by the retaining clips at the appropriate points under the vehicle.
**3** The handbrake is checked for adjustment by measuring the amount of movement possible in the handbrake adjuster plungers. These are located on the inside face of each rear brake backplate **(see illustration)**. The total movement of the two plungers combined should be between 0.5 and 2.0 mm. If the movement measured is outside of this tolerance, the handbrake is in need of adjustment. Adjustment is made altering the position of the in-line cable adjuster sleeve **(see illustration)**.
**4** When adjustment to the handbrake is necessary, a new adjustment sleeve locking pin will be required, and this must therefore be obtained before making the adjustment.
**5** To adjust the handbrake, first ensure that it is fully released, then firmly apply the footbrake a few times to ensure that the rear brake adjustment is taken up by the automatic adjusters. Extract the locking pin from the adjuster sleeve, then turn the sleeve to set the combined movement of the plungers within the tolerance range specified (0.5 to 2.0 mm). Turn the locking nut by hand as tight as is possible (two

**28.3a Handbrake adjustment plunger on drum brake models**

clicks) against the adjustment sleeve. Now grip the locknut with a suitable wrench, and turn it a further two clicks (maximum).
**6** Secure the adjustment by inserting the new lock pin.
**7** Check that the operation of the handbrake is satisfactory, then lower the vehicle to the ground, apply the handbrake and remove the chocks from the front wheels.

### 1996 on drum brake models

*Caution: If the handbrake is incorrectly adjusted, the rear brake automatic adjustment mechanism will not be able to function correctly. This will lead to the brake shoe-to-drum clearance becoming excessive as the shoe linings wear, resulting in excessive brake pedal travel.*

**8** Chock the front wheels.
**9** Fully release the handbrake then apply the footbrake firmly several times to ensure that the self-adjust mechanism is fully adjusted.
**10** Unclip the handbrake lever gaiter to gain access to the adjuster nut on the side of the lever **(see illustration)**.
**11** From the fully-released position, pull the handbrake lever up, noting the number of clicks from the ratchet. The handbrake should be fully applied between three and six clicks. If adjustment is necessary, turn the adjusting nut as required until the correct setting is achieved **(see illustration)**. On completion, clip the gaiter back into position. If after adjustment,

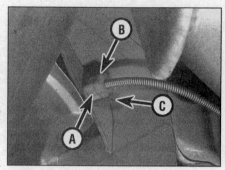

**28.3b Handbrake cable adjuster sleeve (A) locknut (B) and lockpin (C)**

the handbrake operation is still unsatisfactory, the rear brakes may need to be stripped, cleaned and adjusted (see Chapter 9).

### Disc brake models

**12** Chock the front wheels then jack up the rear of the car and support it on axle stands (see *"Jacking and Vehicle Support"*). Fully release the handbrake.
**13** Check that the handbrake cables are correctly routed and secured by the retaining clips at the appropriate points under the vehicle.
**14** Remove the blanking plug from the rear of the brake carrier plate, just below and to the rear of the brake caliper.
**15** With the handbrake released, insert a screwdriver through the blanking plug hole and engage the end of the screwdriver in the teeth of the adjuster wheel. Move the screwdriver up and down to turn the adjuster wheel as necessary, until the wheel is just locked.
**16** Now back off the adjuster wheel until the wheel can be turned freely without binding.
**17** Repeat this procedure on the other brake assembly, then check the operation of the handbrake. Ensure that both wheels are locked when the handbrake lever is applied, and that both are released, with no trace of binding when the lever is fully released.
**18** When all is satisfactory, refit the blanking plugs, and lower the vehicle to the ground. Reapply the handbrake and remove the chocks from the front wheels.

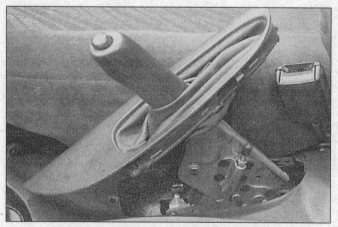

**28.10 Unclip the handbrake lever gaiter and ...**

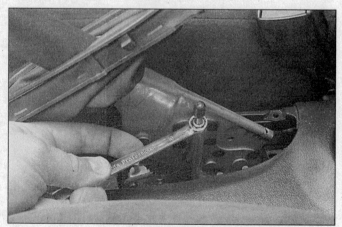

**28.11 ... slacken the handbrake adjuster nut**

# Every 60 000 miles

## 29 Timing belt renewal

Refer to Chapter 2B or 2C as appropriate.

## 30 Fuel filter renewal

30.1a The fuel filter is below and to the rear of the engine, above the driveshafts . . .

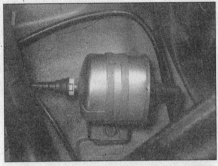

30.1b . . . or under the car at the rear, just forward of the rear suspension assembly

**Warning: Petrol is extremely flammable, so extra precautions must be taken when working on any part of the fuel system. Do not smoke, or allow open flames or bare light bulbs, near the work area. Also, do not work in a garage if a natural gas-type appliance with a pilot light is present. While performing any work on the fuel system, wear safety glasses, and have a suitable (Class B) fire extinguisher on hand. If you spill any fuel on your skin, rinse it off immediately with soap and water.**

1 On fuel injection engines, an in-line fuel filter is provided in the fuel pump outlet line. The filter is located either below and to the rear of the engine, above the driveshafts, or under the car at the rear, just forward of the rear suspension assembly **(see illustrations)**. The renewal procedure is the same for both locations. The filter performs a vital role in keeping dirt and other foreign matter out of the fuel system, and so must be renewed at regular intervals, or whenever you have reason to suspect that it may be clogged. It is always

unpleasant working under a vehicle - pressure-washing or hosing clean the underbody in the filter's vicinity will make working conditions more tolerable, and will reduce the risk of getting dirt into the fuel system.

2 Depressurise the fuel system as described in the relevant Part of Chapter 4.

3 Disconnect the battery negative (earth) lead (refer to Chapter 5A, Section 1).

4 Chock the front or rear wheels as applicable then jack up the front or rear of the car and support it on axle stands (see "Jacking and Vehicle Support").

5 Using rag to soak up any spilt fuel, release the fuel feed and outlet pipe unions from the filter, by squeezing together the protruding locking lugs on each union; and carefully pulling the union off the filter stub. Where the unions are colour-coded, the feed and outlet pipes cannot be confused; where both unions are the same colour, note carefully which pipe is connected to which filter stub, and ensure that they are correctly reconnected on refitting.

6 Noting the arrows and/or other markings on the filter showing the direction of fuel flow (towards the engine), slacken the filter clamp screw and withdraw the filter. Note that the filter will still contain fuel; care should be taken, to avoid spillage and to minimise the risk of fire.

7 On installation, slide the filter into its clamp so that the arrow marked on it faces the correct way, then slide each pipe union on to its (correct) respective filter stub, and press it down until the locking lugs click into their groove. Tighten the clamp screw carefully, until the filter is just prevented from moving; do not overtighten the clamp screw, or the filter casing may be crushed.

8 Refit the fuel pump fuse and reconnect the battery earth terminal, then switch the ignition on and off five times, in order to pressurise the system. Check for any sign of fuel leakage around the filter unions before lowering the vehicle to the ground and starting the engine.

# Every 3 years

## 31 Brake fluid renewal

The procedure is similar to that for the bleeding of the hydraulic system as described in Chapter 9, except that the brake fluid reservoir should be emptied by syphoning, and allowance should be made for the old fluid to be removed from the circuit when bleeding a section of the circuit.

**1**

# Notes

# Chapter 2 Part A:
# HCS & Endura-E engine in-car repair procedures

## Contents

## Degrees of difficulty

| | | | | |
|---|---|---|---|---|
| **Easy,** suitable for novice with little experience  | **Fairly easy,** suitable for beginner with some experience  | **Fairly difficult,** suitable for competent DIY mechanic  | **Difficult,** suitable for experienced DIY mechanic  | **Very difficult,** suitable for expert DIY or professional |

## Specifications

### General

| | |
|---|---|
| Engine type . . . . . . . . . . . . . . . . . . . . . . . . . . . . . . . . . . . . . . . | Four-cylinder, in-line overhead valve |
| Engine code: | |
|   HCS engines: | |
|     Carburettor models . . . . . . . . . . . . . . . . . . . . . . . . . . . . . . | JBD |
|     CFi fuel injection models . . . . . . . . . . . . . . . . . . . . . . . . . | J6A |
|   Endura-E engines . . . . . . . . . . . . . . . . . . . . . . . . . . . . . . . | J4B |
| Capacity . . . . . . . . . . . . . . . . . . . . . . . . . . . . . . . . . . . . . . . . . | 1297 cc |
| Bore . . . . . . . . . . . . . . . . . . . . . . . . . . . . . . . . . . . . . . . . . . . | 73.96 mm |
| Stroke . . . . . . . . . . . . . . . . . . . . . . . . . . . . . . . . . . . . . . . . . | 75.48 mm |
| Compression ratio: | |
|   HCS engines: | |
|     Carburettor models . . . . . . . . . . . . . . . . . . . . . . . . . . . . . | 9.5:1 |
|     CFi fuel injection models . . . . . . . . . . . . . . . . . . . . . . . . . | 8.8:1 |
|   Endura-E engines . . . . . . . . . . . . . . . . . . . . . . . . . . . . . . . | 9.5:1 |
| Firing order . . . . . . . . . . . . . . . . . . . . . . . . . . . . . . . . . . . . . . | 1-2-4-3 (No 1 cylinder at timing chain end) |
| Direction of crankshaft rotation . . . . . . . . . . . . . . . . . . . . . . . . | Clockwise (seen from right-hand side of vehicle) |

### Valves

| | |
|---|---|
| Valve clearance (cold): | |
|   Inlet . . . . . . . . . . . . . . . . . . . . . . . . . . . . . . . . . . . . . . . . | 0.20 mm |
|   Exhaust:* | |
|     Up to 20/11/96 . . . . . . . . . . . . . . . . . . . . . . . . . . . . . . . | 0.30 mm |
|     21/11/96 onward . . . . . . . . . . . . . . . . . . . . . . . . . . . . . | 0.50 mm |

*Note: Later engines can be identified by a label on the cylinder head rocker cover, indicating the revised valve clearance

### Lubrication

| | |
|---|---|
| Engine oil type/specification . . . . . . . . . . . . . . . . . . . . . . . . . . | See "Lubricants, fluids and tyre pressures" on page 0•17 |
| Engine oil capacity . . . . . . . . . . . . . . . . . . . . . . . . . . . . . . . . . | See Chapter 1 Specifications |
| Oil pressure: | |
|   At idle speed . . . . . . . . . . . . . . . . . . . . . . . . . . . . . . . . . . | 0.60 bars |
|   At 2000 rpm . . . . . . . . . . . . . . . . . . . . . . . . . . . . . . . . . . | 1.50 bars |
| Oil pump clearances: | |
|   Outer rotor-to-body . . . . . . . . . . . . . . . . . . . . . . . . . . . . . | 0.14 to 0.26 mm |
|   Inner rotor-to-outer rotor . . . . . . . . . . . . . . . . . . . . . . . . . | 0.051 to 0.127 mm |
|   Rotor endfloat . . . . . . . . . . . . . . . . . . . . . . . . . . . . . . . . | 0.025 to 0.06 mm |

## Torque wrench settings

| | Nm | lbf ft |
|---|---|---|
| Camshaft thrust plate bolts | 11 | 8 |
| Camshaft sprocket bolt | 28 | 21 |
| Crankshaft pulley bolt | 115 | 85 |
| Rocker gear pedestal bolts | 43 | 32 |
| Flywheel bolts | 67 | 49 |
| Sump: | | |
| Stage 1 | 7 | 5 |
| Stage 2 | 10 | 7 |
| Stage 3 (with engine warm) | 10 | 7 |
| Oil pressure switch | 14 | 10 |
| Cylinder head bolts (may be re-used once only): | | |
| Stage 1 | 30 | 22 |
| Stage 2 | Angle-tighten a further 90° | |
| Stage 3 | Angle-tighten a further 90° | |
| Timing chain tensioner | 8 | 6 |
| Timing chain cover | 10 | 7 |
| Crankshaft left-hand oil seal housing | 18 | 13 |
| Rocker cover bolts | 6 | 4 |
| Oil pump | 18 | 13 |
| Oil pump cover | 10 | 7 |
| Engine/transmission mountings: | | |
| Right-hand mounting-to-cylinder block bracket | 120 | 88 |
| Right-hand mounting bracket-to-cylinder block | 69 | 51 |
| Right-hand mounting brace | 69 | 51 |
| Right-hand mounting-to-body | 84 | 62 |
| Left-hand rear mounting bracket-to-transmission | 50 | 37 |
| Left-hand rear mounting bracket-to-mounting | 68 | 50 |
| Left-hand front mounting bracket-to-mounting | 68 | 50 |
| Left-hand front mounting bracket brace | 49 | 36 |

**Note:** *Refer to Part D of this Chapter for remaining torque wrench settings.*

## 1 General information

### How to use this Chapter

This Part of Chapter 2 is devoted to repair procedures possible while the engine is still installed in the vehicle, and includes only the Specifications relevant to those procedures. Similar information concerning the 1.4 and 1.6 litre CVH and PTE engines, and the 1.6 and 1.8 litre Zetec and Zetec-E engines, will be found in Parts B and C of this Chapter respectively. Since these procedures are based on the assumption that the engine is installed in the vehicle, if the engine has been removed from the vehicle and mounted on a stand, some of the preliminary dismantling steps outlined will not apply.

Information concerning engine/ transmission removal and refitting, and engine overhaul, can be found in Part D of this Chapter, which also includes the *Specifications* relevant to those procedures.

### Engine description

The engine is an overhead valve, water-cooled, four cylinder in-line design, designated HCS (High Compression Swirl) or Endura-E. The Endura-E unit was introduced in 1996 and, apart from an aluminium sump and modifications to the inlet manifold and inlet system, is virtually identical to the HCS

engine it replaces. The engine is mounted transversely at the front of the vehicle together with the transmission to form a combined power unit.

The crankshaft is supported in five shell-type main bearings. The connecting rod big-end bearings are also split shell-type, and are attached to the pistons by interference-fit gudgeon pins. Each piston is fitted with two compression rings and one oil control ring.

The camshaft, which runs on bearings within the cylinder block, is chain-driven from the crankshaft, and operates the valves via pushrods and rocker arms. The valves are each closed by a single valve spring, and operate in guides integral in the cylinder head.

The oil pump is mounted externally on the crankcase, incorporates a full-flow oil filter, and is driven by a skew gear on the camshaft. On carburettor versions, the fuel pump is also driven from the camshaft, via an eccentric lobe.

### Repair operations possible with the engine in the car

The following work can be carried out with the engine in the car:

a) *Compression pressure - testing.*
b) *Cylinder head rocker cover - removal and refitting.*
c) *Valve clearances - adjustment.*
d) *Rocker shaft assembly - removal, inspection and refitting.*
e) *Cylinder head - removal and refitting*
f) *Cylinder head and pistons - decarbonising.*

g) *Crankshaft pulley - removal and refitting.*
h) *Crankshaft oil seals - renewal.*
i) *Timing chain, sprockets and tensioner - removal, inspection and refitting.*
j) *Oil filter renewal.*
k) *Oil pump - removal and refitting.*
l) *Sump - removal and refitting.*
m) *Flywheel - removal, inspection and refitting.*
n) *Engine/transmission mountings - inspection and renewal.*

**Note:** *It is possible to remove the pistons and connecting rods (after removing the cylinder head and sump) without removing the engine. However, this is not recommended. Work of this nature is more easily and thoroughly completed with the engine on the bench, as described in Chapter 2D.*

## 2 Compression test - description and interpretation

1 When engine performance is down, or if misfiring occurs which cannot be attributed to the ignition or fuel systems, a compression test can provide diagnostic clues as to the engine's condition. If the test is performed regularly, it can give warning of trouble before any other symptoms become apparent.
2 The engine must be fully warmed-up to operating temperature, the oil level must be correct and the battery must be fully charged. The aid of an assistant will also be required.

**3** On fuel injection engines, refer to Chapter 12 and remove the fuel pump fuse from the fusebox. Now start the engine and allow it to run until it stalls.

**4** Disable the ignition system by disconnecting the 3-pin multi-plug plug from the DIS ignition coil. Remove all the spark plugs with reference to Chapter 1 if necessary.

**5** Fit a compression tester to the No 1 cylinder spark plug hole - the type of tester which screws into the plug thread is to be preferred.

**6** Arrange for an assistant to hold the accelerator pedal fully depressed to the floor, while at the same time cranking the engine over for several seconds on the starter motor. Observe the compression gauge reading. The compression will build up fairly quickly in a healthy engine. Low compression on the first stroke, followed by gradually-increasing pressure on successive strokes, indicates worn piston rings. A low compression on the first stroke which does not rise on successive strokes, indicates leaking valves or a blown head gasket (a cracked cylinder head could also be the cause). Deposits on the underside of the valve heads can also cause low compression. Record the highest gauge reading obtained, then repeat the procedure for the remaining cylinders.

**7** Due to the variety of testers available, and the fluctuation in starter motor speed when cranking the engine, different readings are often obtained when carrying out the compression test. For this reason, actual compression pressure figures are not quoted by Ford. However, the most important factor is that the compression pressures are uniform in all cylinders, and that is what this test is mainly concerned with.

**8** Add some engine oil (about three squirts from a plunger type oil can) to each cylinder through the spark plug holes, and then repeat the test.

**9** If the compression increases after the oil is added, it is indicative that the piston rings are definitely worn. If the compression does not increase significantly, the leakage is occurring at the valves or the head gasket. Leakage past the valves may be caused by burned valve seats and/or faces, or warped, cracked or bent valves.

**10** If two adjacent cylinders have equally low compressions, it is most likely that the head gasket has blown between them. The appearance of coolant in the combustion chambers or on the engine oil dipstick would verify this condition.

**11** If one cylinder is about 20 percent lower than the other, and the engine has a slightly rough idle, a worn lobe on the camshaft could be the cause.

**12** On completion of the checks, refit the spark plugs and reconnect the HT leads and the DIS ignition coil plug. Refit the fuel pump fuse to the fusebox.

## 3 Top Dead Centre (TDC) for No 1 piston - locating

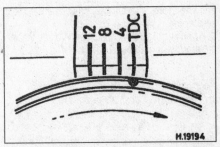

**1** Top dead centre (TDC) is the highest point of the cylinder that each piston reaches as the crankshaft turns. Each piston reaches its TDC position at the end of its compression stroke, and then again at the end of its exhaust stroke. For the purpose of engine timing, TDC at the end of the compression stroke for No 1 piston is used. On the HCS and Endura-E engines, No 1 cylinder is at the crankshaft pulley/timing chain end of the engine. Proceed as follows.

**2** Ensure that the ignition is switched off. Disconnect the HT leads from the spark plugs, then unscrew and remove the plugs as described in Chapter 1.

**3** Turn the engine over by hand (using a spanner on the crankshaft pulley) to the point where the timing mark on the crankshaft pulley aligns with the TDC (0) mark on the timing cover **(see illustration)**. As the pulley mark nears the timing mark, the No 1 piston is simultaneously approaching the top of its cylinder. To ensure that it is on its compression stroke, place a finger over the No 1 cylinder plug hole, and feel to ensure that air pressure exits from the cylinder as the piston reaches the top of its stroke.

**4** A further check to ensure that the piston is on its compression stroke can be made by first removing the air cleaner (refer to the relevant Part of Chapter 4), then unbolting and removing the rocker cover, so that the movement of the valves and rockers can be observed.

**5** With the TDC timing marks on the crankshaft pulley and timing cover in alignment, rock the crankshaft back and forth a few degrees each side of this position, and observe the action of the valves and rockers for No 1 cylinder. When No 1 piston is at the TDC firing position, the inlet and exhaust valve of No 1 cylinder will be fully closed, but the corresponding valves of No 4 cylinder will be seen to rock open and closed.

**6** If the inlet and exhaust valves of No 1 cylinder are seen to rock whilst those of No 4 cylinder are shut, the crankshaft will need to be

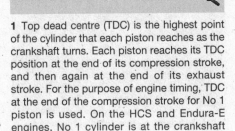

**3.3 Timing mark on the crankshaft pulley aligned with the TDC (0) mark on the timing cover**

turned one full rotation to bring No 1 piston up to the top of its cylinder on the compression stroke.

**7** Once No 1 cylinder has been positioned at TDC on the compression stroke, TDC for any of the other cylinders can then be located by rotating the crankshaft clockwise (in its normal direction of rotation), 180° at a time, and following the firing order (see *Specifications*).

## 4 Cylinder head rocker cover - removal and refitting

### Removal

**1** Where necessary for access, remove the air cleaner as described in the relevant Part of Chapter 4.

**2** Detach the HT leads from the spark plugs. Pull on the connector of each lead (not the lead itself), and note the order of fitting.

**3** Remove the engine oil filler cap and breather hose (where fitted).

**4** Unscrew the four retaining bolts, and lift the rocker cover clear of the cylinder head. Remove the gasket.

### Refitting

**5** Thoroughly clean the rocker cover, and scrape away any traces of old gasket remaining on the cover and cylinder head mating surfaces.

**6** Fit a new gasket to the rocker cover, then refit the rocker cover **(see illustrations)**. Tighten the cover retaining bolts to the

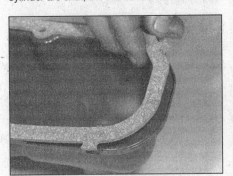

**4.6a Engage tags of rocker cover gasket into the cut-outs in the cover**

**4.6b Refitting the rocker cover**

**2A**

specified torque wrench setting, in a diagonal sequence.

7 Reconnect the HT leads, and refit the air cleaner as described in Chapter 4.

## 5  Valve clearances - checking and adjustment

**Note**: *The valve clearances must be checked and adjusted only when the engine is cold.*

1 The importance of having the valve clearances correctly adjusted cannot be overstressed, as they vitally affect the performance of the engine. If the clearances are too big, the engine will be noisy (characteristic rattling or tapping noises) and engine efficiency will be reduced, as the valves open too late and close too early. A more serious problem arises if the clearances are too small, however. If this is the case, the valves may not close fully when the engine is hot, resulting in serious damage to the engine (eg. burnt valve seats and/or cylinder head warping/cracking). The clearances are checked and adjusted as follows.

2 Set the engine to TDC for No 1 piston, as described in Section 3.

3 Remove the rocker cover as described in Section 4.

4 Starting from the thermostat end of the cylinder head, the valves are numbered as follows:

| Valve No | Cylinder No |
| --- | --- |
| 1 - Exhaust | 1 |
| 2 - Inlet | 1 |
| 3 - Exhaust | 2 |
| 4 - Inlet | 2 |
| 5 - Inlet | 3 |
| 6 - Exhaust | 3 |
| 7 - Inlet | 4 |
| 8 - Exhaust | 4 |

5 Adjust the valve clearances following the sequence given in the following table. Turn the crankshaft pulley 180° (half a turn) after adjusting each pair of valve clearances.

 **HAYNES HiNT** *Turning the engine will be easier if the spark plugs are removed first - see Chapter 1.*

| Valves "rocking" | Valves to adjust |
| --- | --- |
| 7 and 8 | 1 (exhaust), 2 (inlet) |
| 5 and 6 | 3 (exhaust), 4 (inlet) |
| 1 and 2 | 8 (exhaust), 7 (inlet) |
| 3 and 4 | 6 (exhaust), 5 (inlet) |

6 The clearances for the inlet and exhaust valves differ (refer to the *Specifications*). Use a feeler blade of the appropriate thickness to check each clearance between the end of the valve stem and the rocker arm **(see illustration)**. The gauge should be a firm sliding fit between the valve and rocker arm. Where adjustment is necessary, turn the adjuster bolt as required with a ring spanner

**5.6  Adjusting the valve clearances**

to set the clearance to that specified. The adjuster bolts are of stiff-thread type, and require no locking nut.

7 On completion, refit the rocker cover as described in Section 4.

## 6  Cylinder head rocker gear - removal, inspection and refitting

### Removal

1 Remove the rocker cover - see Section 4.
2 Unscrew the four retaining bolts, and lift the rocker gear assembly from the cylinder head. As the assembly is withdrawn, ensure that the pushrods remain seated in their positions in the engine **(see Haynes Hint)**.

### Inspection

3 To dismantle the rocker shaft assembly, extract the split pin from one end of the shaft, then withdraw the spring washers and plain washers from the shaft.
4 Slide off the rocker arms, the support pedestals and coil springs from the shaft, but take care to keep them in their original order of fitting **(see illustration)**.
5 Clean the respective components, and inspect them for signs of excessive wear or damage. Check that the oil lubrication holes in the shaft are clear.
6 Check the rocker shaft and arm pads which bear on the valve stem end faces for wear and scoring, and check each rocker arm on the shaft for excessive wear. Renew any components as necessary.

**6.4  Rocker shaft partially dismantled for inspection**

*If the pushrods are to be removed, keep them in the correct order of fitting by labelling them 1 to 8, starting from the thermostat end of the cylinder head, or locate them in a card.*

### Refitting

7 Apply clean engine oil to the rocker shaft prior to reassembling.
8 Reassemble in the reverse order of dismantling. Make sure that the "flat" on the left-hand end of the rocker shaft is to the same side as the rocker arm adjusting screws (closest to the thermostat end of the cylinder head when fitted) **(see illustration)**. This is essential for the correct lubrication of the cylinder head components.
9 Refit the rocker shaft assembly. As it is fitted, ensure that the rocker adjuster screws engage with their corresponding pushrods.
10 Refit the rocker shaft retaining bolts, hand-tighten them and then tighten them to the specified torque wrench setting. As they are tightened, some of the rocker arms will apply pressure to the ends of the valve stems, and some of the rocker pedestals will not initially be in contact with the cylinder head - these should pull down as the bolts are tightened to their specified torque. If for any reason they do not, avoid the temptation to overtighten in order to pull them into position; loosen off the bolts, and check the cause of the problem. It may be that the rocker adjuster screws require loosening off in order to allow the assembly to be tightened down as required.
11 Adjust the valve clearances as described in Section 5.

**6.8  Flat on the rocker shaft (arrowed) to same side as rocker arm adjusting screws**

## 7 Cylinder head -
### removal and refitting

## Removal

**Note:** *The following procedure describes removal and refitting of the cylinder head complete with inlet and exhaust manifolds. If wished, the manifolds may be removed first, as described in the relevant Part of Chapter 4, and the cylinder head then removed on its own.*

**1** On fuel injection engines, depressurise the fuel system as described in Chapter 4B or D as applicable.
**2** Disconnect the battery negative (earth) lead (refer to Chapter 5A, Section 1).
**3** Refer to Section 4 and remove the rocker cover.
**4** On fuel injection engines, if not already done, remove the air inlet duct from the throttle housing and air cleaner as described in Chapter 4D.
**5** Refer to Chapter 1 and drain the cooling system.
**6** Disconnect the hoses from the thermostat housing.
**7** Disconnect the heater (coolant) hoses from the inlet manifold and CFi unit, where applicable.

>
> **HAYNES HiNT**
> *Whenever you disconnect any vacuum lines, coolant or emissions hoses, wiring connectors and fuel lines, always label them clearly, so that they can be correctly reassembled. Masking tape and/or a touch-up paint applicator work well for marking items. Take instant photos, or sketch the locations of components and brackets.*

**8** Disconnect the accelerator and choke cables as applicable (see Chapter 4A, B or D).
**9** Disconnect the vacuum and breather hoses from the carburettor/CFi unit, throttle housing and inlet manifold as applicable.
**10** Disconnect the fuel feed and return lines at the carburettor, or at the quick-release couplings, then unclip the fuel hoses from the inlet manifold; use rag to soak up any spilt fuel. **Note:** *Do not disturb the threaded couplings at the fuel rail unions (fuel injection engines) unless absolutely necessary; these are sealed at the factory. The quick-release couplings will suffice for all normal service operations.*
**11** Disconnect the HT leads from the spark plugs and the support bracket. Unscrew and remove the spark plugs.
**12** Disconnect the electrical leads from the temperature gauge sender, radiator cooling fan, the engine coolant temperature sender (beneath the inlet manifold), the radio earth

lead on the inlet manifold, and the anti-run-on (anti-dieseling) valve at the carburettor.
**13** Disconnect the remaining wiring multi-plugs from the engine sensors at the inlet manifold and from the oxygen sensor (where fitted) in the exhaust manifold or downpipe.
**14** On Endura-E engines, release the wire clips and unplug the four fuel injector multi-plugs.
**15** On vehicles equipped with a pulse-air system, remove the pulse-air piping and filter assembly as described in Chapter 4E.
**16** Chock the rear wheels then jack up the front of the car and support it on axle stands (see *"Jacking and vehicle support"*).
**17** Undo the retaining nuts, and disconnect the exhaust downpipe from the manifold. Remove the flange gasket. (Note that both the gasket and the joint self-locking nuts must be renewed.) To prevent the exhaust system from being strained, tie the downpipe up using strong wire or a length of cord to support it. Lower the vehicle.
**18** Undo the four retaining bolts and lift clear the rocker gear assembly from the cylinder head.
**19** Lift out the pushrods. Keep them in order of fitting by labelling them 1 to 8, starting from the thermostat end of the cylinder head. Alternatively, push them through a piece of card in their fitted sequence.
**20** Progressively unscrew and loosen off the cylinder head retaining bolts in the reverse sequence to that shown for tightening **(see illustration 7.28a)**. When they are all loosened off, remove the bolts, then lift the cylinder head clear and remove the gasket. The gasket must always be renewed; it should be noted that the cylinder head retaining bolts may be re-used, but only once. They should be marked accordingly with a punch or paint mark. If there is any doubt as to how many times the bolts have been used, they must be renewed.
**21** To dismantle/overhaul the cylinder head, refer to Part D of this Chapter. It is normal for the cylinder head to be decarbonised and the valves to be reground whenever the head is removed.

## Preparation for refitting

**22** The mating faces of the cylinder head and cylinder block must be perfectly clean before refitting the head. Use a hard plastic or wood scraper to remove all traces of gasket and carbon; also clean the piston crowns. Take particular care during the cleaning operations, as aluminium alloy is easily damaged. Also, make sure that the carbon is not allowed to enter the oil and water passages - this is particularly important for the lubrication system, as carbon could block the oil supply to the engine's components. Using adhesive tape and paper, seal the water, oil and bolt holes in the cylinder block **(see Haynes Hint)**.
**23** Check the mating surfaces of the cylinder block and the cylinder head for nicks, deep scratches and other damage. If slight, they may be removed carefully with a file, but if

>
> **HAYNES HiNT**
> *To prevent carbon entering the gap between the pistons and bores, smear a little grease in the gap. After cleaning each piston, use a small brush to remove all traces of grease and carbon from the gap, then wipe away the remainder with a clean rag.*

excessive, machining may be the only alternative to renewal.
**24** If warpage of the cylinder head gasket surface is suspected, use a straight-edge to check it for distortion. Refer to Part D of this Chapter if necessary.
**25** Clean the threads of the cylinder head bolts or fit new ones (as applicable) and clean out the bolt holes in the block. Screwing a bolt into an oil-filled hole can (in extreme cases) cause the block to fracture, due to the hydraulic pressure.

## Refitting

**26** Check that the new cylinder head gasket is the same type as the original, and that the "TOP" (or "OBEN") marking is facing upwards. Locate the new cylinder head gasket onto the top face of the cylinder block and over the dowels. Ensure that it is correctly aligned with the coolant passages and oilways **(see illustration)**.
**27** Lower the cylinder head carefully into position, then insert the retaining bolts and hand-tighten them.
**28** Tightening of the cylinder head bolts must done in three stages, and in the correct sequence **(see illustration)**. First tighten all of the bolts in the sequence shown to the Stage 1 torque setting. When all of the bolts are tightened to the Stage 1 setting, further tighten each bolt (in sequence) through the Stage 2 specified angle of rotation. When the second stage tightening is completed on all of the bolts, further tighten them to the Stage 3 angle setting (in sequence) to complete. Where possible, use an angular torque setting gauge attachment tool for accurate tightening of stages two and three **(see illustrations)**.
**29** Lubricate the pushrods with clean engine oil, and then insert them into their original locations in the engine.

**7.26 Cylinder head gasket top-face marking ("OBEN")**

**2A**

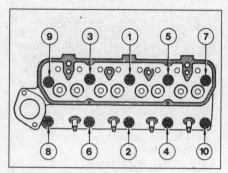

**7.28a Cylinder head bolt tightening sequence**

**7.28b Tightening the cylinder head bolts (Stage 1)**

**7.28c Cylinder head bolt tightening (Stages 2 and 3) using an angle gauge**

**30** Refit the rocker shaft assembly. As it is fitted, ensure that the rocker adjuster screws engage with their corresponding pushrods.

**31** Refit the rocker shaft retaining bolts, hand-tighten them and then tighten them to the specified torque wrench setting. As they are tightened, some of the rocker arms will apply pressure to the ends of the valve stems, and some of the rocker pedestals will not initially be in contact with the cylinder head - these should pull down as the bolts are tightened. If for any reason they do not, avoid the temptation to overtighten in order to pull them into position; loosen off the bolts, and check the cause of the problem. It may be that the rocker adjuster screws require loosening off in order to allow the assembly to be tightened down as required.

**32** Adjust the valve clearances as described in Section 5.

**33** Refit the rocker cover as described in Section 4.

**34** The remainder of the refitting procedure is a reversal of the removal process. Tighten all fastenings to their specified torque setting (where given). Refer to the appropriate Parts of Chapter 4 for details on reconnecting the fuel and exhaust system components. Ensure that all coolant, fuel, vacuum and electrical connections are securely made.

**35** On completion, refill the cooling system and top-up the engine oil (see Chapter 1 and *"Weekly Checks"*). When the engine is restarted, check for any sign of fuel, oil and/or coolant leakage from the various cylinder head joints.

## 8 Crankshaft pulley - removal and refitting

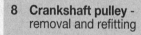

### Removal

**1** Disconnect the battery negative (earth) lead (refer to Chapter 5A, Section 1).

**2** Chock the rear wheels then jack up the front of the car and support it on axle stands (see *"Jacking and vehicle support"*). Remove the right-hand front roadwheel.

**3** Remove the auxiliary drivebelt as described in Chapter 1.

**4** Loosen off the crankshaft pulley retaining bolt. To prevent the crankshaft from turning on HCS engines, unbolt and remove the clutch housing cover plate. Lock the starter ring gear on the flywheel using a large screwdriver or similar tool inserted through the cover plate aperture. On Endura-E engines, remove the starter motor (Chapter 5A) and lock the ring gear through the starter motor aperture.

**5** Fully unscrew the crankshaft pulley bolt, and withdraw the pulley from the right-hand end of the crankshaft. If it does not pull off by hand, lever it free using a pair of suitable levers positioned diagonally opposite each other behind the pulley.

**6** If required, the crankshaft right-hand oil seal can be renewed at this stage, as described in Section 14.

### Refitting

**7** Refitting is a reversal of the removal procedure ensuring that the pulley retaining bolt is tightened to the specified torque setting.

**8** Refit the auxiliary drivebelt as described in Chapter 1, and lower the vehicle to complete.

## 9 Timing chain cover - removal and refitting

### Removal

**1** Remove the sump (see Section 11).

**2** Remove the crankshaft pulley as described in the previous Section.

**3** A combined timing cover and water pump gasket is fitted during production; if this is still in position, it will be necessary to drain the cooling system and remove the water pump as described in Chapter 3. If the water pump and/or the timing cover have been removed at any time, the single gasket used originally will have been replaced by an individual item, in which case the water pump can remain in position.

**4** On Endura-E engines, disconnect the camshaft position sensor wiring multi-plug.

**5** Unscrew the retaining bolts, and carefully prise free the timing chain cover.

**6** Clean the mating faces of the timing chain cover, and the engine.

**7** If necessary, renew the crankshaft right-hand oil seal in the timing cover prior to refitting the cover (see Section 14).

### Refitting

**8** Lightly lubricate the right-hand end of the crankshaft and the radial lip of the timing chain cover oil seal (already installed in the cover). Using a new gasket, fit the timing chain cover, centring it with the aid of the crankshaft pulley - lubricate the seal contact surfaces beforehand. Refit and tighten the retaining bolts to the specified torque setting but, where applicable, leave out the timing cover bolt which also secures the water pump at this stage.

**9** On Endura-E engines, reconnect the camshaft position sensor multi-plug.

**10** Where applicable, refit the water pump as described in Chapter 3.

**11** Refit the crankshaft pulley as described in the previous Section.

**12** Refit the sump as described in Section 11.

## 10 Timing chain, sprockets and tensioner - removal, inspection and refitting

### Removal

**1** Remove the timing chain cover as described in the previous Section.

**2** Remove the oil slinger from the right-hand end of the crankshaft, noting its orientation **(see illustration)**.

**10.2 Oil slinger removal from crankshaft**

**10.3 Chain tensioner arm removal from the pivot pin. Note tensioner retaining bolts (arrowed)**

**10.12a Fit the timing chain to the crankshaft and camshaft sprockets . . .**

## 11 Sump - removal and refitting

**10.12b . . . and check that the timing marks on the sprockets are in alignment**

**10.13 Bend locktabs against the camshaft retaining bolt heads to secure**

**3** Retract the chain tensioner cam back against its spring pressure, then slide the chain tensioner arm from its pivot pin on the right-hand main bearing cap (see illustration).
**4** Unbolt and remove the chain tensioner.
**5** Bend back the lockplate tabs from the camshaft sprocket bolts, then unscrew and remove the bolts. On Endura-E engines, note the fitted position of the camshaft position sensor rotor plate.
**6** Withdraw the sprocket complete with the timing chain.

### Inspection

**7** Examine the teeth on the timing sprockets for any signs of excessive wear or damage.
**8** The timing chain should always be renewed during a major engine overhaul. Slack links and pins are indicative of a worn chain. Unless the chain is known to be relatively new, it should be renewed.
**9** Examine the rubber cushion on the tensioner spring leaf. If grooved or deteriorated, it must be renewed.

### Refitting

**10** Commence reassembly by bolting the timing chain tensioner into position. Check that the face of the tensioner cam is parallel with the face of the cylinder block, ideally using a dial gauge. The maximum permissible error between the two measuring points is 0.2 mm. Release and turn the timing chain tensioner as required to achieve this (if necessary). Refer to the *Specifications* for the correct tightening torque.

**11** Turn the crankshaft so that the timing mark on its sprocket is directly in line with the centre of the camshaft sprocket mounting flange.
**12** Engage the camshaft sprocket with the timing chain, then engage the chain around the teeth of the crankshaft sprocket. Push the camshaft sprocket onto its mounting flange, and check that the sprocket retaining bolt holes are in alignment. Also check that the timing marks of both sprockets face each other. If required, turn the camshaft/sprocket as required to achieve this. It may also be necessary to remove the camshaft from the chain in order to reposition it in the required location in the chain to align the timing marks. This is a "trial and error" procedure, which must be continued until the exact alignment of the bolt holes and the timing marks is made (see illustrations).
**13** Insert and tighten the camshaft sprocket retaining bolts to the specified torque wrench setting. Bend up the tabs of the new lockplate to secure (see illustration). Remember to fit the rotor plate on Endura-E engines.
**14** Retract the timing chain tensioner cam, and then slide the tensioner arm onto its pivot pin. Release the cam so that it bears on the arm.
**15** Refit the oil slinger to the front of the crankshaft sprocket so that its convex side faces the sprocket.
**16** Refit the timing chain cover as described in the previous Section.

### Removal

**1** Disconnect the battery negative (earth) lead (refer to Chapter 5A, Section 1).
**2** Refer Chapter 1 and drain the engine oil. Refit the sump drain plug.
**3** Undo the retaining nuts and detach the exhaust downpipe from the manifold flange. Note that the flange gasket should be renewed on reassembly. Allowing sufficient clearance for sump removal, tie the exhaust downpipe up with a suitable length of wire or cord to prevent the system straining the insulators. On catalytic converter-equipped vehicles, avoid straining the oxygen sensor wiring, where applicable; if necessary, disconnect the sensor's multi-plug.
**4** Remove the starter motor (see Chapter 5A).
**5** Undo the two retaining bolts and remove the clutch housing cover plate. On Endura-E engines, undo the bolts securing the sump flange to the transmission.
**6** On Endura-E engine models with air conditioning, remove the auxiliary drivebelt (Chapter 1), unbolt the compressor from the sump mounting and position the compressor to one side. Do not disconnect any refrigerant hoses.
**7** Undo the eighteen bolts securing the sump to the base of the engine crankcase, then prise free and lower the sump. If the sump is stuck tight to the engine, cut around the flange gasket with a sharp knife, then lightly tap and prise it free. Keep the sump upright as it is lowered, to prevent spillage of any remaining oil in it. Also be prepared for oil drips from the crankcase when the sump is removed.
**8** Remove any dirt and old gasket from the contact faces of the sump and crankcase, and wash the sump out thoroughly before refitting. Check that the mating faces of the sump are not distorted. Check that the oil pick-up strainer is clear, cleaning it if necessary.

### Refitting

#### HCS engines

**9** Remove the old gaskets from the timing chain cover end, and from the flywheel end, and clean their location faces. Apply a dab of sealing compound to the mating faces where the ends of each cork half-gasket are to be fitted (see illustration). Stick the new cork gaskets into position on the block face, using clean thick grease to retain them, then locate the new rubber gaskets into their slots in the timing chain cover and rear oil seal carrier. The lugs of the cork gasket halves fit under the cut-outs in the rubber gaskets (see illustration).
**10** Before offering up the sump, check that the gap between the sump and the oil baffle is

**2A**

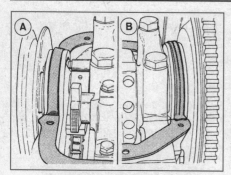

**11.9a Sump gasket fitting details at the timing chain cover end (A) and the flywheel end (B)**

**11.9b Lugs of cork gasket halves to fit under the cut-outs in the rubber gaskets**

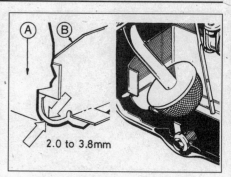

2.0 to 3.8mm

**11.10 Sump (A) and oil baffle (B) clearance details**

between 2.0 and 3.8 mm **(see illustration)**. Do not use a dented or damaged sump, as the indicated dimension is important for correct engine lubrication.

11 Fit the sump into position, and fit the retaining bolts. Initially tighten them all finger-tight, then further tighten them in the sequence shown through Stages 1 and 2, to the torque wrench settings specified **(see illustration)**. Note that different tightening sequences are specified for the tightening stages. Final (Stage 3) tightening is carried out after the engine has been started and warmed up.

12 Refit the lower plate to the front face of the clutch housing.

13 Refit the starter motor.

14 Check that the downpipe and manifold mating faces are clean, then locate a new gasket and reconnect the exhaust downpipe to the manifold. Where applicable, use new self-locking nuts, and tighten securely.

15 Check that the sump drain plug is fitted and tightened to the specified torque, then lower the vehicle to the ground.

16 Refill the engine with oil as described in Chapter 1.

17 Reconnect the battery, then start the engine and run it up to its normal operating temperature. Check that no oil leaks are evident around the sump joint.

18 After the engine has warmed up for approximately 15 minutes, switch it off. Tighten the sump bolts to the Stage 3 torque wrench setting given in the *Specifications*, in the sequence shown in **illustration 11.11**.

**Endura-E engines**

19 Thoroughly clean the sump and cylinder block mating faces.

20 Apply sealing compound (available from Ford dealers) to the cylinder block mating face in the area of the joint between the timing chain cover and cylinder block, and the left-hand oil seal carrier and cylinder block. Also apply sealer into the corners of the semi-circular areas on the timing chain cover and rear oil seal carrier.

21 Locate the one-piece gasket on the sump ensuring that it is correctly positioned, then fit the sump to the cylinder block. Fit the retaining bolts and tighten them initially finger tight.

22 With all the bolts in place, tighten them in the sequence shown through Stages 1 and 2,

to the torque wrench settings specified **(see illustration)**. Note that different tightening sequences are specified for the tightening stages. Final (Stage 3) tightening is carried out after the engine has been started and warmed up.

23 Refit the bolts securing the sump flange to the transmission.

24 Refit the starter motor.

25 Where applicable, refit the air conditioning compressor, then refit the auxiliary drivebelt as described in Chapter 1.

26 Check that the downpipe and manifold mating faces are clean, then locate a new gasket and reconnect the exhaust downpipe to the manifold. Where applicable, use new self-locking nuts, and tighten securely.

27 Check that the sump drain plug is fitted and tightened to the specified torque, then lower the vehicle to the ground.

28 Refill the engine with oil as described in Chapter 1.

29 Reconnect the battery, then start the engine and run it up to its normal operating temperature. Check that no oil leaks are evident around the sump joint.

30 After the engine has warmed up for

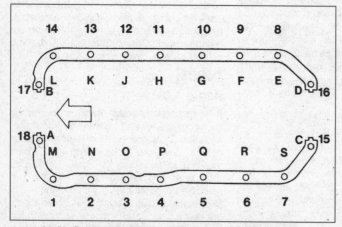

**11.11 Sump bolt tightening sequence (HCS engines) - arrow indicates crankshaft pulley end of engine**
*Refer to Specifications for torque wrench settings*
*Stage 1 - Tighten in alphabetical order*
*Stage 2 - Tighten in numerical order*
*Stage 3 - Tighten in alphabetical order*

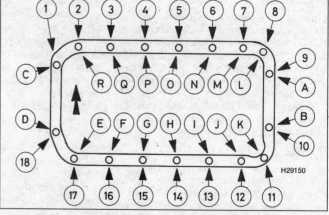

**11.22 Sump bolt tightening sequence (Endura-E engines) - arrow indicates front of car**
*Refer to Specifications for torque wrench settings*
*Stage 1 - Tighten in alphabetical order*
*Stage 2 - Tighten in numerical order*
*Stage 3 - Tighten in alphabetical order*

approximately 15 minutes, switch it off. Tighten the sump bolts to the Stage 3 torque wrench setting given in the *Specifications*, in the sequence shown in **illustration 11.22**.

## 12 Oil pump - removal and refitting

### Removal

1 The oil pump is externally-mounted, on the rear-facing side of the crankcase.
2 Chock the rear wheels then jack up the front of the car and support it on axle stands (see *"Jacking and vehicle support"*).
3 Unscrew and remove the oil filter cartridge. It should unscrew by hand, but will probably be tight. Use a strap wrench to loosen it off, if required. Catch any oil spillage in a suitable container.
4 Undo the three retaining bolts and withdraw the oil pump from the engine **(see illustration)**.
5 Clean all traces of the old gasket from the mating surfaces of the pump and engine.

### Refitting

6 If the original oil pump has been dismantled and reassembled and is to be re-used, or if a new pump is to be fitted, it must first be primed with engine oil prior to fitting. To do this, turn its driveshaft and simultaneously inject clean engine oil into it.
7 Locate a new gasket into position on the pump mounting flange, then insert the pump, engaging the drivegear as it is fitted **(see illustration)**. Fit the retaining bolts, and tighten to the specified torque wrench setting.
8 Fit a new oil filter into position on the oil pump body, as described in Chapter 1.
9 Lower the vehicle to the ground, and top-up the engine oil as described in *"Weekly Checks"*.

## 13 Oil pump - dismantling, inspection and reassembly

### Dismantling

1 To inspect the oil pump components for excessive wear, undo the retaining bolts and remove the cover plate from the pump body. Remove the O-ring seal from the cover face **(see illustration)**.
2 Wipe the exterior of the pump housing clean housing.

### Inspection

3 Noting their orientation, extract and clean the rotors and the inner body of the pump housing. Inspect them for signs of severe scoring or excessive wear, which if evident will necessitate renewal of the complete pump.

12.4 **Unscrewing the oil pump retaining bolts**

4 Using feeler blades, check the clearances between the pump body and the outer rotor, the inner-to-outer rotor clearance, and the amount of rotor endfloat **(see illustrations)**.
5 Check the drivegear for signs of excessive wear or damage.
6 If the clearances measured are outside the specified maximum clearances and/or the drivegear is in poor condition, the complete pump unit must be renewed.

### Reassembly

7 Refit the rotors into the pump (in their original orientation), lubricate the rotors and the new O-ring seal with clean engine oil, and refit the cover. Tighten the retaining bolts to the specified torque wrench setting.

13.1 **Extract the O-ring from the groove in the oil pump**

13.4b **Checking the inner rotor-to-outer rotor clearance**

12.7 **Refitting the oil pump. Note the new gasket**

## 14 Crankshaft oil seals - renewal

### Right-hand oil seal

1 Remove the crankshaft pulley as described in Section 8.
2 Using a suitable claw tool, extract the oil seal from the timing chain cover, but take care not to damage the seal housing. As it is removed, note the fitted orientation of the seal in the cover.
3 Clean the oil seal housing in the timing chain cover. Lubricate the sealing lips of the new seal and the crankshaft stub with clean engine oil.
4 Locate the new seal into position so that it is squarely located on the crankshaft stub and in the housing, and is correctly orientated. Drift it

**2A**

13.4a **Checking the outer body-to-rotor clearance**

13.4c **Checking the rotor endfloat**

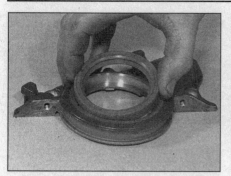

**14.11a Positioning the crankshaft left-hand oil seal in its housing**

**14.11b Fitting the left-hand oil seal housing with a new gasket in position on the rear face of the cylinder block**

into position using a large socket or other suitable tool, or the old seal, until the new seal is flush with the edge of the timing chain cover.

**5** Lightly lubricate the rubbing surface of the crankshaft pulley, then refit the pulley as described in Section 8.

### Left-hand oil seal

**6** Remove the flywheel as described in Section 16.

**7** Using a suitable claw tool, lever the seal from the left-hand seal housing (taking care not to damage the housing). As it is removed, note the fitted orientation of the seal.

**8** Clean the seal housing, the crankshaft left-hand flange face and the flywheel mating surface.

**9** One of two possible methods may be used to insert the new oil seal, depending on the tools available.

**10** If Ford service tool No 21-011 is available, lubricate the crankshaft flange and the oil seal inner lip with clean engine oil. Position the seal onto the service tool (ensuring correct orientation), then press the seal into its housing.

**11** If the service tool is not available, remove the engine sump (Section 11), then unscrew the Torx-head bolts retaining the rear seal housing in position, and remove the seal housing from the rear face of the cylinder block. New gaskets will be required for both the seal housing and the sump when refitting. Clean the seal housing seat and the mating surfaces of the sump and the crankcase. To fit the seal squarely into its housing without damaging either component, place a flat block of wood across the seal, then carefully tap the seal into position in the housing. Do not allow the seal to tilt as it is being fitted. Lubricate the crankshaft flange and the oil seal inner lip with clean engine oil, then with a new gasket located on the seal housing/crankcase face, fit the housing into position. Take care not damage the seal lips as it is passed over the crankshaft rear flange **(see illustrations)**. Centralise the seal on the shaft, then insert and tighten the housing retaining bolts to the specified torque setting. Refit the sump with reference to Section 11.

**12** Check that the crankshaft left-hand flange and the flywheel mating faces are clean, then refit the flywheel as described in Section 16.

## 15 Engine/transmission mountings - inspection and renewal

### Inspection

**1** The engine/transmission mountings seldom require attention, but broken or deteriorated mountings should be renewed immediately, or the added strain placed on the driveline components may cause damage or wear.

**2** During the check, the engine/transmission must be raised slightly, to remove its weight from the mountings.

**3** Chock the rear wheels then jack up the front of the car and support it on axle stands (see *"Jacking and vehicle support"*). Position a jack under the sump, with a large block of wood between the jack head and the sump, then carefully raise the engine/transmission just enough to take the weight off the mountings.

**4** Check the mountings to see if the rubber is cracked, hardened or separated from the metal components. Sometimes, the rubber will split right down the centre.

**5** Check for relative movement between each mounting's brackets and the engine/transmission or body (use a large screwdriver or lever to attempt to move the mountings). If movement is noted, lower the engine and check-tighten the mounting fasteners.

### Renewal

**6** The engine mountings can be removed if the weight of the engine/transmission is supported by one of the following alternative methods.

**7** Either support the weight of the assembly from underneath using a jack and a suitable

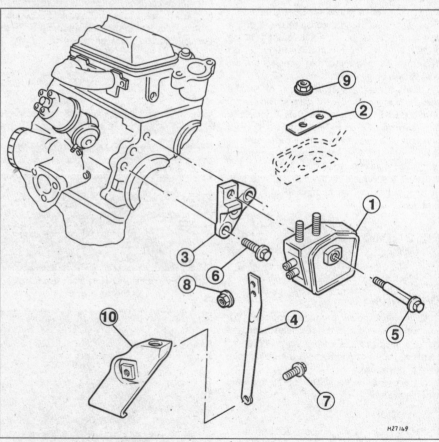

**15.8a Right-hand engine mounting components**

| | | | | | | | |
|---|---|---|---|---|---|---|---|
| 1 | Insulator | 3 | Mounting bracket | 6 | Bolt | 9 | Self-locking nut |
| 2 | Reinforcement plate | 4 | Support | 7 | Bolt | 10 | Insulator |
| | | 5 | Bolt and washer | 8 | Self-locking nut | | |

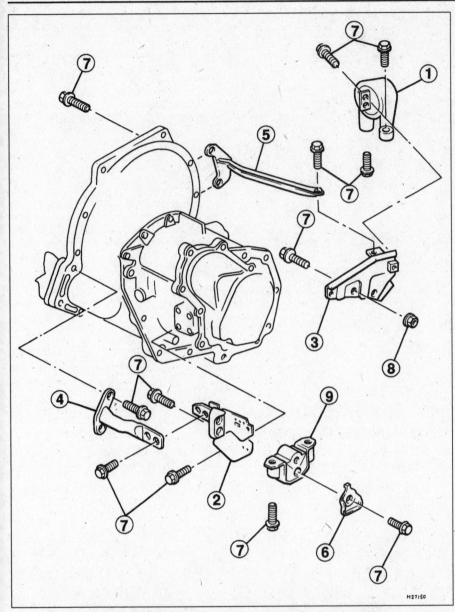

**15.8b Left-hand engine/transmission mounting components**

| 1 | Engine support insulator | 3 | Bracket | 6 | Retainer | 9 | Engine support bracket |
|---|---|---|---|---|---|---|---|
| 2 | Mounting bracket | 4 | Support stay | 7 | Bolt and washer | | |
| | | 5 | Support stay | 8 | Self-locking nut | | |

piece of wood between the jack saddle and the sump (to prevent damage), or from above by attaching a hoist to the engine. A third method is to use a suitable support bar with end pieces which will engage in the water channel each side of the bonnet lid aperture. Using an adjustable hook and chain connected to the engine, the weight of the engine and transmission can then be taken from the mountings.

**8** Once the weight of the engine and transmission is suitably supported, any of the mountings can be unbolted and removed. The accompanying illustrations show the mountings and their attachments, and should

be used for reference **(see illustrations)**. As the mountings are disconnected and removed, note the location and orientation of the fixings and any associated fittings.

**9** Refitting of all mountings is a reversal of the removal procedure. Ensure that the original sequence of washers and associated fittings are correctly fitted.

**10** Do not fully tighten the mounting fasteners until all of the mountings are in position. Check that the mounting rubbers do not twist or distort as the mounting bolts and nuts are tightened to their specified torque wrench settings.

## 16 Flywheel - removal, inspection and refitting

### Removal

**1** Remove the transmission as described in Chapter 7A, then remove the clutch as described in Chapter 6.

**2** Unscrew the six retaining bolts, and remove the flywheel from the left-hand end flange of the crankshaft - take care not to drop the flywheel, as it is heavy. A tool similar to that shown in **illustration 16.5** can be fitted to prevent the flywheel/crankshaft from rotating as the bolts are removed. If on removal, the retaining bolts are found to be in poor condition (stretched threads, etc) they must be renewed.

### Inspection

**3** Inspect the starter ring gear on the flywheel for any broken or excessively-worn teeth. If evident, the ring gear must be renewed; this is a task best entrusted to a Ford dealer or a competent garage. Alternatively, obtain a complete new flywheel.

**4** The clutch friction surface on the flywheel must be carefully inspected for grooving or hairline cracks (caused by overheating). If these conditions are evident, it may be possible to have the flywheel surface-ground to renovate it, providing that the balance is not upset. Regrinding is a task for an automotive engineer. If surface-grinding is not possible, the flywheel must be renewed.

### Refitting

**5** Check that the mating faces of the flywheel and the crankshaft are clean before refitting. Lubricate the threads of the retaining bolts with engine oil before they are screwed into position. Locate the flywheel onto the crankshaft, and insert the bolts. Hand-tighten them initially, then tighten them in a progressive sequence to the specified torque wrench setting **(see illustration)**.

**6** Refit the clutch as described in Chapter 6 and the transmission as described in Chapter 7A.

**2A**

**16.5 Tightening the flywheel retaining bolts to the specified torque**

*Note the "peg" tool locking the ring gear teeth to prevent rotation as the bolts are tightened.*

# Chapter 2 Part B:
# CVH & PTE engine in-car repair procedures

## Contents

## Degrees of difficulty

| Easy, suitable for novice with little experience |  | Fairly easy, suitable for beginner with some experience |  | Fairly difficult, suitable for competent DIY mechanic |  | Difficult, suitable for experienced DIY mechanic | | Very difficult, suitable for expert DIY or professional |  |

## Specifications

### General

Engine type . . . . . . . . . . . . . . . . . . . . . . . . . . . . . . . . . . . . Four-cylinder, in-line overhead camshaft
Engine code:
  1.4 litre CVH engine:
    Carburettor models . . . . . . . . . . . . . . . . . . . . . . . . FUH
    CFi fuel injection models . . . . . . . . . . . . . . . . . . . . F6F
  1.4 litre PTE engine . . . . . . . . . . . . . . . . . . . . . . . . . . F4B
  1.6 litre CVH engine:
    Carburettor models . . . . . . . . . . . . . . . . . . . . . . . . LUK, LUJ
    EFi fuel injection models . . . . . . . . . . . . . . . . . . . . LJE, LJF
Capacity:
  1.4 litre engine . . . . . . . . . . . . . . . . . . . . . . . . . . . . . 1392 cc
  1.6 litre engine . . . . . . . . . . . . . . . . . . . . . . . . . . . . . 1596 cc
Bore:
  1.4 litre engine . . . . . . . . . . . . . . . . . . . . . . . . . . . . . 77.24 mm
  1.6 litre engine . . . . . . . . . . . . . . . . . . . . . . . . . . . . . 79.96 mm
Stroke:
  1.4 litre engine . . . . . . . . . . . . . . . . . . . . . . . . . . . . . 74.30 mm
  1.6 litre engine . . . . . . . . . . . . . . . . . . . . . . . . . . . . . 79.52 mm
Compression ratio:
  1.4 litre CVH engine . . . . . . . . . . . . . . . . . . . . . . . . . 8.5:1
  1.4 litre PTE engine . . . . . . . . . . . . . . . . . . . . . . . . . 9.5:1
  1.6 litre engine:
    Carburettor models . . . . . . . . . . . . . . . . . . . . . . . . 9.5:1
    EFi fuel injection models . . . . . . . . . . . . . . . . . . . . 9.75:1
Firing order . . . . . . . . . . . . . . . . . . . . . . . . . . . . . . . . . . 1-3-4-2 (No 1 cylinder at timing belt end)
Direction of crankshaft rotation . . . . . . . . . . . . . . . . . . . Clockwise (seen from right-hand side of vehicle)

### Cylinder head

Hydraulic tappet bore inside diameter . . . . . . . . . . . . . . . . . . . . . . . 22.235 to 22.265 mm
Camshaft bearing bore diameter:
  Bearing 1 . . . . . . . . . . . . . . . . . . . . . . . . . . . . . . . . . . . 44.738 to 44.808 mm
  Bearing 2 . . . . . . . . . . . . . . . . . . . . . . . . . . . . . . . . . . . 45.033 to 45.058 mm
  Bearing 3 . . . . . . . . . . . . . . . . . . . . . . . . . . . . . . . . . . . 45.283 to 45.308 mm
  Bearing 4 . . . . . . . . . . . . . . . . . . . . . . . . . . . . . . . . . . . 45.533 to 45.558 mm
  Bearing 5 . . . . . . . . . . . . . . . . . . . . . . . . . . . . . . . . . . . 45.783 to 45.808 mm

2B

## Camshaft

Camshaft bearing journal diameter:
| | |
|---|---|
| Bearing 1 | 44.75 mm |
| Bearing 2 | 45.00 mm |
| Bearing 3 | 45.25 mm |
| Bearing 4 | 45.50 mm |
| Bearing 5 | 45.75 mm |
| Camshaft bearing journal-to-cylinder head running clearance | 0.033 to 0.058 mm |
| Camshaft endfloat | 0.05 to 0.13 mm |
| Camshaft thrust plate thickness | 4.99 to 5.01 mm |

## Lubrication

| | |
|---|---|
| Engine oil type/specification | See *"Lubricants, fluids and tyre pressures"* on page 0•17 |
| Engine oil capacity | See Chapter 1 Specifications |

Oil pressure:
| | |
|---|---|
| Idling | 1.0 bar |
| At 2000 rpm | 2.8 bars |

Oil pump clearances:
| | |
|---|---|
| Outer rotor-to-body | 0.060 to 0.190 mm |
| Inner rotor-to-outer rotor | 0.05 to 0.18 mm |
| Rotor endfloat | 0.014 to 0.100 mm |

## Torque wrench settings

| | Nm | lbf ft |
|---|---|---|
| Oil pump to cylinder block | 20 | 14 |
| Oil pump cover | 10 | 7 |
| Oil pump pick-up to cylinder block | 10 | 7 |
| Oil pump pick-up to pump | 10 | 7 |
| Oil cooler threaded sleeve to cylinder block | 57 | 42 |
| Left-hand oil seal housing | 10 | 7 |
| Flywheel | 87 | 64 |
| Cylinder head bolts: | | |
| Stage 1 | 30 | 22 |
| Stage 2 | 50 | 37 |
| Stage 3 | Angle-tighten a further 90° | |
| Stage 4 | Angle-tighten a further 90° | |
| Crankshaft pulley bolt | 108 | 80 |
| Camshaft thrust plate | 11 | 8 |
| Camshaft toothed belt sprocket | 57 | 42 |
| Timing belt tensioner | 18 | 13 |
| Rocker studs in cylinder head | 21 | 15 |
| Rocker arms | 27 | 20 |
| Rocker cover | 7 | 5 |
| Timing belt cover | 10 | 7 |
| Sump: | | |
| Stage 1 | 7 | 5 |
| Stage 2 | 7 | 5 |
| Engine/transmission mountings: | | |
| Right-hand mounting bracket-to-cylinder block | 90 | 66 |
| Right-hand mounting brace | 70 | 52 |
| Right-hand mounting-to-body | 85 | 63 |
| Left-hand rear mounting bracket-to-transmission | 50 | 37 |
| Left-hand rear mounting bracket-to-mounting | 68 | 50 |
| Left-hand front mounting bracket-to-mounting | 68 | 50 |
| Left-hand front mounting bracket brace | 49 | 36 |

**Note:** *Refer to Part D of this Chapter for remaining torque wrench settings.*

## 1  General information

### How to use this Chapter

This Part of Chapter 2 is devoted to repair procedures possible while the engine is still installed in the vehicle, and includes only the Specifications relevant to those procedures. Similar information concerning the 1.3 litre HCS and Endura-E engines, and the 1.6 and 1.8 litre Zetec and Zetec-E engines, will be found in Parts A and C of this Chapter respectively. Since these procedures are based on the assumption that the engine is installed in the vehicle, if the engine has been removed from the vehicle and mounted on a stand, some of the preliminary dismantling steps outlined will not apply.

Information concerning engine/ transmission removal and refitting, and engine overhaul, can be found in Part D of this Chapter, which also includes the Specifications relevant to those procedures.

### Engine description

The engine is a four-cylinder, in-line overhead camshaft type, designated CVH (Compound Valve angle, Hemispherical combustion chamber) or PTE (Pent roof, high

Torque, low Emission). The PTE engine was introduced for 1995 and, apart from modifications to the cylinder head, camshaft and inlet system, is virtually identical to the CVH engine it replaces. The engine is mounted transversely at the front of the vehicle together with the transmission to form a combined power unit.

The crankshaft is supported in five split-shell type main bearings within the cast-iron crankcase. The connecting rod big-end bearings are split-shell type, and the pistons are attached by interference-fit gudgeon pins. Each piston has two compression rings and one oil control ring.

The cylinder head is of light alloy construction, and supports the camshaft in five bearings. Camshaft drive is by a toothed composite rubber timing belt, which is driven by a sprocket on the front end of the crankshaft. The timing belt also drives the water pump, which is mounted below the cylinder head.

Hydraulic cam followers (tappets) operate the rocker arms and valves. The tappets are operated by pressurised engine oil. When a valve closes, the oil passes through a port in the body of the cam follower, through four grooves in the plunger and into the cylinder feed chamber. From the chamber, the oil flows to a ball-type non-return valve and into the pressure chamber. The tension of the coil spring causes the plunger to press against the valve, and so eliminates any free play. As the cam lifts the follower, the oil pressure in the pressure chamber is increased, and the non-return valve closes off the port feed chamber. This in turn provides a rigid link between the cam follower, the cylinder and the plunger. These then rise as a unit to open the valve. The cam follower-to-cylinder clearance allows the specified quantity of oil to pass from the pressure chamber, oil only being allowed past the cylinder bore when the pressure is high during the moment of the valve opening. When the valve closes, the escape of oil will produce a small clearance, and no pressure will exist in the pressure chamber. The feed chamber oil then flows through the non-return valve and into the pressure chamber, so that the cam follower cylinder can be raised by the pressure of the coil spring, eliminating free play until the valve is operated again.

As wear occurs between the rocker arm and the valve stem, the quantity of oil that flows into the pressure chamber will be slightly more than the quantity lost during the expansion cycle of the cam follower. Conversely, when the cam follower is compressed by the expansion of the valve, a slightly smaller quantity of oil will flow into the pressure chamber than was lost.

A rotor-type oil pump is mounted on the timing cover end of the engine, and is driven by a gear on the front end of the crankshaft. A full-flow type oil filter is fitted, and is mounted on the side of the crankcase.

## Repair operations possible with the engine in the car

The following work can be carried out with the engine in the car:

a) Compression pressure - testing.
b) Cylinder head rocker cover - removal and refitting.
c) Timing belt - removal, refitting and adjustment.
d) Camshaft oil seal - renewal.
e) Camshaft - removal and refitting.
f) Cylinder head - removal and refitting.
g) Cylinder head and pistons - decarbonising.
h) Crankshaft pulley - removal and refitting.
i) Crankshaft oil seals - renewal.
j) Oil filter renewal.
k) Sump - removal and refitting.
l) Oil pump - removal and refitting.
m) Flywheel - removal, inspection and refitting.
n) Engine/transmission mountings - removal and refitting.

**Note:** It is possible to remove the pistons and connecting rods (after removing the cylinder head and sump) without removing the engine. However, this is not recommended. Work of this nature is more easily and thoroughly completed with the engine on the bench, as described in Chapter 2D.

## 2 Compression test - description and interpretation

Refer to Section 2 in Part A of this Chapter.

## 3 Top Dead Centre (TDC) for No 1 piston - locating

1 Top dead centre (TDC) is the highest point of the cylinder that each piston reaches as the crankshaft turns. Each piston reaches its TDC position at the end of its compression stroke, and then again at the end of its exhaust stroke. For the purpose of engine timing, TDC on the compression stroke for No 1 piston is used. No 1 cylinder is at the timing belt end of the engine. Proceed as follows.

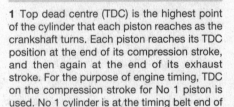

**3.5 Crankshaft pulley notch (arrowed) aligned with the TDC (0) mark on the timing belt cover**

2 Remove the upper timing belt cover as described in Section 7.
3 Chock the rear wheels then jack up the front of the car and support it on axle stands (see "Jacking and vehicle support").
4 Undo the retaining bolts, and remove the cover from the underside of the crankshaft pulley.
5 Fit a spanner onto the crankshaft pulley bolt, and turn the crankshaft in its normal direction of rotation (clockwise, viewed from the pulley end) to the point where the crankshaft pulley timing notch is aligned with the TDC (0) timing mark on the timing belt cover **(see illustration)**.

> **HAYNES HINT** *Turning the engine will be easier if the spark plugs are removed first - see Chapter 1.*

6 Although the crankshaft is now in top dead centre alignment, with piston Nos 1 and 4 at the top of their stroke, the No 1 piston may not be on its compression stroke. To confirm that it is, check that the timing pointer on the camshaft sprocket is exactly aligned with the TDC mark on the front face of the cylinder head **(see illustration)**. If the pointer is not aligned, turn the crankshaft pulley one further complete turn, and all the markings should now align.
7 With the engine set at No 1 piston on TDC compression, refit the crankshaft pulley cover, lower the vehicle and refit the upper timing belt cover.

**2B**

## 4 Cylinder head rocker cover - removal and refitting

### Removal

1 Disconnect the battery negative (earth) lead (refer to Chapter 5A, Section 1).
2 Remove the air cleaner assembly and air inlet components as necessary for access as described in the relevant Part of Chapter 4. Disconnect the crankcase ventilation hose from the rocker cover.
3 Remove the timing belt upper cover as described in Section 7.

**3.6 Camshaft sprocket timing mark aligned with the TDC mark on the front face of the cylinder head**

**4.8a  Fitting a new gasket to the rocker cover**

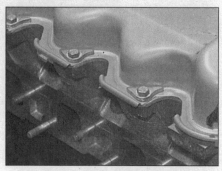

**4.8b  Rocker cover retaining bolts and plate washers**

**4** Referring to the relevant Part of Chapter 4 for details, disconnect the accelerator cable from the throttle linkage and from the adjuster bracket above the rocker cover. Position the cable out of the way.

**5** Where applicable, disconnect the choke cable from the carburettor, referring to Chapter 4A for details.

**6** Unscrew and remove the rocker cover retaining bolts and washers, then lift the cover from the cylinder head. Note that a new rocker cover gasket will be needed on refitting.

### Refitting

**7** Before refitting the rocker cover, clean the mating surfaces of both the cylinder head and the cover.

**8** Locate the new gasket in position, then fit the cover retaining bolts and washers. Ensure that the grooves in the plate washers are facing upwards as they are fitted **(see illustrations)**. Tighten the cover retaining bolts to the specified torque wrench setting. Refer to Chapter 4 for details on reconnecting the accelerator cable, choke cable, air inlet components and air cleaner (as applicable).

**9** Refit the timing belt cover and reconnect the battery earth lead.

## 5  Valve clearances - general information

It is necessary for a clearance to exist between the tip of each valve stem and the valve operating mechanism, to allow for the expansion of the various components as the engine reaches operating temperature.

On most older engine designs, this meant that the valve clearances (also known as "tappet" clearances) had to be checked and adjusted regularly. If the clearances were allowed to be too slack, the engine would be very noisy, its power output would suffer, and its fuel consumption would increase. If the clearances were allowed to be too tight, the engine's power output would be reduced, and the valves and their seats could be severely damaged.

These engines employ hydraulic tappets which use the lubricating system's oil pressure automatically to take up the clearance between each camshaft lobe and its respective valve stem. Therefore, there is no need for regular checking and adjustment of the valve clearances. However, it is essential that only good-quality oil of the recommended viscosity and specification is used in the engine, and that this oil is always changed at the recommended intervals. If this advice is not followed, the oilways and tappets may become clogged with particles of dirt, or deposits of burnt (inferior) engine oil, so that the system cannot work properly; ultimately, one or more of the tappets may fail, and expensive repairs may be required.

On starting the engine from cold, there will be a slight delay while full oil pressure builds up in all parts of the engine, especially in the tappets; the valve components, therefore, may well "rattle" for about 10 seconds or so, and then quieten. This is a normal state of affairs, and is nothing to worry about, provided that all tappets quieten quickly and stay quiet.

After the vehicle has been standing for several days, the valve components may "rattle" for longer than usual, as nearly all the oil will have drained away from the engine's top-end components and bearing surfaces. While this is only to be expected, care must be taken not to damage the engine under these circumstances - avoid high-speed running until all the tappets are refilled with oil and operating normally. With the vehicle

stationary, hold the engine at no more than a fast idle speed (maximum 2000 to 2500 rpm) for 10 to 15 minutes, or until the noise ceases. Do not run the engine at more than 3000 rpm until the tappets are fully recharged with oil and the noise has ceased.

If the valve components are thought to be noisy, or if a light rattle persists from the top end after the engine has warmed up to normal operating temperature, take the vehicle to a Ford dealer for expert advice. Depending on the mileage covered and the usage to which each vehicle has been put, some vehicles may be noisier than others; only a good mechanic experienced in these engines can tell if the noise level is typical for the vehicle's mileage, or if a genuine fault exists. If any tappet's operation is faulty, it must be renewed (Section 11).

## 6  Crankshaft pulley - removal and refitting

### Removal

**1** Disconnect the battery negative (earth) lead (refer to Chapter 5A, Section 1).

**2** Chock the rear wheels then jack up the front of the car and support it on axle stands (see "Jacking and vehicle support").

**3** Unbolt and remove the cover from the underside of the crankshaft pulley.

**4** Remove the auxiliary drivebelt as described in Chapter 1.

**5** If timing belt renewal is also intended, set the engine at TDC as described in Section 3 before removing the crankshaft pulley and retaining bolt.

**6** To prevent the crankshaft from turning as the pulley bolt is loosened off, remove the starter motor as described in Chapter 5A, and then lock the starter ring gear using a suitable lever **(see illustration)**.

**7** Unscrew and remove the crankshaft pulley retaining bolt and its washer. Withdraw the pulley from the end of the crankshaft **(see illustration)**. If necessary, lever it free using a pair of diagonally-opposed levers positioned behind the pulley.

**6.6  Using a suitable bar to lock the flywheel ring gear**

**6.7  Crankshaft pulley removal**

**7.3 Upper timing belt cover removal**

### Refitting

**8** Refit in the reverse order of removal. Tighten the pulley retaining bolt to the specified torque setting, and refer to Chapter 1 for details on refitting the auxiliary drivebelt.
**9** On completion, reconnect the battery earth lead.

### 7 Timing belt covers - removal and refitting

### Removal

**1** Disconnect the battery negative (earth) lead (refer to Chapter 5A, Section 1).
**2** Where applicable, undo the two bolts securing the power steering fluid pipe support clips and ease the pipe away from the upper cover.
**3** Undo the two retaining bolts and remove the upper timing belt cover **(see illustration)**.
**4** Refer to the previous Section for details, and remove the crankshaft pulley.
**5** Unscrew the two bolts securing the lower timing belt cover, and remove it **(see illustration)**.

### Refitting

**6** Refit in the reverse order of removal. Tighten the cover retaining bolts to the specified torque wrench setting.
**7** On completion, reconnect the battery earth lead.

**8.4 Timing belt tensioner retaining bolts (arrowed)**

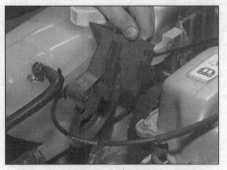

**7.5 Lower timing belt cover removal**

### 8 Timing belt - removal, refitting and adjustment

### Removal

**1** Referring to the previous Sections for details, remove the rocker cover, the crankshaft pulley and the timing belt covers.
**2** Check that the crankshaft is set with the No 1 piston at TDC (on its compression stroke) before proceeding. If necessary, refer to Section 3 for further details.
**3** To check the timing belt for correct adjustment, proceed as described below. To remove the belt, proceed as follows.
**4** Loosen off the two bolts securing the timing belt tensioner. Using a large screwdriver, prise the tensioner to one side to release the timing belt tension. Secure the tensioner in this position by retightening the bolts **(see illustration)**.
**5** If the original timing belt is to be refitted, mark it for direction of travel and also the exact tooth engagement positions on all sprockets. Slip the belt from the camshaft, water pump and crankshaft sprockets **(see illustration)**. Whilst the timing belt is removed, avoid any excessive movement of the sprockets, otherwise the piston crowns and valves may come into contact and be damaged.
**6** If the belt is being removed for reasons other than routine renewal, check it carefully for any signs of uneven wear, splitting, cracks (especially at the roots of the belt teeth) or

**8.5 Timing belt removal**

contamination with oil or coolant. Renew the belt if there is the slightest doubt about its condition. As a safety measure, the belt must be renewed as a matter of course at the intervals given in Chapter 1; if its history is unknown, the belt should be renewed irrespective of its apparent condition whenever the engine is overhauled.

### Refitting and adjustment

**7** Before refitting the belt, check that the crankshaft is still at the TDC position, with the small projection on the belt sprocket front flange aligned with the TDC mark on the oil pump housing **(see illustration)**. Also ensure that the camshaft sprocket is set with its TDC pointer aligned with the corresponding timing mark on the cylinder head. If necessary, adjust the sprockets slightly. As previously mentioned, avoid any excessive movement of the sprockets whilst the belt is removed.
**8** Engage the timing belt teeth with the teeth of the crankshaft sprocket, and then pull the belt vertically upright on its right-hand run. Keep it taut, and engage it with the teeth of the camshaft sprocket. If the original belt is being refitted, check that the belt's direction of travel is correct, and realign the belt-to-sprocket marks made during removal, to ensure that the exact original engagement positions are retained. When the belt is fully fitted on the sprockets, check that the sprocket positions have not altered.
**9** Carefully manoeuvre the belt around the tensioner, and engage its teeth with the water pump sprocket, again ensuring that the TDC positions of the crankshaft and camshaft are not disturbed as the belt is finally located.
**10** Refit the lower timing belt cover, and tighten its retaining bolts to the specified torque setting. Refit the crankshaft pulley, and tighten its retaining bolt to the specified torque setting.
**11** To take up belt slack, loosen off the tensioner and move it towards the front of the car to apply an initial tension to the belt. Secure the tensioner in this position, then remove the flywheel ring gear locking device.
**12** Rotate the crankshaft through two full revolutions in (the normal direction of travel), returning to the TDC position (camshaft

**2B**

**8.7 Sprocket and oil pump housing TDC marks in alignment**

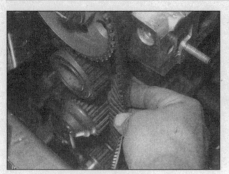

8.13 Checking the tension
of the timing belt

9.13a Refit the camshaft sprocket . . .

9.13b . . . and tighten the retaining bolt to
the specified torque whilst retaining the
sprocket as shown

sprocket-to-cylinder head). Check that the crankshaft pulley notch is aligned with the TDC (0) mark on the lower half of the timing belt cover.

**13** Grasp the belt between the thumb and forefinger, at the midway point between the crankshaft and camshaft sprockets on the right-hand side. If the belt tension is correct, it should just be possible to twist the belt through 90° at this point **(see illustration)**. To adjust the belt, loosen off the tensioner retaining bolts, move the tensioner as required using a suitable screwdriver as a lever, then retighten the retaining bolts. Rotate the crankshaft to settle the belt, then recheck the tension. It may take two or three attempts to get the tension correct. On completion, tighten the tensioner bolts to the specified torque wrench setting.

**14** It should be noted that this setting is approximate, and the belt tension should be rechecked by a Ford dealer with the special tensioner-setting tool at the earliest opportunity.

**15** Refit the starter motor (see Chapter 5A).

**16** Refit the rocker cover (see Section 4) and the upper timing belt cover (see Section 7).

**17** Refit the auxiliary drivebelt, adjust its tension as described in Chapter 1, then refit the crankshaft pulley lower cover.

**18** On completion, reconnect the battery earth lead.

## 9 Timing belt tensioner and sprockets - removal, inspection and refitting

### Tensioner

**1** Set the engine at TDC for No 1 piston on compression as described in Section 3, then refer to Section 7 and remove the timing belt upper cover.

**2** Loosen off the two bolts securing the timing belt tensioner. Using a large screwdriver, prise the tensioner to one side to release the timing belt tension.

**3** Remove the two tensioner bolts, and withdraw the tensioner from behind the timing belt.

**4** Check the condition of the tensioner, ensuring that it rotates smoothly on its bearings, with no signs of roughness or excessive free play. Renew the tensioner if in doubt about its condition.

**5** To refit the tensioner, first check that the engine is still positioned at TDC for No 1 piston on compression, with both the camshaft and crankshaft sprocket timing marks correctly aligned as described in Section 3.

**6** Refit the tensioner, guiding it in position around the timing belt, and secure with the two bolts. Move the tensioner towards the front of the car, to apply an initial tension to the belt. Secure the tensioner in this position.

**7** Adjust the timing belt tension as described in Section 8, paragraphs 12 to 14.

**8** Refit the timing belt upper cover on completion.

### Camshaft sprocket

**9** Set the engine at TDC for No 1 piston on compression as described in Section 3, then refer to Section 7 and remove the timing belt upper cover.

**10** Loosen off the two bolts securing the timing belt tensioner. Using a large screwdriver, prise the tensioner to one side to release the timing belt tension. Slip the timing belt off the camshaft sprocket.

**11** Pass a bar through one of the holes in the camshaft sprocket to prevent the camshaft from rotating, then unscrew and remove the sprocket retaining bolt. Note that this bolt must be renewed when refitting the camshaft sprocket. Remove the sprocket, noting the Woodruff key fitted to the camshaft; if the key is loose, remove it for safekeeping.

**12** Check the condition of the sprocket, inspecting carefully for any wear grooves, pitting or scoring around the teeth.

**13** Install the Woodruff key, then fit the camshaft sprocket with a new retaining bolt. The threads of the bolt should be smeared with thread-locking compound prior to fitting. Tighten the retaining bolt to the specified torque wrench setting **(see illustrations)**.

**14** Check that the engine is still positioned at TDC for No 1 piston on compression, with both the camshaft and crankshaft sprocket

timing marks correctly aligned as described in Section 3.

**15** Slip the timing belt over the camshaft sprocket, then move the tensioner towards the front of the car to apply an initial tension to the belt. Secure the tensioner in this position.

**16** Adjust the timing belt tension as described in Section 8, paragraphs 12 to 14.

**17** Refit the timing belt upper cover on completion.

### Crankshaft sprocket

**18** Remove the timing belt as described in Section 8.

**19** The crankshaft sprocket can now be withdrawn. If it is a tight fit on the crankshaft, a puller or two large screwdrivers can be used to release its grip. Withdraw the thrustwasher and the Woodruff key from the crankshaft.

**20** Check the condition of the sprocket, inspecting carefully for any wear grooves, pitting or scoring around the teeth.

**21** Refit the thrustwasher with its curved side facing outwards, followed by the Woodruff key.

**22** Lubricate the oil seal and the crankshaft sprocket with engine oil, then position the sprocket on the crankshaft with its thrust face facing outwards.

**23** Using the auxiliary drivebelt pulley and its retaining bolt, draw the sprocket fully into position on the crankshaft. Remove the pulley.

**24** Refit the timing belt as described in Section 8.

## 10 Camshaft oil seal - renewal

**1** Remove the camshaft sprocket as described in the previous Section.

**2** The oil seal is now accessible for removal. Note its direction of fitting, then using a suitable screwdriver or a tool with a hooked end to lever and extract the seal from its housing (but take care not to damage the housing with the tool) **(see illustration)**.

**3** Check that the housing is clean before fitting the new seal. Lubricate the lips of the

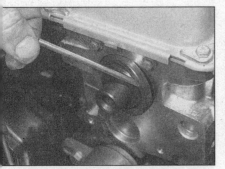
10.2  Camshaft front oil seal removal

10.3  Using a socket to tap the camshaft oil seal into place

11.5a  Undo the rocker arm retaining nut . . .

11.5b  . . . withdraw the guide . . .

11.5c  . . . followed by the rocker arm . . .

11.5d  . . . and spacer plate

11.6a  Removing a hydraulic tappet

11.6b  Store tappets in clearly-marked container filled with oil to prevent oil loss

seal and the running faces of the camshaft with clean engine oil. Carefully locate the seal over the camshaft, and drive it squarely into position using a suitable tube or a socket **(see illustration)**. An alternative method of fitting is to draw it squarely into position using the old sprocket bolt and a suitable distance piece.

4  With the seal fully inserted in its housing, refit the camshaft sprocket as described in the previous Section.

## 11  Camshaft, rocker arms and tappets - removal, inspection and refitting

### Removal

1  Disconnect the battery negative (earth) lead (refer to Chapter 5A, Section 1).
2  Refer to the appropriate earlier Sections in this Chapter, and remove the timing belt upper cover and the rocker cover.
3  On carburettor models, refer to Chapter 4A and remove the fuel pump. On PTE engines, refer to Chapter 4D and remove the camshaft position sensor.

4  Detach, unbolt and remove the ignition coil, its support bracket and the interference capacitor from the end of the cylinder head, as described in Chapter 5B.
5  Undo the retaining nuts and remove the guides, rocker arms and spacer plates **(see illustrations)**. Keep the respective components in their original order of fitting by marking them with a piece of numbered tape, or by using a suitable sub-divided box.
6  Withdraw the hydraulic tappets, again keeping them in their original fitted sequence. The tappets should be placed in an oil bath while removed **(see illustrations)**.
7  Unbolt and remove the lower cover beneath the crankshaft pulley, then with a spanner

2B

**11.10a  Undo the two retaining bolts (arrowed) . . .**

**11.10b  . . . and lift out the camshaft thrust plate**

**11.11a  Pierce the centre of the blanking plug . . .**

**11.11b  . . . and lever it out of the cylinder head**

**11.12  Withdraw the camshaft from the cylinder head**

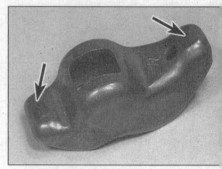

**11.19  Inspect the rocker arm contact points indicated for excessive wear**

engaged on the crankshaft pulley bolt, turn the crankshaft over to set the engine at TDC for No 1 piston on compression (see Section 3).

8 Remove the camshaft sprocket as described in Section 9.

9 Extract the camshaft oil seal as described in Section 10.

10 Before removing the camshaft and its thrust plate, check and take note of the amount of camshaft endfloat, using a dial gauge or feeler blades. With the camshaft endfloat measured and noted, unscrew the two retaining bolts and then extract the camshaft thrust plate from its pocket at the front end of the cylinder head (see illustrations).

11 At the rear end of the cylinder head, pierce the camshaft blanking plug with a suitable tool, and then lever it out of its aperture (see illustrations).

12 Withdraw the camshaft from the cylinder head at the rear (ignition coil) end (see illustration). Take care not to damage the bearings in the cylinder head as the shaft is withdrawn.

## Inspection

13 Clean and inspect the various components removed for signs of excessive wear.

14 Examine the camshaft bearing journals and lobes for damage or wear. If evident, a new camshaft will be required.

15 Compare the previously-measured camshaft endfloat with that specified. If the endfloat is outside of the specified tolerance, the thrust plate must be renewed.

16 The camshaft bearing bore diameters in the cylinder head should be measured and checked against the tolerances specified. A suitable measuring gauge will be required for this, but if this is not available, check for excessive movement between the camshaft journals and the bearings. If the bearings are found to be unacceptably worn, a new cylinder head is the only answer, as the bearings are machined directly into the head.

17 It is seldom that the hydraulic tappets are badly worn in the cylinder head bores but again, if the bores are found to be worn beyond an acceptable level, the cylinder head must be renewed.

18 If the contact surfaces of the cam lobes show signs of depression or grooving, they cannot be renovated by grinding, as the hardened surface will be removed and the overall length of the tappet(s) will be reduced. The self-adjustment point of the tappet will be exceeded as a result, so that the valve adjustment will be affected, resulting in noisy operation. Therefore, renewal of the camshaft is the only remedy in this case.

19 Inspect the rocker arm contact surfaces for excessive wear, and renew if necessary (see illustration).

## Refitting

20 Refitting the camshaft and its associated components is a reversal of the removal procedure, but note the following special points.

21 Lubricate the camshaft bearings, the camshaft and the thrust plate with clean

engine oil prior to fitting them. As the camshaft is inserted, take care not to damage the bearings in the cylinder head. Tighten the camshaft thrust plate retaining bolts to the specified torque. When the thrust plate bolts are tightened, make a final check to ensure that the camshaft endfloat is as specified.

22 A new front oil seal must be fitted after the camshaft has been installed (see previous Section for details). It will also be necessary to insert a new blanking plug into the rear end of the cylinder head. Drive it squarely into position so that it is flush with the head (see illustration).

23 Refer to the procedure in Section 9 when refitting the camshaft sprocket.

24 Refit and tension the timing belt as described in Section 8.

25 Lubricate the hydraulic tappets with hypoid oil before refitting them into their original locations in the cylinder head.

**11.22  Driving a new blanking plug into position**

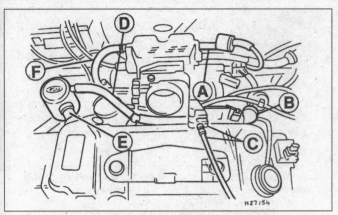

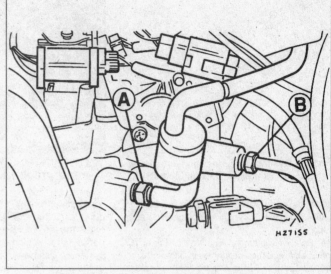

**12.8 Vacuum hoses and throttle cable connections on the 1.6 litre EFi fuel injected engine**

A  Hose to MAP sensor
B  Crankcase ventilation
   breather hose
C  Throttle cable and clip
D  Oil trap hose and T-piece
   connector
E  Hose to oil trap
F  Hose to carbon canister
   solenoid valve

**12.10 Vacuum hose to the MAP sensor (A) and the brake servo unit (B) on the 1.4 litre CFi fuel-injected engine**

26 Lubricate and refit the rocker arms and guides in their original sequence, use new nuts and tighten them to the specified torque setting. It is essential before each rocker arm is installed and its nut tightened, that the respective cam follower is positioned at its lowest point (in contact with the cam base circle). Turn the cam (using the crankshaft pulley bolt) as necessary to achieve this.
27 Refit the rocker cover (see Section 4).
28 Refit the remaining components with reference to the relevant Sections in this Chapter or elsewhere in the manual.
29 Reconnect the battery earth lead.

## 12 Cylinder head -
removal and refitting

### Removal

**Note:** *The following procedure describes removal and refitting of the cylinder head complete with inlet and exhaust manifolds. If wished, the manifolds may be removed first, as described in the relevant Part of Chapter 4, and the cylinder head then removed on its own.*
1 On fuel-injected engines, depressurise the fuel system as described in Chapter 4B.
2 Disconnect the battery negative (earth) lead (refer to Chapter 5A, Section 1).
3 Drain the cooling system (see Chapter 1).
4 Remove the rocker cover (see Section 4).
5 Disconnect the accelerator and choke cables as applicable (refer to Chapter 4).
6 Loosen off the retaining clips and disconnect the upper coolant hose, the expansion tank hose and the heater hose from the thermostat housing. Also disconnect the heater hose from the inlet manifold.
7 On CFi models, disconnect the heated coolant hose from the injector unit.

> **HAYNES HiNT** *Whenever you disconnect any vacuum lines, coolant or emissions hoses, wiring connectors and fuel lines, always label them clearly, so that they can be correctly reassembled. Masking tape and/or a touch-up paint applicator work well for marking items. Take instant photos, or sketch the locations of components and brackets.*

8 On EFi and SEFi models, disconnect the following (see illustration):
a) *The MAP sensor vacuum hose from the inlet manifold upper section (EFi models).*
b) *The carbon canister solenoid valve vacuum hose from the inlet manifold upper section.*
c) *The oil trap vacuum hose at the "T" piece connector.*
d) *The brake servo vacuum hose from the inlet manifold upper section by pressing in the clamp ring and simultaneously pulling the hose free from the connection.*
e) *The coolant hose from the injector intermediate flange and at the thermostat housing.*
9 Disconnect the following fuel supply/return hoses. Plug the hoses and connections, to prevent fuel spillage and the possible ingress of dirt.
a) *On carburettor models, disconnect the fuel supply hose from the pump and the return hose from the carburettor.*
b) *On CFi models, pull free and detach the fuel return hose from the injection unit and the supply hose at the connector.*
c) *On EFi and SEFi models, detach the fuel supply hose from the fuel rail or at the quick-release coupling (where fitted). Disconnect the return line from the fuel pressure regulator or at the quick-release coupling.*

10 On CFi models, disconnect the brake servo vacuum hose from the inlet manifold, the MAP sensor vacuum hose from the sensor, and the carbon canister connecting hose at the injection unit (see illustration).
11 Noting their connections and routings, disconnect the wiring connectors or multi-plugs from the following items, where applicable:
a) *Temperature gauge sender unit.*
b) *DIS ignition coil.*
c) *Coolant temperature sensor.*
d) *Cooling fan thermostatic switch.*
e) *Carburettor.*
f) *Radio earth lead.*
g) *Road speed sensor.*
h) *Fuel injector wiring loom.*
i) *Inlet air temperature sensor.*
12 On CFi models, detach the throttle control motor, throttle position sensor and injector lead multi-plugs (see illustration).

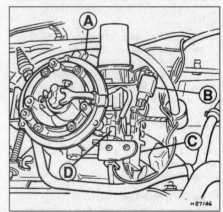

**12.12 Wiring connections to be detached on the 1.4 litre CFi fuel injected engine**

A  Coolant sensor
B  Throttle plate
   control motor
C  Throttle position
   sensor
D  Injector

**2B**

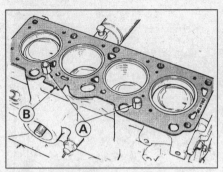

**12.21 Cylinder head location dowels (A) and gasket identification teeth (B)**

**12.27 Fit the cylinder head gasket with the "OBEN/TOP" marking upwards . . .**

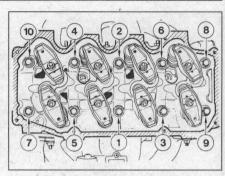

**12.28 Cylinder head bolt tightening sequence**

**13** Where still attached, disconnect the HT leads from the DIS ignition coil and the spark plugs.

**14** Position the engine with No 1 piston at TDC on compression as described in Section 3.

**15** Loosen off the timing belt tensioner retaining bolts, and move the tensioner to release the tension from the drivebelt. Support the belt, and move it clear of the camshaft sprocket.

**16** Chock the rear wheels then jack up the front of the car and support it on axle stands (see *"Jacking and vehicle support"*).

**17** Unscrew the retaining nuts and detach the exhaust downpipe from the manifold. Remove the gasket; note that a new one must be fitted on reassembly. Tie the downpipe up to support it. Where applicable, disconnect the pulse-air supply hose from the check valve. Noting their connections (to ensure correct reassembly), disconnect the appropriate system vacuum hoses at the PVS (three port vacuum switch) under the inlet manifold.

**18** Before it is released and removed, the cylinder head must first have cooled down to room temperature (about 20°C).

**19** Unscrew the cylinder head retaining bolts progressively in the reverse order to that shown for tightening **(see illustration 12.28)**. The cylinder head bolts must be discarded and new bolts obtained for refitting the cylinder head.

**20** Remove the cylinder head complete with its manifolds. If necessary, grip the manifolds and rock it free from the location dowels on the top face of the cylinder block. Do not attempt to tap it sideways or lever between the head and the block top face.

**21** Remove the cylinder head gasket. This must always be renewed; it is essential that the correct type is obtained. Save the old gasket, so that the identification marks (teeth) can be used when ordering the new one **(see illustration)**.

### Preparation for refitting

**22** The mating faces of the cylinder head and cylinder block must be perfectly clean before refitting the head. Use a hard plastic or wood scraper to remove all traces of gasket and carbon; also clean the piston crowns. Take particular care during the cleaning operations,

as aluminium alloy is easily damaged. Also, make sure that the carbon is not allowed to enter the oil and water passages - this is particularly important for the lubrication system, as carbon could block the oil supply to the engine's components. Using adhesive tape and paper, seal the water, oil and bolt holes in the cylinder block.

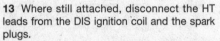

> **HAYNES HiNT** *To prevent carbon entering the gap between the pistons and bores, smear a little grease in the gap. After cleaning each piston, use a small brush to remove all traces of grease and carbon from the gap, then wipe away the remainder with a clean rag.*

**23** Check the mating surfaces of the cylinder block and the cylinder head for nicks, deep scratches and other damage. If slight, they may be removed carefully with a file, but if excessive, machining may be the only alternative to renewal.

**24** If warpage of the cylinder head gasket surface is suspected, use a straight-edge to check it for distortion. Refer to Part D of this Chapter if necessary.

**25** Ensure that new cylinder head bolts are used when refitting and clean out the bolt holes in the block. Screwing a bolt into an oil-filled hole can (in extreme cases) cause the block to fracture, due to the hydraulic pressure.

### Refitting

**26** To prevent the possibility of the valves and pistons coming into contact as the head is fitted, turn the crankshaft over to position No 1 piston approximately 20 mm below its TDC position in the bore.

**27** Locate the cylinder head gasket on the top face of the cylinder block, locating it over the dowels. Ensure that the gasket is fitted the correct way up, as indicated by its "OBEN-TOP" marking **(see illustration)**.

**28** Lower the cylinder head into position, ensuring that it fits over the locating dowels, then insert the new retaining bolts. Hand-tighten the bolts initially, then tighten them in the order shown in the four stages to the specified torque setting **(see illustration)**. Where possible, use an angular torque setting

gauge attachment tool for accurate tightening of stages three and four. Alternatively, after the first two stages, mark the bolt heads with a dab of quick drying paint, so that the paint spots all face the same direction. Now tighten all the bolts in the sequence to the Stage 3 setting, by tightening them through the specified angle. Finally, angle-tighten all the bolts through the Stage 4 angle.

**29** The camshaft sprocket should be positioned so that its TDC index mark pointer is in alignment with the TDC index spot mark on the front end face of the cylinder head **(see illustration 3.6)**.

**30** Now turn the crankshaft pulley to bring its TDC notch in alignment with the TDC (0) indicator on the front face of the timing belt cover, taking the shortest route (not vice-versa) **(see illustration 3.5)**.

**31** Refit the timing belt over the camshaft sprocket, and then tension the belt as described in Section 8.

**32** The remainder of the refitting procedure is a reversal of the removal process. Tighten all fastenings to their specified torque setting (where given). Refer to the appropriate Parts of Chapter 4 for details on reconnecting the fuel and exhaust system components. Ensure that all coolant, fuel, vacuum and electrical connections are securely made.

**33** On completion, refill the cooling system and top-up the engine oil (Chapter 1 and *"Weekly Checks"*). When the engine is restarted, check for any sign of fuel, oil and/or coolant leakages from the various cylinder head joints.

## 13 Sump - removal and refitting

### Removal

**1** Disconnect the battery negative (earth) lead (refer to Chapter 5A, Section 1).

**2** Drain the engine oil (refer to Chapter 1).

**3** Chock the rear wheels then jack up the front of the car and support it on axle stands (see *"Jacking and vehicle support"*).

**4** Where fitted, pull free the oxygen sensor lead multi-plug, and disconnect it. If the engine has been recently run, take particular

13.6a Auxiliary bracing bracket-to-engine bolts (oil filter side) - 1.6 litre engine

13.6b Auxiliary bracing bracket removal from the starter motor side of the engine - 1.6 litre engine

13.7 Removing the clutch cover plate

care against burning when working in the area of the catalytic converter.

5 Undo the retaining nuts, and detach the exhaust downpipe from the manifold. The flange gasket must be renewed when reconnecting. Where applicable, also detach the downpipe at the rear of the catalytic converter, and release it from the front mounting.

6 On 1.6 litre engines, undo the retaining bolts and remove the engine-to-transmission auxiliary bracing brackets (see illustrations).

7 Undo the retaining bolts, and remove the clutch cover plate from the front face of the bellhousing (see illustration).

8 Progressively unscrew the sump retaining bolts and remove them. Support and lower the sump pan, taking care not to spill any oil remaining in it as it is removed. If the sump is stuck to the base of the crankcase, prise it free using screwdriver, but take care not to damage the sump flange face. If it is really stuck in position, check first that all of the bolts are removed, then cut around the sump gasket with a sharp knife to help in freeing the joint.

9 After the sump is removed, further oil will almost certainly continue to drip down from within the crankcase, some old newspapers positioned underneath will soak up the spillage whilst the sump is removed.

10 Clean the sump of old oil and sludge, using paraffin or a suitable engine cleaner solution. Clean any traces of old gasket and sealer from the mating faces of the sump and the crankcase.

## Refitting

11 Smear a suitable sealing compound onto the junctions of the crankcase-to-oil seal carrier at the rear and the crankcase-to-oil pump housing at the front on each side (see illustration).

12 Insert a new rubber seal in the groove in the rear oil seal carrier and the oil pump case. As an aid to correct sump alignment when refitting it, screw ten M6 studs into the cylinder block, in the positions circled in illustration 13.14.

13 Fit a new gasket over the studs. Fit the sump into position, ensuring that the raised spacers sit in the gasket. Insert the bolts into the available holes, and finger-tighten them only at this stage. Now remove the studs and fit the remaining bolts, again finger-tight.

14 Tighten the sump bolts in a progressive, numerical sequence to the specified torque wrench setting (see illustration).

15 Fit the sump drain plug with a new sealing washer, and tighten it to the specified torque wrench setting.

16 Refit the clutch cover plate.

17 Reconnect the exhaust downpipe as described in Chapter 4E.

18 On completion, lower the vehicle, and fill the engine with oil as described in Chapter 1. Reconnect the battery.

## 14 Oil pump - removal and refitting

### Removal

1 Disconnect the battery negative (earth) lead (refer to Chapter 5A, Section 1).

2 Remove the auxiliary drivebelt (Chapter 1).

3 Remove the crankshaft pulley (Section 6), the timing belt covers (Section 7), the timing belt, crankshaft sprocket and thrustwasher (Sections 8 and 9), and the sump (Section 13).

4 Unscrew the retaining nut/bolts and remove the oil pick-up pipe (see illustration).

5 Unbolt and withdraw the oil pump from the front face of the engine. Clean the oil pump for inspection. Refer to Section 15 for the inspection procedures. The oil seal in the oil pump housing should always be renewed (Section 16). Remove the gasket.

### Refitting

6 Before refitting the oil pump and the

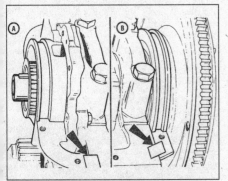

13.11 Sealing compound application points prior to refitting the sump

A Crankcase-to-oil pump housing
B Crankcase-to-rear oil seal carrier

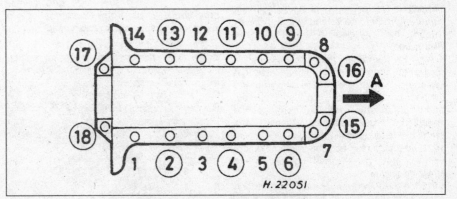

13.14 Sump bolt tightening sequence

A Crankshaft pulley end of engine
Circled numbers indicate locations of studs for correct sump alignment (see text)

2B

**14.4  Removing the oil inlet pipe**

**14.8  Prime the oil pump prior to fitting**

**14.9a  Refit the oil pump**

**14.9b  With the oil pump refitted, remove the protective guide (arrowed)**

associated fittings, clean off the respective mating faces. A new oil pump gasket must be obtained, as well as the seals and gaskets for the other associated components to be refitted. Stick the gasket in place with a little grease.

**7** When refitting the oil pump, precautionary measures must be taken to avoid the possibility of damaging the new oil seal as it is engaged over the shoulder and onto its journal on the crankshaft. Extract the Woodruff key from the groove in the crankshaft, then cut a plastic guide which will furl over and protrude beyond the shoulder of the seal journal on the crankshaft. This will allow the seal to ride over the step, and avoid damaging the seal lip as it is pushed into position on the crankshaft.

**8** If a new oil pump is being fitted or the old pump is to be re-used after cleaning and inspection, first prime the pump by squirting clean engine oil into it, and simultaneously rotating the drivegear a few times **(see illustration)**.

**9** Align the pump gear flats with those on the crankshaft, then fit the oil pump. Check that the sump mating faces of the oil pump and the base of the crankcase are flush each side, then tighten the retaining bolts to the specified torque setting. Remove the protective guide **(see illustrations)**.

**10** Refit the oil pick-up tube to the oil pump, using a new gasket and tighten to the specified torque.

**11** Slide the thrustwasher onto the front end of the crankshaft, then insert the Woodruff key into position in the groove in the crankshaft. The key must be located with its flat edge parallel with the line of the crankshaft, to

ensure that the crankshaft sprocket slides fully into position as it is being refitted.

**12** Refit the sump, crankshaft sprocket, the timing belt, timing belt cover and drivebelt pulley (as described in the appropriate earlier Sections of this Chapter). Refit and adjust the drivebelt as described in Chapter 1.

**13** On completion, lower the vehicle and reconnect the battery.

## 15  Oil pump - dismantling, inspection and reassembly

### Dismantling

**1** The oil pump fitted is a low-friction rotor-type, driven from the front end of the crankshaft. Where a high-mileage engine is being reconditioned, it is recommended that a new oil pump is fitted.

**15.2  Oil pump cover plate retaining screws (arrowed)**

**2** To inspect the rotor assembly, first remove the pump from the engine (Section 14), then undo the retaining screws and remove the cover plate **(see illustration)**. Remove the O-ring seal.

### Inspection

**3** Clean the rotors and the inside of the pump housing, then visually inspect the various components for signs of excessive wear and scoring. Check the pump components for wear using feeler blades in the same manner as that described in Part A of this Chapter, Section 13. Refer to the *Specifications* at the start of this Part for specific details.

### Reassembly

**4** When reassembling the pump, ensure that the inner (driving) and outer (driven) rotors are located with the corresponding indented matchmarks facing the same way **(see illustration)**.

## 16  Crankshaft oil seals - renewal

### Right-hand oil seal

**1** Disconnect the battery negative (earth) lead (refer to Chapter 5A, Section 1).

**2** Chock the rear wheels then jack up the front of the car and support it on axle stands (see *"Jacking and vehicle support"*).

**3** Remove the auxiliary drivebelt as described in Chapter 1.

**4** Remove the crankshaft pulley (Section 6), the timing belt covers (Section 7), the timing belt (Section 8) and crankshaft sprocket, Woodruff key and thrustwasher (Section 9).

**5** The oil seal is now accessible for removal from the front face of the oil pump housing **(see illustration)**. To withdraw the seal, a hooked tool will be required; if available, use Ford special tool No 21-096. Take care not to damage the oil pump housing during removal. As it is removed, note the fitted orientation of the seal in its housing.

**6** Clean the oil pump housing and the crankshaft stub, then lubricate the lips of the new seal and the crankshaft front stub with clean engine oil.

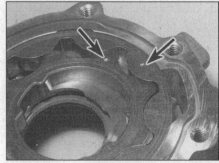

**15.4  Inner and outer rotor matchmarks (arrowed)**

**16.5 Crankshaft right-hand oil seal - seen from below (arrowed)**

**16.18 Rear oil seal removal**

7 The oil seal should be drawn into position using the Ford special tool No 21-093A. Failing this, use a tube of suitable diameter, with the crankshaft pulley bolt and washers. Do not hammer the seal into position. To protect the seal lips as it is fitted onto the crankshaft, cut a thin sheet of plastic to suit and furl it round the front of the crankshaft, over the journal shoulder.

8 When the seal is fully fitted, remove the special tool (or fabricated tool) and withdraw the plastic protector. Check that the crankshaft is still at the TDC position and refit the Woodruff key, thrustwasher and sprocket. Refit and tension the timing belt, then refit the timing belt cover and crankshaft pulley as described in the appropriate Sections earlier in this Chapter.

9 Refit and adjust the auxiliary drivebelt as described in Chapter 1.

10 On completion, lower the vehicle and reconnect the battery.

### Left-hand oil seal

11 With the engine or transmission removed from the vehicle for access, remove the clutch as described in Chapter 6.

12 Remove the flywheel/driveplate as described in Section 18.

13 If available, use Ford special tool No 21-151 or a suitable clawed tool to extract the seal from its housing. If the seal housing is removed from the rear face of the engine, the seal can be removed as described in paragraph 18. As it is removed, note the direction of fitting, and take care not to damage the seal housing as the seal is extracted.

14 Clean the seal housing, the crankshaft flange face, and the flywheel/driveplate mating surfaces.

15 One of two possible methods may be used to insert the new oil seal, depending on the tools available.

16 If Ford special service tool No 21-095 is available, lubricate the seal lips of the seal and its running face on the crankshaft with clean engine oil. Position the seal (correctly orientated) into the special tool, then draw the seal into the housing using two flywheel/driveplate securing bolts so that the seal is against the stop.

17 If the correct Ford service tool is not available, it will be necessary to remove the oil seal carrier housing. To do this, first remove the sump as described in Section 13, then unscrew the seal housing retaining bolts and remove the housing from the face of the crankcase.

18 Drive the old seal from the housing by carefully tapping it from its aperture using a suitable punch as shown **(see illustration)**. As it is removed, note the direction of fitting, and take care not to damage the seal housing as the seal is extracted.

19 New gaskets will be required for the seal housing and sump during reassembly. Clean the mating faces of the seal housing, the crankcase and sump. Insert the new seal squarely into its housing. To avoid damaging the seal or the housing, place a flat piece of wood across the face of the seal, and carefully tap or draw the seal into place. Do not allow the seal to tilt in the housing as it is being fitted.

20 Lubricate the running surface on the crankshaft and the oil seal lip with clean engine oil. Locate a new gasket onto the face of the crankcase, and refit the oil seal housing and seal. To avoid damaging the lips of the seal as it is passed over the end of the crankshaft, cut a thin sheet of plastic to suit and furl it round the rear flange of the crankshaft so that it protrudes, and press the seal over it. With the seal in position, withdraw the plastic protector. Centralise the seal on the shaft, check that the housing-to-sump flange faces are flush to the sump face on the base of the crankcase, then insert and tighten the housing retaining bolts to the specified torque.

21 Refit the sump (see Section 13).

22 Refit the flywheel/driveplate as described in Section 18.

23 Refit the clutch as described in Chapter 6.

24 Refit the engine or transmission, as applicable.

## 17 Engine/transmission mountings - renewal

The procedures for renewing the engine/transmission mountings are much the same as those described for the HCS and Endura-E engines. Refer to Part A, Section 15 for details.

## 18 Flywheel/driveplate - removal, inspection and refitting

### Removal

1 Access to the flywheel (manual transmission) or driveplate (automatic transmission) is gained by first removing the transmission (Chapter 7A or B). On manual transmission models, remove the clutch (Chapter 6).

2 Unscrew and remove the six flywheel/driveplate retaining bolts, and carefully withdraw the flywheel/driveplate from the rear face of the crankshaft. Take care not to drop the flywheel, as it is heavy. Note that the retaining bolts must be renewed when refitting.

### Inspection

3 The inspection procedures for the flywheel/driveplate are the same as those described for the HCS and Endura-E engine in Part A of this Chapter, but note that the grinding procedures do not apply to automatic transmission models (the driveplate cannot be reground).

### Refitting

4 Check that the mating faces of the flywheel/driveplate and crankshaft are clean before refitting.

5 Smear the new retaining bolt threads with thread-locking compound. Fit the flywheel/driveplate into position on the rear end face of the crankshaft. Check that all of the bolt holes in the flywheel/driveplate are in exact alignment with the corresponding bolt holes in the crankshaft, then insert the bolts and tighten them in a progressive sequence to the specified torque wrench setting.

6 Refit the clutch (manual transmission models) as described in Chapter 6.

7 Refit the transmission (according to type) as described in Chapter 7A or B.

**2B**

# Chapter 2 Part C:
# Zetec & Zetec-E engine in-car repair procedures

## Contents

## Degrees of difficulty

| Easy, suitable for novice with little experience |  | Fairly easy, suitable for beginner with some experience |  | Fairly difficult, suitable for competent DIY mechanic |  | Difficult, suitable for experienced DIY mechanic |  | Very difficult, suitable for expert DIY or professional | |
|---|---|---|---|---|---|---|---|---|---|

## Specifications

### General

| | |
|---|---|
| Engine type . . . . . . . . . . . . . . . . . . . . . . . . . . . . . . . . . . . . . . . . . . . | Four-cylinder, in-line, double overhead camshafts |
| Engine code: | |
|   Zetec engines: | |
|     1.6 litre models . . . . . . . . . . . . . . . . . . . . . . . . . . . . . . . . . . . | L1E |
|     1.8 litre models . . . . . . . . . . . . . . . . . . . . . . . . . . . . . . . . . . . | RDA, RQB |
|   Zetec-E engines: | |
|     1.6 litre models . . . . . . . . . . . . . . . . . . . . . . . . . . . . . . . . . . . | L1H, LIK |
|     1.8 litre models . . . . . . . . . . . . . . . . . . . . . . . . . . . . . . . . . . . | RKC |
| Capacity: | |
|   1.6 litre models . . . . . . . . . . . . . . . . . . . . . . . . . . . . . . . . . . . | 1597 cc |
|   1.8 litre models . . . . . . . . . . . . . . . . . . . . . . . . . . . . . . . . . . . | 1796 cc |
| Bore: | |
|   1.6 litre models . . . . . . . . . . . . . . . . . . . . . . . . . . . . . . . . . . . | 76.0 mm |
|   1.8 litre models . . . . . . . . . . . . . . . . . . . . . . . . . . . . . . . . . . . | 80.6 mm |
| Stroke - all models . . . . . . . . . . . . . . . . . . . . . . . . . . . . . . . . . . . . | 88.0 mm |
| Compression ratio: | |
|   Zetec engines: | |
|     1.6 litre models . . . . . . . . . . . . . . . . . . . . . . . . . . . . . . . . . . . | 10.3:1 |
|     1.8 litre models . . . . . . . . . . . . . . . . . . . . . . . . . . . . . . . . . . . | 10.0:1 |
|   Zetec-E engines: | |
|     1.6 litre models . . . . . . . . . . . . . . . . . . . . . . . . . . . . . . . . . . . | 10.3:1 |
|     1.8 litre models . . . . . . . . . . . . . . . . . . . . . . . . . . . . . . . . . . . | 9.8:1 |
| Firing order . . . . . . . . . . . . . . . . . . . . . . . . . . . . . . . . . . . . . . . . . . | 1-3-4-2 (No 1 cylinder at timing belt end) |
| Direction of crankshaft rotation . . . . . . . . . . . . . . . . . . . . . . . . . . . | Clockwise (seen from right-hand side of vehicle) |

### Cylinder head

| | |
|---|---|
| Hydraulic tappet bore inside diameter . . . . . . . . . . . . . . . . . . . . . . | 28.395 to 28.425 mm |

### Camshafts and hydraulic tappets

| | |
|---|---|
| Camshaft bearing journal diameter . . . . . . . . . . . . . . . . . . . . . . . . | 25.960 to 25.980 mm |
| Camshaft bearing journal-to-cylinder head running clearance . . . . . . | 0.020 to 0.070 mm |
| Camshaft endfloat . . . . . . . . . . . . . . . . . . . . . . . . . . . . . . . . . . . . | 0.080 to 0.220 mm |
| Hydraulic tappet diameter . . . . . . . . . . . . . . . . . . . . . . . . . . . . . . . | 28.400 mm |

## Lubrication

| | |
|---|---|
| Engine oil type/specification . . . . . . . . . . . . . . . . . . . . . . . . . . . . . . . . . . . . . | See *"Lubricants, fluids and tyre pressures"* on page 0•17 |
| Engine oil capacity . . . . . . . . . . . . . . . . . . . . . . . . . . . . . . . . . . . . . . . . . . . . . | See Chapter 1 Specifications |
| Oil pressure: | |
|   Idling . . . . . . . . . . . . . . . . . . . . . . . . . . . . . . . . . . . . . . . . . . . . . . . . . . . . . | 1.3 to 2.5 bar |
|   At 4000 rpm . . . . . . . . . . . . . . . . . . . . . . . . . . . . . . . . . . . . . . . . . . . . . . . | 3.7 to 5.5 bars |
| Oil pump clearances . . . . . . . . . . . . . . . . . . . . . . . . . . . . . . . . . . . . . . . . . . . | Not specified |

## Torque wrench settings

| | Nm | lbf ft |
|---|---|---|
| Cylinder head cover bolts: | | |
|   Stage 1 . . . . . . . . . . . . . . . . . . . . . . . . . . . . . . . . . . . . . . . . . . . . . . . . . . . | 2 | 1.5 |
|   Stage 2 . . . . . . . . . . . . . . . . . . . . . . . . . . . . . . . . . . . . . . . . . . . . . . . . . . . | 7 | 5 |
| Camshaft sprocket bolts . . . . . . . . . . . . . . . . . . . . . . . . . . . . . . . . . . . . . . . | 68 | 50 |
| Camshaft bearing cap bolts: | | |
|   Stage 1 . . . . . . . . . . . . . . . . . . . . . . . . . . . . . . . . . . . . . . . . . . . . . . . . . . . | 10 | 7 |
|   Stage 2 . . . . . . . . . . . . . . . . . . . . . . . . . . . . . . . . . . . . . . . . . . . . . . . . . . . | 19 | 14 |
| Cylinder head bolts: | | |
|   Stage 1 . . . . . . . . . . . . . . . . . . . . . . . . . . . . . . . . . . . . . . . . . . . . . . . . . . . | 25 | 18 |
|   Stage 2 . . . . . . . . . . . . . . . . . . . . . . . . . . . . . . . . . . . . . . . . . . . . . . . . . . . | 45 | 33 |
|   Stage 3 . . . . . . . . . . . . . . . . . . . . . . . . . . . . . . . . . . . . . . . . . . . . . . . . . . . | Angle-tighten a further 105° | |
| Timing belt cover fasteners: | | |
|   Upper-to-middle (outer) cover bolts . . . . . . . . . . . . . . . . . . . . . . . . . . . . | 4 | 3 |
|   Cover-to-cylinder head or block bolts . . . . . . . . . . . . . . . . . . . . . . . . . . | 7 | 5 |
|   Cover studs-to-cylinder head or block . . . . . . . . . . . . . . . . . . . . . . . . . . | 10 | 7 |
| Timing belt tensioner bolt . . . . . . . . . . . . . . . . . . . . . . . . . . . . . . . . . . . . . | 38 | 28 |
| Timing belt tensioner backplate locating peg . . . . . . . . . . . . . . . . . . . . . . | 10 | 7 |
| Timing belt tensioner spring retaining pin . . . . . . . . . . . . . . . . . . . . . . . . | 10 | 7 |
| Timing belt guide pulley bolts . . . . . . . . . . . . . . . . . . . . . . . . . . . . . . . . . . | 38 | 28 |
| Water pump pulley bolts . . . . . . . . . . . . . . . . . . . . . . . . . . . . . . . . . . . . . . | 10 | 7 |
| Auxiliary drivebelt idler pulley . . . . . . . . . . . . . . . . . . . . . . . . . . . . . . . . . . | 48 | 35 |
| Alternator mounting bracket-to-cylinder block bolts . . . . . . . . . . . . . . | 47 | 35 |
| Cylinder head support plates: | | |
|   Front plate Torx screws - to power steering pump/air conditioning | | |
|   compressor mounting bracket and cylinder head . . . . . . . . . . . . . . . . | 47 | 35 |
|   Rear plate/engine lifting eye to alternator mounting | | |
|   bracket and cylinder head bolts . . . . . . . . . . . . . . . . . . . . . . . . . . . . . . | 47 | 35 |
| Front engine lifting eye bolt . . . . . . . . . . . . . . . . . . . . . . . . . . . . . . . . . . . | 16 | 12 |
| Exhaust manifold heat shield bolts: | | |
|   Shield-to-cylinder head . . . . . . . . . . . . . . . . . . . . . . . . . . . . . . . . . . . . . | 7 | 5 |
|   Shield/dipstick tube . . . . . . . . . . . . . . . . . . . . . . . . . . . . . . . . . . . . . . . | 10 | 7 |
|   Shield/coolant pipe-to-manifold . . . . . . . . . . . . . . . . . . . . . . . . . . . . . . | 23 | 17 |
| Crankshaft pulley bolt . . . . . . . . . . . . . . . . . . . . . . . . . . . . . . . . . . . . . . . . | 115 | 85 |
| Oil pump-to-cylinder block bolts . . . . . . . . . . . . . . . . . . . . . . . . . . . . . . . | 10 | 7 |
| Oil pick-up pipe-to-pump screws . . . . . . . . . . . . . . . . . . . . . . . . . . . . . . | 10 | 7 |
| Oil baffle/pump pick-up pipe nuts . . . . . . . . . . . . . . . . . . . . . . . . . . . . . . | 19 | 14 |
| Oil filter adapter-to-pump . . . . . . . . . . . . . . . . . . . . . . . . . . . . . . . . . . . . . | 22 | 16 |
| Oil pressure warning light switch . . . . . . . . . . . . . . . . . . . . . . . . . . . . . . . | 27 | 20 |
| Sump bolts . . . . . . . . . . . . . . . . . . . . . . . . . . . . . . . . . . . . . . . . . . . . . . . . . | 21 | 15 |
| Engine (sump) to transmission bolts . . . . . . . . . . . . . . . . . . . . . . . . . . . | 44 | 32 |
| Engine oil drain plug . . . . . . . . . . . . . . . . . . . . . . . . . . . . . . . . . . . . . . . . . | 25 | 18 |
| Coolant pipe-to-sump bolt . . . . . . . . . . . . . . . . . . . . . . . . . . . . . . . . . . . . | 10 | 7 |
| Flywheel/driveplate bolts . . . . . . . . . . . . . . . . . . . . . . . . . . . . . . . . . . . . . | 110 | 81 |
| Crankshaft left-hand oil seal carrier bolts . . . . . . . . . . . . . . . . . . . . . . . | 22 | 16 |
| Engine/transmission mountings: | | |
|   Right-hand mounting bracket-to-cylinder block . . . . . . . . . . . . . . . . . | 90 | 66 |
|   Right-hand mounting brace . . . . . . . . . . . . . . . . . . . . . . . . . . . . . . . . . . | 70 | 52 |
|   Right-hand mounting-to-body . . . . . . . . . . . . . . . . . . . . . . . . . . . . . . . . | 85 | 63 |
|   Left-hand rear mounting bracket-to-transmission . . . . . . . . . . . . . . . | 50 | 37 |
|   Left-hand rear mounting bracket-to-mounting . . . . . . . . . . . . . . . . . . | 68 | 50 |
|   Left-hand front mounting bracket-to-mounting . . . . . . . . . . . . . . . . . . | 68 | 50 |
|   Left-hand front mounting bracket brace . . . . . . . . . . . . . . . . . . . . . . . . | 49 | 36 |

**Note:** *Refer to Part D of this Chapter for remaining torque wrench settings.*

## 1 General information

### How to use this Chapter

This Part of Chapter 2 is devoted to repair procedures possible while the engine is still installed in the vehicle, and includes only the Specifications relevant to those procedures. Similar information concerning the 1.3 litre HCS and Endura-E engines, and the 1.4 and 1.6 litre CVH and PTE engines, will be found in Parts A and B of this Chapter respectively. Since these procedures are based on the assumption that the engine is installed in the vehicle, if the engine has been removed from the vehicle and mounted on a stand, some of the preliminary dismantling steps outlined will not apply.

Information concerning engine/transmission removal and refitting, and engine overhaul, can be found in Part D of this Chapter, which also includes the relevant Specifications.

### Engine description

The Zetec engine, (formerly Zeta), is of sixteen-valve, double overhead camshaft (DOHC), four-cylinder, in-line type, mounted transversely at the front of the vehicle, with the transmission on its left-hand end. The Zetec-E engine is virtually identical to the Zetec unit apart from revisions to the intake system and emission control system components.

Apart from the plastic timing belt covers and the cast-iron cylinder block/crankcase, all major engine castings are of aluminium alloy.

The crankshaft runs in five main bearings, the centre main bearing's upper half incorporating thrustwashers to control crankshaft endfloat. The connecting rods rotate on horizontally-split bearing shells at their big-ends. The pistons are attached to the connecting rods by gudgeon pins which are an interference fit in the connecting rod small-end eyes. The aluminium alloy pistons are fitted with three piston rings: two compression rings and an oil control ring. After manufacture, the cylinder bores and piston skirts are measured and classified into three grades, which must be carefully matched together, to ensure the correct piston/cylinder clearance; no oversizes are available to permit reboring.

The inlet and exhaust valves are each closed by coil springs; they operate in guides which are shrink-fitted into the cylinder head, as are the valve seat inserts.

Both camshafts are driven by the same toothed timing belt, each operating eight valves via self-adjusting hydraulic tappets, thus eliminating the need for routine checking and adjustment of the valve clearances. Each camshaft rotates in five bearings that are line-bored directly in the cylinder head and the (bolted-on) bearing caps; this means that the bearing caps are not available separately from the cylinder head, and must not be interchanged with caps from another engine.

The water pump is bolted to the right-hand end of the cylinder block, inboard of the timing belt, and is driven with the power steering pump and alternator by a flat "polyvee"-type auxiliary drivebelt from the crankshaft pulley.

When working on this engine, note that Torx-type (both male and female heads) and hexagon socket (Allen head) fasteners are widely used; a good selection of bits and adapters will be required, so that these can be unscrewed and tightened to the torque wrench settings specified without damage.

Lubrication is by means of an eccentric-rotor trochoidal pump, which is mounted on the crankshaft right-hand end, and draws oil through a strainer located in the sump. The pump forces oil through an externally-mounted full-flow cartridge-type filter - on some versions of the engine, an oil cooler is fitted to the oil filter mounting, so that clean oil entering the engine's galleries is cooled by the main engine cooling system.

### Repair operations possible with the engine in the car

The following work can be carried out with the engine in the car:

a) Compression pressure - testing.
b) Cylinder head cover - removal and refitting.
c) Timing belt covers - removal and refitting.
d) Timing belt - renewal.
e) Timing belt tensioner and sprockets - removal and refitting.
f) Camshaft oil seals - renewal.
g) Camshafts and hydraulic tappets - removal and refitting.
h) Cylinder head - removal and refitting.
i) Cylinder head and pistons - decarbonising.
j) Sump - removal and refitting.
k) Crankshaft oil seals - renewal.
l) Oil pump - removal and refitting.
m) Flywheel/driveplate - removal and refitting.
n) Engine/transmission mountings - removal and refitting.

**Note:** It is possible to remove the pistons and connecting rods (after removing the cylinder head and sump) without removing the engine. However, this is not recommended. Work of this nature is more easily and thoroughly completed with the engine on the bench, as described in Chapter 2D.

## 2 Compression test - description and interpretation

Refer to Section 2 in Part A of this Chapter.

## 3 Top Dead Centre (TDC) for No 1 piston - locating

1 Top dead centre (TDC) is the highest point of the cylinder that each piston reaches as the crankshaft turns. Each piston reaches its TDC position at the end of its compression stroke, and then again at the end of its exhaust stroke. For the purpose of engine timing, TDC on the compression stroke for No 1 piston is used. No 1 cylinder is at the timing belt end of the engine. Proceed as follows.
2 Disconnect the battery negative (earth) lead (refer to Chapter 5A, Section 1).
3 Chock the rear wheels then jack up the front of the car and support it on axle stands (see "Jacking and vehicle support"). Remove the right-hand roadwheel.
4 Remove the auxiliary drivebelt cover (see Chapter 1) to expose the crankshaft pulley and timing marks.
5 Fit a spanner onto the crankshaft pulley bolt, and turn the crankshaft in its normal direction of rotation (clockwise, viewed from the pulley end).

> **HAYNES HINT** *Turning the engine will be easier if the spark plugs are removed first - see Chapter 1.*

6 Note the two pairs of notches in the inner and outer rims of the crankshaft pulley. In the normal direction of crankshaft rotation the first pair of notches are irrelevant to the vehicles covered in this manual, while the second pair indicate TDC when aligned with the rear edge of the raised mark on the sump. Rotate the crankshaft clockwise until the second pair of notches align with the edge of the sump mark; use a straight edge extended out from the sump if greater accuracy is required **(see illustrations)**.

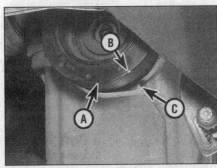

3.6a Do not use crankshaft pulley's first pair of notches "A" - align second pair of notches "B" with raised rib on sump "C"...

3.6b ... use a straight edge extended out from the sump (arrowed) if greater accuracy is required

**2C**

**4.5 Disconnecting crankcase breather hose from cylinder head cover union**

**4.7 Removing cylinder head cover**

**4.9 Ensure gasket is located correctly in cover groove**

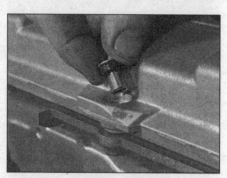

**4.10 Ensure rubber seal is fitted to each cover bolt spacer, as shown**

7 Nos 1 and 4 cylinders are now at TDC, one of them on the compression stroke. Remove the oil filler cap; if No 4 cylinder exhaust cam lobe is pointing to the rear of the vehicle and slightly downwards, it is No 1 cylinder that is correctly positioned. If the lobe is pointing horizontally forwards, rotate the crankshaft one full turn (360°) clockwise until the pulley notches align again, and the lobe is pointing to the rear and slightly down. No 1 cylinder will then be at TDC on the compression stroke.

8 Once No 1 cylinder has been positioned at TDC on the compression stroke, TDC for any of the other cylinders can then be located by rotating the crankshaft clockwise 180° at a time and following the firing order (see *Specifications*).

9 With the engine set at No 1 piston on TDC compression, refit the drivebelt cover and the roadwheel, then lower the vehicle and refit the spark plugs.

## 4 Cylinder head cover - removal and refitting

### Removal

1 Disconnect the battery negative (earth) lead (refer to Chapter 5A, Section 1).
2 Remove the air inlet components as necessary for access as described in the Chapter 4D.
3 Disconnect the accelerator cable from the throttle linkage as described in Chapter 4D.

4 Remove the timing belt upper cover (see Section 7).
5 Disconnect the crankcase breather hose from the cylinder head cover union **(see illustration)**.
6 Unplug the HT leads from the spark plugs and withdraw them, unclipping the leads from the cover.
7 Working progressively, unscrew the cylinder head cover retaining bolts, noting the spacer sleeve and rubber seal at each, then withdraw the cover **(see illustration)**.
8 Discard the cover gasket; this *must* be renewed whenever it is disturbed. Check that the sealing faces are undamaged, and that the rubber seal at each retaining bolt is serviceable; renew any worn or damaged seals.

### Refitting

9 On refitting, clean the cover and cylinder head gasket faces carefully, then fit a new

**6.4a Unscrew pulley bolt to release crankshaft pulley**

gasket to the cover, ensuring that it locates correctly in the cover grooves **(see illustration)**.
10 Refit the cover to the cylinder head, then insert the rubber seal and spacer sleeve at each bolt location **(see illustration)**. Start all bolts finger-tight, ensuring that the gasket remains seated in its groove.
11 Working in a diagonal sequence from the centre outwards, and in two stages (see *Specifications*), tighten the cover bolts to the specified torque wrench setting.
12 Refit the HT leads, clipping them into place so that they are correctly routed; each is numbered, and can also be identified by the numbering on its respective coil terminal.
13 Reconnect the crankcase breather hose, and refit the timing belt upper cover. Reconnect and adjust the accelerator cable, then refit the air inlet components (see Chapter 4D).

## 5 Valve clearances - general information

Refer to Section 5 in Part B of this Chapter.

## 6 Crankshaft pulley - removal and refitting

### Removal

1 Remove the auxiliary drivebelt - either remove the drivebelt completely, or just secure it clear of the crankshaft pulley, depending on the work to be carried out (see Chapter 1).
2 If necessary, rotate the crankshaft until the timing marks align (see Section 3).
3 The crankshaft must now be locked to prevent its rotation while the pulley bolt is unscrewed. To do this, remove the starter motor (Chapter 5A) and lock the starter ring gear teeth using a suitable screwdriver.
4 Unscrew the pulley bolt and remove the pulley **(see illustrations)**.

### Refitting

5 Refitting is the reverse of the removal procedure; ensure that the pulley's keyway is

**6.4b Ensure pulley is located on crankshaft Woodruff key on reassembly**

aligned with the crankshaft's locating key, and tighten the pulley bolt to the specified torque wrench setting.

## 7 Timing belt covers - removal and refitting

### Upper cover

**1** Unscrew the cover's two mounting bolts and withdraw it **(see illustration)**.
**2** Refitting is the reverse of the removal procedure; ensure that the cover edges engage correctly with each other, and note the torque wrench setting specified for the bolts.

### Middle cover

**3** Unscrew the nut securing the power steering pipe support clip to the stud at the rear of the middle cover. Lift the power steering fluid reservoir upwards out of its mounting bracket and move it clear, as far as the hoses will allow, for access. If insufficient clearance is obtained, disconnect the fluid unions as necessary, and collect the fluid in a suitable container. Plug or cover any disconnected unions.
**4** Slacken the water pump pulley bolts.
**5** Remove the timing belt upper cover.
**6** Remove the auxiliary drivebelt (Chapter 1).
**7** Unbolt and remove the water pump pulley.
**8** Unscrew the middle cover fasteners (one bolt at the front, one at the lower rear, one stud at the top rear) and withdraw the cover.
**9** Refitting is the reverse of the removal procedure. Ensure that the cover edges engage correctly with each other, and note the torque wrench settings specified for the various fasteners.
**10** If the power steering hoses where disconnected, bleed the system as described in Chapter 10 after reconnection.

### Lower cover

**11** Remove the crankshaft pulley (see Section 6).
**12** Unscrew the three cover securing bolts, and withdraw it **(see illustration)**.
**13** Refitting is the reverse of the removal procedure; ensure the cover edges engage correctly with each other, and note the torque wrench settings specified for the various fasteners.

### Inner shield

**14** Remove the timing belt, its tensioner components and the camshaft sprockets (see Sections 8 and 9).
**15** The shield is secured to the cylinder head by two bolts at the top, and by two studs lower down; unscrew these and withdraw the shield **(see illustration)**.
**16** Refitting is the reverse of the removal procedure; note the torque wrench settings specified for the various fasteners.

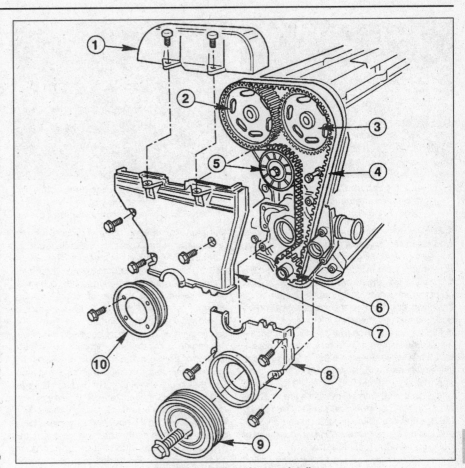

**7.1 Timing belt and cover details**

| | | | |
|---|---|---|---|
| 1 | Timing belt upper cover | 6 | Crankshaft toothed pulley |
| 2 | Inlet camshaft toothed pulley | 7 | Timing belt middle cover |
| 3 | Exhaust camshaft toothed pulley | 8 | Timing belt lower cover |
| 4 | Timing belt | 9 | Crankshaft pulley |
| 5 | Timing belt tensioner | 10 | Water pump pulley |

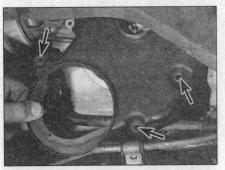

**7.12 Removing timing belt lower cover - bolt locations arrowed**

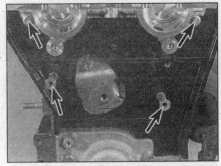

**7.15 Timing belt inner shield fasteners (arrowed)**

## 8 Timing belt - removal, refitting and adjustment

**Note:** To carry out this operation, a new timing belt (where applicable), a new cylinder head cover gasket, and some special tools (see text) will be required. If the timing belt is being removed for the first time since the vehicle left the factory, a tensioner spring and retaining pin must be obtained for fitting on reassembly.

### Removal

**1** Disconnect the battery negative (earth) lead (refer to Chapter 5A, Section 1).
**2** Slacken the water pump pulley bolts.
**3** Remove the cylinder head cover (see Section 4).

**2C**

**8.8 Fit camshaft-aligning tool to ensure engine is locked with Nos 1 and 4 cylinders at TDC**

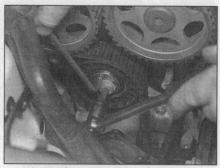

**8.12 Slacken the tensioner bolt, and use an Allen key to rotate the tensioner away from the timing belt**

**4** Remove the spark plugs, covering their holes with clean rag, to prevent dirt or other foreign bodies from dropping in (see Chapter 1).

**5** Remove the auxiliary drivebelt (Chapter 1).

**6** Position the engine with No 1 piston at TDC on compression as described in Section 3.

**7** Unbolt and remove the water pump pulley and the auxiliary drivebelt idler pulley.

**8** Obtain Ford service tool 21-162, or fabricate a substitute alternative from a strip of metal 5 mm thick (while the strip's thickness *is* critical, its length and width are not, but should be approximately 180 to 230 mm by 20 to 30 mm). Check that Nos 1 and 4 cylinders are at TDC - No 1 on the compression stroke - by resting this tool on the cylinder head mating surface, and sliding it into the slot in the left-hand end of both camshafts **(see illustration)**. The tool should slip snugly into both slots while resting on the cylinder head mating surface; if one camshaft is only slightly out of alignment, it is permissible to use an open-ended spanner to rotate the camshaft gently and carefully until the tool will fit.

**9** If both camshaft slots (they are machined significantly off-centre) are below the level of the cylinder head mating surface, rotate the crankshaft through one full turn clockwise and fit the tool again; it should now fit as described in the previous paragraph.

**10** With the camshaft aligning tool remaining in place, remove the crankshaft pulley. *Do not use the locked camshafts to prevent the crankshaft from rotating - use only the locking method described in Section 6.*

**11** Remove the timing belt lower and middle covers (see Section 7).

**12** With the camshaft-aligning tool still in place, slacken the tensioner bolt, and use an Allen key inserted into its centre to rotate the tensioner clockwise as far as possible away from the belt; retighten the bolt to secure the tensioner clear of the timing belt **(see illustration)**.

**13** If the timing belt is to be re-used, use white paint or similar to mark its direction of rotation, and note from the manufacturer's markings which way round it is fitted. Withdraw the belt. *Do not* rotate the crankshaft until the timing belt is refitted.

**14** If the belt is being removed for reasons other than routine renewal, check it carefully for

any signs of uneven wear, splitting, cracks (especially at the roots of the belt teeth) or contamination with oil or coolant. Renew the belt if there is the slightest doubt about its condition. As a safety measure, the belt must be renewed as a matter of course at the intervals given in Chapter 1; if its history is unknown, the belt should be renewed irrespective of its apparent condition whenever the engine is overhauled. Similarly, check the tensioner spring (where fitted), renewing it if there is any doubt about its condition. Check also the sprockets for signs of wear or damage, and ensure that the tensioner and guide pulleys rotate smoothly on their bearings; renew any worn or damaged components. If signs of oil or coolant contamination are found, trace the source of the leak and rectify it, then wash down the engine timing belt area and related components, to remove all traces of oil or coolant.

### Refitting and adjustment

**15** On reassembly, temporarily refit the crankshaft pulley, to check that the crankshaft is still positioned at TDC for No 1 piston on compression, then ensure that both camshafts are aligned at TDC by the special tool (paragraph 8). If the engine is being reassembled after major dismantling, both camshaft sprockets should be free to rotate on their respective camshafts; if the timing belt alone is being renewed, both sprockets should still be securely fastened.

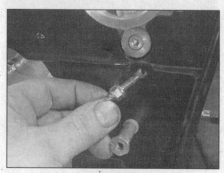

**8.17a Fitting tensioner spring retaining pin**

**16** A holding tool will be required to prevent the camshaft sprockets from rotating while their bolts are slackened and retightened; either obtain Ford service tool 15-030A, or fabricate a suitable substitute **(see Tool Tip)**. **Note:** *Do not use the camshaft-aligning tool (whether genuine Ford or not) to prevent rotation while the camshaft sprocket bolts are slackened or tightened; the risk of damage to the camshaft concerned and to the cylinder head is far too great. Use only a forked holding tool applied directly to the sprockets, as described.*

**TOOL TiP** *To make a camshaft sprocket holding tool, obtain two lengths of steel strip about 6 mm thick by 30 mm wide or similar, one 600 mm long, the other 200 mm long (all dimensions approximate). Bolt the two strips together to form a forked end, leaving the bolt slack so that the shorter strip can pivot freely. At the end of each "prong" of the fork, bend the strips through 90° about 50 mm from their ends to act as the fulcrums; these will engage with the holes in the sprockets. It may be necessary to grind or cut off their sides slightly to allow them to fit the sprocket holes.*

**17** If it is being fitted for the first time, screw the timing belt tensioner spring retaining pin into the cylinder head, tightening it to the specified torque wrench setting. Unbolt the tensioner, hook the spring on to the pin and the tensioner backplate, then refit the tensioner, engaging its backplate on the locating peg **(see illustrations)**.

**18** In all cases, slacken the tensioner bolt (if necessary), and use an Allen key inserted into its centre to rotate the tensioner clockwise as far as possible against spring tension, then retighten the bolt to secure the tensioner **(see illustration)**.

**19** Fit the timing belt; if the original is being refitted, ensure that the marks and notes made on removal are followed, so that the belt is refitted the same way round, and to run in the same direction. Starting at the crankshaft

**8.17b Hook spring onto tensioner and refit as shown - engage tensioner backplate on locating peg (arrowed) . . .**

8.18 . . . then use Allen key to position tensioner so that timing belt can be refitted

8.20 Slacken tensioner bolt to give initial belt tension

8.23 Using forked holding tool while camshaft toothed pulley bolt is tightened

8.24 When setting is correct, tighten tensioner bolt to specified torque setting

sprocket, work anti-clockwise around the camshaft sprockets and tensioner, finishing off at the rear guide pulley. The front run, between the crankshaft and the exhaust camshaft sprockets, *must* be kept taut, without altering the position either of the crankshaft or of the camshaft(s) - if necessary, the position of the camshaft sprockets can be altered by rotating each on its camshaft (which remains fixed by the aligning tool). Where the sprocket is still fastened, use the holding tool described above to prevent the sprocket from rotating while its retaining bolt is slackened - the sprocket can then be rotated on the camshaft until the belt will slip into place; retighten the sprocket bolt.

20 When the belt is in place, slacken the tensioner bolt gently until the spring pulls the tensioner against the belt; the tensioner should be retained correctly against the timing belt inner shield and cylinder head, but must be just free to respond to changes in belt tension **(see illustration)**.

21 Tighten both camshaft sprocket bolts (or check that they are tight, as applicable) and remove the camshaft-aligning tool. Temporarily refit the crankshaft pulley, and rotate the crankshaft through two full turns clockwise to settle and tension the timing belt, returning the crankshaft to the TDC position described previously. Refit the camshaft-aligning tool; it should slip into place as described in paragraph 8. If all is well, proceed to paragraph 24 below.

22 If one camshaft is only just out of line, fit the forked holding tool to its sprocket, adjust

its position as required, and check that any slack created has been taken up by the tensioner; rotate the crankshaft through two further turns clockwise, and refit the camshaft-aligning tool to check that it now fits as it should. If all is well, proceed to paragraph 24 below.

23 If either camshaft is significantly out of line, use the holding tool to prevent its sprocket from rotating while its retaining bolt is slackened - the camshaft can then be rotated (gently and carefully, using an open-ended spanner) until the camshaft-aligning tool will slip into place; take care not to disturb the relationship of the sprocket to the timing belt. Without disturbing the sprocket's new position on the camshaft, tighten the sprocket bolt to its specified torque wrench setting **(see illustration)**. Remove the camshaft-aligning tool, rotate the crankshaft through two further turns clockwise, and refit the tool to check that it now fits as it should.

24 When the timing belt has been settled at its correct tension, and the camshaft-aligning tool fits correctly when the crankshaft pulley notches are exactly aligned, tighten the tensioner bolt to its specified torque wrench setting **(see illustration)**. Fitting the forked holding tool to the spokes of each sprocket in turn, check that the sprocket bolts are tightened to their specified torque wrench setting. Remove the camshaft-aligning tool, rotate the crankshaft through two further turns clockwise, and refit the tool to make a final check that it fits as it should.

25 The remainder of the reassembly procedure is the reverse of removal, ensuring that all fasteners are tightened to the specified torque.

## 9 Timing belt tensioner and sprockets - removal, inspection and refitting

### Tensioner

**Note:** *If the tensioner is being removed for the first time since the vehicle left the factory, a tensioner spring and retaining pin must be obtained for fitting on reassembly.*

1 While it is possible to reach the tensioner once the timing belt upper and middle covers only have been removed, the whole procedure outlined below must be followed, to ensure that the valve timing is correctly reset once the belt's tension has been disturbed.

2 Release the tension from the timing belt as described in Section 8, paragraphs 1 to 12.

3 Unscrew the tensioner bolt and withdraw the tensioner, unhooking the spring, if fitted **(see illustration)**. Check the tensioner spring, and renew it if there is any doubt about its condition.

4 On reassembly, if it is being fitted for the first time, screw the timing belt tensioner spring retaining pin into the cylinder head, tightening it to the specified torque wrench setting. Hook the spring onto the pin and the tensioner backplate, then refit the tensioner, engaging its backplate on the locating peg.

5 Use an Allen key inserted into its centre to rotate the tensioner clockwise as far as possible against spring tension, then tighten the bolt to secure the tensioner.

6 Reassemble, checking the camshaft alignment (valve timing) and setting the timing belt tension, as described in paragraphs 20 to 25 of Section 8.

### Camshaft and crankshaft sprockets

7 While it may be possible to remove any of these sprockets once the relevant belt covers have been removed, the complete timing belt removal/refitting procedure (see Section 8) must be followed, to ensure that the valve timing is correctly reset once the belt's tension has been disturbed.

9.3 Removing timing belt tensioner

2C

**9.8 Note "FRONT" marking on outside face of crankshaft toothed pulley - note which way round the thrustwasher behind is fitted**

**10.5 Using socket and toothed pulley bolt to install camshaft oil seal**

**10.6 Alternatively, seal can be inserted when camshaft bearing cap is unbolted**

**8** With the timing belt removed, the camshaft sprockets can be detached once their retaining bolts have been unscrewed as described in paragraph 16 of Section 8. The crankshaft sprocket can be pulled off the end of the crankshaft, once the crankshaft pulley and the timing belt have been removed. Note the "FRONT" marking identifying the sprocket's outboard face, and the thrustwasher behind it; note which way round the thrustwasher is fitted **(see illustration)**. Note the sprocket-locating Woodruff key; if this is loose, it should be removed for safe storage with the sprocket.
**9** Check the sprockets as described in paragraph 14 of Section 8.
**10** Refitting is a reversal of removal.

### Timing belt guide pulleys

**11** Remove the timing belt covers (Section 7).
**12** Unbolt and withdraw the pulley(s); check their condition as described in paragraph 14 of Section 8.
**13** Refitting is the reverse of the removal procedure; tighten the pulley bolts to the specified torque wrench setting.

## 10 Camshaft oil seals - renewal

**Note:** *While it is possible to reach either oil seal, once the respective sprocket has been removed (see Section 9) to allow the seal to be prised out, this procedure is not recommended. Not only are the seals very soft, making this difficult to do without risk of damage to the seal housing, but it would be very difficult to ensure that the valve timing and the timing belt's tension, once disturbed, are correctly reset. Owners are advised to follow the whole procedure outlined below.*
**1** Release the tension from the timing belt as described in Section 8, paragraphs 1 to 12.
**Note:** *If the timing belt is found to be contaminated by oil, remove it completely as described, then renew the oil seal (see below). Wash down the engine timing belt area and all related components, to remove all traces of oil. Fit a new belt on reassembly.*

**2** If the timing belt is still clean, slip it off the sprocket, taking care not to twist it too sharply; use the fingers only to handle the belt. *Do not* rotate the crankshaft until the timing belt is refitted. Cover the belt, and secure it so that it is clear of the working area and cannot slip off the remaining sprocket.
**3** Unfasten the sprocket bolt and withdraw the sprocket (see Section 9).
**4** Unbolt the camshaft right-hand bearing cap, and withdraw the defective oil seal. Clean the seal housing, and polish off any burrs or raised edges, which may have caused the seal to fail in the first place.
**5** To fit a new seal, Ford recommend the use of their service tool 21-009B, with a bolt (10 mm thread size, 70 mm long) and a washer, to draw the seal into place when the camshaft bearing cap is bolted down; a substitute can be made using a suitable socket **(see illustration)**. Grease the seal lips and periphery to ease installation, and draw the seal into place until it is flush with the housing/bearing cap outer edge. Refit the bearing cap, using sealant and tightening the cap bolts as described in Section 11.
**6** For most owners, the simplest answer will be to grease the seal lips, and to slide it onto the camshaft (until it is flush with the housing's outer edge). Refit the bearing cap, using sealant and tightening the cap bolts as described in Section 11 **(see illustration)**. Take care to ensure that the seal remains absolutely square in its housing, and is not distorted as the cap is tightened down.
**7** Refit the sprocket to the camshaft, tightening the retaining bolt loosely, then slip

**11.3 Using forked holding tool while camshaft toothed pulley bolt is slackened**

the timing belt back onto the sprocket (refer to paragraphs 16 and 19 of Section 8) and tighten the bolt securely.
**8** The remainder of the reassembly procedure, including checking the camshaft alignment (valve timing) and setting the timing belt tension, is as described in paragraphs 20 to 25 of Section 8.

## 11 Camshafts and hydraulic tappets - removal, inspection and refitting

### Removal

**1** Release the tension from the timing belt as described in Section 8, paragraphs 1 to 12.
**2** Either remove the timing belt completely (Section 8, paragraphs 13 and 14) or slip off the camshaft sprockets, taking care not to twist it too sharply; use the fingers only to handle the belt. Cover the belt, and secure it so that it is clear of the working area. *Do not* rotate the crankshaft until the timing belt is refitted.
**3** Unfasten the sprocket bolts as described in Section 8, paragraph 16, and withdraw the sprockets; while both are the same and could be interchanged, it is good working practice to mark them so that each is refitted only to its original location **(see illustration)**.
**4** Working in the sequence shown, slacken progressively, by half a turn at a time, the camshaft bearing cap bolts **(see illustration)**. Work only as described, to release gradually

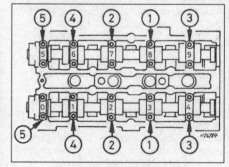

**11.4 Camshaft bearing cap slackening sequence**
**Note:** *Viewed from front of vehicle, showing bearing cap numbers*

11.5a Note locating dowels when removing camshaft bearing caps

11.5b Inlet camshaft has lobe for camshaft position sensor

11.6a Removing hydraulic tappets

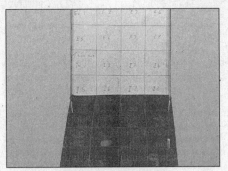

11.6b Hydraulic tappets must be stored as described in text

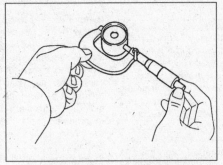

11.8 Use a micrometer to measure diameter of hydraulic tappets

and evenly the pressure of the valve springs on the caps.

5 Withdraw the caps, noting their markings and the presence of the locating dowels, then remove the camshafts and withdraw their oil seals. The inlet camshaft can be identified by the reference lobe for the camshaft position sensor; therefore, there is no need to mark the camshafts (see illustrations).

6 Obtain sixteen small, clean containers, and number them 1 to 16. Using a rubber sucker, withdraw each hydraulic tappet in turn, invert it to prevent oil loss, and place it in its respective container, which should then be filled with clean engine oil (see illustrations). Do not interchange the hydraulic tappets, or the rate of wear will be much increased. Do not allow them to lose oil, or they will take a long time to refill on restarting the engine, resulting in incorrect valve clearances.

### Inspection

7 With the camshafts and hydraulic tappets removed, check each for signs of obvious wear (scoring, pitting etc) and for ovality, and renew if necessary.

8 Measure the outside diameter of each tappet (see illustration) - take measurements at the top and bottom of each tappet, then a second set at right-angles to the first; if any measurement is significantly different from the others, the tappet is tapered or oval (as applicable) and must be renewed. If the necessary equipment is available, measure the inside diameter of the corresponding cylinder head bore. Compare the measurements

obtained to those given in the *Specifications* of this Chapter; if the tappets or the cylinder head bores are excessively worn, new tappets and/or a new cylinder head will be required.

9 If the engine's valve components have sounded noisy, particularly if the noise persists after initial start-up from cold, there is reason to suspect a faulty hydraulic tappet. Only a good mechanic experienced in these engines can tell whether the noise level is typical, or if renewal of one or more of the tappets is warranted. If faulty tappets are diagnosed, and the engine's service history is unknown, it is always worth trying the effect of renewing the engine oil and filter (see Chapter 1), using *only* good-quality engine oil of the recommended viscosity and specification, before going to the expense of renewing any of the tappets - refer also to the advice in Section 5 of this Chapter.

10 Visually examine the camshaft lobes for score marks, pitting, galling (wear due to rubbing) and evidence of overheating (blue, discoloured areas). Look for flaking away of the hardened surface layer of each lobe. If any such signs are evident, renew the component concerned.

11 Examine the camshaft bearing journals and the cylinder head bearing surfaces for signs of obvious wear or pitting. If any such signs are evident, renew the component concerned.

12 Using a micrometer, measure the diameter of each journal at several points. If the diameter of any one journal is less than the specified value, renew the camshaft.

13 To check the bearing journal running clearance, remove the hydraulic tappets, use a suitable solvent and a clean lint-free rag to clean carefully all bearing surfaces, then refit the camshafts and bearing caps with a strand of Plastigage across each journal. Tighten the bearing cap bolts to the specified torque wrench setting (do not rotate the camshafts), then remove the bearing caps and use the scale provided to measure the width of the compressed strands. Scrape off the Plastigage with your fingernail or the edge of a credit card - don't scratch or nick the journals or bearing caps.

14 If the running clearance of any bearing is found to be worn to beyond the specified service limits, fit a new camshaft and repeat the check; if the clearance is still excessive, the cylinder head must be renewed.

15 To check camshaft endfloat, remove the hydraulic tappets, clean the bearing surfaces carefully, and refit the camshafts and bearing caps. Tighten the bearing cap bolts to the specified torque wrench setting, then measure the endfloat using a DTI (Dial Test Indicator, or dial gauge) mounted on the cylinder head so that its tip bears on the camshaft right-hand end.

16 Tap the camshaft fully towards the gauge, zero the gauge, then tap the camshaft fully away from the gauge, and note the gauge reading. If the endfloat measured is found to be at or beyond the specified service limit, fit a new camshaft and repeat the check; if the clearance is still excessive, the cylinder head must be renewed.

**2C**

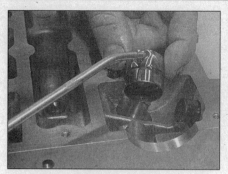

11.17  Oil liberally when refitting hydraulic tappets

11.19  Apply sealant to mating surface of camshaft right-hand bearing caps

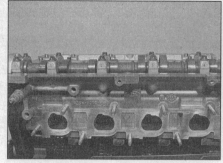

11.20  Etched marks on camshaft bearing caps must be arranged as shown, and face outwards

## Refitting

**17** On reassembly, liberally oil the cylinder head hydraulic tappet bores and the tappets **(see illustration)**. Note that if new tappets are being fitted, they must be charged with clean engine oil before installation. Carefully refit the tappets to the cylinder head, ensuring that each tappet is refitted to its original bore, and is the correct way up. Some care will be required to enter the tappets squarely into their bores.

**18** Liberally oil the camshaft bearings and lobes. Ensuring that each camshaft is in its original location, refit the camshafts, locating each so that the slot in its left-hand end is approximately parallel to, and just above, the cylinder head mating surface.

**19** Ensure that the locating dowels are pressed firmly into their recesses, and check that all mating surfaces are completely clean, unmarked and free from oil. Apply a thin film of suitable sealant (Ford recommend Loctite 518) to the mating surfaces of each camshaft's right-hand bearing cap **(see illustration)**. Referring to paragraph 6 of Section 10, some owners may wish to fit the new camshaft oil seals at this stage.

**20** All camshaft bearing caps have a single-digit identifying number etched on them **(see illustration)**. The exhaust camshaft's bearing caps are numbered in sequence 0 to 4, the inlet's 5 to 9; **see illustration 11.21a** for details. Each cap is to be fitted so that its numbered side faces outwards, to the front (exhaust) or to the rear (inlet).

**21** Ensuring that each cap is kept square to the cylinder head as it is tightened down, and working in the sequence shown, tighten the camshaft bearing cap bolts slowly and by one turn at a time, until each cap touches the cylinder head **(see illustration)**. Next, go round again in the same sequence, tightening the bolts to the first stage torque wrench setting specified, then once more, tightening them to the second stage setting. Work only as described, to impose gradually and evenly the pressure of the valve springs on the caps. Fit the camshaft-aligning tool; it should slip into place as described in paragraph 8 of Section 8 **(see illustration)**.

**22** Wipe off all surplus sealant, so that none is left to find its way into any oilways. Follow the sealant manufacturer's instructions as to the time needed for curing; usually, at least an hour must be allowed between application of the sealant and starting the engine.

**23** If using Ford's recommended procedure, fit new oil seals to the camshafts as described in paragraph 5 of Section 10.

**24** Using the marks and notes made on dismantling to ensure that each is refitted to its original camshaft, refit the sprockets to the camshafts, tightening the retaining bolts loosely. Slip the timing belt back onto the sprockets (refer to paragraph 19 of Section 8) and tighten the bolts to the specified torque setting - use the forked holding tool described in paragraph 16 of Section 8.

**25** The remainder of the reassembly procedure, including checking the camshaft alignment (valve timing) and setting the timing belt tension, is as described in paragraphs 15 to 25 of Section 8.

## 12 Cylinder head - removal and refitting

### Removal

**Note:** *The following text assumes that the cylinder head will be removed with both inlet and exhaust manifolds attached. This simplifies the procedure, but makes it a bulky and heavy assembly to handle - an engine hoist will be required, to prevent the risk of injury, and to prevent damage to any delicate components as the assembly is removed and refitted. If it is wished first to remove the manifolds, refer to Chapters 4D and 4E, then amend the following procedure accordingly.*

**1** Depressurise the fuel system (Chapter 4D).

**2** Disconnect the battery negative (earth) lead (refer to Chapter 5A, Section 1).

**3** Refer to Chapter 4D and remove the air inlet components.

**4** Equalise the pressure in the fuel tank by removing the filler cap, then undo the fuel feed and return lines connecting the engine to the chassis (see Chapter 4D). Plug or cap all open fittings.

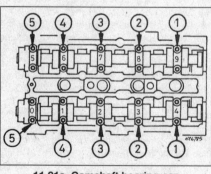

11.21a  Camshaft bearing cap tightening sequence
**Note:** *Viewed from front of vehicle - locate bearing caps according to etched numbers, aligned as described in text*

11.21b  Fit camshaft-aligning tool to set TDC position while camshaft toothed pulleys are refitted

> **HAYNES HiNT** *Whenever you disconnect any vacuum lines, coolant or emissions hoses, wiring connectors and fuel lines, always label them clearly, so that they can be correctly reassembled. Masking tape and/or a touch-up paint applicator work well for marking items. Take instant photos, or sketch the locations of components and brackets.*

**5** Disconnect the accelerator cable from the throttle linkage as described in Chapter 4D. Secure the cable clear of the engine/transmission.

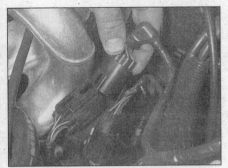

**12.8a Unplug engine wiring loom connector alongside the inlet manifold**

**12.8b Unplug connectors (arrowed) to disconnect ignition coil wiring**

**12.13 Disconnect all coolant hoses from thermostat housing**

6 Remove the auxiliary drivebelt (Chapter 1).

7 Refer to Chapter 10 and remove the power steering pump. Releasing its wire clip, unplug the power steering pressure switch electrical connector, then unbolt the earth lead from the cylinder head rear support plate/engine lifting eye.

8 Remove the three screws securing the wiring "rail" to the rear of the manifold. Releasing its wire clip, unplug the large electrical connector (next to the fuel pressure regulator) to disconnect the engine wiring from the main loom (see illustration). Unplug the electrical connectors on each side of the ignition coil, and the single connector from beneath the front of the thermostat housing, to disconnect the coil and coolant temperature gauge sender wiring (see illustration).

9 Marking or labelling them as they are unplugged, disconnect the vacuum hoses as follows:

a) One from the rear of the throttle housing (only the one hose - there is no need to disconnect the second hose running to the fuel pressure regulator).

b) One from the union on the inlet manifold's left-hand end.

c) The braking system vacuum servo unit hose (see Chapter 9 for details).

10 Unbolt both parts of the exhaust manifold heat shield. Either remove the dipstick and tube, or swing them out of the way.

11 Unscrew the single bolt securing the pulse-air filter housing to the engine/transmission front mounting bracket, then disconnect its vacuum hose.

12 Drain the cooling system (see Chapter 1).

13 Disconnect all coolant hoses from the thermostat housing (see illustration).

14 Unscrew the two nuts to disconnect the exhaust system front downpipe from the manifold (Chapter 4E); disconnect the oxygen sensor wiring, so that it is not strained by the weight of the exhaust system.

15 Support the weight of the engine/transmission using a trolley jack, with a wooden spacer to prevent damage to the sump.

16 Remove the timing belt and both camshafts (see Sections 8 and 11); if the cylinder head is to be dismantled, withdraw the hydraulic tappets.

17 Remove the timing belt inner shield (see Section 7).

18 Working in the *reverse* of the sequence shown in **illustration 12.29a**, slacken the ten cylinder head bolts progressively and by one turn at a time; a Torx key (TX 55 size) will be required. Remove each bolt in turn, and ensure that new replacements are obtained for reassembly; these bolts are subjected to severe stresses and so must be renewed, regardless of their apparent condition, whenever they are disturbed.

19 Lift the cylinder head away; use assistance if possible, as it is a heavy assembly. Remove the gasket, noting the two dowels, and discard it.

## Preparation for refitting

20 The mating faces of the cylinder head and cylinder block must be perfectly clean before refitting the head. Use a hard plastic or wood scraper to remove all traces of gasket and carbon; also clean the piston crowns. Take particular care during the cleaning operations, as aluminium alloy is easily damaged. Also, make sure that the carbon is not allowed to enter the oil and water passages - this is particularly important for the lubrication system, as carbon could block the oil supply to the engine's components. Using adhesive tape and paper, seal the water, oil and bolt holes in the cylinder block. To prevent carbon entering the gap between the pistons and bores, smear a little grease in the gap. After cleaning each piston, use a small brush to remove all traces of grease and carbon from the gap, then wipe away the remainder with a clean rag.

21 Check the mating surfaces of the cylinder block and the cylinder head for nicks, deep scratches and other damage. If slight, they may be removed carefully with a file, but if excessive, machining may be the only alternative to renewal.

22 If warpage of the cylinder head gasket surface is suspected, use a straight-edge to check it for distortion. Refer to Part D of this Chapter if necessary.

## Refitting

23 Wipe clean the mating surfaces of the cylinder head and cylinder block. Check that the two locating dowels are in position in the cylinder block, and that all cylinder head bolt holes are free from oil.

24 Position a new gasket over the dowels on the cylinder block surface, so that the "TOP/OBEN" mark is uppermost, and with the tooth (or teeth, according to engine size) protruding from the front edge (see illustration).

25 Temporarily refit the crankshaft pulley, and rotate the crankshaft anti-clockwise so that No 1 cylinder's piston is lowered to approximately 20 mm before TDC, thus avoiding any risk of valve/piston contact and damage during reassembly.

26 As the cylinder head is such a heavy and awkward assembly to refit with manifolds, it is helpful to make up a pair of guide studs from two 10 mm (thread size) studs approximately 90 mm long, with a screwdriver slot cut in one end - two old cylinder head bolts with their heads cut off would make a good starting point. Screw these guide studs, screwdriver slot upwards to permit removal, into the bolt holes at diagonally-opposite corners of the cylinder block surface (or into those where the locating dowels are fitted, as shown); ensure that approximately 70 mm of stud protrudes above the gasket.

27 Refit the cylinder head, sliding it down the guide studs (if used) and locating it on the dowels. Unscrew the guide studs (if used) when the head is in place.

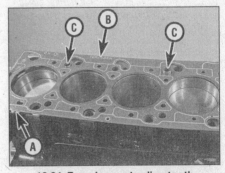

**12.24 Ensuring protruding tooth (or teeth) "A" are at front and marking "B" is upwards, locate new cylinder head gasket on dowels "C"**

**2C**

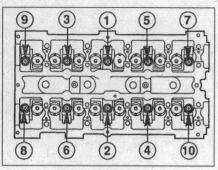

**12.29a Cylinder head bolt tightening sequence**
Note: *Viewed from rear of vehicle*

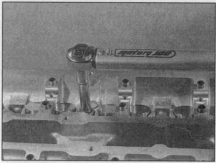

**12.29b Tightening cylinder head bolts (Stages 1 and 2) using torque wrench . . .**

**12.29c . . . and to Stage 3 using angle gauge**

**28** Fit the new cylinder head bolts dry (*do not oil their threads*); carefully enter each into its hole and screw it in, by hand only, until finger-tight.

**29** Working progressively and in the sequence shown, use first a torque wrench, then an ordinary socket extension bar and an angle gauge, to tighten the cylinder head bolts in the stages given in the *Specifications* of this Chapter **(see illustrations). Note:** *Once tightened correctly, following this procedure, the cylinder head bolts do not require check-tightening, and must* **not** *be re-torqued.*

**30** Refit the hydraulic tappets (if removed), the camshafts, their oil seals and sprockets (see Sections 11, 10 and 9, as appropriate). Temporarily refit the crankshaft pulley, and rotate the crankshaft clockwise to return the pulley notches to the TDC position described in Section 3.

**31** Refit the timing belt and covers, checking the camshaft alignment (valve timing) and setting the timing belt tension, as described in Section 8.

**32** The remainder of reassembly is the reverse of the removal procedure, noting the following points:
  a) *Tighten all fasteners to the torque wrench settings specified.*
  b) *Refill the cooling system, and top-up the engine oil (see Chapter 1 and "Weekly Checks").*
  c) *Check all disturbed joints for signs of oil or coolant leakage, once the engine has been restarted and warmed-up to normal operating temperature.*
  d) *If the power steering hoses where disconnected, bleed the system as described in Chapter 10 after reconnection.*

## 13 Sump - removal and refitting

### Removal

**Note:** *The full procedure outlined below must be followed, so that the mating surfaces can be cleaned and prepared to achieve an oil-*tight joint on reassembly, and so that the sump can be aligned correctly; depending on your skill and experience, and the tools and facilities available, it may be that this task can be carried out only with the engine removed from the vehicle. Note that the sump gasket must be renewed whenever it is disturbed.

**1** Disconnect the battery negative (earth) lead (refer to Chapter 5A, Section 1).

**2** Drain the engine oil, then clean and refit the engine oil drain plug, tightening it to the specified torque wrench setting. Although not strictly necessary as part of the dismantling procedure, owners are advised to remove and discard the oil filter, so that it can be renewed with the oil (see Chapter 1).

**3** Refer to Chapter 5A and remove the starter motor.

**4** Remove the auxiliary drivebelt cover (see Chapter 1).

**5** Unplug the electrical connector(s) to disconnect the oxygen sensor.

**6** Unscrew the nuts to disconnect the exhaust system front downpipe from the manifold, then either unhook all the system's rubber mountings and withdraw the complete exhaust system from under the vehicle, or remove only the downpipe/catalytic converter (see Chapter 4E for details).

**7** Unscrew the sump-to-transmission bolts, also any securing the engine/transmission lower adapter plate.

**8** Progressively unscrew the sump retaining bolts. Break the joint by striking the sump with the palm of the hand, then lower the sump and withdraw it with the engine/transmission lower adapter plate (where fitted); note the presence of any shims between the sump and transmission.

**9** Remove and discard the sump gasket; this must be renewed as a matter of course whenever it is disturbed.

**10** While the sump is removed, take the opportunity to remove the oil pump pick-up/strainer pipe and to clean it (Section 14).

### Refitting

**11** On reassembly, thoroughly clean and degrease the mating surfaces of the cylinder block/crankcase and sump, then use a clean rag to wipe out the sump and the engine's interior. If the oil pump pick-up/strainer pipe was removed, fit a new gasket and refit the pipe, tightening its screws to the specified torque wrench setting. Fit the new gasket to the sump mating surface so that the gasket fits into the sump groove **(see illustration)**.

**12** If the sump is being refitted with the engine/transmission still connected and in the vehicle, proceed as follows:
  a) *Check that the mating surfaces of the sump, the cylinder block/crankcase and the transmission are absolutely clean and flat. Any shims found on removal of the sump must be refitted in their original locations.*
  b) *Apply a thin film of suitable sealant (Ford recommend Hylosil 102) to the junctions of the cylinder block/crankcase with the oil pump and the crankshaft left-hand oil seal carrier. Without delay - the sump bolts must be fully tightened within 10 to 20 minutes of applying the sealant - offer up the sump and engine/transmission lower adapter plate, and refit the bolts, tightening them lightly at first.*
  c) *Ensuring that the engine/transmission lower adapter plate is correctly located, firmly press the sump against the transmission, and tighten the transmission-to-sump (ie, engine) bolts to the specified torque wrench setting.*
  d) *Without disturbing the position of the sump, and working in a diagonal sequence from the centre outwards, tighten the sump bolts to the specified torque wrench setting.*
  e) *Proceed to paragraph 14.*

**13.11 Ensure gasket is located correctly in sump groove**

**13.13a Apply sealant (arrowed) as directed when refitting sump**

**13.13b Checking alignment of sump with cylinder block/crankcase**

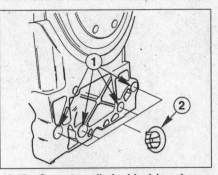

**13.13c Sump-to-cylinder block/crankcase alignment shims**
*1 Fitting points on sump    2 Shim*

**13** If the sump is being refitted with the engine and transmission separated (in or out of the vehicle), proceed as follows:

a) *Apply a thin film of suitable sealant (Ford recommend Hylosil 102) to the junctions of the cylinder block/crankcase with the oil pump and the crankshaft left-hand oil seal carrier (see illustration). Without delay - the sump bolts must be fully tightened within 10 to 20 minutes of applying the sealant - offer up the sump to the cylinder block/crankcase, and insert the sump bolts, tightening them lightly at first.*

b) *Using a suitable straight edge to check alignment across the flat-machined faces of each, move the sump as necessary so that its left-hand face - including any shims found on removal - is flush with that of the cylinder block/crankcase (see illustration). Without disturbing the position of the sump, and working in a diagonal sequence from the centre outwards, tighten the sump bolts to the specified torque wrench setting.*

c) *Check again that both faces are flush before proceeding; if necessary, unbolt the sump again, clean the mating surfaces, and repeat the full procedure to ensure that the sump is correctly aligned.*

d) *If it is not possible to achieve exact alignment by moving the sump, shims are available in thicknesses of 0.25 mm (colour-coded yellow) or 0.50 mm (colour-coded black) to eliminate the discrepancy (see illustration).*

**14** The remainder of reassembly is the reverse of the removal procedure, noting the following points.

a) *Tighten all fasteners to the torque wrench settings specified.*

b) *Always renew any self-locking nuts disturbed on removal.*

c) *Refill the cooling system (see Chapter 1).*

d) *Refill the engine with oil, remembering that you are advised to fit a new filter (see Chapter 1).*

e) *Check for signs of oil or coolant leaks once the engine has been restarted and warmed-up to normal operating temperature.*

## 14 Oil pump - removal, inspection and refitting

### Removal

**Note:** *While this task is theoretically possible when the engine is in place in the vehicle, in practice, it requires so much preliminary dismantling, and is so difficult to carry out due to the restricted access, that owners are advised to remove the engine from the vehicle first. Note, however, that the oil pump pressure relief valve can be removed with the engine in situ - see paragraph 8.*

**1** Remove the timing belt (see Section 8).

**2** Withdraw the crankshaft sprocket and the thrustwasher behind it, noting which way round the thrustwasher is fitted (Section 9).

**3** Remove the sump (see Section 13).

**4** Undo the screws securing the oil pump pick-up/strainer pipe to the pump, then unscrew the nut and withdraw the oil pump pick-up/strainer pipe. Discard the gasket.

**5** Unbolt the pump from the cylinder block/crankcase **(see illustration)**. Withdraw and discard the gasket, and remove the crankshaft right-hand oil seal. Thoroughly clean and degrease all components, particularly the mating surfaces of the pump, the sump, and the cylinder block/crankcase.

### Inspection

**6** Unscrew the Torx screws, and remove the pump cover plate; noting any identification

marks on the rotors, withdraw the rotors **(see illustration)**.

**7** Inspect the rotors for obvious signs of wear or damage, and renew if necessary; if either rotor, the pump body, or its cover plate are scored or damaged, the complete oil pump assembly must be renewed.

**8** The oil pressure relief valve can be dismantled, if required, without disturbing the pump. Chock the rear wheels then jack up the front of the car and support it on axle stands (see "Jacking and vehicle support"). Remove the front right-hand roadwheel and auxiliary drivebelt cover (see Chapter 1) to provide access to the valve.

**9** Unscrew the threaded plug, and recover the valve spring and plunger **(see illustrations)**. If the plug's sealing O-ring is worn or damaged, a new one must be obtained, to be fitted on reassembly.

**10** Reassembly is the reverse of the dismantling procedure; ensure the spring and valve are refitted the correct way round, and tighten the threaded plug securely.

### Refitting

**11** The oil pump must be primed on installation, by pouring clean engine oil into it, and rotating its inner rotor a few turns.

**12** Using grease to stick the new gasket in place on the cylinder block/crankcase, and rotating the pump's inner rotor to align with the flats on the crankshaft, refit the pump and insert the bolts, tightening them lightly at first **(see illustration)**.

**13** Using a suitable straight edge and feeler

**14.5 Unscrew bolts (arrowed) to remove oil pump**

**14.6 Withdrawing oil pump inner rotor**

**2C**

14.9a Unscrew threaded plug - seen through right-hand wheel arch . . .

14.9b . . . to withdraw oil pressure relief valve spring and plunger

14.12 Use new gasket when refitting oil pump

14.13 Checking the alignment of the oil pump (see text)

14.16 Use new gasket when refitting oil pick-up pipe to pump

**2** Drive the oil seal out of the pump from behind **(see illustration)**.

**3** Clean the seal housing and crankshaft, polishing off any burrs or raised edges, which may have caused the seal to fail in the first place.

**4** Refit the oil pump (see Section 14). Grease the lips and periphery of the new seal, to ease installation.

**5** To fit a new seal, Ford recommend the use of their service tool 21-093A, with the crankshaft pulley bolt, to draw the seal into place; an alternative can be arranged using a socket of suitable size, with a washer to match the crankshaft pulley bolt **(see illustration)**.

**6** If such tools are not available, press the seal squarely into place by hand; tap it in until it is flush with the pump housing, using a soft-faced mallet and a socket with an outside diameter only slightly smaller than the seal's **(see illustration)**. This approach requires great care, to ensure that the seal is fitted squarely, without distortion or damage.

**7** Wash off any traces of oil. The remainder of reassembly is the reverse of the removal procedure, referring to the relevant text for details where required. Check for signs of oil leakage when the engine is restarted.

gauges, check that the pump is both centred *exactly* around the crankshaft, and aligned squarely so that its (sump) mating surface is exactly the same amount - between 0.3 and 0.8 mm - below that of the cylinder block/crankcase on each side of the crankshaft **(see illustration)**. Being careful not to disturb the gasket, move the pump into the correct position, and tighten its bolts to the specified torque wrench setting.

**14** Check that the pump is correctly located; if necessary, unbolt it again, and repeat the full procedure to ensure that the pump is correctly aligned.

**15** Fit a new crankshaft right-hand oil seal (see Section 15).

**16** Using grease to stick the gasket in place on the pump, refit the pick-up/strainer pipe, tightening its screws and nut to their specified torque wrench settings **(see illustration)**.

**17** The remainder of reassembly is the reverse of the removal procedure, referring to the relevant text for details where required.

### 15 Crankshaft oil seals - renewal

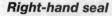

**Note:** *Don't try to prise these seals out without removing the oil pump or seal carrier - the seals are too soft, and the amount of space available is too small, for this to be possible without considerable risk of damage to the seal housing and/or the crankshaft journal. Follow exactly the procedure given below.*

#### Right-hand seal

**1** Remove the oil pump (see Section 14).

#### Left-hand seal

**8** Remove the transmission (see the relevant Part of Chapter 7).

**9** Where appropriate, remove the clutch (Chapter 6).

15.2 Driving out crankshaft right-hand oil seal

15.5 Socket of correct size can be used to replace Ford service tool, drawing new seal into place as described

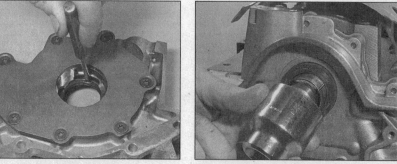
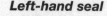

15.6 If seal is tapped into place as shown, exercise great care to prevent seal from being damaged or distorted

**15.12 Unscrew bolts (arrowed) to remove crankshaft left-hand oil seal carrier . . .**

**15.13 . . . and ensure carrier is properly supported when driving out used oil seal - note notches provided in carrier for drift**

**15.15 Use new gasket when refitting left-hand oil seal carrier**

**15.16 Aligning oil seal carrier as described in text**

**15.18 Using guide made from thin sheet of plastic to slide oil seal lips over crankshaft shoulder**

**10** Unbolt the flywheel/driveplate (see Section 16).

**11** Remove the sump (see Section 13).

**12** Unbolt the oil seal carrier **(see illustration)**. Remove and discard its gasket.

**13** Supporting the carrier evenly on wooden blocks, drive the oil seal out of the carrier from behind **(see illustration)**.

**14** Clean the seal housing and crankshaft, polishing off any burrs or raised edges, which may have caused the seal to fail in the first place. Clean also the mating surfaces of the cylinder block/crankcase and carrier, using a scraper to remove all traces of the old gasket - be careful not to scratch or damage the material of either - then use a suitable solvent to degrease them.

**15** Use grease to stick the new gasket in place on the cylinder block/crankcase, then offer up the carrier **(see illustration)**.

**16** Using a suitable straight edge and feeler gauges, check that the carrier is both centred *exactly* around the crankshaft, and aligned squarely so that its (sump) mating surface is exactly the same amount - between 0.3 and 0.8 mm - below that of the cylinder block/crankcase on each side of the crankshaft. Being careful not to disturb the gasket, move the carrier into the correct position, and tighten its bolts to the specified torque wrench setting **(see illustration)**.

**17** Check that the carrier is correctly located; if necessary, unbolt it again, and repeat the full procedure to ensure that the carrier is correctly aligned.

**18** Ford's recommended method of seal fitting is to use service tool 21-141, with two flywheel bolts to draw the seal into place. If this is not available, make up a guide from a thin sheet of plastic or similar, lubricate the lips of the new seal and the crankshaft shoulder with grease, then offer up the seal, with the guide feeding the seal's lips over the crankshaft shoulder **(see illustration)**. Press the seal evenly into its housing by hand only, and use a soft-faced mallet gently to tap it into place until it is flush with the surrounding housing.

**19** Wipe off any surplus oil or grease; the remainder of the reassembly procedure is the reverse of dismantling, referring to the relevant text for details where required. Check for signs of oil leakage when the engine is restarted.

### 16 Flywheel/driveplate - removal, inspection and refitting

#### Removal

**1** Remove the transmission (see the relevant Part of Chapter 7).

**2** Where appropriate, remove the clutch (Chapter 6).

**3** Use a centre-punch or paint to make alignment marks on the flywheel/driveplate and crankshaft, to ensure correct alignment during refitting.

**4** Prevent the flywheel/driveplate from turning by locking the ring gear teeth, or by bolting a strap between the flywheel/driveplate and the cylinder block/crankcase. Slacken the bolts evenly until all are free.

**5** Remove each bolt in turn, and ensure new replacements are obtained for reassembly; these bolts are subjected to severe stresses, and so must be renewed, regardless of their apparent condition, whenever they are disturbed.

**6** Noting the reinforcing plate (automatic transmission models only), withdraw the flywheel/driveplate; do not drop it - it is very heavy.

#### Inspection

**7** Clean the flywheel/driveplate to remove grease and oil. Inspect the surface for cracks, rivet grooves, burned areas and score marks. Light scoring can be removed with emery cloth. Check for cracked and broken ring gear teeth. Lay the flywheel/driveplate on a flat surface, and use a straight edge to check for warpage.

**8** Clean and inspect the mating surfaces of the flywheel/driveplate and the crankshaft. If the crankshaft left-hand seal is leaking, renew it (see Section 15) before refitting the flywheel/driveplate.

**9** While the flywheel/driveplate is removed, clean carefully its inboard (right-hand) face, particularly the recesses which serve as the reference points for the crankshaft speed/position sensor. Clean the sensor's tip, and check that the sensor is securely fastened.

#### Refitting

**10** On refitting, ensure that the engine/transmission adapter plate is in place (where necessary), then fit the flywheel/driveplate to the crankshaft so that all bolt holes align - it will fit only one way - check this using the marks made on removal. Do not forget the reinforcing plate (automatic transmission models).

**11** Lock the flywheel/driveplate by the method used on dismantling. Working in a diagonal sequence to tighten them evenly, and increasing to the final amount in two or

**2C**

three stages, tighten the new bolts to the specified torque wrench setting.

**12** The remainder of reassembly is the reverse of the removal procedure, referring to the relevant text for details where required.

## 17 Engine/transmission mountings - inspection and renewal

### General

**1** The engine/transmission mountings seldom require attention, but broken or deteriorated mountings should be renewed immediately, or the added strain placed on the driveline components may cause damage or wear.

**2** The mounting arrangement varies considerably depending on whether manual or automatic transmission is fitted, and if manual transmission is fitted, whether it is the iB5 type or MTX-75 type. This also has a significant bearing on the amount of peripheral dismantling necessary for access to the mountings, which will have to be assessed according to model.

### Inspection

**3** During the check, the engine/transmission must be raised slightly, to remove its weight from the mountings.

**4** Chock the rear wheels then jack up the front of the car and support it on axle stands (see *"Jacking and vehicle support"*). Position a jack under the sump, with a large block of wood between the jack head and the sump, then carefully raise the engine/transmission just enough to take the weight off the mountings.

 **Warning: DO NOT place any part of your body under the engine when it is supported only by a jack!**

**5** Check the mountings to see if the rubber is cracked, hardened or separated from the metal components. Sometimes, the rubber will split right down the centre.

**6** Check for relative movement between each mounting's brackets and the engine/transmission or body (use a large screwdriver or lever to attempt to move the mountings). If movement is noted, lower the engine and check-tighten the mounting fasteners.

### Renewal

#### Left-hand front mounting

**7** Position a jack under the transmission, with a block of wood between the jack head and the sump. Raise the jack to just take the weight off the mounting.

**8** Undo the two bolts securing the mounting to the body side member, and the two bolts securing the mounting to the transmission bracket **(see illustration)**. Withdraw the mounting from its location.

**9** Refitting is the reversal of removal, tightening the retaining bolts to the specified torque.

#### Left-hand rear mounting

**10** Remove the air cleaner assembly as described in Chapter 4D.

**11** Position a jack under the transmission, with a block of wood between the jack head and the transmission. Raise the jack to just take the weight off the mounting.

**12** Undo the nuts and bolts securing the mounting brackets to the top of the transmission and to the mounting itself **(see illustration)**. Remove the mounting brackets from the transmission.

**13** Undo the two bolts, one from above and one from below, securing the mounting to the body. Remove the mounting from under the brake servo unit.

**14** Refitting is the reversal of removal, tightening the retaining bolts to the specified torque.

### Right-hand mounting

**15** Chock the rear wheels then jack up the front of the car and support it on axle stands (see *"Jacking and vehicle support"*). For preference, raise the car on ramps.

**16** Drain the engine oil, and remove the oil filter (see Chapter 1).

**17** Undo the two upper bolts and one lower bolt, and remove the mounting support brace.

**18** Undo the two upper nuts securing the mounting to the body **(see illustration)**.

**19** Undo the two lower nuts securing the mounting to the engine bracket **(see illustration)**. Manipulate the mounting, complete with damper weight, out from under the car.

**20** Refitting is the reversal of removal, tightening the retaining nuts and bolts to the specified torque.

**17.8 Engine/transmission left-hand front mounting attachments**

**17.12 Engine/transmission left-hand rear mounting and mounting bracket attachments**

**17.18 Engine right-hand mounting-to-body retaining nuts**

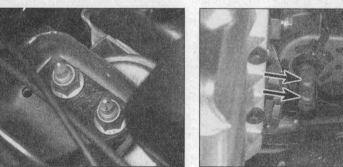
**17.19 Engine right-hand mounting-to-engine bracket retaining bolts (arrowed)**

# Chapter 2 Part D:
# Engine removal and overhaul procedures

## Contents

## Degrees of difficulty

| **Easy,** suitable for novice with little experience |  | **Fairly easy,** suitable for beginner with some experience | | **Fairly difficult,** suitable for competent DIY mechanic |  | **Difficult,** suitable for experienced DIY mechanic | | **Very difficult,** suitable for expert DIY or professional | |

## Specifications

### HCS and Endura-E engines

#### Cylinder head

Maximum permissible gasket surface distortion
(measured over full length) ................................... 0.15 mm
Valve seat angle (inlet and exhaust) ........................... 45º
Valve seat width (inlet and exhaust) ........................... 1.18 to 1.75 mm*
*The inlet and exhaust valves have special inserts which cannot be recut using conventional tools.*

#### Valves - general

| | Inlet | Exhaust |
|---|---|---|
| Valve length | 103.7 to 104.4 mm | 104.2 to 104.7 mm |
| Valve head diameter | 34.40 to 34.60 mm | 28.90 to 29.10 mm |
| Valve stem diameter | 7.0 mm | 7.0 mm |
| Valve stem-to-guide clearance | 0.020 to 0.069 mm | 0.046 to 0.095 mm |

#### Cylinder block

Cylinder bore diameter:
    Standard 1 ........................................ 73.94 to 73.95 mm
    Standard 2 ........................................ 73.50 to 73.96 mm
    Standard 3 ........................................ 73.96 to 73.97 mm
    Oversize 0.5 mm ................................... 74.50 to 74.51 mm
    Oversize 1.0 mm ................................... 75.00 to 75.01 mm
Camshaft endfloat ...................................... 0.02 to 0.19 mm

#### Pistons and piston rings

Piston diameter:
    Standard 1 ........................................ 73.91 to 73.92 mm
    Standard 2 ........................................ 73.92 to 73.93 mm
    Standard 3 ........................................ 73.93 to 73.94 mm
    Oversize 0.5 mm ................................... 74.46 to 74.49 mm
    Oversize 1.0 mm ................................... 74.96 to 74.99 mm
Piston-to-cylinder bore clearance ......................... 0.015 to 0.050 mm
Piston ring end gap - installed:
    Top compression ring ............................... 0.25 to 0.45 mm
    Second compression ring ............................ 0.45 to 0.75 mm
    Oil control ring ................................... 0.20 to 0.40 mm

**2D**

## Pistons and piston rings (continued)

Piston ring-to-groove clearance:
Compression rings . . . . . . . . . . . . . . . . . . . . . . . . . . . . . . . . . . . . . . 0.20 mm (maximum)
Oil control ring . . . . . . . . . . . . . . . . . . . . . . . . . . . . . . . . . . . . . . . . . 0.10 mm (maximum)
Ring gap position:
Top compression ring . . . . . . . . . . . . . . . . . . . . . . . . . . . . . . . . . . . Offset 180° from oil control ring gap
Second compression ring . . . . . . . . . . . . . . . . . . . . . . . . . . . . . . . . . Offset 90° from oil control ring gap
Oil control ring . . . . . . . . . . . . . . . . . . . . . . . . . . . . . . . . . . . . . . . . . Aligned with gudgeon pin

## Gudgeon pin

Length . . . . . . . . . . . . . . . . . . . . . . . . . . . . . . . . . . . . . . . . . . . . . . . . 63.3 to 64.6 mm
Diameter:
White colour code . . . . . . . . . . . . . . . . . . . . . . . . . . . . . . . . . . . . . . 18.026 to 18.029 mm
Red colour code . . . . . . . . . . . . . . . . . . . . . . . . . . . . . . . . . . . . . . . 18.029 to 18.032 mm
Blue colour code . . . . . . . . . . . . . . . . . . . . . . . . . . . . . . . . . . . . . . . 18.032 to 18.035 mm
Yellow colour code . . . . . . . . . . . . . . . . . . . . . . . . . . . . . . . . . . . . . 18.035 to 18.038 mm
Clearance in piston . . . . . . . . . . . . . . . . . . . . . . . . . . . . . . . . . . . . . 0.008 to 0.014 mm
Interference fit in connecting rod . . . . . . . . . . . . . . . . . . . . . . . . . . . 0.016 to 0.048 mm

## Crankshaft and bearings

Main bearing journal diameter:
Standard . . . . . . . . . . . . . . . . . . . . . . . . . . . . . . . . . . . . . . . . . . . . . 56.980 to 57.000 mm
0.254 mm undersize . . . . . . . . . . . . . . . . . . . . . . . . . . . . . . . . . . . . 56.726 to 56.746 mm
0.508 mm undersize (HCS only) . . . . . . . . . . . . . . . . . . . . . . . . . . . 56.472 to 56.492 mm
0.762 mm undersize (HCS only) . . . . . . . . . . . . . . . . . . . . . . . . . . . 56.218 to 56.238 mm
Main bearing journal-to-shell running clearance . . . . . . . . . . . . . . . 0.009 to 0.056 mm
Crankpin (big-end) bearing journal diameter:
Standard . . . . . . . . . . . . . . . . . . . . . . . . . . . . . . . . . . . . . . . . . . . . . 40.99 to 41.01 mm
0.254 mm undersize . . . . . . . . . . . . . . . . . . . . . . . . . . . . . . . . . . . . 40.74 to 40.76 mm
0.508 mm undersize (HCS only) . . . . . . . . . . . . . . . . . . . . . . . . . . . 40.49 to 40.51 mm
0.762 mm undersize (HCS only) . . . . . . . . . . . . . . . . . . . . . . . . . . . 40.24 to 40.26 mm
Crankpin (big-end) bearing journal-to-shell running clearance . . . . . . . 0.006 to 0.060 mm
Crankshaft endfloat . . . . . . . . . . . . . . . . . . . . . . . . . . . . . . . . . . . . 0.075 to 0.285 mm
Thrustwasher thickness:
Standard . . . . . . . . . . . . . . . . . . . . . . . . . . . . . . . . . . . . . . . . . . . . . 2.80 to 2.85 mm
Oversize . . . . . . . . . . . . . . . . . . . . . . . . . . . . . . . . . . . . . . . . . . . . . 2.99 to 3.04 mm

## Torque wrench settings

| | Nm | lbf ft |
|---|---|---|
| Main bearing cap . . . . . . . . . . . . . . . . . . . . . . . . . . . . . . . . . . . . . | 95 | 70 |
| *Crankpin (big-end) bearing cap bolts: | | |
| Stage 1 . . . . . . . . . . . . . . . . . . . . . . . . . . . . . . . . . . . . . . . . . . . . | 4 | 3 |
| Stage 2 . . . . . . . . . . . . . . . . . . . . . . . . . . . . . . . . . . . . . . . . . . . . | Angle-tighten a further 90° | |
| Engine-to-transmission bolts . . . . . . . . . . . . . . . . . . . . . . . . . . . . | 40 | 30 |

*New bolts must be used
**Note:** *Refer to Part A of this Chapter for remaining torque wrench settings.*

## *CVH and PTE engines*

## Cylinder head

Maximum permissible gasket surface distortion (measured
over full length) . . . . . . . . . . . . . . . . . . . . . . . . . . . . . . . . . . . . . . . 0.15 mm
Camshaft bearing bore diameters in cylinder head (standard):
Bearing 1 . . . . . . . . . . . . . . . . . . . . . . . . . . . . . . . . . . . . . . . . . . . . 44.783 to 44.808 mm
Bearing 2 . . . . . . . . . . . . . . . . . . . . . . . . . . . . . . . . . . . . . . . . . . . . 45.033 to 45.058 mm
Bearing 3 . . . . . . . . . . . . . . . . . . . . . . . . . . . . . . . . . . . . . . . . . . . . 45.283 to 45.308 mm
Bearing 4 . . . . . . . . . . . . . . . . . . . . . . . . . . . . . . . . . . . . . . . . . . . . 45.533 to 45.558 mm
Bearing 5 . . . . . . . . . . . . . . . . . . . . . . . . . . . . . . . . . . . . . . . . . . . . 45.783 to 45.808 mm
Camshaft bearing bore diameters in cylinder head (oversize):
Bearing 1 . . . . . . . . . . . . . . . . . . . . . . . . . . . . . . . . . . . . . . . . . . . . 45.188 to 45.163 mm
Bearing 2 . . . . . . . . . . . . . . . . . . . . . . . . . . . . . . . . . . . . . . . . . . . . 45.438 to 45.413 mm
Bearing 3 . . . . . . . . . . . . . . . . . . . . . . . . . . . . . . . . . . . . . . . . . . . . 45.668 to 45.663 mm
Bearing 4 . . . . . . . . . . . . . . . . . . . . . . . . . . . . . . . . . . . . . . . . . . . . 45.938 to 45.913 mm
Bearing 5 . . . . . . . . . . . . . . . . . . . . . . . . . . . . . . . . . . . . . . . . . . . . 46.188 to 46.163 mm
Valve tappet bore diameter (standard) . . . . . . . . . . . . . . . . . . . . . . . 22.235 to 22.265 mm
Valve tappet bore diameter (oversize) . . . . . . . . . . . . . . . . . . . . . . . 22.489 to 22.519 mm
Valve seat angle (inlet and exhaust) . . . . . . . . . . . . . . . . . . . . . . . . 44°30' to 45°30'
Valve seat width (inlet and exhaust) . . . . . . . . . . . . . . . . . . . . . . . . . 1.75 to 2.32 mm*

*The cylinder head has valve seat rings on the exhaust side. These valve seats cannot be recut with conventional tools.

## Valves - general

|  | Inlet | Exhaust |
|---|---|---|
| Valve length: | | |
| 1.4 litre engine | 136.29 to 136.75 mm | 132.97 to 133.43 mm |
| 1.6 litre engine | 134.54 to 135.00 mm | 131.57 to 132.03 mm |
| Valve head diameter: | | |
| 1.4 litre engine | 39.90 to 40.10 mm | 33.90 to 34 10 mm |
| 1.6 litre engine | 41.90 to 42.10 mm | 36.90 to 37.10 mm |
| Valve stem diameter (standard) | 8.025 to 8.043 mm | 7.999 to 8.017 mm |
| Valve stem diameter (0.2 mm oversize) | 8.225 to 8.243 mm | 8.199 to 8.217 mm |
| Valve stem diameter (0.4 mm oversize) | 8.425 to 8.443 mm | 8.399 to 8.417 mm |
| Valve stem-to-guide clearance | 0.020 to 0.063 mm | 0.046 to 0.089 mm |

## Cylinder block

Cylinder bore diameter:
1.4 litre engine:
| | |
|---|---|
| Standard 1 | 77.22 to 77.23 mm |
| Standard 2 | 77.23 to 77.24 mm |
| Standard 3 | 77.24 to 77.25 mm |
| Standard 4 | 77.25 to 77.26 mm |
| Oversize A | 77.51 to 77.52 mm |
| Oversize B | 77.52 to 77.53 mm |
| Oversize C | 77.53 to 77.54 mm |

1.6 litre engine:
| | |
|---|---|
| Standard 1 | 79.94 to 79.95 mm |
| Standard 2 | 79.95 to 79.96 mm |
| Standard 3 | 79.96 to 79.97 mm |
| Standard 4 | 79.97 to 79.98 mm |
| Oversize A | 80.23 to 80.24 mm |
| Oversize B | 80.24 to 80.25 mm |
| Oversize C | 80.25 to 80.26 mm |

## Pistons and piston rings

Piston diameter (production):
1.4 litre engine:
| | |
|---|---|
| Standard 1 | 77.190 to 77.200 mm |
| Standard 2 | 77.200 to 77.210 mm |
| Standard 3 | 77.210 to 77.220 mm |
| Standard 4 | 77.220 to 77.230 mm |
| Oversize A | 77.480 to 77.490 mm |
| Oversize B | 77.490 to 77.500 mm |
| Oversize C | 77.500 to 77.510 mm |

1.6 litre carburettor engine:
| | |
|---|---|
| Standard 1 | 79.910 to 79.920 mm |
| Standard 2 | 79.920 to 79.930 mm |
| Standard 3 | 79.930 to 79.940 mm |
| Standard 4 | 79.940 to 79.950 mm |
| Oversize A | 80.200 to 80.210 mm |
| Oversize B | 80.210 to 80.220 mm |
| Oversize C | 80.220 to 80.230 mm |

1.6 litre EFi fuel injection engine:
| | |
|---|---|
| Standard 1 | 79.915 to 79.925 mm |
| Standard 2 | 79.925 to 79.935 mm |
| Standard 3 | 79.935 to 79.945 mm |
| Standard 4 | 79.945 to 79.955 mm |
| Oversize A | 80.205 to 80.215 mm |
| Oversize B | 80.215 to 80.225 mm |
| Oversize C | 80.225 to 80.235 mm |

Piston-to-cylinder bore clearance:
| | |
|---|---|
| 1.4 litre engine | 0.020 to 0.040 mm |
| 1.6 litre carburettor engine | 0.020 to 0.040 mm |
| 1.6 litre EFi fuel injection engine | 0.015 to 0.035 mm |

Piston ring end gaps - installed:
| | |
|---|---|
| Compression rings | 0.30 to 0.50 mm |

Oil control rings:
| | |
|---|---|
| 1.4 litre engine | 0.40 to 1.40 mm |
| 1.6 litre carburettor engine | 0.40 to 1.40 mm |
| 1.6 litre EFi fuel injection engine | 0.25 to 0.40 mm |

2D

## Gudgeon pins

Length:
| | |
|---|---|
| 1.4 litre engine | 63.000 to 63.800 mm |
| 1.6 litre carburettor engine | 66.200 to 67.000 mm |
| 1.6 litre EFi fuel injection engine | 63.000 to 63.800 mm |

Diameter:
| | |
|---|---|
| White colour code | 20.622 to 20.625 mm |
| Red colour code | 20.625 to 20.628 mm |
| Blue colour code | 20.628 to 20.631 mm |
| Yellow colour code | 20.631 to 20.634 mm |
| Clearance in piston | 0.005 to 0.011 mm |
| Interference fit in connecting rod | 0.013 to 0.045 mm |

## Crankshaft and bearings

Main bearing journal diameter:
| | |
|---|---|
| Standard | 57.98 to 58.00 mm |
| 0.25 mm undersize | 57.73 to 57.75 mm |
| 0.50 mm undersize | 57.48 to 57.50 mm |
| 0.75 mm undersize | 57.23 to 57.25 mm |
| Main bearing journal-to-shell running clearance | 0.011 to 0.058 mm |

Crankpin (big-end) bearing journal diameter:
| | |
|---|---|
| Standard | 47.89 to 47.91 mm |
| 0.25 mm undersize | 47.64 to 47.66 mm |
| 0.50 mm undersize | 47.39 to 47.41 mm |
| 0.75 mm undersize | 47.14 to 47.16 mm |
| 1.00 mm undersize | 46.89 to 46.91 mm |
| Crankpin (big-end) bearing journal-to-shell running clearance | 0.006 to 0.060 mm |
| Crankshaft endfloat | 0.09 to 0.30 mm |

Thrustwasher thickness:
| | |
|---|---|
| Standard | 2.301 to 2.351 mm |
| Oversize | 2.491 to 2.541 mm |

## Torque wrench settings

| | Nm | lbf ft |
|---|---|---|
| Main bearing caps | 95 | 70 |
| Crankpin (big-end) bearing caps | 33 | 24 |
| Engine-to-transmission bolts | 40 | 30 |

**Note:** *Refer to Part B of this Chapter for remaining torque wrench settings.*

## *Zetec and Zetec-E engines*

## Cylinder head

| | |
|---|---|
| Maximum permissible gasket surface distortion | 0.10 mm |
| Valve seat included angle | 90° |
| Valve guide bore | 6.060 to 6.091 mm |

## Valves - general

| | Inlet | Exhaust |
|---|---|---|
| Valve length | 96.870 to 97.330 mm | 96.470 to 96.930 mm |
| Valve head diameter: | | |
| 1.6 litre engine | 26.0 mm | 24.5 mm |
| 1.8 litre engine | 32.0 mm | 28.0 mm |
| Valve stem diameter | 6.028 to 6.043 mm | 6.010 to 6.025 mm |
| Valve stem-to-guide clearance | 0.017 to 0.064 mm | 0.035 to 0.081 mm |

## Cylinder block

Cylinder bore diameter:

1.6 litre engine:
| | |
|---|---|
| Class 1 | 76.000 to 76.010 mm |
| Class 2 | 76.010 to 76.020 mm |
| Class 3 | 76.020 to 76.030 mm |

1.8 litre engine:
| | |
|---|---|
| Class 1 | 80.600 to 80.610 mm |
| Class 2 | 80.610 to 80.620 mm |
| Class 3 | 80.620 to 80.630 mm |

## Pistons and piston rings

Piston diameter

1.6 litre engine:

| | |
|---|---|
| Class 1 | 75.975 to 75.985 mm |
| Class 2 | 75.985 to 75.995 mm |
| Class 3 | 75.995 to 76.005 mm |

1.8 litre engine:

| | |
|---|---|
| Class 1 | 80.570 to 80.580 mm |
| Class 2 | 80.580 to 80.590 mm |
| Class 3 | 80.590 to 80.600 mm |
| Oversizes - all engines | None available |
| Piston-to-cylinder bore clearance | Not specified |

Piston ring end gaps - installed:

| | |
|---|---|
| Compression rings | 0.30 to 0.50 mm |

Oil control ring:

| | |
|---|---|
| 1.6 litre engine | 0.25 to 1.00 mm |
| 1.8 litre engine | 0.38 to 1.14 mm |

## Gudgeon pin

Diameter:

| | |
|---|---|
| White colour code/piston crown marked "A" | 20.622 to 20.625 mm |
| Red colour code/piston crown marked "B" | 20.625 to 20.628 mm |
| Blue colour code/piston crown marked "C" | 20.628 to 20.631 mm |
| Clearance in piston | 0.010 to 0.016 mm |
| Interference fit in connecting rod | 0.011 to 0.042 mm |

## Crankshaft and bearings

| | |
|---|---|
| Main bearing journal standard diameter | 57.980 to 58.000 mm |
| Main bearing journal-to-shell running clearance | 0.011 to 0.058 mm |
| Main bearing shell undersizes available | 0.02 mm, 0.25 mm |
| Crankpin (big-end) bearing journal standard diameter | 46.890 to 46.910 mm |
| Crankpin (big-end) bearing journal-to-shell running clearance | 0.016 to 0.070 mm |
| Big-end bearing shell undersizes available | 0.02 mm, 0.25 mm |
| Crankshaft endfloat | 0.090 to 0.310 mm |

## Torque wrench settings

| | Nm | lbf ft |
|---|---|---|
| Main bearing cap bolts and nuts | 80 | 59 |
| Crankpin (big-end) bearing cap bolts: | | |
| Stage 1 | 18 | 13 |
| Stage 2 | Angle-tighten a further 90° | |
| Piston-cooling oil jet/blanking plug Torx screws | 10 | 7 |
| Cylinder block and head oilway blanking plugs: | | |
| M6 x 10 | 10 | 7 |
| M10 x 11.5 - in block | 24 | 17 |
| 1/4 PTF plug - in block | 25 | 18 |
| Power steering pump/air conditioning compressor mounting bracket-to-cylinder block bolts | 47 | 35 |
| Exhaust manifold heat shield bracket-to-cylinder block bolts | 32 | 24 |
| Crankcase breather system: | | |
| Oil separator-to-cylinder block bolts | 10 | 7 |
| Pipe-to-cylinder head bolt | 23 | 17 |
| Transmission-to-engine bolts | 40 | 30 |

**Note:** *Refer to Part C of this Chapter for remaining torque wrench settings.*

## 1 General information

Included in this Part of Chapter 2 are details of removing the engine/transmission from the car and general overhaul procedures for the cylinder head, cylinder block/crankcase and all other engine internal components.

The information given ranges from advice concerning preparation for an overhaul and the purchase of replacement parts, to detailed step-by-step procedures covering removal, inspection, renovation and refitting of engine internal components.

After Section 6, all instructions are based on the assumption that the engine has been removed from the car. For information concerning in-car engine repair, as well as the removal and refitting of those external components necessary for full overhaul, refer to Part A, B or C of this Chapter (as applicable) and to Section 6. Ignore any preliminary dismantling operations described in Part A, B or C that are no longer relevant once the engine has been removed from the car.

## 2 Engine/transmission removal - preparation and precautions

If you have decided that an engine must be removed for overhaul or major repair work, several preliminary steps should be taken.

**2D**

Locating a suitable place to work is extremely important. Adequate work space, along with storage space for the car, will be needed. If a workshop or garage is not available, at the very least, a flat, level, clean work surface is required.

If possible, clear some shelving close to the work area and use it to store the engine components and ancillaries as they are removed and dismantled. In this manner the components stand a better chance of staying clean and undamaged during the overhaul. Laying out components in groups together with their fixing bolts, screws etc will save time and avoid confusion when the engine is refitted.

Clean the engine compartment and engine/transmission before beginning the removal procedure; this will help visibility and help to keep tools clean.

On two of the engines covered in this manual, the unit can only be withdrawn by removing it complete with the transmission; the vehicle's body must be raised and supported securely, sufficiently high that the engine/transmission can be unbolted as a single unit and lowered to the ground; the engine/transmission can then be withdrawn from under the vehicle and separated. On all engines, an engine hoist or A-frame will be necessary. Make sure the equipment is rated in excess of the combined weight of the engine and transmission.

The help of an assistant should be available; there are certain instances when one person cannot safely perform all of the operations required to remove the engine from the vehicle. Safety is of primary importance, considering the potential hazards involved in this kind of operation. A second person should always be in attendance to offer help in an emergency. If this is the first time you have removed an engine, advice and aid from someone more experienced would also be beneficial.

Plan the operation ahead of time. Before starting work, obtain (or arrange for the hire of) all of the tools and equipment you will need. Access to the following items will allow the task of removing and refitting the engine/transmission to be completed safely and with relative ease: an engine hoist - rated in excess of the combined weight of the engine/transmission, a heavy-duty trolley jack,

complete sets of spanners and sockets as described at the rear this manual, wooden blocks, and plenty of rags and cleaning solvent for mopping up spilled oil, coolant and fuel. A selection of different sized plastic storage bins will also prove useful for keeping dismantled components grouped together. If any of the equipment must be hired, make sure that you arrange for it in advance, and perform all of the operations possible without it beforehand; this may save you time and money.

Plan on the vehicle being out of use for quite a while, especially if you intend to carry out an engine overhaul. Read through the whole of this Section and work out a strategy based on your own experience and the tools, time and workspace available to you. Some of the overhaul processes may have to be carried out by a Ford dealer or an engineering works - these establishments often have busy schedules, so it would be prudent to consult them before removing or dismantling the engine, to get an idea of the amount of time required to carry out the work.

When removing the engine from the vehicle, be methodical about the disconnection of external components. Labelling cables and hoses as they are removed will greatly assist the refitting process.

Always be extremely careful when lifting the engine/transmission assembly from the engine bay. Serious injury can result from careless actions. If help is required, it is better to wait until it is available rather than risk personal injury and/or damage to components by continuing alone. By planning ahead and taking your time, a job of this nature, although major, can be accomplished successfully and without incident.

## 3 Engine - removal and refitting (HCS and Endura-E engines)

⚠️ **Warning: Petrol is extremely flammable, so take extra precautions when disconnecting any part of the fuel system. Don't smoke, or allow naked flames or bare light bulbs, in or near the work area, and don't work in a garage where a natural-gas appliance (such as a clothes dryer or water**

*heater) is installed. If you spill petrol on your skin, rinse it off immediately. Have a fire extinguisher rated for petrol fires handy, and know how to use it.*

**Note:** *Read through the entire Section, as well as reading the advice in the preceding Section, before beginning this procedure. The engine is removed separately from the transmission and is lifted upwards and out of the engine compartment.*

### Removal

**1** On fuel injection engines, depressurise the fuel system (see Chapter 4B or 4D).

**2** Disconnect the battery negative (earth) lead (refer to Chapter 5A, Section 1).

**3** Referring to Chapter 1 for details, drain the coolant and engine oil. Refit the drain plug to the sump on completion.

**4** Remove the bonnet (see Chapter 11).

**5** Remove the air cleaner assembly or air inlet components as described in the relevant Part of Chapter 4.

**6** Release the clips and detach the following coolant hoses. Allow for coolant spillage as the hoses are detached (**see illustrations**):

a) *All hoses at the thermostat housing.*
b) *Bottom hose from the radiator to the water pump.*
c) *Heater hoses at the bulkhead and water pump.*
d) *Inlet manifold coolant supply hose (where applicable).*

**HAYNES HiNT** *Whenever you disconnect any vacuum lines, coolant or emissions hoses, wiring connectors and fuel lines, always label them clearly, so that they can be correctly reassembled. Masking tape and/or a touch-up paint applicator work well for marking items. Take instant photos, or sketch the locations of components and brackets.*

**7** Disconnect the fuel trap vacuum hose from the inlet manifold.

**8** Disconnect the brake servo unit vacuum hose from the inlet manifold, by pushing the hose retainer in towards the manifold and simultaneously pulling free the hose (**see illustration**).

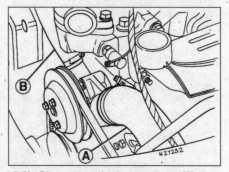

**3.6a Disconnect the overflow hose (A) and top hose (B) from the thermostat housing**

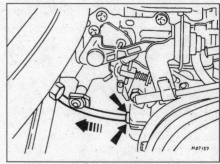

**3.6b Disconnect the bottom hose (A) and the heater hose (B) from the water pump**

**3.8 Detach the servo vacuum hose from the manifold**

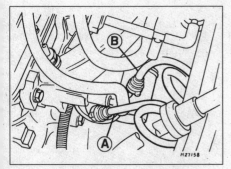

**3.10 Fuel supply (A) and return (B) hose connections at the fuel pump**

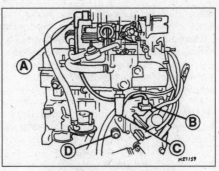

**3.11a Wiring connections to the HCS engine**

A  *Idle cut-off valve*
B  *DIS ignition coil*
C  *Engine coolant temperature sensor*
D  *Oil pressure switch*

**3.11b Engine crankshaft position sensor and multi-plug**

**9** Refer to the relevant Part of Chapter 4 for details, and detach the accelerator cable. Where applicable, detach the choke cable from the carburettor.

**10** Compress the quick-release couplings at the sides, and detach the fuel supply hose and return hose from the fuel pump, CFi unit or fuel rail **(see illustration)**. Allow for fuel spillage as the hoses are disconnected, and plug the exposed ends to prevent further spillage and the ingress of dirt. Position the hoses out of the way.

**11** Note their locations and disconnect the wiring from the following **(see illustrations)**:

a) *Coolant temperature gauge sender unit.*
b) *The oil pressure switch.*
c) *The radio earth lead.*
d) *The cooling fan thermostatic switch.*
e) *The DIS ignition coil.*
f) *The crankshaft speed/position sensor.*
g) *The engine coolant temperature sensor.*
h) *The idle cut-off valve.*

**12** Disconnect the remaining wiring multi-plugs from the engine sensors at the inlet manifold and from the oxygen sensor (where fitted) in the exhaust manifold or downpipe.

**13** On Endura-E engines, release the wire clips and unplug the four fuel injector multi-plugs.

**14** Chock the rear wheels then jack up the front of the car and support it on axle stands (see *"Jacking and vehicle support"*).

**15** Unscrew the retaining nuts, and detach the exhaust downpipe from the exhaust manifold. Remove the seal from the joint flange.

**16** Refer to Chapter 5A for details, and remove the starter motor.

**17** Undo the two retaining bolts, and remove the clutch lower cover plate.

**18** Unscrew the retaining bolt, and detach the gearshift stabiliser from the transmission.

**19** Unscrew and remove the engine/transmission flange attachment bolts and also the bolt fitted from the front, securing the earth lead (from the underside) **(see illustration)**.

**20** Unscrew and remove the single bolt securing the engine mounting brace to the crossmember **(see illustration)**.

**21** Check that the appropriate underside attachments are disconnected and out of the way, then lower the vehicle to the ground.

**22** Unbolt and remove the heat shield from the exhaust manifold.

**23** Attach a suitable hoist to the engine. It is possible to fabricate lifting eyes to connect the hoist to the engine, but make sure that they are strong enough, and connect them to the inlet and exhaust manifold at diagonally-opposite ends of the engine.

**24** With the hoist securely connected, take the weight of the engine, then unscrew the two retaining nuts to detach the engine mounting from the apron panel, and the single bolt to disconnect it at the mounting bracket.

**25** Locate a jack under the transmission, and raise it to take the weight of the transmission.

**26** Unscrew and remove the remaining engine-to-transmission retaining bolts on the upper flange.

**27** Check around the engine to ensure that all of the relevant fixings and attachments are disconnected and out of the way for the removal.

**28** Enlist the aid of an assistant, then move the engine forwards and away from the transmission, whilst simultaneously raising the transmission. When the engine is separated from the transmission, carefully guide it up and out of the engine compartment. Do not allow the weight of the engine to hang on the transmission input shaft at any point during the removal (or refitting) of the engine. When the engine sump is clear of the vehicle, swing the power unit out of the way, and lower it onto a trolley (if available). Unless a mobile hoist is being used, it will be necessary to move the vehicle rearwards and out of the way in order to allow the engine to be lowered for removal. In this instance, ensure that the weight of the transmission is well supported as the vehicle is moved.

**29** While the engine is removed, check the mountings; renew them if they are worn or damaged. Similarly, check the condition of all coolant and vacuum hoses and pipes (see Chapter 1); components that are normally hidden can now be checked properly, and should be renewed if there is any doubt at all about their condition. Also, consider over-hauling the clutch components (see Chapter 6). It is regarded by many as good practice to renew the clutch assembly as a matter of course, whenever major engine overhaul work is carried out. Check also the condition of all components disturbed on removal, and renew any that are damaged or worn.

### Refitting

**30** Refitting is in general, a reversal of the removal procedure, but the following special points should be noted.

**31** Before coupling the engine to the transmission, apply a thin smear of high-melting-point grease onto the transmission input shaft splines. If the clutch has been removed, ensure that the clutch disc is centralised, and disconnect the clutch cable from the release lever on the transmission casing.

**2D**

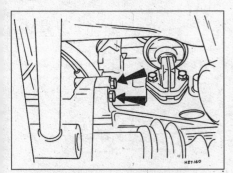

**3.19 Engine-to-transmission flange attachment bolts (arrowed)**

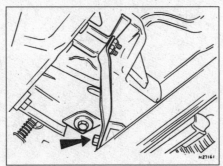

**3.20 Mounting brace-to-crossmember bolt (arrowed)**

**32** Tighten all fixings to their recommended torque wrench settings.

**33** Check that the mating faces are clean, and fit a new exhaust downpipe-to-manifold gasket and self-locking nuts when reconnecting this joint.

**34** Ensure that all wiring connections are correctly and securely made.

**35** Remove the plugs from the fuel lines before reconnecting them correctly and securely.

**36** Reconnect and adjust the accelerator and choke cables as described in Chapter 4. The refitting details for the air cleaner components are also given in that Chapter.

**37** Renew any coolant hoses (and/or retaining clips) that are not in good condition.

**38** Refer to Chapter 6 for details on reconnecting the clutch cable.

**39** When the engine is fully refitted, check that the various hoses are connected, and then refill the engine oil and coolant levels as described in Chapter 1 and *"Weekly Checks"*.

**40** When engine refitting is completed, refer to Section 19 for the engine start-up procedures.

---

### 4    Engine/transmission - removal and refitting (CVH and PTE engines)

⚠️ **Warning: Petrol is extremely flammable, so take extra precautions when disconnecting any part of the fuel system. Don't smoke, or allow naked flames or bare light bulbs, in or near the work area, and don't work in a garage where a natural-gas appliance (such as a clothes dryer or water heater) is installed. If you spill petrol on your skin, rinse it off immediately. Have a fire extinguisher rated for petrol fires handy, and know how to use it.**

**Note:** *Read through the entire Section, as well as reading the advice in the preceding Section, before beginning this procedure. The engine and transmission are removed as a unit, lowered to the ground and removed from underneath, then separated outside the vehicle.*

### Removal

**1** On all fuel injection engines, refer to Chapter 4B, C or D as applicable and depressurise the fuel system.

**2** Disconnect the battery negative (earth) lead (refer to Chapter 5A, Section 1).

**3** Referring to Chapter 1 for details, drain the coolant and the engine and gearbox oil. Refit the drain plugs on completion.

**4** Refer to Chapter 11 for details, and remove the bonnet.

**5** Remove the air cleaner assembly and air inlet components as described in the relevant Part of Chapter 4.

**6** Release the retaining clips and detach the coolant top hose, the heater hose and the radiator overflow hose from the thermostat housing. Disconnect the coolant hose from the inlet manifold, and the bottom hose from the water pump and/or the radiator **(see illustrations)**. On 1.4 litre CFi fuel injection models, also disconnect the coolant hose from the injection unit. On EFi and SEFi fuel injection models, detach the heater hose Y-connector. Allow for coolant spillage as they are detached.

> **HAYNES HiNT** *When disconnecting vacuum lines, coolant or emissions hoses, wiring connectors and fuel lines, always label them clearly, so they can be correctly reassembled. Masking tape and/or a touch-up paint applicator work well for marking items. Take instant photos, or sketch the locations of components and brackets.*

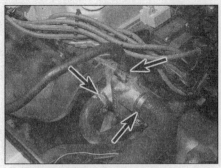

**4.6a  Coolant hose connections to the thermostat (arrowed)**

**7** Refer to the relevant Part of Chapter 4 for details, and disconnect the accelerator cable from the throttle linkage and support/adjuster bracket. Where applicable, also disconnect the choke cable. Position the cable(s) out of the way.

**8** On carburettor models, disconnect the fuel supply hose from the fuel pump, and the return hose from the carburettor.

**9** On CFi models, detach the fuel hose at the injector/pressure regulator unit, and the return line, by compressing the couplings whilst pulling the hoses free from their connections. On EFi and SEFi models, unscrew the union nut to detach the fuel line from the fuel rail; release the retaining clip to detach the return pipe from the pressure regulator. Plug the exposed ends of the hoses and connections, to prevent fuel spillage and the ingress of dirt. Position the hoses out of the way.

**10** Press the clamp ring inwards, and simultaneously pull free the brake servo hose from the inlet manifold. Position it out of the way.

**11** On CFi and EFi models, detach the vacuum hose from the MAP sensor, and the hose between the carbon canister and the fuel injection unit **(see illustration)**.

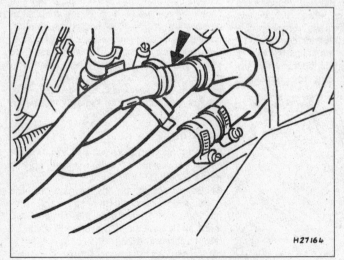

**4.6b  Heater coolant hoses and Y-connector on 1.6 litre EFi fuel injection models**

**4.11  Vacuum hose to MAP sensor (A) and brake servo (B)**

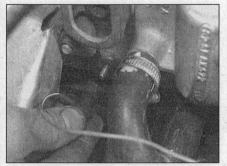

**4.12a  Disconnect the wiring at the temperature gauge sender unit . . .**

**4.12b  . . . the oil pressure switch . . .**

**4.12c  . . . and the crankshaft position sensor**

**12** Note their connections and routings, and detach the following wiring connections, according to model **(see illustrations)**:
 a) *Coolant temperature sender unit.*
 b) *Oil pressure switch.*
 c) *DIS ignition coil unit.*
 d) *Coolant temperature sensor.*
 e) *Cooling fan thermostatic switch.*
 f) *Carburettor.*
 g) *Earth lead (radio).*
 h) *Reversing light switch (from transmission).*
 i) *Crankshaft position sensor.*
 j) *Earth leads from transmission and engine.*

**13** Disconnect the wiring at the following additional items specific to fuel injection models only.
 a) *Inlet air temperature sensor.*
 b) *Vehicle speed sensor.*
 c) *Throttle plate control motor (CFi models).*
 d) *Throttle position sensor.*
 e) *Injector harness connector.*
 f) *Idle speed control valve (EFi and SEFi models).*

**14** Unscrew the retaining bolt and detach the bracket locating the wiring and coolant hoses above the transmission.

**15** Disconnect the speedometer drive cable from the transmission.

**16** On manual transmission models, disconnect the clutch cable from the release lever at the transmission (see Chapter 6 for details). Position the cable out of the way.

**17** Unscrew the two retaining bolts, and detach the engine/transmission mounting from the mounting bracket **(see illustration)**.

**4.17  Engine/transmission mounting bracket bolts (arrowed)**

**18** Chock the rear wheels then jack up the front of the car and support it on axle stands (see *"Jacking and vehicle support"*). Allow sufficient clearance under the vehicle to withdraw the engine and transmission from under the front end.

**19** Where applicable on catalytic converter-equipped vehicles, release the multi-plug from the bracket and disconnect the wiring connector from the oxygen sensor in the exhaust downpipe.

**20** Undo the three retaining nuts, detach the exhaust downpipe from the manifold, and collect the gasket from the flange joint. Now disconnect the exhaust downpipe from the rest of the system, and remove it from the vehicle. Where applicable, disconnect the pulse-air supply hose from the check valve. Noting their connections (to ensure correct reassembly), detach the appropriate system vacuum hoses at the PVS (three-port vacuum switch) under the inlet manifold.

**21** Where fitted, undo the four retaining nuts and two bolts securing the front part of the exhaust heat shield to the floor, then remove the heat shield.

**22** Note their connections, and detach the wiring from the starter motor and the alternator. Unbolt and remove the starter motor.

### Manual transmission models

**23** On 4-speed models, select 2nd gear; on 5-speed models, select 4th gear, to assist in correct adjustment of the gearchange during reassembly. If it is likely that the gear lever will

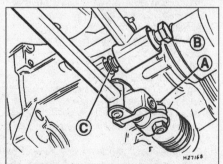

**4.23  Manual transmission shift rod clamp bolt (A), stabiliser-to-transmission bolt (B) and washer (C)**

be moved from this position before refitting, mark the relative position of the transmission shift rod and the selector shaft before separating them. Undo the clamp bolt, and then pull free and detach the shift rod from the selector shaft **(see illustration)**.

**24** Unscrew the retaining bolt, and detach the shift rod stabiliser from the transmission. As it is detached, note the washer located between the stabiliser and the transmission. Tie the stabiliser and the shift rod up out of the way.

### Automatic transmission models

**25** Unclip and detach the wiring connector from the starter inhibitor switch (on the transmission housing).

**26** Referring to Chapter 7B, Section 6 for details, unhook the accelerator (cam plate) cable from the carburettor or fuel injection unit (as applicable) at the transmission end of the cable. Undo the retaining bolt and detach the cable sheath bracket from the transmission. Detach the cam plate cable from the link.

**27** Undo the two nuts from the selector cable bracket which connects it to the lever on the selector shaft. Disconnect the yoke from the lever on the selector shaft and the cable from the lever.

**28** Unscrew the union nuts, and disconnect the oil cooler feed and return pipes from the transmission. Allow for a certain amount of spillage, and plug the connections to prevent the ingress of dirt.

### All models

**29** Note the direction of fitting, unscrew the retaining nut and withdraw the Torx-type clamp bolt securing the lower suspension arm to the spindle carrier on each side.

**30** Refer to Chapter 10 for details, and detach the right-hand track rod end balljoint from the spindle carrier.

**31** Insert a suitable lever between the right-hand driveshaft inner joint and the transmission housing, and prise free the driveshaft from the transmission; be prepared for oil spillage from the transmission case through the vacated driveshaft aperture. As it is being prised free, simultaneously pull the roadwheel outwards on that side, to enable the driveshaft inboard end to separate from the transmission. Once it is free, suspend and support the driveshaft from

**2D**

**4.34 Remove the brace between the transmission left front mounting bracket and the transmission flange**

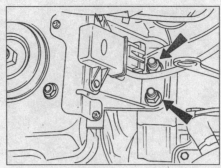

**4.38 Right-hand engine mounting bracket and MAP sensor on EFi models**

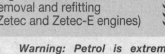

## 5 Engine/transmission - removal and refitting (Zetec and Zetec-E engines)

the steering gear, to prevent unnecessary strain being placed on the driveshaft joints. The outer joint must not be angled in excess of 45°, the inner joint no more than 20°, or the joints may be damaged. Refer to Chapter 8 for further details if necessary.

**32** Insert a suitable plastic plug (or if available, an old driveshaft joint), into the transmission driveshaft aperture, to immobilise the gears of the differential unit.

**33** Proceed as described above in paragraphs 30 to 32, and disconnect the left-hand driveshaft from the transmission.

**34** Unscrew the retaining bolts, and remove the brace between the transmission left front mounting bracket and the transmission flange **(see illustration)**.

**35** Connect a suitable lift hoist and sling to the engine, connecting to the lifting eyes. When securely connected, take the weight of the engine/transmission so that the tension is relieved from the mountings.

**36** Unscrew the two retaining bolts, and detach the transmission front mounting from the side member.

**37** Unscrew the three retaining bolts, and remove the auxiliary drivebelt cover from under the crankshaft pulley.

**38** Unscrew the two retaining nuts, and detach the right-hand engine mounting from the suspension strut mounting. On EFi engines, remove the MAP sensor **(see illustration)**.

**39** The engine/transmission should now be ready for removal from the vehicle. Check that all of the associated connections and fittings are disconnected from the engine and transmission, and positioned out of the way.

**40** Enlist the aid of an assistant to help steady and guide the power unit down through the engine compartment as it is removed. If available, position a suitable engine trolley or crawler board under the engine/transmission so that when lowered, the power unit can be withdrawn from the front end of the vehicle, and then moved to the area where it is to be cleaned and dismantled. On automatic transmission models, particular care must be taken not to damage the transmission fluid pan (sump) during the removal and subsequent refitting processes.

**41** Carefully lower the engine and transmission, ensuring that no fittings become snagged. Detach the hoist and remove the power unit from under the vehicle.

**42** Referring to the relevant Part of Chapter 7, separate the transmission from the engine.

**43** While the engine/transmission is removed, check the mountings; renew them if they are worn or damaged. Similarly, check the condition of all coolant and vacuum hoses and pipes (see Chapter 1). Components that are normally hidden can now be checked properly, and should be renewed if there is any doubt at all about their condition. Where the vehicle is fitted with manual transmission, take the opportunity to inspect the clutch components (see Chapter 6). It is regarded by many as good working practice to renew the clutch assembly as a matter of course, whenever major engine overhaul work is carried out. Check also the condition of all components (such as the transmission oil seals) disturbed on removal, and renew any that are damaged or worn.

### Refitting

**44** Refitting is a reversal of removal, however note the following additional points:

a) *Refer to the applicable Chapters and Sections as for removal.*

b) *Fit new spring clips to the grooves in the inboard end of the right- and left-hand driveshaft joints. Lubricate the splines with transmission oil prior to fitting.*

c) *Renew the exhaust flange gasket when reconnecting the exhaust. Ensure that all wires are routed clear of the exhaust system and, on catalytic converter models, ensure that the heat shields are securely and correctly fitted.*

d) *Ensure that all earth lead connections are clean and securely made.*

e) *Tighten all nuts and bolts to the specified torque.*

f) *Fit a new oil filter, and refill the engine and transmission with oil, with reference to Chapter 1.*

g) *Refill the cooling system with reference to Chapter 1.*

**45** When engine and transmission refitting is complete, refer to the procedures described in Section 19 before restarting the engine.

> ⚠ *Warning: Petrol is extremely flammable, so take extra precautions when disconnecting any part of the fuel system. Don't smoke, or allow naked flames or bare light bulbs, in or near the work area, and don't work in a garage where a natural-gas appliance (such as a clothes dryer or water heater) is installed. If you spill petrol on your skin, rinse it off immediately. Have a fire extinguisher rated for petrol fires handy, and know how to use it.*

**Note:** *Read through the entire Section, as well as reading the advice in the preceding Section, before beginning this procedure. The engine and transmission are removed as a unit, lowered to the ground and removed from underneath, then separated outside the vehicle.*

### Removal

**1** Park the vehicle on firm, level ground, apply the handbrake firmly, and slacken the nuts securing both front roadwheels.

**2** Depressurise the fuel system as described in Chapter 4D.

**3** Disconnect the battery negative (earth) lead (refer to Chapter 5A, Section 1).

**4** Place protective covers on the wings, then remove the bonnet (see Chapter 11).

**5** Drain the cooling system and the engine oil (see Chapter 1). On the MTX-75 transmission only, position a suitable container beneath the transmission, then unscrew the drain plug and drain the oil. Refit and tighten the plug on completion.

**6** Remove the air inlet components and the complete air cleaner assembly as described in Chapter 4D.

**7** Equalise the pressure in the fuel tank by removing the filler cap, then release the fuel feed and return quick-release couplings, and pull the hoses off the fuel pipes. Plug or cap all open fittings.

> **HAYNES HINT** *Whenever you disconnect any vacuum lines, coolant or emissions hoses, wiring connectors and fuel lines, always label them clearly, so that they can be correctly reassembled. Masking tape and/or a touch-up paint applicator work well for marking items. Take instant photos, or sketch the locations of components and brackets.*

**8** Disconnect the accelerator cable from the throttle linkage as described in Chapter 4D. Secure the cable clear of the engine/transmission.

**9** Releasing its wire clip, unplug the power steering pressure switch electrical connector,

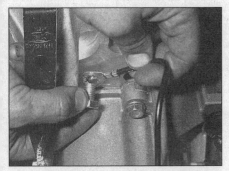

**5.11 Unbolt the engine/transmission-to-body earth lead from the transmission**

**5.14a Disconnect the wiring multi-plug from the ignition coil . . .**

**5.14b . . . the radio interference suppressor . . .**

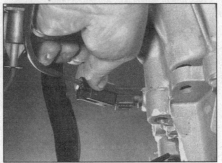

**5.14c . . . and the reversing light switch**

then disconnect the earth cable from the engine lifting eye. Refit the bolt after disconnecting the cable.

10 Marking or labelling all components as they are disconnected, disconnect the vacuum hoses as follows:

a) *From the rear of the inlet manifold.*

b) *The braking system vacuum servo unit hose - from the inlet manifold (see Chapter 9 for details).*

c) *While you are there, trace the vacuum line from the pulse-air filter housing, and disconnect it from the pulse-air solenoid valve.*

d) *Secure all these hoses so that they won't get damaged as the engine/transmission is removed.*

11 Unbolt the engine/transmission-to-body earth lead from the transmission **(see illustration)**. Disconnect the speedometer drive cable (see Chapter 12) and secure it clear of the engine/transmission.

12 Disconnect the additional earth strap at the top of the engine/transmission flange, and the adjacent bolt securing the wiring harness clip.

13 Where the vehicle is fitted with manual transmission, disconnect the clutch cable (see Chapter 6).

14 Marking or labelling all components as they are disconnected, disconnect the engine wiring connectors as follows **(see illustrations)**:

a) *The multi-plug from the DIS ignition coil.*

b) *The radio interference suppressor from the DIS ignition coil.*

c) *The reversing light switch multi-plug.*

d) *The engine main wiring loom multi-plug behind the DIS ignition coil.*

e) *The crankshaft speed/position sensor and vehicle speed sensor multi-plugs.*

f) *The oxygen sensor multi-plug.*

15 Unbolt the exhaust manifold heat shield, and lift it clear.

16 Remove the auxiliary drivebelt (Chapter 1).

17 Marking or labelling all components as they are disconnected and catching as much as possible of the escaping coolant in the drain tray, disconnect the cooling system hoses and pipes as follows:

a) *The coolant hoses at the thermostat housing.*

b) *The coolant hose at the metal cross pipe lower connection.*

c) *The radiator top and bottom hoses.*

18 Undo the nut securing the power steering pump pressure pipe clip to the timing belt cover. Release the unions and clips, and disconnect the pump pressure and return lines. Collect the fluid in a suitable container, and plug the disconnected unions. Lift the power steering fluid reservoir out of its bracket, and move it clear of the engine.

19 Chock the rear wheels then jack up the front of the car and support it on axle stands (see *"Jacking and vehicle support"*). Remove the front roadwheels.

20 Refer to Chapter 5 if necessary, and disconnect the wiring from the starter motor and alternator.

21 Disconnect the oil pressure switch wiring connector.

22 On automatic transmission models, disconnect the starter inhibitor switch wiring and disconnect the selector cable (see Chapter 7B). Secure the cable clear of the engine/transmission.

23 On models with manual transmission, disconnect the gearchange linkage and transmission support rod from the rear of the transmission - make alignment marks as they are disconnected **(see illustrations)**.

24 On automatic transmission models, clean around the unions, then disconnect the fluid pipes from the transmission. Plug the openings in the transmission and the pipe unions after removal.

25 Unscrew the nuts to disconnect the exhaust system front downpipe from the manifold. Undo the nuts securing the catalytic converter to the rear part of the exhaust system, and remove the converter and downpipe assembly.

26 Where the vehicle is fitted with air conditioning, refer to Chapter 3 and disconnect any components that are likely to impede removal of the engine/transmission from below.

⚠️ *Warning: Do not disconnect the refrigerant hoses.*

27 Disconnect both anti-roll bar links from their respective suspension struts, and both track rod end ball joints from their spindle carriers (see Chapter 10).

28 Noting the direction of fitting, unscrew the retaining nut and withdraw the Torx-type clamp bolt securing the lower suspension arm to the spindle carrier on each side.

**2D**

**5.23a Disconnect the gearchange linkage . . .**

**5.23b . . . and transmission support rod**

**29** Insert a suitable lever between the right-hand driveshaft inner joint and the transmission housing, and prise free the driveshaft from the transmission; be prepared for oil spillage from the transmission case through the vacated driveshaft aperture. As it is being prised free, simultaneously pull the spindle carrier outwards on that side to enable the driveshaft inboard end to separate from the transmission. Once it is free, suspend and support the driveshaft from the steering gear, to prevent unnecessary strain being placed on the driveshaft joints. The outer joint must not be angled in excess of 45°, the inner joint no more than 20°. Refer to Chapter 8 for further details if necessary.

**30** Insert a suitable plastic plug (or if available, an old driveshaft joint), into the transmission driveshaft aperture, to immobilise the gears of the differential unit.

**31** Proceed as described above in paragraphs 29 and 30, and disconnect the left-hand driveshaft from the transmission.

**32** Remove the oil filter, referring to Chapter 1 if necessary.

**33** Undo the two upper bolts and one lower bolt, and remove the right-hand engine mounting support brace.

**34** Connect a suitable lift hoist and sling to the engine, connecting to the lift eyes. When securely connected, take the weight of the engine/transmission so that the tension is relieved from the mountings.

**35** From above, undo the two bolts securing the left-hand rear mounting to the transmission bracket.

**36** Undo the two nuts securing the right-hand mounting to the body adjacent to the suspension strut tower.

**37** Undo the two bolts securing the left-hand front mounting to the body side member.

**38** The engine/transmission should now be hanging on the hoist only, with all components which connect it to the rest of the vehicle disconnected or removed, and secured well clear of the unit. Make a final check that this is the case.

**39** Lower the engine/transmission to the ground, and withdraw it from under the vehicle.

**40** Referring to the relevant Part of Chapter 7, separate the transmission from the engine.

**41** While the engine/transmission is removed, check the mountings; renew them if they are worn or damaged. Similarly, check the condition of all coolant and vacuum hoses and pipes (see Chapter 1); components that are normally hidden can now be checked properly, and should be renewed if there is any doubt at all about their condition. Where the vehicle is fitted with manual transmission, take the opportunity to overhaul the clutch components (see Chapter 6). It is regarded by many as good working practice to renew the clutch assembly as a matter of course, whenever major engine overhaul work is carried out. Check also the condition of all components (such as the transmission oil

seals) disturbed on removal, and renew any that are damaged or worn.

## Refitting

**42** Refitting is a reversal of removal, however note the following additional points:
a) Refer to the applicable Chapters and Sections as for removal.
b) Fit new spring clips to the grooves in the inboard end of the right- and left-hand driveshaft joints. Lubricate the splines with transmission oil prior to fitting.
c) Renew the exhaust flange gaskets when reconnecting the exhaust. Ensure that all wires are routed clear of the exhaust system, and that the heat shields are securely and correctly fitted.
d) Ensure that all earth lead connections are clean and securely made.
e) Tighten all nuts and bolts to the specified torque.
f) Fit a new oil filter, and refill the engine and transmission with oil, with reference to Chapter 1.
g) Refill the cooling system with reference to Chapter 1.
h) Bleed the power steering system with reference to Chapter 10.

**43** When engine and transmission refitting is complete, refer to the procedures described in Section 19 before restarting the engine.

## 6 Engine overhaul - preliminary information

It is much easier to dismantle and work on the engine if it is mounted on a portable engine stand. These stands can often be hired from a tool hire shop. Before the engine is mounted on a stand, the flywheel/driveplate should be removed so that the stand bolts can be tightened into the end of the cylinder block/crankcase.

If a stand is not available, it is possible to dismantle the engine with it suitably supported on a sturdy workbench or on the floor. Be careful not to tip or drop the engine when working without a stand.

If you intend to obtain a reconditioned engine, all ancillaries must be removed first, to be transferred to the replacement engine (just as they will if you are doing a complete engine overhaul yourself). These components include the following:
a) Alternator and mounting brackets.
b) DIS ignition coil unit (and mounting bracket), HT leads and spark plugs.
c) The thermostat and housing cover.
d) Carburettor/fuel injection system components.
e) Inlet and exhaust manifolds.
f) Oil filter.
g) Fuel pump.
h) Engine mountings.
i) Flywheel/driveplate.
j) Water pump.

**Note:** When removing the external components from the engine, pay close attention to details that may be helpful or important during refitting. Note the fitted positions of gaskets, seals, washers, bolts and other small items.

If you are obtaining a "short" engine (cylinder block/crankcase, crankshaft, pistons and connecting rods all assembled), then the cylinder head, timing chain/belt (together with tensioner, tensioner and idler pulleys and covers) sump and oil pump will have to be removed also.

If a complete overhaul is planned, the engine can be dismantled in the order given below, referring to Part A, B or C of this Chapter unless otherwise stated.
a) Inlet and exhaust manifolds.
b) Timing chain/belt, tensioner and sprockets.
c) Cylinder head.
d) Flywheel/driveplate.
e) Sump.
f) Oil pump.
g) Pistons (with connecting rods).
h) Crankshaft.
i) Camshaft and tappets (HCS and Endura-E engines).

## 7 Cylinder head - dismantling

**Note:** New and reconditioned cylinder heads are available from the manufacturers, and from engine overhaul specialists. Due to the fact that some specialist tools are required for the dismantling and inspection procedures, and new components may not be readily available, it may be more practical and economical for the home mechanic to purchase a reconditioned head, rather than to dismantle, inspect and recondition the original head.

**1** Remove the cylinder head as described in Part A, B or C of this Chapter (as applicable).

**2** If not already done, remove the inlet and exhaust manifolds with reference to the relevant Part of Chapter 4.

**3** Proceed as follows according to engine type.

### HCS and Endura-E engines

**4** Valve removal should commence with No 1 valve (nearest the timing chain end).

**5** To remove the valve springs and valves from the cylinder head, a standard valve spring compressor will required. Fit the spring compressor to the first valve and spring to be removed. Assuming that all of the valves and springs are to be removed, start by compressing the No 1 valve (nearest the timing cover end) spring. Take care not to damage the valve stem with the compressor, and do not over-compress the spring, or the valve stem may bend. When tightening the compressor, it may be found that the spring retainer does not release and the collets are then difficult to remove. In this instance, remove the

**7.6  Compress the valve spring to remove the collets**

**7.7a  Remove the valve spring retainer and spring . . .**

**7.7b  . . . followed by the valve**

**7.8  Prise off the valve stem oil seal**

**7.9  Use a labelled plastic bag to store and identify valve components**

### Zetec and Zetec-E engines

**17** Remove the camshafts and hydraulic tappets as described in Part C of this Chapter, being careful to store the hydraulic tappets as described.

**18** Using a valve spring compressor, compress each valve spring in turn until the split collets can be removed. A special valve spring compressor will be required, to reach into the deep wells in the cylinder head without risk of damaging the hydraulic tappet bores; such compressors are now widely available from most good motor accessory shops. Release the compressor, and lift off the spring upper seat and spring.

**19** If, when the valve spring compressor is screwed down, the spring upper seat refuses to free and expose the split collets, gently tap the top of the tool, directly over the upper seat, with a light hammer. This will free the seat.

**20** Withdraw the valve through the combustion chamber. If it binds in the guide (won't pull through), push it back in, and de-burr the area around the collet groove with a fine file or whetstone; take care not to mark the hydraulic tappet bores.

**21** Ford recommend the use of their service tool 21-160 to extract the valve spring lower seat/stem oil seals; while this is almost indispensable if the seals are to be removed without risk of damage to the cylinder head, a serviceable substitute can be made from a strong spring of suitable size. Screw on the tool or spring so that it bites into the seal, then draw the seal off the valve guide (see illustrations).

compressor, then press a piece of tube (or a socket of suitable diameter) so that it does not interfere with the removal of the collets, against the retainer's outer rim. Tap the tube (or socket) with a hammer to unsettle the components.

**6** Refit the compressor, and wind it in to enable the collets to be extracted (see illustration).

**7** Loosen off the compressor, and remove the retainer and spring. Withdraw the valve from the cylinder head (see illustrations).

**8** Prise up and remove the valve stem seal (see illustration).

**9** Repeat the removal procedure with each of the remaining seven valve assemblies in turn. As they are removed, keep the individual valves and their components together, and in their respective order of fitting, by placing them in a separate labelled bag (see illustration).

### CVH and PTE engines

**10** Remove the camshaft, rocker arms and tappets as described in Part B of this Chapter, being careful to store the hydraulic tappets as described.

**11** Valve removal should commence with No 1 valve (nearest the timing belt end).

**12** Using a standard valve spring compressor, compress the valve spring (and upper retainer) just enough to enable the split collets to be released from the groove in the top of the valve stem, then separate and extract the split collets from the valve. Do not compress the spring any further than is necessary, or the valve stem may bend. If the valve spring retainer does not release from the collets as the spring is compressed, remove the compressor, and position a piece of suitable tube over the end of

the retainer, so that it does not impinge on the collets. Place a small block of wood under the valve head (with the head resting face down on the workbench), then tap the end of the tube with a hammer. Now refit the compressor tool, and compress the valve spring. The collets should release.

**13** Extract the split collets, then slowly unscrew, release and remove the compressor.

**14** Withdraw the upper retainer and the valve spring from the valve stem, then remove the valve from the underside of the cylinder head. Use a suitable screwdriver to prise free and remove the valve stem oil seal from the guide.

**15** Remove the lower retainer.

**16** Repeat the removal procedure with each of the remaining valve assemblies in turn. As they are removed, keep the valves and their associated components together, and in the originally-installed order, by placing them in a separate labelled bag (see illustration 7.9).

**7.21a  Ford service tool in use to remove valve spring lower seat/stem oil seals . . .**

**7.21b  . . . can be replaced by home-made tool if suitable spring can be found**

**2D**

**7.23 Cylinder head oil-retaining valve (arrowed)**

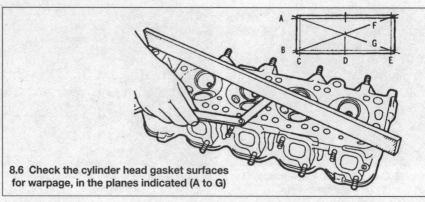

**8.6 Check the cylinder head gasket surfaces for warpage, in the planes indicated (A to G)**

**22** It is essential that the valves are kept together with their collets, spring seats and springs, and in their correct sequence (unless they are so badly worn that they are to be renewed). If they are going to be kept and used again, place them in a labelled polythene bag or similar small container **(see illustration 7.9)**. Note that No 1 valve is nearest to the timing belt end of the engine.

**23** If the oil-retaining valve is to be removed (to flush out the cylinder head oil galleries thoroughly), seek the advice of a Ford dealer as to how it can be extracted; it may be that the only course of action involves destroying the valve as follows. Screw a self-tapping screw into its ventilation hole, and use the screw to provide purchase with which the valve can be drawn out; a new valve must be purchased and pressed into place on reassembly **(see illustration)**.

**8  Cylinder head and valve components** - cleaning and inspection

**1** Thorough cleaning of the cylinder head and valve components, followed by a detailed inspection, will enable you to decide how much valve service work must be carried out during the engine overhaul. **Note:** *If the engine has been severely overheated, it is best to assume that the cylinder head is warped, and to check carefully for signs of this.*

### Cleaning

**2** Scrape away all old gasket material and sealing compound from the cylinder head.
**3** Scrape away the carbon from the combustion chambers and ports, then wash the cylinder head thoroughly with paraffin or a suitable solvent.
**4** Scrape off any heavy carbon deposits that may have formed on the valves, then use a power-operated wire brush to remove deposits from the valve heads and stems.

### Inspection

**Note:** *Be sure to perform all the following inspection procedures before concluding that the services of a machine shop or engine overhaul specialist are required. Make a list of all items that require attention.*

### Cylinder head

**5** Inspect the head very carefully for cracks, evidence of coolant leakage, and other damage. If cracks are found, a new cylinder head should be obtained.
**6** Use a straight edge and feeler blade to check that the cylinder head gasket surface is not distorted **(see illustration)**. If it is, it may be possible to re-surface it.
**7** Examine the valve seats in each of the combustion chambers. If they are severely pitted, cracked or burned, then they will need to be renewed or re-cut by an engine overhaul specialist. If they are only slightly pitted, this can be removed by grinding-in the valve heads and seats with fine valve-grinding compound, as described below.
**8** If the valve guides are worn, indicated by a side-to-side motion of the valve, new guides must be fitted. Measure the diameter of the existing valve stems (see below) and the bore of the guides, then calculate the clearance, and compare the result with the specified value; if the clearance is excessive, renew the valves or guides as necessary.
**9** The renewal of valve guides is best carried out by an engine overhaul specialist.
**10** If the valve seats are to be re-cut, this must be done *only after* the guides have been renewed.

### Valves

**11** Examine the head of each valve for pitting, burning, cracks and general wear, and check the valve stem for scoring and wear ridges. Rotate the valve, and check for any obvious indication that it is bent. Look for pits

and excessive wear on the tip of each valve stem. Renew any valve that shows any such signs of wear or damage.
**12** If the valve appears satisfactory at this stage, measure the valve stem diameter at several points, using a micrometer **(see illustration)**. Any significant difference in the readings obtained indicates wear of the valve stem. Should any of these conditions be apparent, the valve(s) must be renewed.
**13** If the valves are in satisfactory condition, they should be ground (lapped) into their respective seats, to ensure a smooth gas-tight seal. If the seat is only lightly pitted, or if it has been re-cut, fine grinding compound *only* should be used to produce the required finish. Coarse valve-grinding compound should *not* be used unless a seat is badly burned or deeply pitted; if this is the case, the cylinder head and valves should be inspected by an expert, to decide whether seat re-cutting, or even the renewal of the valve or seat insert, is required.
**14** Valve grinding is carried out as follows. Place the cylinder head upside-down on a bench, with a block of wood at each end to give clearance for the valve stems.
**15** Smear a trace of (the appropriate grade of) valve-grinding compound on the seat face, and press a suction grinding tool onto the valve head. With a semi-rotary action, grind the valve head to its seat, lifting the valve occasionally to redistribute the grinding compound **(see illustration)**. A light spring placed under the valve head will greatly ease this operation.
**16** If coarse grinding compound is being used, work only until a dull, matt even surface

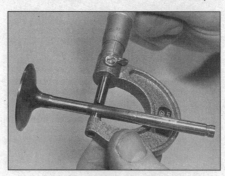

**8.12 Measuring the diameter of a valve stem**

**8.15 Grinding-in a valve seat**

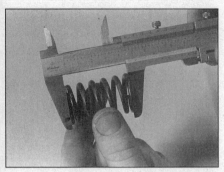

**8.18 Checking the valve spring free length**

is produced on both the valve seat and the valve, then wipe off the used compound, and repeat the process with fine compound. When a smooth unbroken ring of light grey matt finish is produced on both the valve and seat, the grinding operation is complete. *Do not grind in the valves any further than absolutely necessary, or the seat will be prematurely sunk into the cylinder head.*

17  When all the valves have been ground-in, carefully wash off *all* traces of grinding compound, using paraffin or a suitable solvent, before reassembly of the cylinder head.

## Valve components

18  Examine the valve springs for signs of damage and discolouration, and also measure their free length **(see illustration)**. If possible, compare each of the existing springs with a new component.

19  Stand each spring on a flat surface, and check it for squareness. If any of the springs are damaged, distorted, or have lost their tension, obtain a complete set of new springs.

20  Check the spring upper seats and collets for obvious wear and cracks. Any questionable parts should be renewed, as extensive damage will occur if they fail during engine operation. Any damaged or excessively-worn parts must be renewed; the valve spring lower seat/stem oil seals must be renewed as a matter of course whenever they are disturbed.

21  Check the rocker gear components and hydraulic tappets as described in earlier parts of this Chapter according to engine type.

---

## 9  Cylinder head - reassembly

1  Before reassembling the cylinder head, first ensure that it is perfectly clean, and that no traces of grinding paste are left in the head or on the valves and guides. Use compressed air, if available, to blow out all the oil holes and passages.

2  Commence reassembly of the cylinder head by lubricating the valve stems and guides with clean engine oil.

### *HCS and Endura-E engines*

3  Insert the first valve into its guide. Wipe the oil from the top of the valve stem, then wind some insulation tape over the split collet location groove, to protect the new valve stem seal as it is fitted over the valve and into position. As the seal is fitted, support the valve to prevent it from falling out; push the seal down the valve, and locate it flush to the valve guide. Press the seal down firmly and evenly using a suitable diameter tube or socket, and take care not to distort the seal as it is located. Check that the seal spring is correctly located to ensure that it seals correctly, then remove the tape from the valve stem **(see illustrations)**.

4  Locate the valve spring and its retainer over the valve stem, and engage the valve spring compressor. Compress the spring and retainer just enough to allow the split collets to be inserted in the location groove in the

valve stem. Holding the collets in position, slowly release and remove the valve spring compressor.

**HAYNES HiNT** *A little grease applied to the collet groove will help retain them in position.*

5  Repeat the operation on the remaining valves, ensuring that each valve is fitted in its appropriate location.

6  On completion, support the cylinder head on a suitable piece of wood, and lightly strike the end of each valve stem in turn with a plastic- or copper-faced hammer to fractionally open the valve and seat the valve components.

### *CVH and PTE engines*

7  Working on one valve at a time, fit the lower retainer into position **(see illustration)**.

8  Check for correct orientation, then fit the new oil seal into position over the guide. Drive or press the seal squarely into place, using a suitable tube or socket **(see illustration)**.

9  To protect the seal lips from being damaged by the collet grooves in the valve stem as it is passed through the seal, wipe any oil from the stem at the top, and mask the split collet groove on the stem with insulating tape. Lubricate the lips of the valve stem seal, and insert the valve **(see illustration)**.

10  Remove the tape from the grooved section of the valve stem, then locate the spring and the upper retainer over the valve.

11  Locate the valve spring compressor into

**2D**

**9.3a  Tape the end of the valve stem before fitting the valve stem seal**

**9.3b  Press the seal into position using a suitable socket**

**9.7  Fit the lower retainer**

**9.8  Locate the seal, and tap it into position over the guide**

**9.9  Insert the valve into its guide**

**9.11 Insert the split collets into the groove in the valve stem**

**9.16 Valve spring pressure is sufficient to seat lower seat/stem oil seals on reassembly**

**9.18 Apply a small dab of grease to each collet before installation - it will hold them in place on the valve stem**

position, and compress the spring and cup down the valve stem so that the collet's groove is exposed above the upper retainer. Lightly grease the collet's groove in the stem, (to retain the collets in position) then locate the split collets into the groove in the stem. Slowly release and remove the valve spring compressor. As the compressor is released, ensure that the collets remain fully seated in the groove, and the upper retainer rides up over them to secure them in position **(see illustration)**.

**12** Repeat the above operations on the remaining valves, ensuring that each valve assembly is returned to its original position, or where new valves have been fitted, onto the seat to which it was ground.

**13** When all of the valves have been fitted, support the cylinder head on a wooden block, and using a plastic or copper-faced hammer, lightly tap the end of each valve stem in turn to seat the respective valve assemblies.

**14** Refit the camshaft, tappets and rocker arms to the cylinder head as described in Part B of this Chapter.

### Zetec and Zetec-E engines

**15** Beginning at one end of the head, lubricate and install the first valve. Apply molybdenum disulphide-based grease or clean engine oil to the valve stem, and refit the valve. Where the original valves are being re-used, ensure that each is refitted in its original guide. If new valves are being fitted, insert them into the locations to which they have been ground.

**16** Fit the plastic protector supplied with new valve spring lower seat/stem oil seals to the end of the valve stem, then put the new seal squarely on top of the guide, and leave it there; the action of refitting the valve spring presses the lower seat/stem oil seal into place **(see illustration)**.

**17** Refit the valve spring and upper seat.

**18** Compress the spring with a valve spring compressor, and carefully install the collets in the stem groove. Apply a small dab of grease to each collet to hold it in place if necessary **(see illustration)**. Slowly release the compressor, and make sure the collets seat properly.

**19** When the valve is installed, place the cylinder head flat on the bench and, using a hammer and interposed block of wood, tap the end of the valve stem gently, to settle the components.

**20** Repeat the procedure for the remaining valves. Be sure to return the components to their original locations - don't mix them up!

**21** Refit the hydraulic tappets as described in Part C of this Chapter.

### 10 Camshaft and tappets -
removal, inspection and refitting (HCS and Endura-E engines)

#### Removal

**1** Refer to the applicable Sections in Part A of this Chapter and remove the cylinder head, timing chain and camshaft sprocket, and the sump.

**2** Invert the engine so that it is supported on its cylinder head face (on a clean work area). This is necessary to make all of the tappets slide to the top of their stroke, thus allowing the camshaft to be withdrawn. Rotate the camshaft through a full turn, to ensure that all of the tappets slide up their bores, clear of the camshaft.

**3** Before removing the camshaft, check its endfloat using a dial gauge mounted on the front face of the engine or feeler blades. Pull the camshaft fully towards the front (timing chain) end of the engine, then insert feeler blades between the camshaft sprocket flange and the camshaft thrust plate to assess the endfloat clearance **(see illustration)**. The camshaft endfloat must be as specified.

**4** Undo the two retaining bolts, and remove the camshaft thrust plate.

**5** Carefully withdraw the camshaft from the front end of the engine **(see illustration)**.

**6** Extract each tappet in turn. Keep them in order of fitting by inserting them in a card with eight holes in it, numbered 1 to 8 (from the timing chain end of the engine). A valve grinding suction tool will be found to be useful for the removal of tappets **(see illustration)**.

#### Inspection

**7** Examine the camshaft bearing journals and lobes for damage or excessive wear. If evident, the camshaft must be renewed.

**8** Examine the camshaft bearing internal surfaces for signs of damage or excessive wear. If evident, the bearings must be renewed by a Ford dealer.

**10.3 Checking the camshaft endfloat**

**10.5 Withdrawing the camshaft from the front of the engine**

**10.6 Tappet withdrawal using a valve grinding tool suction cup**

**10.15 Refitting the camshaft thrust plate**

**11.6 Removing the oil baffle to provide access to crankshaft and bearings**

**11.7 Each connecting rod and big-end bearing cap will have a flat-machined surface visible from the front (exhaust) side of the engine, with the cylinder number etched in it**

**9** If not carried out on removal, check the camshaft endfloat as described in paragraph 3. If the endfloat is exceeds the specified tolerance, renew the thrust plate.

**10** It is seldom that the tappets wear excessively in their bores, but it is likely that after a high mileage, the cam lobe contact surfaces will show signs of depression or grooving.

**11** Where this condition is evident, renew the tappets. Grinding out the grooves and wear marks will reduce the thickness of the surface hardening, and will accelerate further wear.

### Refitting

**12** To refit the tappets and the camshaft, it is essential that the crankcase is inverted.

**13** Lubricate their bores and the tappets. Insert each tappet fully into its original bore in the cylinder block.

**14** Lubricate the camshaft bearings, camshaft and thrust plate, then insert the camshaft into the crankcase from the timing case end.

**15** Fit the thrust plate and tighten the retaining bolts to the specified torque setting **(see illustration)**. Check that the camshaft is able to rotate freely, and that the endfloat is as specified.

---

### 11 Piston/connecting rod assemblies - removal and inspection

### Removal

#### HCS and Endura-E engines

**1** Refer to Part A of this Chapter and remove the cylinder head and sump, then remove the oil pick-up pipe and strainer.

**2** Temporarily refit the crankshaft pulley, so that the crankshaft can be rotated. Check that the connecting rod big-end caps have adjacent matching numbers facing towards the camshaft side of the engine. If no marks can be seen, make your own before disturbing any of the components, so that you can be certain of refitting each piston/connecting rod assembly the right way round, to its correct (original) bore, with the cap also the right way round.

#### CVH and PTE engines

**3** Refer to Part B of this Chapter and remove the cylinder head and sump, then remove the oil pick-up pipe and strainer.

**4** Temporarily refit the crankshaft pulley, so the crankshaft can be rotated. Check that the connecting rods have identification numbers - these should be found on the exhaust side of the big-ends. No 1 assembly is at the timing belt end of the engine. If no marks can be seen, make your own before disturbing any of the components, so that you can be certain of refitting each piston/ connecting rod assembly the right way round, to its correct (original) bore, with the cap also the right way round.

#### Zetec and Zetec-E engines

**5** Refer to Part C of this Chapter and remove the cylinder head and sump.

**6** Undo the screws securing the oil pump pick-up/strainer pipe to the pump, then unscrew the four nuts, and withdraw the oil pump pick-up/strainer pipe and oil baffle **(see illustration)**.

**7** Temporarily refit the crankshaft pulley, so that the crankshaft can be rotated. Note that each piston/connecting rod assembly can be identified by its cylinder number (counting from the timing belt end of the engine) etched into the flat-machined surface of both the connecting rod and its cap. The numbers are visible from the front (exhaust side) of the engine **(see illustration)**. Furthermore, each piston has an arrow stamped into its crown, pointing towards the timing belt end of the engine. If no marks can be seen, make your own before disturbing any of the components, so that you can be certain of refitting each piston/connecting rod assembly the right way round, to its correct (original) bore, with the cap also the right way round.

#### All engines

**8** Use your fingernail to feel if a ridge has formed at the upper limit of ring travel (about a quarter-inch down from the top of each cylinder). If carbon deposits or cylinder wear have produced ridges, they must be completely removed with a special tool. Follow the tool manufacturer's instructions provided. Failure to remove the ridges before attempting to remove the piston/connecting rod assemblies may result in piston ring breakage.

**9** Slacken each of the big-end bearing cap bolts half a turn at a time, until they can be removed by hand. Remove the No 1 cap and bearing shell. Don't drop the shell out of the cap.

**10** Remove the upper bearing shell, and push the connecting rod/piston assembly out through the top of the engine. Use a wooden hammer handle to push on the connecting rod's bearing recess. If resistance is felt, double-check that all of the ridge was removed from the cylinder.

**11** Repeat the procedure for the remaining cylinders.

**12** After removal, reassemble the big-end bearing caps and shells on their respective connecting rods, and refit the bolts finger-tight. Leaving the old shells in place until reassembly will help prevent the bearing recesses from being accidentally nicked or gouged. New shells should be used on reassembly.

### Inspection

**13** Before the inspection process can begin, the piston/connecting rod assemblies must be cleaned, and the original piston rings removed from the pistons.

**14** Carefully expand the old rings over the top of the pistons. The use of two or three old feeler blades will be helpful in preventing the rings dropping into empty grooves **(see illustration)**. Be careful not to scratch the piston with the ends of the ring. The rings are

**11.14 Using feeler blades to remove piston rings**

**2D**

brittle, and will snap if they are spread too far. They are also very sharp - protect your hands and fingers. Note that the third ring may incorporate an expander. Always remove the rings from the top of the piston. Keep each set of rings with its piston if the old rings are to be re-used.

15 Scrape away all traces of carbon from the top of the piston. A hand-held wire brush (or a piece of fine emery cloth) can be used, once the majority of the deposits have been scraped away.

16 Remove the carbon from the ring grooves in the piston, using an old ring. Break the ring in half to do this (be careful not to cut your fingers - piston rings are sharp). Be careful to remove only the carbon deposits - do not remove any metal, and do not nick or scratch the sides of the ring grooves.

17 Once the deposits have been removed, clean the piston/connecting rod assembly with paraffin or a suitable solvent, and dry thoroughly. Make sure that the oil return holes in the ring grooves are clear.

18 If the pistons and cylinder liners/bores are not damaged or worn excessively, the original pistons can be refitted. Normal piston wear shows up as even vertical wear on the piston thrust surfaces, and slight looseness of the top ring in its groove. New piston rings should always be used when the engine is reassembled.

19 Carefully inspect each piston for cracks around the skirt, around the gudgeon pin holes, and at the piston ring "lands" (between the ring grooves).

20 Look for scoring and scuffing on the piston skirt, holes in the piston crown, and burned areas at the edge of the crown. If the skirt is scored or scuffed, the engine may have been suffering from overheating, and/or abnormal combustion which caused excessively high operating temperatures. The cooling and lubrication systems should be checked thoroughly. Scorch marks on the sides of the pistons show that blow-by has occurred. A hole in the piston crown, or burned areas at the edge of the piston crown, indicates that abnormal combustion (pre-ignition, knocking, or detonation) has been occurring. If any of the above problems exist, the causes must be investigated and corrected, or the damage will occur again. The causes may include incorrect ignition timing, or a carburettor or fuel injection system fault.

21 Corrosion of the piston, in the form of pitting, indicates that coolant has been leaking into the combustion chamber and/or the crankcase. Again, the cause must be corrected, or the problem may persist in the rebuilt engine.

22 Check the piston-to-rod clearance by twisting the piston and rod in opposite directions. Any noticeable play indicates excessive wear, which must be corrected. The piston/connecting rod assemblies should be taken to a Ford dealer or engine reconditioning

11.24 Check that the connecting rod oilway on CVH engines is clear

specialist to have the pistons, gudgeon pins and rods checked, and new components fitted as required.

23 Don't attempt to separate the pistons from the connecting rods (even if non-genuine replacements are found elsewhere). This is a task for a Ford dealer or similar engine reconditioning specialist, due to the special heating equipment, press, mandrels and supports required to do the job. If the piston/connecting rod assemblies do require this sort of work, have the connecting rods checked for bend and twist, since only such engine repair specialists will have the facilities for this purpose.

24 Check the connecting rods for cracks and other damage. Also on CVH engines, check that the oilway in the base of the connecting rod is clear by probing with a piece of wire (see illustration). Temporarily remove the big-end bearing caps and the old bearing shells, wipe clean the rod and cap bearing recesses, and inspect them for nicks, gouges and scratches. After checking the rods, replace the old shells, slip the caps into place, and tighten the bolts finger-tight.

## 12 Crankshaft - removal and inspection

### Removal

**Note:** The crankshaft can be removed only after the engine has been removed from the vehicle. It is assumed that the transmission,

12.1 Checking crankshaft endfloat with a dial gauge

flywheel/driveplate, timing belt/chain, cylinder head, sump, oil pump pick-up/strainer, oil baffle, oil pump, and piston/connecting rod assemblies, have already been removed. The crankshaft left-hand oil seal carrier/housing must be unbolted from the cylinder block/crankcase before proceeding with crankshaft removal.

1 Before the crankshaft is removed, check the endfloat. Mount a DTI (Dial Test Indicator, or dial gauge) with the stem in line with the crankshaft and just touching the crankshaft (see illustration).

2 Push the crankshaft fully away from the gauge, and zero it. Next, lever the crankshaft towards the gauge as far as possible, and check the reading obtained. The distance that the crankshaft moved is its endfloat; if it is greater than specified, check the crankshaft thrust surfaces for wear. If no wear is evident, new thrustwashers should correct the endfloat.

3 If no dial gauge is available, feeler blades can be used. Gently lever or push the crankshaft all the way towards the right-hand end of the engine. Slip feeler blades between the crankshaft and the main bearing incorporating the thrustwashers to determine the clearance.

### HCS and Endura-E engines

4 Check that the main bearing caps have marks to indicate their respective fitted positions in the block. They also have arrow marks pointing towards the timing chain cover end of the engine to indicate correct orientation (see illustration).

5 Unscrew the retaining bolts, and remove the main bearing caps. If the caps are reluctant to separate from the block face, lightly tap them free using a plastic- or copper-faced hammer. If the bearing shells are likely to be used again, keep them with their bearing caps for safekeeping. However, unless the engine is known to be of low mileage, it is recommended that they be renewed.

6 Lift the crankshaft out from the crankcase, then extract the upper bearing shells and side thrustwashers. Keep them with their respective caps for correct repositioning if they are to be used again.

7 Remove the crankshaft oil seals from the timing cover and the rear oil seal housing.

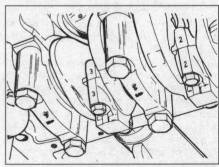

12.4 Connecting rod big-end bearing cap and main bearing cap markings

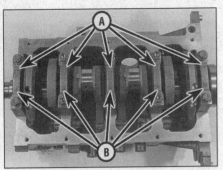

**12.12 Crankshaft main bearing cap arrows point to timing belt end of engine (A), and bearing numbers (B) are consecutive from timing belt end**

**12.22 Measure the diameter of each crankshaft journal at several points, to detect taper and out-of-round conditions**

## 13 Cylinder block/crankcase - cleaning and inspection

### CVH and PTE engines

**8** Check that each main bearing cap is numerically marked for position. Each cap should also have an arrow marking to indicate its direction of fitting (arrow points to the timing belt end).

**9** Unscrew the retaining bolts, and remove the main bearing caps. As they are removed, keep each bearing shell with its cap (in case they are to used again). Note that the bearing shells in the main bearing caps are plain (no groove). It is recommended that the shells be renewed, unless the engine is known to be of low mileage.

**10** Lift out the crankshaft from the crankcase.

**11** Remove each bearing shell in turn from the crankcase, and keep them in order of fitting. Note that the upper shell halves are grooved. Also remove the semi-circular thrustwasher from each side of the central main bearing web, and keep them in their order of fitting.

### Zetec and Zetec-E engines

**12** Check the main bearing caps, to see if they are marked to indicate their locations (see illustration). They should be numbered consecutively from the timing belt end of the engine - if not, mark them with number-stamping dies or a centre-punch. The caps will also have an embossed arrow pointing to the timing belt end of the engine. Noting the different fasteners (for the oil baffle nuts) used on caps 2 and 4, slacken the cap bolts a quarter-turn at a time each, starting with the left- and right-hand end caps and working toward the centre, until they can be removed by hand.

**13** Gently tap the caps with a soft-faced hammer, then separate them from the cylinder block/crankcase. If necessary, use the bolts as levers to remove the caps. Try not to drop the bearing shells if they come out with the caps.

**14** Carefully lift the crankshaft out of the engine.

**15** Remove each bearing shell in turn from the cylinder block/crankcase, and keep them in order of fitting.

### Inspection

**16** Clean the crankshaft, and dry it with compressed air if available.

> ⚠️ **Warning: Wear eye protection when using compressed air! Be sure to clean the oil holes with a pipe cleaner or similar probe.**

**17** Check the main and crankpin (big-end) bearing journals for uneven wear, scoring, pitting and cracking.

**18** Big-end bearing wear is accompanied by distinct metallic knocking when the engine is running (particularly noticeable when the engine is pulling from low speed) and some loss of oil pressure.

**19** Main bearing wear is accompanied by severe engine vibration and rumble - getting progressively worse as engine speed increases - and again by loss of oil pressure.

**20** Check the bearing journal for roughness by running a finger lightly over the bearing surface. Any roughness (which will be accompanied by obvious bearing wear) indicates that the crankshaft requires regrinding (where possible) or renewal.

**21** Remove all burrs from the crankshaft oil holes with a stone, file or scraper.

**22** Using a micrometer, measure the diameter of the main bearing and crankpin (big-end) journals, and compare the results with the *Specifications* at the beginning of this Chapter (see illustration).

**23** By measuring the diameter at a number of points around each journal's circumference, you will be able to determine whether or not the journal is out-of-round. Take the measurement at each end of the journal, near the webs, to determine if the journal is tapered.

**24** If the crankshaft journals are damaged, tapered, out-of-round, or worn beyond the limits specified in this Chapter, the crankshaft must be taken to an engine overhaul specialist, who will regrind it, and who can supply the necessary undersize bearing shells.

**25** Check the oil seal journals at each end of the crankshaft for wear and damage. If either seal has worn an excessive groove in its journal, consult an engine overhaul specialist, who will be able to advise whether a repair is possible, or whether a new crankshaft is necessary.

### Cleaning

**1** Prior to cleaning, remove all external components and senders. On the HCS and Endura-E engines, make sure that the camshaft and tappets are removed before carrying out thorough cleaning of the block. On the CVH and PTE engines, remove the engine ventilation cap from the recess in the rear corner of the cylinder block and if still fitted, undo the retaining screw and withdraw the engine speed sensor from the bellhousing face. On the Zetec and Zetec-E engines, unbolt the piston-cooling oil jets or blanking plugs (as applicable); note that Ford state that the piston-cooling oil jets (where fitted) must be renewed whenever the engine is dismantled for full overhaul (see illustrations).

**2** Remove all oil gallery plugs (where fitted). The plugs are usually very tight - they may have to be drilled out, and the holes re-tapped. Use new plugs when the engine is reassembled. Drill a small hole in the centre of each core plug, and pull them out with a car bodywork dent puller (see illustration).

*Caution: The core plugs (also known as freeze or soft plugs) may be difficult or impossible to retrieve if they are driven into the block coolant passages.*

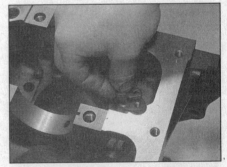

**13.1a Unbolt blanking plugs (where fitted) to clean out oilways . . .**

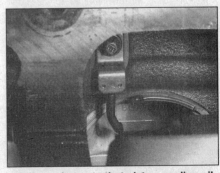

**13.1b . . . but note that piston-cooling oil jets (where fitted) must be renewed as a matter of course whenever engine is overhauled - Zetec and Zetec-E engines**

**2D**

**13.2 The core plugs should be removed with a puller - if they're driven into the block, they may be impossible to retrieve**

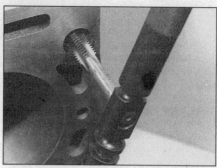

**13.6 All bolt holes in the block should be cleaned and restored with a tap**

3 If any of the castings are extremely dirty, all should be steam-cleaned.

4 After the castings are returned from steam-cleaning, clean all oil holes and oil galleries one more time. Flush all internal passages with warm water until the water runs clear, then dry thoroughly, and apply a light film of oil to all machined surfaces, to prevent rusting. If you have access to compressed air, use it to speed the drying process, and to blow out all the oil holes and galleries.

 **Warning: Wear eye protection when using compressed air!**

5 If the castings are not very dirty, you can do an adequate cleaning job with hot soapy water (as hot as you can stand!) and a stiff brush. Take plenty of time, and do a thorough job. Regardless of the cleaning method used, be sure to clean all oil holes and galleries very thoroughly, and to dry all components completely; protect the machined surfaces as described above, to prevent rusting.

6 All threaded holes must be clean and dry, to ensure accurate torque readings during reassembly; now is also a good time to clean and check the threads of all principal bolts - however, note that some, such as the cylinder head and flywheel/driveplate bolts, are to be renewed as a matter of course whenever they are disturbed. Run the proper-size tap into each of the holes, to remove rust, corrosion, thread sealant or sludge, and to restore damaged threads **(see illustration)**. If possible, use compressed air to clear the holes of debris produced by this operation; a good alternative is to inject aerosol-applied water-dispersant lubricant into each hole, using the long spout usually supplied.

 **Warning: Wear eye protection when cleaning out these holes in this way, and be sure to dry out any excess liquid left in the holes.**

7 When all inspection and repair procedures are complete (see below) and the block is ready for reassembly, apply suitable sealant to the new oil gallery plugs, and insert them into the holes in the block. Tighten them securely. After coating the sealing surfaces of the new core plugs with suitable sealant, install them in the cylinder block/crankcase. Make sure they are driven in straight and

seated properly, or leakage could result. Special tools are available for this purpose, but a large socket with an outside diameter that will just slip into the core plug, used with an extension and hammer, will work just as well.

8 On the Zetec and Zetec-E engines, refit the blanking plugs or (new) piston-cooling oil jets (as applicable), tightening their Torx screws to the torque wrench setting specified. On all engines, refit all other external components removed, referring to the relevant Chapter of this manual for further details where required. Refit the main bearing caps, and tighten the bolts finger-tight.

9 If the engine is not going to be reassembled right away, cover it with a large plastic bag to keep it clean; protect the machined surfaces as described above, to prevent rusting.

## Inspection

10 Visually check the castings for cracks and corrosion. Look for stripped threads in the threaded holes. If there has been any history of internal coolant leakage, it may be worthwhile having an engine overhaul specialist check the cylinder block/crankcase for cracks with special equipment. If defects are found, have them repaired, if possible, or renew the assembly.

11 Check each cylinder bore for scuffing and scoring.

12 The cylinder bores must be measured with all the crankshaft main bearing caps bolted in place (without the crankshaft and

bearing shells), and tightened to the specified torque wrench settings. Measure the diameter of each cylinder at the top (just under the ridge area), centre and bottom of the cylinder bore, parallel to the crankshaft axis. Next, measure each cylinder's diameter at the same three locations across the crankshaft axis **(see illustration)**. Note the measurements obtained.

13 Measure the piston diameter at right-angles to the gudgeon pin axis, just above the bottom of the skirt; again, note the results **(see illustration)**.

14 If it is wished to obtain the piston-to-bore clearance, measure the bore and piston skirt as described above, and subtract the skirt diameter from the bore measurement. If the precision measuring tools shown are not available, the condition of the pistons and bores can be assessed, though not quite as accurately, by using feeler blades as follows. Select a feeler blade of thickness equal to the specified piston-to-bore clearance, and slip it into the cylinder along with the matching piston. The piston must be positioned exactly as it normally would be. The feeler blade must be between the piston and cylinder on one of the thrust faces (at right-angles to the gudgeon pin bore). The piston should slip through the cylinder (with the feeler blade in place) with moderate pressure; if it falls through or slides through easily, the clearance is excessive, and a new piston will be required. If the piston binds at the lower end of the cylinder, and is loose toward the top, the cylinder is tapered. If tight spots are encountered as the piston/feeler blade is rotated in the cylinder, the cylinder is out-of-round (oval).

15 Repeat these procedures for the remaining pistons and cylinder bores.

16 Compare the results with the *Specifications* at the beginning of this Chapter; if any measurement is beyond the dimensions specified for that class (check the piston crown marking to establish the class of piston fitted), or if any bore measurement is significantly different from the others (indicating that the bore is tapered or oval), the piston or bore is excessively-worn.

17 Worn pistons must be renewed; on some

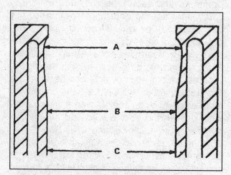

**13.12 Measure the diameter of each cylinder just under the wear ridge (A), at the centre (B) and at the bottom (C)**

**13.13 Measure the piston skirt diameter at right-angles to the gudgeon pin axis, just above the base of the skirt**

engines, the pistons are available as Ford replacement parts only as part of the complete piston/connecting rod assembly. See a Ford dealer or engine reconditioning specialist for advice.

**18** If any of the cylinder bores are badly scuffed or scored, or if they are excessively-worn, out-of-round or tapered, the usual course of action would be to have the cylinder block/crankcase rebored, and to fit new, oversized, pistons on reassembly. See a Ford dealer or engine reconditioning specialist for advice.

**19** If the bores are in reasonably good condition and not excessively-worn, then it may only be necessary to renew the piston rings.

**20** If this is the case, the bores should be honed, to allow the new rings to bed in correctly and provide the best possible seal. Honing is an operation that will be carried out for you by an engine reconditioning specialist.

**21** After all the machining operations have been carried out, the entire block/crankcase must be washed very thoroughly with warm soapy water to remove all traces of abrasive grit produced during the machining operations. When completely clean, rinse it thoroughly and dry it, then lightly oil all exposed machined surfaces to prevent rusting.

**22** The cylinder block/crankcase should now be completely clean and dry, with all components checked for wear or damage, and repaired or overhauled as necessary. Refit as many ancillary components as possible, for safekeeping. If reassembly is not to start immediately, cover the block with a large plastic bag to keep it clean.

## 14 Main and big-end bearings - inspection

**1** Even though the main and big-end bearing shells should be renewed during the engine overhaul, the old shells should be retained for close examination, as they may reveal valuable information about the condition of the engine **(see illustration)**.

**2** Bearing failure occurs because of lack of lubrication, the presence of dirt or other foreign particles, overloading the engine, and corrosion. Regardless of the cause of bearing failure, it must be corrected before the engine is reassembled, to prevent it from happening again.

**3** When examining the bearing shells, remove them from the cylinder block/crankcase and main bearing caps, and from the connecting rods and the big-end bearing caps, then lay them out on a clean surface in the same general position as their location in the engine. This will enable you to match any bearing problems with the corresponding crankshaft journal. *Do not* touch any shell's bearing surface with your fingers while checking it, or the delicate surface may be scratched.

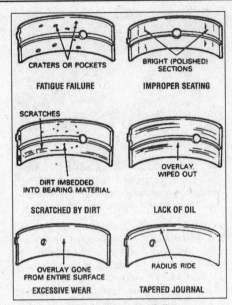

14.1 Typical bearing failures

**4** Dirt or other foreign matter gets into the engine in a variety of ways. It may be left in the engine during assembly, or it may pass through filters or the crankcase ventilation system. It may get into the oil, and from there into the bearings. Metal chips from machining operations and normal engine wear are often present. Abrasives are sometimes left in engine components after reconditioning, especially when parts are not thoroughly cleaned using the proper cleaning methods. Whatever the source, these foreign objects often end up embedded in the soft bearing material, and are easily recognised. Large particles will not embed in the material, and will score or gouge the shell and journal. The best prevention for this cause of bearing failure is to clean all parts thoroughly, and to keep everything spotlessly-clean during engine assembly. Frequent and regular engine oil and filter changes are also recommended.

**5** Lack of lubrication (or lubrication breakdown) has a number of inter-related causes. Excessive heat (which thins the oil), overloading (which squeezes the oil from the bearing face) and oil leakage (from excessive bearing clearances, worn oil pump or high engine speeds) all contribute to lubrication breakdown. Blocked oil passages, which usually are the result of misaligned oil holes in a bearing shell, will also starve a bearing of oil, and destroy it. When lack of lubrication is the cause of bearing failure, the bearing material is wiped or extruded from the shell's steel backing. Temperatures may increase to the point where the steel backing turns blue from overheating.

**6** Driving habits can have a definite effect on bearing life. Full-throttle, low-speed operation (labouring the engine) puts very high loads on bearings, which tends to squeeze out the oil film. These loads cause the shells to flex, which produces fine cracks in the bearing

face (fatigue failure). Eventually, the bearing material will loosen in pieces, and tear away from the steel backing.

**7** Short-distance driving leads to corrosion of bearings, because insufficient engine heat is produced to drive off condensed water and corrosive gases. These products collect in the engine oil, forming acid and sludge. As the oil is carried to the engine bearings, the acid attacks and corrodes the bearing material.

**8** Incorrect shell refitting during engine assembly will lead to bearing failure as well. Tight-fitting shells leave insufficient bearing running clearance, and will result in oil starvation. Dirt or foreign particles trapped behind a bearing shell result in high spots on the bearing, which lead to failure.

**9** *Do not* touch any shell's bearing surface with your fingers during reassembly; there is a risk of scratching the delicate surface, or of depositing particles of dirt on it.

## 15 Engine overhaul - reassembly sequence

**1** Before reassembly begins ensure that all new parts have been obtained and that all necessary tools are available. Read through the entire procedure to familiarise yourself with the work involved, and to ensure that all items necessary for reassembly of the engine are at hand. In addition to all normal tools and materials, jointing and thread locking compound will be needed during engine reassembly. For general-purpose applications, it is recommended that Loctite 275 setting sealer or Hylomar PL32M non-setting sealer be used for joints where required, and Loctite 270 for stud and bolt thread-locking. For specific applications on the Zetec and Zetec-E engines, Hylosil 102 for the cylinder block/crankcase-to-sump/oil pump/oil seal carrier joints, and Loctite 518 for the camshaft right-hand bearing caps should be used. These are recommended by, and obtained from, Ford dealers. In all other cases, provided the relevant mating surfaces are clean and flat, new gaskets will be sufficient to ensure joints are oil-tight. *Do not* use any kind of silicone-based sealant on any part of the fuel system or inlet manifold, and *never* use exhaust sealants upstream of the catalytic converter.

**2** In order to save time and avoid problems, engine reassembly can be carried out in the following order (as applicable).

a) *Engine ventilation cap (CVH and PTE engines).*
b) *Tappets and camshaft (HCS and Endura-E engines).*
c) *Crankshaft and main bearings.*
d) *Pistons and connecting rods.*
e) *Oil pump.*
f) *Sump.*
g) *Flywheel/driveplate.*
h) *Cylinder head.*
i) *Timing sprockets and chain/belt.*

**2D**

*j) Engine external components.*

**3** Ensure that everything is clean prior to reassembly. As mentioned previously, dirt and metal particles can quickly destroy bearings and result in major engine damage. Use clean engine oil to lubricate during reassembly.

## 16 Piston rings - refitting

**1** Before installing new piston rings, check the end gaps. Lay out each piston set with a piston/connecting rod assembly, and keep them together as a matched set from now on.
**2** Insert the top compression ring into the first cylinder, and square it up with the cylinder walls by pushing it in with the top of the piston. The ring should be near the bottom of the cylinder, at the lower limit of ring travel.
**3** To measure the end gap, slip feeler blades between the ends of the ring, until a gauge equal to the gap width is found. The feeler blade should slide between the ring ends with a slight amount of drag. Compare the measurement to the value given in the *Specifications* in this Chapter; if the gap is larger or smaller than specified, double-check to make sure you have the correct rings before proceeding. If you are assessing the condition of used rings, have the cylinder bores checked and measured by a Ford dealer or similar engine reconditioning specialist, so that you can be sure of exactly which component is worn, and seek advice as to the best course of action to take.
**4** If the end gap is still too small, it must be opened up by careful filing of the ring ends using a fine file. If it is too large, this is not as serious, unless the specified limit is exceeded, in which case very careful checking is required of the dimensions of all components, as well as of the new parts.
**5** Repeat the procedure for each ring that will be installed in the first cylinder, and for each ring in the remaining cylinders. Remember to keep rings, pistons and cylinders matched up.
**6** Refit the piston rings as follows. Where the original rings are being refitted, use the marks or notes made on removal, to ensure that each ring is refitted to its original groove and the same way up. New rings generally have their top surfaces identified by markings (often an indication of size, such as "STD", or the word "TOP") - the rings must be fitted with such markings uppermost **(see illustration)**.
**Note:** *Always follow the instructions printed on the ring package or box - different manufacturers may require different approaches. Do not mix up the top and second compression rings, as they usually have different cross-sections.*
**7** The oil control ring (lowest one on the piston) is usually installed first. It is composed of three separate elements. Slip the spacer/expander into the groove. If an anti-rotation tang is used, make sure it is

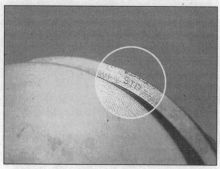

**16.6 Look for etched markings ("STD" - indicating a standard-sized ring - shown here) identifying piston ring top surface**

inserted into the drilled hole in the ring groove. Next, install the lower side rail. Don't use a piston ring installation tool on the oil ring side rails, as they may be damaged. Instead, place one end of the side rail into the groove between the spacer/expander and the ring land, hold it firmly in place, and slide a finger around the piston while pushing the rail into the groove. Next, install the upper side rail in the same manner.
**8** After the three oil ring components have been installed, check that both the upper and lower side rails can be turned smoothly in the ring groove.
**9** The second compression (middle) ring is installed next, followed by the top compression ring - ensure that their marks are uppermost, and be careful not to confuse them. Don't expand either ring any more than necessary to slide it over the top of the piston.
**10** On the HCS and Endura-E engines, when all of the rings are fitted to each piston, arrange them so that the gaps are positioned as described in the *Specifications* at the start of this Chapter.
**11** On the CVH and PTE engines, when all of the rings are fitted to each piston, arrange them so that the gaps are spaced at 120° intervals, with no gaps positioned above the gudgeon pin hole.
**12** On the Zetec and Zetec-E engines, when all the rings are fitted to each piston, space the ring gaps (including the elements of the oil control ring) uniformly around the piston at 120° intervals.

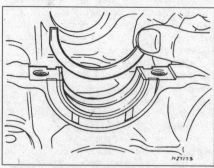

**17.5 Place the crankshaft thrustwashers into position in the crankcase so that their oil grooves are facing outwards**

## 17 Crankshaft - refitting and main bearing running clearance check

**1** It is assumed at this point that the cylinder block/crankcase and crankshaft have been cleaned and repaired or reconditioned as necessary. Position the engine upside-down.
**2** Remove the main bearing cap bolts, and lift out the caps. Lay the caps out in the proper order, to ensure correct installation.
**3** If they're still in place, remove the old bearing shells from the block and the main bearing caps. Wipe the bearing recesses of the block and caps with a clean, lint-free cloth. They must be kept spotlessly-clean!

### *Main bearing clearance check*
#### HCS and Endura-E engines

**4** Wipe clean the main bearing shell seats in the crankcase, and clean the backs of the bearing shells. Insert the respective upper shells (dry) into position in the crankcase. Note that the upper shells have grooves in them (the lower shells are plain, and have a wider location lug). Where the old main bearings are being refitted, ensure that they are located in their original positions. Make sure that the tab on each bearing shell fits into the notch in the block or cap.
**Caution: Don't hammer the shells into place, and don't damage the bearing faces. No lubrication should be used at this time.**
**5** Place the crankshaft thrustwashers into position in the crankcase, so that their oil grooves are facing outwards (away from the central web) **(see illustration)**.

#### CVH and PTE engines

**6** Wipe clean the main bearing shell seats in the crankcase, and clean the backs of the bearing shells. Insert the respective upper shells (dry) into position in the crankcase. Note that with the exception of the front main bearing, the upper shells have grooves in them (the lower half bearings are plain). The upper and lower front shells are narrower in section, and both have an oil groove in them. Where the old main bearings are being refitted, ensure that they are located in their original positions **(see illustration)**. Make sure

**17.6 Fit the bearing shells to the main bearing housings in the crankcase**

17.7 Fit the crankcase ventilation cap and its retaining spring

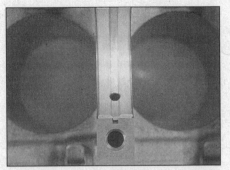

17.9 Tab on each bearing shell must engage with notch in block or cap, and oil holes in upper shells must align with block oilways

17.11 Lay the Plastigage strips (arrowed) on the main bearing journals, parallel to the crankshaft centre-line

that the tab on each bearing shell fits into the notch in the block or cap.

*Caution: Don't hammer the shells into place, and don't damage the bearing faces. No lubrication should be used at this time.*

7 Relocate the crankcase ventilation cap and its retaining spring into position in the crankcase (see illustration).

8 Place the crankshaft thrustwashers into position in the crankcase so that their oil grooves are facing outwards (away from the central web).

### Zetec and Zetec-E engines

9 Wipe clean the main bearing shell seats in the crankcase, and clean the backs of the new main bearing shells. Fit the shells with an oil groove in each main bearing location in the block; note the thrustwashers integral with the No 3 (centre) main bearing upper shell. Fit the other shell from each bearing set in the corresponding main bearing cap. Make sure the tab on each bearing shell fits into the notch in the block or cap. Also, the oil holes in the block must line up with the oil holes in the bearing shell (see illustration).

*Caution: Don't hammer the shells into place, and don't damage the bearing faces. No lubrication should be used at this time.*

### All engines

10 Clean the bearing surfaces of the shells in the block, and the crankshaft main bearing journals with a clean, lint-free cloth. Check or clean the oil holes in the crankshaft, as any dirt here can go only one way - straight through the new bearings.

11 Once you're certain the crankshaft is clean, carefully lay it in position in the main bearings. Trim several pieces of the appropriate-size Plastigage (they must be slightly shorter than the width of the main bearings), and place one piece on each crankshaft main bearing journal, parallel with the crankshaft centre-line (see illustration).

12 Clean the bearing surfaces of the cap shells, and install the caps in their respective positions (don't mix them up) with the arrows pointing to the timing chain/belt end of the engine. Don't disturb the Plastigage.

13 Working on one cap at a time, from the centre main bearing outwards (and ensuring

17.15 Compare the width of the crushed Plastigage to the scale on the envelope to determine the main bearing running clearance

that each cap is tightened down squarely and evenly onto the block), tighten the main bearing cap bolts to the specified torque. Don't rotate the crankshaft at any time during this operation!

14 Remove the bolts, and carefully lift off the main bearing caps. Keep them in order. Don't disturb the Plastigage or rotate the crankshaft. If any of the main bearing caps are difficult to remove, tap them gently from side-to-side with a soft-faced mallet to loosen them.

15 Compare the width of the crushed Plastigage on each journal with the scale printed on the Plastigage envelope to obtain the main bearing running clearance (see illustration). Check the *Specifications* to make sure that the clearance is correct.

16 If the clearance is not as specified, seek the advice of a Ford dealer or similar engine reconditioning specialist - if the crankshaft journals are in good condition, it may be possible simply to renew the shells to achieve the correct clearance. If this is not possible, the crankshaft must be reground by a specialist who can supply the necessary undersized shells. First though, make sure no dirt or oil was between the bearing shells and the caps or block when the clearance was measured. If the Plastigage is wider at one end than the other, the journal may be tapered.

17 Carefully scrape all traces of the Plastigage material off the main bearing journals and the bearing surfaces. Be very careful not to scratch the bearing - use your fingernail or the edge of a credit card.

17.20 Refit the crankshaft after checking bearing clearances

### Final crankshaft refitting

18 Carefully lift the crankshaft out of the engine. Clean the bearing surfaces of the shells in the block, then apply a thin, uniform layer of clean molybdenum disulphide-based grease, engine assembly lubricant, or clean engine oil to each surface. Coat the thrustwasher surfaces as well.

19 Lubricate the crankshaft oil seal journals with molybdenum disulphide-based grease, engine assembly lubricant, or clean engine oil.

20 Make sure the crankshaft journals are clean, then lay the crankshaft back in place in the block (see illustration). Clean the bearing surfaces of the shells in the caps, then lubricate them. Install the caps in their respective positions, with the arrows pointing to the timing belt/chain end of the engine.

21 Working on one cap at a time, from the centre main bearing outwards (and ensuring that each cap is tightened down squarely and evenly onto the block), tighten the main bearing cap bolts to the specified torque wrench setting.

22 Rotate the crankshaft a number of times by hand, to check for any obvious binding.

23 Check the crankshaft endfloat (refer to Section 12). It should be correct if the crankshaft thrust faces aren't worn or damaged.

24 Refit the crankshaft left-hand oil seal carrier, and install a new seal (see Part A, B or C of this Chapter according to engine type).

**2D**

## 18 Piston/connecting rod assemblies - refitting and big-end bearing clearance check

**Note:** *On the HCS and Endura-E engines, new big-end bearing cap retaining bolts will be required for reassembly.*

1 Before refitting the piston/connecting rod assemblies, the cylinder bores must be perfectly clean, the top edge of each cylinder must be chamfered, and the crankshaft must be in place.

2 Remove the big-end bearing cap from No 1 cylinder connecting rod (refer to the marks noted or made on removal). Remove the original bearing shells, and wipe the bearing recesses of the connecting rod and cap with a clean, lint-free cloth. They must be kept spotlessly-clean!

### Big-end bearing running clearance check

3 Clean the back of the new upper bearing shell, fit it to the connecting rod, then fit the other shell of the bearing set to the big-end bearing cap. Make sure that the tab on each shell fits into the notch in the rod or cap recess **(see illustration)**.
**Caution: Don't hammer the shells into place, and don't damage the bearing face. Don't lubricate the bearing at this time.**

4 It's critically important that all mating surfaces of the bearing components are perfectly clean and oil-free when they're assembled.

5 Position the piston ring gaps as described in Section 16, lubricate the piston, and rings with clean engine oil, and attach a piston ring compressor to the piston. Leave the skirt protruding about a quarter-inch, to guide the piston into the cylinder bore. The rings must be compressed until they're flush with the piston.

6 Rotate the crankshaft until No 1 crankpin (big-end) journal is at BDC (Bottom Dead Centre), and apply a coat of engine oil to the cylinder walls.

7 Arrange the No 1 piston/connecting rod assembly so that the arrow on the piston crown points to the timing belt/chain end of the engine. Gently insert the assembly into the No 1 cylinder bore, and rest the bottom edge of the ring compressor on the engine block.

8 Tap the top edge of the ring compressor to make sure it's contacting the block around its entire circumference.

9 Gently tap on the top of the piston with the end of a wooden hammer handle **(see illustration)**, while guiding the connecting rod's big-end onto the crankpin. The piston rings may try to pop out of the ring compressor just before entering the cylinder bore, so keep some pressure on the ring compressor. Work slowly, and if any resistance is felt as the piston enters the cylinder, stop immediately. Find out what's binding, and fix it before proceeding. *Do not*, for any reason, force the piston into the cylinder - you might break a ring and/or the piston.

10 To check the big-end bearing running clearance, cut a piece of the appropriate-size Plastigage slightly shorter than the width of the connecting rod bearing, and lay it in place on the No 1 crankpin (big-end) journal, parallel with the crankshaft centre-line **(see illustration 17.11)**.

11 Clean the connecting rod-to-cap mating surfaces, and refit the big-end bearing cap. Tighten the cap bolts evenly - on the HCS, Endura-E, Zetec and Zetec-E engines, first use a torque wrench to tighten the bolts to the Stage 1 torque setting, then use an ordinary socket extension bar and an angle gauge to tighten the bolts further through the Stage 2 angle **(see illustration)**. On the CVH and PTE engines, tighten the bolts progressively to the specified torque; further angle-tightening is not required on these engines. Use a thin-wall socket, to avoid erroneous torque readings that can result if the socket is wedged between the cap and nut. If the socket tends to wedge itself between the nut and the cap, lift up on it slightly until it no longer contacts the cap. Don't rotate the crankshaft at any time during this operation!

12 Unscrew the bolts and detach the cap, being very careful not to disturb the Plastigage.

13 Compare the width of the crushed Plastigage to the scale printed on the Plastigage envelope, to obtain the running clearance **(see illustration 17.15)**. Compare it to the *Specifications*, to make sure the clearance is correct.

14 If the clearance is not as specified, seek the advice of a Ford dealer or similar engine reconditioning specialist - if the crankshaft journals are in good condition it may be possible simply to renew the shells to achieve the correct clearance. If this is not possible, the crankshaft must be reground by a specialist, who can also supply the necessary undersized shells. First though, make sure that no dirt or oil was trapped between the bearing shells and the connecting rod or cap when the clearance was measured. Also, recheck the crankpin diameter. If the Plastigage was wider at one end than the other, the crankpin journal may be tapered.

15 Carefully scrape all traces of the Plastigage material off the journal and the bearing surface. Be very careful not to scratch the bearing - use your fingernail or the edge of a credit card.

### Final piston/connecting rod refitting

16 Make sure the bearing surfaces are perfectly clean, then apply a uniform layer of clean molybdenum disulphide-based grease, engine assembly lubricant, or clean engine oil, to both of them. You'll have to push the piston into the cylinder to expose the bearing surface of the shell in the connecting rod.

17 Slide the connecting rod back into place on the crankpin (big-end) journal, refit the big-end bearing cap, and then tighten the bolts as described above.

18 Repeat the entire procedure for the remaining piston/connecting rod assemblies.

19 The important points to remember are:

a) *Keep the backs of the bearing shells and the recesses of the connecting rods and caps perfectly clean when assembling them.*

b) *Make sure you have the correct piston/rod assembly for each cylinder - use the etched cylinder numbers to identify the front-facing side of both the rod and its cap.*

c) *The arrow on the piston crown must face the timing belt/chain end of the engine.*

**18.3 Tab on each big-end bearing shell must engage with notch in connecting rod or cap**

**18.9 The piston can be driven gently into the cylinder bore with the end of a wooden or plastic hammer handle**

**18.11 Angle-tightening the big-end bolts using the correct tool**

---


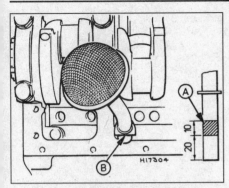

**18.21 Oil inlet pipe refitting details on the HCS engine**

A  *Area of sealant application - dimensions in mm*
B  *Edge must be parallel with engine longitudinal axis*

d) *Lubricate the cylinder bores with clean engine oil.*

e) *Lubricate the bearing surfaces when refitting the big-end bearing caps after the running clearance has been checked.*

**20** After all the piston/connecting rod assemblies have been properly installed, rotate the crankshaft a number of times by hand, to check for any obvious binding.

**21** On the HCS and Endura-E engines, if the oil pick-up pipe and strainer was removed, this is a good time to refit it. First clean the joint area, then coat the area indicated with the specified activator (available from Ford dealers) **(see illustration)**. Wait for a period of ten minutes, then smear the shaded area with the specified adhesive and immediately press the inlet pipe into position in the crankcase.

## 19  Engine - initial start-up after overhaul

**1** With the engine refitted in the vehicle, double-check the engine oil and coolant levels. Make a final check that everything has been reconnected, and that there are no tools or rags left in the engine compartment.

**2** With the spark plugs removed and the ignition system disabled by unplugging the ignition coil's electrical connector, remove the fuel pump fuse (fuel injection engines) to disconnect the fuel pump (see Chapter 12). Turn the engine on the starter until the oil pressure warning light goes out.

**3** Refit the spark plugs, and connect all the spark plug (HT) leads (Chapter 1). Reconnect the ignition coil. On fuel injection engines, refit the fuel pump fuse, switch on the ignition and listen for the fuel pump; it will run for a little longer than usual, due to the lack of pressure in the system.

**4** Start the engine, noting that this also may take a little longer than usual, due to the fuel system components being empty.

**5** While the engine is idling, check for fuel, coolant and oil leaks. Don't be alarmed if there are some odd smells and smoke from parts getting hot and burning off oil deposits. If the hydraulic tappets (where applicable) have been disturbed, some valve gear noise may be heard at first; this should disappear as the oil circulates fully around the engine, and normal pressure is restored in the tappets.

**6** Keep the engine idling until hot water is felt circulating through the top hose, check that it idles reasonably smoothly and at the usual speed, then switch it off.

**7** After a few minutes, recheck the oil and coolant levels, and top-up as necessary ("*Weekly checks*").

**8** If they were tightened as described, there is no need to re-tighten the cylinder head bolts once the engine has first run after reassembly - in fact, Ford state that the bolts *must not* be re-tightened.

**9** If new components such as pistons, rings or crankshaft bearings have been fitted, the engine must be run-in for the first 500 miles (800 km). Do not operate the engine at full-throttle, or allow it to labour in any gear during this period. It is recommended that the oil and filter be changed at the end of this period.

**2D**

# Chapter 3
# Cooling, heating and air conditioning systems

## Contents

## Degrees of difficulty

| Easy, suitable for novice with little experience |  | Fairly easy, suitable for beginner with some experience |  | Fairly difficult, suitable for competent DIY mechanic |  | Difficult, suitable for experienced DIY mechanic |  | Very difficult, suitable for expert DIY or professional | |
|---|---|---|---|---|---|---|---|---|---|

## Specifications

**Coolant**

Mixture type . . . . . . . . . . . . . . . . . . . . . . . . . . . . . . . . . . . . . . . . . . See Chapter 1
Cooling system capacity . . . . . . . . . . . . . . . . . . . . . . . . . . . . . . . . . See Chapter 1

**System pressure**

Pressure test . . . . . . . . . . . . . . . . . . . . . . . . . . . . . . . . . . . . . . . . . . 1.2 bars - should hold this pressure for at least 10 seconds

**Expansion tank filler cap**

Pressure rating . . . . . . . . . . . . . . . . . . . . . . . . . . . . . . . . . . . . . . . . . 1.2 bars approximately - see cap for actual value

**Thermostat**

Starts to open . . . . . . . . . . . . . . . . . . . . . . . . . . . . . . . . . . . . . . . . . . 85°C to 89°C

**Coolant temperature sensor**

Resistance:
   At 0°C . . . . . . . . . . . . . . . . . . . . . . . . . . . . . . . . . . . . . . . . . . . . . 89 to 102 kilohms
   At 20°C . . . . . . . . . . . . . . . . . . . . . . . . . . . . . . . . . . . . . . . . . . . . 35 to 40 kilohms
   At 100°C . . . . . . . . . . . . . . . . . . . . . . . . . . . . . . . . . . . . . . . . . . . 1.9 to 2.5 kilohms
   At 120°C . . . . . . . . . . . . . . . . . . . . . . . . . . . . . . . . . . . . . . . . . . . 1.0 to 1.4 kilohms

**Air conditioning system**

Refrigerant . . . . . . . . . . . . . . . . . . . . . . . . . . . . . . . . . . . . . . . . . . . . R12 or R134a

3

## Torque wrench settings

| | Nm | lbf ft |
|---|---|---|
| Thermostat housing to cylinder head: | | |
| HCS and Endura-E engines | 17 to 21 | 13 to 16 |
| CVH engines | 9 to 12 | 6 to 9 |
| PTE engines | 9 | 6 |
| Zetec engines | 17 to 21 | 13 to 16 |
| Water outlet to thermostat housing (Zetec engines) | 9 to 12 | 6 to 9 |
| Water pump pulley | 10 | 7 |
| Water pump retaining bolts: | | |
| HCS and Endura-E engines | 8 | 6 |
| CVH and PTE engines | 8 | 6 |
| Zetec and Zetec-E engines | 18 | 13 |
| Coolant temperature gauge sender | 6 | 4 |
| Coolant temperature sensor: | | |
| HCS engine | 23 | 17 |
| CVH engine: | | |
| 1.4 litre models | 19 | 14 |
| 1.6 litre models | 15 | 11 |
| PTE engine | 15 | 11 |
| Zetec and Zetec-E engines | 15 | 11 |
| Radiator retaining bolts | 23 | 17 |
| Cooling fan motor-to-shroud | 10 | 7 |
| Cooling fan shroud-to-radiator | 4 | 3 |
| Heater housing to body | 9 | 6 |
| Air conditioning system components: | | |
| Condenser to side member | 9 | 6 |
| Shroud to radiator | 4 | 3 |
| Dehydrator to radiator bracket | 4 | 3 |
| High pressure switch to dehydrator | 15 | 11 |
| Expansion valve to evaporator | 4 | 3 |
| Air conditioner housing to cowl panel | 6 | 4 |
| Low and high pressure pipes to compressor | 23 | 17 |
| Low pressure liquid pipe to expansion valve | 6 | 4 |
| Dehydrator connecting pipe to condenser | 17 | 13 |
| Pipes to dehydrator | 17 | 13 |
| Compressor to bracket | 24 | 18 |
| Compressor driveplate to compressor | 14 | 10 |

## 1 General information and precautions

### General information

#### Engine cooling system

The cooling system is of the pressurised type consisting of a belt-driven pump, aluminium crossflow radiator, expansion tank, electric cooling fan and a thermostat. The system functions as follows. Cold coolant in the bottom of the radiator passes through the bottom hose to the water pump, where it is pumped around the cylinder block and head passages. After cooling the cylinder bores, combustion surfaces and valve seats, the coolant reaches the underside of the thermostat, which is initially closed. The coolant passes through the heater and inlet manifold and is returned to the water pump.

When the engine is cold, the coolant circulates through the cylinder block, cylinder head, heater and inlet manifold. When the coolant reaches a predetermined temperature, the thermostat opens, and the coolant then passes through the top hose to the radiator.

As the coolant circulates through the radiator, it is cooled by the inrush of air when the car is in forward motion. Airflow is supplemented by the action of the electric cooling fan when necessary. Upon reaching the bottom of the radiator, the coolant is now cooled, and the cycle is repeated.

When the engine is at normal operating temperature, the coolant expands, and some of it is displaced into the expansion tank. This coolant collects in the tank, and is returned to the radiator when the system cools.

The electric cooling fan, mounted behind the radiator, is controlled by a thermostatic switch. At a predetermined coolant temperature, the switch contacts close, thus actuating the fan.

#### Heating system

The heating system consists of a blower fan and heater matrix (radiator) located in the heater unit, with hoses connecting the heater matrix to the engine cooling system. Hot engine coolant is circulated through the heater matrix. When the heater temperature control on the facia is operated, a flap door opens to expose the heater matrix to the passenger compartment. Air entering the vehicle passes over the matrix and is thus heated - the supply of air can be supplemented by operating the blower fan as required.

#### Air conditioning system

See Section 13.

### Precautions

⚠ **Warning: DO NOT attempt to remove the expansion tank filler cap, or to disturb any part of the cooling system, while it or the engine is hot, as there is a very great risk of scalding. If the expansion tank filler cap must be removed before the engine and radiator have fully cooled down (even though this is not recommended) the pressure in the cooling system must first be released. Cover the cap with a thick layer of cloth, to avoid scalding, and slowly unscrew the filler cap until a hissing sound can be heard. When the hissing has stopped, showing that pressure is released, slowly unscrew the filler cap further until it can be removed; if more hissing sounds are heard, wait until they have stopped before unscrewing the cap completely. At all times, keep well away from the filler opening.**

⚠ **Warning: Do not allow antifreeze to come in contact with your skin, or with the painted surfaces of the vehicle. Rinse off spills immediately with plenty of water. Never leave antifreeze** lying around in an open container, or in a puddle in the driveway or on the garage floor. Children and pets are attracted by its sweet smell, but antifreeze can be fatal if ingested.

⚠️ *Warning: If the engine is hot, the electric cooling fan may start rotating even if the engine is not running, so be careful to keep hands, hair and loose clothing well clear when working in the engine compartment.*

⚠️ *Warning: Refer to Section 13 for precautions to be observed when working on vehicles equipped with air conditioning.*

## 2  Antifreeze -
### general information

**Note:** *Refer to the warnings given in Section 1 of this Chapter before proceeding.*

The cooling system should be filled with a water/ethylene glycol-based antifreeze solution, of a strength which will prevent freezing down to at least -25°C, or lower if the local climate requires it. Antifreeze also provides protection against corrosion, and increases the coolant boiling point.

The cooling system should be maintained according to the schedule described in Chapter 1. If antifreeze is used that is not to Ford's specification, old or contaminated coolant mixtures are likely to cause damage, and encourage the formation of corrosion and scale in the system. Use distilled water with the antifreeze, if available - if not, be sure to use only soft water. Clean rainwater is suitable.

Before adding antifreeze, check all hoses and hose connections, because antifreeze tends to leak through very small openings. Engines don't normally consume coolant, so if the level falls regularly, find the cause and correct it.

The exact mixture of antifreeze-to-water which you should use depends on the relative weather conditions. The mixture should contain at least 40% antifreeze, but not more than 70%. Consult the mixture ratio chart on the antifreeze container before adding coolant. Hydrometers are available at most automotive accessory shops to test the coolant. Use only good-quality ethylene-glycol-based antifreeze which meets the vehicle manufacturer's specifications.

## 3  Cooling system hoses -
### disconnection and renewal

**Note:** *Refer to the warnings given in Section 1 of this Chapter before starting work.*

**1** If the checks described in Chapter 1 reveal a faulty hose, it must be renewed as follows.
**2** First drain the cooling system (refer to Chapter 1); if the antifreeze is not due for renewal, the drained coolant may be re-used, if it is collected in a clean container.
**3** To disconnect any hose, use a pair of pliers to release the spring clamps (or a screwdriver to slacken screw-type clamps), then move them along the hose clear of the union. Carefully work the hose off its stubs. The hoses can be removed with relative ease when new - on an older car, they may have stuck.
**4** If a hose proves stubborn, try to release it by rotating it on its unions before attempting to work it off. Gently prise the end of the hose with a blunt instrument (such as a flat-bladed screwdriver), but do not apply too much force, and take care not to damage the pipe stubs or hoses. Note in particular that the radiator hose unions are fragile; do not use excessive force when attempting to remove the hoses.

> **HAYNES HiNT**
> *If all else fails, cut the hose with a sharp knife, then slit it so that it can be peeled off in two pieces. Although this may prove expensive if the hose is otherwise undamaged, it is preferable to buying a new radiator.*

**5** When refitting a hose, first slide the clamps onto the hose, then work the hose onto its unions.

> **HAYNES HiNT**
> *If the hose is stiff, use a little soapy water as a lubricant, or soften the hose by soaking it in hot water. Do not use oil or grease, which may attack the rubber.*

**6** Work each hose end fully onto its union, then check that the hose is settled correctly and is properly routed. Slide each clip along the hose until it is behind the union flared end, before tightening it securely.
**7** Refill the system with coolant (see Chapter 1).
**8** Check for leaks as soon as possible after disturbing any part of the cooling system.

## 4  Thermostat -
### removal, testing and refitting

**Note:** *Refer to the warnings given in Section 1 of this Chapter before starting work.*

### Removal

**1** Disconnect the battery negative (earth) lead (refer to Chapter 5A, Section 1).
**2** Drain the cooling system (see Chapter 1).

#### HCS, Endura-E, CVH and PTE engines

**3** Loosen the clips, and disconnect the radiator top hose, expansion tank hose and, where applicable, the heater hose from the thermostat housing **(see illustrations)**.
**4** Disconnect the thermostatic switch wire multi-plug from the thermostat housing.
**5** Unscrew the retaining bolts, and remove the thermostat housing **(see illustration)**.
**6** Remove the gasket from the mating face of the thermostat housing, then using suitable pliers, compress the thermostat retaining clip and remove it from the housing. Extract the thermostat from the housing (noting its direction of fitting) and where applicable, remove the O-ring seal **(see illustrations)**.

#### Zetec and Zetec-E engines

**7** Disconnect the expansion tank hose and the radiator top hose from the thermostat housing's water outlet.

**3**

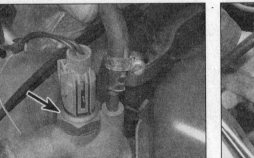

**4.3a Detaching the expansion tank top hose from the thermostat housing on the HCS engine. Thermostatic switch is also shown (arrowed)**

**4.3b Detaching the heater hose from the thermostat housing (CVH engine shown)**

**4.5 Removing the thermostat housing (CVH engine shown)**

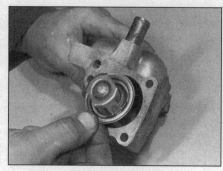

**4.6a Release the retaining clip . . .**

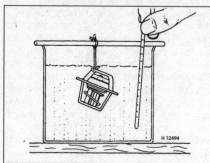

**4.6b . . . extract the thermostat . . .**

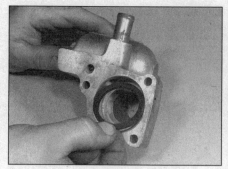

**4.6c . . . and where applicable, remove the O-ring seal**

**4.8 Unscrew the retaining bolts, and remove the water outlet from the thermostat housing**

**4.15 Testing the thermostat**

### Thermostat test

**14** If the thermostat remains in the open position at room temperature, it is faulty, and must be renewed as a matter of course.

**15** To test it fully, suspend the (closed) thermostat on a length of string in a container of cold water, with a thermometer beside it; ensure that neither touches the side of the container **(see illustration)**.

**16** Heat the water, and check the temperature at which the thermostat begins to open; compare this value with that specified. It's not possible to check the fully-open temperature, because this occurs above the boiling point of water at normal atmospheric pressure. If the temperature at which the thermostat began to open was as specified, then it is most likely that the thermostat is all right. Remove the thermostat, and allow it to cool down; check that it closes fully.

**17** If the thermostat does not open and close as described, if it sticks in either position, or if it does not open at the specified temperature, it must be renewed.

### Refitting

#### All models

**18** Refitting is a reversal of removal. Clean the mating surfaces carefully, and renew the thermostat's O-ring seal or housing gasket, as applicable **(see illustration)**.

**19** On Zetec and Zetec-E engines, ensure that the thermostat is fitted with its air bleed valve uppermost **(see illustration)**.

**20** Tighten the thermostat housing/water outlet bolts to the specified torque.

**21** Refill the cooling system (see Chapter 1).

**22** Start the engine and allow it to reach normal operating temperature, then check for leaks and proper thermostat operation.

**4.18 Use a new gasket when refitting the thermostat housing**

**4.19 Ensure that the thermostat is fitted as shown**

**8** Unscrew the retaining bolts, and remove the water outlet from the thermostat housing **(see illustration)**.

**9** Withdraw the thermostat from the housing noting the position of the air bleed valve, and how the thermostat is installed (which end is facing outwards).

### Testing

#### General check

**10** Before assuming the thermostat is to blame for a cooling system problem, check the coolant level, auxiliary drivebelt tension and condition (see Chapter 1) and temperature gauge operation.

**11** If the engine seems to be taking a long time to warm up (based on heater output or temperature gauge operation), the thermostat is probably stuck open. Renew the thermostat.

**12** If the engine runs hot, use your hand to check the temperature of the radiator top hose. If the hose isn't hot, but the engine is, the thermostat is probably stuck closed, preventing the coolant inside the engine from escaping to the radiator - renew the thermostat.

*Caution: Don't drive the vehicle without a thermostat. The lack of a thermostat will slow warm-up time. The engine management system's ECU will then stay in its warm-up mode for longer than necessary, causing emissions and fuel economy to suffer.*

**13** If the radiator top hose is hot, it means that the coolant is flowing and the thermostat is open. Consult *"Fault finding"* in the *Reference Section* at the end of this manual to assist in tracing possible cooling system faults.

---

**5 Radiator electric cooling fan assembly** - testing, removal and refitting

**Note:** *Refer to the warnings given in Section 1 of this Chapter before starting work.*

### Testing

**1** If it is suspected that the cooling fan is not

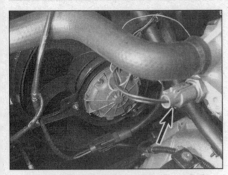

5.2a Cooling fan thermostatic switch location (arrowed) in the thermostat housing (CVH engine shown)

5.2b Cooling fan thermostatic switch location (arrowed) in the radiator top hose (Zetec engine shown)

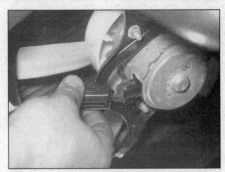

5.5a Detach the cooling fan motor wiring connector . . .

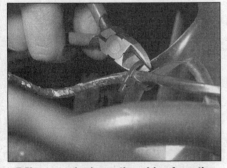

5.5b . . . and release the wiring from the shroud/motor support arm . . .

5.5c . . . and from the locating clip

5.6 Cooling fan shroud-to-radiator retaining nut

operating when high engine temperature would normally require it to do so, first check the relevant fuses and relays (see Chapter 12).
2 Detach the wiring multi-plug from the thermostatic switch, which is located either in the thermostat housing or in the radiator top hose (see illustrations). Using a suitable piece of wire, bridge the two connections within the plug. Switch the ignition on and check if the cooling fan operates. If the fan now operates, the thermostatic switch is at fault, and should be renewed as described in Section 6. Remove the bridging wire from the plug, and reconnect the wiring connector to complete the test.
3 If the fan failed to operate in the previous test, either the fan motor is at fault, or there is a fault in the wiring loom (see Chapter 12 for testing details).

### Removal

**Note:** Refer to Section 14 for removal and refitting procedures on models equipped with air conditioning.
4 Disconnect the battery negative (earth) lead (refer to Chapter 5A, Section 1).
5 Detach the wiring multi-plug from the fan motor, and the additional in-line wiring connector on the side of the shroud on later models. Unclip and remove the wiring from the retaining clips on the shroud (see illustrations). Also where applicable, disconnect the coolant heater hose from the location clips on the cooling fan shroud, or unscrew the metal coolant pipe retaining bolts.

6 Unscrew the two nuts (one each side) securing the cooling fan shroud to the radiator (see illustration).
7 Lift the fan unit complete with its shroud so that the shroud is clear of the radiator attachments, then lower and remove the assembly from underneath the vehicle (see illustration). Take care not to damage the core of the radiator as the fan assembly is withdrawn. On later models it may be necessary to unbolt the engine stabiliser bar to allow clearance for the assembly to be removed.
8 If required, the fan motor can be detached from the shroud by unscrewing the three retaining nuts (see illustration).

### Refitting

9 Refitting is a reversal of the removal procedure. Tighten the shroud-to-radiator

5.7 Withdrawing the cooling fan shroud and motor from under the vehicle

nuts and the fan-to-shroud nuts to the specified torque. Ensure that the wiring connection is cleanly and securely made, and locate the loom in the retaining clips.

**3**

### 6 Cooling system electrical switches and sensors - testing, removal and refitting

**Note:** Refer to the warnings given in Section 1 of this Chapter before starting work.

## Coolant temperature gauge sender

### Testing

1 If the coolant temperature gauge is inoperative, check the fuses first (refer to Chapter 12).

5.8 Fan motor-to-shroud nuts (arrowed)

**2** If the gauge indicates overheating at any time, consult the *"Fault finding"* in the *Reference Section* at the end of this manual, to assist in tracing possible cooling system faults.
**3** If the gauge indicates overheating shortly after the engine is started from cold, unplug the coolant temperature sender's electrical connector. The sender is located below the thermostat housing on HCS and Endura-E engines, adjacent to the thermostat housing on CVH and PTE engines, and on the forward-facing side of the thermostat housing on Zetec and Zetec-E engines. If the gauge reading now drops, renew the sender. If the reading remains high, the wire to the gauge may be shorted to earth, or the gauge is faulty.
**4** If the gauge fails to indicate after the engine has been warmed up (approximately 10 minutes) and the fuses are known to be sound, switch off the engine. Unplug the sender's electrical connector, and use a jumper wire to ground the connector to a clean earth point (bare metal) on the engine. Switch on the ignition without starting the engine. If the gauge now indicates Hot, renew the sender.
**5** If the gauge still does not work, the circuit may be open, or the gauge may be faulty. See Chapter 12 for additional information.

### Removal

**6** Refer to the relevant Part of Chapter 4 and remove the air cleaner or air inlet hoses, according to engine type as necessary, to gain access to the sender unit.
**7** Drain the cooling system (see Chapter 1).
**8** On Zetec and Zetec-E engines, disconnect the expansion tank coolant hose and the radiator top hose from the thermostat housing's water outlet.
**9** Unplug the electrical connector from the sender unit.
**10** Unscrew the sender and withdraw it.

### Refitting

**11** Clean as thoroughly as possible the sender unit location, then apply a light coat of sealant to the sender's threads. Screw in the sender, tighten it to the specified torque, and plug in the electrical connector.
**12** Reconnect the hoses, and refit any components disconnected for access. Refill or top-up the cooling system (see *"Weekly Checks"* or Chapter 1) and run the engine. Check for leaks and proper gauge operation.

### Engine coolant temperature sensor

#### Testing

**13** Disconnect the battery negative (earth) lead (see Chapter 5A, Section 1).
**14** Locate the coolant temperature sensor, which will be found below the inlet manifold on HCS and Endura-E engines, on the side or centre of the inlet manifold on CVH and PTE engines, or on top of the thermostat housing on Zetec and Zetec-E engines. Once located,

refer to the relevant Part of Chapter 4 and remove the air cleaner or air inlet hoses, according to engine type as necessary, to improve access to the sensor unit.
**15** Unplug the electrical connector from the sensor.
**16** Using an ohmmeter, measure the resistance between the sensor terminals. Depending on the temperature of the sensor tip, the resistance measured will vary, but should be within the broad limits given in the *Specifications* of this Chapter. If the sensor's temperature is varied - by removing it (see below) and placing it in a freezer for a while, or by warming it gently - its resistance should alter accordingly.
**17** If the results obtained show the sensor to be faulty, renew it.
**18** On completion, plug in the connector and refit any components removed for access, then reconnect the battery.

### Removal

**19** Disconnect the battery negative (earth) lead (see Chapter 5A, Section 1).
**20** Locate the sensor as described previously, and remove any components as necessary for access.
**21** Drain the cooling system (see Chapter 1).
**22** Unplug the electrical connector from the sensor.
**23** Unscrew the sensor and withdraw it.

### Refitting

**24** Clean as thoroughly as possible the sensor location, then apply a light coat of sealant to the sensor's threads. Refit and tighten the sensor to the specified torque wrench setting, and plug in its electrical connector.
**25** Refit any components disconnected for access then refill the cooling system (see Chapter 1).

### Radiator electric cooling fan thermostatic switch

#### Testing

**26** Refer to the procedures contained in Section 5.

#### Removal

**27** Disconnect the battery negative (earth) lead (refer to Chapter 5A, Section 1).

**7.6a Detach the top hose . . .**

**28** Drain the cooling system (see Chapter 1).
**29** Disconnect the wiring multi-plug from the thermostatic switch, and then unscrew the switch from the thermostat housing or radiator top hose, as applicable. Remove the sealing washer.

### Refitting

**30** Refitting is a reversal of removal, but fit a new sealing washer and tighten the switch securely. Refill the cooling system as described in Chapter 1, then reconnect the battery.

---

**7  Radiator and expansion tank -** removal, inspection and refitting

**Note:** *Refer to the warnings given in Section 1 of this Chapter before starting work.*

### Radiator

#### Removal

> **HAYNES HINT** *If leakage is the reason for removing the radiator, bear in mind that minor leaks can often be cured using a radiator sealant without removing the radiator.*

**1** Disconnect the battery negative (earth) lead (refer to Chapter 5A, Section 1).
**2** On carburettor engines, refer to Chapter 4A and remove the air cleaner inlet if necessary, for access.
**3** Drain the cooling system (see Chapter 1).
**4** Remove the cooling fan assembly as described in Section 5.
**5** Chock the rear wheels then jack up the front of the car and support it on axle stands (see *"Jacking and vehicle support"*).
**6** Loosen off their retaining clips, and detach the top, bottom and expansion tank hoses from the radiator **(see illustrations)**.
**7** On later models, remove the wheel arch liner extensions each side, if fitted.
**8** Where applicable, disconnect the automatic transmission fluid cooling pipes from the

**7.6b . . . the bottom hose and expansion tank hose from the radiator**

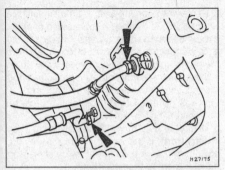

**7.8a Automatic transmission fluid cooling pipe connections to the radiator (arrowed)**

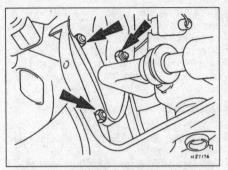

**7.8b Air conditioner condenser retaining nuts (arrowed)**

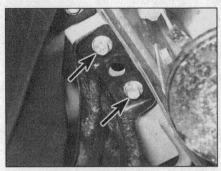

**7.9 Radiator retaining bolts (arrowed)**

**7.10a Radiator mounting rubber**

**7.10b Drilling out a radiator-to-splash shield rivet**

radiator - be prepared for fluid loss **(see illustration)**. As they are disconnected, plug the fluid hoses and connections, to prevent further loss of fluid and the ingress of dirt into the system. If air conditioning is fitted, remove the splash shield (see paragraph 10), then undo the three retaining nuts and detach the air conditioning condenser from the side of the radiator side deflector **(see illustration)**.

**9** Unscrew the two retaining bolts on each side of the radiator (underneath the radiator), then supporting it, lower the radiator clear of the mounting studs at the top, and carefully withdraw it from underneath the front end of the vehicle **(see illustration)**.

**10** Detach the rubber mounts, the side deflectors and the bottom mounting from the radiator. If required, the splash shield can be removed from the radiator by undoing the six retaining screws or drilling out the pop-rivets and extracting the retaining clips (according to type) **(see illustrations)**.

**11** With the radiator removed, it can be inspected for leaks and damage. If it needs repair, have a radiator specialist or dealer service department perform the work, as special techniques are required.

**12** Insects and dirt can be removed from the radiator with a garden hose or a soft brush. Don't bend the cooling fins as this is done.

### Refitting

**13** Refitting is a reversal of removal, but check the mounting bushes, and if necessary renew them. If the splash shield was detached from the base of the radiator, refit it using new pop-rivets and retaining clips or screws, according

to type. Refill the cooling system with reference to Chapter 1. On automatic transmission models check, and if necessary top-up, the automatic transmission fluid level (Chapter 1).

### Expansion tank

#### Removal

**14** Partially drain the cooling system, so that the coolant level drops below the expansion tank. Refer to Chapter 1 for details.

**15** Where fitted, withdraw the power steering fluid reservoir from the side of the expansion tank, and move it aside as far as the hoses will permit.

**16** Before disconnecting the coolant hoses from the expansion tank, it is advisable to clamp them just short of their connections to the expansion tank, to prevent spillage of coolant and the ingress of air when they are detached.

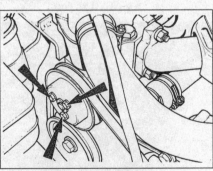

**8.3 Slacken the water pump drivebelt pulley retaining bolts (arrowed) while the drivebelt is still in place**

**17** Loosen off the coolant hose clips at the expansion tank, and detach the hoses from it. If they are not clamped, secure them so that their ends are raised, to minimise coolant spillage.

**18** Unscrew the two retaining screws, and remove the expansion tank from the inner wing panel.

### Refitting

**19** Refit in the reverse order of removal. Top-up the cooling system as described in *"Weekly Checks"*.

## 8 Water pump (HCS and Endura-E engines) - removal and refitting

**Note:** *Refer to the warnings given in Section 1 of this Chapter before starting work.*

### Removal

**1** Disconnect the battery negative (earth) lead (refer to Chapter 5A, Section 1).

**2** Drain the cooling system (see Chapter 1).

**3** Slacken the water pump pulley retaining bolts, then remove the auxiliary drivebelt as described in Chapter 1 **(see illustration)**.

**4** Remove the retaining bolts, and remove the drivebelt pulley from the water pump.

**5** Loosen off the coolant hose securing clips, and disconnect the hoses from the water pump.

**6** Unscrew the retaining bolts, and withdraw the water pump from the engine **(see illustration)**.

**8.6 Unscrew the water pump retaining bolts (arrowed)**

**3**

## Refitting

**7** Clean all traces of gasket from the engine and the water pump mating faces. Ensure that the mating faces are clean and dry. Note that the water pump gasket fitted during production is integral with the timing cover gasket, and this will need to be cut away using a sharp knife, keeping as close to the timing cover as possible.

**8** No provision is made for the repair of the water pump; if it is noisy or defective in any way, it must be renewed.

**9** Refitting is a reversal of the removal procedure. Use a new gasket, lightly smeared with jointing compound, and tighten the retaining bolts to the specified torque.

**10** Refit and adjust the auxiliary drivebelt as described in Chapter 1.

**11** Refill the cooling system as described in Chapter 1, and reconnect the battery.

### 9 Water pump (CVH and PTE engines) - removal and refitting

**Note:** *Refer to the warnings given in Section 1 of this Chapter before starting work.*

## Removal

**1** Disconnect the battery negative (earth) lead (refer to Chapter 5A, Section 1).

**2** Drain the cooling system (see Chapter 1).

**3** Remove the timing belt and tensioner (see Chapter 2B). If the belt is fouled with coolant, it must be renewed as a matter of course.

**9.4 Detach the coolant hose from the water pump**

**10.5 Unscrew the bolts (arrowed) to remove the water pump**

**4** Loosen off the coolant hose retaining clip, and detach the coolant hose from the water pump **(see illustration)**.

**5** Unscrew and remove the four bolts securing the water pump to the front end face of the cylinder block, and then withdraw the pump from the vehicle **(see illustration)**.

## Refitting

**6** Clean the engine water pump mating faces. Ensure that the mating faces are clean and dry.

**7** No provision is made for the repair of the water pump; if it is noisy or defective in any way, it must be renewed.

**8** Refitting is a reversal of the removal procedure. Tighten the retaining bolts to the specified torque, and ensure that the coolant hose connection to the water pump is securely made.

**9** Refit the timing belt and tensioner as described in Chapter 2B.

**10** Refill the cooling system as described in Chapter 1, and reconnect the battery.

### 10 Water pump (Zetec and Zetec-E engines) - removal and refitting

**Note:** *Refer to the warnings given in Section 1 of this Chapter before starting work.*

## Removal

**1** Disconnect the battery negative (earth) lead (refer to Chapter 5A, Section 1).

**2** Drain the cooling system (see Chapter 1).

**9.5 Removing the water pump from the CVH engine**

**10.6 Always use a new gasket, and clean all mating surfaces carefully**

**3** Remove the timing belt and tensioner (see Chapter 2C). If the belt is fouled with coolant, it must be renewed as a matter of course.

**4** Disconnect the radiator bottom hose from the pump union. It is easier to reach this union if the power steering pump is unbolted and moved aside, as described in Chapter 10. There is no need to disconnect any of the power steering system hoses.

**5** Unbolt and remove the water pump **(see illustration)**. If the pump is to be renewed, unbolt the timing belt guide pulleys, and transfer them to the new pump.

## Refitting

**6** Clean the mating surfaces carefully; the gasket must be renewed whenever it is disturbed **(see illustration)**.

**7** On refitting, use grease to stick the new gasket in place, refit the pump, and tighten the pump bolts to the specified torque.

**8** The remainder of refitting is a reversal of the removal procedure. Refit the timing belt and tensioner as described in Chapter 2C, noting that a new tensioner spring and retaining pin must be fitted if the timing belt has been removed for the first time. Tighten all fasteners to the specified torque, and refill the system with coolant as described in Chapter 1.

### 11 Heater/ventilation components - removal and refitting

## Heater blower motor

### Removal

**1** Disconnect the battery negative (earth) lead (refer to Chapter 5A, Section 1).

**2** For improved access, refer to the relevant Part of Chapter 4 for details, and remove the air cleaner components (where applicable).

**3** Peel back the seal strip from the top edge of the bulkhead.

**4** Cut the ties and detach the hose and wiring loom from the bulkhead.

**5** Undo the six retaining bolts, and remove the cover from the air chamber **(see illustration)**.

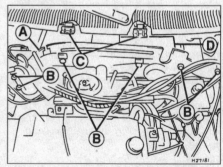

**11.5 Air chamber and associated components**

*A Bulkhead cover*  
*B Cover bolts*  
*C Blower cover guides*  
*D Blower cover*

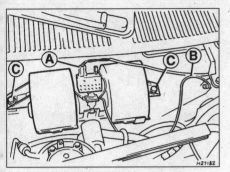

**11.7 Heater blower motor unit**

A  *Resistor multi-plug*   C  *Blower unit*
B  *Earth lead*                      *securing nuts*

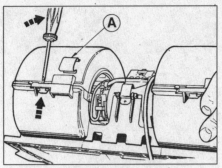

**11.8 Heater blower unit
locking clip (A) removal**

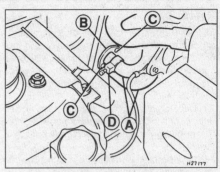

**11.15 Coolant heater hose connections to
heater at bulkhead**

A  *Coolant hoses*   C  *Screws*
B  *Cover plate*        D  *Clip*

**6** Release the heater blower cover from its guides, and remove it.
**7** Disconnect the wires from the blower motor, then undo the two retaining nuts and withdraw the blower motor from the air chamber **(see illustration)**.
**8** To remove the motor from its housing, prise free the locking clips and release the securing lugs using a pin punch **(see illustration)**. Detach the connector from the blower resistor unit, bend the retaining tabs up, and then separate the motor (with resistor) from the retainer. Remove the motor from the housing.

### Refitting

**9** Refitting is a reversal of the removal procedure. When reassembling the blower motor housing covers, ensure that the locating lugs are fully engaged.

## Heater blower motor resistor

### Removal

**10** On models without air conditioning, carry out the operations described in paragraphs 1 to 5 above. On models with air conditioning, Remove the cover of the resistor by releasing the retaining clips.
**11** Detach the wiring connector and the multi-plug from the resistor unit. Bend up the securing tabs, or unscrew the two retaining bolts (as applicable) and remove the resistor from its location.

### Refitting

**12** Refit in the reverse order of removal.

## Heater unit and matrix

### Removal

**13** Disconnect the battery negative (earth) lead (refer to Chapter 5A, Section 1).
**14** Drain the cooling system (see Chapter 1).
**15** Undo the retaining clips, and detach the heater coolant supply and return hoses at their bulkhead connections **(see illustration)**.
**16** A small amount of coolant (about half a litre), will have remained in the heater matrix after draining. In order to prevent the possibility of the coolant spilling onto the carpets during the removal of the heater, it is advisable to blow through one of the

connections to eject the remaining coolant out through the other open connection.
**17** Undo the two retaining screws, and detach the heater matrix cover plate and gasket from the bulkhead.
**18** Undo the two retaining screws, and remove the upper steering column shroud.
**19** Similarly, undo the four screws and remove the lower steering column shroud.
**20** Refer to Chapter 10 and remove the steering wheel.
**21** Undo the single retaining screw, and withdraw the multi-function switch from the steering column. Disconnect the wiring multi-plugs.
**22** On 1996 models onward, pull off the three operating knobs from the heater controls.
**23** Undo the two retaining screws from the underside top edge of the instrument panel bezel and withdraw the bezel, releasing it from the location clips each side and underneath (refer to Chapter 12 for details). On later models, disconnect the bezel wiring multi-plugs.
**24** Refer to Chapter 12 for details, and remove the radio/cassette unit from the facia.
**25** Undo the two retaining screws, and remove the stowage unit from under the radio/cassette aperture.
**26** Peel back the front door weatherstrip (seal) from the "A" pillar adjacent to the facia. Undo the retaining screw, and remove the "A" pillar trim. Repeat the procedure on the opposite side.

**27** Referring to Chapter 11, undo the facia retaining screws as necessary.
**28** Refer to Chapter 11 for details, and remove the centre console.
**29** Pull free the covers from the right- and left-hand heater control levers, then unclip and disconnect the cables from their connections on the heater unit each side.
**30** Prise free the cover from each of the three facia securing bolt apertures on the top face of the facia, also the cover from the radio/cassette recess.
**31** Unscrew and remove the Torx-type retaining bolts, and pull the facia rearwards to partially withdraw it, taking care not to stretch the wiring harnesses under the facia (see Chapter 11).
**32** Where fitted unbolt the two heater unit support struts.
**33** Pull free the footwell air vent from the heater housing connection.
**34** Pull free the air ducts from the heater housing connections (two each side, and two in the centre).
**35** Undo the two retaining nuts, and disconnect the heater housing from the cowl panel by withdrawing it downwards and removing it from the side **(see illustration)**.
**36** To remove the heater matrix (radiator) from the heater unit, undo the two retaining screws and carefully withdraw it **(see illustration)**.

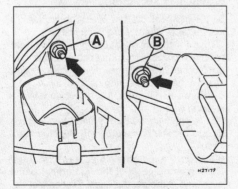

**11.35 Left-hand (A) and right-hand (B)
heater housing securing nuts (arrowed)**

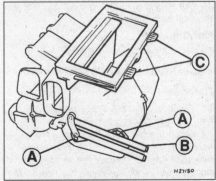

**11.36 Heater unit showing matrix
retaining screws (A), matrix (B)
and unit locating lugs (C)**

**3**

## Refitting

**37** Refitting is a reversal of the removal procedure. When fitting the heater unit into position, engage the lugs of its flange with the support bracket on the cowl panel, and guide the matrix into position through the opening in the bulkhead.

**38** Check that all wiring, coolant hose and air duct connections are securely made. Tighten the housing retaining nuts to the specified torque.

**39** On completion, refill the cooling system as described in Chapter 1, then reconnect the battery.

## Face-level air vent (right-hand)

### Removal (pre-1996 models)

**40** Disconnect the battery negative (earth) lead (refer to Chapter 5A, Section 1).

**41** Undo the two retaining screws from its upper edge, and withdraw the instrument panel surround.

**42** Undo the two retaining screws, and withdraw the face-level vent from the facia. Where applicable, detach the wiring connectors from the switches in the panel.

### Removal (1996 models onward)

**43** Disconnect the battery negative (earth) lead (refer to Chapter 5A, Section 1).

**44** Undo the two retaining screws, and remove the upper steering column shroud.

**45** Similarly, undo the four retaining screws and remove the lower steering column shroud.

**46** Refer to Chapter 10 and remove the steering wheel.

**47** Carefully prise free the three heater/fresh air and blower/air conditioning switch control knobs.

**48** Undo the two retaining screws from the underside top edge of the instrument panel bezel. Release the bezel from the retaining clips (two at the top, four along the bottom, and one at the side furthest away from the steering wheel). Use a screwdriver with protective pad or cloth to prevent damage to the bezel and facia when releasing the clips. Withdraw the bezel and disconnect the wiring multi-plugs

**49** Release the retaining clips and remove the vent from the facia.

### Refitting

**50** Refitting is the reversal of removal.

## Face-level air vent (left-hand)

### Removal

**51** Disconnect the battery negative (earth) lead (refer to Chapter 5A, Section 1).

**52** Open the glovebox lid, then unscrew the vent retaining screw from the underside of the box roof (directly under the vent). Carefully prise free and remove the vent **(see illustration)**.

### Refitting

**53** Refitting is the reversal of removal.

**11.52 Prising free the left-hand side vent**

**11.56b . . . undo the retaining screws . . .**

## Face-level air vent (centre)

### Removal (pre-1996 models)

**54** Disconnect the battery negative (earth) lead (refer to Chapter 5A, Section 1).

**55** Undo the two retaining screws from its upper edge, and withdraw the instrument panel surround.

**56** Carefully prise free the three heater/fresh air and blower/air conditioning switch control knobs. Loosen off the centre air vent retaining screws, and partially withdraw the air vent unit just enough to allow access to the wiring connectors on the inside face of the unit **(see illustrations)**.

**57** Where applicable, disconnect the wiring multi-plugs from the heated rear window and rear foglight or heated windscreen switches, then remove the centre air vent unit.

### Removal (1996 models onward)

**58** Disconnect the battery negative (earth) lead (refer to Chapter 5A, Section 1).

**59** Undo the two retaining screws, and remove the upper steering column shroud.

**60** Similarly, undo the four screws and remove the lower steering column shroud.

**61** Refer to Chapter 10 and remove the steering wheel.

**62** Carefully prise free the three heater/fresh air and blower/air conditioning switch control knobs.

**63** Undo the two retaining screws from the underside top edge of the instrument panel bezel and withdraw the bezel. Disconnect the wiring multi-plugs and remove the bezel.

**64** Release the retaining clips and remove the vent from the facia.

**11.56a Prise free the control knobs . . .**

**11.56c . . . and partially withdraw the air vent unit**

### Refitting

**65** Refitting is the reversal of removal.

## 12 Heater/air conditioning controls - removal and refitting

## Heater/air conditioning control panel

### Removal

**1** Remove the centre face-level air vent as described in the previous Section.

**2** Pull free the covers, then disconnect the control cables from each side of the heater unit. The right-hand side cable operates the temperature control valve, and the left-hand cable operates the air distribution valve **(see illustration)**.

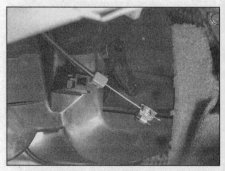

**12.2 Heater temperature control cable connection on the right-hand side of the heater unit**

**12.3a Control panel retaining screws (arrowed)**

**12.3b Control panel removal**

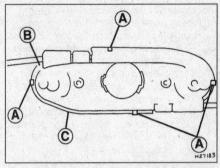

**12.6 Heater control unit retaining tabs (A), cover (B) and baseplate (C)**

3 Undo the two screws securing the heater control panel to the facia. Withdraw the panel from the facia just enough to allow the heater blower/air conditioning switch wiring plug to be detached, then fully withdraw the control panel, and feed the control cables through the facia aperture (see illustrations).

### Refitting

4 Refit in the reverse order of removal. Ensure that the control cables are correctly re-routed (with no tight bends). Check that the cables and the wiring connectors are securely refitted.

## Heater/air conditioning control cables

### Removal

5 Remove the control panel as previously described.
6 Bend the retaining tabs straight, and then detach the cover from the baseplate to open the heater control unit (see illustration).
7 Cut the cable retaining clips free, then release the cables from the toothed guide strips to remove them. Note that the retaining clips will need to be renewed during reassembly.

### Refitting

8 Refitting is a reversal of the removal procedure.

## 13 Air conditioning system - general information and precautions

### General information

The air conditioning system consists of a condenser mounted in front of the radiator, an evaporator mounted adjacent to the heater matrix, a compressor mounted on the engine, a dehydrator, and the plumbing connecting all of the above components (see illustration).

A blower fan forces the warmer air of the passenger compartment through the evaporator core (rather like a radiator in reverse), transferring the heat from the air to the refrigerant. The liquid refrigerant boils off into low-pressure vapour, taking the heat with it when it leaves the evaporator.

### Precautions

⚠️ *Warning: The air conditioning system is under high pressure. Do not loosen any fittings or remove any components until after the system has been discharged. Air conditioning refrigerant should be properly discharged into an approved type of container, at a dealer service department or an automotive air conditioning repair facility capable of handling the refrigerant safely. Always wear eye protection when disconnecting air conditioning system fittings.*

When an air conditioning system is fitted, it is necessary to observe the following special precautions whenever dealing with any part of the system, its associated components, and any items which necessitate disconnection of the system:

a) *While the refrigerant used on later models - R134a - is less harmful to the environment than the previously-used R12, both are very dangerous substances. They must not come into contact with the skin or eyes, or there is a risk of frostbite. They must also not be discharged in an enclosed space, as there is a risk of suffocation. The refrigerant is heavier than air, and so must never be discharged over a pit.*

b) *The refrigerant must not be allowed to come in contact with a naked flame, otherwise a poisonous gas will be created - under certain circumstances, this can form an explosive mixture with air. For similar reasons, smoking in the presence of refrigerant is highly dangerous, particularly if the vapour is inhaled through a lighted cigarette.*

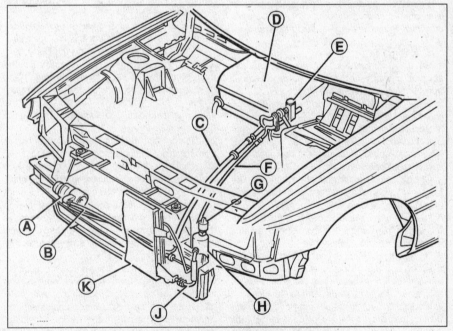

**13.1 Air conditioning system layout**

| | | |
|---|---|---|
| A  Compressor | D  Evaporator and blower | H  Dehydrator |
| B  Compressor-to-condenser pipe | E  Expansion valve | J  Dehydrator-to-condenser pipe |
| C  Compressor-to-expansion valve | F  Expansion valve-to-dehydrator pipe | K  Condenser |
| | G  High-pressure switch | |

3

c) *Never discharge the system to the atmosphere - R134a is not an ozone-depleting ChloroFluoroCarbon (CFC) as is R12, but is instead a hydrofluorocarbon, which causes environmental damage by contributing to the "greenhouse effect" if released into the atmosphere.*

d) *R134a refrigerant must not be mixed with R12; the system uses different seals (now green-coloured, previously black) and has different fittings requiring different tools, so that there is no chance of the two types of refrigerant becoming mixed accidentally.*

e) *If for any reason the system must be disconnected, entrust this task to your Ford dealer or a refrigeration engineer.*

f) *It is essential that the system be professionally discharged prior to using any form of heat - welding, soldering, brazing, etc - in the vicinity of the system, before having the vehicle oven-dried at a temperature exceeding 70°C after repainting, and before disconnecting any part of the system.*

## 14  Air conditioning system components - removal and refitting

**Warning: Refer to the precautions given in the previous Section before proceeding.**

**Note:** *This Section refers to the components of the air conditioning system itself - refer to Sections 11 and 12 for details of components common to the heating/ventilation system.*

### Condenser

**1** Have the refrigerant discharged at a dealer service department or an automotive air conditioning repair facility.

**2** Disconnect the battery negative (earth) lead (see Chapter 5A, Section 1).

**3** Secure the radiator to the front body panel using string or wire to prevent it dropping when the mounting bracket is removed in a subsequent operation.

**4** Chock the rear wheels then jack up the front of the car and support it on axle stands (see *"Jacking and vehicle support"*).

**5** Undo the six plastic screws, and remove the cover from under the condenser/radiator mounting bracket.

**6** Using the Ford service tool 34-001, disconnect the refrigerant lines from the condenser. Immediately cap the open fittings, to prevent the entry of dirt and moisture.

**7** Undo the two bolts and one nut securing the dehydrator to the condenser/radiator mounting bracket, and move the dehydrator to one side.

**8** Undo the two bolts each side securing the condenser/radiator mounting bracket to the body side members.

**9** Detach the condenser and mounting bracket from the right-hand then the left-hand upper radiator mountings, and withdraw the assembly from under the car.

**10** Release the clips and remove the air deflector from the condenser, then undo the two nuts and remove the mounting bracket. If required, unscrew the two mountings.

**11** Refitting is the reversal of removal.

**12** Have the system evacuated, charged and leak-tested by the specialist who discharged it.

### Evaporator and blower motor

**13** Have the refrigerant discharged at a dealer service department or an automotive air conditioning repair facility.

**14** Disconnect the battery negative (earth) lead (refer to Chapter 5A, Section 1), followed by the positive lead, then remove the battery from its location.

**15** For improved access, refer to the relevant Part of Chapter 4 for details, and remove the air cleaner components (where applicable).

**16** Peel back the seal strip from the top edge of the bulkhead.

**17** Cut the ties and detach the hose and wiring loom from the bulkhead.

**18** Undo the three bolts, and detach the air conditioning pipe gasket retaining plate complete with gasket, from the bulkhead.

**19** Undo the six retaining bolts, and remove the cover from the air chamber.

**20** Release the evaporator housing cover from its guides and remove it.

**21** Undo the retaining bolt, and disconnect the compressor low-pressure pipe and the dehydrator liquid pipe from the front of the expansion valve.

**22** Disconnect the blower motor resistor multi-plug, and disconnect the blower motor earth lead at the connection on the body.

**23** At the vacuum reservoir, disconnect the multi-plugs for the vacuum motor switch and de-ice switch, and detach the two vacuum hoses. Undo the screw and remove the vacuum reservoir assembly from the evaporator housing.

**24** Disconnect the two condensation hoses from the front of the evaporator housing.

**25** Undo the two bolts and two nuts, and remove the evaporator housing from the car.

**26** From the side of the evaporator housing, release the vacuum motor linkage clamp screw, then undo the two nuts and remove the vacuum motor. Undo the two screws securing the de-ice switch, and withdraw the switch sensor.

**27** Disconnect the blower motor resistor wiring plug, then undo the three screws and withdraw the evaporator housing cover.

**28** Undo the two screws, release all the retaining clips securing the upper and lower halves of the evaporator housing, and lift off the upper half.

**29** Undo the two screws, and detach the expansion valve from the side of the evaporator. Recover the valve seals.

**30** Lift the evaporator out of the lower half of the housing.

**31** To remove the blower motor, undo the securing bolt from the motor retaining strap, and lift out the motor.

**32** Refitting is a reversal of the removal procedure, but use new seals where applicable, and tighten all fastenings to the specified torque wrench settings (where given).

**33** Have the system evacuated, charged and leak-tested by the specialist who discharged it.

### Compressor

**34** Have the refrigerant discharged at a dealer service department or an automotive air conditioning repair facility.

**35** Disconnect the battery negative (earth) lead (see Chapter 5A, Section 1).

**36** Chock the rear wheels then jack up the front of the car and support it on axle stands (see *"Jacking and vehicle support"*).

**37** Remove the auxiliary drivebelt (see Chapter 1).

**38** Undo the six plastic screws, and remove the cover from under the condenser/radiator mounting bracket.

**39** Disconnect the compressor clutch wiring multi-plug, then undo the retaining bolt to detach the compressor high- and low-pressure pipes.

**40** Undo the four bolts, and remove the compressor from its mounting bracket.
**Note:** *Keep the compressor level during handling and storage. If the compressor has seized, or if you find metal particles in the refrigerant lines, the system must be flushed out by an air conditioning technician, and the dehydrator must be renewed.*

**41** Refit the compressor in the reverse order of removal; renew all seals disturbed.

**42** Have the system evacuated, charged and leak-tested by the specialist that discharged it.

### Dehydrator

**43** Have the refrigerant discharged at a dealer service department or an automotive air conditioning repair facility.

**44** Disconnect the battery negative (earth) lead (see Chapter 5A, Section 1).

**45** Unscrew the pipe to the expansion valve and the compressor connecting pipe at the dehydrator.

**46** Disconnect the high-pressure switch multi-plug, then remove the high-pressure switch.

**47** Chock the rear wheels then jack up the front of the car and support it on axle stands (see *"Jacking and vehicle support"*).

**48** Undo the six plastic screws, and remove the cover from under the condenser/radiator mounting bracket.

**49** Undo the two bolts and one nut securing the dehydrator to the condenser/radiator mounting bracket, and remove the dehydrator from under the vehicle.

**50** Refit the dehydrator in the reverse order of removal; renew all seals disturbed.

**51** Have the system evacuated, charged and leak-tested by the specialist that discharged it.

### Electric cooling fan motor

**52** Disconnect the battery negative (earth) lead (refer to Chapter 5A, Section 1).

**53** Detach the wiring multi-plugs from the air conditioning fan motor and the motor resistor. Cut free the cable-ties securing the wires to the bracket.

**54** Working from above, unscrew the left-hand retaining nut from the fan motor support frame. Apply the handbrake, then raise and support the vehicle, then working from underneath, unscrew and remove the right-hand retaining nut from the support frame.

**55** Undo the four retaining bolts, and detach the transmission brace (where fitted) from the bearer and transmission flange.

**56** Remove the starter motor (Chapter 5A).

**57** Detach and remove the exhaust downpipe (Chapter 4E).

**58** Lift the support frame and fan motor from the mounting each side, and withdraw it from underneath the vehicle. If required, undo the three retaining nuts and detach the fan unit from the support frame.

**59** Refit in the reverse order of removal. Tighten all fastenings to their specified torque wrench settings (where given). Ensure that all wiring connections are securely made and, where applicable, relocate the wiring using new cable-ties.

### De-ice switch

**60** Disconnect the battery negative (earth) lead (refer to Chapter 5A, Section 1), followed by the positive lead, then remove the battery from its location.

**61** For improved access, refer to the relevant Part of Chapter 4 and remove the air cleaner components (where applicable).

**62** Peel back the seal strip from the top edge of the bulkhead.

**63** Cut the ties and detach the hose and wiring loom from the bulkhead.

**64** Undo the three bolts, and detach the air conditioning pipe gasket retaining plate complete with gasket, from the bulkhead.

**65** Undo the six retaining bolts, and remove the cover from the air chamber.

**66** Release the evaporator housing cover from its guides and remove it.

**67** At the vacuum reservoir, disconnect the multi-plugs for the vacuum motor switch and de-ice switch, and detach the two vacuum hoses. Undo the screw, and remove the vacuum reservoir assembly from the evaporator housing.

**68** Undo the two bolts and two nuts, and remove the evaporator housing from the vehicle.

**69** Undo the two screws securing the de-ice switch, and withdraw the switch from the housing.

**70** Refitting is a reversal of the removal procedure.

### Air conditioning control switch

**71** The switch is located in the main heating and ventilation control panel. Remove the control panel from the facia as described in Section 12, then unclip the air conditioning/blower motor switch from the control unit.

**72** Disconnect the wiring multi-plug and the light lead from the switch.

**73** Refit in the reverse order of removal.

### Vacuum motor switch

**74** Disconnect the battery negative (earth) lead (refer to Chapter 5A, Section 1), followed by the positive lead, then remove the battery from its location.

**75** Detach the wiring multi-plug from the vacuum motor switch, then undo the two retaining screws and remove the switch from the vacuum reservoir.

**76** Refit in the reverse order of removal, but ensure that the seal is seated correctly.

### Vacuum motor

**77** Disconnect the battery negative (earth) lead (refer to Chapter 5A, Section 1), followed by the positive lead, then remove the battery from its location.

**78** For improved access, refer to Chapter 4 for details, and remove the air cleaner (where applicable).

**79** Peel back the seal strip from the top edge of the bulkhead.

**80** Cut the ties and detach the hose and wiring loom from the bulkhead.

**81** Undo the three bolts, and detach the air conditioning pipe gasket retaining plate complete with gasket, from the bulkhead.

**82** Undo the six retaining bolts and remove the cover from the air chamber.

**83** Release the evaporator housing cover from its guides and remove it.

**84** From the side of the evaporator housing, release the vacuum motor linkage clamp screw, then undo the two nuts and remove the vacuum motor. As it is withdrawn, detach the vacuum hose.

**85** Refit in the reverse order of the removal. Ensure that the vacuum hose and wiring connections are securely made. Renew the cable-ties to relocate the wiring to the bulkhead cover.

### Vacuum reservoir

**86** Proceed as described in paragraphs 77 to 83 inclusive above, then continue as follows.

**87** Detach the two vacuum hoses from the vacuum reservoir. Detach the wiring multi-plug from the vacuum motor switch, then undo the retaining screw and remove the vacuum reservoir from the evaporator housing.

**88** Undo the two screws and remove the vacuum motor switch from the reservoir.

**89** Refit in the reverse order of the removal. Ensure that the vacuum hose and wiring connections are securely made. Renew the cable-ties to relocate the wiring to the bulkhead cover.

**3**

# Chapter 4  Part A:
# Fuel system - carburettor engines

## Contents

Accelerator cable (manual transmission models) -
  removal, refitting and adjustment ........................ 3
Accelerator (cam plate) cable
  (CTX automatic transmission models) - adjustment .......... 4
Accelerator pedal - removal and refitting ................... 5
Air cleaner - removal and refitting ........................ 2
Air cleaner element renewal ...................See Chapter 1
Automatic choke (Weber TLD carburettor) - adjustment ......... 21
Automatic choke (Weber TLD carburettor) -
  removal, inspection and refitting ...................... 22
Carburettor (Weber TLD) - fast idle speed adjustment .......... 19
Carburettor (Weber TLD) - description ..................... 18
Carburettor (Weber TLD) - dismantling, cleaning,
  inspection and reassembly ........................... 24
Carburettor (Weber TLD) - removal and refitting ............. 23
Carburettor (Weber TLDM) - description .................... 12
Carburettor (Weber TLDM) - dismantling, cleaning,
  inspection and reassembly ........................... 17
Carburettor (Weber TLDM) - fast idle speed adjustment ........ 13
Carburettor (Weber TLDM) - removal and refitting ............. 16
Choke cable - removal, refitting and adjustment ............. 6
Exhaust system check ..........................See Chapter 1
Fuel gauge sender unit - removal and refitting ............... 9
Fuel pump - testing, removal and refitting ................... 7
Fuel tank - removal, inspection and refitting ................ 8
Fuel tank filler pipe - removal and refitting ................ 11
General fuel system checks ......................See Chapter 1
Idle speed and mixture check and adjustment ........See Chapter 1
Inlet manifold - removal and refitting ..................... 25
Needle valve and float (Weber TLD carburettor) -
  removal, refitting and adjustment ...................... 20
Needle valve and float (Weber TLDM carburettor) -
  removal, refitting and adjustment ...................... 14
Throttle kicker unit (Weber TLDM carburettor) - removal, refitting
  and adjustment ................................... 15
Roll-over valve - removal and refitting .................... 10
Underbody fuel/brake line check ..................See Chapter 1
Underbonnet check for fluid leaks and hose condition ..See Chapter 1

**4A**

## Degrees of difficulty

**Easy,** suitable for novice with little experience  | **Fairly easy,** suitable for beginner with some experience  | **Fairly difficult,** suitable for competent DIY mechanic  | **Difficult,** suitable for experienced DIY mechanic | **Very difficult,** suitable for expert DIY or professional

## Specifications

**General**

System type ................................ Rear-mounted fuel tank, mechanical fuel pump, single Weber carburettor

**Carburettor**

Type ..................................... Twin choke, downdraught
Application:
  1.3 HCS engines ........................ Weber 2V TLDM
  1.4 and 1.6 CVH engines ................. Weber 2V TLD
Choke type ............................... Manual or automatic

**Fuel grade**

Fuel octane requirement .................... 95 RON unleaded

**Fuel pump**

Delivery pressure .......................... 0.24 to 0.38 bars

## Carburettor data

### Weber TLDM carburettor

| | | |
|---|---|---|
| Idle speed and mixture settings | See Chapter 1 | |
| Fast idle speed | 2500 rpm | |
| Float height | 28 to 30 mm | |
| Throttle kicker operating speed (automatic transmission) | 1800 to 2000 rpm | |

| | Primary | Secondary |
|---|---|---|
| Venturi diameter | 19 | 20 |
| Main jet | 90 | 122 |
| Emulsion jet | F113 | F75 |
| Air correction jet | 185 | 130 |

### Weber TLD carburettor

| | | |
|---|---|---|
| Idle speed and mixture settings | See Chapter 1 | |

Float height:

| | | |
|---|---|---|
| 1.4 litre | 31.0 ± 0.5 mm | |
| 1.6 litre (without air conditioning) | 31.0 ± 0.5 mm | |
| 1.6 litre (with air conditioning) | 29.0 ± 0.5 mm | |

Choke vacuum pull-down:

| | | |
|---|---|---|
| 1.4 litre | 3.1 ± 0.5 mm | |
| 1.6 litre | 2.7 ± 0.5 mm | |

Choke fast idle (on kickdown step):

| | | |
|---|---|---|
| 1.4 litre | 1900 ± 50 rpm | |
| 1.6 litre (with manual steering) | 1750 ± 50 rpm | |
| 1.6 litre (with power steering) | Module-controlled | |

| Venturi diameter: | Primary | Secondary |
|---|---|---|
| 1.4 litre | 20 | 22 |
| 1.6 litre | 21 | 23 |

| Main jet: | | |
|---|---|---|
| 1.4 litre | 107 | 140 |
| 1.6 litre (without air conditioning) | 115 | 140 |
| 1.6 litre (with air conditioning) | 115 | 127 |

| Emulsion tube | | |
|---|---|---|
| 1.4 litre | F105 | F75 |
| 1.6 litre (without air conditioning) | F105 | 157 |
| 1.6 litre (with air conditioning) | F105 | 171 |

| Air correction jet: | | |
|---|---|---|
| 1.4 litre | 195 | 170 |
| 1.6 litre (without air conditioning) | 180 | 150 |
| 1.6 litre (with air conditioning) | 185 | 125 |

| Throttle kicker speed: | | |
|---|---|---|
| 1.4 litre | 1400 rpm | |
| 1.6 litre | 1300 rpm | |

### Torque wrench settings

| | Nm | lbf ft |
|---|---|---|
| Fuel pump | 18 | 13 |
| Inlet manifold | 18 | 13 |

## 1 General information and precautions

### General information

The fuel system on all models with carburettor induction comprises a rear-mounted fuel tank, a mechanical diaphragm fuel pump, a carburettor and an air cleaner.

The fuel tank is mounted at the rear, under the floorpan behind the rear seats. The tank has a "ventilation-to-atmosphere system" through a combined roll-over/anti-trickle fill valve assembly, located in the left-hand rear wheel arch. A filler neck sensing pipe, integral with the fuel tank filler pipe, will shut off the fuel pump filler gun when the predetermined maximum level of fuel is reached in the tank, so preventing spillage and wastage. A conventional fuel level sender unit is mounted in the top face of the fuel tank.

One of two fuel pump types will be fitted, depending on the engine type. On HCS engines, the fuel pump is operated by a pivoting rocker arm; one end rests on an eccentric lobe on the engine camshaft, and the other end is attached to the fuel pump diaphragm. The pump fitted to the CVH engine is operated by a separate pushrod, one end rests on an eccentric lobe on the engine camshaft, and the other rests on the pump actuating rod which operates the diaphragm. Both types of mechanical pump incorporate a nylon filter, and are of sealed type (they cannot be serviced or overhauled).

A twin-choke Weber carburettor is fitted, further details being given later in this Chapter.

The air cleaner incorporates a "waxstat" controlled air inlet, supplying either hot air from a shroud mounted around the exhaust manifold, or cool air from a duct in the front of the vehicle.

### Precautions

⚠ *Warning: Petrol is extremely flammable - great care must be taken when working on any part of the fuel system. Do not smoke or allow any naked flames or uncovered light bulbs near the work area. Note that gas powered domestic appliances with pilot flames, such as heaters, boilers and tumble dryers, also present a fire hazard - bear this in mind if you are working in an area where*

**2.4a Disconnecting the oil separator/ crankcase ventilation hose from the air cleaner (CVH engine)**

**2.4b Disconnecting the vacuum hose from the inlet manifold (CVH engine)**

**2.4c Disconnecting the inlet air temperature sensor connector (CVH engine)**

*such appliances are present. Always keep a suitable fire extinguisher close to the work area and familiarise yourself with its operation before starting work. Wear eye protection when working on fuel systems and wash off any fuel spilt on bare skin immediately with soap and water. Note that fuel vapour is just as dangerous as liquid fuel; a vessel that has just been emptied of liquid fuel will still contain vapour and can be potentially explosive. Petrol is a highly dangerous and volatile liquid, and the precautions necessary when handling it cannot be overstressed.*

*Many of the operations described in this Chapter involve the disconnection of fuel lines, which may cause an amount of fuel spillage. Before commencing work, refer to the above Warning and the information in "Safety first" at the start of this manual.*

*When working with fuel system components, pay particular attention to cleanliness - dirt entering the fuel system may cause blockages which will lead to poor running.*

Certain adjustment points in the fuel system are protected by tamperproof caps, plugs or seals. In some territories, it is an offence to drive a vehicle with broken or missing tamperproof seals. Before disturbing a tamperproof seal, first check that no local or national laws will be broken by doing so, and fit a new tamperproof seal after adjustment is complete, where required by law. Do not break tamperproof seals on any vehicle whilst it is still under warranty.

Carburettors are delicate instruments, and care must be taken not to disturb any components unnecessarily. Before attempting work on a carburettor, ensure that the relevant spares are available; it should be noted that a complete strip down of a carburettor is unlikely to cure a fault which is not immediately obvious, without introducing new problems. If persistent problems occur, it is recommended that the services of a Ford dealer or a carburettor specialist are sought. Most dealers will be able to provide carburettor rejetting and servicing facilities. Where necessary, it may be possible to purchase a reconditioned carburettor.

## 2 Air cleaner - removal and refitting

**Note:** *Air cleaner element renewal and air cleaner temperature control system checks are described in Chapter 1.*

### Removal

1 Disconnect the battery negative (earth) lead (refer to Chapter 5A, Section 1).
2 On CVH engine models, pull free and release the accelerator cable from the locating clip on the side of the air cleaner.
3 Undo the three bolts, and partially lift the air cleaner from the carburettor so that the hose and wiring connections to the underside of the air cleaner body are accessible.
4 Note their connections and routings, then

detach the wiring and hoses from the underside of the air cleaner. On CVH engines, also disconnect the vacuum hose from the inlet manifold **(see illustrations)**.
5 Lift the air cleaner from the carburettor.
6 If required, the inlet air temperature sensor can be unscrewed and removed from the base of the air cleaner (where fitted).

### Refitting

7 Refit in the reverse order of removal. Renew any hoses that are perished or cracked, and ensure that all fittings are securely and correctly reconnected.

## 3 Accelerator cable (manual transmission models) - removal, refitting and adjustment

### Removal

1 Disconnect the battery negative (earth) lead (refer to Chapter 5A, Section 1).
2 Working inside the vehicle, disconnect the cable from the top of the accelerator pedal, release the grommet and pull the cable free from the pedal **(see illustration)**. Withdraw the cable through the engine side of the bulkhead.
3 Remove the air cleaner (see Section 2).
4 Detach the inner cable from the carburettor linkage **(see illustrations)**.

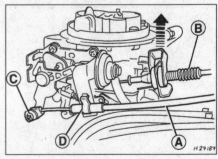

**3.4b Cable connections to the carburettor on the HCS engine**

A  Choke cable
B  Accelerator cable
C  Choke cable inner cable connection
D  Choke cable support bracket connection

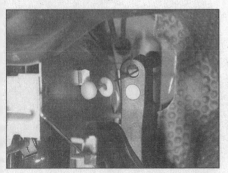

**3.2 Disconnecting the accelerator cable from the pedal**

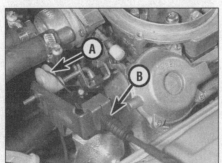

**3.4a Accelerator inner (A) and outer (B) cable connection to the CVH engine**

**4A**

**5** Prise free the retaining clip, detach the outer cable from the support bracket, and remove the cable.

### Refitting and adjustment

**6** To refit the cable, feed the inner cable through the bulkhead, and reconnect the inner cable to the accelerator pedal.

**7** Locate the grommet in the bulkhead, then push the outer cable into it to secure it in the bulkhead.

**8** Lubricate the cable grommet at the carburettor end with a mild soapy solution, then reconnect the cable to the carburettor. Locate the outer cable by pulling it towards the rocker cover.

**9** Have an assistant depress the accelerator pedal fully, and hold it in this position. The outer cable should be seen to move in its grommet. Refit the securing clip to the bracket, then release the accelerator pedal.

**10** Depress the accelerator pedal, then release it and check that the throttle opens and shuts fully. Further adjust if necessary before refitting the air cleaner and reconnecting the battery.

### 4  Accelerator (cam plate) cable (CTX automatic transmission models) - adjustment

**1** Refer to Section 2 and remove the air cleaner.

**2** Release the cable by pressing the orange (or red) button on the cable auto adjuster mechanism. As the cable is released, it will be heard to click. The cable shoulder will now be seen to protrude from the adjuster mechanism by approximately 20 mm (see illustration).

**3** Turn the cam plate by hand so that the throttle moves to the fully-open position. Now release the cam plate and close the throttle. The cable will automatically adjust as required, and the adjuster will be heard to click as it makes the adjustment. The cable shoulder will now be seen to protrude from the auto adjuster mechanism by approximately 10 mm.

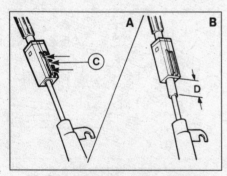

**4.2  Cam plate cable release showing cable taut (A) and released (B). Also shown are the release button (C) and 20 mm pre-adjustment/10 mm post-adjustment minimum protrusion (D)**

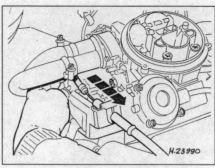

**4.4  Remove the clip from the cable adjusting sleeve at the carburettor bracket, and pull the adjusting sleeve right out**

**4** Remove the clip from the cable adjusting sleeve at the carburettor bracket, and pull the adjusting sleeve right out (see illustration).

**5** Have an assistant fully depress the accelerator pedal, then refit the clip to the cable adjusting sleeve. Release the pedal.

**6** Depress the accelerator pedal once or twice, to check that the throttle opens fully. If necessary, repeat paragraphs 4 and 5.

**7** Refit the air cleaner as described in Section 2, and reconnect the battery earth lead.

### 5  Accelerator pedal - removal and refitting

### Removal

**1** Disconnect the battery negative (earth) lead (refer to Chapter 5A, Section 1).

**2** Peel back the carpet and insulation from the driver's footwell to allow access to the accelerator pedal.

**3** Detach the accelerator cable from the pedal (see Section 3), then release the circlip from the pivot shaft and remove the accelerator pedal.

### Refitting

**4** Refit in the reverse order of removal. On completion, check the action of the pedal and the cable to ensure that the throttle has full unrestricted movement, and fully returns when released.

**5** Reconnect the battery earth lead.

### 6  Choke cable - removal, refitting and adjustment

### Removal

**1** Disconnect the battery negative (earth) lead (refer to Chapter 5A, Section 1).

**2** Refer to Section 2 and remove the air cleaner.

**3** Carefully prise free the choke inner cable from its linkage connection on the carburettor, then release the outer cable from the support bracket.

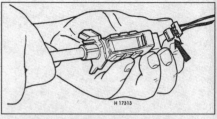

**6.6  Disconnecting the wiring connector from the choke control (control unit removed for clarity)**

**4** Release the choke control knob from the cable by depressing the retaining pin on the underside of the knob.

**5** Undo the choke control-to-trim retaining collar.

**6** Undo and remove the screw securing the choke control recessed trim, and remove the trim and cable control. Detach the "choke on" warning light lead from the control, then withdraw the choke cable from the facia trim (passing it through the bulkhead) (see illustration).

### Refitting

**7** To refit the cable, first pass it through the bulkhead and trim panel, then refit the retaining collar and attach the wiring connector. Fit the trim recess to the main trim panel, and tighten the retaining screw to secure. Push the knob into position on the choke cable control so that it is felt to lock into engagement.

**8** Reconnect the inner choke cable to the carburettor linkage.

**9** Pull the choke control knob fully out (to the full-on position). Return to the carburettor end, and move the choke lever by hand to its full-on position; hold it there whilst simultaneously reconnecting the outer cable to its support bracket.

### Adjustment

**10** To check that the choke cable is correctly adjusted, the control knob must be pulled out to the full-on position and the choke lever must be in contact with its stop (see illustration). Adjust as required if necessary.

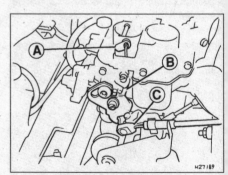

**6.10  Choke cable adjustment**

*A  Choke lever*
*B  Full choke stop*
*C  Cable in "full-on" position*

11 Press the choke knob fully in (to the off position), then check that the choke linkage at the carburettor has fully returned to its off position and the choke valve plate in the carburettor is at a right angle (90°) to the venturi.

12 Refit the air cleaner.

13 Reconnect the battery, turn the ignition on, operate the choke and check that the choke warning light operates correctly.

## 7 Fuel pump - testing, removal and refitting

**Note:** *Refer to the warning note in Section 1 before proceeding.*

### Testing

1 Access to the fuel pump on HCS engine models is best gained from underneath the vehicle **(see illustrations)**. Apply the handbrake, then raise and support it on axle stands at the front end (see *"Jacking and Vehicle Support"*).

2 The fuel pump may be tested by disconnecting the fuel feed pipe from the carburettor, and placing the pipe's open end in a suitable container.

3 Detach the multi-plug from the DIS ignition coil, to prevent the engine from firing.

4 Actuate the starter motor. If the fuel pump is in good working order, regular well-defined spurts of fuel should eject from the open end of the disconnected fuel pipe.

5 If this does not occur, and there is fuel in the tank, the pump is defective and must be renewed. The fuel pump is a sealed unit, and cannot be repaired.

### Removal

6 Two types of mechanical fuel pump are fitted, the application depending on the engine type. Some models may also be fitted with a fuel vapour separator; if this is removed, its hoses should be labelled to avoid the possibility of confusion and incorrect attachment on refitting.

7 To remove the fuel pump, first disconnect the battery negative (earth) lead (refer to Chapter 5A, Section 1).

8 Where applicable, remove the air cleaner to improve access to the fuel pump (Section 2).

9 Disconnect the fuel hoses from the fuel pump, noting their respective connections for refitting. Where quick-release couplings are used on the fuel hoses, release the protruding locking lugs on each union, by squeezing them together and carefully pulling the coupling apart. Use rag to soak up any spilt fuel. Where the unions are colour-coded, the pipes cannot be confused. Where both unions are the same colour, note carefully which pipe is connected to which, and ensure that they are correctly reconnected on refitting. Plug the hoses to prevent fuel spillage and the ingress of dirt.

**7.1a Underside view of the fuel pump fitted to the HCS engine**

**7.1b Fuel pump location on the CVH engine**

**7.10 Fuel pump removal from the CVH engine**

**7.11 Withdrawing the fuel pump pushrod from the CVH engine**

10 Unscrew and remove the retaining bolts or nuts (as applicable) and remove the fuel pump **(see illustration)**.

11 Recover the gasket/spacer and if required, withdraw the pump operating pushrod (CVH engines only) **(see illustration)**.

12 Thoroughly clean the mating faces on the pump and engine.

### Refitting

13 Refit in the reverse order of removal. Be sure to use a new gasket, and tighten the securing bolts/nuts to the specified torque. Ensure that the hoses are correctly and securely reconnected. If they were originally secured with crimped type hose clips, discard them and fit screw clamp type clips. Where quick-release couplings are fitted, press them together until the locking lugs snap into their groove.

14 When the engine is restarted, check the pump connections for any signs of fuel leaks.

## 8 Fuel tank - removal, inspection and refitting

**Note:** *Refer to the warning note in Section 1 before proceeding.*

### Removal

1 Run the fuel level as low as possible prior to removing the tank.

2 Disconnect the battery negative (earth) lead (refer to Chapter 5A, Section 1).

3 Remove the fuel filler cap, then syphon or pump out the remaining fuel from the fuel tank

(there is no drain plug). The fuel must be emptied into a suitable container for storage.

4 Chock the front wheels, then raise and support the vehicle on axle stands at the rear (see *"Jacking and Vehicle Support"*).

### Hatchback, Saloon and Estate models

5 Undo the two bolts securing the fuel filler pipe to the vehicle underbody.

6 Disconnect the handbrake cable locating strap from the vent hose pipe stub on the rear of the fuel tank **(see illustration)**. Undo the clip and disconnect the vent hose from the pipe stub.

7 Undo the screw securing the upper end of the fuel filler pipe to the body inside the filler flap opening. On models without a filler flap, release the filler pipe surround using a screwdriver, then rotate the retaining ring clockwise to release the filler pipe from the body.

**8.6 Handbrake cable locating strap on the fuel tank pipe connection**

**4A**

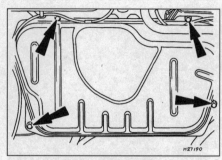

**8.8  Fuel tank retaining bolt locations (arrowed)**

8  Support the underside of the fuel tank to hold it in position, then remove the four tank retaining bolts **(see illustration)**.

9  Partially lower the fuel tank, and detach the roll-over valve tube from the tank top surface. Also disconnect the fuel gauge sender unit wiring multi-plug and the fuel hoses. Where quick-release couplings are used on the fuel hoses, release the protruding locking lugs on each union, by squeezing them together and carefully pulling the coupling apart. Note that the fuel supply hose couplings are identified by a white colour band and the return hose couplings by a yellow colour band.

10  Slowly lower the tank, complete with filler pipe, and remove it from under the vehicle. With the tank removed, detach the filler pipe, if required.

### Van models

11  Disconnect the fuel gauge sender unit wiring at the in-line connector.

12  Support the underside of the fuel tank to hold it in position, then remove the two tank retaining strap bolts.

13  Release the three clips and detach the vent pipe from the tank.

14  Undo the screw securing the upper end of the fuel filler pipe to the body inside the filler flap opening. On models without a filler flap, release the filler pipe surround using a screwdriver, then rotate the retaining ring clockwise to release the filler pipe from the body.

15  Undo the two front retaining bolts then partially lower the fuel tank.

16  Slacken the clip and disconnect the vent pipe from the tank.

17  Detach the roll-over valve tube from the tank top surface and disconnect the two fuel hoses. Where quick-release couplings are used on the fuel hoses, release the protruding locking lugs on each union, by squeezing them together and carefully pulling the coupling apart. Note that the fuel supply hose couplings are identified by a white colour band and the return hose couplings by a yellow colour band.

18  Slowly lower the tank, complete with filler pipe, and remove it from under the vehicle. With the tank removed, detach the filler pipe, if required.

### Inspection

19  Whilst removed, the fuel tank can be inspected for damage or deterioration. Removal of the sender unit (see Section 9) will allow a partial inspection of the interior. If the tank is contaminated with sediment or water, swill it out with clean petrol. Do not under any circumstances undertake any repairs on a leaking or damaged fuel tank; this work must be carried out by a professional who has experience in this critical and potentially-dangerous work.

20  Whilst the fuel tank is removed from the vehicle, it should not be placed in an area where sparks or open flames could ignite the fumes coming out of the tank. Be especially careful inside garages where a natural-gas type appliance is located, because the pilot light could cause an explosion.

21  Check the condition of the filler pipe seal in the fuel tank, and renew it if necessary.

### Refitting

#### All models

22  Refitting is a reversal of the removal procedure. Apply a light smear of grease to the filler pipe seal, to ease fitting. Ensure that all connections are securely fitted. Where quick-release fuel couplings are fitted, press them together until the locking lugs snap into their groove. If evidence of contamination was found, do not return any previously-drained fuel to the tank unless it is carefully filtered first.

## 9  Fuel gauge sender unit - removal and refitting

**Note:** *Ford specify the use of their service tool 23-014 or 23-026 (a large box spanner with projecting teeth to engage the fuel gauge sender unit retaining ring's slots) for this task. While alternatives are possible, in view of the difficulty experienced in removing and refitting the sender unit, owners are strongly advised to obtain the correct tool before starting work. The help of an assistant will be required. Refer to the warning note in Section 1 before proceeding.*

### Removal

1  Remove the fuel tank as described in Section 8.

2  Engage the special tool into the sender unit then carefully turn the sender unit and release it from the tank **(see illustration)**.

**9.2  Sender unit removal from the fuel tank using special tool No 23-014**

**10.3  Roll-over valve location on fuel filler pipe**

### Refitting

3  Refit the sender unit in the reverse order of removal. Be sure to fit a new seal, and lubricate it with a smear of grease to prevent it from distorting when fitting the sender unit.

## 10  Roll-over valve - removal and refitting

**Note:** *Refer to the warning note in Section 1 before proceeding.*

### Removal

1  Disconnect the battery negative (earth) lead (refer to Chapter 5A, Section 1).

2  Chock the front wheels then jack up the rear of the car and support it on axle stands (see *"Jacking and Vehicle Support"*). Remove the rear wheel on the fuel filler cap side to improve the access under the wheel arch.

3  Undo the retaining screw, withdraw the roll-over valve from the filler pipe, detach the vent hoses and remove the valve **(see illustration)**.

### Refitting

4  Refit in the reverse order of removal.

## 11  Fuel tank filler pipe - removal and refitting

**Note:** *Refer to the warning note in Section 1 before proceeding.*

### Removal

1  Refer to Section 8 and remove the fuel tank.

2  Detach the roll-over valve clamp, undo the filler pipe securing screws, then lower the pipe from the vehicle.

### Refitting

3  Refit in the reverse order of removal. Lubricate the filler pipe seal to ease assembly prior to fitting.

4  When the fuel tank is refitted, refill with fuel, and check for any signs of leaks from the filler pipe and associated connections.

## 12 Carburettor (Weber TLDM) - description

The carburettor is of twin venturi, downdraught type, featuring a fixed size main jet system, adjustable idle system, a mechanically-operated accelerator pump, and a vacuum-operated power valve. A manually-operated cold start choke is fitted, and a throttle kicker is utilised on some models.

In order to comply with emission control regulations and maintain good fuel consumption, the main jets are calibrated to suit the 1/4 to 3/4 throttle range. The power valve is therefore only used to supply additional fuel during full-throttle conditions.

The accelerator pump is fitted to ensure a smooth transmission from the idle circuit to the main jet system. As the accelerator pedal is depressed, a linkage moves the diaphragm within the accelerator pump, and a small quantity of fuel is injected into the venturi, to prevent a momentary weak mixture and resultant engine hesitation.

The manually-operated choke features a vacuum-operated pull-down mechanism which controls the single choke plate under certain vacuum conditions.

The throttle kicker (where fitted) acts as an idle speed compensator, which operates when required under certain operating conditions to prevent stalling.

An anti-dieselling (fuel cut-off) solenoid is fitted to prevent the possibility of the engine running on after the ignition is switched off.

Adjustment procedures are described in Chapter 1, but it is important to note that accurate adjustments can only be made using the necessary equipment.

## 13 Carburettor (Weber TLDM) - fast idle speed adjustment

**Note:** *Before carrying out any carburettor adjustments, ensure that the spark plug gaps are set as specified, and that all electrical and vacuum connections are secure. To carry out checks and adjustments, an accurate*

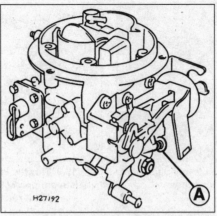

**13.4 Fast idle adjuster screw location (A) in the Weber TLDM carburettor**

*tachometer and an exhaust gas analyser (CO meter) will be required.*

**1** Check the idle speed and mixture settings are as specified (as described in Chapter 1). These must be correct before checking/adjusting the fast idle speed.
**2** Switch the engine off, then remove the air cleaner as described in Section 2.
**3** Actuate the choke by pulling the control knob fully out, then start the engine and note the engine fast idle speed. Compare it with the specified speed.
**4** If adjustment is required, turn the fast idle adjuster screw clockwise to decrease, or anti-clockwise to increase, the fast idle speed **(see illustration)**.
**5** Recheck the fast idle and basic idle speeds.
**6** On completion of the adjustment, stop the engine, detach the tachometer and CO meter, reconnect the radiator cooling fan lead, and refit the air cleaner.

## 14 Needle valve and float (Weber TLDM carburettor) - removal, refitting and adjustment

**Note:** *Refer to the warning note in Section 1 before proceeding. New gaskets and a washer (seal) will be required when reassembling. A tachometer and an exhaust gas analyser (CO meter) will also be required to check the idle speed and mixture settings on completion.*

### Removal and refitting

**1** Disconnect the battery negative (earth) lead (refer to Chapter 5A, Section 1).
**2** Remove the air cleaner (see Section 2).
**3** Clean the exterior of the carburettor, then disconnect the fuel supply hose and the anti-dieselling solenoid wiring.
**4** Disconnect the choke control cable.
**5** Undo and remove the six retaining screws (four of which are Torx type) and carefully lift the carburettor upper body clear.
**6** Invert and support the upper body of the carburettor for access to the float and pivot. Lightly tap out the float pivot pin, then withdraw the float, taking care not to distort the arms of the float **(see illustrations)**.
**7** Unscrew the needle valve housing, and extract it from the carburettor upper body **(see illustration)**. Collect the washer from the threads of the needle valve housing.
**8** Clean and inspect the components for signs of damage or wear, particularly the pivot holes in the float arm. Check the float for signs of leakage, by shaking it to see if it contains fuel. Clean the float chamber and jets (refer to Section 17 for details). Renew any components as necessary.
**9** Fit a new washer over the needle valve housing threads, and then carefully screw the valve unit into position in the upper body.
**10** Refit the needle valve, float and retaining pin, ensuring that the tag on the float engages with the ball and clip of the needle valve.
**11** Before refitting the upper body to the carburettor, check and if necessary adjust the float level as described in paragraphs 16 to 18. Also check the float and needle valve for free movement.
**12** Clean the gasket contact faces, then locate a new gasket and refit the upper body to the carburettor.
**13** Reconnect the fuel supply hose, anti-dieselling solenoid wiring and the choke cable. Adjust the choke cable (Section 6). If the fuel hose was originally secured with a crimped type clip, discard it and fit a screw clamp type.
**14** Refit the air cleaner (see Section 2).
**15** Reconnect the battery earth lead, then restart the engine and check the idle speed and mixture settings. Adjust if necessary as described in Chapter 1.

**4A**

**14.6a Slide out the float retaining pin . . .**

**14.6b . . . then detach the float and needle valve**

**14.7 Remove the needle valve housing and its washer**

**14.17 Checking the float level adjustment (TLD carburettor shown)**

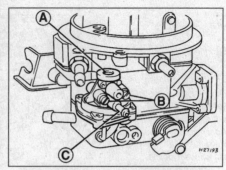

**15.9 Throttle kicker unit showing adjustment point (A), vacuum take-off (C) and unit retaining screws (B)**

## Float level adjustment

**16** With the carburettor upper body removed as described in paragraphs 1 to 5 inclusive, proceed as follows.

**17** Support the carburettor upper body vertically, ensuring that the needle valve is shut off. Locate the new upper body gasket onto the carburettor upper body, then measure the distance between the gasket and the bottom of the float **(see illustration)**.

**18** If the measurement is not as specified, adjust the setting by carefully bending the tag on the float as required, then recheck.

**19** Refit with reference to paragraphs 12 to 15 inclusive.

## 15 Throttle kicker unit (Weber TLDM carburettor) - removal, refitting and adjustment

**Note:** *A tachometer and exhaust gas analyser (CO meter) will be required to check and make any adjustment necessary.*

### Removal and refitting

**1** Disconnect the battery negative (earth) lead (refer to Chapter 5A, Section 1).

**2** Refer to Section 2 and remove the air cleaner.

**3** Detach the vacuum hose from the kicker unit. Undo the two retaining screws, detach the linkage and remove the kicker unit.

**4** Refitting the kicker unit is a reversal of the removal procedure. If the unit is to be checked for adjustment, loosely locate the air cleaner, reconnect the inlet air temperature sensor multi-plug and the battery earth lead, then proceed as follows.

### Adjustment

**5** Start and run the engine up to its normal operating temperature (at which point the cooling fan will start to operate) then switch the engine off.

**6** Remove the air cleaner again, then detach the wiring connector of the cooling fan thermostatic switch. Bridge the terminals in the connector with a suitable piece of wire, in order to actuate the cooling fan and keep it

running. Start the engine and run it at 3000 rpm for 30 seconds to stabilise it, then release the throttle and check (and if necessary adjust) the idle speed and mixture settings as described in Chapter 1. Stop the engine.

**7** Detach the vacuum hose between the throttle kicker and the inlet manifold at source (but not the vacuum supply to the ignition module). Connect a new length of vacuum hose directly between the manifold and the kicker unit.

**8** Restart the engine and check the engine speed. The throttle kicker should increase the engine speed above its normal idle. Check the speed registered against the specified throttle kicker operating speed.

**9** If required, the throttle kicker speed can be adjusted by prising free the tamperproof plug and the adjustment screw turned as necessary **(see illustration)**.

**10** When the adjustment is complete, stop the engine, fit a new tamperproof plug, disconnect the temporary vacuum hose (between the manifold and the kicker unit) and reconnect the original hose (between the carburettor and the kicker unit).

**11** Remove the bridging wire, and reconnect the cooling fan thermostatic switch multi-plug. Refit and secure the air cleaner, and disconnect the tachometer and CO meter to complete.

## 16 Carburettor (Weber TLDM) - removal and refitting

**Note:** *Refer to the warning note in Section 1 before proceeding. New gaskets will be required on refitting, and a tachometer and an exhaust gas analyser will be required on completion.*

### Removal

**1** Disconnect the battery negative (earth) lead (refer to Chapter 5A, Section 1).

**2** Remove the air cleaner (see Section 2).

**3** Disconnect the accelerator cable from the carburettor (Section 3).

**4** Disconnect the choke cable from the carburettor (Section 6).

**5** Disconnect the fuel hose from the carburettor, and plug its end to prevent fuel spillage and the ingress of dirt. If a crimped type hose clip is fitted, cut it free, but take care not to damage the hose. Crimped clips must be discarded and replaced with screw clamp type clips during refitting.

**6** Disconnect the wiring from the anti-dieselling solenoid.

**7** Unscrew and remove the four carburettor-to-manifold retaining Torx head screws, then carefully lift the carburettor from the manifold.

### Refitting

**8** Clean the carburettor and manifold gasket mating faces.

**9** Refit in the reverse order of removal. Fit a new gasket, and tighten the retaining screws securely. Ensure that the fuel supply hose connection to the carburettor is securely fitted, using a new screw clamp retaining clip.

**10** Reconnect the accelerator cable, and adjust it as described in Section 3.

**11** Reconnect the choke cable, and adjust it as described in Section 6.

**12** Refer to Section 2 and refit the air cleaner.

**13** When the battery is reconnected, start the engine and check the idle speed and mixture settings as described in Chapter 1.

## 17 Carburettor (Weber TLDM) - dismantling, cleaning, inspection and reassembly

**Note:** *Refer to the warning note in Section 1 before proceeding. Check parts availability before dismantling. If possible, obtain an overhaul kit containing all the relevant gaskets, seals, etc, required for reassembly prior to dismantling the carburettor.*

### Dismantling

**1** With the carburettor removed from the vehicle, prepare a clean, flat work surface prior to commencing dismantling. The following procedures may be used for partial or complete dismantling, as required.

## Cleaning and inspection

**16** Wash the carburettor components, drillings and passages with clean petrol, then blow them dry using a low-pressure air line. A high-pressure air line must not be applied to the accelerator pump discharge assembly or the pump supply valve, as they each contain a rubber Vernay valve, and these can easily be damaged under high pressure. *Never use a piece of wire for cleaning purposes.*

**17** Examine all of the carburettor components for signs of damage or wear, paying particular attention to the diaphragms, throttle spindle and plates, needle valve and mixture screw; the power valve jet is adjacent to the primary main jet. Renew all diaphragms, sealing washers and gaskets as a matter of course.

## Reassembly

**18** Refit the throttle housing to the carburettor main body (fitting a new gasket), and secure with its retaining screws.

**19** Refit the fuel mixture screw. Make an initial adjustment by screwing it fully in (but do not overtighten or screw it onto its seat), then unscrew it two full turns.

**20** Where fitted, reassemble the throttle kicker, ensuring that its diaphragm lies flat, and that the relative position of the operating link to the kicker cover is correct.

**21** Fit the power valve, ensuring that its diaphragm lies flat and the vacuum gallery aligns with the diaphragm and housing.

**22** Refit the accelerator pump. Take care not to damage the valve as it is inserted, and check that the O-ring seal is correctly located on the end of the valve. Check that the valve is not trapped by the spring.

**23** Refit the accelerator pump discharge jet. Take care not to damage the valve and/or the O-ring seal, and ensure that they are correctly located.

**24** Commence reassembly of the upper body by inserting the emulsion tubes and the air correction jets into their respective ports (as noted during removal).

**25** Screw the anti-dieselling solenoid into position. Ensure that the aluminium washer is fitted, and take care not to overtighten the valve.

**26** Refit the needle valve and the float, and adjust the float setting as described in Section 14.

**27** Refit the choke control mechanism, and secure with its three retaining screws.

**28** Locate a new gasket onto the mating face, then refit the carburettor upper body to the main body. As they are reassembled, take care not to snag the float on the carburettor main body. Fit and tighten the retaining screws to secure.

**29** With the carburettor reassembled, refit it to the vehicle and adjust it as described in Chapter 1. Where applicable, check and adjust the throttle kicker setting.

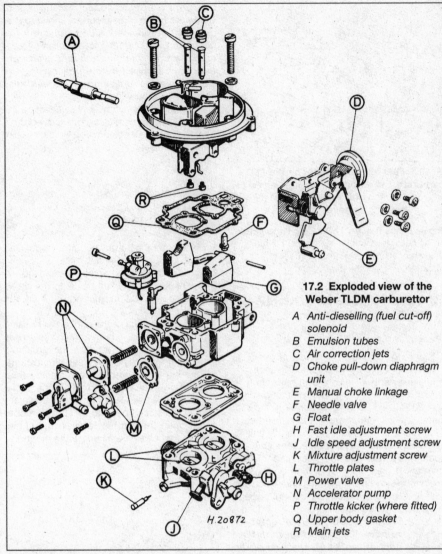

**17.2 Exploded view of the Weber TLDM carburettor**

A   Anti-dieselling (fuel cut-off) solenoid
B   Emulsion tubes
C   Air correction jets
D   Choke pull-down diaphragm unit
E   Manual choke linkage
F   Needle valve
G   Float
H   Fast idle adjustment screw
J   Idle speed adjustment screw
K   Mixture adjustment screw
L   Throttle plates
M   Power valve
N   Accelerator pump
P   Throttle kicker (where fitted)
Q   Upper body gasket
R   Main jets

H.20872

**4A**

**2** Clean the exterior of the carburettor, then undo the six retaining screws and lift the upper carburettor body from the lower section **(see illustration)**.

**3** Remove the float and needle valve from the carburettor upper body, as described in Section 14.

**4** Unscrew and remove the anti-dieselling solenoid from the upper body, but ensure that the seal washer is removed together with the valve.

**5** Undo the three screws securing the choke mechanism, and detach it.

**6** Unscrew and remove the two air correction jets from the underside of the upper body. Note the size and location of each, to ensure correct refitting.

**7** Invert the upper body so that the emulsion tubes can fall out of their apertures (above the air correction jets). Remove the emulsion tubes from their locations, again having noted the size and location of each.

**8** Unscrew and remove the main jets, again having noted their fitted positions.

**9** Dismantle the carburettor lower (main) body as follows.

**10** Prise free the accelerator pump discharge tube, but take care not to damage it or the carburettor body.

**11** Undo the four screws securing the accelerator pump; remove the cover, followed by the diaphragm and return spring. The valve should come out on the end of the return spring. Check that the valve is complete and with its O-ring seal (where applicable).

**12** Undo the three retaining screws, and remove the power valve unit. Remove the cover and return spring, followed by the diaphragm.

**13** Where fitted, undo the retaining screws and remove the throttle kicker unit from the lower (main) body.

**14** Prise free and remove the tamperproof seal, then unscrew and remove the fuel mixture screw.

**15** Undo the retaining screws, and remove the throttle housing from the carburettor main body.

4A•10 Fuel system - carburettor engines

## 18 Carburettor (Weber TLD) - description

This carburettor incorporates many of the features of the TLDM type fitted to 1.3 litre HCS engines. The main differences are that the secondary venturi (barrel) is vacuum-operated, and that a coolant-heated automatic choke control system is fitted.

The choke system is fully automatic. When the engine is cold, the bi-metal spring which controls the position of the choke plate is fully wound up, and holds the plate closed. As the engine warms up, the bi-metal spring is heated by the coolant and begins to unwind, thereby progressively opening the choke plate. A vacuum-operated pull-down mechanism controls the choke plate under certain operating conditions, and an internal fast idle system is incorporated.

The carburettors used on cars with CTX automatic transmission have a throttle position sensor and throttle plate (idle speed) control motor for additional control of certain engine functions. A similar system is used on cars equipped with air conditioning.

## 19 Carburettor (Weber TLD) - fast idle speed adjustment

**Note:** *Before carrying out any carburettor adjustments, ensure that the spark plug gaps are set as specified, and that all electrical and vacuum connections are secure. To carry out checks and adjustments, an accurate tachometer and an exhaust gas analyser (CO meter) will be required.*

1 Check that the idle speed and mixture settings are as specified (as described in Chapter 1). These must be correct before checking/adjusting the fast idle speed.
2 Switch the engine off, then remove the air cleaner as described in Section 2.
3 With the engine at its normal operating temperature and a tachometer connected in accordance with its manufacturer's instructions, hold the throttle linkage partly open, then close the choke plate until the fast idle adjustment screw aligns with the 4th step on the fast idle cam **(see illustration)**. Release the throttle linkage so that the fast idle speed adjustment screw rests on the cam. Release the choke plate. The linkage will hold it in the fast idle speed setting position, as long as the accelerator pedal is not depressed.
4 Without touching the accelerator pedal, start the engine and record the fast idle speed achieved. If adjustment is required, turn the fast idle speed adjuster screw until the specified fast idle speed is obtained.
5 When the throttle linkage is opened, the choke plate should return to its fully-open position. If this does not happen, either the

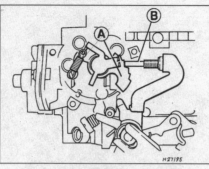

**19.3 Fast idle adjustment on the TLD carburettor showing the adjuster screw (B) on 4th step of the fast idle cam (A) (housing removed for clarity)**

engine is not at normal operating temperature, or the automatic choke mechanism is faulty.
6 Switch off the engine and disconnect the tachometer. Refit the air cleaner.

## 20 Needle valve and float (Weber TLD carburettor) - removal, refitting and adjustment

1 Refer to Section 14 and proceed as described, noting the following difference.
2 In paragraph 4, ignore the instruction to detach the choke cable (an automatic choke is fitted to the TLD type carburettor). Instead, clamp the coolant supply and return hoses which lead to the automatic choke unit to minimise coolant loss, then ensure that the cooling system is not pressurised (see Chapter 1). Identify then detach both of the coolant hoses at the automatic choke housing **(see illustration)**. Catch any coolant spillage in a suitable container.

⚠️ *Warning: DO NOT attempt to remove the expansion tank filler cap, or to disturb any part of the cooling system, while it or the engine is hot, as there is a very great risk of scalding. If the expansion tank filler cap must be removed before the engine and radiator have fully cooled down (even though this is not recommended) the pressure in the cooling system must first be released. Cover the cap with a thick layer of cloth, to avoid scalding, and slowly unscrew the filler*

**20.2 Coolant hose connections to the automatic choke unit**

*cap until a hissing sound can be heard. When the hissing has stopped, showing that pressure is released, slowly unscrew the filler cap further until it can be removed; if more hissing sounds are heard, wait until they have stopped before unscrewing the cap completely. At all times, keep well away from the filler opening.*
3 On completion, reconnect the hoses to the automatic choke unit, and remove the clamps from the hoses. Check and top-up the coolant level on completion (see *"Weekly Checks"* and Chapter 1).

## 21 Automatic choke (Weber TLD carburettor) - adjustment

1 Disconnect the battery negative (earth) lead (refer to Chapter 5A, Section 1).
2 Remove the air cleaner (see Section 2).
3 Disconnect the coolant hoses to the choke unit as described in paragraph 2 of the previous Section.
4 Note the position of the choke coil housing alignment marks, then undo the three retaining screws and withdraw the automatic choke bi-metal coil housing **(see illustration)**.
5 Remove the inner heat shield **(see illustration)**. To check and adjust the choke vacuum pull-down, secure the choke plate lever in the closed position by fitting a rubber band, open the throttle to allow the choke plate to fully close, then release the throttle.

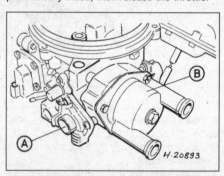

**21.4 Automatic choke unit on the Weber TLD carburettor, showing the pull-down diaphragm housing (A) and the choke bi-metal spring housing (B)**

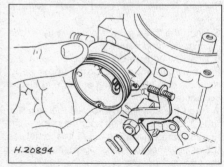

**21.5 Removing the inner heat shield from the automatic choke housing**

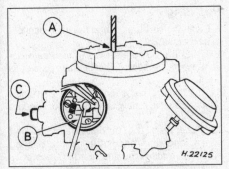

**21.6  Choke plate pull-down adjustment on the Weber TLD carburettor**

A  *Twist drill*
B  *Screwdriver in contact with operating arm*
C  *Adjuster screw*

6 Using a screwdriver, push the operating arm to the right against its spring, and measure the clearance between the lower edge of the choke plate and the venturi using a twist drill or other suitable gauge rod **(see illustration)**. Where the clearance is outside that specified, remove the plug from the diaphragm housing, and turn the adjuster screw (now exposed) in the required direction.
7 Fit a new diaphragm housing plug and remove the rubber band.
8 Refit the heat shield so that its slotted hole engages over the choke housing peg.
9 Refit the bi-metal coil housing by first connecting the bi-metal spring to the choke lever (ensuring correct engagement), locate the housing and hand-tighten the three retaining screws. Rotate the housing to align the index line on the housing with the dot mark on the choke main body, then retighten the retaining screws **(see illustration)**.
10 Reconnect the coolant hoses with reference to paragraph 3 in the previous Section.
11 Refit the air cleaner as described in Section 2.

## 22  Automatic choke (Weber TLD carburettor) - removal, inspection and refitting

**Note:** *Refer to the warning note in Section 1 before proceeding. A new carburettor upper body gasket will be required when reassembling. On completion, a tachometer will be required to check the fast idle speed adjustment.*

### Removal

1 Disconnect the battery negative (earth) lead (refer to Chapter 5A, Section 1).
2 Remove the air cleaner as described in Section 2.
3 To prevent excess coolant loss, clamp the coolant supply and return hoses to the automatic choke unit, and ensure that the cooling system is not pressurised (see Chapter 1). Identify then detach both of the

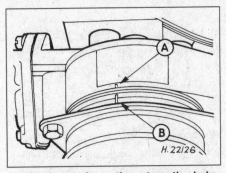

**21.9  Index marks on the automatic choke housing (B) and body (A) should be in alignment**

coolant hoses at the automatic choke housing. Catch any coolant spillage in a suitable container.

⚠️ *Warning: DO NOT attempt to remove the expansion tank filler cap, or to disturb any part of the cooling system, while it or the engine is hot, as there is a very great risk of scalding. If the expansion tank filler cap must be removed before the engine and radiator have fully cooled down (even though this is not recommended) the pressure in the cooling system must first be released. Cover the cap with a thick layer of cloth, to avoid scalding, and slowly unscrew the filler cap until a hissing sound can be heard. When the hissing has stopped, showing that pressure is released, slowly unscrew the filler cap further until it can be removed; if more hissing sounds are heard, wait until they have stopped before unscrewing the cap completely. At all times, keep well away from the filler opening.*

4 Detach the fuel pipe and the anti-dieselling solenoid wiring connector. Any crimped type hose clips must be replaced with a screw clamp type clips during reassembly.
5 Unscrew and remove the retaining screws (two conventional, and four Torx type), then lift the carburettor upper body clear and remove it.
6 Note the position of the choke housing alignment marks, then undo the three

retaining screws and remove the choke bi-metal coil unit. Remove the internal heat shield.
7 To remove the automatic choke unit, undo the three retaining screws and detach the choke link from the operating lever.
8 Undo the three retaining screws to remove the vacuum diaphragm unit.
9 If dismantling the choke mechanism any further, note the component fitment as an aid to reassembly, but do not detach the choke spindle **(see illustration)**.

### Inspection

10 Clean and inspect all components for wear, damage and/or distortion. Pay particular attention to the condition of the vacuum (pull-down) diaphragm and the choke housing O-ring. Renew any items that are defective (or suspect).

### Refitting

11 Reassemble the automatic choke mechanism, making references to the notes taken during dismantling **(see illustration 22.9)**. Note that no lubricants must be used.
12 Refit the vacuum unit, making reference to the notes taken during dismantling. Ensure that the diaphragm is lying flat before tightening the housing retaining screws.
13 Locate the O-ring (ensuring that it is correctly seated), then reconnect the choke link. Refit the automatic choke unit, and secure with the retaining screws. Check and adjust the choke vacuum pull-down as described in the previous Section (paragraphs 5 and 6).
14 Refit the inner heat shield, ensuring that the location peg is securely engaged in its notch.
15 Refit the automatic choke housing and the bi-metal spring unit as described in the previous Section (paragraph 9).
16 Refit the carburettor upper body, ensuring that a new gasket is used and that the mating surfaces are clean. Fit the retaining screws to secure.
17 Reconnect the fuel hose to the carburettor, using new screw type hose clips to secure it.

**4A**

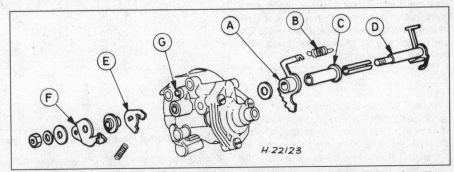

**22.9  Automatic choke unit and associated components on the Weber TLD carburettor**

A  *Operating link/fast idle cam*
B  *Fast idle cam return spring*
C  *Spindle*
D  *Connecting rod and lever assembly*
E  *Pull-down link*
F  *Actuating lever*
G  *Automatic choke housing*

**18** Reconnect the anti-dieselling solenoid wiring connector.
**19** Reconnect the coolant hoses to the automatic choke unit, then check and if necessary top-up the cooling system as described in Chapter 1.
**20** Reconnect the battery earth lead, then check and adjust the fast idle speed as described in Section 19.
**21** Refit the air cleaner (Section 2).

## 23 Carburettor (Weber TLD) - removal and refitting

**Note:** *Refer to the warning note in Section 1 before proceeding. New gaskets will be required on refitting and a tachometer and an exhaust gas analyser will be required on completion.*

### Removal

**1** Disconnect the battery negative (earth) lead (refer to Chapter 5A, Section 1).
**2** Remove the air cleaner as described in Section 2.
**3** Release any pressure remaining in the cooling system (see Chapter 1), and then detach the two coolant hoses from the automatic choke unit. Catch any coolant spillage in a suitable container. Identify each hose for subsequent refitting, then plug their ends or position them as high as possible to prevent coolant leakage.

⚠ **Warning: DO NOT attempt to remove the expansion tank filler cap, or to disturb any part of the cooling system, while it or the engine is hot, as there is a very great risk of scalding. If the expansion tank filler cap must be removed before the engine and radiator have fully cooled down (even though this is not recommended) the pressure in the cooling system must first be released. Cover the cap with a thick layer of cloth, to avoid scalding, and slowly unscrew the filler cap until a hissing sound can be heard. When the hissing has stopped, showing that pressure is released, slowly unscrew the filler cap further until it can be removed; if more hissing sounds are heard, wait until they have stopped before unscrewing the cap completely. At all times, keep well away from the filler opening.**

**4** Disconnect the accelerator cable from the linkage at the carburettor, as described in Section 3.
**5** Detach the anti-dieselling solenoid wiring connector. Where applicable, also detach the idle speed control motor multi-plug and the throttle position sensor wiring multi-plug.
**6** Detach the fuel feed hose at the carburettor. As it is detached, plug the end of the hose to prevent excessive fuel spillage and the ingress of dirt. Where a crimped type hose clip is fitted, cut it free, taking care not to damage the hose; a new screw clamp type

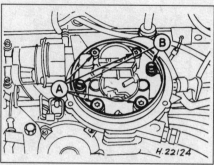

**23.8 Weber TLD carburettor showing the four Torx-type screws (A). The two conventional screws (B) hold the upper and lower carburettor body sections together**

clip will need to be obtained to replace the crimped clip during reassembly.
**7** Disconnect the relevant vacuum pipes from the carburettor. As they are detached, label them to ensure correct reassembly.
**8** Unscrew and remove the four Torx-type retaining screws, and carefully lift clear the carburettor from the inlet manifold **(see illustration)**. Remove the gasket.

### Refitting

**9** Clean the carburettor and the inlet manifold mating faces.
**10** Refit the carburettor in the reverse order of removal, ensuring that a new gasket is fitted.
**11** If they are perished or were damaged during removal, renew the fuel and/or vacuum hoses.
**12** Reconnect the automatic choke unit hoses, and then check/top-up the cooling system if required, as described in Chapter 1.
**13** Finally, check the idle speed and fuel mixture settings, and adjust if necessary as described in Chapter 1.

## 24 Carburettor (Weber TLD) - dismantling, cleaning, inspection and reassembly

**1** Proceed as described in Section 17 for the TLDM carburettor, but refer to the appropriate illustrations for the TLD type carburettor **(see illustrations)**. The following differences should also be observed:

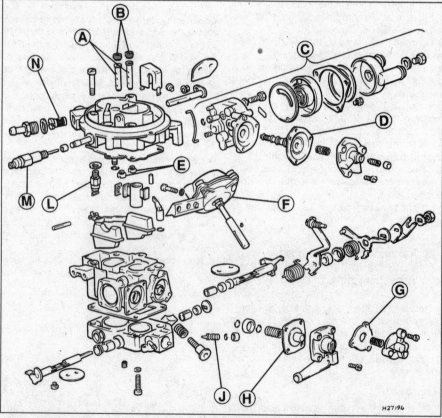

**24.1a Exploded view of the Weber TLD type carburettor as fitted to the 1.6 litre engine**

A  Emulsion tubes
B  Air correction jets
C  Automatic choke unit
D  Choke pull-down diaphragm
E  Main jets
F  Secondary barrel diaphragm
G  Power valve diaphragm
H  Accelerator pump diaphragm
J  Mixture screw
L  Needle valve
M  Anti dieselling (fuel cut-off) solenoid
N  Fuel supply filter

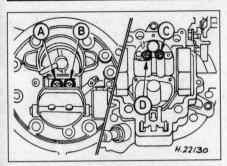

**24.1b  Jet arrangement in the upper body of the Weber TLD carburettor**

A  *Primary air correction jet*
B  *Secondary air correction jet*
C  *Secondary main jet*
D  *Primary main jet*

a) *When refitting the adjuster screw, make the initial adjustment by screwing it fully into position (without overtightening it), then unscrewing it by three full turns.*
b) *Refer to Section 20 to adjust the needle valve and float.*
c) *When the carburettor is reassembled and refitted, check and adjust it as described in Chapter 1.*

## 25  Inlet manifold - removal and refitting

**Note:** *Refer to the warning note in Section 1 before proceeding.*

### Removal

**1** Drain the cooling system as described in Chapter 1.
**2** Remove the carburettor as described in Section 16 or 23 as applicable.
**3** Noting their locations, disconnect the coolant, vacuum and breather hoses from the manifold.
**4** Disconnect the wiring multi-plugs from the engine sensors at the inlet manifold. Disconnect the radio earth lead at the inlet manifold connector.
**5** Undo the retaining nuts, and withdraw the manifold from the cylinder head. Remove the gasket.
**6** With the manifold removed, clean all traces of the old gasket from the mating surfaces of the manifold and the cylinder head.

### Refitting

**7** Refitting is the reversal of removal. Use a new gasket, and tighten the retaining nuts to the specified torque. Refit the remainder of the components with reference to the appropriate Chapters of this manual. On completion, refill the cooling system as described in Chapter 1.

**4A**

# Chapter 4 Part B:
# Fuel system - central fuel injection (CFi) engines

## Contents

**4B**

## Degrees of difficulty

| | | | | |
|---|---|---|---|---|
| **Easy,** suitable for novice with little experience  | **Fairly easy,** suitable for beginner with some experience  | **Fairly difficult,** suitable for competent DIY mechanic  | **Difficult,** suitable for experienced DIY mechanic | **Very difficult,** suitable for expert DIY or professional |

## Specifications

### General
System type . . . . . . . . . . . . . . . . . . . . . . . . . . . . . . . . . . . . . . . . . . Central Fuel injection (CFi)
Application . . . . . . . . . . . . . . . . . . . . . . . . . . . . . . . . . . . . . . . . . . . 1.3 litre HCS and 1.4 litre CVH engines

### Fuel grade
Fuel octane requirement . . . . . . . . . . . . . . . . . . . . . . . . . . . . . . . . . 95 RON unleaded

### Fuel system data
Regulated fuel pressure - engine running at idle speed . . . . . . . . . . . . 1.0 ± 0.1 bars
Hold pressure - engine stopped after 1 minute . . . . . . . . . . . . . . . . . 0.5 bars minimum

### Torque wrench settings

| | Nm | lbf ft |
|---|---|---|
| CFi unit-to-inlet manifold . . . . . . . . . . . . . . . . . . . . . . . . . . . . . . | 14 | 10 |
| Inlet manifold . . . . . . . . . . . . . . . . . . . . . . . . . . . . . . . . . . . . . . . | 18 | 13 |
| Inlet air temperature sensor . . . . . . . . . . . . . . . . . . . . . . . . . . . . . | 23 | 17 |
| Oxygen sensor . . . . . . . . . . . . . . . . . . . . . . . . . . . . . . . . . . . . . . | 60 | 44 |

## 1 General information and precautions

### General information

The fuel system consists of a fuel tank (mounted under the body, beneath the rear seats), fuel hoses, an electric fuel pump mounted in the fuel tank, and a central fuel injection (CFi) system.

Fuel is supplied from the tank by an integral electric fuel pump (and combined fuel gauge sender unit). The fuel is passed through an in-line filter within the engine compartment, then to the fuel injection unit. The fuel is maintained at the required operating pressure by a pressure regulator unit.

The CFi unit itself is a relatively simple device when compared with a conventional carburettor. Fuel is injected by a single solenoid valve (fuel injector) which is mounted centrally on top of the unit. It is this feature which gives the system CFi (or Central Fuel Injection) its name **(see illustration)**.

The injector is energised by an electrical signal sent from the engine management electronic control unit (ECU). When energised, the injector pintle is lifted from its seat, and atomised fuel is delivered into the inlet manifold under pressure. The electrical signals take two forms of current - a high current to open the injector, and a low current to hold it open for the duration required. At idle speed, the injector is pulsed at every other inlet stroke, rather than with every stroke as during normal operation.

The air-to-fuel mixture ratio is regulated by the engine management ECU, based on inputs from the various engine sensors. No adjustments to the fuel mixture are possible.

The throttle plate control motor (mounted on the side of the CFi unit) regulates the idle speed by reacting to the signals sent by the ECU. The signals are calculated by the values and information provided from the engine sensors. When the throttle position sensor indicates that the throttle is closed, the ECU enters the idle speed mode or dashpot mode (according to engine speed). The ECU maintains the idle speed at a constant value, making minor adjustments as necessary for different loads and conditions. The base idle speed can only be adjusted by a dealer or fuel injection specialist with the necessary equipment to link up to the engine management ECU.

To prevent the engine from running on (or dieselling) when it is switched off, the ECU sends a signal to the throttle plate control motor, to fully close the throttle plate and return it to its preset position ready for restarting. When the ignition is switched on to restart the engine, the motor repositions the throttle plate to the position required according to the prevailing conditions.

The ECU is the heart of the entire engine management system, controlling the fuel injection, ignition and emissions control systems. The ECU receives information from various sensors to determine engine temperature, speed and load, and the quantity of air entering the engine. The sensors also inform the ECU of throttle position, inlet air temperature and exhaust gas oxygen content. All the information supplied to the ECU is computed and compared with pre-set values stored in the ECU memory, to determine the required period of injection.

Information on engine speed is supplied to the ECU by the crankshaft position sensor. This is an inductive pulse generator bolted (in a separate bracket) to the cylinder block/crankcase, to scan the ridges between 36 holes machined in the inboard (right-hand) face of the flywheel/driveplate. As each ridge passes the sensor tip, a signal is generated, which is used by the ECU to determine engine speed.

The ridge between the 35th and 36th holes (corresponding to 90° BTDC) is missing - this step in the incoming signals is used by the ECU to determine crankshaft (ie, piston) position.

Engine temperature information is supplied by the coolant temperature sensor. This component is an NTC (Negative Temperature Coefficient) thermistor - that is, a semi-conductor whose electrical resistance decreases as its temperature increases. It provides the ECU with a constantly-varying (analogue) voltage signal, corresponding to the temperature of the engine coolant. This is used to refine the calculations made by the ECU, when determining the correct amount of fuel required to achieve the ideal air/fuel mixture ratio.

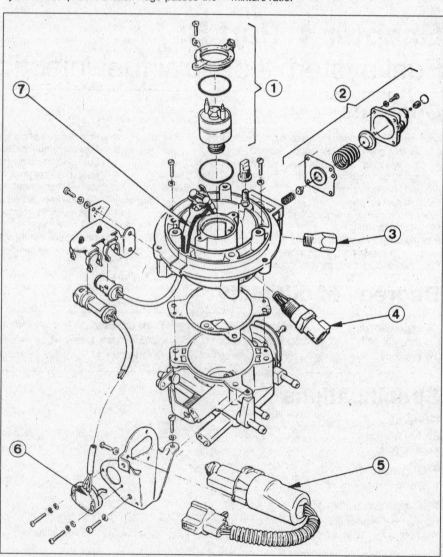

**1.3 Exploded view of the CFi unit**

1  Fuel injection unit
2  Fuel pressure regulator unit
3  Fuel feed connector
4  Inlet air temperature sensor
5  Throttle plate control motor
6  Throttle position sensor
7  Fuel injector wiring

Inlet air temperature information is supplied by the inlet air temperature sensor. This component is also an NTC thermistor - see the previous paragraph - providing the ECU with a signal corresponding to the temperature of air passing into the engine. This is used to refine the calculations made by the ECU, when determining the correct amount of fuel required to achieve the ideal air/fuel mixture ratio.

A throttle position sensor is mounted on the end of the throttle valve spindle, to provide the ECU with a constantly-varying (analogue) voltage signal corresponding to the throttle opening. This allows the ECU to register the driver's input when determining the amount of fuel required by the engine.

Road speed is monitored by the vehicle speed sensor. This component is a Hall-effect generator, mounted on the transmission's speedometer drive. It supplies the ECU with a series of pulses corresponding to the vehicle's road speed, enabling the ECU to control features such as the fuel shut-off on the overrun, and to provide information for the trip computer, adaptive damping and cruise control systems (where fitted).

A manifold absolute pressure sensor measures inlet manifold vacuum, and supplies this information to the ECU for calculation of engine load at any given throttle position.

Where power steering is fitted, a pressure-operated switch is screwed into the power steering system's high-pressure pipe. Its contacts are normally closed, opening when the system reaches the specified pressure - on receiving this signal, the ECU increases the idle speed, to compensate for the additional load on the engine.

The oxygen sensor in the exhaust system provides the ECU with constant feedback - "closed-loop" control - which enables it to adjust the mixture to provide the best possible conditions for the catalytic converter to operate.

## Precautions

⚠️ *Warning: Petrol is extremely flammable - great care must be taken when working on any part of the fuel system. Do not smoke or allow any naked flames or uncovered light bulbs near the work area. Note that gas powered domestic appliances with pilot flames, such as heaters, boilers and tumble dryers, also present a fire hazard - bear this in mind if you are working in an area where such appliances are present. Always keep a suitable fire extinguisher close to the work area and familiarise yourself with its operation before starting work. Wear eye protection when working on fuel systems and wash off any fuel spilt on bare skin immediately with soap and water. Note that fuel vapour is just as dangerous as liquid fuel; a vessel that has just been emptied of liquid fuel will still contain* vapour and can be potentially explosive. Petrol is a highly dangerous and volatile liquid, and the precautions necessary when handling it cannot be overstressed.

*Many of the operations described in this Chapter involve the disconnection of fuel lines, which may cause an amount of fuel spillage. Before commencing work, refer to the above Warning and the information given in "Safety first" at the beginning of this manual.*

*When working with fuel system components, pay particular attention to cleanliness - dirt entering the fuel system may cause blockages which will lead to poor running.*

**Note:** *Residual pressure will remain in the fuel lines long after the vehicle was last used, when disconnecting any fuel line, it will be necessary to depressurise the fuel system as described in Section 2.*

## 2 Fuel system - depressurisation

**Note:** *Refer to the warning note in Section 1 before proceeding.*

⚠️ *Warning: The following procedure will merely relieve the pressure in the fuel system - remember that fuel will still be present in the system components, and take precautions accordingly before disconnecting any of them.*

1 The fuel system referred to in this Chapter is defined as the fuel tank and tank-mounted fuel pump/fuel gauge sender unit, the fuel filter, the fuel injector, fuel pressure regulator, and the metal pipes and flexible hoses of the fuel lines between these components. All these contain fuel, which will be under pressure while the engine is running and/or while the ignition is switched on.

2 The pressure will remain for some time after the ignition has been switched off, and must be relieved before any of these components is disturbed for servicing work.

3 The simplest depressurisation method is to disconnect the fuel pump electrical supply - either by removing the fuel pump fuse (see Chapter 12), or by lifting the red button on the fuel cut-off switch (see Section 11) - and to allow the engine to idle until it dies through lack of fuel pressure. Turn the engine over once or twice on the starter to ensure that all pressure is released, then switch off the ignition; do not forget to refit the fuse (or depress the red button, as appropriate) when work is complete.

4 Note that, once the fuel system has been depressurised and drained (even partially), it will take significantly longer to restart the engine - perhaps several seconds of cranking - before the system is refilled and pressure restored.

## 3 Fuel lines and fittings - general information

**Note:** *Refer to the warning note in Section 1 before proceeding.*

### Disconnecting and connecting quick-release couplings

1 Quick-release couplings are employed at many of the unions in the fuel feed and return lines.

2 Before disconnecting any fuel system component, relieve the residual pressure in the system (see Section 2), and equalise tank pressure by removing the fuel filler cap.

⚠️ *Warning: This procedure will merely relieve the increased pressure necessary for the engine to run - remember that fuel will still be present in the system components, and take precautions accordingly before disconnecting any of them.*

3 Release the protruding locking lugs on each union, by squeezing them together and carefully pulling the coupling apart. Use rag to soak up any spilt fuel. Where the unions are colour-coded, the pipes cannot be confused. Where both unions are the same colour, note carefully which pipe is connected to which, and ensure that they are correctly reconnected on refitting.

4 To reconnect one of these couplings, press them together until the locking lugs snap into their groove. Switch the ignition on and off five times to pressurise the system, and check for any sign of fuel leakage around the disturbed coupling before attempting to start the engine.

### Checking

5 Checking procedures for the fuel lines are included in Chapter 1.

### Component renewal

6 If any damaged sections are to be renewed, use original-equipment replacement hoses or pipes, constructed from exactly the same material as the section being replaced. Do not install substitutes constructed from inferior or inappropriate material; this could cause a fuel leak or a fire.

7 Before detaching or disconnecting any part of the fuel system, note the routing of all hoses and pipes, and the orientation of all clamps and clips. Replacement sections must be installed in exactly the same manner.

8 Before disconnecting any part of the fuel system, be sure to relieve the fuel system pressure (see Section 2), and equalise tank pressure by removing the fuel filler cap. Also disconnect the battery negative (earth) lead - see Chapter 5A, Section 1. Cover the fitting being disconnected with a rag, to absorb any fuel that may spray out.

**4B**

## 4 Air cleaner assembly and air inlet components - removal and refitting

**Note:** *Air cleaner element renewal is described in Chapter 1.*

### Air cleaner assembly

1 Disconnect the battery negative (earth) lead (refer to Chapter 5A, Section 1).
2 Undo the retaining bolts and partially lift the air cleaner from the CFi unit, so that the hose and wiring connections to the underside of the air cleaner body are accessible.
3 Note their connections and routings, then detach the wiring and hoses from the underside of the air cleaner.
4 Lift the air cleaner clear from the CFi unit.
5 Refit in the reverse order of removal.
6 Renew any hoses that are perished or cracked, and ensure that all fittings are securely and correctly reconnected.

### Air inlet components

7 The air cleaner inlet spout and related components are removed with the air cleaner assembly as described above.

## 5 Accelerator cable - removal, refitting and adjustment

### Removal

1 Disconnect the battery negative (earth) lead (refer to Chapter 5A, Section 1).
2 Fold back the carpet and insulation in the driver's footwell to gain access to the accelerator pedal.
3 Detach the accelerator cable from the pedal.
4 Remove the air cleaner assembly as described in Section 4.
5 Working at the throttle housing end of the cable, pivot the throttle quadrant by hand to release the tension from the cable, then detach the inner cable nipple from the throttle lever.
6 Detach the outer cable from the adjuster/support bracket, then remove the cable.

### Refitting and adjustment

7 Refit in the reverse order of removal. When the cable is reconnected at each end, have an assistant depress the accelerator, and check that the throttle fully opens and shuts without binding. Ensure that there is a small amount of slack in the inner cable when the throttle is fully released. If adjustment is required, release the outer cable retaining clip from the cable at the adjustment/support bracket, slide the cable through the adjuster grommet to the point required, then refit the retaining clip to secure it in the set position.

## 6 Accelerator pedal - removal and refitting

Refer to Part A, Section 5.

## 7 Fuel pump/fuel pressure - checking

**Note:** *Refer to the warning in Section 1.*

### Fuel pump operation check

1 Switch on the ignition, and listen for the fuel pump (the sound of an electric motor running, audible from beneath the rear seats). Assuming there is sufficient fuel in the tank, the pump should start and run for approximately one or two seconds, then stop, each time the ignition is switched on. **Note:** *If the pump runs continuously all the time the ignition is switched on, the electronic control system is running in the backup (or "limp-home") mode referred to by Ford as "Limited Operation Strategy" (LOS). This almost certainly indicates a fault in the ECU itself, and the vehicle should therefore be taken to a Ford dealer for a full test of the complete system, using the correct diagnostic equipment; do not waste time or risk damaging the components by trying to test the system without such facilities.*
2 Listen for fuel return noises from the fuel pressure regulator. It should be possible to feel the fuel pulsing in the regulator and in the feed hose from the fuel filter.
3 If the pump does not run at all, check the fuse, relay and wiring (see Chapter 12). Check also that the fuel cut-off switch has not been activated and if so, reset it.

### Fuel pressure check

4 A fuel pressure gauge will be required for this check and should be connected in the fuel line between the fuel filter and the CFi unit; follow the gauge maker's instructions.
5 Start the engine and allow it to idle. Note the gauge reading as soon as the pressure stabilises, and compare it with the figures given for regulated fuel pressure in the Specifications. If the pressure is high, check for a restricted fuel return line. If the pressure is low, renew the fuel pressure regulator.

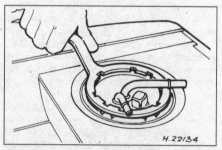

**9.2 Fuel pump/sender unit removal from the fuel tank using Ford special tool 23-026**

6 Switch off the engine, and check that after one minute, the hold pressure has not fallen below that specified. If it has, check the seals on the fuel injector (see Section 13) and renew them if they appear in any way suspect. If the seals are okay, then the fuel pressure regulator or CFi unit are suspect.
7 Carefully disconnect the fuel pressure gauge, depressurising the system first as described in Section 2.
8 Run the engine, and check for fuel leaks.

## 8 Fuel tank - removal, inspection and refitting

1 Proceed as described in Part A, Section 8, but before disconnecting the battery, relieve the residual pressure in the fuel system (see Section 2), and equalise tank pressure by removing the fuel filler cap.

## 9 Fuel pump/fuel gauge sender unit - removal and refitting

**Note:** *Refer to the warning note in Section 1 before proceeding. Ford specify the use of their service tool 23-014 or 23-026 (a large box spanner with projecting teeth to engage the fuel pump/sender unit retaining ring's slots) for this task. While alternatives are possible, in view of the difficulty experienced in removing and refitting the pump/sender unit, it is strongly advised that the correct tool is obtained before starting work.*

### Removal

1 A combined fuel pump and fuel gauge sender unit are located in the top face of the fuel tank. The combined unit can only be detached and withdrawn from the tank after the tank is released and lowered from under the vehicle. Refer to Section 8 and remove the fuel tank, then proceed as follows.
2 With the fuel tank removed, the pump/sender unit can be unscrewed using the special tool **(see illustration)**.
3 Withdraw the unit upwards from the tank **(see illustration)**, and detach the seal ring. The seal ring must be renewed whenever the pump/sender unit is withdrawn from the tank.

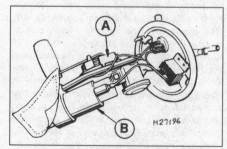

**9.3 In-tank fuel pump (B) and sender unit (A)**

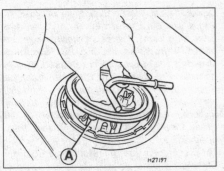

9.4 Fuel pump/sender unit refitting to the tank, showing position of locating lug (A)

## Refitting

4 Refit in the reverse order of removal. Lightly coat the new unit seal ring with grease to ease fitting, and ensure the seal is not distorted as the unit is fitted into position. Insert the unit so that the lug of the unit is in engagement with the slot in the tank aperture, then turn the unit to lock and secure (see illustration).

## 10 Roll-over valve - removal and refitting

Refer to Part A, Section 10.

## 11 Fuel cut-off switch - removal and refitting

## Removal

1 Disconnect the battery negative (earth) lead (refer to Chapter 5A, Section 1).
2 Remove the front footwell side cowl trim panel on the driver's side (see Chapter 11).
3 Undo the retaining screws and withdraw the cut-off (inertia) switch unit from the body (see illustration). As it is withdrawn, disconnect the wiring connector to the switch.

## Refitting

4 Reconnect the wiring connector to the switch, ensuring that it is felt to snap securely into position.
5 Relocate the switch, and refit the screws to secure it.
6 Reset the switch by pushing the top button down, then refit the side cowl trim panel.
7 Reconnect the battery and restart the engine to ensure that the switch has reset.

## 12 Fuel injection system - checking

Note: Refer to the warning note in Section 1 before proceeding.
1 If a fault appears in the fuel injection system, first ensure that all the system wiring connectors are securely connected and free

11.3 Fuel cut-off switch location in the driver's footwell

of corrosion. Ensure that the fault is not due to poor maintenance; ie, check that the air cleaner filter element is clean, the spark plugs are in good condition and correctly gapped, the valve clearances are correctly adjusted, the cylinder compression pressures are correct, the ignition timing is correct (where adjustable), and that the engine breather hoses are clear and undamaged, referring to Chapters 1, 2 and 5 for further information.
2 If these checks fail to reveal the cause of the problem, the vehicle should be taken to a suitably-equipped Ford dealer for testing. A wiring block connector is incorporated in the engine management circuit, into which a special electronic diagnostic tester can be plugged. The tester will locate the fault quickly and simply, alleviating the need to test all the system components individually, which is a time-consuming operation that also carries a risk of damaging the ECU.

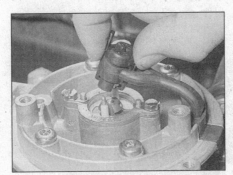

13.4 Disconnect the multi-plug from the injector

13.5b . . . and remove the injector retaining collar

## 13 Fuel injection system components - removal and refitting

Note: Refer to the warning note in Section 1 before proceeding.

## Fuel injector

1 Relieve the residual pressure in the fuel system (see Section 2), and equalise tank pressure by removing the fuel filler cap.

⚠️ Warning: This procedure will merely relieve the increased pressure necessary for the engine to run - remember that fuel will still be present in the system components, and take precautions accordingly before disconnecting any of them.
2 Disconnect the battery negative (earth) lead (refer to Chapter 5A, Section 1).
3 Refer to Section 4 and remove the air cleaner.
4 Release the injector feed wiring multi-plug, and detach it from the injector (pulling on the plug - not the wire) (see illustration).
5 Bend over the locking tabs retaining the injector screws, then undo and remove the screws. Withdraw the injector retaining collar, then carefully withdraw the injector from the CFi unit (noting its orientation) followed by its seal (see illustrations).
6 Refit in the reverse order of removal. Always use new seals in the CFi unit and the retaining collar, and lightly lubricate them with clean engine oil prior to assembly. Take care

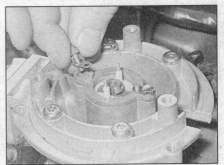

13.5a Remove the injector retaining collar bolt and locktab . . .

13.5c Withdraw the injector from the CFi unit

**4B**

**13.5d  Injector seal location (arrowed) in the CFi unit**

**13.5e  Withdrawing the seal from the injector retaining collar**

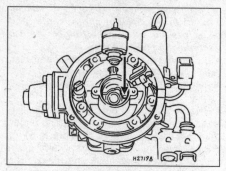

**13.6  Injector location peg position (arrowed)**

**13.8  Fuel pressure regulator and retaining screws (arrowed) - shown in situ**

not to damage the seals as they are fitted and as the injector is fitted, check that the location peg engages correctly **(see illustration)**.

## Fuel pressure regulator

**7**  Refer to paragraphs 14 to 22 in this Section and remove the CFi unit from the vehicle.

**8**  Unscrew and remove the four regulator retaining screws, and remove the regulator **(see illustration)**. As they are removed, note the fitting positions and the orientation of the components. **Do not** (unless absolutely necessary) attempt to prise out the plug or adjust the screw in the centre of the housing (if no plug is fitted), as this will alter the system pressure.

**9**  Examine the components, and renew any that are defective or suspect.

**10**  To refit, position the regulator on its side, then insert the small spring, the valve, diaphragm (ensuring that it seats correctly), large spring, cup and then the regulator cover. Insert and tighten the retaining screws, but take care not overtighten them, or the cover will be distorted.

**11**  Carefully place the ball into position on the spring cup, and ensure that it seats correctly.

**12**  If removed, fit the central Allen type adjuster screw, hand-tighten it and then unscrew it (from the hand-tight position) three full turns to make a provisional adjustment.

**13**  Refit the CFi unit in accordance with paragraphs 23 to 25 in this Section, but note that further checks for fuel leaks must be made with the engine running. The fuel

system pressure must be checked by a Ford dealer or other suitable specialist at the earliest opportunity.

## CFi unit

**14**  Relieve the residual pressure in the fuel system (see Section 2), and equalise tank pressure by removing the fuel filler cap.

⚠️ *Warning: This procedure will merely relieve the increased pressure necessary for the engine to run - remember that fuel will still be present in the system components, and take precautions accordingly before disconnecting any of them.*

**15**  Disconnect the battery negative (earth) lead (refer to Chapter 5A, Section 1).

**16**  Refer to Section 4 and remove the air cleaner.

**17**  Position a suitable drain tray under the coolant hose connections to the CFi unit. Ensure that the cooling system is not pressurised (see Chapter 1), then detach the hoses from the unit. Plug or clamp the hoses to prevent further coolant spillage whilst the hoses are detached.

⚠️ *Warning: DO NOT attempt to remove the expansion tank filler cap, or to disturb any part of the cooling system, while it or the engine is hot, as there is a very great risk of scalding. If the expansion tank filler cap must be removed before the engine and radiator have fully cooled down (even though this is not recommended) the pressure in the cooling system must first be released.*

*Cover the cap with a thick layer of cloth, to avoid scalding, and slowly unscrew the filler cap until a hissing sound can be heard. When the hissing has stopped, showing that pressure is released, slowly unscrew the filler cap further until it can be removed; if more hissing sounds are heard, wait until they have stopped before unscrewing the cap completely. At all times, keep well away from the filler opening.*

**18**  Disconnect the fuel return pipe from the CFi unit.

**19**  Refer to Section 5 and disconnect the accelerator cable from the CFi unit.

**20**  Disconnect the inlet air temperature sensor, throttle plate control motor and throttle position sensor wiring multi-plug connectors.

**21**  Disconnect the vacuum hose from the CFi unit.

**22**  Unscrew and remove the four retaining screws, and remove the CFi unit from the inlet manifold **(see illustration)**. Remove the gasket.

**23**  Clean the CFi unit and the inlet manifold mating faces.

**24**  Refit in the reverse order of removal. Tighten the retaining bolts to the specified torque wrench setting. Check and top-up the cooling system as required (see *"Weekly Checks"* and Chapter 1).

**25**  When the CFi unit is refitted, turn the ignition on and off at least five times to pressurise the system, and check carefully for leaks.

## Throttle plate control motor

**26**  Disconnect the battery negative (earth) lead (refer to Chapter 5A, Section 1).

**27**  Refer to Section 4 and remove the air cleaner.

**28**  Detach the wiring multi-plugs from the throttle position sensor and the throttle plate control motor, and release the retaining clips on the bracket **(see illustrations)**.

**29**  Undo and remove the motor support bracket screws, and remove the bracket complete with the motor from the CFi unit **(see illustration)**.

**30**  Undo the motor retaining screws and remove it from the support bracket.

**13.22  CFi unit retaining screws (arrowed)**

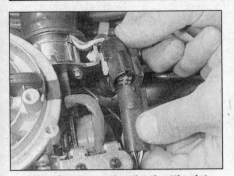

**13.28a  Disconnecting the throttle plate control motor multi-plug**

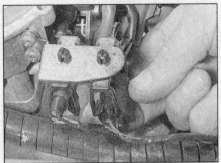

**13.28b  Releasing the throttle position sensor multi-plug from the retaining clip**

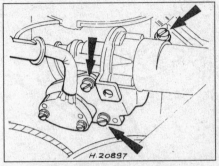

**13.29  Throttle plate control motor retaining screws (arrowed)**

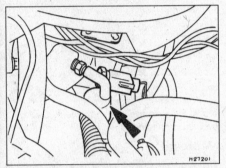

**13.32  Fuel trap location (arrowed) in MAP sensor vacuum hose**

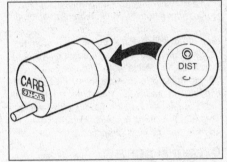

**13.34  Fuel trap orientation markings**

**13.36  ECU location behind the side cowl kick panel in the passenger's footwell**

31  Refit in the reverse order of removal, but note the following points:

a)  *When refitting the motor and its support bracket to the injector unit, the throttle position sensor must locate on the accelerator linkage, and the bracket must align with the pegs.*

b)  *On completion, the idle speed should be checked by a Ford garage or fuel injection specialist who has the required equipment to link up with the engine management ECU.*

## Fuel trap

32  A fuel trap is fitted to the Manifold Absolute Pressure (MAP) sensor hose **(see illustration)**.

33  To remove the fuel trap, first disconnect the battery negative (earth) lead (refer to Chapter 5A, Section 1), then disconnect the vacuum hoses from the fuel trap and withdraw it.

34  Refit in the reverse order of removal. It is important to ensure that the trap is correctly orientated, with the "CARB" mark on one end face towards the inlet manifold, and the "DIST" mark towards the MAP sensor **(see illustration)**.

## ECU

**Note:** *The ECU is fragile. Take care not to drop it, or subject it to any other kind of impact. Do not subject it to extremes of temperature, or allow it to get wet.*

35  Disconnect the battery negative (earth) lead (refer to Chapter 5A, Section 1).

36  Working inside the vehicle, remove the side cowl kick panel from the front passenger's footwell to gain access to the ECU **(see illustration)**.

37  Release the ECU from its retaining bracket **(see illustration)**, then unscrew the retaining bolt and remove the wiring multi-plug.

38  Refitting is the reverse of the removal procedure.

## Crankshaft position sensor

39  Refer to Chapter 5B.

## Coolant temperature sensor

40  Refer to Chapter 3.

## Inlet air temperature sensor

41  Remove the air cleaner assembly as described in Section 4.

**13.37  Release the ECU from its retaining bracket, then unscrew the retaining bolt and remove the wiring multi-plug**

42  Releasing its clip, unplug the sensor's electrical connector, then unscrew the sensor from the CFi unit.

43  Refitting is the reverse of the removal procedure. Be particularly careful to tighten the sensor to the specified torque wrench setting; if it is overtightened, its tapered thread may crack the resonator.

## Throttle position sensor

44  Remove the air cleaner assembly as described in Section 4.

45  Releasing its wire clip, unplug the potentiometer's electrical connector. Remove the retaining screws, and withdraw the unit from the throttle housing **(see illustration)**. *Do not force the sensor's centre to rotate past its normal operating sweep; the unit will be seriously damaged.*

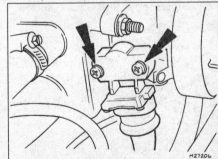

**13.45  Throttle position sensor securing screws (arrowed)**

**4B**

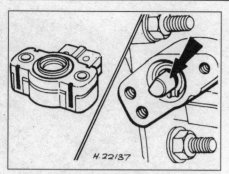

13.46 Align the throttle position sensor "D" section on the throttle shaft (arrowed) when refitting

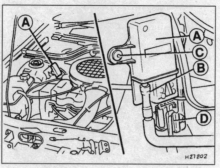

13.48 Manifold absolute pressure (MAP) sensor location and connections

A  MAP sensor        C  Retaining screw(s)
B  Vacuum hose       D  Wiring multi-plug

13.52 Power steering pressure switch location at right-hand rear of engine

46 Refitting is the reverse of the removal procedure, noting the following points:
a) Ensure that the potentiometer is correctly orientated (see illustration), by locating its centre on the D-shaped throttle shaft (throttle closed), and aligning the potentiometer body so that the bolts pass easily into the throttle housing.
b) Tighten the screws evenly and securely (but do not overtighten them, or the potentiometer body will be cracked).

### Vehicle speed sensor

47 The sensor is mounted at the base of the speedometer drive cable, and is removed with the speedometer drive pinion. Refer to the relevant Section of Chapter 7A or B, as applicable.

### Manifold absolute pressure sensor

48 The sensor is located at the rear of the engine compartment, on the right-hand side (see illustration).
49 Disconnect the wiring multi-plug, and detach the vacuum hose from the base of the sensor.
50 Undo the two retaining screws, and withdraw the sensor from its location.
51 Refitting is the reverse of the removal procedure.

### Power steering pressure switch

52 Releasing its clip, unplug the switch's electrical connector, then unscrew the switch

(see illustration). Place some rag underneath, to catch any spilt fluid. If a sealing washer is fitted, renew it if it is worn or damaged.
53 Refitting is a reverse of removal; tighten the switch securely, then top-up the fluid reservoir (see "Weekly Checks") to replace any fluid lost from the system, and bleed out any trapped air (see Chapter 10).

### Oxygen sensor

Note: The sensor is delicate, and will not work if it is dropped or knocked, if its power supply is disrupted, or if any cleaning materials are used on it.
54 Release the sensor's electrical connector from its bracket either on the engine/transmission front mounting or in front of the exhaust manifold, and unplug it to disconnect the sensor.
55 Raise and support the front of the vehicle if required to remove the sensor from underneath (see "Jacking and Vehicle Support"). Unscrew the sensor from the exhaust system front downpipe; collect the sealing washer (where fitted).
56 On refitting, clean the sealing washer (where fitted) and renew it if it is damaged or worn. Apply a smear of anti-seize compound to the sensor's threads, to prevent them from welding themselves to the downpipe in service. Refit the sensor, tightening it to its specified torque wrench setting; a slotted socket will be required to do this. Reconnect the wiring, and refit the connector plug.

### 14 Inlet manifold - removal and refitting

Note: Refer to the warning note in Section 1 before proceeding.

### Removal

1 Drain the cooling system as described in Chapter 1.
2 Remove the CFi unit as described in Section 13.
3 Noting their locations, disconnect the coolant, vacuum and breather hoses from the manifold.
4 Disconnect the wiring multi-plugs from the engine sensors at the inlet manifold. Disconnect the radio earth lead at the inlet manifold connector.
5 Undo the retaining bolts, and withdraw the manifold from the cylinder head. Remove the gasket.
6 With the manifold removed, clean all traces of the old gasket from the mating surfaces of the manifold and the cylinder head.

### Refitting

7 Refitting is the reversal of removal. Use a new gasket, and tighten the retaining bolts to the specified torque. Refit the remainder of the components with reference to the appropriate Chapters of this manual.

# Chapter 4 Part C: Fuel system - electronic fuel injection (EFi) engines

## Contents

## Degrees of difficulty

| | | | | |
|---|---|---|---|---|
| **Easy,** suitable for novice with little experience  | **Fairly easy,** suitable for beginner with some experience  | **Fairly difficult,** suitable for competent DIY mechanic  | **Difficult,** suitable for experienced DIY mechanic | **Very difficult,** suitable for expert DIY or professional |

## Specifications

### General

| | |
|---|---|
| System type ............................................... | Electronic Fuel injection (EFi) |
| Application ............................................... | 1.6 litre CVH engines |

### Fuel grade

| | |
|---|---|
| Fuel octane requirement ................................... | 95 RON unleaded |

### Fuel system data

| | |
|---|---|
| Idle speed and mixture settings ........................... | See Chapter 1 |
| Fuel pump pressure - engine not running ................... | 3.0 bars minimum |
| Regulated fuel pressure - engine running at idle speed ........ | 3.0 ± 0.1 bars |
| Hold pressure - engine stopped after two minutes ............ | Not less than 0.8 bars below regulated pressure |

### Torque wrench settings

| | Nm | lbf ft |
|---|---|---|
| Idle speed control valve bolts ......................... | 4 | 3 |
| Fuel pressure regulator bolts ......................... | 10 | 7 |
| Fuel rail bolts ................................. | 23 | 17 |
| Inlet air temperature sensor ......................... | 23 | 17 |
| Inlet manifold ................................. | 18 | 13 |
| Oxygen sensor ................................. | 60 | 44 |

## 1  General information and precautions

### General information

The fuel system consists of a fuel tank (mounted under the body, beneath the rear seats), fuel hoses, an electric fuel pump mounted in the fuel tank, and an electronic fuel injection system.

Fuel is supplied under pressure from the fuel pump to the fuel distributor rail mounted on top of the inlet manifold **(see illustration)**. The fuel rail acts as a pressurised fuel reservoir for the fuel injectors. The electro-mechanical injectors have only "on" or "off" positions, the volume of fuel being injected to meet the engine operating conditions being determined by the length of time that the injectors are opened. The volume of fuel required for one power stroke is determined by the engine management electronic control unit (ECU), and is divided by two equal amounts. The first half of the required volume is injected into the static air ahead of the inlet valve one complete engine revolution before the inlet valve is due to open. After one further revolution, the inlet valve opens and the required fuel volume is injected into the air flow being drawn into the cylinder. The fuel will therefore be consistently injected to two inlet valves simultaneously at a particular crankshaft position.

The volume of air drawn into the engine is governed by the air filter unit and other variable operating factors. These variables are assessed by the engine management ECU and the corresponding signals are produced to actuate the injectors accordingly.

The engine base idle speed can be adjusted (if required), by turning the adjuster screw (covered by a tamperproof cap) in the throttle housing. Provision for adjusting the fuel mixture is made by the mixture screw in the potentiometer unit mounted on the bulkhead.

The ECU is the heart of the entire engine management system, controlling the fuel injection, ignition and emissions control systems. The ECU receives information from various sensors to determine engine temperature, speed and load, and the quantity of air entering the engine. The sensors also inform the ECU of throttle position, inlet air temperature and exhaust gas oxygen content. All the information supplied to the ECU is computed and compared with pre-set values stored in the ECU memory, to determine the required period of injection.

Information on engine speed is supplied to the ECU by the crankshaft position sensor. This is an inductive pulse generator bolted (in a separate bracket) to the cylinder block/crankcase, to scan the ridges between 36 holes machined in the inboard (right-hand) face of the flywheel/driveplate. As each ridge passes the sensor tip, a signal is generated, which is used by the ECU to determine engine speed.

The ridge between the 35th and 36th holes (corresponding to 90° BTDC) is missing - this step in the incoming signals is used by the ECU to determine crankshaft (ie, piston) position.

Engine temperature information is supplied by the coolant temperature sensor. This component is an NTC (Negative Temperature Coefficient) thermistor - that is, a semi-conductor whose electrical resistance decreases as its temperature increases. It provides the ECU with a constantly-varying (analogue) voltage signal, corresponding to the temperature of the engine coolant. This is used to refine the calculations made by the ECU, when determining the correct amount of fuel required to achieve the ideal air/fuel mixture ratio.

Inlet air temperature information is supplied by the inlet air temperature sensor. This component is also an NTC thermistor - see the previous paragraph - providing the ECU with a signal corresponding to the temperature of air passing into the engine. This is used to refine the calculations made by the ECU, when determining the correct amount of fuel required to achieve the ideal air/fuel mixture ratio.

A throttle position sensor is mounted on the end of the throttle valve spindle, to provide the ECU with a constantly-varying (analogue) voltage signal corresponding to the throttle opening. This allows the ECU to register the driver's input when determining the amount of fuel required by the engine.

Road speed is monitored by the vehicle speed sensor. This component is a Hall-effect generator, mounted on the transmission's speedometer drive. It supplies the ECU with a series of pulses corresponding to the vehicle's road speed, enabling the ECU to control features such as the fuel shut-off on the overrun, and to provide information for the trip computer, adaptive damping and cruise control systems (where fitted).

A manifold absolute pressure sensor measures inlet manifold vacuum, and supplies this information to the ECU for calculation of engine load at any given throttle position.

Where power steering is fitted, a pressure-operated switch is screwed into the power steering system's high-pressure pipe. Its contacts are normally closed, opening when the system reaches the specified pressure - on receiving this signal, the ECU increases the idle speed, to compensate for the additional load on the engine.

The oxygen sensor in the exhaust system provides the ECU with constant feedback - "closed-loop" control - which enables it to adjust the mixture to provide the best possible conditions for the catalytic converter to operate.

**1.2  General view of the fuel injection system arrangement on the 1.6 litre EFi model**

1  Throttle housing
2  Upper inlet manifold section
3  Wiring loom connector
4  Inlet air temperature sensor
5  Wiring harness ducting
6  Fuel distributor rail
7  Lower section of inlet manifold
8  Cylinder head
9  Fuel injector
10  Fuel pressure regulator
11  Vacuum hose
12  Air inlet duct

### Precautions

 **Warning: Petrol is extremely flammable - great care must be taken when working on any part of the fuel system. Do not smoke or allow any naked flames or uncovered light bulbs near the work area. Note that gas powered**

domestic appliances with pilot flames, such as heaters, boilers and tumble dryers, also present a fire hazard - bear this in mind if you are working in an area where such appliances are present. Always keep a suitable fire extinguisher close to the work area and familiarise yourself with its operation before starting work. Wear eye protection when working on fuel systems and wash off any fuel spilt on bare skin immediately with soap and water. Note that fuel vapour is just as dangerous as liquid fuel; a vessel that has just been emptied of liquid fuel will still contain vapour and can be potentially explosive. Petrol is a highly dangerous and volatile liquid, and the precautions necessary when handling it cannot be overstressed.

Many of the operations described in this Chapter involve the disconnection of fuel lines, which may cause an amount of fuel spillage. Before commencing work, refer to the above Warning and the information in "Safety first" at the start of this manual.

When working with fuel system components, pay particular attention to cleanliness - dirt entering the fuel system may cause blockages which will lead to poor running.

**Note:** Residual pressure will remain in the fuel lines long after the vehicle was last used, when disconnecting any fuel line, it will be necessary to depressurise the fuel system as described in Section 2.

### 2  Fuel system - depressurisation

Refer to Part B, Section 2.

### 3  Fuel lines and fittings - general information

Refer to Part B, Section 3.

### 4  Air cleaner assembly and air inlet components - removal and refitting

**Note:** Air cleaner element renewal is described in Chapter 1.

#### Air cleaner assembly

1 Disconnect the battery negative (earth) lead (refer to Chapter 5A, Section 1).
2 Undo the retaining nut at the front, then loosen off the air duct-to-filter housing clip screw, and detach the air duct from the housing.
3 Unscrew and remove the two retaining nuts on the underside of the housing (that secure it to the location studs).

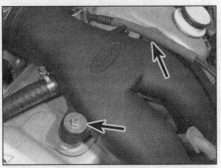

**4.8  Undo the two retaining bolts (arrowed) and remove the air inlet duct from the rocker cover**

4 Disconnect the hose at the base of the unit (to the inlet manifold) and lift the air cleaner clear.
5 Refit in the reverse order of removal. Ensure that the air hose and duct are securely located.

#### Air inlet components

6 Disconnect the HT leads from the spark plugs, labelling them if necessary to avoid confusion on refitting.
7 Slacken the retaining clips, and detach the air inlet hose and breather hose from the air inlet duct.
8 Undo the two retaining bolts, and remove the air inlet duct from the rocker cover (see illustration).
9 Slacken the retaining clip, and remove the air inlet hose from the air cleaner assembly.
10 Refitting is the reverse of the removal procedure.

### 5  Accelerator cable - removal, refitting and adjustment

#### Removal

1 Disconnect the battery negative (earth) lead (refer to Chapter 5A, Section 1).
2 Fold back the carpet and insulation in the driver's footwell to gain access to the accelerator pedal.
3 Detach the accelerator cable from the pedal.

**5.4  Disconnecting the accelerator inner cable from the throttle quadrant**

4 Working at the throttle housing end of the cable, pivot the throttle quadrant by hand to release the tension from the cable, then detach the inner cable nipple from the throttle lever (see illustration).
5 Detach the outer cable from the adjuster/support bracket, then remove the cable (see illustration).

#### Refitting and adjustment

6 Refit in the reverse order of removal. When the cable is reconnected at each end, have an assistant depress the accelerator, and check that the throttle fully opens and shuts without binding. Ensure that there is a small amount of slack in the inner cable when the throttle is fully released. If adjustment is required, release the outer cable retaining clip from the cable at the adjustment/support bracket, slide the cable through the adjuster grommet to the point required, then refit the retaining clip to secure it in the set position.

### 6  Accelerator pedal - removal and refitting

Refer to Part A, Section 5.

### 7  Fuel pump/fuel pressure - checking

**Note:** Refer to the warning note in Section 1 before proceeding.

#### Fuel pump operation check

1 Switch on the ignition, and listen for the fuel pump (the sound of an electric motor running, audible from beneath the rear seats). Assuming there is sufficient fuel in the tank, the pump should start and run for approximately one or two seconds, then stop, each time the ignition is switched on. **Note:** If the pump runs continuously all the time the ignition is switched on, the electronic control system is running in the backup (or "limp-home") mode referred to by Ford as "Limited Operation Strategy" (LOS). This almost certainly indicates a fault in the ECU itself, and the vehicle should therefore be taken to a Ford

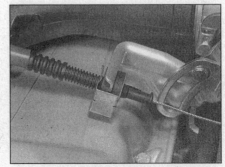

**5.5  Accelerator outer cable location at the adjuster/support bracket**

**4C**

dealer for a full test of the complete system, using the correct diagnostic equipment; do not waste time or risk damaging the components by trying to test the system without such facilities.

**2** Listen for fuel return noises from the fuel pressure regulator. It should be possible to feel the fuel pulsing in the regulator and in the feed hose from the fuel filter.

**3** If the pump does not run at all, check the fuse, relay and wiring (see Chapter 12). Check also that the fuel cut-off switch has not been activated and if so, reset it.

### Fuel pressure check

**4** A fuel pressure gauge will be required for this check and should be connected in the fuel line between the fuel filter and the fuel rail, in accordance with the gauge maker's instructions.

**5** Disconnect the wiring from the E-DIS ignition coil and the fuel injectors.

**6** Switch the ignition on and off twice, and check that the pump pressure is as listed in the Specifications.

**7** If the pressure is not as specified, check the fuel system for leaks or damage. If the system appears okay, renew the fuel pump.

**8** Reconnect the wiring to the ignition coil and fuel injectors.

**9** If the pump pressure was satisfactory, start the engine and allow it to idle. Disconnect the vacuum hose at the fuel pressure regulator, and plug the hose. Note the gauge reading as soon as the pressure stabilises, and compare it with the figures given for regulated fuel pressure in the Specifications.

**10** If the regulated fuel pressure is not as specified, remove the plug from the top of the fuel pressure regulator, and using an Allen key, adjust the pressure regulator as necessary.

**11** Switch off the engine, and check that the fuel pressure stays at the specified hold pressure for two minutes after the engine is turned off.

**12** Carefully disconnect the fuel pressure gauge, depressurising the system first as described in Section 2. Reconnect the ignition coil and fuel injector wiring. Reconnect the vacuum hose.

**13** Run the engine, and check that there are no fuel leaks.

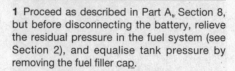

## 8 Fuel tank - removal, inspection and refitting

**1** Proceed as described in Part A, Section 8, but before disconnecting the battery, relieve the residual pressure in the fuel system (see Section 2), and equalise tank pressure by removing the fuel filler cap.

## 9 Fuel pump/fuel gauge sender unit - removal and refitting

Refer to Part B, Section 9.

## 10 Roll-over valve - removal and refitting

Refer to Part A, Section 10.

## 11 Fuel cut-off switch - removal and refitting

Refer to Part B, Section 11.

## 12 Fuel injection system - checking

Refer to Part B, Section 12.

## 13 Fuel injection system components - removal and refitting

**Note:** *Refer to the warning note in Section 1 before proceeding.*

### Fuel rail and injectors

**Note:** *For simplicity, and to ensure that the necessary absolute cleanliness on reassembly, the following procedure describes the removal of the fuel rail assembly, complete with the*

injectors and pressure regulator, so that the injectors can be serviced individually on a clean work surface. It is also possible to remove and refit an individual injector, once the fuel system has been depressurised and the battery has been disconnected. If this approach is followed, read through the complete procedure, and work as described in the relevant paragraphs, depending on the amount of preliminary dismantling required. Be careful not to allow any dirt to enter the system.

**1** Relieve the residual pressure in the fuel system (see Section 2), and equalise tank pressure by removing the fuel filler cap.

⚠️ **Warning: This procedure will merely relieve the increased pressure necessary for the engine to run - remember that fuel will still be present in the system components, and take precautions accordingly before disconnecting any of them.**

**2** Disconnect the battery negative (earth) lead (refer to Chapter 5A, Section 1).

**3** Loosen off the retaining clip, and detach the hot-air hose duct from the exhaust manifold **(see illustration)**.

**4** Disconnect the ignition HT lead connectors from the spark plugs, and release the leads from their locating grooves in the air inlet duct. Position them out of the way.

**5** Unscrew the retaining nuts and the bolt, and detach the accelerator cable support bracket at the throttle housing.

**6** Disconnect the wiring connector from the throttle position sensor.

**7** Unscrew the four retaining bolts, and remove the throttle housing and its mating face gasket **(see illustration)**.

**8** Disconnect the wiring multi-plug from the engine coolant temperature sensor and the air inlet temperature sensor.

**9** Disconnect the wiring connectors from the fuel injectors, then undo the two retaining nuts and detach the wiring harness from the fuel rail **(see illustrations)**.

**10** Unscrew the fuel supply pipe at the fuel rail. Plug the rail and pipe, to prevent further fuel spillage and the possible ingress of dirt.

**11** Disconnect the fuel return and vacuum pipes from the pressure regulator, and catch any fuel spillage in a clean cloth.

**12** Unscrew the fuel rail securing bolts, and

**13.3  Disconnecting the hot-air duct from the exhaust manifold**

**13.7  Throttle housing retaining bolt locations (arrowed)**

**13.9a  Disconnect the wiring connector from each injector . . .**

**13.9b . . . undo the wiring harness nuts . . .**

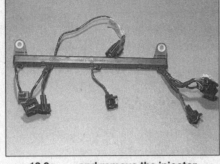

**13.9c . . . and remove the injector wiring harness**

**13.12a Remove the injector rail retaining bolts . . .**

**13.12b . . . release each injector . . .**

**13.12c . . . and withdraw the fuel rail and injectors**

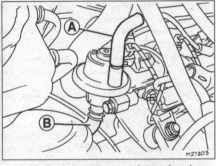

**13.20 Fuel pressure regulator showing vacuum pipe (A) and return pipe connections (B)**

**13.24 Idle speed control valve and wiring connector**

carefully withdraw the rail (complete with injectors) from the engine **(see illustrations).**
**13** Detach the fuel injectors from the fuel rail, then remove the upper and lower seal from each injector. All seals must be renewed (even if only one injector is to be renewed).
**14** Prior to refitting the injectors, ensure that all mating surfaces are perfectly clean. Lubricate the new injector seals with clean engine oil to ease their assembly to the injectors.
**15** Refitting is a reversal of the removal procedure. Refer to the Specifications at the start of this Chapter for the tightening torques. When refitting the fuel rail, ensure that the injectors are correctly located. Ensure that the mating surfaces of the throttle housing are perfectly clean before assembling.
**16** On completion, restart the engine and check the various fuel connections for any signs of leaks.

### Fuel pressure regulator

**17** Relieve the residual pressure in the fuel system (see Section 2), and equalise tank pressure by removing the fuel filler cap.

⚠ *Warning: This procedure will merely relieve the increased pressure necessary for the engine to run - remember that fuel will still be present in the system components, and take precautions accordingly before disconnecting any of them.*

**18** Disconnect the battery negative (earth) lead (refer to Chapter 5A, Section 1).
**19** Release the fuel return pipe securing clip, and detach the pipe from the regulator.
**20** Pull free the vacuum pipe from the regulator connector **(see illustration).**
**21** Unscrew the two retaining bolts and remove the regulator. Remove the old sealing ring for renewal.

**22** Refit in the reverse order of removal. Lubricate the new seal ring with clean engine oil to ease assembly. When the regulator is refitted and the fuel and vacuum lines are reconnected, turn the ignition on and off five times (without cranking the engine) and check for fuel leaks before restarting the engine.

### Idle speed control valve

**23** Disconnect the battery negative (earth) lead (refer to Chapter 5A, Section 1).
**24** Unplug the valve's electrical connector **(see illustration).**
**25** Undo the four retaining screws, and remove the idle speed control valve.
**26** Refitting is a reversal of the removal procedure. Ensure that the mating faces of the valve and inlet manifold are clean before reassembling.
**27** When the valve is refitted, restart the engine and check that there are no induction leaks. Run the engine until its normal operating temperature is reached, and check that the idle speed is stable. Stop the engine, connect up a tachometer in accordance with its maker's instructions, then restart the engine and check that the idle speed is as specified with all electrical items (lights, heater blower motor, etc) switched off, then on. The idle speed should remain the same. Switch off the electrical items, turn the engine off and detach the tachometer to complete the test.

### Throttle housing

**28** Relieve the residual pressure in the fuel system (see Section 2), and equalise tank pressure by removing the fuel filler cap.

⚠ *Warning: This procedure will merely relieve the increased pressure necessary for the engine to run - remember that fuel will still be present in the system components, and take precautions accordingly before disconnecting any of them.*

**29** Disconnect the battery negative (earth) lead (refer to Chapter 5A, Section 1).
**30** Loosen off the retaining clip, and detach the hot-air duct from the exhaust manifold **(see illustration 13.3).**
**31** Disconnect the ignition HT lead connectors from the spark plugs, and release the leads from their locating grooves in the air inlet duct. Position them out of the way.

**4C**

**32** Unscrew the retaining nuts and the bolt, and detach the accelerator cable support bracket at the throttle housing.

**33** Disconnect the vacuum hoses from the inlet manifold and the fuel pressure regulator.

**34** Detach the wiring connections from the idle speed control valve, the temperature sensor and the harness connector.

**35** Disconnect the fuel return hose from the pressure regulator unit.

**36** Unscrew the throttle housing-to-manifold retaining bolts, and unbolt the throttle housing support bracket bolts **(see illustration 13.7)**. Remove the throttle housing and gasket.

**37** Refit in the reverse order of removal. Check that the mating faces are clean, and fit a new gasket.

### ECU

**Note:** *The ECU is fragile. Take care not to drop it, or subject it to any other kind of impact. Do not subject it to extremes of temperature, or allow it to get wet.*

**38** Disconnect the battery negative (earth) lead (refer to Chapter 5A, Section 1).

**39** Working inside the vehicle, remove the side cowl kick panel from the front passenger's footwell to gain access to the ECU.

**40** Release the ECU from its retaining bracket, then unscrew the retaining bolt and remove the wiring multi-plug.

**41** Refitting is the reverse of the removal procedure.

### Crankshaft position sensor

**42** Refer to Chapter 5B.

### Coolant temperature sensor

**43** Refer to Chapter 3.

### Inlet air temperature sensor

**44** Remove the air inlet ducting as described in Section 4.

**45** Releasing its clip, unplug the sensor's electrical connector, then unscrew the sensor from the inlet manifold.

**46** Refitting is the reverse of the removal procedure.

### Throttle position sensor

**47** Remove the air inlet ducting as described in Section 4.

**48** Releasing its wire clip, unplug the sensorÕs electrical connector. Remove the retaining screws, and withdraw the unit from the throttle housing. *Do not* force the sensor's centre to rotate past its normal operating sweep; the unit will be seriously damaged.

**49** Refitting is the reverse of the removal procedure, noting the following points:

a) *Ensure that the potentiometer is correctly orientated, by locating its centre on the D-shaped throttle shaft (throttle closed), and aligning the potentiometer body so that the bolts pass easily into the throttle housing.*

b) *Tighten the screws evenly and securely (but do not overtighten them, or the potentiometer body will be cracked).*

### Vehicle speed sensor

**50** The sensor is mounted at the base of the speedometer drive cable, and is removed with the speedometer drive pinion. Refer to the relevant Section of Chapter 7A or B, as applicable.

### Manifold absolute pressure sensor

**51** The sensor is located at the rear of the engine compartment, on the right-hand side.

**52** Disconnect the wiring multi-plug, and detach the vacuum hose from the base of the sensor.

**53** Undo the two retaining screws, and withdraw the sensor from its location.

**54** Refitting is the reverse of the removal procedure.

### Power steering pressure switch

**55** Releasing its clip, unplug the switch's electrical connector, then unscrew the switch. Place a wad of rag underneath, to catch any spilt fluid. If a sealing washer is fitted, renew it if it is worn or damaged.

**56** Refitting is the reverse of the removal procedure; tighten the switch securely, then top-up the fluid reservoir (see *"Weekly Checks"*) to replace any fluid lost from the system, and bleed out any trapped air (see Chapter 10).

### Oxygen sensor

**Note:** *The sensor is delicate, and will not work if it is dropped or knocked, if its power supply is disrupted, or if any cleaning materials are used on it.*

**57** Release the sensor's electrical connector from its bracket on the engine/transmission front mounting, and unplug it to disconnect the sensor.

**58** Raise and support the front of the vehicle if required to remove the sensor from underneath (see *"Jacking and Vehicle Support"*). Unscrew the sensor from the exhaust system front downpipe; collect the sealing washer (where fitted).

**59** On refitting, clean the sealing washer (where fitted) and renew it if it is damaged or worn. Apply a smear of anti-seize compound to the sensor's threads, to prevent them from welding themselves to the downpipe in service. Refit the sensor, tightening it to its specified torque wrench setting; a slotted socket will be required to do this. Reconnect the wiring, and refit the connector plug.

## 14 Inlet manifold - removal and refitting

**Note:** *Refer to the warning note in Section 1 before proceeding.*

### Removal

**1** The inlet manifold is a two-piece assembly comprising an upper and lower section bolted together.

**2** Drain the cooling system with reference to Chapter 1.

**3** Depressurise the fuel system as described in Section 2.

**4** Disconnect the battery negative (earth) lead (refer to Chapter 5A, Section 1).

**5** Remove the air inlet duct (Section 4) and disconnect the accelerator cable from the throttle linkage (Section 5).

**6** Remove the fuel injectors and fuel rail as described in Section 13.

**7** Noting their locations, disconnect the coolant, vacuum and breather hoses from the manifold.

**8** Disconnect the wiring multi-plugs from the engine sensors at the inlet manifold.

**9** Undo the retaining bolts, and withdraw the manifold from the cylinder head. Note the location of the engine lifting bracket and earth lead, where fitted. Remove the gasket.

**10** With the manifold removed, clean all traces of the old gasket from the mating surfaces of the manifold and the cylinder head.

### Refitting

**11** Refitting is the reversal of removal. Use a new gasket, and tighten the retaining bolts to the specified torque. Refit the remainder of the components with reference to the appropriate Chapters of this manual. Refill the cooling system as described in Chapter 1 on completion.

# Chapter 4 Part D: Fuel system - sequential electronic fuel injection (SEFi) engines

## Contents

## Degrees of difficulty

| | | | | |
|---|---|---|---|---|
| **Easy,** suitable for novice with little experience  | **Fairly easy,** suitable for beginner with some experience  | **Fairly difficult,** suitable for competent DIY mechanic  | **Difficult,** suitable for experienced DIY mechanic | **Very difficult,** suitable for expert DIY or professional |

## Specifications

### General

System type . . . . . . . . . . . . . . . . . . . . . . . . . . . . . . . . . . . . . . . . . . . Sequential Electronic Fuel injection (SEFi)
Application . . . . . . . . . . . . . . . . . . . . . . . . . . . . . . . . . . . . . . . . . . . . 1.3 litre Endura-E engines, 1.4 litre PTE engines,
  1.6 and 1.8 litre Zetec and Zetec-E engines

### Fuel grade

Fuel octane requirement . . . . . . . . . . . . . . . . . . . . . . . . . . . . . . . . . 95 RON unleaded

### Fuel system data

**Fuel pressure**

Regulated fuel pressure - engine running at idle speed:*
  Pressure regulator vacuum hose connected . . . . . . . . . . . . . . . . . 2.1 ± 0.2 bars
  Pressure regulator vacuum hose disconnected . . . . . . . . . . . . . . . 2.7 ± 0.2 bars
Hold pressure - engine stopped after five minutes* . . . . . . . . . . . . . 1.8 bars minimum

*The figures quoted are specific to the Zetec and Zetec-E engines. No values are quoted by the manufacturer for the Endura-E and PTE engines, however they are likely to be similar.

## Torque wrench settings

| | Nm | lbf ft |
|---|---|---|
| **Endura-E engines** | | |
| Inlet manifold to cylinder head | 18 | 13 |
| Crankshaft position sensor | 6 | 4 |
| Camshaft position sensor | 10 | 7 |
| Oxygen sensor | 60 | 44 |
| **PTE engines** | | |
| Inlet air duct to cylinder head cover | 10 | 7 |
| Inlet manifold to cylinder head | 18 | 13 |
| Inlet manifold upper to lower sections | 18 | 13 |
| Inlet air temperature sensor | 15 | 11 |
| Fuel rail-to-lower inlet manifold | 23 | 17 |
| Camshaft position sensor | 6 | 4 |
| Oxygen sensor | 60 | 44 |
| **Zetec and Zetec-E engines** | | |
| Throttle housing-to-inlet manifold screws | 10 | 7 |
| Inlet manifold to cylinder head | 18 | 13 |
| Idle speed control valve bolts | 6 | 4 |
| Fuel pressure regulator bolts | 6 | 4 |
| Fuel injector bolts | 6 | 4 |
| Fuel rail-to-inlet manifold bolts | 10 | 7 |
| Camshaft position sensor | 8 | 6 |
| Oxygen sensor | 60 | 44 |

## 1  General information and precautions

### General information

The fuel system consists of a fuel tank (mounted under the body, beneath the rear seats), fuel hoses, an electric fuel pump mounted in the fuel tank, and a sequential electronic fuel injection system.

The electric fuel pump supplies fuel under pressure to the fuel rail, which distributes fuel evenly to all injectors. A pressure regulator controls the system pressure in relation to inlet tract depression. From the fuel rail, fuel is injected into the inlet ports, just above the inlet valves, by four fuel injectors. The system also includes features such as the flushing of fresh (ie, cold) fuel around each injector on start-up, thus improving hot starts.

The amount of fuel supplied by the injectors is precisely controlled by the engine management electronic control unit (ECU). The ECU uses the signals derived from the crankshaft position sensor and the camshaft position sensor, to trigger each injector separately in cylinder firing order (sequential injection), with benefits in terms of better fuel economy and lower exhaust emissions.

The ECU is the heart of the entire engine management system, controlling the fuel injection, ignition and emissions control systems. The ECU receives information from various sensors which is then computed and compared with pre-set values stored in the ECU memory, to determine the required period of injection.

Engine speed information is supplied to the ECU by the crankshaft position sensor. This is an inductive pulse generator bolted to the cylinder block/crankcase, to scan the ridges between 36 holes machined in the inboard (right-hand) face of the flywheel/driveplate. As each ridge passes the sensor tip, a signal is generated, which is used by the ECU to determine engine speed. The ridge between the 35th and 36th holes (corresponding to 90° BTDC) is missing - this step in the incoming signals is used by the ECU to determine crankshaft (ie, piston) position.

The camshaft position sensor is located in the cylinder head on PTE, Zetec and Zetec-E engines, so that it registers with a lobe on the camshaft. On Endura-E engines the sensor is attached to the timing chain cover and registers with a rotor plate bolted to the camshaft sprocket. The camshaft position sensor functions in the same way as the crankshaft position sensor, producing a series of pulses; this gives the ECU a reference point, to enable it to determine the firing order, and operate the injectors in the appropriate sequence.

The mass air flow sensor is based on a "hot-wire" system, sending the ECU a constantly-varying (analogue) voltage signal corresponding to the mass of air passing into the engine. Since air mass varies with temperature (cold air being denser than warm), measuring air mass provides the ECU with a very accurate means of determining the correct amount of fuel required to achieve the ideal air/fuel mixture ratio.

Engine temperature information is supplied by the coolant temperature sensor. This component is an NTC (Negative Temperature Coefficient) thermistor - that is, a semiconductor whose electrical resistance decreases as its temperature increases. It provides the ECU with a constantly-varying (analogue) voltage signal, corresponding to the temperature of the engine coolant. This is used to refine the calculations made by the ECU, when determining the correct amount of fuel required to achieve the ideal air/fuel mixture ratio.

Inlet air temperature information is supplied by the inlet air temperature sensor. This component is also an NTC thermistor - see the previous paragraph - providing the ECU with a signal corresponding to the temperature of air passing into the engine. This is used to refine the calculations made by the ECU, when determining the correct amount of fuel required to achieve the ideal air/fuel mixture ratio.

A throttle position sensor is mounted on the end of the throttle valve spindle, to provide the ECU with a constantly-varying (analogue) voltage signal corresponding to the throttle opening. This allows the ECU to register the driver's input when determining the amount of fuel required by the engine.

Road speed is monitored by the vehicle speed sensor. This component is a Hall-effect generator, mounted on the transmission's speedometer drive. It supplies the ECU with a series of pulses corresponding to the vehicle's road speed, enabling the ECU to control features such as the fuel shut-off on the overrun, and to provide information for the trip computer, adaptive damping and cruise control systems (where fitted).

Where power steering is fitted, a pressure-operated switch is screwed into the power steering system's high-pressure pipe. Its contacts are normally closed, opening when the system reaches the specified pressure - on receiving this signal, the ECU increases the idle speed, to compensate for the additional load on the engine.

The oxygen sensor in the exhaust system provides the ECU with constant feedback - "closed-loop" control - which enables it to adjust the mixture to provide the best possible conditions for the catalytic converter to operate.

The air inlet side of the system consists of an air cleaner housing, the mass air flow sensor, an inlet hose and duct, and a throttle housing.

The throttle valve inside the throttle housing is controlled by the driver, through the accelerator pedal. As the valve opens, the amount of air that can pass through the system increases. As the throttle valve opens further, the mass air flow sensor signal alters, and the ECU opens each injector for a longer duration, to increase the amount of fuel delivered to the inlet ports.

Both the idle speed and mixture are under the control of the ECU, and cannot be adjusted. Not only can they not be adjusted, they cannot even be checked, except with the use of special Ford diagnostic equipment.

## Precautions

⚠️ *Warning: Petrol is extremely flammable - great care must be taken when working on any part of the fuel system. Do not smoke or allow any naked flames or uncovered light bulbs near the work area. Note that gas powered domestic appliances with pilot flames, such as heaters, boilers and tumble dryers, also present a fire hazard - bear this in mind if you are working in an area where such appliances are present. Always keep a suitable fire extinguisher close to the work area and familiarise yourself with its operation before starting work. Wear eye protection when working on fuel systems and wash off any fuel spilt on bare skin immediately with soap and water. Note that fuel vapour is just as dangerous as liquid fuel; a vessel that has just been emptied of liquid fuel will still contain vapour and can be potentially explosive. Petrol is a highly dangerous and volatile liquid, and the precautions necessary when handling it cannot be overstressed.*

*Many of the operations described in this Chapter involve the disconnection of fuel lines, which may cause an amount of fuel*

*spillage. Before commencing work, refer to the above Warning and the information in "Safety first" at the start of this manual.*

*When working with fuel system components, pay particular attention to cleanliness - dirt entering the fuel system may cause blockages which will lead to poor running.*

**Note:** *Residual pressure will remain in the fuel lines long after the vehicle was last used, when disconnecting any fuel line, it will be necessary to depressurise the fuel system as described in Section 2.*

### 2  Fuel system - depressurisation

Refer to Part B, Section 2.

### 3  Fuel lines and fittings - general information

Refer to Part B, Section 3.

### 4  Air cleaner assembly and air inlet components - removal and refitting

## Air cleaner assembly

**Note:** *The air cleaner assembly is basically the*

same on all engines with sequential electronic fuel injection. The following procedure is a general guide to cover all types.

1 Disconnect the battery negative (earth) lead (refer to Chapter 5A, Section 1).
2 Detach the crankcase breather hose from the air cleaner housing (see illustration).
3 Disconnect the mass air flow sensor wiring multi-plug, then release the clips and withdraw the sensor, complete with inlet hose, from the air cleaner cover (see illustrations). Carefully position the mass air flow sensor and hose assembly to one side.
4 Detach the air inlet duct from the air cleaner housing.
5 Unscrew the air cleaner housing retaining nut(s), then pull the housing sharply upwards to release the locating pegs from their rubber grommets. Remove the assembly from the car.
6 Refitting is the reverse of the removal procedure. Ensure that the housing pegs seat fully in their grommets, and that the air inlet duct is correctly located.

## Air inlet components

7 Where applicable, disconnect the wiring multi-plug at the inlet air temperature sensor in the air inlet hose (see illustration). Slacken the hose clips at each end, and detach the air inlet hose from the inlet duct or throttle housing, and from the mass air flow sensor (see illustration). On some engines, there is a small projection on the end of the hose, which engages with a cut-out in the inlet duct to ensure correct orientation when refitting.

**4D**

4.2  Detach the crankcase breather hose from the air cleaner housing

4.3a  Disconnect the mass air flow sensor wiring multi-plug . . .

4.3b  . . . release the two clips and withdraw the sensor, complete with inlet hose

4.7a  Disconnect the wiring multi-plug at the inlet air temperature sensor in the air inlet hose (Zetec-E engine shown)

4.7b  Detach air inlet hose from inlet duct. Note small projection on end of the hose which engages with a cut-out in inlet duct

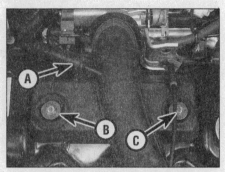

**4.8a Where an additional inlet duct is fitted over the top of the engine, disconnect the ventilation hose (A), and undo the two nuts or bolts (B and C) . . .**

**4.8b . . . or undo the two nuts (arrowed) and lift off the inlet duct retaining strap**

**8** Where an additional inlet duct is fitted over the top of the engine, disconnect the ventilation hose, undo the two nuts or bolts and, where fitted, lift off the air inlet duct retaining strap **(see illustrations)**. On PTE engines it may be beneficial to disconnect the HT leads from the spark plugs to facilitate removal. Withdraw the inlet duct from the throttle housing.

**9** Refitting is the reverse of the removal procedure, but ensure correct orientation of the inlet hose by aligning the projections and cut-outs. Tighten the inlet air duct to cylinder head cover fastenings to the specified torque (PTE engines).

## 5 Accelerator cable - removal, refitting and adjustment

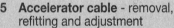

### Removal

**1** Disconnect the battery negative (earth) lead (refer to Chapter 5A, Section 1).
**2** Fold back the carpet and insulation in the driver's footwell to gain access to the accelerator pedal.
**3** Detach the accelerator cable from the pedal.
**4** Remove the air inlet components as necessary for access to the cable attachment at the throttle housing (see Section 4).
**5** Working at the throttle housing end of the cable, pivot the throttle quadrant by hand to

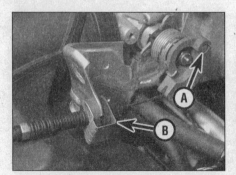

**5.5 Accelerator cable attachment at the throttle quadrant (A) and at the adjuster/support bracket (B)**

release the tension from the cable, then detach the inner cable nipple from the throttle lever **(see illustration)**.
**6** Detach the outer cable from the adjuster/support bracket, either by removing the retaining clip, or by turning the outer cable end fitting 45° anti-clockwise, then remove the cable **(see illustration)**.

### Refitting

**7** Refit in the reverse order of removal. When the cable is reconnected at each end, adjust the cable as follows.

### Adjustment

**8** Locate the cable adjuster - this is either at the adjuster/support bracket, or further along the cable, over the top of the engine. Remove the metal clip and lubricate the adjuster grommet with soapy water.
**9** Remove any slack by pulling the cable outer as far as possible out of the adjuster. Have an assistant depress the accelerator pedal fully - the cable outer will move back into the adjuster - and hold it there while the clip is refitted.
**10** Check that the throttle quadrant moves smoothly and easily from the fully-closed to the fully-open position and back again as the assistant depresses and releases the accelerator pedal. Re-adjust the cable if required.
**11** On completion, refit any air cleaner components removed for access.

**5.6 With this type of cable attachment, release the outer cable by turning the end fitting (arrowed) 45° anti-clockwise**

## 6 Accelerator pedal - removal and refitting

Refer to Part A, Section 5.

## 7 Fuel pump/fuel pressure - checking

**Note:** *Refer to the warning note in Section 1 before proceeding.*

### Fuel pump operation check

**1** Switch on the ignition, and listen for the fuel pump (the sound of an electric motor running, audible from beneath the rear seats). Assuming there is sufficient fuel in the tank, the pump should start and run for approximately one or two seconds, then stop, each time the ignition is switched on. **Note:** *If the pump runs continuously all the time the ignition is switched on, the electronic control system is running in the backup (or "limp-home") mode referred to by Ford as "Limited Operation Strategy" (LOS). This almost certainly indicates a fault in the ECU itself, and the vehicle should therefore be taken to a Ford dealer for a full test of the complete system, using the correct diagnostic equipment; do not waste time or risk damaging the components by trying to test the system without such facilities.*
**2** Listen for fuel return noises from the fuel pressure regulator. It should be possible to feel the fuel pulsing in the regulator and in the feed hose from the fuel filter.
**3** If the pump does not run at all, check the fuse, relay and wiring (see Chapter 12). Check also that the fuel cut-off switch has not been activated and if so, reset it.

### Fuel pressure check

**4** A fuel pressure gauge will be required for this check and should be connected in the fuel line between the fuel filter and the fuel rail, in accordance with the gauge maker's instructions. On Zetec and Zetec-E engines, a pressure gauge equipped with an adapter to suit the Schrader-type valve on the fuel rail pressure test/release fitting (identifiable by its blue plastic cap, and located on the union of the fuel feed line and the fuel rail) will be required. If the Ford special tool 29-033 is available, the tool can be attached to the valve, and a conventional-type pressure gauge attached to the tool.
**5** If using the service tool, ensure that its tap is turned fully anti-clockwise, then attach it to the valve. Connect the pressure gauge to the service tool. If using a fuel pressure gauge with its own adapter, connect it in accordance with its maker's instructions **(see illustration)**.
**6** Start the engine and allow it to idle. Note the gauge reading as soon as the pressure

**7.5 Fuel pressure gauge connected to the fuel line**

stabilises, and compare it with the regulated fuel pressure figures listed in the Specifications.

a) *If the pressure is high, check for a restricted fuel return line. If the line is clear, renew the fuel pressure regulator.*

b) *If the pressure is low, pinch the fuel return line. If the pressure now goes up, renew the fuel pressure regulator. If the pressure does not increase, check the fuel feed line, the fuel pump and the fuel filter.*

**7** Detach the vacuum hose from the fuel pressure regulator; the gauge pressure should increase. Note the increase in pressure, and compare it with the Specifications. If the pressure increase is not as specified, check the vacuum hose and pressure regulator.

**8** Reconnect the regulator vacuum hose, and switch off the engine. Verify that the hold pressure stays at the specified level for five minutes after the engine is turned off.

**9** Carefully disconnect the fuel pressure gauge, depressurising the system first as described in Section 2. Be sure to cover the fitting with a rag before slackening it. Mop up any spilt petrol if necessary.

**10** Run the engine, and check that there are no fuel leaks.

## 8 Fuel tank - removal, inspection and refitting

Proceed as described in Part A, Section 8, but before disconnecting the battery, relieve the residual pressure in the fuel system (see Section 2), and equalise tank pressure by removing the fuel filler cap.

## 9 Fuel pump/fuel gauge sender unit - removal and refitting

Refer to Part B, Section 9.

## 10 Roll-over valve - removal and refitting

Refer to Part A, Section 10.

## 11 Fuel cut-off switch - removal and refitting

Refer to Part B, Section 11.

## 12 Fuel injection system - checking

Refer to Part B, Section 12.

## 13 Fuel injection system components - removal and refitting

**Note:** *Refer to the warning note in Section 1 before proceeding.*

### Throttle housing

**1** Relieve the residual pressure in the fuel system (see Section 2), and equalise tank pressure by removing the fuel filler cap.

⚠️ *Warning: This procedure will merely relieve the increased pressure necessary for the engine to run - remember that fuel will still be present in the system components, and take precautions accordingly before disconnecting any of them.*

**2** Disconnect the battery negative (earth) lead (refer to Chapter 5A, Section 1).

**3** Proceed as follows, according to engine.

### Endura-E engines

**4** Remove the air inlet components as described in Section 4.

**5** Disconnect the accelerator cable from the throttle linkage (see Section 5).

**6** Disconnect the throttle position sensor multi-plug.

**7** Noting their locations, disconnect any vacuum hoses from the throttle housing.

**8** Remove the throttle housing mounting screws, then detach the throttle housing and gasket from the inlet manifold. Discard the gasket - this must be renewed whenever it is disturbed.

**9** Refit in the reverse order of removal. Check that the mating faces are clean, and fit a new gasket. Adjust the accelerator cable as described in Section 5 on completion.

### PTE engines

**10** Remove the air inlet components as described in Section 4.

**11** Disconnect the accelerator cable from the throttle linkage (see Section 5).

**12** Unscrew the retaining bolts, and detach the accelerator cable support bracket at the throttle housing.

**13** Disconnect the vacuum hoses from the inlet manifold and the fuel pressure regulator.

**14** Detach the wiring connections from the idle speed control valve, the temperature sensor and the harness connector.

**13.21 Throttle housing mounting screw locations (arrowed)**

**15** Disconnect the fuel return hose from the pressure regulator unit.

**16** Unscrew the throttle housing-to-manifold retaining bolts, and unbolt the throttle housing support bracket bolts. Remove the throttle housing and gasket. Discard the gasket - this must be renewed whenever it is disturbed.

**17** Refit in the reverse order of removal. Check that the mating faces are clean, and fit a new gasket. Adjust the accelerator cable as described in Section 5 on completion.

### Zetec and Zetec-E engines

**18** Remove the air inlet components as described in Section 4.

**19** Disconnect the accelerator cable from the throttle linkage (see Section 5).

**20** Disconnect the throttle position sensor multi-plug.

**21** Remove the throttle housing mounting screws, then detach the throttle housing and gasket from the inlet manifold **(see illustration)**. Discard the gasket - this must be renewed whenever it is disturbed.

**22** Refit in the reverse order of removal. Check that the mating faces are clean, and fit a new gasket. Adjust the accelerator cable as described in Section 5 on completion.

### Fuel rail and injectors

**Note:** *The following procedure is applicable mainly to the Zetec and Zetec-E engines; specific information for the Endura-E and PTE engines was not available at the time of writing. However, apart from minor differences in component attachments, all engines covered in this Chapter are very similar in this area.*

**23** Relieve the residual pressure in the fuel system (see Section 2), and equalise tank pressure by removing the fuel filler cap.

⚠️ *Warning: This procedure will merely relieve the increased pressure necessary for the engine to run - remember that fuel will still be present in the system components, and take precautions accordingly before disconnecting any of them.*

**24** Disconnect the battery negative (earth) lead - see Chapter 5A, Section 1.

**25** Remove the air inlet components as described in Section 4.

**26** Disconnect the accelerator cable from the throttle linkage (see Section 5).

**13.32 Undo the three bolts (arrowed) to release the fuel rail from the manifold**

**13.39 Disconnect the vacuum hose and undo the bolts (arrowed) to withdraw the fuel pressure regulator**

**13.43 Unscrew the three retaining bolts (arrowed) and withdraw the idle speed control valve from the inlet manifold**

**27** Disconnect the throttle position sensor multi-plug.

**28** Remove the throttle housing screws, then detach the throttle housing and gasket from the inlet manifold. Discard the gasket - this must be renewed whenever it is disturbed.

**29** Detach the crankcase breather hose from the cylinder head cover, and the fuel pressure regulator vacuum hose from the inlet manifold.

**30** Releasing the wire clips, unplug the four fuel injector multi-plugs and the inlet air temperature sensor multi-plug.

**31** Refer to Section 3 and disconnect the fuel feed and return lines at the quick-release couplings, then unclip the fuel hoses from the inlet manifold; use rag to soak up any spilt fuel. **Note:** *Do not disturb the threaded couplings at the fuel rail unions unless absolutely necessary; these are sealed at the factory. The quick-release couplings will suffice for all normal service operations.*

**32** Unscrew the three bolts securing the fuel rail **(see illustration)**. Withdraw the rail, carefully prising it out of the inlet manifold, and draining any remaining fuel into a suitable clean container. Note the seals between the rail noses and the manifold; these must be renewed whenever the rail is removed.

**33** Clamping the rail carefully in a vice fitted with soft jaws, unscrew the two bolts securing each injector, and withdraw the injectors. Place each in a clean, labelled storage container.

**34** If the injector(s) are being renewed, discard the old injector, the nose seal and the O-rings. If only the injector O-rings are being renewed, and it is intended that the same injectors will be re-used, remove the old nose seal and O-rings, and discard them.

**35** Refitting is the reverse of the removal procedure, noting the following points:

a) *Lubricate each nose seal and O-ring with clean engine oil on installation.*

b) *Locate each injector carefully in the fuel rail recess, ensuring the locating tab on the injector head fits into the slot provided in the rail. Tighten the bolts to the specified torque setting.*

c) *Fit a new seal to each fuel rail nose, and ensure that the seals are not displaced as the rail is refitted. Ensure that the fuel rail is settled fully in the manifold before tightening the bolts.*

d) *Ensure the hoses and wiring are routed correctly, and secured on reconnection by any clips or ties provided.*

e) *Adjust the accelerator cable (Section 5).*

f) *On completion, switch the ignition on and off five times, to activate the fuel pump and pressurise the system, without cranking the engine. Check for signs of fuel leaks around all disturbed unions and joints before attempting to start the engine.*

### Fuel pressure regulator

**36** Relieve the residual pressure in the fuel system (see Section 2), and equalise tank pressure by removing the fuel filler cap.

⚠️ **Warning: This procedure will merely relieve the extra pressure necessary for the engine to run - remember that fuel will still be present in the system, and take precautions before disconnecting any of them.**

**37** Disconnect the battery negative (earth) lead - see Chapter 5A, Section 1.

**38** Disconnect the vacuum hose and fuel return hose from the regulator.

**39** Unscrew the two regulator bolts **(see illustration)** then use clean rag to soak up any spilt fuel, and withdraw the regulator.

**40** Refitting is the reverse of the removal procedure, noting the following points:

a) *Renew the regulator sealing O-ring whenever the regulator is disturbed. Lubricate the new O-ring with clean engine oil on installation.*

b) *Locate the regulator carefully in the fuel rail recess, and tighten the bolts to the specified torque setting.*

c) *On completion, switch the ignition on and off five times, to activate the fuel pump and pressurise the system, without cranking the engine. Check for signs of fuel leaks around all disturbed unions and joints before attempting to start the engine.*

### Idle speed control valve

**41** Disconnect the battery negative (earth) lead (refer to Chapter 5A, Section 1).

**42** Disconnect the valve's wiring multi-plug.

**43** Unscrew the three retaining bolts, and withdraw the valve from the inlet manifold **(see illustration)**.

**44** Refitting is the reverse of the removal procedure, noting the following points:

a) *Clean the mating surfaces carefully, and always fit a new gasket whenever the valve is disturbed.*

b) *Once the wiring and battery are reconnected, start the engine and allow it to idle. When it has reached normal operating temperature, check that the idle speed is stable, and that no induction (air) leaks are evident. Switch on all electrical loads (headlights, heated rear window, etc), and check that the idle speed is still satisfactory.*

### Mass air flow sensor

**45** Releasing its wire clip, unplug the electrical connector from the sensor **(see illustration)**.

**46** Release the two clips and detach the sensor from the air cleaner cover **(see illustration)**.

**47** Slacken the clamp securing the sensor to the air inlet hose, and withdraw the sensor.

**13.45 Disconnect the mass air flow sensor electrical connector . . .**

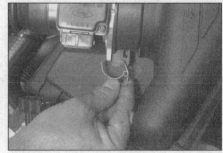

**13.46 . . . then release the two clips and detach the sensor from the air cleaner cover**

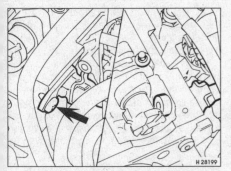

**13.54 Camshaft position sensor location in cylinder head with retaining screw (arrowed) - cylinder head cover shown removed for clarity**

**13.62 Throttle position sensor location in the throttle housing**

**13.68 Oxygen sensor location in the exhaust system downpipe**

**48** Refitting is the reverse of the removal procedure. Ensure that the sensor and air cleaner cover are seated correctly and securely fastened, so there are no air leaks.

## ECU

**Note:** *The ECU is fragile. Take care not to drop it, or subject it to any other kind of impact. Do not subject it to extremes of temperature, or allow it to get wet.*

**49** Disconnect the battery negative (earth) lead (refer to Chapter 5A, Section 1). Working inside the vehicle, remove the side cowl kick panel from the front passenger's footwell to gain access to the ECU.
**50** On later models, drill out the rivet and remove the security shield over the ECU. Release the ECU from its retaining bracket, then unscrew the retaining bolt and remove the wiring multi-plug.
**51** Refitting is the reverse of the removal procedure but, where applicable, secure the security shield using a new rivet.

## Crankshaft position sensor

**52** Refer to Chapter 5B.

## Camshaft position sensor

**53** Where applicable, release the fuel feed and return hoses from their clip.
**54** Releasing its wire clip, unplug the sensor's electrical connector. Remove the retaining screw, and withdraw the sensor from the cylinder head or timing chain cover; be prepared for slight oil loss **(see illustration)**.
**55** Refitting is the reverse of the removal procedure, noting the following points:

a) *Apply petroleum jelly or clean engine oil to the sensor's sealing O-ring.*
b) *Locate the sensor fully in the cylinder head, and wipe off any surplus lubricant before securing it.*
c) *Tighten the screw to the specified torque wrench setting.*

## Coolant temperature sensor

**56** Refer to Chapter 3.

## Inlet air temperature sensor

**57** The sensor is located in the air cleaner casing on Endura-E engines, in the inlet

manifold on PTE and Zetec engines, and in the air inlet hose on Zetec-E engines.
**58** Remove the air cleaner assembly or air inlet ducting as necessary (refer to Section 4) to gain access to the sensor.
**59** Releasing its clip, unplug the sensor's electrical connector, then either unscrew the sensor or withdraw it from its locating grommet, as applicable.
**60** Refitting is the reverse of the removal procedure.

## Throttle position sensor

**61** Remove the air cleaner assembly or air inlet ducting as necessary (refer to Section 4) to gain access to the sensor.
**62** Releasing its wire clip, unplug the sensor's electrical connector. Remove the retaining screws, and withdraw the unit from the throttle housing **(see illustration)**. *Do not force the sensor's centre to rotate past its normal operating sweep; the unit will be seriously damaged.*
**63** Refitting is the reverse of the removal procedure, noting the following points:

a) *Ensure that the sensor is correctly orientated, by locating its centre on the D-shaped throttle shaft (throttle closed), and aligning the sensor body so that the bolts pass easily into the throttle housing.*
b) *Tighten the screws evenly and securely (but do not overtighten them, or the potentiometer body will be cracked).*

## Vehicle speed sensor

**64** The sensor is mounted at the base of the speedometer drive cable, and is removed with the speedometer drive pinion. Refer to the relevant Section of Chapter 7A or B, as applicable.

## Power steering pressure switch

**65** Releasing its clip, unplug the switch's electrical connector, then unscrew the switch. Place a wad of rag underneath, to catch any spilt fluid. If a sealing washer is fitted, renew it if it is worn or damaged.
**66** Refitting is the reverse of the removal procedure; tighten the switch securely, then top-up the fluid reservoir (see *"Weekly Checks"*) to replace any fluid lost from the system, and bleed out any trapped air (see Chapter 10).

## Oxygen sensor

**Note:** *The sensor is delicate, and will not work if it is dropped or knocked, if its power supply is disrupted, or if any cleaning materials are used on it.*

**67** Release the sensor's electrical connector from its bracket on the engine/transmission front mounting, and unplug it to disconnect the sensor.
**68** Raise and support the front of the vehicle if required to remove the sensor from underneath (see *"Jacking and Vehicle Support"*). Unscrew the sensor from the exhaust system front downpipe; collect the sealing washer (where fitted) **(see illustration)**.
**69** On refitting, clean the sealing washer (where fitted) and renew it if it is damaged or worn. Apply a smear of anti-seize compound to the sensor's threads, to prevent them from welding themselves to the downpipe in service. Refit the sensor, tightening it to its specified torque wrench setting; a slotted socket will be required to do this. Reconnect the wiring, and refit the connector plug.

**4D**

**14 Inlet manifold -** removal and refitting

**Note:** *Refer to the warning note in Section 1 before proceeding.*

## Removal

### Endura-E engines

**1** Depressurise the fuel system (Section 2).
**2** Disconnect the battery negative (earth) lead (refer to Chapter 5A, Section 1).
**3** Remove the air inlet duct (see Section 4) and disconnect the accelerator cable from the throttle linkage (see Section 5).
**4** Mark their locations then disconnect the HT leads from the spark plugs. Release the leads from the clips on the inlet manifold.
**5** Remove the fuel injectors and fuel rail as described in Section 13.
**6** Noting their locations, disconnect the coolant, vacuum and breather hoses from the manifold and throttle housing.
**7** Disconnect the wiring multi-plugs from the engine sensors at the inlet manifold.

**8** Undo the seven retaining bolts, and withdraw the manifold from the cylinder head. Remove the gasket.

**9** With the manifold removed, clean all traces of the old gasket from the mating surfaces of the manifold and the cylinder head.

### PTE engines

**10** The inlet manifold is a two-piece assembly comprising an upper and lower section bolted together.

**11** Drain the cooling system with reference to Chapter 1.

**12** Depressurise the fuel system (Section 2).

**13** Disconnect the battery negative (earth) lead (refer to Chapter 5A, Section 1).

**14** Remove the air inlet duct (Section 4) and disconnect the accelerator cable from the throttle linkage (Section 5).

**15** Remove the fuel injectors and fuel rail as described in Section 13.

**16** Noting their locations, disconnect the coolant, vacuum and breather hoses from the manifold.

**17** Disconnect the wiring multi-plugs from the engine sensors at the inlet manifold.

**18** Undo the retaining bolts, and withdraw the manifold from the cylinder head. Note the location of the engine lifting bracket and earth lead, where fitted. Remove the gasket.

**19** With the manifold removed, clean all traces of the old gasket from the mating surfaces of the manifold and the cylinder head.

### Zetec and Zetec-E engines

**20** Depressurise the fuel system as described in Section 2.

**21** Disconnect the battery negative (earth) lead (refer to Chapter 5A, Section 1).

**22** Remove the air inlet duct (see Section 4) and disconnect the accelerator cable from the throttle linkage (see Section 5).

**23** Disconnect the crankcase breather hose from the cylinder head cover union.

**24** Unbolt the upper part of the exhaust manifold heat shield.

**25** On Zetec-E engines, Slacken the sleeve nut securing the EGR pipe to the manifold, remove the screws securing the pipe to the ignition coil bracket, then unscrew the sleeve nut securing the pipe to the EGR valve.

**26** Remove the two screws securing the wiring "rail" to the top of the manifold - this is simply so that it can be moved as required to reach the manifold bolts. Unplug the electrical connectors at the camshaft position sensor and the coolant temperature sensor, then unclip the wiring from the ignition coil bracket, and secure it to the manifold.

**27** Remove the three screws securing the wiring "rail" to the rear of the manifold. Releasing its wire clip, unplug the large electrical connector (next to the fuel pressure regulator) to disconnect the wiring of the manifold components from the engine wiring loom.

**28** Marking or labelling them as they are unplugged, disconnect the vacuum hoses at the manifold and throttle housing.

**29** Equalise the pressure in the fuel tank by removing the filler cap, then undo the fuel feed and return lines connecting the engine to the chassis. Plug or cap all open fittings.

**30** Unbolt the earth lead from the cylinder head rear support plate/engine lifting eye, then unscrew the bolt securing the support plate/lifting eye.

**31** Unscrew the nuts and bolts securing the manifold to the cylinder head, and withdraw it. Take care not to damage vulnerable components as the manifold assembly is manoeuvred out of the engine compartment.

**32** With the manifold removed, clean all traces of the old gasket from the mating surfaces of the manifold and the cylinder head.

### Refitting

#### All engines

**33** Refitting is the reverse of the removal procedure, noting the following points:

a) *Fit a new gasket, then locate the manifold on the head and install the nuts and bolts.*

b) *Tighten the nuts/bolts in three or four equal steps to the specified torque, working from the centre outwards, to avoid warping the manifold.*

c) *Refit the remaining parts in the reverse order of removal - tighten all fasteners to the torque wrench settings specified (where given).*

d) *Where drained, refill the cooling system as described in Chapter 1.*

e) *Before starting the engine, check the accelerator cable for correct adjustment and the throttle linkage for smooth operation (Section 5).*

f) *When the engine is fully warmed-up, check for signs of fuel, inlet and/or vacuum leaks.*

# Chapter 4 Part E:
# Exhaust and emission control systems

## Contents

## Degrees of difficulty

| | | | | |
|---|---|---|---|---|
| **Easy,** suitable for novice with little experience  | **Fairly easy,** suitable for beginner with some experience  | **Fairly difficult,** suitable for competent DIY mechanic | **Difficult,** suitable for experienced DIY mechanic | **Very difficult,** suitable for expert DIY or professional |

## Specifications

| Torque wrench settings | Nm | lbf ft |
|---|---|---|
| Pulse-air system piping-to-exhaust manifold sleeve nuts . . . . . . . . . . . | 32 | 24 |
| EGR pipe to EGR valve sleeve nut . . . . . . . . . . . . . . . . . . . . . . . . . . . . | 55 | 41 |
| EGR pipe to exhaust manifold sleeve nut . . . . . . . . . . . . . . . . . . . . . | 73 | 54 |
| Exhaust manifold to cylinder head: | | |
|    HCS and Endura-E engines . . . . . . . . . . . . . . . . . . . . . . . . . . . . . . | 23 | 17 |
|    CVH and PTE engines . . . . . . . . . . . . . . . . . . . . . . . . . . . . . . . . . . | 16 | 12 |
|    Zetec and Zetec-E engines . . . . . . . . . . . . . . . . . . . . . . . . . . . . . . | 16 | 12 |

## 1 General information

### Exhaust system

**1** The exhaust system is composed of an exhaust manifold, the front downpipe and catalytic converter (where fitted), and a main section incorporating two silencers. The service replacement exhaust system consists of three sections: the front downpipe/catalytic converter, the intermediate pipe and front silencer, and the tailpipe and rear silencer. The system is suspended throughout its entire length by rubber mountings.

### Emission control systems

**2** To minimise pollution of the atmosphere from incompletely-burned and evaporating gases, and to maintain good driveability and fuel economy, a number of emissions control systems are used on these vehicles. They include the following:

a) *The engine management system (comprising both fuel and ignition sub-systems) itself.*

b) *Positive Crankcase Ventilation (PCV) system.*

c) *Evaporative emissions control (EVAP) system.*

d) *Exhaust Gas Recirculation (EGR) system*

e) *Pulse-AIR (PAIR) system.*

f) *Catalytic converter.*

**3** The operation of the systems is described in the following paragraphs.

### Positive crankcase ventilation system

**4** The function of the crankcase ventilation system is to reduce the emissions of unburned hydrocarbons from the crankcase, and to minimise the formation of oil sludge. By ensuring that a depression is created in the crankcase under most operating conditions, particularly at idle, and by positively inducing fresh air into the system, the oil vapours and "blow-by" gases collected in the crankcase are drawn from the crankcase, through the air cleaner or oil separator, into the inlet tract, to be burned by the engine during normal combustion.

**5** On HCS engines, the system consists of a vented oil filler cap (with an integral mesh filter) and a hose connecting it to a connector on the underside of the air cleaner housing. A further hose leads from the adapter/filter to the inlet manifold. Under conditions of idle and part-load, the emissions gases are directed into the inlet manifold, and dispensed with in the combustion process. Additional air is supplied

through two small orifices next to the mushroom valve in the air cleaner housing, the object of which is to prevent high vacuum build-up. Under full-load conditions, when the inlet manifold vacuum is weak, the mushroom valve opens, and the emissions are directed through the air cleaner housing into the engine induction system and thence into the combustion chambers. This arrangement eliminates any fuel mixture control problems. The operating principles for the system used on the Endura-E engine are basically the same as just described with revisions to the component locations and hose arrangement.

**6** On CVH and PTE engines, a closed-circuit type crankcase ventilation system is used, the function of which is basically the same as that described for the HCS engine type, but the breather hose connects directly to the rocker cover. The oil filler cap incorporates a separate filter in certain applications.

**7** On Zetec and Zetec-E engines, the crankcase ventilation system main components are the oil separator mounted on the front (radiator) side of the cylinder block/crankcase, and the Positive Crankcase Ventilation (PCV) valve set in a rubber grommet in the separator's left-hand upper end. The associated pipework consists of a crankcase breather pipe and two flexible hoses connecting the PCV valve to a union on the left-hand end of the inlet manifold,

**4E**

and a crankcase breather hose connecting the cylinder head cover to the air cleaner assembly. A small foam filter in the air cleaner prevents dirt from being drawn directly into the engine.

## Evaporative emissions control system

**8** This system is fitted to minimise the escape of unburned hydrocarbons into the atmosphere. Fuel evaporative emissions control systems are limited on vehicles meeting earlier emissions regulations; carburettor float chambers are vented internally, whilst fuel tanks vent to atmosphere through a combined roll-over/anti-trickle-fill valve. On vehicles meeting the more stringent emissions regulations, the fuel tank filler cap is sealed, and a charcoal canister is used to collect and store petrol vapours generated in the tank when the vehicle is parked. When the engine is running, the vapours are cleared from the canister (under the control of the ECU via the canister-purge solenoid valve) into the inlet tract, to be burned by the engine during normal combustion.

**9** To ensure that the engine runs correctly when it is cold and/or idling, and to protect the catalytic converter from the effects of an over-rich mixture, the canister-purge solenoid valve is not opened by the ECU until the engine is fully warmed-up and running under part-load; the solenoid valve is then switched on and off, to allow the stored vapour to pass into the inlet tract.

## Exhaust gas recirculation system

**10** This system, fitted to Zetec-E engines reduces the emissions of oxides of nitrogen ($NO_x$). This is achieved by recirculating some of the exhaust gases through the EGR valve back to the inlet manifold. This has the effect of lowering combustion temperatures.

**11** The system consists of the EGR valve, the EGR exhaust gas pressure differential sensor, the EGR solenoid valve, the system ECU and various sensors. The ECU is programmed to produce the ideal EGR valve lift for all operating conditions.

## Pulse-air system

**12** This system consists of the pulse-air solenoid valve (fuel injection models), the pulse-air valve itself, the delivery tubing, a pulse-air filter, and on some models, a check valve. The system injects filtered air directly into the exhaust ports, using the pressure variations in the exhaust gases to draw air through from the filter housing; air will flow into the exhaust only when its pressure is below atmospheric. The pulse-air valve allows gases to flow only one way, so there is no risk of hot exhaust gases flowing back into the filter.

**13** The system's primary function is raise exhaust gas temperatures on start-up, thus reducing the amount of time taken for the catalytic converter to reach operating temperature. Until this happens, the system reduces emissions of unburned hydrocarbon particles (HC) and carbon monoxide (CO) by ensuring that a considerable proportion of

these substances remaining in the exhaust gases after combustion are burned up, either in the manifold itself or in the catalytic converter.

**14** To ensure that the system does not upset the smooth running of the engine under normal driving conditions, it is linked by the pulse-air solenoid valve to the ECU on fuel injection models, so that it only functions during engine warm-up, when the oxygen sensor is not influencing the fuel/air mixture ratio. On carburettor models, a temperature-sensitive ported vacuum switch shuts the system off when normal engine operating temperature is reached.

## Catalytic converter

**15** Catalytic converters have been introduced on all models in the range, to meet the various emissions regulations.

**16** The catalytic converter is located in the exhaust system, and operates in conjunction with an exhaust gas oxygen sensor to reduce exhaust gas emissions. The catalytic converter uses precious metals (platinum and palladium or rhodium) as catalysts to speed up the reaction between the pollutants and the oxygen in the vehicle's exhaust gases, CO and HC being oxidised to form $H_2O$ and $CO_2$ and (in the three-way type of catalytic converter) $NO_x$ being reduced to $N_2$. **Note:** *The catalytic converter is not a filter in the physical sense; its function is to promote a chemical reaction, but it is not itself affected by that reaction.*

**17** The converter consists of an element (or "substrate") of ceramic honeycomb, coated with a combination of precious metals in such a way as to produce a vast surface area over which the exhaust gases must flow; the whole being mounted in a stainless-steel box. A simple "oxidation" (or "two-way") catalytic converter can deal with CO and HC only, while a "reduction" (or "three-way") catalytic converter can deal with CO, HC and $NO_x$. Three-way catalytic converters are further sub-divided into "open-loop" (or "unregulated") converters, which can remove 50 to 70% of pollutants and "closed-loop" (also known as "controlled" or "regulated") converters, which can remove over 90% of pollutants.

**18** In order for a closed-loop catalytic converter to operate effectively, the air/fuel mixture must be very accurately controlled, and this is achieved by measuring the oxygen content of the exhaust gas. The oxygen sensor transmits information on the exhaust gas oxygen content to the ECU, which adjusts the air/fuel mixture strength accordingly.

**19** The sensor has a built-in heating element which is controlled by the ECU, in order to bring the sensor's tip to an efficient operating temperature as rapidly as possible. The sensor's tip is sensitive to oxygen, and sends the ECU a varying voltage depending on the amount of oxygen in the exhaust gases; if the inlet air/fuel mixture is too rich, the sensor sends a high-voltage signal. The voltage falls as the mixture weakens. Peak conversion

efficiency of all major pollutants occurs if the inlet air/fuel mixture is maintained at the chemically-correct ratio for the complete combustion of petrol - 14.7 parts (by weight) of air to 1 part of fuel (the "stoichiometric" ratio). The sensor output voltage alters in a large step at this point, the ECU using the signal change as a reference point, and correcting the inlet air/fuel mixture accordingly by altering the fuel injector pulse width (injector opening time).

**20** Removal and refitting procedures for the oxygen sensor are given in Parts B, C and D of this Chapter according to fuel system type.

---

## 2 Exhaust system - repair

⚠️ *Warning: Inspection and repair of exhaust system components should be done only after enough time has elapsed to allow the system to cool completely. This applies particularly to the catalytic converter, which runs at very high temperatures. Also, when working under the vehicle, make sure it is securely supported on axle stands (see "Jacking and Vehicle Support").*

**1** If the exhaust system components are extremely corroded or rusted together, they will probably have to be cut from the exhaust system. The most convenient way of accomplishing this is to have a quick-fit exhaust repair specialist remove the corroded sections. Alternatively, you can simply cut off the old components with a hacksaw. If you do decide to tackle the job at home, be sure to wear eye protection, to protect your eyes from metal chips, and work gloves, to protect your hands. If the production-fit system is still fitted, it must be cut at the points shown **(see illustrations)** for the service-replacement system sections to fit.

**2** Here are some simple guidelines to apply when repairing the exhaust system:

a) *Work from the back to the front when removing exhaust system components.*

b) *Apply penetrating fluid to the exhaust system component fasteners, to make them easier to remove.*

c) *Use new gaskets, rubber mountings and clamps when installing exhaust system components.*

d) *Apply anti-seize compound to the threads of all exhaust system fasteners during reassembly.*

e) *Note that on some models, the downpipe is secured to the manifold by two bolts, with a coil spring, spring seat and self-locking nut on each. On refitting, tighten the nuts until they stop on the bolt shoulders; the pressure of the springs will then suffice to make a gas-tight joint. Do not overtighten the nuts to cure a leak - the bolts will shear. Renew the gasket and the springs if a leak is found.*

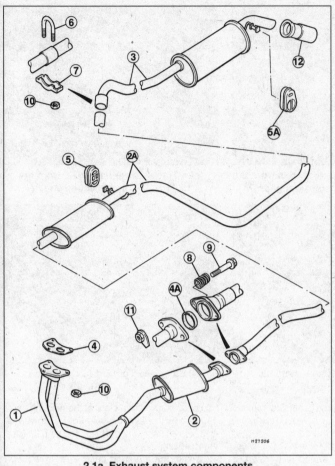

**2.1a  Exhaust system components as fitted to carburettor engine models**

| | | |
|---|---|---|
| 1 Front downpipe | 4A Sealing ring | 10 Self-locking nut |
| 2 Front silencer section | 5 Rubber mounting | 11 Nut |
| 2A Centre section | 5A Rubber mounting | 12 Rear silencer outlet trim (1.4 and 1.6 engines only) |
| 3 Rear silencer section | 6 U-bolt | |
| 4 Gasket | 7 Clamp | |
| | 8 Spring | |
| | 9 Bolt | |

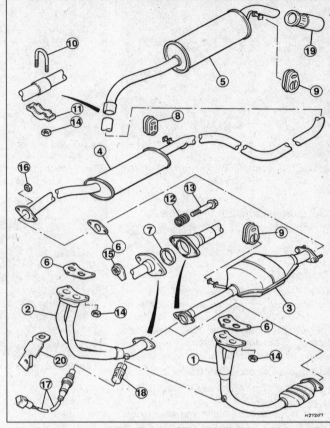

**2.1b  Exhaust system fitted to the CFi fuel injection engine models (EFi and SEFi systems similar)**

| | | |
|---|---|---|
| 1 Front downpipe (manual transmission) | 6 Gasket | 15 Self-locking nut |
| | 7 Sealing ring | 16 Nut |
| | 8 Rubber mounting | 17 Oxygen sensor |
| 2 Front downpipe (CTX transmission) | 9 Rubber mounting | 18 Heat shield |
| | 10 U-bolt | 19 Rear silencer outlet trim |
| 3 Catalytic converter | 11 Clamp | |
| 4 Front silencer | 12 Spring | 20 Bracket |
| 5 Rear silencer (tailpipes differ) | 13 Bolt | |
| | 14 Nut | |

f) Be sure to allow sufficient clearance between newly-installed parts and all points on the underbody, to avoid overheating the floorpan, and possibly damaging the interior carpet and insulation. Pay close attention to the catalytic converter and its heat shield.

⚠ **Warning: The catalytic converter operates at extremely high temperatures, and takes a long time to cool. Wait until it's completely cool before attempting to remove the converter. Failure to do so could result in serious burns.**

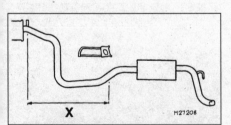

**2.1c  Cut at points indicated (according to model) when renewing the rear silencer - carburettor engine models**

*X = 720 mm (all models except Van)*
*X = 914 mm (Van models)*

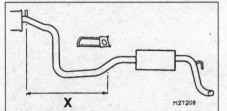

**2.1d  Cut at points indicated when renewing the rear silencer on HCS and CVH engines with CFi and EFi systems**

*X = 720 mm*

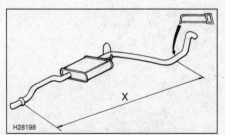

**2.1e  Cut at points indicated when renewing the rear silencer on Zetec engine with SEFi system**

*X = 1717 mm*

**4E**

3.2a Exhaust manifold shroud/heat shield (HCS engine)

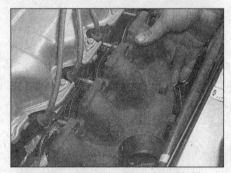

3.2b Removing the hot-air shroud from the 1.6 litre CVH carburettor engine

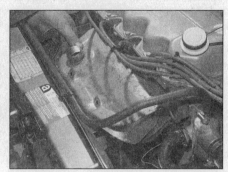

3.2c Hot air shroud removal from the 1.6 litre CVH fuel injection engine

## 3 Exhaust manifold - removal, inspection and refitting

### Removal

**Note:** *Never work on or near the exhaust system and in particular, the catalytic converter (where fitted), while it is still hot. If this is unavoidable, wear thick gloves, and protect yourself from burns should you accidentally touch a hot exhaust component.*

#### All engines except Zetec and Zetec-E

1 Disconnect the battery negative (earth) lead - see Chapter 5A, Section 1.
2 The exhaust manifold is secured to the cylinder head by studs and nuts, and is similarly attached to the exhaust downpipe. A shroud/heat shield is bolted to the manifold, to direct exhaust-heated air into the air inlet system when the engine is cold. Access to the exhaust manifold retaining nuts is gained by first removing this shroud (see illustrations).
3 On vehicles equipped with a pulse-air system, remove the pulse-air piping as described in Section 8.
4 On catalytic converter equipped vehicles with an oxygen sensor fitted to the exhaust front downpipe, remove the sensor as described in Part B, Section 13.
5 Support the exhaust downpipe on a jack or suitable blocks, and undo the downpipe-to-manifold retaining nuts. Separate the pipe from the manifold, and remove the gasket. On

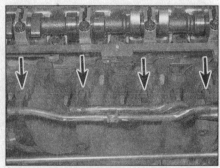

3.6a Removing the exhaust manifold . . .

3.6b . . . and gasket (CVH engine)

catalytic converter-equipped vehicles with an oxygen sensor fitted to the exhaust downpipe, take care not to stretch the sensor wiring; if necessary, disconnect the sensor's multi-plug.
6 Undo the retaining nuts, and withdraw the manifold from the cylinder head studs. Remove the manifold gasket (see illustrations).

#### Zetec and Zetec-E engines

**Note:** *In addition to the new gasket and any other parts, tools or facilities needed to carry out this operation, a new plastic guide sleeve will be required on reassembly.*

7 Disconnect the battery negative (earth) lead - see Chapter 5A, Section 1.
8 Remove the air inlet hose and duct as described in Part D of this Chapter.
9 Drain the cooling system (see Chapter 1).
10 Disconnect the coolant hose and the coolant pipe/hose from the thermostat

housing; secure them clear of the working area.
11 Unbolt the exhaust manifold heat shield, and withdraw both parts of the shield (see illustration).
12 While the manifold can be removed with the pulse-air system components attached - unbolt the filter housing and disconnect its vacuum hose if this is to be done - it is easier to remove the pulse-air assembly first, as described in Section 8 (see illustration).
13 Unplug the oxygen sensor electrical connector, to avoid straining its wiring. Unscrew the nuts to disconnect the exhaust system front downpipe from the manifold.
14 Remove the nuts and detach the manifold and gasket (see illustration). When removing the manifold with the engine in the vehicle, additional clearance can be obtained by unscrewing the studs from the cylinder head; a female Torx-type socket will be required.

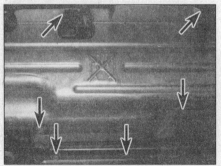

3.11 Exhaust manifold heat shield upper part bolts (arrowed) (Zetec engine)

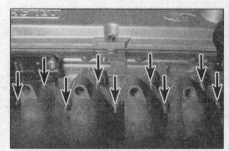

3.12 Pulse-air system (sleeve nuts arrowed) need not be removed

3.14 Unscrew nuts (arrowed) to remove exhaust manifold on Zetec engines

**3.17a Renew exhaust system downpipe-to-manifold gasket to prevent leaks**

**3.17b Showing exhaust downpipe-to-manifold securing bolts - note coil spring, and shoulder on bolt**

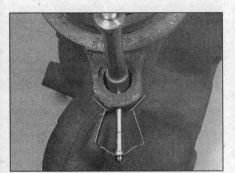

**3.17c Release spring clip to extract securing bolt from manifold, when required**

**3.19 Fit plastic guide sleeve to stud (arrowed) when refitting exhaust manifold to Zetec engines**

**15** Always fit a new gasket on reassembly, to carefully-cleaned components. *Do not attempt to re-use the original gasket.*

## Inspection

**16** Use a scraper to remove all traces of old gasket material and carbon deposits from the manifold and cylinder head mating surfaces. Provided both mating surfaces are clean and flat, a new gasket will be sufficient to ensure that the joint is gas-tight. *Do not use any kind of exhaust sealant upstream of the catalytic converter, where fitted.*

**17** Note that on some models, the downpipe is secured to the manifold by two bolts, with a coil spring, spring seat and self-locking nut on each. On refitting, tighten the nuts until they stop on the bolt shoulders; the pressure of the springs will then suffice to make a gas-tight joint **(see illustrations)**.

**18** Do not overtighten the nuts to cure a leak - the bolts will shear; renew the gasket and the springs if a leak is found. The bolts themselves are secured by spring clips to the manifold, and can be renewed easily if damaged.

## Refitting

**19** Refitting is the reverse of the removal procedure, noting the following points:

a) *Position a new gasket over the cylinder head studs, and on Zetec and Zetec-E engines, fit a new plastic guide sleeve to the stud nearest to the thermostat*

housing, so that the manifold will be correctly located **(see illustration)**. **Do not** refit the manifold without this sleeve.

b) *Refit the manifold, and finger-tighten the mounting nuts.*

c) *Working from the centre out, and in three or four equal steps, tighten the nuts to the torque wrench settings given in the Specifications.*

d) *Refit the remaining parts in the reverse order of removal. Tighten all fasteners to the specified torque wrench settings where given.*

e) *Where drained, refill the cooling system (see Chapter 1).*

f) *Run the engine, and check for exhaust leaks. Check the coolant level when fully warmed-up to normal operating temperature.*

## 4 Catalytic converter - general information and precautions

**1** The catalytic converter is a reliable and simple device, which needs no maintenance in itself, but there are some facts of which an owner should be aware if the converter is to function properly for its full service life.

a) *DO NOT use leaded petrol in a vehicle equipped with a catalytic converter - the lead will coat the precious metals,*

reducing their converting efficiency, and will eventually destroy the converter.

b) *Always keep the ignition and fuel systems well-maintained in accordance with the manufacturer's schedule (see Chapter 1).*

c) *If the engine develops a misfire, do not drive the vehicle at all (or at least as little as possible) until the fault is cured.*

d) *DO NOT push - or tow-start the vehicle - this will soak the catalytic converter in unburned fuel, causing it to overheat when the engine does start.*

e) *DO NOT switch off the ignition at high engine speeds, ie do not "blip" the throttle immediately before switching off.*

f) *DO NOT use fuel or engine oil additives - these may contain substances harmful to the catalytic converter.*

g) *DO NOT continue to use the vehicle if the engine burns oil to the extent of leaving a visible trail of blue smoke.*

h) *Remember that the catalytic converter operates at very high temperatures. DO NOT, therefore, park the vehicle in dry undergrowth, over long grass or piles of dead leaves, after a long run.*

i) *Remember that the catalytic converter is FRAGILE. Do not strike it with tools during servicing work.*

j) *In some cases, a sulphurous smell (like that of rotten eggs) may be noticed from the exhaust. This is common to many catalytic converter-equipped vehicles. Once the vehicle has covered a few thousand miles, the problem should disappear. Low quality fuel with a high sulphur content will exacerbate this effect.*

k) *The catalytic converter used on a well-maintained and well-driven vehicle should last for between 50 000 and 100 000 miles. If the converter is no longer effective, it must be renewed.*

## 5 Positive crankcase ventilation system - checking and component renewal

### Checking

**1** Checking procedures for the system components are included in Chapter 1.

### Component renewal

**Air cleaner components**

**2** See the relevant part of this Chapter.

**Positive Crankcase Ventilation (PCV) valve**

**3** The valve is plugged into the oil separator on Zetec engines **(see illustration)**. Depending on the tools available, access to the valve may be possible once the pulse-air assembly has been removed (see Section 8). If this is not feasible, proceed as outlined in paragraph 4 below.

**4E**

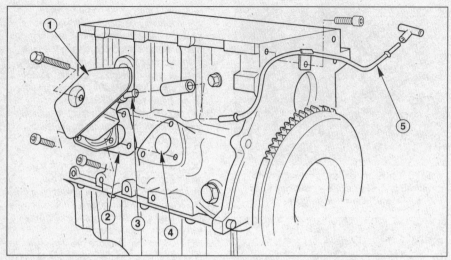

**5.3 Crankcase ventilation system oil separator and related components on Zetec engines**

| | |
|---|---|
| 1 Oil separator | 4 Cylinder block/crankcase opening |
| 2 Gasket | 5 Breather pipe and hose |
| 3 PCV valve | |

## Oil separator

**4** Remove the exhaust manifold (refer to Section 3). The Positive Crankcase Ventilation (PCV) valve can now be unplugged and flushed, or renewed, as required, as described in Chapter 1.

**5** Unbolt the oil separator from the cylinder block/crankcase, and withdraw it; remove and discard the gasket.

**6** Flush out or renew the oil separator, as required (see Chapter 1).

**7** Refitting is the reverse of the removal procedure, but use a new gasket between the oil separator and cylinder block. Refill the cooling system (see Chapter 1). Run the engine, check for exhaust leaks, and check the coolant level when it is fully warmed-up.

---

## 6 Evaporative emissions control system - checking and component renewal

### Checking

**1** Poor idle, stalling and poor driveability can be caused by an inoperative canister-purge solenoid valve, a damaged canister, split or cracked hoses, or hoses connected to the wrong fittings. Check the fuel filler cap for a damaged or deformed gasket.

**2** Fuel loss or fuel odour can be caused by liquid fuel leaking from fuel lines, a cracked or damaged canister, an inoperative canister-purge solenoid valve, or disconnected, misrouted, kinked or damaged vapour or control hoses.

**3** Inspect each hose attached to the canister for kinks, leaks and cracks along its entire length. Repair or renew as necessary.

**4** Inspect the canister. If it is cracked or damaged, renew it. Look for fuel leaking from

the bottom of the canister. If fuel is leaking, renew the canister, and check the hoses and hose routing.

**5** If the canister-purge solenoid valve is thought to be faulty, unplug its electrical connector and disconnect its vacuum hoses. Connect a battery directly across the valve terminals. Check that air can flow through the valve passages when the solenoid is thus energised, and that nothing can pass when the solenoid is not energised.

**6** Further testing should be left to a dealer service department.

### Component renewal

#### Charcoal canister-purge solenoid valve

**7** The solenoid is located at the front right-hand side of the engine compartment, near the headlight unit, on all engines except Zetec and Zetec-E **(see illustration)**. On Zetec and

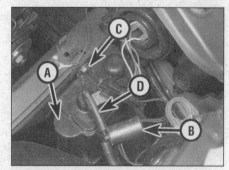

**6.7 Location of the charcoal canister-purge solenoid valve and associated components on HCS and CVH engines**

| | |
|---|---|
| A | Charcoal canister |
| B | Purge solenoid valve |
| C | Canister retaining bolt |
| D | Canister vapour hose |

Zetec-E engines, the valve is clipped to the bulkhead, behind the engine on the right-hand side. Locate the solenoid, then remove any components as necessary to improve access.

**8** Disconnect the battery negative (earth) lead (refer to Chapter 5A, Section 1), then unplug the valve's electrical connector. Unclip the valve from its location, then disconnect its vacuum hoses and withdraw it.

**9** Refitting is the reverse of the removal procedure.

### Charcoal canister

**10** Disconnect the battery negative (earth) lead (refer to Chapter 5A, Section 1).

**11** The canister is located in the forward section of the right-hand wheel arch (beneath the coolant expansion reservoir). Access to the top of the unit is made by removing the coolant expansion reservoir. Access to the underside of the unit is gained by raising the vehicle at the front and removing the roadwheel on the right-hand side (see "Jacking and Vehicle Support").

**12** Disconnect the hose from the unit, and plug it to prevent the ingress of dirt.

**13** Undo the retaining screws, and withdraw the unit from under the wheel arch.

**14** Refit in the reverse order of removal. Unplug the hose before reconnecting it, and ensure that it is clean and securely connected.

---

## 7 Exhaust gas recirculation system - checking and component renewal

**Note:** The following procedures should be considered as the limit of work that can be undertaken on this system. Any further testing or component renewal should be entrusted to a dealer service department.

### Checking

#### EGR valve

**1** Start the engine and allow it to idle.

**2** Detach the vacuum hose from the EGR valve, and attach a hand vacuum pump in its place.

**3** Apply vacuum to the EGR valve. Vacuum should remain steady, and the engine should run poorly.

a) If the vacuum doesn't remain steady and the engine doesn't run poorly, renew the EGR valve and recheck it.

b) If the vacuum remains steady but the engine doesn't run poorly, remove the EGR valve and check the valve and the inlet manifold for blockage. Clean or renew parts as necessary, and recheck.

#### EGR system

**4** Any further checking requires special tools and test equipment and should be left to a dealer service department.

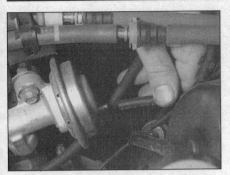

**7.7 Disconnecting the vacuum hose from the EGR valve**

**7.8 Undo the two mounting bolts and withdraw the EGR valve from the inlet manifold**

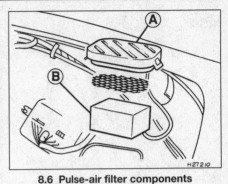

**8.6 Pulse-air filter components on CVH engines**

*A Filter housing lid    B Filter element*

## Component renewal

> ⚠ **Warning: These components will be very hot when the engine is running. Always allow the engine to cool down fully before starting work to prevent the possibility of burns.**

### EGR valve and pipe

**Note:** *To ensure that the gas tight integrity of the EGR system, the EGR pipe must be renewed whenever the EGR valve or the pipe itself are disturbed.*

**5** Disconnect the battery negative (earth) lead (refer to Chapter 5A, Section 1).

**6** Refer to Part D of this Chapter and remove the air inlet components.

**7** Detach the vacuum hose and unscrew the sleeve nut securing the EGR pipe to the valve **(see illustration)**.

**8** Undo the two mounting bolts and withdraw the valve from the inlet manifold **(see illustration)**. Note the valve's gasket; this must be renewed whenever the valve is disturbed.

**9** Undo the three bolts and lift off the exhaust manifold heat shield.

**10** Detach the two EGR pressure transducer hoses from the EGR pipe.

**11** Unscrew the sleeve nut securing the EGR pipe to the exhaust manifold and remove the pipe.

**12** Clean the mating faces of the EGR valve and manifold ensuring that all traces of old gasket and carbon deposits are removed. Take care not to allow debris from cleaning to enter the manifold or EGR valve. Obtain a new gasket and EGR pipe for refitting.

**13** Refit in the reverse order of removal, bearing in mind the following points:

a) Fit the new EGR pipe to the exhaust manifold first, and tighten its sleeve nut finger tight only. Tighten this nut and the sleeve nut at the EGR valve to the specified torque once the EGR valve has been refitted.

b) Use a new gasket when refitting the EGR valve.

## 8 Pulse-air system - checking and component renewal

### Checking

**1** Poor idle, stalling, backfiring and poor driveability can be caused by a fault in the pulse-air system.

**2** Inspect the vacuum pipe/hose for kinks, leaks and cracks along its entire length. Repair or renew as necessary.

**3** Inspect the filter housing and piping. If either is cracked or damaged, renew it.

**4** If the pulse-air solenoid valve is thought to be faulty, unplug its electrical connector and disconnect its vacuum hoses. Connect a battery directly across the valve terminals, and check that air can flow through the valve passages when the solenoid is thus energised, and that nothing can pass when the solenoid is not energised.

**5** Further testing should be left to a dealer service department.

### Component renewal

**Pulse-air filter and housing (CVH engines)**

**6** Detach the lid from the filter body, and lift

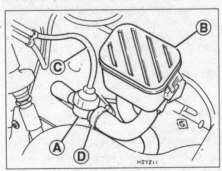

**8.9 Pulse-air valve and connections on CVH engines**

*A Pulse-air valve*
*B Pulse-air filter housing*
*C Vacuum hose*
*D Air hose securing clamp*

out the filter element from the housing **(see illustration)**. If required, the housing can be removed by detaching the air hoses from the base of the unit and withdrawing the unit from the vehicle.

**7** Refit in the reverse order of removal.

### Pulse-air valve (CVH engines)

**8** Disconnect the battery negative (earth) lead (refer to Chapter 5A, Section 1).

**9** Detach the vacuum hoses from the valve **(see illustration)**.

**10** Loosen off the air hose clamp, and detach the air hose from the valve.

**11** Detach the remaining air hose. Note the orientation of the valve, and remove it from the vehicle.

**12** When refitting the valve, ensure that it is fitted the correct way round. Refitting is otherwise a reversal of removal the removal procedure.

### Pulse-air check valve (CVH engines)

 **4E**

**13** Disconnect the battery negative (earth) lead (refer to Chapter 5A, Section 1).

**14** Detach the air hoses from the check valve **(see illustration)**.

**15** Hold the lower tube nut at the base of the valve firm with a suitable spanner, and unscrew the valve using a spanner fitted on the upper nut.

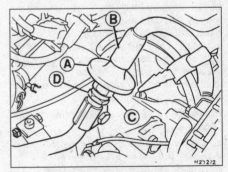

**8.14 Pulse-air check valve and connections on CVH engines**

*A Check valve*
*B Air hose*
*C Check valve upper nut*
*D Lower tube nut*

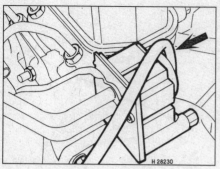

8.18 Vacuum hose connection (arrowed) to pulse-air valve on HCS engines

8.24 Disconnect the vacuum hose from the base of the filter housing . . .

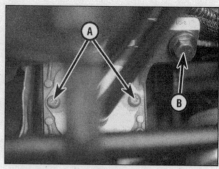

8.26 . . . then undo screws "A" to disconnect the piping and mounting bolt "B" to release the housing

8.27a Remove the four screws to release the filter housing top from the base . . .

8.27b . . . and withdraw the foam filter for cleaning, if required

16 Refit in the reverse order of removal. Ensure that the valve is correctly positioned before fully tightening the tube nut against the valve nut.

## Pulse-air valve, filter and housing (HCS engines)

17 Disconnect the battery negative (earth) lead (refer to Chapter 5A, Section 1).
18 Disconnect the vacuum hose from the rear of the pulse-air valve assembly (see illustration).
19 Undo the retaining screws, and withdraw the air-valve, filter and housing assembly from the mounting bracket.
20 To dismantle the filter housing, undo the four screws and separate the top from the base of the housing; extract the foam filter, and clean it in a suitable solvent. If any of the housing's components are worn or damaged, the assembly must be renewed.
21 Refitting is the reverse of the removal procedure.

## Pulse-air valve, filter and housing (Zetec engines)

22 Disconnect the battery negative (earth) lead (refer to Chapter 5A, Section 1).
23 Chock the rear wheels then jack up the front of the car and support it on axle stands (see "Jacking and Vehicle Support").
24 Disconnect the vacuum hose from the base of the filter housing (see illustration).
25 Remove the air cleaner air inlet ducting for access (refer to Part D of this Chapter).

26 Remove the filter housing-to-piping securing screws, unscrew the mounting bolt, then withdraw the housing (see illustration).
27 To dismantle the filter housing, undo the four screws and separate the top from the base of the housing. Extract the foam filter, and clean it in a suitable solvent (see illustrations). If any of the housing's components are worn or damaged, the assembly must be renewed.
28 Refitting is the reverse of the removal procedure.

## Pulse-air solenoid valve

29 Disconnect the battery negative (earth) lead (refer to Chapter 5A, Section 1).
30 Releasing its wire clip, unplug the electrical connector, then release the valve from its mounting bracket. Withdraw the valve, then label and disconnect the two vacuum hoses.
31 Refitting is the reverse of the removal procedure; ensure that the hoses are correctly reconnected.

## Pulse-air piping (HCS and CVH engines)

32 Disconnect the battery negative (earth) lead (refer to Chapter 5A, Section 1).
33 Remove the air cleaner if necessary for improved access (refer to Part A, B or C of this Chapter, as applicable).
34 Disconnect the vacuum hose from the pulse-air valve.
35 Unbolt and detach the air tube from its

fixing to the exhaust manifold, cylinder head and transmission, according to engine type.
36 Loosen off the four nuts securing the air delivery tubes to the cylinder head exhaust ports, then carefully withdraw the delivery tubes as a unit (see illustration). Do not apply undue force to the tubes as they are detached.
37 Carefully clean the piping, particularly its threads and those of the manifold. Remove all traces of corrosion, which might prevent the pipes seating properly, causing air leaks when the engine is restarted.
38 On refitting, insert the piping carefully into the cylinder head ports, taking care not to bend or distort it. Apply anti-seize compound to the threads, and tighten the retaining sleeve nuts while holding each pipe firmly in its port.

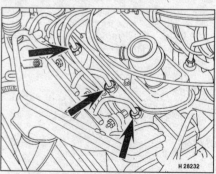

8.36 Pulse-air piping retaining nuts (arrowed) on HCS engines

**39** The remainder of the refitting procedure is the reverse of removal.

### Pulse-air piping (Zetec engines)

**40** Disconnect the battery negative (earth) lead (refer to Chapter 5A, Section 1).

**41** Remove the air cleaner air inlet ducting for access (refer to Part D of this Chapter).

**42** Unbolt the exhaust manifold heat shield; unclip the coolant hose to allow the upper part to be withdrawn.

**43** Chock the rear wheels then jack up the front of the car and support it on axle stands (see *"Jacking and Vehicle Support"*).

**44** Disconnect the vacuum hose at the base of the pulse-air filter housing.

**45** Unscrew the two bolts securing the pipe assembly to the support bracket and the four nuts securing the pipes into the exhaust manifold. Remove the pipes and filter housing as an assembly, taking care not to distort them **(see illustration)**.

**46** Carefully clean the piping, particularly its threads and those of the manifold. Remove all traces of corrosion, which might prevent the pipes seating properly, causing air leaks when the engine is restarted.

**47** On refitting, insert the piping carefully into the exhaust manifold ports, taking care not to bend or distort it. Apply anti-seize compound to the threads, and tighten the retaining sleeve nuts while holding each pipe firmly in its port; if a suitable spanner is available, tighten the sleeve nuts to the specified torque wrench setting.

**8.45 Removing the pulse-air piping on Zetec engines**

**48** The remainder of the refitting procedure is the reverse of removal.

**4E**

# Chapter 5 Part A:
# Starting and charging systems

## Contents

## Degrees of difficulty

| Easy, suitable for novice with little experience  | Fairly easy, suitable for beginner with some experience  | Fairly difficult, suitable for competent DIY mechanic | Difficult, suitable for experienced DIY mechanic | Very difficult, suitable for expert DIY or professional 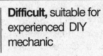 |
|---|---|---|---|---|

## Specifications

### General
System type ......................................... 12 volt, negative earth

### Battery
Rating - Cold cranking/Reserve capacity ...................... 270 A/50 RC, 360 A/60 RC, 500 A/70 RC, 590 A/90 RC or 650 A/130 RC

Charge condition:
Poor ................................................ 12.5 volts
Normal ............................................. 12.6 volts
Good ............................................... 12.7 volts

### Alternator
Make/type:
Bosch .............................................. K1-55A, K1-70A or NC 14V 60-90A
Magneti-Marelli ..................................... A127/55 or 127/70
Mitsubishi ......................................... A5T or A002T
Output (nominal at 13.5 volts with engine speed of 6000 rpm) ....... 55, 70 or 90 amps
Regulating voltage at 4000 rpm engine speed and 3 to 7 amp load ... 14.0 to 14.6 volts
Minimum brush length:
Bosch and Magneti-Marelli ............................. 5.0 mm
Mitsubishi ......................................... 3.0 mm

### Starter motor
Make/type:
Bosch .............................................. DM, DW or EV
Magneti-Marelli ..................................... M79 or M80R
Nippondenso ........................................ No type numbers given
Minimum brush length:
Bosch and Magneti-Marelli ............................. 8.0 mm
Nippondenso ........................................ 10.0 mm

### Torque wrench settings

| | Nm | lbf ft |
|---|---|---|
| Alternator mounting bolts | 25 | 18 |
| Alternator adjustment bolts | 22 | 16 |
| Alternator pulley nut: | | |
| With key | 50 | 37 |
| Without key | 60 | 44 |
| Starter motor mounting bolts | 35 | 26 |
| Starter motor support bracket bolt | 25 | 18 |

5A

## 1 General information, precautions and battery disconnection

### General information

The engine electrical system consists mainly of the charging and starting systems. Because of their engine-related functions, these components are covered separately from the body electrical devices such as the lights, instruments, etc (which are covered in Chapter 12). Information on the ignition system is covered in Part B of this Chapter.

The electrical system is of the 12-volt negative earth type.

The battery is of the low maintenance or "maintenance-free" (sealed for life) type and is charged by the alternator, which is belt-driven from the crankshaft pulley.

The starter motor is of the pre-engaged type incorporating an integral solenoid. On starting, the solenoid moves the drive pinion into engagement with the flywheel ring gear before the starter motor is energised. Once the engine has started, a one-way clutch prevents the motor armature being driven by the engine until the pinion disengages from the flywheel.

### Precautions

Further details of the various systems are given in the relevant Sections of this Chapter. While some repair procedures are given, the usual course of action is to renew the component concerned. The owner whose interest extends beyond mere component renewal should obtain a copy of the "Automobile Electrical & Electronic Systems Manual", available from the publishers of this manual.

It is necessary to take extra care when working on the electrical system to avoid damage to semi-conductor devices (diodes and transistors), and to avoid the risk of personal injury. In addition to the precautions given in "Safety first!" at the beginning of this manual, observe the following when working on the system:

*Always remove rings, watches, etc before working on the electrical system.* Even with the battery disconnected, capacitive discharge could occur if a component's live terminal is earthed through a metal object. This could cause a shock or nasty burn.

*Do not reverse the battery connections.* Components such as the alternator, electronic control units, or any other components having semi-conductor circuitry could be irreparably damaged.

If the engine is being started using jump leads and a slave battery, connect the batteries *positive-to-positive* and *negative-to-negative* (see "Booster battery (jump) starting"). This also applies when connecting a battery charger.

Never disconnect the battery terminals, the alternator, any electrical wiring or any test instruments when the engine is running.

Do not allow the engine to turn the alternator when the alternator is not connected.

Never "test" for alternator output by "flashing" the output lead to earth.

Never use an ohmmeter of the type incorporating a hand-cranked generator for circuit or continuity testing.

Always ensure that the battery negative lead is disconnected when working on the electrical system.

Before using electric-arc welding equipment on the car, disconnect the battery, alternator and components such as the fuel injection/ignition electronic control unit to protect them from the risk of damage.

### Battery disconnection

Several systems fitted to the vehicle require battery power to be available at all times, either to ensure that their continued operation (such as the clock) or to maintain control unit memories (such as that in the engine management system's ECU) which would be wiped if the battery were to be disconnected. Whenever the battery is to be disconnected therefore, first note the following, to ensure that there are no unforeseen consequences of this action:

a) *First, on any vehicle with central locking, it is a wise precaution to remove the key from the ignition, and to keep it with you, so that it does not get locked in, if the central locking should engage accidentally when the battery is reconnected.*

b) *On cars equipped with an engine management system, the system's ECU will lose the information stored in its memory - referred to by Ford as the "KAM" (Keep-Alive Memory) - when the battery is disconnected. This includes idling and operating values, and any fault codes detected - in the case of the fault codes, if it is thought likely that the system has developed a fault for which the corresponding code has been logged, the vehicle must be taken to a Ford dealer for the codes to be read, using the special diagnostic equipment necessary for this. Whenever the battery is disconnected, the information relating to idle speed control and other operating values will have to be re-programmed into the unit's memory. The ECU does this by itself, but until then, there may be surging, hesitation, erratic idle and a generally inferior level of performance. To allow the ECU to relearn these values, start the engine and run it as close to idle speed as possible until it reaches its normal operating temperature, then run it for approximately two minutes at 1200 rpm. Next, drive the vehicle as far as necessary - approximately 5 miles of varied driving conditions is usually sufficient - to complete the relearning process.*

c) *If the battery is disconnected while the alarm system is armed or activated, the alarm will remain in the same state when the battery is reconnected. The same applies to the engine immobiliser system (where fitted).*

d) *If a Ford "Keycode" audio unit is fitted, and the unit and/or the battery is disconnected, the unit will not function again on reconnection until the correct security code is entered. Details of this procedure, which varies according to the unit and model year, are given in the "Ford Audio Systems Operating Guide" supplied with the vehicle when new, with the code itself being given in a "Radio Passport" and/or a "Keycode Label" at the same time. Ensure you have the correct code before you disconnect the battery. For obvious security reasons, the procedure is not given in this manual. If you do not have the code or details of the correct procedure, but can supply proof of ownership and a legitimate reason for wanting this information, the vehicle's selling dealer may be able to help.*

Devices known as "memory-savers" (or "code-savers") can be used to avoid some of the above problems. Precise details vary according to the device used. Typically, it is plugged into the cigarette lighter, and is connected by its own wires to a spare battery; the vehicle's own battery is then disconnected from the electrical system, leaving the "memory-saver" to pass sufficient current to maintain audio unit security codes and ECU memory values, and also to run permanently-live circuits such as the clock, all the while isolating the battery in the event of a short-circuit occurring while work is carried out.

⚠️ **Warning: Some of these devices allow a considerable amount of current to pass, which can mean that many of the vehicle's systems are still operational when the main battery is disconnected. If a "memory-saver" is used, ensure that the circuit concerned is actually "dead" before carrying out any work on it!**

## 2 Electrical fault finding - general information

Refer to Chapter 12.

## 3 Battery - testing and charging

### Standard and low maintenance battery - testing

1 If the vehicle covers a small annual mileage, it is worthwhile checking the specific gravity of the electrolyte every three months to

determine the state of charge of the battery. Use a hydrometer to make the check and compare the results with the following table.

| | Above 25°C | Below 25°C |
|---|---|---|
| Fully-charged | 1.210 to 1.230 | 1.270 to 1.290 |
| 70% charged | 1.170 to 1.190 | 1.230 to 1.250 |
| Discharged | 1.050 to 1.070 | 1.110 to 1.130 |

Note that the specific gravity readings assume an electrolyte temperature of 15°C (60°F); for every 10°C (18°F) below 15°C (60°F) subtract 0.007. For every 10°C (18°F) above 15°C (60°F) add 0.007.

2 If the battery condition is suspect, first check the specific gravity of electrolyte in each cell. A variation of 0.040 or more between any cells indicates loss of electrolyte or deterioration of the internal plates.

3 If the specific gravity variation is 0.040 or more, the battery should be renewed. If the cell variation is satisfactory but the battery is discharged, it should be charged as described later in this Section.

### Maintenance-free battery - testing

4 In cases where a "sealed for life" maintenance-free battery is fitted, topping-up and testing of the electrolyte in each cell is not possible. The condition of the battery can therefore only be tested using a battery condition indicator or a voltmeter.

5 If testing the battery using a voltmeter, connect the voltmeter across the battery and compare the result with those given in the *Specifications* under "charge condition". The test is only accurate if the battery has not been subjected to any kind of charge for the previous six hours. If this is not the case, switch on the headlights for 30 seconds, then wait four to five minutes before testing the battery after switching off the headlights. All other electrical circuits must be switched off, so check that the doors and tailgate are fully shut when making the test.

6 If the voltage reading is less than 12.2 volts, then the battery is discharged, whilst a reading of 12.2 to 12.4 volts indicates a partially discharged condition.

7 If the battery is to be charged, remove it from the vehicle (Section 4) and charge it as described later in this Section.

### Standard and low maintenance battery - charging

**Note:** *The following is intended as a guide only. Always refer to the manufacturer's recommendations (often printed on a label attached to the battery) before charging a battery.*

8 Charge the battery at a rate of 3.5 to 4 amps and continue to charge the battery at this rate until no further rise in specific gravity is noted over a four hour period.

9 Alternatively, a trickle charger charging at the rate of 1.5 amps can safely be used overnight.

10 Specially rapid "boost" charges which are claimed to restore the power of the battery in 1 to 2 hours are not recommended, as they can cause serious damage to the battery plates through overheating.

11 While charging the battery, note that the temperature of the electrolyte should never exceed 37.8°C (100°F).

### Maintenance-free battery - charging

**Note:** *The following is intended as a guide only. Always refer to the manufacturer's recommendations (often printed on a label attached to the battery) before charging a battery.*

12 This battery type takes considerably longer to fully recharge than the standard type, the time taken being dependent on the extent of discharge, but it can take anything up to three days.

13 A constant voltage type charger is required, to be set, when connected, to 13.9 to 14.9 volts with a charger current below 25 amps. Using this method, the battery should be usable within three hours, giving a voltage reading of 12.5 volts, but this is for a partially discharged battery and, as mentioned, full charging can take considerably longer.

14 If the battery is to be charged from a fully discharged state (condition reading less than 12.2 volts), have it recharged by your Ford dealer or local automotive electrician, as the charge rate is higher and constant supervision during charging is necessary.

---

**4  Battery** - removal and refitting

**Note:** *Refer to the precautions in Section 1 before starting work.*

### Removal

1 Undo the retaining nut, then detach the earth leads from the stud of the battery negative (earth) terminal post **(see illustration)**. This is the terminal to disconnect before working on, or disconnecting, any electrical component on the vehicle.

2 Pivot up the plastic cover from the positive terminal, then unscrew the positive lead

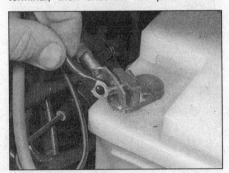

**4.1  Detaching the earth leads from the stud of the battery negative (earth) terminal post**

retaining nut on the terminal. Detach the positive lead from the terminal.

3 Unscrew the two battery clamp bolts, and remove the clamp from the front of the battery.

4 Lift the battery from the tray, keeping it upright and taking care not to let it touch any clothing. Be careful - it's heavy.

5 Clean the battery terminal posts, clamps and the battery casing. If the bulkhead is rusted as a result of battery acid spilling onto it, clean it thoroughly and re-paint with reference to "*Weekly checks*".

6 If you are renewing the battery, make sure that you get one that is identical, with the same dimensions, amperage rating, cold cranking rating, etc. Dispose of the old battery in a responsible fashion. Most local authorities have facilities for the collection and disposal of such items - batteries contain sulphuric acid and lead, and should not be simply thrown out with the household rubbish!

### Refitting

7 Refitting is a reversal of removal. Smear the battery terminals with a petroleum-based jelly prior to reconnecting. Always connect the positive terminal clamp first and the negative terminal clamp last.

---

**5  Charging system** - testing

**Note:** *Refer to the precautions in Section 1 before starting work.*

1 If the ignition warning light fails to illuminate when the ignition is switched on, first check the alternator wiring connections for security. If satisfactory, check that the warning light bulb has not blown, and that the bulbholder is secure in its location in the instrument panel. If the light still fails to illuminate, check the continuity of the warning light feed wire from the alternator to the bulbholder. If all is satisfactory, the alternator is at fault and should be renewed or taken to an auto-electrician for testing and repair.

2 If the ignition warning light illuminates when the engine is running, stop the engine and check that the drivebelt is correctly tensioned (see Chapter 1) and that the alternator connections are secure. If all is so far satisfactory, have the alternator checked by an auto-electrician for testing and repair.

3 If the alternator output is suspect even though the warning light functions correctly, the regulated voltage may be checked as follows.

4 Connect a voltmeter across the battery terminals and start the engine.

5 Increase the engine speed until the voltmeter reading remains steady; the reading should be approximately 13.5 to 14.6 volts.

6 Switch on as many electrical accessories (eg, the headlights, heated rear window and heater blower) as possible, and check that the

**5A**

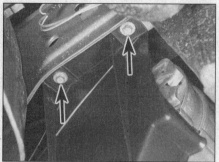

6.3 Two of the drivebelt guard retaining bolts (arrowed)

6.6 Alternator and lower mounting/pivot bolts (HCS engine shown)

6.9 Alternator removal (CVH engine shown)

alternator maintains the regulated voltage at around 13 to 14 volts.

7 If the regulated voltage is not as stated, the fault may be due to worn brushes, weak brush springs, a faulty voltage regulator, a faulty diode, a severed phase winding or worn or damaged slip rings. The alternator should be renewed or taken to an auto-electrician for testing and repair.

## 6  Alternator - removal and refitting

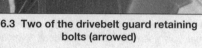

### Removal

1 Disconnect the battery negative (earth) lead (refer to Section 1).

2 Chock the rear wheels then jack up the front of the car and support it on axle stands (see "Jacking and vehicle support").

3 Where applicable, undo the retaining bolts and remove the drivebelt splash guard (see illustration).

### Alternator with V-belt drive and manual adjustment

4 On models fitted with a sliding arm type adjuster strap, unscrew and remove the top (adjuster) bolt from the strap.

5 On models fitted with a "rack-and-pinion" type adjuster, unscrew and remove the central (locking) bolt whilst, at the same time, loosening the (adjuster) nut.

6 Loosen off, but do not yet remove, the lower mounting bolts (see illustration), pivot the alternator inwards towards the engine to slacken the tension of the drivebelt, then disengage the drivebelt from the pulleys and remove it.

7 Where applicable, detach and remove the alternator heat shield.

8 Where applicable, detach and remove the phase terminal and the splash cover.

9 Supporting the weight of the alternator from underneath, unscrew and remove the mounting bolts. Lower the alternator; noting the connections, detach the wiring and remove the alternator from the vehicle (see illustration).

### Alternator with flat "polyvee" belt drive and automatic adjustment

10 Fit a ring spanner onto the drivebelt tensioner, and rotate it clockwise to loosen off the tension from the drivebelt. Note the routing of the drivebelt, then disengage the belt from the pulleys and remove it.

11 On pre-1996 model year Zetec engines detach the following components for access to the alternator:

a) Disconnect the oxygen sensor wiring multi-plug, then undo the two nuts and separate the exhaust downpipe from the manifold. Support the downpipe to avoid straining the exhaust system mountings.

b) Remove the bottom guard from the radiator. This is secured in position by clips or pop-rivets. In the latter instance, it will be necessary to carefully drill the rivets out in order to remove the guard.

c) Position a jack under the radiator support bracket. The bracket must be partially lowered on the right-hand side, and although the coolant hoses should be able to take the weight and strain of the radiator assembly and bracket, the jack will prevent the possibility of an older hose splitting.

d) Unscrew and remove the radiator support bracket retaining bolts on the right-hand side, then loosen off (but do not remove) the securing bolts on the left-hand side.

e) Unscrew and remove the alternator retaining bolts. Withdraw the alternator from its mounting bracket, disconnect the

wiring then lower the radiator/support bracket just enough to allow the alternator to be removed.

12 On all other models, unscrew the alternator upper mounting bolt(s) and disconnect the alternator wiring. Unscrew the lower bolt(s) and remove the alternator from the engine.

### Refitting

13 Refit in the reverse order of removal. Refit the drivebelt, and ensure that it is correctly re-routed around the pulleys. Adjust the tension of the drivebelt (according to type) as described in Chapter 1.

## 7  Alternator brushes and voltage regulator - renewal

1 Disconnect the battery negative (earth) lead (refer to Section 1).

2 Remove the alternator from the vehicle as described in the previous Section.

### Bosch K1-55A and K1-70A

3 Remove the two screws securing the combined brush box/regulator unit, and withdraw the assembly from the rear of the alternator (see illustrations).

4 Check the brush lengths (see illustration). If either is less than, or close to, the minimum specified length, renew them by unsoldering the brush wiring connectors and withdrawing the brushes and their springs.

7.3a Undo the retaining screws and . . .

7.3b . . . withdraw the brush box/regulator unit (Bosch K1 alternator)

**7.4 Measuring the brush lengths (Bosch K1 alternator)**

**7.7 Remove the three screws, and withdraw the plastic end cover (Bosch NC alternator)**

**7.9 Remove the regulator/brush holder from the end frame (Bosch NC alternator)**

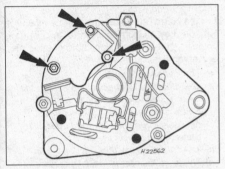

**7.14 Regulator/brush box retaining screws on the Magneti-Marelli alternator**

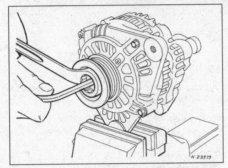

**7.18 Pulley nut removal on the Mitsubishi alternator**

5 Clean the slip rings with a solvent-moistened cloth, then check for signs of scoring, burning or severe pitting. If evident, the slip rings should be attended to by an automobile electrician.
6 Refit in the reverse order of removal.

### Bosch NC 14V 60-90A

7 Remove the three screws, and withdraw the plastic end cover (see illustration).
8 Remove the two voltage regulator/brush holder mounting screws.
9 Remove the regulator/brush holder from the end frame (see illustration).
10 Measure the exposed length of each brush, and compare it to the minimum length listed in the Specifications. If the length of either brush is less than the specified minimum, renew the assembly.
11 Make sure that each brush moves smoothly in the brush holder.
12 Check that the slip rings - the ring of copper on which each brush bears - are clean. Wipe them with a solvent-moistened cloth; if either appears scored or blackened, take the alternator to a repair specialist for advice.
13 Refit in the reverse order of removal.

### Magneti-Marelli

14 Remove the three screws securing the regulator/brush box unit on the rear face of the alternator, partially withdraw the assembly, detach the field connector, and remove the unit from the alternator (see illustration).
15 If the brushes are worn beyond the

minimum allowable length specified, a new regulator and brush box unit must be fitted; the brushes are not available separately.
16 Clean the slip rings with a solvent-

moistened cloth, then check for signs of scoring, burning or severe pitting. If evident, the slip rings should be attended to by an automobile electrician.
17 Refit in the reverse order of removal.

### Mitsubishi

18 Hold the pulley nut stationary using an 8 mm Allen key, unscrew the pulley nut and remove the washer (see illustration).
19 Withdraw the pulley, cooling fan, spacer and dust shield from the rotor shaft.
20 Mark the relative fitted positions of the front housing, stator and rear housing (to ensure correct re-alignment when reassembling). Unscrew the through-bolts and remove the front housing from the rotor shaft, followed by the dust seal and the thin spacer (see illustrations).

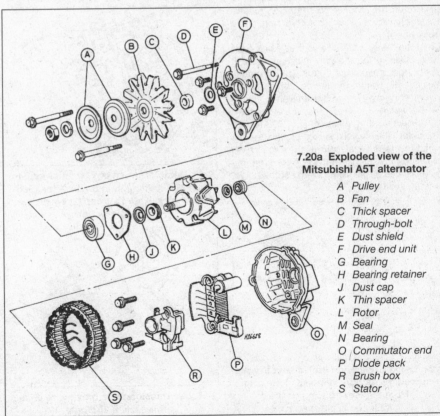

**7.20a Exploded view of the Mitsubishi A5T alternator**

A Pulley
B Fan
C Thick spacer
D Through-bolt
E Dust shield
F Drive end unit
G Bearing
H Bearing retainer
J Dust cap
K Thin spacer
L Rotor
M Seal
N Bearing
O Commutator end
P Diode pack
R Brush box
S Stator

**5A**

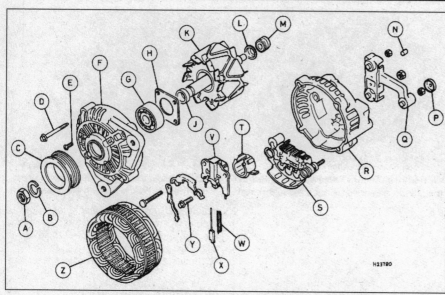

**7.20b Exploded view of the AOO2T Mitsubishi alternator**

| | | | | | |
|---|---|---|---|---|---|
| A | Pulley nut | G | Bearing | S | Rectifier |
| B | Spring washer | H | Bearing retaining | T | Dust cover |
| C | Pulley | | plate | V | Regulator |
| D | Through-bolt | J | Spacer | W | Brush spring |
| E | Retainer plate | K | Rotor | X | Brush |
| | screw | L | Spacer | Y | Regulator screw |
| F | Drive end housing | M | Slip ring end | Z | Stator |
| | | | bearing | | |
| | | N | Plug | | |
| | | P | Cap | | |
| | | Q | Terminal insulator | | |
| | | R | Slip ring end | | |
| | | | housing | | |

**21** Remove the rotor from the rear housing and the stator. If difficulty is experienced, heat the rear housing with a 200-watt soldering iron for three or four minutes **(see illustration)**.

**22** Unbolt the rectifier/brush box and stator assembly from the rear housing **(see illustration)**.

**23** Unsolder the stator and brush box from the rectifier, using the very minimum of heat. Use a pair of pliers as a heat sink to reduce the heat transference to the diodes (overheating may cause diode failure).

**24** Renew the brushes if they are worn down to, or beyond, the minimum specified length. Unsolder the brush wires at the points indicated **(see illustration)**, then solder the new brush leads so that the wear limit line projects 2 to 3 mm from the end of the holder **(see illustration)**.

**25** Clean the slip rings with a solvent-moistened cloth, then check for signs of scoring, burning or severe pitting. If evident, the slip rings should be attended to by an automobile electrician.

**26** Refit in the reverse order of removal. Insert a piece of wire through the access hole in the rear housing to hold the brushes in the retracted position as the rotor is refitted **(see illustration)**. Do not forget to release the brushes when assembled.

## 8 Starting system - testing

**Note:** Refer to the precautions in Section 1 before starting work.

**1** If the starter motor fails to operate when the ignition key is turned to the appropriate position, the following possible causes may be to blame.

a) The battery is faulty.
b) The electrical connections between the switch, solenoid, battery and starter motor are somewhere failing to pass the necessary current from the battery through the starter to earth.
c) The solenoid is faulty.
d) The starter motor is mechanically or electrically defective.

**2** To check the battery, switch on the headlights. If they dim after a few seconds, this indicates that the battery is discharged - recharge (see Section 3) or renew the battery. If the headlights glow brightly, operate the

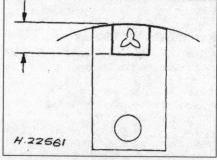

**7.22 Rectifier/brush box (1) and regulator unit (3) retaining nuts on the Mitsubishi alternator. Note that cap (2) covers the regulator nut**

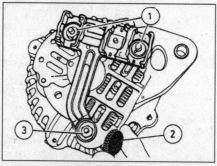

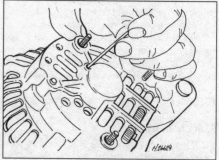

**7.24b Fitted position of new brush on a Mitsubishi alternator**

**7.21 Using a soldering iron to heat the slip ring end housing for removal of the rotor from the rear housing on the Mitsubishi alternator**

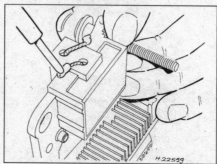

**7.24a Unsoldering a brush wire on a Mitsubishi alternator**

**7.26 Use a length of wire rod to hold brushes in the retracted position when reassembling the rotor to the housing on the Mitsubishi alternator**

ignition switch and observe the lights. If they dim, then this indicates that current is reaching the starter motor, therefore the fault must lie in the starter motor. If the lights continue to glow brightly (and no clicking sound can be heard from the starter motor solenoid), this indicates that there is a fault in the circuit or solenoid - see following paragraphs. If the starter motor turns slowly when operated, but the battery is in good condition, then this indicates that either the starter motor is faulty, or there is considerable resistance somewhere in the circuit.

3 If a fault in the circuit is suspected, disconnect the battery leads (including the earth connection to the body), the starter/solenoid wiring and the engine/transmission earth strap. Thoroughly clean the connections, and reconnect the leads and wiring, then use a voltmeter or test lamp to check that full battery voltage is available at the battery positive lead connection to the solenoid, and that the earth is sound. Smear petroleum jelly around the battery terminals to prevent corrosion - corroded connections are amongst the most frequent causes of electrical system faults.

4 If the battery and all connections are in good condition, check the circuit by disconnecting the wire from the solenoid blade terminal. Connect a voltmeter or test lamp between the wire end and a good earth (such as the battery negative terminal), and check that the wire is live when the ignition switch is turned to the "start" position. If it is, then the circuit is sound - if not the circuit wiring can be checked as described in Chapter 12.

5 The solenoid contacts can be checked by connecting a voltmeter or test lamp between the battery positive feed connection on the starter side of the solenoid, and earth. When the ignition switch is turned to the "start" position, there should be a reading or lighted bulb, as applicable. If there is no reading or lighted bulb, the solenoid is faulty and should be renewed.

6 If the circuit and solenoid are proved sound, the fault must lie in the starter motor. In this event, it may be possible to have the starter motor overhauled by a specialist, but check on the cost of spares before proceeding, as it may prove more economical to obtain a new or exchange motor.

9.4a  Starter motor and wiring connections (CVH engine shown)

9.4b  Oxygen sensor wiring multi-plug connector and location bracket

9.5a  Starter motor support bracket bolt

9.5b  Starter motor removal (CVH engine shown)

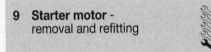
## 9  Starter motor - removal and refitting

### Removal

1 Disconnect the battery negative (earth) lead (refer to Section 1).

2 Chock the rear wheels then jack up the front of the car and support it on axle stands (see "Jacking and vehicle support"). Remove the front roadwheels.

3 Undo the two retaining nuts, and remove the starter motor heat shield (where fitted).

4 Prise free the cap, if fitted, then unscrew the nuts to disconnect the wiring from the starter/solenoid terminals. Where applicable, disconnect the oxygen sensor wiring multi-plug from the locating bracket (see illustrations).

5 Unscrew and remove the starter motor retaining bolts at the transmission/clutch housing and, where applicable, also unbolt

and detach the support bracket. Withdraw the starter motor from its mounting, and remove it from the vehicle (see illustrations).

### Refitting

6 Refitting is a reversal of removal. Tighten the retaining bolts to the specified torque. Ensure that the wiring is securely reconnected to the starter motor (and solenoid) and is routed clear of the exhaust downpipe.

## 10  Starter motor - testing and overhaul

If the starter motor is thought to be suspect, it should be removed from the vehicle and taken to an auto-electrician for testing. Most auto-electricians will be able to supply and fit brushes at a reasonable cost. However, check on the cost of repairs before proceeding as it may prove more economical to obtain a new or exchange motor.

**5A**

# Chapter 5 Part B: Ignition system

## Contents

## Degrees of difficulty

| | | | | |
|---|---|---|---|---|
| **Easy,** suitable for novice with little experience  | **Fairly easy,** suitable for beginner with some experience  | **Fairly difficult,** suitable for competent DIY mechanic | **Difficult,** suitable for experienced DIY mechanic | **Very difficult,** suitable for expert DIY or professional |

## Specifications

**Ignition coil**

| | |
|---|---|
| Output . . . . . . . . . . . . . . . . . . . . . . . . . . . . . . . . . . . . . . . . . . . . . . . | 37.0 kilovolts (minimum) |
| Primary resistances - measured at coil connector terminal pins . . . . . . | 0.50 ± 0.05 ohms |
| **Spark plugs** . . . . . . . . . . . . . . . . . . . . . . . . . . . . . . . . . . . . . . . . . . . . | See Chapter 1 Specifications |

| **Torque wrench setting** | Nm | lbf ft |
|---|---|---|
| Ignition coil retaining screws . . . . . . . . . . . . . . . . . . . . . . . . . . . . . . . | 6 | 4 |

---

## 1 General information and precautions

### General information

The main ignition system components include the ignition switch, the battery, the crankshaft speed/position sensor, the ignition module, the coil, the primary (low tension/LT) and secondary (high tension/HT) wiring circuits, and the spark plugs.

A Distributorless Ignition System (DIS) is used on all carburettor engines, and an Electronic Distributorless Ignition System (E-DIS) on all fuel injection engines. With these systems, the main functions of the conventional distributor are replaced by the computerised ignition module and a coil unit. The coil unit combines a double-ended pair of coils - each time a coil receives an ignition signal, two sparks are produced, at each end of the secondary windings. One spark goes to a cylinder on compression stroke and the other goes to the corresponding cylinder on its exhaust stroke. The first will give the correct power stroke, but the second spark will have no effect (a "wasted spark"), occurring as it does during exhaust conditions.

On carburettor engines, the ignition module receives signals provided by information sensors which monitor various engine functions (such as crankshaft speed/position, coolant temperature, inlet air temperature, etc). This information allows the ignition module to generate the optimum ignition timing setting under all operating conditions.

On fuel injection engines, the ignition module operates in conjunction with the fuel system Electronic Control Unit (ECU), and together with the various information sensors and emission control components, forms the complete engine management package.

The information contained in this Chapter concentrates on the ignition-related components of the engine management system. Information covering the fuel, exhaust and emission control components can be found in the applicable Parts of Chapter 4.

### Precautions

When working on the ignition system, take the following precautions:

a) *Do not keep the ignition on for more than 10 seconds if the engine will not start.*

b) *If a separate tachometer is ever required for servicing work, consult a dealer service department before buying a tachometer for use with this vehicle - some tachometers may be incompatible with this type of ignition system - and always connect it in accordance with the equipment manufacturer's instructions.*

c) *Never connect the ignition coil terminals to earth. This could result in damage to the coil and/or the ignition module.*

d) *Do not disconnect the battery when the engine is running.*

e) *Make sure that the ignition module is properly earthed.*

f) *Refer to the warning at the beginning of the next Section concerning HT voltage.*

## 2 Ignition system - testing

⚠️ *Warning: Voltages produced by an electronic ignition system are considerably higher than those produced by conventional ignition systems. Extreme care must be taken when working on the system with the ignition switched on. Persons with surgically-implanted cardiac pacemaker devices should keep well clear of the ignition circuits, components and test equipment.*

**Note:** *Refer to the precautions given in Section 1 of Part A of this Chapter before starting work. Always switch off the ignition before disconnecting or connecting any component and when using a multi-meter to check resistances.*

1 If the engine turns over but won't start, disconnect the (HT) lead from any spark plug, and attach it to a calibrated tester (available at most automotive accessory shops). Connect the clip on the tester to a good earth - a bolt or metal bracket on the engine. If you're unable to obtain a calibrated ignition tester, have the check carried out by a Ford dealer service department or similar. Any other form of testing (such as jumping a spark from the end of an HT lead to earth) is not recommended, because of the risk of personal injury, or of damage to the ignition module.

2 Crank the engine, and watch the end of the tester to see if bright blue, well-defined sparks occur.

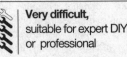

**5B**

**3** If sparks occur, sufficient voltage is reaching the plug to fire it. Repeat the check at the remaining plugs, to ensure that all leads are sound and that the coil is serviceable. However, the plugs themselves may be fouled or faulty, so remove and check them as described in Chapter 1.

**4** If no sparks or intermittent sparks occur, the spark plug lead(s) may be defective - check them as described in Chapter 1.

**5** If there's still no spark, check the coil's electrical connector, to make sure it's clean and tight. Check for full battery voltage to the coil at the connector's centre terminal. Check the coil itself (see Section 3). Make any necessary repairs, then repeat the check again.

**6** The remainder of the system checks should be left to a dealer service department or other qualified repair facility, as there is a chance that the ignition module may be damaged if tests are not performed properly.

**3.7  Disconnecting the multi-plug from the ignition coil**

**3.9  Disconnecting an HT lead from the ignition coil (CVH engine shown)**

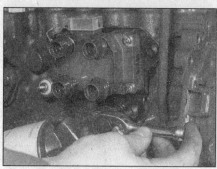

**3.10a  Unbolting the ignition coil from the HCS engine**

**3.10b  Removing the ignition coil from the CVH engine (leaving the HT leads attached)**

## 3  Ignition coil - checking, removal and refitting

### Check

**1** Having checked that full battery voltage is available at the centre terminal of the coil's electrical connector (see Section 2), disconnect the battery negative (earth) lead (refer to Part A, Section 1).

**2** Unplug the coil's electrical connector, if not already disconnected.

**3** Using an ohmmeter, measure the resistance of the coil's primary windings, connecting the meter between the connector terminal pins as follows. Measure first from one outer pin to the centre pin, then from the other outer pin to the centre. Compare the readings with the coil primary resistance listed in the *Specifications*.

**4** Disconnect the spark plug (HT) leads - note their connections or label them carefully, as described in Chapter 1. Use the meter to check that there is continuity (ie, a resistance corresponding to that of the coil secondary winding) between each pair of (HT) lead terminals; Nos 1 and 4 terminals are connected by their secondary winding, as are Nos 2 and 3. Now switch to the highest resistance scale, and check that there is no continuity between either pair of terminals and the other - ie, there should be infinite resistance between terminals 1 and 2, or 4 and 3 - and between any terminal and earth.

**5** If either of the above tests yield resistance values outside the specified amount, or results other than those described, renew the coil. Any further testing should be left to a dealer service department or other qualified repair facility.

### Removal

**6** Disconnect the battery negative (earth) lead (refer to Part A, Section 1).

**7** Disconnect the coil main electrical connector and (where fitted) the electrical connector to the suppressor **(see illustration)**.

**8** The coil can be removed with the HT leads left attached, in which case disconnect the leads from their respective spark plugs and from the location clips in the rocker cover or air inlet duct (as applicable). If preferred, the HT leads can be disconnected from the coil. First check that both the ignition HT leads and their fitted positions are clearly marked numerically to ensure correct refitting. Spot mark them accordingly if necessary, using quick-drying paint.

**9** If disconnecting the HT leads from the spark plugs, always pull them free by gripping on the connector, not the lead. To detach the leads from the ignition coil, compress the retaining arms of each lead connector at the coil, and detach each lead in turn **(see illustration)**.

**10** Unscrew the Torx-type retaining screws, and remove the coil from its mounting on the engine **(see illustrations)**.

### Refitting

**11** Refitting is the reverse of the removal procedure. Ensure that the spark plug (HT) leads are correctly reconnected, and tighten the coil screws to the specified torque setting.

## 4  Ignition module (carburettor engines) - removal and refitting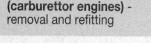

### Removal

**1** The ignition module is on the engine compartment left-hand inner wing panel.

**2** Disconnect the battery negative (earth) lead (refer to Part A, Section 1).

**3** Detach the vacuum hose from the module **(see illustration)**.

**4** According to type, either compress the locktab securing the wiring multi-plug in position, or where applicable, undo the retaining bolt, then withdraw the plug from the module **(see illustration)**.

**5** Undo the retaining screws, and remove the module from the inner wing panel.

**4.3  Ignition module showing vacuum hose and multi-plug arrangement (CVH carburettor engine shown)**

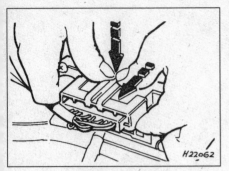

**4.4 Multi-plug removal from the ignition module**

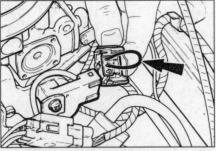

**4.9 Bridge the earth signal and ground terminals in the throttle position sensor multi-plug with a length of wire (arrowed)**

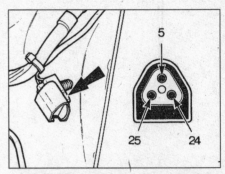

**4.10 Ignition module service connector (arrowed) and terminal identification**

## Refitting

**6** Refitting is the reverse of the removal procedure. If working on a 1.6 litre CVH engine model with power steering, air conditioning and/or automatic transmission, the following procedure must be followed before starting the engine.

**7** When a new module is fitted, or when certain carburettor or engine components have been changed, it is necessary to clear the module memory and allow it to "learn" new engine parameters for its correct operation. This is done as follows.

**8** With the ignition switched off, disconnect the throttle position sensor multi-plug on the side of the carburettor.

**9** Using a short length of wire, bridge the earth signal terminal and ground terminal in the wiring multi-plug **(see illustration)**.

**10** Locate the ignition module service connector, which is a small multi-plug (like the throttle position sensor multi-plug) joined to the main wiring loom by three wires. The service connector will be located either adjacent to the ignition module or on the engine compartment bulkhead near the carburettor **(see illustration)**.

**11** If the service connector multi-plug has a wire connected to its centre terminal (pin 5), disconnect the wire.

**12** Switch on the ignition, but do not crank the engine on the starter.

**13** Connect one end of a suitable length of wire to the multi-plug centre terminal (pin 5), and hold the other end of the wire on a good earth point for 5 seconds only.

**14** Switch off the ignition, and remove the earthing wire from pin 5 of the multi-plug.

**15** Remove the bridge wire from the throttle position sensor multi-plug, and reconnect the multi-plug.

**16** Start the engine and allow it to idle. The idle speed will be initially high, but will then settle back to a stable idle condition.

**17** Switch off the ignition and, if pin 5 of the service connector had a wire connected to it originally, reconnect the wire.

## 5  Ignition module (fuel injection engines) - removal and refitting

### Removal

**1** The ignition module is located on the engine compartment left-hand inner wing panel.

**2** Disconnect the battery negative (earth) lead (refer to Part A, Section 1).

**3** Disconnect the wiring multi-plug from the module, pulling on the plug, not the wire **(see illustration)**.

**4** Undo the two retaining screws, and remove the module from the inner wing panel.

### Refitting

**5** Refit in the reverse order of removal. On completion, reconnect the battery and restart the engine.

## 6  Ignition timing - checking

The ignition timing is controlled by the ignition module (acting in conjunction with the ECU on fuel injection engines), and cannot be adjusted.

Not only can the ignition timing not be adjusted, it cannot be checked either, except with the use of special diagnostic equipment - this makes it a task for a Ford dealer.

## 7  Crankshaft position sensor - removal and refitting

### Removal

**1** Disconnect the battery negative (earth) lead.

**2** Chock the rear wheels then jack up the front of the car and support it on axle stands (see *"Jacking and vehicle support"*).

**3** On Zetec or Zetec-E engines, remove the starter motor (see Part A of this Chapter).

**4** Compress the retaining clip and pull free the wiring multi-plug connector from the sensor unit, but take care to pull on the connector, not the lead **(see illustration)**.

**5** Undo the Torx-type screw, and withdraw the sensor from its location in the cylinder block bellhousing flange **(see illustration)**.

### Refitting

**6** Refitting is the reversal of removal.

**5B**

**5.3 Ignition module and wiring connection on the 1.6 litre EFi fuel-injected engine**

**7.4 Disconnecting the wiring connector from the crankshaft position sensor**

**7.5 Crankshaft position sensor shown removed from engine**

# Notes

# Chapter 6 Clutch

## Contents

## Degrees of difficulty

|  **Easy,** suitable for novice with little experience |  **Fairly easy,** suitable for beginner with some experience |  **Fairly difficult,** suitable for competent DIY mechanic |  **Difficult,** suitable for experienced DIY mechanic | **Very difficult,** suitable for expert DIY or professional |
|---|---|---|---|---|

## Specifications

### General

| | | |
|---|---|---|
| Type . . . . . . . . . . . . . . . . . . . . . . . | Diaphragm spring, single dry plate, cable operation | |
| Pedal free play: | | |
| Pre-1996 models . . . . . . . . . . . . . . . | Automatic adjustment | |
| 1996 models on . . . . . . . . . . . . . . . | 150 ± 5 mm (RHD) | 145± 5 mm (LHD) |
| Disc diameter: | | |
| 1.3 and 1.4 litre engines . . . . . . . . . | 190 mm | |
| 1.6 litre engines . . . . . . . . . . . . . . . | 220 mm | |
| 1.8 litre engines: | | |
| With B5 and iB5 transmission . . . . . | 220 mm | |
| With MTX-75 transmission . . . . . . . | 240 mm | |

### Torque wrench settings

| | Nm | lbf ft |
|---|---|---|
| Clutch cover (pressure plate) to flywheel . . . . . . . . . . . | 30 | 22 |
| Clutch release lever to lever shaft . . . . . . . . . . . . | 25 | 18 |

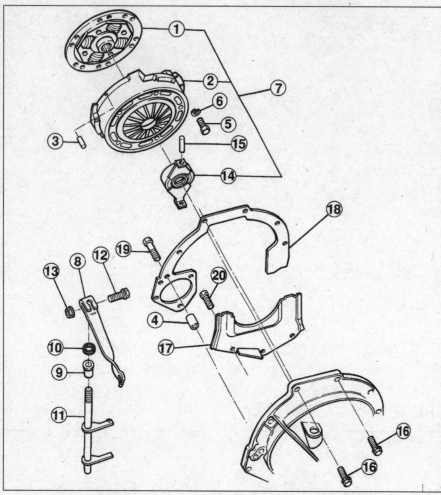

**1.1 Exploded view of the clutch and associated components**

| | | |
|---|---|---|
| 1 Clutch disc (driven plate) | 8 Release lever | 16 Bolts |
| 2 Clutch cover and pressure plate unit | 9 Bush | 17 Clutch housing cover plate (lower) |
| 3 Dowel | 10 Seal | 18 Clutch housing intermediate plate (upper) |
| 4 Dowel | 11 Clutch release shaft | |
| 5 Bolt | 12 Bolt | 19 Bolt |
| 6 Lockwasher | 13 Nut | 20 Bolt |
| 7 Clutch repair kit | 14 Clutch release bearing | |
| | 15 Pin | |

## 1 General information

All manual transmission models are equipped with a cable-operated single dry plate diaphragm spring clutch assembly. The unit consists of a clutch disc (or driven plate), a steel cover (doweled and bolted to the rear face of the flywheel, it contains the pressure plate and diaphragm spring) and a release mechanism (see illustration).

The clutch disc is free to slide along the splines of the transmission input shaft, and is held in position between the flywheel and the pressure plate by the pressure of the diaphragm spring. Friction lining material is riveted to the clutch disc, which has a spring cushioned hub to absorb transmission shocks and help ensure a smooth take-up of the drive.

The clutch is actuated by a cable, controlled by the clutch pedal. The clutch release mechanism consists of a release arm and bearing, which is in permanent contact with the fingers of the diaphragm spring. Depressing the clutch pedal actuates the release arm by means of the cable. The arm pushes the release bearing against the diaphragm fingers, so moving the centre of the diaphragm spring inwards. As the centre of the spring is pushed in, the outside of the spring pivots out, so moving the pressure plate backwards and disengaging its grip on the clutch disc.

When the pedal is released, the diaphragm spring forces the pressure plate back into contact with the friction linings on the clutch disc. The disc is now firmly held between the pressure plate and the flywheel, thus transmitting engine power to the transmission.

On pre-1996 models, wear of the friction material on the clutch disc is automatically compensated for by a self-adjusting mechanism attached to the clutch pedal; this arrangement is replaced by a manual adjuster on later models. The self-adjusting mechanism consists of a toothed segment, a notched pawl and a tension spring. One end of the clutch cable is attached to the segment which is free to pivot on the pedal, but is kept in tension by the spring. As the pedal is depressed, the pawl contacts the segment, thus locking it and allowing the pedal to pull the cable and operate the clutch. As the pedal is released, the tension spring causes the segment to move free of the pawl and rotate slightly, thus taking up any free play that may exist in the cable.

## 2 Clutch cable - removal and refitting

### Removal

**1** At the transmission end, disengage the clutch cable from the release lever by gripping the inner cable with pliers, pulling it forwards to disengage the cable nipple from the release lever. Take care not to damage the cable if it is to be re-used. Disengage the outer cable from the support lug on top of the bellhousing (see illustrations).

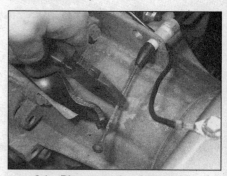

**2.1a Disengage the clutch cable from the lever . . .**

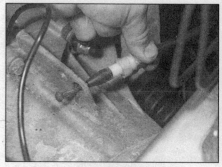

**2.1b . . . and withdraw the cable through the locating lug**

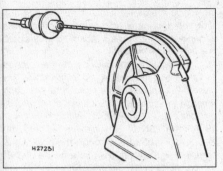

**2.3 Clutch cable connection at the pedal end**

**2** Working from the driver's footwell, unhook the segment tension spring from its pedal location.

**3** Release the cable from the pedal segment so that it may be withdrawn through the engine compartment **(see illustration)**.

**4** Pull the cable through the aperture in the bulkhead, and withdraw it from the engine compartment.

## Refitting

**5** To refit the cable, thread it through from the engine compartment and fit the inner cable over the segment, engaging the nipple to secure it. Reconnect the tension spring.

**6** Reconnect the cable at the transmission end, passing it through the support lug on the top of the transmission and engaging it with the release lever.

**7** On models with a self-adjusting clutch, operate the clutch and check it for satisfactory operation. On models with a manually adjusted clutch, check and if necessary adjust the clutch pedal free play as described in Chapter 1.

## 3 Clutch pedal - removal and refitting

### Removal

**1** Disconnect the battery negative (earth) lead (refer to Chapter 5A, Section 1).

**2** Disconnect the clutch cable at the transmission end by slipping the cable nipple out of the release fork and disengaging the outer cable from the bracket on the bellhousing.

**3** Referring to Chapter 12 for details, detach the fusebox and the relay multi-plugs, then position the fusebox unit out of the way to allow access to the clutch pedal.

**4** Release the clutch cable from the pedal (see Section 2).

**5** Release the brake stop light switch in a clockwise direction, and extract it from the pedal bracket.

**6** Release the clip securing the brake pedal connecting rod.

**7** Release the retaining clip from the end of the pedal shaft, then slide the shaft through

**3.8a Clutch pedal and self-adjusting cable components**

A Pawl
B Pawl tension spring
C Pedal connecting rod and clip
D Pedal/shaft bushes
E Clutch pedal
F Toothed segment tension spring
G Toothed segment

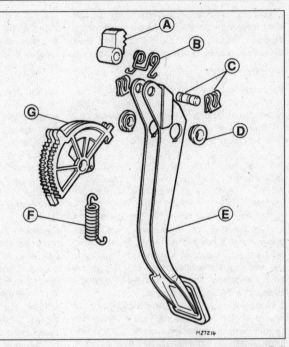

(away from the steering column) and remove the brake pedal, the spacer sleeves and the clutch pedal.

**8** The pedal can now be dismantled as necessary by prising out the bushes, the tension spring or the adjustment mechanism as applicable **(see illustrations)**.

## Refitting

**9** Refitting is a reversal of the removal procedure. Apply a little grease to the pedal shaft and bushes, and ensure that the bushes are correctly located. On models with a self-adjusting clutch, do not refit the toothed segment tension spring into position until after the pedal is fitted onto the shaft. The pawl and its tension spring must be fitted so that the

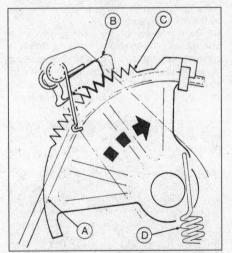

**3.8b Clutch cable self-adjusting mechanism**

A Clutch cable
B Pawl
C Toothed segment
D Tension spring

pawl is bearing on the toothed segment. Pull the spring into position using a suitable length of temporarily-attached wire **(see illustration)**.

**10** On models with a self-adjusting clutch, operate the clutch and check it for satisfactory operation. On models with a manually adjusted clutch, check and if necessary adjust the clutch pedal free play as described in Chapter 1.

## 4 Clutch assembly - removal, inspection and refitting

⚠ *Warning: Dust created by clutch wear and deposited on the clutch components may contain asbestos, which is a health hazard. DO NOT blow it out with compressed air, or inhale any of it. DO NOT use petrol or petroleum-based solvents to clean off the dust. Brake system cleaner or methylated spirit should be used to flush the dust into*

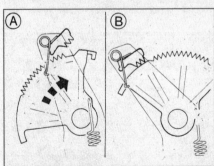

**3.9 Positioning the clutch self-adjuster mechanism prior to refitting the pedal**

A Lift pawl and turn the segment
B Pawl bearing on smooth section of segment

**6**

*a suitable receptacle. After the clutch components are wiped clean with rags, dispose of the contaminated rags and cleaner in a sealed, marked container.*

## Removal

**1** Access to the clutch may be gained in one of two ways. Depending on the engine fitted, either the engine or engine/transmission can be removed as described in Chapter 2D, and where applicable, the transmission separated from the engine, or the engine may be left in the car and the transmission removed independently, as described in Chapter 7A.

**2** Having separated the transmission from the engine, check if there are any marks identifying the relation of the clutch cover to the flywheel. If not, make your own marks using a dab of paint or a scriber. These marks will be used if the original cover is refitted, and will help to maintain the balance of the unit. A new cover may be fitted in any position allowed by the locating dowels.

**3** Unscrew and remove the six clutch cover retaining bolts, working in a diagonal sequence and slackening the bolts only a few turns at a time. If necessary, the flywheel may be held stationary using a wide-bladed screwdriver, inserted in the teeth of the starter ring gear and resting against part of the cylinder block.

**4** Ease the clutch cover off its locating dowels. Be prepared to catch the clutch disc, which will drop out as the cover is removed. Note which way round the disc is fitted **(see illustration)**.

## Inspection

**5** The most common problem which occurs in the clutch is wear of the clutch disc. However, all the clutch components should be inspected at this time, particularly if the vehicle has covered a high mileage. Unless the clutch components are known to be virtually new, it is worth renewing them all as a set (disc, pressure plate and release bearing). Renewing a worn clutch disc by itself is not always satisfactory, especially if the old disc was slipping and causing the pressure plate to overheat. Not renewing the release bearing is a false economy - it's bound to wear out eventually, and all the preliminary dismantling

will have to be repeated if it's not renewed with the rest of the clutch.

**6** Examine the linings of the clutch disc for wear and loose rivets, and the disc hub and rim for distortion, cracks, broken torsion springs, and worn splines. The surface of the friction linings may be highly glazed, but as long as the friction material pattern can be clearly seen, and the rivet heads are at least 1 mm below the lining surface, this is satisfactory. If there is any sign of oil contamination, indicated by shiny black discoloration, the disc must be renewed, and the source of the contamination traced and rectified. This will be a leaking crankshaft oil seal or transmission input shaft oil seal. The renewal procedure for the former is given in the appropriate Part of Chapter 2; renewal of the transmission input shaft oil seal should be entrusted to a Ford dealer, as it involves major dismantling and the renewal of the clutch release bearing guide tube, using a press.

**7** Check the machined faces of the flywheel and pressure plate. If either is grooved, or heavily scored, renewal is necessary. The pressure plate must also be renewed if any cracks are apparent, or if the diaphragm spring is damaged, or its pressure suspect. Pay particular attention to the tips of the spring fingers, where the release bearing acts upon them.

**8** With the transmission removed, it is also advisable to check the condition of the release bearing, as described in Section 5. Having got this far, it is almost certainly worth renewing it.

## Refitting

**9** It is important that no oil or grease is allowed to come into contact with the friction material of the clutch disc or the pressure plate and flywheel faces. To ensure this, it is advisable to refit the clutch assembly with clean hands, and to wipe down the pressure plate and flywheel faces with a clean rag before assembly begins.

**10** Begin reassembly by placing the clutch disc against the flywheel, ensuring that it is correctly orientated. It may be marked "flywheel side" **(see illustration)**, but if not, position it with the word "schwungradseite" stamped in the disc face towards the flywheel.

**11** Place the clutch cover over the dowels, refit the retaining bolts, and tighten them finger-tight so that the clutch disc is gripped, but can still be moved.

**12** The clutch disc must now be centralised so that, when the engine and transmission are mated, the splines of the input shaft will pass through the splines in the centre of the clutch disc hub.

**13** Centralisation can be carried out by inserting a round bar through the hole in the centre of the clutch disc, so that the end of the bar rests in the innermost hole in the rear end of the crankshaft. Move the bar sideways or up and down to move the clutch disc in whichever direction is necessary to achieve centralisation.

**14** Centralisation can then be checked by removing the bar and viewing the clutch disc hub in relation to the diaphragm spring fingers. When the disc hub appears exactly in the centre of the circle created by the diaphragm spring fingers, the position is correct.

**15** An alternative and more accurate method of centralisation is to use a commercially-available clutch-aligning tool, obtainable from most accessory shops **(see illustration)**.

**16** Once the clutch is centralised, progressively tighten the cover bolts in a diagonal sequence to the torque setting given in the *Specifications*.

**17** Ensure that the input shaft splines, clutch disc splines and release bearing guide sleeve are clean. Apply a thin smear of high-melting-point grease to the input shaft splines and the release bearing guide sleeve. Only use a very small amount of grease, otherwise the excess will inevitably find its way onto the friction linings when the vehicle is in use.

**18** The engine/transmission can now be refitted by referring to the relevant Chapters of this manual.

## 5 Clutch release bearing - removal, inspection and refitting

**Note:** *Refer to the warning at the beginning of Section 4 before proceeding.*

**4.4 Removing the clutch cover and disc from the flywheel**

**4.10 Clutch disc orientation markings**

**4.15 Centralising the clutch disc using a clutch aligning tool**

5.2 Withdrawing the
clutch release bearing

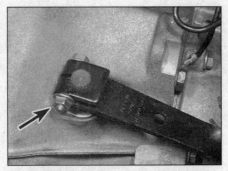

6.2 Clutch release lever-to-shaft connection
with clamp bolt and nut (arrowed)

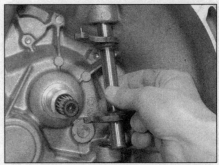

6.5 Removing the clutch release shaft

## Removal

**1** Separate the engine and transmission as described in the previous Section.
**2** Withdraw the release bearing from its guide sleeve by turning the release arm **(see illustration)**.

## Inspection

**3** Check the bearing for smoothness of operation, and renew it if there is any sign of harshness or roughness as the bearing is spun. Do not attempt to dismantle, clean or lubricate the bearing.
**4** As mentioned earlier, it is worth renewing the release bearing as a matter of course, unless it is known to be in perfect condition.

## Refitting

**5** Refitting of the clutch release bearing is a reversal of the removal procedure, making sure that it is correctly located on the release arm fork. It is helpful to slightly lift the release arm while locating the bearing on its guide sleeve. Keep the fork in contact with the plastic shoulders on the bearing (where fitted) as the bearing is being located.

## 6 Clutch release shaft and bush - removal and refitting

## Removal

**1** Remove the clutch release bearing as described in the previous Section.
**2** Unscrew the clamp bolt securing the release arm to the shaft **(see illustration)**. Mark the relative position of the shaft to the arm, then withdraw the arm from the shaft.

The shaft has a master spline, to ensure that the arm is fitted correctly.
**3** Remove the protective cap from around the top of the release shaft splines to allow access to the bush.
**4** Extract the bush by gently levering it from the housing using a pair of screwdrivers, then lift it out over the splines of the shaft.
**5** With the bush removed, the release shaft can be withdrawn (if required) by lifting it from its lower bearing bore, manoeuvring it sideways and withdrawing it **(see illustration)**.

## Refitting

**6** Refit in the reverse order of removal. Slide the bush over the shaft, and locate it so that it is flush in the upper housing, then fit the protective cap.
**7** Refit the release bearing as described in the previous Section.

**6**

# Notes

# Chapter 7 Part A:
# Manual transmission

## Contents

## Degrees of difficulty

| Easy, suitable for novice with little experience | Fairly easy, suitable for beginner with some experience | Fairly difficult, suitable for competent DIY mechanic | Difficult, suitable for experienced DIY mechanic | Very difficult, suitable for expert DIY or professional |
|---|---|---|---|---|
|  |  | 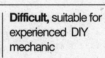 |  | |

## Specifications

### Transmission type/application
1.3, 1.4 and 1.6 litre engine models . . . . . . . . . . . . . . . . . . . . . . . . . . B5 type, 4- or 5-speed, or iB5 type, 5-speed
1.8 litre engine models . . . . . . . . . . . . . . . . . . . . . . . . . . . . . . . . . . . B5 or iB5 type, 5-speed, or MTX-75 type, 5-speed

### Gear ratios (typical)
B5 and iB5 transmission:
1st . . . . . . . . . . . . . . . . . . . . . . . . . . . . . . . . . . . . . . . . 3.15:1
2nd . . . . . . . . . . . . . . . . . . . . . . . . . . . . . . . . . . . . . . . 1.91:1
3rd . . . . . . . . . . . . . . . . . . . . . . . . . . . . . . . . . . . . . . . 1.28:1
4th . . . . . . . . . . . . . . . . . . . . . . . . . . . . . . . . . . . . . . . 0.95:1
5th . . . . . . . . . . . . . . . . . . . . . . . . . . . . . . . . . . . . . . . 0.75:1
Reverse . . . . . . . . . . . . . . . . . . . . . . . . . . . . . . . . . . . . 3.62:1
Final drive . . . . . . . . . . . . . . . . . . . . . . . . . . . . . . . . . . 3.82:1, 3.84:1, 4.06:1 or 4.27:1 (according to model)
MTX-75 transmission:
1st . . . . . . . . . . . . . . . . . . . . . . . . . . . . . . . . . . . . . . . 3.23:1
2nd . . . . . . . . . . . . . . . . . . . . . . . . . . . . . . . . . . . . . . 2.13:1
3rd . . . . . . . . . . . . . . . . . . . . . . . . . . . . . . . . . . . . . . 1.48:1
4th . . . . . . . . . . . . . . . . . . . . . . . . . . . . . . . . . . . . . . 1.11:1
5th . . . . . . . . . . . . . . . . . . . . . . . . . . . . . . . . . . . . . . 0.85:1
Reverse . . . . . . . . . . . . . . . . . . . . . . . . . . . . . . . . . . . . 3.46:1
Final drive . . . . . . . . . . . . . . . . . . . . . . . . . . . . . . . . . . 3.82:1 or 3.84:1 (according to model)

### Torque wrench settings

| | Nm | lbf ft |
|---|---|---|
| Reversing light switch | 18 | 13 |
| Engine-to-transmission bolts | 44 | 32 |
| Clutch housing cover plate bolts | 40 | 30 |
| Left-hand rear mounting bracket-to-transmission | 50 | 37 |
| Left-hand rear mounting bracket-to-mounting | 68 | 50 |
| Left-hand front mounting bracket-to-mounting | 68 | 50 |
| Left-hand front mounting bracket brace | 49 | 36 |
| Gearshift stabiliser rod-to-transmission | 55 | 41 |
| Gearshift rod to transmission selector shaft | 23 | 17 |
| Gearshift linkage clamp bolt | 16 | 12 |
| Gearshift housing-to-floor | 10 | 7 |
| Gearshift stabiliser rod-to-housing | 7 | 5 |

## 1 General information

Three types of manual transmission are available. Most models are equipped with a 4- or 5-speed unit designated "B5" or iB5. Certain Zetec and Zetec-E-engined models are equipped with a 5-speed unit designated "MTX-75". The transmission is mounted transversely in the engine bay, bolted directly to the engine.

All types feature a compact, two-piece, light-weight aluminium alloy housing, containing both the transmission and the differential assemblies.

The transmission is lubricated independently of the engine, the capacity differing according to type (see Chapter 1). The transmission and differential both share the same lubricating oil. Torque from the transmission output shaft is transmitted to the crownwheel (which is bolted to the differential unit), and then from the differential gears to the driveshafts.

Gearshift is by means of a floor-mounted gear lever, connected by a remote control housing and gearshift rod to the transmission selector shaft.

## 2 Gearchange linkage - adjustment

### B5 and iB5 type transmission

**1** Chock the rear wheels then jack up the front of the car and support it on axle stands (see "Jacking and vehicle support").
**2** On 4-speed models, select 2nd gear; on 5-speed models, select 4th gear.
**3** Working from underneath the vehicle, loosen off the gearshift rod-to-gear selector shaft clamp bolt, and disengage the shift rod from the transmission selector shaft **(see illustrations)**. Slide the selector shaft back and forth to find its central position, then turn the selector shaft to the right and left to find the central position in the transverse plane. Hold the selector shaft in the centralised position, then insert a suitable rod (or punch) into the hole in the selector shaft in the transmission, and move it as far forwards as possible **(see illustration)**.
**4** Insert a fabricated "lock pin" adjustment tool (from the left-hand side), and secure it in position with a sturdy elastic band or similar **(see illustration)**.
**5** Check that the selector shaft coupling surfaces are free of grease, then reconnect the gearshift rod onto the transmission selector shaft, and secure it by tightening the clamp bolt to the specified torque setting.
**6** Extract the locking pin, then check for the satisfactory engagement of all gears, selecting each gear in turn to confirm that the

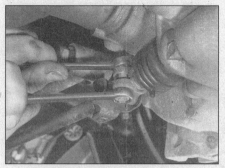

**2.3a Loosen off the clamp bolt . . .**

**2.3b . . . and disengage the gearshift rod from the selector shaft**

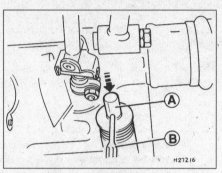

**2.3c Gearchange linkage/mechanism adjustment**
*A Selector shaft    B Rod or punch*

mechanism has been correctly reset. Further minor adjustment may be required.
**7** With the adjustment correctly made, lower the vehicle to complete.

### MTX-75 type transmission

**Note:** *The special Ford tool 16-064 will be required in order to carry out the following adjustment. This tool is simply a slotted ring which locks the gear lever in the neutral position during adjustment. If the tool is not available, adjustment is still possible by proceeding on a trial-and-error basis, preferably with the help of an assistant to hold the gear lever in the neutral position.*
**8** Prise free and release the gear lever surround and gaiter from the centre console, and remove it upwards from the gear lever.
**9** Chock the rear wheels then jack up the front of the car and support it on axle stands (see "Jacking and vehicle support"). Remove the front roadwheels. Move the gear lever to the neutral position.
**10** Working beneath the vehicle, loosen the clamp bolt on the gearchange linkage located behind the transmission.
**11** From inside the car, slacken the four nuts securing the gearchange housing to the body, and align the housing so that it is unstressed. This is particularly important if the adjustment operation is being carried out after removal and refitting of the engine/transmission. Retighten the four bolts.
**12** With the gear lever still in neutral, fit the special Ford tool 16-064 over the gear lever, and locate it in the recess in the lever retaining housing on top of the transmission. Twist the

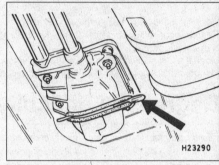

**2.4 Gear lever locked in position by fabricated tool with elastic band to secure it**

tool clockwise to lock the lever in the neutral position. Take care during the adjustment not to move the gear lever or displace the adjustment tool.
**13** Check that the front part of the gearchange linkage from the transmission is in neutral. It will be necessary to move the linkage slightly forwards and backwards to determine that it is in the correct position.
**14** Recheck that the adjustment tool is still correctly fitted to the gear lever, then tighten the clamp bolt on the gearchange linkage to the specified torque.
**15** Remove the adjustment tool from the gear lever.
**16** Lower the vehicle to the ground, then refit the gear lever boot.

## 3 Gearchange linkage and gear lever - removal and refitting

### Removal

#### B5 and iB5 type transmission

**1** Working inside the car, first engage 2nd gear (4-speed transmission) or 4th gear (5-speed transmission). This will provide the correct re-engagement and adjustment for the gearchange mechanism during reassembly.
**2** Unscrew and remove the gear lever knob.
**3** Prise free and release the gear lever surround and gaiter from the centre console, and remove it upwards from the gear lever. If required, the

**3.3a Disengage the gear lever-to-console boot for access to the unit retaining nuts**

**3.3b Remove the lever gaiter to inspect the gear lever balljoint from above**

**3.4 Four gear lever retaining nuts (arrowed)**

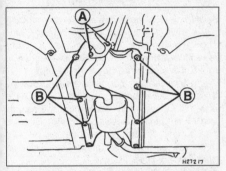

**3.6 Detach the exhaust system at the front joint (A) and the heatshield from the points indicated (B) on catalytic converter models**

**3.8 Unscrewing the stabiliser-to-transmission bolt. Note washer (arrowed)**

14 Unscrew the bolt securing the gearchange support rod to the bracket on the rear of the transmission.

15 Support the weight of the gearchange linkage assembly, unscrew the mounting nuts, and lower the assembly from the underbody.

### Refitting

#### All models

16 Refitting is a reversal of removal, but lubricate the pivot points with grease. Before lowering the vehicle from the axle stands, check and if necessary adjust the gearchange linkage as described in Section 2. Tighten the fastenings to the specified torque setting, where given.

gear lever-to-selector unit can be prised free and withdrawn to inspect the selector balljoint from above **(see illustrations)**.

4 Loosen off the four gear lever retaining nuts **(see illustration)**.

5 Chock the rear wheels then jack up the front of the car and support it on axle stands (see *"Jacking and vehicle support"*).

6 Working beneath the vehicle, release the flexible exhaust pipe mountings, and disconnect the exhaust system from the downpipe. On catalytic converter models, also detach the heat shield from the underside of the floorpan to allow access to the underside of the gear lever for its removal **(see illustration)**. When detaching the exhaust system refer to Chapter 4E for details.

7 Mark the relative fitted positions of the selector shaft and gearshift rod, then undo the clamp bolt and separate the shaft from the rod.

8 Unscrew and remove the gearshift rod stabiliser retaining bolt. Note the position of the washer as the bolt is withdrawn **(see illustration)**. Support the gear lever assembly from underneath, and have an assistant unscrew and remove the four gear lever retaining nuts within the vehicle, then lower and withdraw the gearchange mechanism from underneath the vehicle.

#### MTX-75 type transmission

9 Unscrew and remove the gear lever knob, then prise free and release the gear lever surround and gaiter from the centre console,

and remove it upwards from the gear lever.

10 Chock the rear wheels then jack up the front of the car and support it on axle stands (see *"Jacking and vehicle support"*). Move the gear lever to its neutral position.

11 Working beneath the vehicle, remove the exhaust downpipe and catalytic converter, with reference to Chapter 4E. Detach the heat shield from the underside of the floorpan, to allow access to the underside of the gear lever for its removal.

12 Unscrew the bolt securing gearchange linkage to the selector shaft on the rear of the transmission **(see illustration)**.

13 Mark the position of the gearchange linkage front and rear sections in relation to each other. Loosen the clamp bolt and remove the front section **(see illustration)**.

---

### 4  Speedometer drive pinion - removal and refitting

### Removal

#### B5 and iB5 type transmission

1 Disconnect the battery negative (earth) lead (refer to Chapter 5A, Section 1).

2 Undo the retaining nut, and withdraw the speedometer cable from the drive pinion or vehicle speed sensor in the top face of the transmission **(see illustration)**. If a vehicle speed sensor is fitted, use two spanners to loosen the nut - one to counterhold the sensor, and the other to unscrew the cable nut.

**7A**

**3.12 Unscrew the bolt securing the gearchange linkage to the selector shaft on the rear of the transmission**

**3.13 Removing the gearchange linkage front section**

**4.2 Disconnecting the speedometer cable from the pinion**

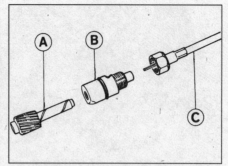

**4.5 Speedometer drive pinion (A) pinion bearing (B) and drive cable (C)**

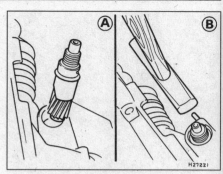

**4.15 Insert the speedometer drive pinion/bearing (A) and secure with a new retaining pin (B)**

**3** Where applicable, disconnect the wiring from the vehicle speed sensor, then unscrew the sensor from the top of the drive pinion.
**4** Grip the drive pinion retaining pin with self-locking grips or pliers, and withdraw it from the drive pinion housing.
**5** Pull the drive pinion and bearing out of the housing, but take care not to tilt it, because the pinion and bearing are not secured and can easily be separated if the pinion is snagged **(see illustration)**.
**6** Using a small screwdriver, prise the O-ring from the groove in the bearing; obtain a new one for reassembly.
**7** Wipe clean the drive pinion and bearing, also the seating bore in the transmission casing.

**MTX-75 type transmission**

**8** Access to the drive pinion may be gained from the top of the engine, or from below by raising the front of the vehicle and reaching up over the top of the transmission. If the latter method is used, make sure that the vehicle is supported adequately on axle stands (see *"Jacking and vehicle support"*).
**9** Unscrew the nut, and disconnect the speedometer cable from the vehicle speed sensor on the transmission. Use two spanners to loosen the nut - one to counterhold the sensor, and the other to unscrew the cable nut.
**10** Disconnect the wiring from the vehicle speed sensor, then unscrew the sensor from the top of the drive pinion.
**11** Using a pair of grips, pull out the drive pinion retaining roll pin from the transmission casing.
**12** Withdraw the speedometer drive pinion and bearing from the top of the transmission.
**13** Using a small screwdriver, prise the O-ring from the groove in the bearing; obtain a new one for reassembly.
**14** Wipe clean the drive pinion and bearing, also the seating bore in the transmission casing.

**Refitting**

**All models**

**15** Refitting is a reversal of the removal procedure, but lightly oil the new O-ring

before inserting the assembly in the transmission casing. Drive in the retaining roll pin using a hammer **(see illustration)**.

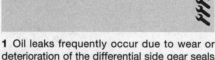

**5 Oil seals** - renewal

**1** Oil leaks frequently occur due to wear or deterioration of the differential side gear seals and/or the gearchange selector shaft oil seal and speedometer drive pinion O-ring. Renewal of these seals is relatively easy, since the repairs can be performed without removing the transmission from the vehicle.

*Differential side gear oil seals*

**2** The differential side gear oil seals are located at the sides of the transmission, where the driveshafts enter the transmission. If leakage at the seal is suspected, raise the vehicle and support it securely on axle stands (see *"Jacking and vehicle support"*). If the seal is leaking, oil will be found on the side of the transmission below the driveshaft.
**3** Refer to Chapter 8 and remove the appropriate driveshaft.
**4** Wipe clean the old oil seal and, if working on the B5 or iB5 type transmission, note its orientation and measure its fitted depth below the casing edge. This is necessary to determine the correct fitted position of the new oil seal. On the MTX-75 type transmission, the seal fitted depth is determined by a seating in the transmission casing.

**5.5 Levering out an old driveshaft oil seal**

**5** Using a large screwdriver or lever, carefully prise the oil seal out of the transmission casing, taking care not to damage the casing **(see illustration)**. If the oil seal is reluctant to move, it is sometimes helpful to carefully drive it *into* the transmission a little way, applying the force at one point only. This will have the effect of swivelling the seal out of the casing, and it can then be pulled out. If the oil seal is particularly difficult to remove, an oil seal removal tool may be obtained from a garage or accessory shop.
**6** Wipe clean the oil seal seating in the transmission casing.
**7** Dip the new oil seal in clean oil, then press it a little way into the casing by hand, making sure that it is square to its seating.
**8** Using suitable tubing or a large socket, carefully drive the oil seal fully into the casing up to its previously-noted fitted depth, or until it contacts the seating **(see illustration)**.
**9** Refit the driveshaft with reference to Chapter 8.

*Gearchange selector shaft oil seal*

**10** Apply the handbrake, then jack up the front of the vehicle and support it on axle stands.
**11** Unscrew the bolt securing the gearchange linkage to the shaft on the rear of the transmission. Pull off the linkage and remove the rubber boot.
**12** Using a suitable tool or grips, pull the oil seal out of the transmission casing. Ford technicians use a slide hammer, with an end

**5.8 Driving a new driveshaft oil seal into position using a suitable socket**

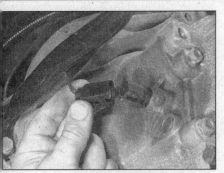

**6.2 Disconnecting the reversing light switch lead**

fitting which locates over the oil seal extension. In the absence of this tool, if the oil seal is particularly tight, drill one or two small holes in the oil seal, and screw in self-tapping screws. The oil seal can then be removed from the casing by pulling on the screws.

13 Wipe clean the oil seal seating in the transmission.

14 Dip the new oil seal in clean oil, then press it a little way into the casing by hand, making sure that it is square to its seating.

15 Using suitable tubing or a large socket, carefully drive the oil seal fully into the casing.

16 Locate the rubber boot over the selector shaft.

17 Refit the gearchange linkage to the shaft on the rear of the transmission, and tighten the bolt to the specified torque setting.

18 If necessary, adjust the gearchange linkage as described in Section 2 of this Chapter.

### Speedometer drive pinion oil seal

19 The procedure is covered in Section 4 of this Chapter.

## 6 Reversing light switch - removal and refitting

### Removal

**B5 and iB5 type transmission**

1 Chock the rear wheels then jack up the front of the car and support it on axle stands (see *"Jacking and vehicle support"*).

2 Disconnect the wiring from the reversing light switch **(see illustration)**.

3 Unscrew the switch from the side of the transmission, and remove the washer.

### MTX-75 type transmission

4 Disconnect the wiring leading to the reversing light switch on the top of the transmission.

5 Unscrew the mounting bolts, and remove the reversing light switch from the cover housing on the transmission.

### *Refitting*

**B5 and iB5 type transmission**

6 Clean the location in the transmission, and the threads of the switch.

7 Insert the switch together with a new washer, and tighten it to the specified torque wrench setting.

8 Reconnect the wiring.

9 Check and top-up the transmission oil level if necessary, with reference to Chapter 1.

10 Lower the vehicle to the ground.

### MTX-75 type transmission

11 Refitting is a reversal of the removal procedure.

## 7 Manual transmission (B5 and iB5 type) - removal and refitting

**Note:** *Read through this procedure before starting work to see what is involved, particularly in terms of lifting equipment. Depending on the facilities available, the home mechanic may prefer to remove the engine and transmission together, then separate them on the bench, as described in Chapter 2D.*

### *Removal*

1 The manual transmission is removed downwards from the engine compartment, after disconnecting it from the engine. Due to the weight of the unit, it will be necessary to have a suitable method of supporting the transmission as it is lowered during removal

and subsequently raised during its refitting. A trolley jack fitted with a suitable saddle to support the transmission as it is removed will be ideal, but failing this, an engine lift hoist and sling will suffice. The weight of the engine will also need to be supported whilst the transmission is detached from it - an engine support bar fitted in the front wing drain channel each side is ideal for this purpose, but care must be taken not to damage the wings or their paintwork. If this type of tool is not available (or cannot be fabricated), the engine can be supported by blocks or a second jack from underneath.

2 Disconnect the battery negative (earth) lead (refer to Chapter 5A, Section 1).

3 Refer to the applicable Part of Chapter 4 and remove the air cleaner and air inlet components as necessary for access to the transmission. Disconnect the clutch cable from the clutch release lever as described in Chapter 6.

4 Undo the retaining nut, and detach the speedometer drive cable from the transmission. Also where applicable, disconnect the speed sensor lead multi-plug. Position the cable (and where applicable, the sensor lead) out of the way.

5 Unbolt and disconnect the radio earth strap from the transmission.

6 Extract the transmission breather tube from the aperture in the chassis side member.

7 On 4-speed models, engage 2nd gear. On 5-speed models, engage 4th gear. This will ease realignment and adjustment of the gearchange linkage during the refitting procedures.

8 Unscrew and remove the three upper transmission-to-engine flange bolts. Note that one bolt secures the main earth strap to the battery, and one bolt retains the coolant hose locating strap **(see illustration)**.

9 Unscrew and remove the two nuts securing the left-hand rear engine/transmission mounting bracket to the transmission **(see illustration)**.

10 Apply the handbrake, then raise the vehicle at the front. Support it on axle stands at a sufficient height to allow the transmission to be withdrawn from under the front end (see *"Jacking and vehicle support"*).

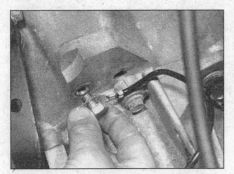

**7.8 Detaching the earth strap from the transmission**

**7.9 Unscrew the two engine/transmission mounting bracket nuts (arrowed)**

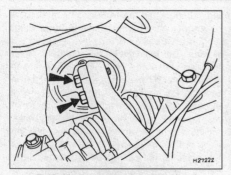

**7.13 Unscrew the rear left-hand mounting bolts (arrowed)**

**7.14 Unscrew the front left-hand mounting bolts (arrowed)**

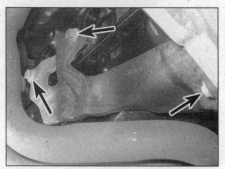

**7.17a On 1.6 litre CVH engine models, undo the retaining bolts (arrowed) . . .**

**7.17b . . . and remove the engine-to-transmission bracing plates**

**11** If fitting an engine lifting bar to support the engine on HCS engine models, unscrew and remove the No 4 spark plug, to prevent it from damage.

**12** Fit the engine support bar, or failing this, position a jack under the engine. Whichever is used, raise the engine so that its weight is taken from the mountings.

**13** Undo the two retaining bolts, and detach the rear left-hand engine/transmission mounting bracket from the engine/transmission **(see illustration)**.

**14** Similarly, undo the two retaining bolts and detach the front left-hand engine/transmission mounting bracket from the engine/transmission **(see illustration)**.

**15** Disconnect the lead connector from the reversing light switch.

**16** Detach the wiring, and then unbolt and withdraw the starter motor. See Chapter 5A for full details.

**17** On 1.6 litre CVH engine models, undo the seven engine/transmission housing bracing bolts, and remove the bracing plate from each side **(see illustrations)**. Unbolt and remove the adapter plate.

**18** On 1.3 and 1.4 litre models, undo the retaining bolts and remove the engine/transmission adapter plate.

**19** Before disconnecting the gearshift rod, mark the relative fitted positions of the gearshift rod and the selector shaft, as a guide for refitting and adjustment.

**20** Undo the gearshift rod stabiliser-to-transmission retaining bolt. Separate the stabiliser from the transmission (noting the washer fitted between the stabiliser and the

transmission). Tie the gearshift rod and stabiliser up out of the way.

**21** Referring to Chapter 10 for details, detach the track rod end balljoint from the steering arm on the left-hand side, and the suspension arm-to-spindle carrier balljoint on the left and right-hand sides.

**22** Insert a suitable lever between the driveshaft inner CV joint and the transmission, and carefully lever the driveshaft free from the transmission. Lever against the reinforcement rib to avoid damaging the transmission housing, and have an assistant pull the suspension strut outwards on the side being detached, to assist in the driveshaft withdrawal from the transmission. As the driveshaft is withdrawn, be prepared for escaping oil.

**23** When the driveshaft is detached from the transmission, tie it up out of the way. Do not allow the inner CV joint to be angled more than 17°, and do not force the outer CV joint past its stop, or the joints may be damaged.

**24** Repeat the above procedure and detach the driveshaft on the opposite side. After removal of both driveshafts, plug the apertures in the differential (or preferably and if available, insert old CV joints) to prevent further oil leakage, and to immobilise the differential gears.

**25** Partially lower the engine and transmission, then unscrew the retaining nut and remove the engine/transmission mounting bracket from the transmission.

**26** Unscrew and remove the remaining engine-to-transmission retaining bolts. Note that two bolts on the bulkhead side also

secure the mounting bracket stay. Make a final check to ensure that all of the transmission connections have been detached and are positioned out of the way.

**27** Check that the engine remains securely supported. The method of supporting the transmission during its removal is largely a matter of personal choice and/or the facilities available. It can be supported from above, and lowered (using a conventional hoist) onto a trolley for withdrawal from under the vehicle **(see illustration)**. Failing this, it can be supported underneath with a suitable trolley jack, and withdrawn from under the front end. Whichever method is employed, engage the aid of an assistant to help guide the transmission down and clear of the surrounding components in the engine compartment.

**28** Withdraw the transmission from the engine, taking care not to allow the weight of the transmission to rest on the input shaft at any time. Once the input shaft is clear of the clutch unit, the transmission can be lowered and manoeuvred down through the engine compartment, and then withdrawn from underneath the vehicle.

### Refitting

**29** Refitting is a reversal of removal, but note the following additional points:

a) *Make sure that all mating faces are clean.*

b) *Apply a smear of high-melting-point grease to the splines of the transmission input shaft. Do not apply too much, otherwise there is the possibility of the grease contaminating the clutch friction disc.*

c) *On 1.3 and 1.4 litre models, ensure that the engine adapter plate is correctly seated on the locating dowels on the engine.*

d) *Fit new snap-rings to the grooves in the inner end of each driveshaft CV joint, and ensure that they are felt to snap fully into engagement as they are fitted into position in the transmission.*

e) *Locate the left-hand engine/transmission mounting bracket over the three studs, and fit the retaining nut from underneath.*

**7.27 Supporting the weight of the transmission from above during its removal using a fabricated bracket bolted to the transmission**

*f) Temporarily lower the vehicle, then raise the engine/transmission to align the mounting brackets on the left-hand side with the threaded holes in the rubber mountings. Refit the two bolts securing the front left engine/transmission mounting bracket, then repeat this procedure and secure the rear left-hand bracket. The vehicle can then be raised and supported on axle stands at the front end again, to allow the remaining refitting operations to be carried out.*

*g) Refer to Chapters 8 and 10 for details on reconnecting the driveshafts to the transmission and the suspension arm/ steering balljoint and track rod end balljoint.*

*h) Reconnect and adjust the gearchange linkage as described in Section 2.*

*i) Tighten all nuts and bolts to the specified torque settings.*

*j) Replenish the transmission oil, and check the level with reference to Chapter 1.*

*k) On models with a self-adjusting clutch, operate the clutch and check it for satisfactory operation. On models with a manually adjusted clutch, check and if necessary adjust the clutch pedal free play as described in Chapter 1.*

## 8  Manual transmission (MTX-75 type) - removal and refitting

**Note:** *Read through this procedure before starting work to see what is involved, particularly in terms of lifting equipment. Depending on the facilities available, the home mechanic may prefer to remove the engine and transmission together, then separate them on the bench, as described in Chapter 2D.*

### Removal

**1** The manual transmission is removed downwards from the engine compartment, after disconnecting it from the engine. Due to the weight of the unit, it will be necessary to have a suitable method of supporting the transmission as it is lowered during removal, and subsequently raised during its refitting. A trolley jack fitted with a suitable saddle to support the transmission as it is removed will be ideal, but failing this, an engine lift hoist and sling will suffice. The weight of the engine will also need to be supported whilst the transmission is detached from it - an engine support bar fitted in the front wing drain channel each side is ideal for this purpose, but care must be taken not to damage the wings or their paintwork. If this type of tool is not available (or cannot be fabricated), the engine can be supported by blocks or a second jack from underneath.

**2** Disconnect the battery negative (earth) lead (refer to Chapter 5A, Section 1).

**3** If necessary, the bonnet may be removed as described in Chapter 11, for better access, and for fitting the engine lifting hoist.

**8.7 Unscrew the upper transmission-to-engine flange bolts (1), noting the location of the earth lead and the cable/hose clips. Unscrew the additional earth lead bolt (2)**

**4** Refer to the applicable Part of Chapter 4 and remove the air cleaner and air inlet components as necessary for access to the transmission.

**5** Disconnect the clutch cable from the release lever and the transmission bracket, with reference to Chapter 6.

**6** Disconnect the wiring multi-plug from the reversing light switch on the transmission.

**7** Unscrew the upper transmission-to-engine flange bolts, noting the location of the earth lead and the cable/hose clips **(see illustration)**.

**8** Unscrew the bolt securing the earth lead to the top of the transmission.

**9** Disconnect the vehicle speed sensor multi-plug.

**10** Disconnect the oxygen sensor multi-plug, and release the cable-tie.

**11** Unscrew and remove the starter motor upper mounting bolt, noting that an earth cable is attached to it.

**12** Chock the rear wheels then jack up the front of the car and support it on axle stands (see *"Jacking and vehicle support"*). Remove the front roadwheels.

**13** Working on each side of the vehicle in turn, unscrew the nut and disconnect the anti-roll bar link from the suspension strut.

**14** Extract the split pins, then unscrew the nuts securing the track rod end balljoints to the steering arms on each side. Release the balljoints from the steering arms, using a balljoint separator tool.

**15** Working on each side in turn, note which way round the front suspension lower arm balljoint clamp bolt is fitted, then unscrew and remove it from the spindle carrier.

**16** Lever the balljoint down from the spindle carrier - if it is tight, prise the joint open carefully using a large flat-bladed tool. Take care not to damage the balljoint seal during the separation procedure.

**17** Insert a suitable lever between the right-hand driveshaft inner joint and the transmission case (with a thin piece of wood against the case), then prise free the joint from the differential. If it proves reluctant to move, strike the lever firmly with the palm of the hand.

**18** Be careful not to damage the adjacent components, and be prepared for some oil spillage.

**19** Move the right-hand spindle carrier outwards, at the same time withdrawing the driveshaft inner joint from the transmission. Tie the driveshaft up out of the way, ensuring that the driveshaft is kept as straight as possible. Do not allow the inner CV joint to be angled more than 17° and do not force the outer CV joint past its stop, or the joints may be damaged.

**20** Repeat the previous procedure on the left-hand side, to remove the left-hand driveshaft inner joint from the transmission. After removal of both driveshafts, plug the aperture in the differential (or preferably and if available, insert old CV joints) to prevent further oil leakage, and to immobilise the differential gears.

**21** Undo the bolts and release the catalytic converter from the rear exhaust system.

**22** Undo the two nuts, recover the springs, and separate the exhaust downpipe from the manifold. Release the exhaust mounting bracket, and remove the catalytic converter.

**23** Remove the starter motor with reference to Chapter 5A.

**24** Unscrew the bolt securing the gearchange linkage to the selector shaft on the rear of the transmission.

**25** Mark the position of the gearchange linkage front and rear sections, then unscrew the clamp bolt. Slide the two sections together, to release the linkage from the selector shaft on the rear of the transmission.

**26** Unscrew the mounting bolt, and disconnect the gearchange support rod from the bracket on the rear of the transmission.

**27** Fit the engine support bar, or failing this, position a jack under the engine. Whichever is used, raise the engine so that its weight is taken from the mountings.

**28** Unscrew the bolts, and detach the front left-hand engine mounting from the body.

**29** Disconnect the crankshaft position sensor multi-plug, and using a flexi-head socket bar, unscrew the flange bolt securing the pulse-air system filter housing **(see illustration)**.

**8.29 Disconnect the crankshaft position sensor multi-plug (1), and the flange bolt securing the pulse-air system filter housing (2)**

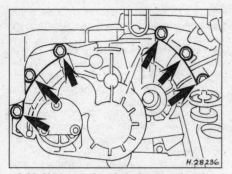

**8.32 Unscrew the six bolts securing the left-hand mounting brackets to the transmission (arrowed)**

**8.35 Remove the remaining flange bolts (arrowed) securing the transmission to the engine**

**30** Disconnect the speedometer drive cable from the vehicle speed sensor on the transmission.

**31** Unscrew the bolts, and remove the engine/transmission left-hand rear mounting.

**32** Lower the engine/transmission to the level of the left-hand body side member, then unscrew the six bolts securing the left-hand mounting brackets to the transmission **(see illustration)**. Remove both brackets.

**33** Make a final check to ensure that all of the transmission connections have been detached and are positioned out of the way.

**34** Check that the engine remains securely supported. The method of supporting the transmission during its removal is largely a matter of personal choice and/or the facilities available. It can be supported from above, and lowered (using a conventional hoist) onto a trolley for withdrawal from under the vehicle. Failing this, it can be supported underneath with a suitable trolley jack, and withdrawn from under the front end. Whichever method is employed, engage the aid of an assistant to help guide the transmission down and clear of the surrounding components in the engine compartment.

**35** Remove the remaining flange bolts securing the transmission to the engine **(see illustration)**.

**36** Withdraw the transmission from the engine, taking care not to allow the weight of the transmission to rest on the input shaft at any time. Once the input shaft is clear of the clutch, the transmission can be lowered and manoeuvred down through the engine compartment and withdrawn from underneath the vehicle.

### Refitting

**37** Refitting is a reversal of removal, but note the following additional points:

a) Make sure that all mating faces are clean.

b) Apply a smear of high-melting-point grease to the splines of the transmission input shaft. Do not apply too much, otherwise there is the possibility of the grease contaminating the clutch friction disc.

c) Fit new snap-rings to the grooves in the inner end of each driveshaft, and ensure that they are felt to snap fully into engagement as they are fitted into position in the transmission.

d) Ensure that all the engine/transmission mountings are aligned without being stressed. Tighten the mounting bolts lightly initially, then when all are installed, go back and tighten them to the specified torque.

e) Refer to Chapters 8 and 10 for details on reconnecting the driveshafts to the transmission and the suspension arm/steering balljoint and track rod end balljoint.

f) Use a new gasket when reconnecting the catalytic converter to the exhaust system.

g) Reconnect and adjust the gearchange linkage as described in Section 2.

h) Tighten all nuts and bolts to the specified torque settings.

i) Replenish the transmission oil, and check the level with reference to Chapter 1.

j) On models with a self-adjusting clutch, operate the clutch and check it for satisfactory operation. On models with a manually adjusted clutch, check and if necessary adjust the clutch pedal free play as described in Chapter 1.

## 9 Manual transmission overhaul - general

No work can be carried out to the transmission until the engine/transmission has been removed from the car and cleaned externally.

Overhauling a manual transmission is a difficult and involved job for the DIY home mechanic. In addition to dismantling and reassembling many small parts, clearances must be precisely measured and, if necessary, changed by selecting shims and spacers. Internal transmission components are also often difficult to obtain, and in many instances, are extremely expensive. Because of this, if the transmission develops a fault or becomes noisy, the best course of action is to have the unit overhauled by a specialist repairer, or to obtain an exchange reconditioned unit.

Nevertheless, it is not impossible for the more experienced mechanic to overhaul the transmission, provided the special tools are available, and that the job is done in a deliberate step-by-step manner so that nothing is overlooked.

The tools necessary for an overhaul may include internal and external circlip pliers, bearing pullers, a slide hammer, a set of pin punches, a dial test indicator, and possibly a hydraulic press. In addition, a large, sturdy workbench and a vice will be required.

During dismantling of the transmission, make careful notes of how each component is fitted, to make reassembly easier and accurate.

Before dismantling the transmission, it will help if you have some idea which area is malfunctioning. Certain problems can be closely related to specific areas in the transmission, which can make component examination and replacement easier.

# Chapter 7 Part B:
# Automatic transmission

## Contents

## Degrees of difficulty

| | | | | |
|---|---|---|---|---|
| **Easy,** suitable for novice with little experience  | **Fairly easy,** suitable for beginner with some experience  | **Fairly difficult,** suitable for competent DIY mechanic  | **Difficult,** suitable for experienced DIY mechanic | **Very difficult,** suitable for expert DIY or professional 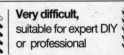 |

## Specifications

| Torque wrench settings | Nm | lbf ft |
|---|---|---|
| Transmission fluid cooling pipes to fluid cooler . . . . . . . . . . . . . . . . . . | 20 | 15 |
| Transmission fluid cooling pipe connections at transmission . . . . . . . . | 22 | 17 |
| Starter inhibitor switch . . . . . . . . . . . . . . . . . . . . . . . . . . . . . . . . . . . . | 12 | 9 |
| Transmission-to-engine flange bolts . . . . . . . . . . . . . . . . . . . . . . . . . . | 44 | 32 |
| Torsional vibration damper to flywheel . . . . . . . . . . . . . . . . . . . . . . . | 30 | 22 |
| Lower engine adapter plate (clutch housing cover) . . . . . . . . . . . . . . | 10 | 7 |
| Selector lever housing to floor . . . . . . . . . . . . . . . . . . . . . . . . . . . . . | 10 | 7 |
| Selector cable bracket to transmission housing . . . . . . . . . . . . . . . . . | 40 | 30 |
| Selector lever rod-to-lever guide . . . . . . . . . . . . . . . . . . . . . . . . . . . | 22 | 16 |
| Left-hand rear mounting bracket-to-transmission . . . . . . . . . . . . . . . . | 51 | 38 |
| Left-hand rear mounting bracket-to-mounting . . . . . . . . . . . . . . . . . . | 68 | 50 |
| Left-hand front mounting bracket-to-mounting . . . . . . . . . . . . . . . . . . | 68 | 50 |
| Left-hand front mounting bracket brace . . . . . . . . . . . . . . . . . . . . . . . | 51 | 38 |

## 1 General information and precautions

The CTX transmission is an automatic transmission providing continuously-variable drive over the entire speed range. Torque from the engine is transmitted to the transmission via an input shaft and a multiplate wet clutch (rather than a conventional torque converter employed on most automatic transmissions).

A steel thrust-link drivebelt made of disc-shaped steel elements transmits the torque from the primary cone pulley (driven by the engine) to the secondary cone pulley. The secondary cone pulley is linked by a series of gears to the final drive gear which drives the differential unit and the driveshafts.

The continuous variation in ratio is produced by altering the diameter of the path followed by the drivebelt around the two cone pulleys. This alteration of the drivebelt path is produced by an hydraulic control system which moves one half of each cone pulley in an axial direction. The secondary pulley cone is also spring-loaded, to keep the drivebelt at the required tension needed to transmit the torque. The hydraulic control system is governed by the position of the transmission selector lever, the accelerator and the load resistance encountered (such as up or down gradients), as well as road speed.

The selector lever is connected to the transmission selector shaft by a cable.

A gear-type pump delivers fluid (according to the input speed) to the hydraulic control system. A transmission fluid cooler is located in the side tank of the engine coolant radiator.

As with more conventional automatic transmission systems, the CTX type has a parking mechanism. The parking pawl engages with the teeth on the outside of the secondary pulley. A starter inhibitor switch prevents the engine from being started in selector positions R, D or L.

When accelerating, the engine speed may sound higher than would normally be expected, similar to a slipping clutch on a manual transmission vehicle. The reverse is true when decelerating, with the engine speed dropping faster than the comparable drop in road speed. These are normal characteristics of the CTX transmission.

### Precautions

When the vehicle is parked and left with the engine running, or when any checks and/or adjustments are being carried out, the handbrake must be applied and the selector lever moved to the P position.

Do not allow the engine speed to rise above the normal idle speed when the vehicle is stationary with the selector lever in the R, D or L position.

The engine must not run at more than 3000 rpm with the selector lever in the R, D or L position when the driving (front) roadwheels are clear of the ground.

If the vehicle is to be towed with the front wheels on the road, move the selector lever to position N. If the distance that the vehicle is to be towed is no more than 30 miles (50 km), it can be towed up to a maximum towing speed of 30 mph (50 kph). Ideally, the vehicle should always be towed on a trailer or dolly with the front wheels clear of the road - where the towing distance exceeds 30 miles (50 km), this is essential.

**7B**

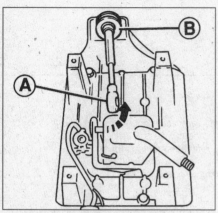

**2.3 Selector cable-to-lever connection, showing connecting eye (A) and retaining clip (B)**

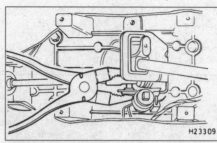

**2.8 Reconnecting the selector cable eye**

---

## 2 Selector cable - removal, refitting and adjustment

### Removal

**1** Unscrew and remove the selector lever knob. Unclip and detach the selector gate cover, followed by its locating frame (see Chapter 11).

**2** Slide the front seats fully forward. Referring to Chapter 11, undo the two retaining screws at the rear and the four screws at the front, then lift clear the centre console, guiding it up over the handbrake lever.

**3** Using a suitable screwdriver as a lever, prise free the plastic connecting eye of the selector lever from the cable, then prise free the cable retaining clip, and withdraw the cable from the selector housing. If necessary, cut the carpet at the front to allow extra access **(see illustration)**.

**4** Chock the rear wheels then jack up the front of the car and support it on axle stands (see *"Jacking and vehicle support"*). Remove the front roadwheels.

**5** Working underneath the vehicle, release the retaining clip and pin, and detach the cable from the selector shaft lever and the transmission housing bracket.

**6** Pull free the rubber gaiter from the floor, and then withdraw the selector cable from the vehicle.

### Refitting

**7** Feed the selector cable up through the floor, refit the rubber gaiter, then lower the vehicle to the ground.

**8** Reconnect the selector cable to the lever and housing, ensuring that the annular bead of the cable eye faces the end of the pin. Use a suitable pair of pliers to press the pin in until it is heard to clip into engagement **(see illustration)**.

**9** The selector lever must now be moved to the "P" position, and the vehicle then raised and supported at the front end again.

**10** Reconnect the cable to the transmission, then adjust the cable as follows before refitting the centre console and selector gate assembly.

### Adjustment

**11** The vehicle must be raised and supported on axle stands at the front end to make the cable adjustment check.

**12** With the selector lever set in the "P" position, the parking pawl engaged and the gears immobilised, check that the lever/selector shaft drilling and the cable yoke are in alignment, and that the connecting pin is an easy fit. If required, draw the bellows back from the yoke, and screw the yoke in the appropriate direction to reposition it on the cable so that the pin fits freely. Fit the pin and retaining clip, then relocate the bellows.

**13** The vehicle can now be lowered to the ground.

---

## 3 Gear selector mechanism - removal and refitting

### Removal

**1** Refer to Section 2, paragraphs 1 to 3 inclusive, to disconnect the cable from the selector housing unit.

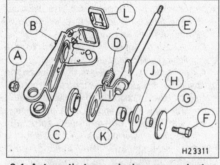

**3.4 Automatic transmission gear selector mechanism components**

| | |
|---|---|
| A Nut | G Steel washer |
| B Selector lever guide | H Spacer bush |
| C Guide bush | J Spacer washer (plastic) |
| D Spring | K Bush |
| E Selector lever | L Plastic guide |
| F Pivot pin | |

**2** Pull free the quadrant illumination light bulbholder, then undo the four retaining bolts and remove the selector housing unit.

**3** To remove the selector lever from the housing, release the clip and extract the lever pivot pin.

**4** To remove the selector lever rod from the guide, detach the spring, unscrew the retaining pin nut, withdraw the pin, nut and washer, and withdraw the lever rod **(see illustration)**.

### Refitting

**5** Reassemble and refit in the reverse order of removal. When refitting the selector lever and bushes to the housing, ensure that the wide side of the bush guide faces up.

---

## 4 Speedometer drive pinion - removal and refitting

### Removal

**1** Disconnect the battery negative (earth) lead (refer to Chapter 5A, Section 1).

**2** Undo the retaining nut, and withdraw the speedometer cable from the drive pinion or vehicle speed sensor in the top face of the transmission **(see illustration)**. If a vehicle speed sensor is fitted, use two spanners to loosen the nut - one to counterhold the sensor, and the other to unscrew the cable nut.

**3** Where applicable, disconnect the wiring from the vehicle speed sensor, then unscrew the sensor from the top of the drive pinion.

**4** Grip the drive pinion retaining roll pin with self-locking grips or pliers, and withdraw it from the drive pinion housing.

**5** Pull the drive pinion and bearing out of the housing, but take care not to tilt it, because the pinion and bearing are not secured and can easily be separated if the pinion is snagged.

**6** Using a small screwdriver, prise the O-ring from the groove in the bearing; obtain a new one for reassembly.

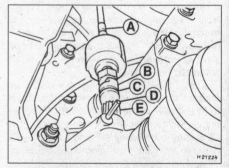

**4.2 Speedometer drive pinion and cable location in the automatic transmission**

| | |
|---|---|
| A Speedometer drive cable | C O-ring |
| | D Roll pin |
| B Drive pinion bearing | E Drive pinion |

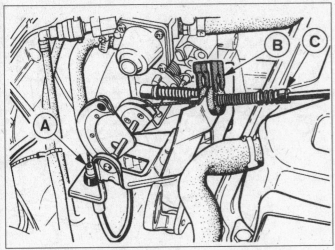
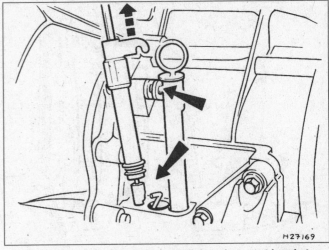

**6.7a Cam plate cable connections to the carburettor**
*A Cam plate cable    B Clip    C Cable adjuster sleeve*

**6.7b Detach the cam plate cable link and support bracket
as indicated**

**7** Wipe clean the drive pinion and bearing, also the seating bore in the transmission casing.

### Refitting

**8** Refitting is a reversal of the removal procedure, but lightly oil the new O-ring before inserting the assembly in the transmission. Drive in the retaining roll pin as far as the stop. When fitted, it should protrude by approximately 5.0 mm.

## 5  Fluid seals - renewal
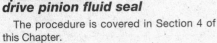

### Differential side gear fluid seals

The procedure is the same as that for the B5 and iB5 type manual transmissions (refer to Chapter 7A, Section 5).

### Speedometer drive pinion fluid seal

The procedure is covered in Section 4 of this Chapter.

## 6  Automatic transmission - removal and refitting

**Note:** *This Section describes the removal of the automatic transmission, leaving the engine in position in the car. However, if an adequate hoist is available, it may be easier to remove both the engine and the transmission together as described in Chapter 2D, and then to separate the transmission from the engine on the bench.*

### Removal

**1** The automatic transmission is removed downwards from the engine compartment, after disconnecting it from the engine. Due to

the weight of the unit, it will be necessary to have a suitable method of supporting the transmission as it is lowered during removal, and subsequently raised during its refitting. A trolley jack fitted with a suitable saddle to support the transmission as it is removed will be ideal, but failing this, an engine lift hoist and sling will suffice. The weight of the engine will also need to be supported whilst the transmission is detached from it. An engine support bar fitted in the front wing drain channel on each side is ideal for this purpose, but care must be taken not to damage the wings or their paintwork. If this type of tool is not available (or cannot be fabricated), the engine can be supported by blocks or a second jack from underneath.
**2** Disconnect the battery negative (earth) lead (refer to Chapter 5A, Section 1).
**3** Remove the air cleaner and air inlet components as described in the relevant Part of Chapter 4.
**4** Disconnect the speedometer drive cable from the transmission.
**5** Unclip and disconnect the starter inhibitor switch wire.
**6** Disconnect and separate the speed sensor connector halves (near to the brake master cylinder).
**7** Release the cam plate operating cable from the throttle linkage, then undo the retaining

bolt and detach the cable support bracket from the transmission. Detach the cam plate cable link **(see illustrations)**.
**8** Unscrew and remove the upper transmission-to-engine flange bolts.
**9** Unscrew the two retaining bolts, and remove the transmission rear mounting bracket.
**10** Drain the automatic transmission fluid as described in Chapter 1.
**11** Chock the rear wheels then jack up the front of the car and support it on axle stands (see *"Jacking and vehicle support"*). Remove the front roadwheels.
**12** Remove the starter motor as described in Chapter 5A.
**13** Undo the two selector cable bracket retaining bolts, disconnect the yoke from the lever and detach the selector cable from the lever on the transmission selector shaft.
**14** Disconnect the starter/inhibitor and the reversing light lead from their connections at the transmission.
**15** Undo the three retaining bolts, and remove the lower cover plate from the lower front end face of the transmission **(see illustration)**.
**16** Undo the fluid cooler-to-transmission union nuts at the transmission end, and tie the pipes up out of the way **(see illustration)**. Allow for fluid spillage as they are detached,

**7B**

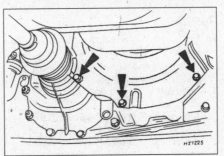

**6.15 Lower cover plate retaining bolts (arrowed)**

**6.16 Fluid cooler pipe union connections at the transmission (arrowed)**

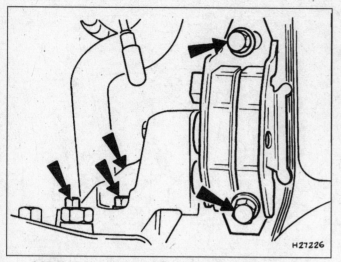

**6.22 Undo the retaining bolts indicated, and remove the transmission front bracket**

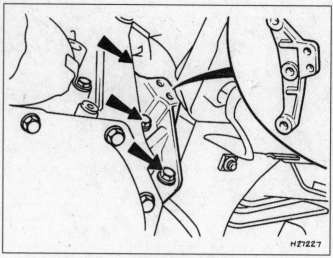

**6.23 Undo the retaining bolts indicated, and remove the transmission rear bracket**

and plug the hose and transmission union connections to prevent the ingress of dirt.

**17** Refer to Chapter 10 and detach the track rod end balljoint from the steering arm on the left-hand side, and the suspension arm-to-spindle carrier balljoint on the left and right-hand sides.

**18** Insert a suitable lever between the driveshaft inner CV joint and the transmission, and carefully lever the driveshaft free from the transmission. Lever against the reinforcement rib, to avoid damaging the transmission housing. Have an assistant pull the suspension strut outwards on the side being detached, to assist in the driveshaft withdrawal from the transmission. As the driveshaft is withdrawn, be prepared for escaping fluid.

**19** When the driveshaft is detached from the transmission, tie it up out of the way, but do not allow the inner CV joint to be angled more than 20° and the outer joints by more than 45°, or the joints may be damaged.

**20** Repeat the above procedure and detach the driveshaft on the opposite side. After removal of both driveshafts, plug the apertures in the differential (or preferably, and if available, insert old CV joints) to prevent further fluid leakage, and to immobilise the differential gears.

**21** The weight of the engine must now be supported independently from the mountings. This can be achieved by suspending it with a support bar located in the front wing drain channel each side, by using a conventional hoist and sling method, or by supporting it from the underside with a jack or blocks. Whichever method is used, raise the hoist to just take the weight of the engine.

**22** Unscrew the five retaining bolts, and remove the front transmission mounting bracket **(see illustration)**.

**23** Slightly release the weight of the engine

from the support, then undo the three retaining bolts and detach the rear support bracket from the transmission **(see illustration)**. Take care not to damage the transmission sump pan during this operation.

**24** Check that the engine remains securely supported. The method of supporting the transmission during its removal is largely a matter of personal choice and/or the facilities available. It can be supported from above, and lowered (using a conventional hoist) onto a trolley for withdrawal from under the vehicle. Failing this, it can be supported underneath with a suitable trolley jack, and withdrawn from under the front end. Whichever method is employed, engage the aid of an assistant to help guide the transmission down and clear of the surrounding components in the engine compartment.

**25** Unscrew and remove the remaining engine-to-transmission retaining bolts, noting the location of the earth strap.

**26** Check that all of the associated fittings are disconnected, and are positioned out of the way.

**27** Separate the transmission from the engine. The transmission can then be lowered and simultaneously manoeuvred down through the engine compartment, and withdrawn from underneath the vehicle.

### Refitting

**28** Refitting is a reversal of removal, but note the following additional points:

a) *Do not apply any grease or lubricant to the input shaft splines, as it could adversely effect the operation of the damper.*

b) *New snap-rings must be fitted to the inboard end of each driveshaft before reconnecting them to the transmission. Refer to Chapter 8 for further refitting details.*

c) *Tighten all nuts and bolts to the specified torque wrench settings (where applicable).*

d) *Refer to Chapter 10 for details on reconnecting the track rod end balljoint and the suspension arm balljoint assemblies to the steering arm/knuckle unit.*

e) *If necessary, adjust the selector cable with reference to Section 2.*

f) *When refitting the fluid cooler, check that the temporary plugs have been removed and that the connections are cleanly made.*

g) *Fill the automatic transmission with fluid (see Chapter 1).*

h) *Adjust the accelerator cable and (where applicable) the choke cable, with reference to the relevant Part of Chapter 4.*

## 7  Automatic transmission overhaul - general

In the event of a fault occurring on the transmission, it is first necessary to determine whether it is of an electrical, mechanical or hydraulic nature, and to do this, special test equipment is required. It is therefore essential to have the work carried out by a Ford dealer if a transmission fault is suspected.

Do not remove the transmission from the car for possible repair before professional fault diagnosis has been carried out, since most tests require the transmission to be in the vehicle.

## 8  Starter inhibitor switch - removal and refitting

Refer to Chapter 12, Section 4 for details.

# Chapter 8 Driveshafts

## Contents

## Degrees of difficulty

| | | | | |
|---|---|---|---|---|
| **Easy,** suitable for novice with little experience  | **Fairly easy,** suitable for beginner with some experience  | **Fairly difficult,** suitable for competent DIY mechanic  | **Difficult,** suitable for experienced DIY mechanic  | **Very difficult,** suitable for expert DIY or professional |

## Specifications

### Type

All 1.3 litre and 1.4 litre models, except those fitted with
  automatic transmission and/or ABS . . . . . . . . . . . . . . . . . . . . . . . . . 23-spline driveshaft
1.4 litre models with automatic transmission and/or ABS,
  and all 1.6 and 1.8 litre models . . . . . . . . . . . . . . . . . . . . . . . . . . . . 25-spline driveshaft

### Lubrication

Driveshaft joint grease type . . . . . . . . . . . . . . . . . . . . . . . . . . . . . . . . Supplied with repair kit
Outer joint grease quantity:
  1.3 litre (except Van) . . . . . . . . . . . . . . . . . . . . . . . . . . . . . . . . . . . . 30 grams
  All other models (except models with MTX75 transmission) . . . . . . . 40 grams
  Models with MTX75 transmission . . . . . . . . . . . . . . . . . . . . . . . . . . . 50 grams
Inner joint grease quantity:
  All models (except models with MTX75 transmission) . . . . . . . . . . . 95 grams
  Models with MTX75 transmission . . . . . . . . . . . . . . . . . . . . . . . . . . . 150 grams

| Torque wrench settings | Nm | lbf ft |
|---|---|---|
| Hub/driveshaft retaining nut: | | |
| M20 x 1.5 (23-spline driveshaft) . . . . . . . . . . . . . . . . . . . . . . . . . . | 220 | 162 |
| M22 x 1.5 (25-spline driveshaft) . . . . . . . . . . . . . . . . . . . . . . . . . . | 235 | 173 |
| Roadwheel nuts . . . . . . . . . . . . . . . . . . . . . . . . . . . . . . . . . . . . . . . | 85 | 63 |

**8**

## 1  General information

Drive is transmitted from the differential to the front wheels by means of two unequal-length steel driveshafts. On certain models, one or both of the driveshafts incorporate a vibration/harmonic damper, which is either bolted or pressed in position on the shaft.

Each driveshaft consists of three main components - the sliding tripod type inner CV joint, the main driveshaft (which is splined at each end) and a fixed type outer CV joint **(see illustration)**. The inner end section of the tripod type joint is secured in the differential by the engagement of a snap-ring, whilst the outer (ball and cage type) CV joint is secured in the front hub by the stub axle nut. The nut has a shouldered outer section which is peened over to lock it in position.

On most models the only repairs possible are the renewal of the rubber gaiters and the renewal of the inner joint spiders. Wear or damage to the outer constant velocity joints or the driveshaft splines can only be rectified by fitting a complete new driveshaft assembly. On certain later models, the outer CV joint may be available separately; seek the advice of a Ford dealer if component renewal is anticipated.

## 2  Driveshafts - removal and refitting

### Removal

**1** Remove the wheel trim from the front roadwheel on the side concerned, then using a small pin punch, peen back the locking portion of the front hub/driveshaft nut. Loosen off the nut about half-a-turn.

**2** Loosen off the front roadwheel retaining nuts on the side concerned.

**3** Chock the rear wheels then jack up the front of the car and support it on axle stands (see *"Jacking and vehicle support"*). Remove the appropriate roadwheel, and unscrew and remove the hub/driveshaft retaining nut and washer **(see illustration)**.

**4** Undo the two bolts, and remove the brake caliper from the spindle carrier. Support the caliper from above, to prevent the hydraulic hose from being strained or distorted.

**5** Detach the relevant track rod end balljoint from the steering arm (see Chapter 10).

**6** Remove the Torx-head pinch-bolt and nut securing the lower suspension arm balljoint to the spindle carrier. As it is withdrawn, note the fitted direction of the bolt (to ensure correct refitting). Lever the suspension arm downwards to detach it from the spindle carrier unit. Refer to Chapter 10 for the full procedure.

**7** Release the driveshaft from its location in the hub by pulling the spindle carrier outwards, away from the centre of the vehicle. Do not fully withdraw the shaft from the hub at this stage, but ensure that it is free to be withdrawn when required. If it is tight in the hub, lightly tap its outer end with a soft-faced hammer, or use a conventional puller and spacer as shown **(see illustration)**.

**8** Insert a suitable lever between the inner driveshaft joint and the transmission case, adjacent to a reinforcing rib, then prise free the inner joint from the differential **(see illustration)**. If it proves reluctant to move,

**2.3 Remove the hub/driveshaft retaining nut and washer**

**2.7 Driveshaft separation from the front wheel hub using a conventional puller. Note the spacer location (arrowed)**

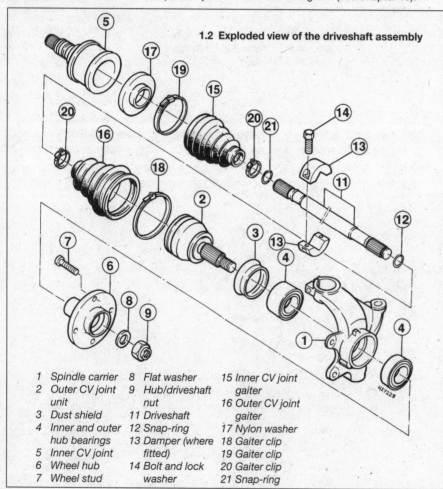

**1.2 Exploded view of the driveshaft assembly**

| | | |
|---|---|---|
| 1  Spindle carrier | 8  Flat washer | 15 Inner CV joint gaiter |
| 2  Outer CV joint unit | 9  Hub/driveshaft nut | 16 Outer CV joint gaiter |
| 3  Dust shield | 11 Driveshaft | 17 Nylon washer |
| 4  Inner and outer hub bearings | 12 Snap-ring | 18 Gaiter clip |
| 5  Inner CV joint | 13 Damper (where fitted) | 19 Gaiter clip |
| 6  Wheel hub | 14 Bolt and lock washer | 20 Gaiter clip |
| 7  Wheel stud | | 21 Snap-ring |

**2.8 Levering the driveshaft free from the transmission**

**2.10 Prising free the snap-ring from the groove in the inner end of the driveshaft**

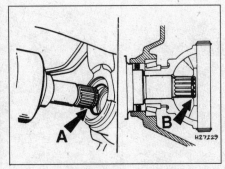

**2.13 Snap-ring (A) must be renewed and fully engage in groove (B)**

strike the lever firmly with the palm of the hand. Be careful not to damage the adjacent components, and be prepared for oil spillage from the transmission case through the vacated driveshaft aperture. If possible, plug the aperture (or preferably, and if available, insert an old CV joint) to prevent leakage and to immobilise the differential gears. Do not allow the inner tripod joint to bend more than 17° on manual transmission models, or 20° on automatic transmission models, or it may be damaged. The outer joint must not be bent past its stop (more than 45°).

9 Withdraw the driveshaft from the hub, and remove it as a unit from the vehicle. If the driveshaft on the opposing side is to be removed also, the differential must be immobilised by the insertion of an old CV joint or a suitable shaft before the other shaft is removed.

10 Remove the snap-ring from the groove in the splines of the inner joint tripod housing **(see illustration)**. *This snap-ring must be renewed each time the driveshaft is withdrawn from the differential. The hub/driveshaft retaining nut and the track rod end balljoint split pin must also be renewed when refitting the driveshaft.*

### Refitting

11 Fit a new snap-ring to the groove in the splines of the inner joint tripod housing.

12 Smear the splines at the wheel hub end of the shaft with grease, then insert it into the spindle carrier. Use the old nut and retaining washer to assist in drawing the shaft into position, and as it is fitted, rotate the brake disc to assist in centralising the wheel bearings.

13 Remove the temporarily-fitted plug (or the old CV joint) from the differential housing. Lightly smear the oil seal lips in the differential housing with grease, then insert the inner driveshaft joint. Align the splines, and push it into position so that the snap-ring is clearly felt to engage in the groove of the differential side gear **(see illustration)**.

14 Reconnect the suspension lower arm balljoint to the spindle carrier. Insert the pinch-bolt (in its original direction of fitting), ensure that the bolt is fully engaged in the groove of the ballstud, then fit and tighten the

retaining nut to the specified torque wrench setting (Chapter 10).

15 Reconnect the track rod end balljoint to the steering arm as described in Chapter 10.

16 Refit the brake caliper unit to the spindle carrier, and tighten the retaining bolts to the specified torque (see Chapter 9).

17 Refit the roadwheel, and lightly tighten its retaining nuts.

18 Fit a new hub nut and washer, and tighten the nut as much possible at this stage. As the nut is being tightened, rotate the roadwheel to ensure that the wheel bearings seat correctly.

19 Lower the vehicle to the ground, then tighten the hub nut to the specified torque wrench setting. Using a pin punch, stake-lock the nut in the groove in the end of the axle stub.

20 Tighten the roadwheel nuts to the specified torque setting.

21 Check the level of the transmission oil, and top-up if necessary with the recommended lubricant (see Chapter 1).

### 3 Driveshaft inner CV joint gaiter - renewal

1 The inner CV joint gaiter can only be renewed once the inner CV joint has been detached at the transmission end. This can be done with the driveshaft fully removed (as described in Section 2), or by leaving it in situ in the wheel hub. The latter method is described below. If it is wished to fully remove the driveshaft, refer to Section 2 for details,

then proceed as described in paragraphs 6 to 14 inclusive in this Section to renew the gaiter.

2 Loosen off the front roadwheel nuts on the side concerned.

3 Chock the rear wheels then jack up the front of the car and support it on axle stands (see *"Jacking and vehicle support"*). Remove the appropriate roadwheel.

4 Detach the track rod end balljoint from the steering arm as described in Chapter 10.

5 Remove the Torx-head pinch-bolt and nut securing the lower suspension arm balljoint to the spindle carrier. As it is withdrawn, note the fitted direction of the bolt (to ensure correct refitting). Lever the suspension arm downwards to detach it from the spindle carrier.

6 Note the direction of fitting of the inner joint gaiter retaining clips, then release the clips from the gaiter, and slide the gaiter back along the driveshaft (away from the transmission) together with the large nylon washer. **(see illustration)**.

7 Get an assistant to help pull the suspension strut outwards, and separate the driveshaft and tripod from the tripod housing. With the driveshaft disconnected at the inner end, do not allow the outer CV joint to be angled past its stop (see paragraph 8 in the previous Section).

8 Wipe the grease from the tripod joint assembly.

9 Prise free the snap-ring retaining the tripod on the inner end of the driveshaft **(see illustration)**. Check if the inner end face of the driveshaft and the tripod are "match-marked"

**8**

**3.6 Release and withdraw the gaiter from the inner CV joint housing**

**3.9 Remove the snap-ring from the tripod end of the driveshaft**

3.11a  Fit the new gaiter over the inboard end of the driveshaft . . .

3.11b  . . . and locate the nylon washer (note its orientation)

**2** Loosen off the front roadwheel nuts on the side concerned.

**3** Check that the handbrake is fully applied, then jack up the front of the vehicle and support it on axle stands. Remove the roadwheel.

**4** Detach the track rod end balljoint from the steering arm as described in Chapter 10.

**5** Remove the Torx-head pinch-bolt and nut securing the lower suspension arm balljoint to the spindle carrier. As it is withdrawn, note the fitted direction of the bolt (to ensure correct refitting). Lever the suspension arm downwards to detach it from the spindle carrier.

**6** Note the direction of fitting of the outer CV joint gaiter retaining clips, then release the clips from the gaiter, and slide the gaiter back along the driveshaft (towards the transmission end).

**7** To disconnect the driveshaft from the outer CV joint, first wipe away the grease from the joint. Using suitable circlip pliers, expand the snap-ring, and have an assistant simultaneously pull the CV joint outwards (or when in situ, pull the suspension strut outwards) to separate the driveshaft from the CV joint **(see illustration)**. Whilst the driveshaft is detached at the outer end, do not allow the inner (tripod) joint to be angled beyond 17° on manual transmission models, or 20° on automatic transmission models, or the joint may be damaged.

**8** Withdraw the gaiter from the driveshaft.

**9** Clean the driveshaft. Note: *The CV joint retaining snap-ring, the track rod end balljoint split pin and the gaiter retaining clips must be renewed.*

**10** Slide the new gaiter along on the shaft to allow access for reassembly of the outer CV joint.

**11** Locate a new snap-ring into position in the outer CV joint, then lubricate the joint with some of the specified grease **(see illustrations)**.

**12** Engage the driveshaft with the CV joint, and push them together so that the circlip engages in the groove of the driveshaft **(see illustration)**. If the task is being carried out with the spindle carrier attached, pull the suspension strut outwards, and guide the driveshaft into the CV joint. Progressively

3.12  Tripod refitted onto the driveshaft with the match-marks aligned (arrowed)

3.14  Special pliers are required to securely clamp the inner gaiter clip on the driveshaft

for position, then remove the tripod from the shaft, followed by the large nylon washer and the old gaiter.

**10** Clean the driveshaft. Note that the joint retaining snap-ring, the track rod end balljoint split pin and the gaiter retaining clips must be renewed on reassembly.

**11** Slide the new gaiter into position on the shaft to allow sufficient access for reassembly of the tripod joint. Locate the large nylon washer over the shaft and into the gaiter **(see illustrations)**.

**12** Refit the tripod on the driveshaft. It must be fitted with the chamfered edge leading (towards the driveshaft), and with the match-marks aligned **(see illustration)**. Secure it in position using a new snap-ring. Ensure that the snap-ring is fully engaged in its groove.

**13** Refit the driveshaft and tripod to the tripod housing, then pack the housing with the specified type and quantity of grease.

**14** Move the gaiter along the driveshaft, and locate it over the joint and onto its inner and outer seatings. Ensure that it is correctly seated and not twisted or distorted, then fit the new retaining clips. The fitted direction of the clips must be as noted during removal. The inner clip is a pinch-clamp type, secured using special pliers as shown **(see illustration)**. In the event of such pliers not being available, the gaiter can be secured at this point by a suitable nylon cable-tie.

**15** Reconnect the suspension lower arm balljoint to the spindle carrier. Insert the pinch-bolt (in its original direction of fitting), ensure that the bolt is fully engaged in the groove of the ballstud, then fit and tighten the

retaining nut to the specified torque setting (Chapter 10).

**16** Reconnect the track rod end balljoint to the steering arm as described in Chapter 10.

**17** Refit the roadwheel and its retaining nuts, then lower the vehicle to the ground. Tighten the roadwheel nuts to the specified torque.

## 4  Driveshaft outer CV joint gaiter - renewal

**1** The outer CV joint gaiter can be renewed with the driveshaft fully removed or with it in situ in the wheel hub, but with the outer CV joint disconnected. If the driveshaft has already been removed, proceed as described in paragraphs 6 to 14 inclusive to renew the outer CV joint gaiter.

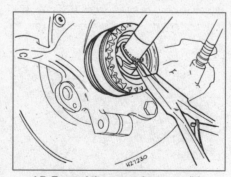

4.7  Expand the snap-ring to enable the driveshaft to be withdrawn from the outer CV joint

4.11a  Locate the new snap-ring (arrowed) in the outer CV joint . . .

**4.11b . . . partially lubricate the joint . . .**

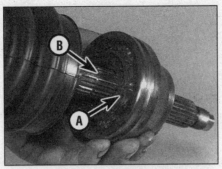

**4.12 . . . and reassemble the shaft to the joint so that the circlip (A) engages in the groove in the shaft (B)**

release the suspension until the shaft is fully engaged with the joint, and the snap-ring engages in the groove in the driveshaft.

**13** Pack the joint with the remainder of the specified grease.

**14** Move the gaiter along the driveshaft, and locate it over the joint and onto its inner and outer seatings. Check that it is correctly seated and not twisted or distorted, then fit new retaining clips. The fitted direction of the clips must be as noted during removal.

**15** Reconnect the suspension lower arm balljoint to the spindle carrier. Insert the pinch-bolt (in its original direction of fitting), ensure that the bolt is fully engaged in the groove of the ballstud, then fit and tighten the retaining nut to the specified torque wrench setting (Chapter 10).

**16** Reconnect the track rod end balljoint to the steering arm as described in Chapter 10.

**17** Refit the roadwheel and tighten its nuts, then lower the vehicle to the ground. Tighten the roadwheel nuts to the specified torque wrench setting.

## 5 Driveshafts - inspection and overhaul

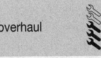

**1** Remove the driveshaft as described in Section 2.

**2** Clean away all external dirt and grease from the driveshaft and gaiters.

**3** Note the direction of fitting of the inner and outer CV joint gaiter retaining clips, then release the clips from the gaiters, and slide the gaiters along the driveshaft towards the centre.

**4** Wipe the grease from the inner and outer CV joints.

**5** Withdraw the inner joint tripod housing from the driveshaft, then prise free the snap-ring retaining the tripod on the inboard end of the driveshaft. Check if the inner end face of the driveshaft and the tripod are "match-marked" for position, then remove the tripod from the shaft, followed by the large nylon washer and the gaiter.

**6** Using suitable circlip pliers, expand the snap-ring and have an assistant simultaneously pull the outboard joint outwards to separate the shaft from the joint.

**7** If removing the vibration damper from the right-hand driveshaft, mark its relative position on the shaft before unbolting it.

**8** Thoroughly clean the joint components, and examine them for wear or damage. A repair kit may resolve a minor problem, but extensive wear or damage will necessitate renewal of the component concerned or the complete driveshaft.

**9** Where the joints and possibly even the gaiters, are found to be in a serviceable condition, it will still be necessary to renew the CV joint retaining snap-rings, the gaiter retaining clips, and also to obtain the recommended type and quantity of CV joint grease.

**10** Reassembly of the joints is as described in Section 3 (paragraphs 10 to 14) for the inner CV joint, and Section 4 (paragraphs 9 to 14) for the outer CV joint. If the vibration damper unit was removed from the right-hand driveshaft, ensure that it is refitted in the same position as noted during removal.

**11** Refit the driveshaft on completion as described in Section 2.

**8**

# Chapter 9
# Braking system

## Contents

## Degrees of difficulty

| | | | | |
|---|---|---|---|---|
| **Easy,** suitable for novice with little experience  | **Fairly easy,** suitable for beginner with some experience  | **Fairly difficult,** suitable for competent DIY mechanic  | **Difficult,** suitable for experienced DIY mechanic | **Very difficult,** suitable for expert DIY or professional |

## Specifications

### Front brakes

| | |
|---|---|
| Type . . . . . . . . . . . . . . . . . . . . . . . . . . . . . . . . . . . . . . . . . . . . | Solid or ventilated disc, with single-piston sliding calipers |
| Disc diameter . . . . . . . . . . . . . . . . . . . . . . . . . . . . . . . . . . . . . | 240.0 or 260.0 mm |
| Disc thickness: | |
|    Solid disc . . . . . . . . . . . . . . . . . . . . . . . . . . . . . . . . . . . | 10.0 mm |
|    Ventilated disc . . . . . . . . . . . . . . . . . . . . . . . . . . . . . . . . | 20.0 or 24.0 mm |
| Minimum disc thickness: | |
|    Solid disc . . . . . . . . . . . . . . . . . . . . . . . . . . . . . . . . . . . | 8.0 mm |
|    Ventilated disc . . . . . . . . . . . . . . . . . . . . . . . . . . . . . . . . | 18.0 or 22.0 mm |
| Maximum disc run-out (disc fitted) . . . . . . . . . . . . . . . . . . . . . | 0.1 mm |
| Minimum brake pad lining thickness . . . . . . . . . . . . . . . . . . . . | 1.5 mm |
| Maximum disc thickness variation . . . . . . . . . . . . . . . . . . . . . . | 0.015 mm |

### Rear drum brakes

| | |
|---|---|
| Type . . . . . . . . . . . . . . . . . . . . . . . . . . . . . . . . . . . . . . . . . . | Drum with leading and trailing shoes and automatic adjusters |
| Nominal drum diameter . . . . . . . . . . . . . . . . . . . . . . . . . . . . . | 180.0, 203.0 or 228.6 mm according to model |
| Maximum drum diameter . . . . . . . . . . . . . . . . . . . . . . . . . . . . | 1.0 mm above nominal diameter |
| Minimum brake lining thickness . . . . . . . . . . . . . . . . . . . . . . . | 1.0 mm |

### Rear disc brakes

| | |
|---|---|
| Type . . . . . . . . . . . . . . . . . . . . . . . . . . . . . . . . . . . . . . . . . . | Solid disc with twin-piston fixed calipers |
| Disc diameter . . . . . . . . . . . . . . . . . . . . . . . . . . . . . . . . . . . . | 270.0 mm |
| Disc thickness . . . . . . . . . . . . . . . . . . . . . . . . . . . . . . . . . . . | 10.0 mm |
| Minimum disc thickness . . . . . . . . . . . . . . . . . . . . . . . . . . . . . | 8.0 mm |
| Maximum disc run-out (disc fitted) . . . . . . . . . . . . . . . . . . . . . | 0.1 mm |
| Minimum brake pad lining thickness . . . . . . . . . . . . . . . . . . . . | 1.5 mm |
| Maximum disc thickness variation . . . . . . . . . . . . . . . . . . . . . . | 0.015 mm |

9

## Torque wrench settings

| | Nm | lbf ft |
|---|---|---|
| Master cylinder to servo | 23 | 17 |
| Servo unit to bracket/bulkhead | 25 | 18 |
| Drum/hub to rear axle flange | 66 | 49 |
| Caliper anchor bracket to spindle carrier | 58 | 43 |
| Caliper piston housing to anchor bracket: | | |
|    Bendix caliper | 50 | 37 |
|    Teves caliper | 23 | 17 |
| Rear caliper mounting bolts | 58 | 43 |
| Rear wheel cylinder to backplate | 15 | 11 |
| Brake hose bracket to suspension strut | 18 | 13 |
| ABS hydraulic unit to bracket: | | |
|    Pre-1996 models | 23 | 17 |
|    1996 models onward | 10 | 7 |
| ABS wheel speed sensor bolts | 10 | 7 |
| Roadwheel nuts | 85 | 63 |

## 1 General information

The braking system is of the diagonally split, dual-circuit hydraulic type, with servo assistance to the front disc brakes and rear drum/disc brakes. The dual-circuit hydraulic system is a safety feature - in the event of a malfunction somewhere in one of the hydraulic circuits, the other circuit continues to operate, providing at least some braking effort. Under normal circumstances, both brake circuits operate in unison, to provide efficient braking.

The master cylinder (and the vacuum servo unit to which it is bolted) is located on the left-hand side of the bulkhead in the engine compartment. On all right-hand drive variants, they are jointly operated via a transverse cross-link from the brake pedal.

Brake pressure control valves are fitted in-line to each rear brake circuit, their function being to regulate the braking force available at each rear wheel, reducing the possibility of the rear wheels locking up under heavy braking. Van models also have a "light-laden" valve incorporated into the rear braking circuits for the same reason.

The front brake discs are of the ventilated type on all 1.6 litre, 1.8 litre and ABS-equipped models, and all later fuel injection models. Solid discs are fitted on all other models. The front brake calipers are of single sliding piston type mounted on the front spindle carriers each side.

Each rear brake shoe assembly is operated by a twin-piston wheel cylinder. The leading brake shoe in each brake unit has a thicker lining than the trailing shoe, so that they wear proportionally. To take up the brake adjustment as the linings wear, each rear brake assembly incorporates an automatic adjuster mechanism.

On models fitted with rear disc brakes, the brake calipers are of twin-piston fixed type, with handbrake operation by means of separate handbrake shoes operating within a "drum-in-disc" arrangement.

The cable-operated handbrake acts on both rear brakes, to provide an independent means of brake operation.

An anti-lock braking system (ABS) is available on some models, and has many of the components in common with the conventional braking system. Further details on ABS can be found later in this Chapter.

**Note:** *When servicing any part of the system, work carefully and methodically; also observe scrupulous cleanliness when overhauling any part of the hydraulic system. Always renew components (in axle sets, where applicable) if in doubt about their condition, and use only genuine Ford replacement parts, or at least those of known good quality. Note the warnings given in "Safety first" and at relevant points in this Chapter concerning the dangers of asbestos dust and hydraulic fluid.*

## 2 Front brake pads - renewal

⚠️ *Warning: Disc brake pads MUST be renewed on both front wheels at the same time - NEVER renew the pads on only one wheel, as uneven braking may result. The front brake calipers will be of Bendix or Teves manufacture, and if they or their component parts require renewal, ensure that the correct type is fitted. Dust created by wear of the pads may contain asbestos, which is a health hazard. Never blow it out with compressed air, and do not inhale any of it. DO NOT use petroleum-based solvents to clean brake parts - use brake cleaner or methylated spirit only. DO NOT allow any brake fluid, oil or grease to contact the brake pads or disc. Also refer to the warning in Section 16 concerning the dangers of hydraulic fluid.*

1 Chock the rear wheels then jack up the front of the car and support it on axle stands (see "Jacking and vehicle support"). Remove the front roadwheels.

### Bendix caliper

2 Extract the R-clip from the cross-pin, and withdraw the pin from the base of the caliper **(see illustrations)**.

3 Undo the nut, and release the brake hose support bracket from the suspension strut **(see illustration)**.

4 Swing the caliper upwards to allow access

2.2a Extract the R-clip from the cross-pin . . .

2.2b . . . and withdraw the pin from the base of the caliper

2.3 Undo the retaining nut (arrowed) and release the brake hose support bracket from the suspension strut

**2.5 Withdraw the inner and outer brake pads from the anchor bracket**

to the brake pads, and if necessary, tie the caliper up in the raised position.

**5** Withdraw the inner and outer brake pads from the anchor bracket **(see illustration)**. If the old pads are to be refitted, ensure that they are identified so that they can be returned to their original positions.

**6** Brush the dust and dirt from the caliper and piston, but *do not inhale it, as it is a health hazard*. Inspect the dust cover around the piston for damage and for evidence of fluid leaks, which if found will necessitate caliper overhaul as described in Section 3. Inspect the anti-rattle plate for corrosion, and if necessary renew it.

**7** If new brake pads are to be fitted, the caliper piston will need to be pushed back into its housing, to allow for the extra pad thickness - use a C-clamp to do this. Note that, as the piston is pressed back into the bore, it will displace the fluid in the system, causing the fluid level in the brake master cylinder reservoir to rise and possibly overflow.

To avoid this possibility, a small quantity of fluid should be syphoned from the reservoir. If any brake fluid is spilt onto the bodywork, hoses or adjacent components in the engine compartment, wipe it clean without delay.

**8** Prior to refitting, check that the pads and the disc are clean. Where new pads are to be installed, peel the protective backing paper from them. If the old pads are to be refitted, ensure that they are correctly located as noted during their removal.

**9** Locate the inner and outer brake pads into position in the caliper anchor bracket.

**10** Lower the caliper down, insert the cross-pin and fit the R-clip to secure.

**11** Reconnect the brake hose bracket to the suspension strut, ensuring the brake hose is not twisted, stretched or distorted in any way. Tighten the brake hose support bracket nut to the specified torque setting.

**12** Repeat the procedure on the opposite front brake.

**13** Before lowering the vehicle, check that the fluid level in the brake master cylinder reservoir is up to the Maximum mark, and top-up with the specified fluid if required (see *"Weekly Checks"*). Depress the brake pedal a few times to position the pads against the disc, then recheck the fluid level in the reservoir and further top-up the fluid level if necessary.

**14** Refit the roadwheels, then lower the vehicle to the ground. Tighten the roadwheel retaining nuts to the specified torque.

**15** To allow the new brake pads to bed-in properly and reach full efficiency, a running-in period of approximately 100 miles or so should be observed before hard use and heavy braking.

### Teves caliper

**16** Hold the caliper support spring with a pair of pliers, and prise it out of its location in the caliper housing using a screwdriver **(see illustration)**.

**17** Prise free the blanking plugs from the caliper upper and lower mounting bolts. Unscrew the bolts, then withdraw the caliper from the anchor bracket **(see illustrations)**. Suitably support the caliper to avoid straining the brake hose.

**18** Withdraw the pads from the caliper piston housing or anchor bracket. The outer pad will normally remain in position in the anchor bracket, but the inner pad will stay attached to the piston in the caliper, and may need to be carefully prised free **(see illustrations)**. If the old pads are to be refitted, ensure that they are identified so that they can be returned to their original positions.

**2.16 Hold the caliper support spring with a pair of pliers, and prise it out of its location in the caliper housing using a screwdriver**

**2.17a Prise free the blanking plugs from the caliper upper and lower mounting bolts**

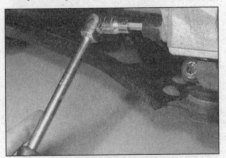

**2.17b Using a suitable Allen key socket bit . . .**

**2.17c . . . unscrew and remove the bolts . . .**

**2.17d . . . then withdraw the caliper from the anchor bracket and disc**

**2.18a Withdraw the outer pad from the anchor bracket . . .**

**2.18b . . . and the inner pad from the piston in the caliper**

**9**

**19** Brush the dust and dirt from the caliper and piston, but *do not inhale it, as it is a health hazard*. Inspect the dust cover around the piston for damage and for evidence of fluid leaks, which if found will necessitate caliper overhaul as described in Section 3.

**20** If new brake pads are to be fitted, the caliper piston will need to be pushed back into its housing, to allow for the extra pad thickness - use a C-clamp to do this. Note that, as the piston is pressed back into the bore, it will displace the fluid in the system, causing the fluid level in the brake master cylinder reservoir to rise and possibly overflow. To avoid this possibility, a small quantity of fluid should be syphoned from the reservoir. If any brake fluid is spilt onto the bodywork, hoses or adjacent components in the engine compartment, wipe it clean without delay.

**21** Prior to refitting, check that the pads and the disc are clean. Where new pads are to be installed, peel the protective backing paper from them. If the old pads are to be refitted, ensure that they are correctly located as noted during their removal.

**22** Locate the inner and outer brake pad into position in the caliper. Relocate the caliper into position on the anchor bracket, and insert the mounting bolts.

**23** Tighten the mounting bolts to the specified torque, and refit the blanking plugs. Relocate the caliper support spring.

**24** Repeat the procedure on the opposite front brake.

**25** Before lowering the vehicle, check that the fluid level in the brake master cylinder reservoir is up to the Maximum level mark, and top-up with the specified fluid type if required (see *"Weekly Checks"*). Depress the brake pedal a few times to position the pads against the disc, then recheck the fluid level in the reservoir and further top-up the fluid level if necessary.

**26** Refit the roadwheels, then lower the vehicle to the ground. Tighten the roadwheel retaining nuts to the specified torque.

**27** To allow the new brake pads to bed-in and reach full efficiency, a running-in period of approximately 100 miles or so should be observed before hard use and heavy braking.

## 3 Front brake caliper - removal, overhaul and refitting

**Note:** *Before starting work, refer to the warning at the beginning of Section 16 concerning the dangers of hydraulic fluid, and to the warning at the beginning of Section 2 concerning the dangers of asbestos dust.*

### Removal

**1** Chock the rear wheels then jack up the front of the car and support it on axle stands (see *"Jacking and vehicle support"*). Remove the front roadwheels.

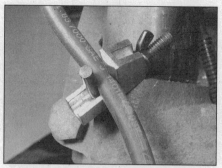
**3.2 Brake hose clamp fitted to the front flexible brake hose**

**3.8 Brake caliper anchor bracket securing bolts (arrowed)**

**2** Fit a brake hose clamp to the flexible brake hose leading to the front brake caliper. This will minimise brake fluid loss during subsequent operations **(see illustration)**.

### Bendix caliper

**3** Unscrew the brake hose-to-caliper banjo union bolt, and recover the copper sealing washers **(see illustration)**. Cover or plug the open hydraulic unions to keep them clean.

**4** Extract the R-clip from the cross-pin at the base of the caliper, and withdraw the cross-pin.

**5** Prise free the blanking plug from the caliper-to-anchor bracket pivot bolt at the top, then support the caliper and unscrew the bolt.

**6** Withdraw the caliper from anchor bracket and brake pads, and remove it from the car.

**7** To remove the caliper anchor bracket, first withdraw the brake pads. If they are likely to be re-used, mark them for identification (inner and outer, right- or left-hand as applicable) to ensure that they are installed in their original locations when refitting.

**8** Unscrew the two retaining bolts, and withdraw the anchor bracket from the spindle carrier **(see illustration)**.

### Teves caliper

**9** Loosen (but do not completely unscrew) the union on the caliper end of the flexible brake hose **(see illustration)**.

**10** Remove the front brake pads as described in Section 2.

**11** Support the caliper in one hand, and prevent the brake hose from turning with the

**3.3 Unscrew the brake hose-to-caliper banjo union bolt (arrowed) and recover the copper sealing washers**

**3.9 Loosening the flexible brake hose at the caliper**

other hand. Unscrew the caliper from the hose, making sure that the hose is not twisted unduly or strained. Once the caliper is detached, cover or plug the open hydraulic unions to keep them clean.

**12** If required, the caliper anchor bracket can be unbolted and removed from the spindle carrier.

### Overhaul

#### Bendix and Teves calipers

**13** With the caliper on the bench, wipe away all traces of dust and dirt, but *avoid inhaling the dust, as it is a health hazard*.

**14** Remove the piston from its bore by applying low air pressure (from a foot pump, for example) into the caliper hydraulic fluid hose port. In the event of a high-pressure air hose being used, keep the pressure as low as possible, to enable the piston to be extracted, but to avoid the piston being ejected too quickly and being damaged. Position a suitable piece of wood between the caliper frame and the piston to prevent this possibility. Any fluid remaining in the caliper will probably be ejected with the piston.

**15** Using a suitable hooked tool, carefully extract the dust cover from its groove in the piston and the seal from its groove in the caliper bore, but take care not to scratch or damage the piston and/or the bore in the caliper.

**16** Clean all the parts in methylated spirit or clean brake fluid, and wipe dry using a clean

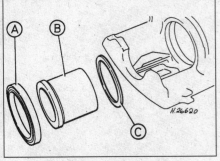

**3.16 Bendix front brake caliper components showing the dust cover (A), piston (B) and piston seal (C)**

lint-free cloth (see illustration). Inspect the piston and caliper bore for signs of damage, scuffing or corrosion. If these conditions are evident, renew the caliper body assembly.

**17** If the components are in satisfactory condition, a repair kit which includes a new seal and dust cover must be obtained.

**18** Lubricate the piston bore in the caliper and the seal with clean brake fluid. Carefully fit the seal in the caliper bore, using fingers only (no tools) to manipulate it into position in its groove. When in position, check that it is not distorted or twisted.

**19** Locate the dust cover over the piston so that its inner diameter is engaged in the piston groove. Smear the area behind the piston groove with the special lubricating grease supplied in the repair kit, then insert the piston into the caliper. Push the piston into position in the bore, and simultaneously press the dust cover into the piston housing so that it is seated correctly (see illustration). Take particular care not to distort or damage the seal or cover as they are fitted.

## Refitting

### Bendix caliper

**20** If the anchor bracket was removed, fit it into position on the spindle carrier, and tighten the retaining bolts to the specified torque.

**21** Locate the brake pads into the anchor bracket. Where new pads are to be installed, peel the protective backing paper from them. If the old pads are to be refitted, ensure that they are correctly located in their original positions as noted during their removal.

**22** Refit the caliper to the anchor bracket, and loosely locate the caliper-to-anchor bracket pivot bolt. Swing the unit down, and insert the cross-pin and its R-clip. Tighten the caliper-to-anchor bracket bolt to the specified torque.

**23** Unplug the hydraulic hose, and check that the unions are clean. Reconnect the hose to the caliper, using new copper washers if necessary. Tighten the brake hose union banjo bolt, then turn the steering from lock-to-lock to ensure that the hose does not foul on the wheel housing or suspension components.

**3.19 Piston and dust seal in position in the caliper**

**24** Bleed the brake hydraulic system as described in Section 16. Providing suitable precautions were taken to minimise loss of fluid, it should only be necessary to bleed the relevant front brake.

**25** Refit the roadwheel, lower the vehicle to the ground, and then tighten the wheel nuts to the specified torque.

### Teves caliper

**26** If the anchor bracket was removed, fit it into position on the spindle carrier, and tighten the retaining bolts to the specified torque.

**27** Unplug the hydraulic hose, and check that the unions are clean. Reconnect the caliper to the hose so that the hose is not twisted or strained. The hose union connection can be fully tightened when the caliper is refitted.

**28** Refit the brake pads as described in Section 2.

**29** The brake hydraulic hose can now be fully tightened. When secured, turn the steering from lock-to-lock to ensure that the hose does not foul on the wheel housing or suspension components.

**30** Bleed the brake hydraulic system as described in Section 16. Providing suitable precautions were taken to minimise loss of fluid, it should only be necessary to bleed the relevant front brake.

**31** Refit the roadwheel, lower the vehicle to the ground, then tighten the wheel nuts to the specified torque.

**4.3 Checking the brake disc thickness using a micrometer**

## 4  Front brake disc - inspection, removal and refitting

**Note:** *Before starting work, refer to the warning at the beginning of Section 2 concerning the dangers of asbestos dust.*

### Inspection

**Note:** *If a disc requires renewal, BOTH front discs should be renewed or reground at the same time to ensure even and consistent braking. New brake pads should also be fitted.*

**1** Chock the rear wheels then jack up the front of the car and support it on axle stands (see *"Jacking and vehicle support"*). Remove the appropriate front roadwheel.

**2** Temporarily refit two of the wheel nuts to diagonally-opposite studs, with the flat sides of the nuts against the disc. Tighten the nuts progressively, to hold the disc firmly.

**3** Scrape any corrosion from the disc. Rotate the disc, and examine it for deep scoring, grooving or cracks. Using a micrometer, measure the thickness of the disc in several places (see illustration). Light wear and scoring is normal, but if excessive, the disc should be removed, and either reground by a specialist, or renewed. If regrinding is undertaken, at least the minimum thickness must be maintained. Obviously, if the disc is cracked, it must be renewed.

**4** Using a dial gauge, check that the disc run-out, measured at a point 10.0 mm from the outer edge of the disc, does not exceed the limit given in the *Specifications*. To do this, fix the measuring equipment, and rotate the disc, noting the variation in measurement as the disc is rotated (see illustration). The difference between the minimum and maximum measurements recorded is the disc run-out.

> **HAYNES HiNT**
> *If a dial gauge is not available, check the run-out by placing a fixed pointer near the outer edge, in contact with the disc face. Rotate the disc and measure the maximum displacement of the pointer with feeler blades.*

**4.4 Checking the brake disc run-out using a dial gauge**

**9**

**5** If the run-out is greater than the specified amount, check for variations of the disc thickness as follows. Mark the disc at eight positions 45° apart, then using a micrometer, measure the disc thickness at the eight positions, 15.0 mm in from the outer edge. If the variation between the minimum and maximum readings is greater than the specified amount, the disc should be renewed.

### Removal

**6** Remove the caliper and its anchor bracket with reference to Section 3, but do not disconnect the hydraulic brake hose. Suspend the caliper assembly from the front suspension coil spring, taking care to avoid straining the brake hose.
**7** Remove the wheel nuts which were temporarily refitted in paragraph 2.
**8** Using a Torx-type socket bit or driver, unscrew the screw securing the disc to the hub, and withdraw the disc. If it is tight, lightly tap its rear face with a hide or plastic mallet.

### Refitting

**9** Refit the disc in a reversal of the removal sequence. If new discs are being fitted, first remove their protective coating. Ensure complete cleanliness of the hub and disc mating faces and tighten the screw securely.
**10** Refit the caliper/anchor bracket with reference to Section 3.
**11** Refit the roadwheel, lower the vehicle to the ground, and tighten the wheel nuts to the specified torque.

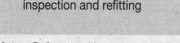

## 5 Rear brake drum - removal, inspection and refitting

**Note:** *Before starting work, refer to the warning at the beginning of Section 6 concerning the dangers of asbestos dust.*

### Removal

**1** Chock the front wheels then jack up the rear of the car and support it on axle stands (see *"Jacking and vehicle support"*). Remove the appropriate rear roadwheel. On pre-1996 models, release the handbrake. On 1996 on models, unclip the handbrake lever gaiter to gain access to the adjuster nut on the side of the lever and slacken the cable right off.
**2** On all except Van models, undo the four bolts securing the drum/hub to the rear axle flange, then withdraw the drum/hub from the axle **(see illustrations)**. If the brake drum is stuck on the shoes, remove the rubber access plug from the inside face of the brake backplate, and release the automatic brake adjuster by levering the release catch on the adjuster pawl through the backplate.
**3** On Van models, prise free the drum retaining clip from the wheel nut stud, then withdraw the drum over the studs and remove it. Note that the retaining clip must be renewed during reassembly.

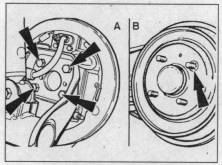

**5.2a  Rear brake drum/hub securing methods**

*A  Brake drum/hub retaining bolts*
*B  Brake drum retaining clip on Van models*

**4** With the brake drum removed, brush or wipe the dust from the drum, brake shoes, wheel cylinder and backplate. *Take great care not to inhale the dust, as it may contain asbestos.*
**5** If required, remove the hub from the drum (where applicable) - see Chapter 10.

### Inspection

**Note:** *If a brake drum requires renewal, BOTH rear drums should be renewed at the same time to ensure even and consistent braking. New brake shoes should also be fitted.*
**6** Clean the inside surfaces of the brake drum and hub, then examine the internal surface of the brake drum for signs of scoring or cracks. If any deterioration of the friction surface is evident, renewal of the drum is necessary. To detach the hub from the drum (where applicable), refer to Chapter 10.

### Refitting

**7** Check that the automatic brake adjuster is fully retracted, then according to type, refit the drum/hub to the axle. Tighten the retaining bolts to the specified torque, or fit the drum over the wheel studs, and press a new retaining clip over one of the studs.

#### Pre 1996 models

**8** With the brake drum refitted, refit the roadwheel. Fully depress the brake pedal several times, to actuate the rear brake adjuster and take up the adjustment. Check that the rear wheels spin freely when the brakes are released, then apply the handbrake, lower the vehicle and tighten the wheel nuts to the specified torque.

#### 1996 on models

**9** With the brake drum refitted, refit the roadwheel. Adjust the handbrake cable, as described in Chapter 1. Fully depress the brake pedal several times, to actuate the rear brake adjuster and take up the adjustment. Check that the rear wheels spin freely when the brakes are released, then apply the handbrake, lower the vehicle and tighten the wheel nuts to the specified torque.

**5.2b  Removing the rear brake drum/hub**

## 6 Rear brake shoes - renewal

> **Warning: Drum brake shoes MUST be renewed on both rear wheels at the same time - NEVER renew the shoes on only one wheel, as uneven braking may result. Also, the dust created by wear of the shoes may contain asbestos, which is a health hazard. Never blow it out with compressed air, and don't inhale any of it. An approved filtering mask should be worn when working on the brakes. DO NOT use petroleum-based solvents to clean brake parts - use brake cleaner or methylated spirit only.**

**1** Remove the rear brake drum with reference to Section 5.
**2** Note the fitted positions of the springs and the adjuster strut.
**3** Remove the shoe steady springs by depressing and turning them through 90° **(see illustration)**. Remove the springs and pins.
**4** Pull the leading brake shoe from the bottom anchor, and disconnect the lower return spring **(see illustration)**.
**5** Move the bottom ends of the brake shoes towards each other, then disconnect the tops of the shoes from the wheel cylinder. Be careful not to damage the wheel cylinder rubber boots. To prevent the wheel cylinder pistons from being accidentally ejected, fit a suitable elastic band (or wire) lengthways over the cylinder/pistons **(see illustrations)**.

**6.3  Removing a shoe steady spring**

6.4  Disengage the leading brake shoe from the bottom anchor . . .

6.5a  . . . then from the wheel cylinder at the top

6.5b  Elastic band fitted round the wheel cylinder to prevent piston ejection

6.7a  Disconnecting the handbrake cable from the trailing brake shoe

6.7b  Disconnecting the support spring from the strut

6.8  Disconnecting the strut from the leading brake shoe

**6** Disconnect the upper return (pull-off) spring from the brake shoes.

**7** Unhook the handbrake cable from the handbrake operating lever on the trailing shoe. Disconnect the support spring from the strut, twist the trailing shoe through 90°, and detach it from the strut (see illustrations).

**8** Disconnect the strut from the leading shoe. As the strut is pulled from the shoe, the automatic adjuster will operate and release the pawl from the shoe (see illustration).

**9** Clean the adjuster strut and its associated components.

**10** Clean the backplate, then apply a little high-melting-point grease to the shoe contact points on the backplate and the lower anchor plate (see illustration).

**11** Transfer the strut and the upper return spring onto the new leading shoe (see illustration).

**12** Locate the other end of the upper return spring into the new trailing shoe, then twisting the shoe, engage the strut support spring and strut. When reconnected, check that the cam and pawl of the automatic adjuster have engaged (see illustrations).

**13** Remove the elastic band (or wire retainer) from the wheel cylinder. Reconnect the handbrake cable to the operating lever on the trailing shoe, and refit the trailing shoe assembly into position on the backplate. As the shoe is engaged over the wheel cylinder, be careful not to damage the rubber dust cover.

**14** Reconnect the lower return spring to the trailing shoe and, checking that the handbrake operating lever is resting on the lever stop

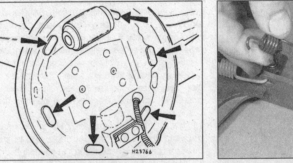

6.10  Brake shoe contact points (arrowed) to be lubricated on the backplate

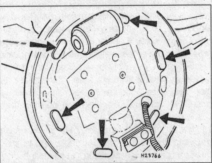

6.12a  . . . and trailing shoe

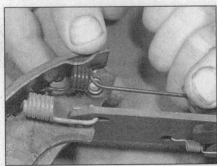

6.11  Reconnect the upper return spring to the leading . . .

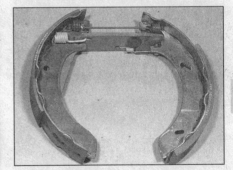

6.12b  Brake shoes, strut and upper springs reconnected

head (not wedged against the side), locate the shoe in the bottom anchor plate. Refit the steady pin, spring and cup to secure the shoe in position.

**15** Offer the leading shoe onto the backplate

and insert its steady pin, spring and cup to hold it in place.

**16** Reconnect the lower return spring to the leading shoe, using a screwdriver to stretch the spring end into the location hole.

**9**

**17** Refit the upper return spring, using a screwdriver to stretch the spring end into the location hole.

**18** Check that the brake shoes and their associated components are correctly refitted, then refit the brake drum with reference to Section 5.

**19** Repeat the procedure on the remaining rear brake.

## 7 Rear wheel cylinder - removal, overhaul and refitting

**Note:** *Before starting work, refer to the warning at the beginning of Section 16 concerning the dangers of hydraulic fluid.*

### Removal

**1** Remove the brake drum as described in Section 5.

**2** Pull the brake shoes apart at the top end, so that they are just clear of the wheel cylinder. The automatic adjuster will hold the shoes in this position so that the cylinder can be withdrawn.

**3** Using a brake hose clamp or self-locking wrench with protected jaws, clamp the flexible brake hose forward of the shock absorber (midway between the hose protective sleeve and the hose rigid connection bracket on the underside of the body). This will minimise brake fluid loss during subsequent operations.

**4** Wipe away all traces of dirt around the brake hose union at the rear of the wheel cylinder, then loosen off the hose-to-wheel cylinder union nut **(see illustration)**.

**5** Unscrew the two bolts securing the wheel cylinder to the backplate.

**6** Withdraw the wheel cylinder from the backplate so that it is clear of the brake shoes, then holding the brake hose steady to prevent it twisting, unscrew and detach the wheel cylinder from the hose. Plug the hose, to prevent the possible ingress of dirt and to minimise further fluid loss whilst the cylinder is detached from it.

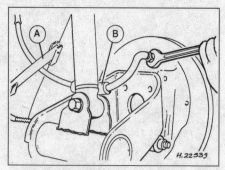

**7.4 Disconnecting the hydraulic hose from the rear wheel cylinder. Note the hose clamp (A) and the protective sleeve on the hose (B)**

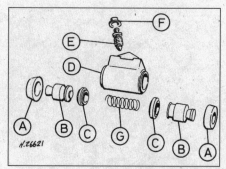

**7.9 Rear wheel cylinder components**

| | |
|---|---|
| A Dust cover | E Bleed nipple |
| B Piston | F Dust cap |
| C Piston seal | G Spring |
| D Cylinder body | |

### Overhaul

**7** Clean the external surfaces of the cylinder, then pull free the dust cover from each end of the cylinder.

**8** The pistons and seals will probably shake out; if not, use a foot pump to apply air pressure through the hydraulic union and eject them.

**9** Clean the pistons and the cylinder by washing in fresh hydraulic fluid or methylated spirits (not petrol, paraffin or any other mineral-based fluid). Examine the surfaces of the pistons and the cylinder bores. Look for any signs of rust, scoring or metal-to-metal rubbing, which if evident, will necessitate renewal of the wheel cylinder **(see illustration)**.

**10** Begin reassembly by lubricating the first piston in clean hydraulic fluid. Manipulate its new seal into position so that its raised lip faces away from the brake shoe bearing face of the piston.

**11** Insert the piston into the cylinder from the opposite end of the cylinder body, and push it through to its normal location in the bore.

**12** Insert the spring into the cylinder, then fit the second new seal into position on the second piston (as described for the first) and fit the second piston into the wheel cylinder. Take care not to damage the lip of the seal as the piston is inserted into the cylinder - additional lubrication and a slight twisting action may help. Only use fingers (no tools) to manipulate the piston and seal into position.

**13** Fit the new dust covers to each end of the piston.

### Refitting

**14** Wipe clean the backplate, and remove the plug from the end of the hydraulic hose. Carefully screw the cylinder onto the hose connector, and then fit the cylinder onto the backplate. Tighten the retaining bolts to securely, then fully tighten the hydraulic hose union.

**15** Retract the automatic brake adjuster mechanism so that the brake shoes engage with the pistons of the wheel cylinder.

**16** Remove the clamp from the flexible brake

hose. Ensure that the protective sleeve on the hose is adjacent to the shock absorber **(see illustration 7.4)**.

**17** Refit the brake drum with reference to Section 5.

**18** Bleed the brake hydraulic system as described in Section 16. Providing suitable precautions were taken to minimise loss of fluid, it should only be necessary to bleed the relevant rear brake.

## 8 Rear brake backplate - removal and refitting

### Drum brake models

#### Removal

**1** On Hatchback/Saloon/Estate models, remove the brake drum/hub assembly as described in Section 5. On Van models, remove the brake drum as described in Section 5, then remove the rear hub assembly as described in Chapter 10.

**2** Remove the rear brake shoes as described in Section 6.

**3** Remove the wheel cylinder from the backplate as described in Section 7.

**4** Compress the three retaining lugs, and release the handbrake cable from the backplate by pushing it back through the plate.

**5** Drill out the pop-rivets securing the backplate to the rear axle, and remove the backplate.

#### Refitting

**6** Refit in the reverse order of removal. Check that the plate is correctly located (with the wheel cylinder aperture at the top) before riveting it into position.

**7** Refit the handbrake cable, and ensure that the retaining lugs are secure.

**8** Refit the wheel cylinder as described in Section 7.

**9** Refit the rear brake shoes as described in Section 6.

**10** Refit the brake drum/hub as described in Section 5, or the rear hub assembly as described in Chapter 10, according to model.

**11** On completion, bleed the brake hydraulic system as described in Section 16.

### Disc brake models

#### Removal

**12** Remove the rear brake disc as described in Section 11, then remove the rear hub assembly as described in Chapter 10.

**13** Remove the handbrake shoes as described in Section 19.

**14** Drill out the pop-rivets securing the backplate to the rear axle, and remove the backplate.

#### Refitting

**15** Refit in the reverse order of removal, securing the backplate with new pop-rivets.

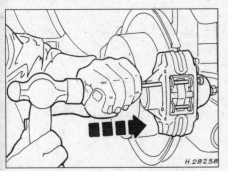

9.2 Drift out the two rear brake pad retaining pins using a punch

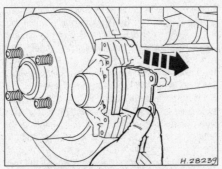

9.3 Withdraw the inner and outer rear brake pads from the caliper

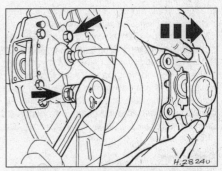

10.5 Undo the two caliper retaining bolts and withdraw the caliper from the disc

16 Refit the handbrake shoes as described in Section 19.

17 Refit the rear brake disc as described in Section 11, and the rear hub assembly as described in Chapter 10.

## 9 Rear brake pads - renewal

**Warning: Disc brake pads must be renewed on BOTH rear wheels at the same time - NEVER renew the pads on only one wheel, as uneven braking may result. Dust created by wear of the pads may contain asbestos, which is a health hazard. Never blow it out with compressed air, and do not inhale any of it. DO NOT use petroleum-based solvents to clean brake parts - use brake cleaner or methylated spirit only. DO NOT allow any brake fluid, oil or grease to contact the brake pads or disc. Also refer to the warning in Section 16 concerning the dangers of hydraulic fluid.**

1 Chock the front wheels then jack up the rear of the car and support it on axle stands (see "Jacking and vehicle support"). Remove the rear roadwheels.

2 Using a hammer and suitable punch, drift out the two brake pad retaining pins, and lift away the anti-rattle plate (see illustration).

3 Withdraw the inner and outer brake pads from the caliper (see illustration). If the old pads are to be refitted, ensure that they are identified so that they can be returned to their original positions.

4 Brush the dust and dirt from the caliper and pistons, but do not inhale it, as it is a health hazard. Inspect the dust cover around the pistons for damage and for evidence of fluid leaks, which if found will necessitate caliper overhaul as described in Section 10. Inspect the anti-rattle plate for corrosion, and if necessary renew it.

5 If new brake pads are to fitted, the caliper pistons will need to be pushed back into their bores, to allow for the extra pad thickness. Use a C-clamp or suitably-protected screwdriver as a lever to do this. Note that, as the pistons are pressed back, they will displace the fluid in the

system, causing the fluid level in the brake master cylinder reservoir to rise and possibly overflow. To avoid this possibility, a little fluid should be syphoned from the reservoir. If any brake fluid is spilt onto the bodywork, hoses or adjacent components within the engine compartment, wipe it clean without delay.

6 Prior to refitting, check that the pads and the disc are clean. Where new pads are to be installed, peel the protective backing paper from them. If the old pads are to be refitted, ensure that they are correctly located as noted during their removal.

7 Locate the inner and outer brake pads into position in the caliper, and refit the upper retaining pin.

8 Locate the anti-rattle plate in position, and refit the lower retaining pin.

9 Repeat the procedure on the opposite rear brake assembly.

10 Before lowering the vehicle, check the that the fluid level in the brake master cylinder reservoir is up to the "Maximum" level mark, and top-up with the specified fluid type if required (see "Weekly Checks"). Depress the brake pedal a few times to position the pads against the disc, then recheck the fluid level in the reservoir and further top-up the fluid level if necessary.

11 Refit the roadwheels, then lower the vehicle to the ground. Tighten the roadwheel retaining nuts to the specified torque.

12 To allow the new brake pads to bed-in and reach full efficiency, a running-in period of approximately 100 miles or so should be observed before hard use and heavy braking.

## 10 Rear brake caliper - removal, overhaul and refitting

**Note:** Before starting work, refer to the warning at the beginning of Section 16 concerning the dangers of hydraulic fluid, and to the warning at the beginning of Section 9 concerning the dangers of asbestos dust.

### Removal

1 Chock the front wheels then jack up the rear of the car and support it on axle stands (see "Jacking and vehicle support"). Remove the appropriate rear roadwheel.

2 Remove the rear brake pads as described in Section 9.

3 Fit a brake hose clamp to the flexible brake hose leading to the rear brake caliper. This will minimise brake fluid loss during subsequent operations.

4 Loosen (but do not completely unscrew) the union on the caliper end of the flexible brake hose.

5 Undo the two caliper retaining bolts, and withdraw the caliper from the disc (see illustration).

6 Support the caliper in one hand, and prevent the brake hose from turning with the other hand. Unscrew the caliper from the hose, making sure that the hose is not twisted unduly or strained. Once the caliper is detached, cover or plug the open hydraulic unions to keep them clean.

### Overhaul

7 With the caliper on the bench, wipe away all traces of dust and dirt, but avoid inhaling the dust, as it is a health hazard.

8 Remove the pistons from their bores by applying air pressure from a foot pump into the caliper hydraulic fluid hose port. In the event of a high-pressure air hose being used, keep the pressure as low as possible, to avoid the pistons being ejected too quickly and being damaged. Any fluid remaining in the caliper will probably be ejected with the pistons.

9 Using a suitable hooked tool, carefully extract the dust covers from their grooves in the pistons, and the seals from their grooves in the caliper bore, but take care not to scratch or damage the pistons and/or the bores in the caliper.

10 Clean all parts in methylated spirit or clean brake fluid, and wipe dry using a clean lint-free cloth. Inspect the pistons and caliper bores for signs of damage, scuffing or corrosion; if these conditions are evident, renew the caliper assembly.

11 If the components are in satisfactory condition, a repair kit which includes new seals and dust covers must be obtained.

12 Lubricate the caliper bores and the seals with clean brake fluid, and carefully fit the seals in the caliper bore. Use the fingers only (no tools) to manipulate them into position in

**9**

their grooves. When in position, check that the seals are not distorted or twisted.

**13** Locate the dust covers over the pistons so that their inner diameters are engaged in the piston grooves. Insert the pistons into the caliper. Push the pistons into position in the bore, and simultaneously press the dust covers into the caliper so that they are seated correctly. Take particular care not to distort or damage the seals or dust cover as they are fitted.

### Refitting

**14** Unplug the hydraulic hose, check that the unions are clean, then reconnect the caliper to the hose, reversing the disconnection procedure so that the hose is not twisted or strained. The hose union connection can be fully tightened when the caliper is refitted.

**15** Slide the caliper over the brake disc, and secure with the two retaining bolts tightened to the specified torque.

**16** The brake hydraulic hose can now be fully tightened. When secured, ensure that the hose does not foul on the wheel arch or suspension components.

**17** Refit the brake pads as described in Section 9.

**18** Bleed the brake hydraulic system as described in Section 16. Providing suitable precautions were taken to minimise loss of fluid, it should only be necessary to bleed the relevant rear brake.

**19** Refit the roadwheel, lower the vehicle to the ground, and then tighten the wheel nuts to the specified torque.

---

### 11 Rear brake disc - inspection, removal and refitting

**Note:** *Before starting work, refer to the warning at the beginning of Section 9 concerning the dangers of asbestos dust.*

### Inspection

**Note:** *If a disc requires renewal, BOTH rear discs should be renewed or reground at the same time to ensure even and consistent braking. New brake pads should also be fitted.*

**1** Chock the front wheels then jack up the rear of the car and support it on axle stands (see *"Jacking and vehicle support"*). Remove the appropriate rear roadwheel.

**2** Remove the brake pads as described in Section 9, then undo the two brake caliper retaining bolts. Withdraw the caliper from the disc, and tie it up using string or wire from a convenient location. Avoid straining the brake hose.

**3** Temporarily refit two of the wheel nuts to diagonally-opposite studs, with the flat sides of the nuts against the disc. Tighten the nuts progressively, to hold the disc firmly.

**4** Scrape any corrosion from the disc. Rotate the disc, and examine it for deep scoring, grooving or cracks. Using a micrometer,

measure the thickness of the disc in several places. Light wear and scoring is normal, but if excessive, the disc should be removed, and either reground by a specialist, or renewed. If regrinding is undertaken, the minimum thickness must be maintained. Obviously, if the disc is cracked, it must be renewed.

**5** Using a dial gauge, check that the disc run-out, measured at a point 10.0 mm from the outer edge of the disc, does not exceed the limit given in the *Specifications*. To do this, fix the measuring equipment, and rotate the disc, noting the variation in measurement as the disc is rotated **(see illustration 4.4).** The difference between the minimum and maximum measurements recorded is the disc run-out.

*If a dial gauge is not available, check the run-out by placing a fixed pointer near the outer edge, in contact with the disc face. Rotate the disc and measure the maximum displacement of the pointer with feeler blades.*

**6** If the run-out is greater than the specified amount, check for variations of the disc thickness as follows. Mark the disc at eight positions 45° apart, then using a micrometer, measure the disc thickness at the eight positions, 15.0 mm in from the outer edge. If the variation between the minimum and maximum readings is greater than the specified amount, the disc should be renewed.

### Removal

**7** With the caliper removed as previously described, remove the wheel nuts which were temporarily refitted in paragraph 3.

**8** Ensure that the handbrake is fully released, then using a Torx-type socket bit or driver, unscrew the screw securing the disc to the hub and withdraw the disc. If it is tight, lightly tap its rear face with a hide or plastic mallet.

### Refitting

**9** Refit the disc in a reversal of the removal sequence. If new discs are being fitted, first remove their protective coating. Ensure complete cleanliness of the hub and disc mating faces, and tighten the screw securely.

**10** Refit the caliper and secure with the retaining bolts tightened to the specified torque.

**11** Refit the rear brake pads as described in Section 9.

**12** Refit the roadwheel, lower the vehicle to the ground, and tighten the wheel nuts to the specified torque.

---

### 12 Master cylinder - removal, overhaul and refitting

**Note:** *Before starting work, refer to the warning at the beginning of Section 16 concerning the dangers of hydraulic fluid.*

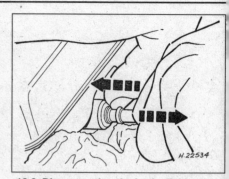

**12.2 Disconnecting the brake fluid return pipes from the reservoir on ABS models**

### Removal

**1** Disconnect the wiring multi-plug from the fluid level warning indicator in the reservoir filler cap, then remove the filler cap from the reservoir. Note that the filler cap must not be inverted. The reservoir should now be emptied by siphoning or drawing out the fluid with a pipette.

**2** Identify each brake pipe and its connection to the master cylinder. Unscrew the fluid line to master cylinder union nuts and disconnect the fluid lines. On models equipped with ABS, when disconnecting the fluid return pipes from the reservoir, press the retaining boss into the reservoir and pull free the fluid line **(see illustration).** Plug the connections and tape over the pipe ends, to prevent the entry of dust and dirt.

**3** Unscrew the mounting nuts and withdraw the master cylinder from the servo unit.

### Overhaul

**4** With the master cylinder removed, empty any remaining fluid from it, and clean it externally.

**5** Secure the master cylinder in a vice fitted with soft-faced jaws to avoid damaging the cylinder.

**6** Withdraw the hydraulic fluid reservoir from the top of the master cylinder by pulling and rocking it free from its retaining seals.

**7** Extract the reservoir seals from the top face of the master cylinder.

**8** Extract the circlip from its groove in the inner port at the rear of the master cylinder.

**9** Pull free the primary piston from the rear end of the master cylinder bore, together with the spacer, seal and steel washer.

**10** Extract the secondary piston assembly by shaking or lightly tapping it free from the cylinder **(see illustration).**

**11** To dismantle the primary piston and to remove its seal, undo the retaining screw and detach the spring from the piston. Lever the seal retainer tabs free using a suitable screwdriver and remove the seal. As it is removed, note the fitted direction of the seal on the piston **(see illustrations).**

**12** To dismantle the secondary piston, pull free the spring (note its orientation), remove the seal retainer using the same method as that for the primary piston seal, and remove the seal (noting its direction of fitting). Prise

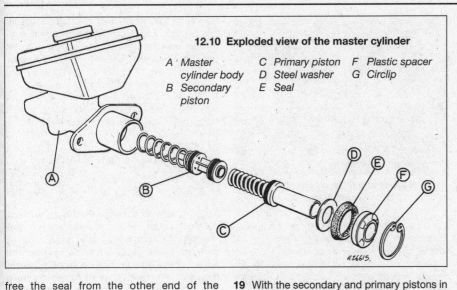

**12.10 Exploded view of the master cylinder**

| | | |
|---|---|---|
| A | Master cylinder body | C Primary piston |
| B | Secondary piston | D Steel washer |
| | | E Seal |
| | | F Plastic spacer |
| | | G Circlip |

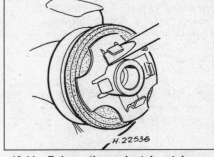

**12.11a Release the seal retainer tabs on the primary piston**

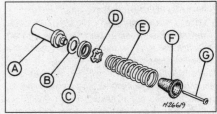

**12.11b Primary piston components**

| | |
|---|---|
| A Piston | E Spring |
| B Shim | F Boot |
| C Seal | G Retaining screw |
| D Seal retainer | |

free the seal from the other end of the secondary piston, again noting its direction of fitting (see illustration).

**13** Wash all components of the cylinder in methylated spirit or clean hydraulic brake fluid of the specified type. Do not use any other type of cleaning fluid.

**14** Inspect the master cylinder and piston assemblies for any signs of excessive wear or damage. Deep scoring in the cylinder bore and/or on the piston surfaces will necessitate a new master cylinder being fitted.

**15** If the cylinder is in a serviceable condition, obtain a cylinder seals/repair kit. Once removed, the seals must always be renewed.

**16** Check that all components are perfectly clean before they refitted. Smear them in new brake fluid of the specified type as they are assembled. *Do not allow grease, old fluid or any other lubricant to contact the components during reassembly.*

**17** Reassemble each piston in the reverse order of dismantling. Ensure that the seals are correctly orientated, and that the retainers are securely fitted.

**18** Lubricate the pistons before refitting them to the cylinder and as they are inserted, use a twisting action to assist in pushing them into position.

**19** With the secondary and primary pistons in position, fit the steel washer, a new seal, and the spacer; secure them with the circlip. Ensure that the circlip is fully engaged into its retaining groove in the rear end of the cylinder.

## Refitting

**20** Before refitting the master cylinder, clean the mounting faces.

**21** Refitting is a reversal of removal. Ensure that the vacuum servo unit seal is in position, and tighten the master cylinder retaining nuts to the specified torque. Finally bleed the hydraulic system as described in Section 16.

## 13 Brake pedal - removal and refitting

## Removal

**1** Disconnect the battery negative (earth) lead (refer to Chapter 5A, Section 1).

**2** Working inside the car, move the driver's seat fully to the rear, to allow maximum working area.

**3** Disconnect the wiring connector from the stop-light switch, then twist the switch and release it from the mounting bracket.

**4** Using a suitable hooked tool, extract the circlip from the pedal cross-link (see illustration).

**5** Prise free and remove the retaining clip securing the pedal-to-cross-link rod.

**6** Press the brake pedal pivot shaft through the mounting box just far enough then release and remove the pedal and spacers.

**7** Prise the bushes out from each side of the brake pedal, and renew them if necessary (see illustration).

## Refitting

**8** Prior to refitting, apply a small amount of molybdenum disulphide grease to the brake pedal pivot shaft.

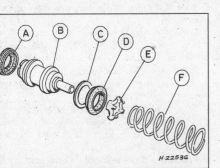

**12.12 Secondary piston components**

| | |
|---|---|
| A Seal | D Seal |
| B Piston | E Seal retainer |
| C Shim | F Spring |

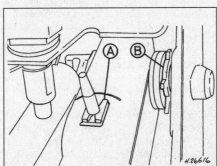

**13.4 Brake pedal-to-cross-link circlip (A) and the brake pedal cross-link retaining clip (B)**

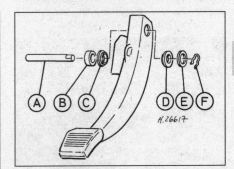

**13.7 Brake pedal components**

| | |
|---|---|
| A Pivot shaft | D Bush |
| B Spacer | E Washer |
| C Bush | F Clip |

**9**

**9** Refit in the reverse order to removal. Ensure that the pedal bushes are correctly located, and that the pedal shaft "D" section locates in the pedal box right-hand support.

**10** On completion, refit the stop-light switch, and adjust it as described in Chapter 12.

## 14 Brake pedal-to-servo cross-link - removal and refitting

### Removal

**1** Disconnect the battery negative (earth) lead (refer to Chapter 5A, Section 1).

**2** Remove the vacuum servo unit (Section 17).

**3** Where necessary, remove the air cleaner components as described in the relevant Part of Chapter 4 to allow increased access to the cross-link assembly.

**4** Working inside the vehicle, prise free and remove the retaining clip from the brake pedal-to-cross-link pushrod.

**5** Arrange for an assistant to support the weight of the cross-link assembly on the engine compartment side of the bulkhead. Fold down the bulkhead trim covering in the footwell on each side, to allow access to the cross-link support bracket securing nuts on the bulkhead. Unscrew the nuts on each side of the bulkhead, and remove the cross-link assembly from the bulkhead in the engine compartment **(see illustration)**.

**6** Clean the linkage components, and examine the bushes for excessive wear. Renew the bushes if necessary.

### Refitting

**7** Refitting of the cross-link assembly is a reversal of the removal procedure. Refer to Section 17 to refit the vacuum servo unit.

**8** On completion, bleed the brake hydraulic system as described in Section 16.

## 15 Hydraulic pipes and hoses - renewal
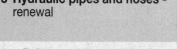

**Note:** *Before starting work, refer to the warning at the beginning of Section 16 concerning the dangers of hydraulic fluid.*

**14.5 Brake system cross-link mounting to the bulkhead**

**15.1 Brake hose clamp fitted to minimise fluid loss**

**1** If any pipe or hose is to be renewed, minimise hydraulic fluid loss by removing the master cylinder reservoir cap, placing a piece of plastic film over the reservoir and sealing it with an elastic band. Flexible hoses can be sealed, if required, using a proprietary brake hose clamp **(see illustration)**; metal brake pipe unions can be plugged (if care is taken not to allow dirt into the system) or capped immediately they are disconnected. Place a wad of rag under any union that is to be disconnected, to catch any spilt fluid.

**2** If a flexible hose is to be disconnected, unscrew the brake pipe union nut before removing the spring clip which secures the hose to its mounting. Depending upon the make of the particular caliper, the other end of the hose may be connected simply by screwing it into its tapped hole or by using a hollow bolt with banjo end fitting. Use a new copper sealing washer on each side of the banjo union.

**3** To unscrew the union nuts, it is preferable to obtain a brake pipe spanner of the correct size; these are available from most large motor accessory shops. Failing this, a close-fitting open-ended spanner will be required, though if the nuts are tight or corroded, their flats may be rounded-off if the spanner slips. In such a case, a self-locking wrench is often the only way to unscrew a stubborn union, but it follows that the pipe and the damaged nuts must be renewed on reassembly. Always clean a union and surrounding area before disconnecting it. If disconnecting a component with more than one union, make a careful note of the connections before disturbing any of them.

**4** If a brake pipe is to be renewed, it can be obtained, cut to length and with the union nuts and end flares in place, from Ford dealers. All that is then necessary is to bend it to shape, following the line of the original, before fitting it to the car. Alternatively, most motor accessory shops can make up brake pipes from kits, but this requires very careful measurement of the original, to ensure that the replacement is of the correct length. The safest answer is usually to take the original to the shop as a pattern.

**5** Before refitting, blow through the new pipe or hose with dry compressed air. Do not

overtighten the union nuts. It is not necessary to exercise brute force to obtain a sound joint.

**6** If flexible rubber hoses are renewed, ensure that the pipes and hoses are correctly routed, with no kinks or twists, and that they are secured in the clips or brackets provided.

**7** After fitting, bleed the hydraulic system as described in Section 16, wash off any spilt fluid, and check carefully for fluid leaks.

## 16 Hydraulic system - bleeding

⚠ *Warning: Brake fluid is poisonous; wash off immediately and thoroughly in the case of skin contact, and seek immediate medical advice if any fluid is swallowed or gets into the eyes. Certain types of hydraulic fluid are inflammable, and may ignite when allowed into contact with hot components; when servicing any hydraulic system, it is safest to assume that the fluid IS inflammable, and to take precautions against the risk of fire as though it is petrol that is being handled. Hydraulic fluid is also an effective paint stripper, and will attack plastics; if any is spilt, it should be washed off immediately, using copious quantities of clean water. Finally, it is hygroscopic (it absorbs moisture from the air). The more moisture is absorbed by the fluid, the lower its boiling point becomes, leading to a dangerous loss of braking under hard use. Old fluid may be contaminated and unfit for further use. When topping-up or renewing the fluid, always use the recommended type, and ensure that it comes from a freshly-opened sealed container.*

**1** The correct operation of any hydraulic system is only possible after removing all air from the components and circuit; and this is achieved by bleeding the system.

**2** During the bleeding procedure, add only clean, unused hydraulic fluid of the recommended type; never re-use fluid that has already been bled from the system. Ensure that sufficient fluid is available before starting work.

**3** If there is any possibility of incorrect fluid being already in the system, the brake components and circuit must be flushed completely with uncontaminated, correct fluid, and new seals should be fitted throughout the system.

**4** If hydraulic fluid has been lost from the system, or air has entered because of a leak, ensure that the fault is cured before proceeding further.

**5** Park the vehicle on level ground, and apply the handbrake. Switch off the engine, then (where applicable) depress the brake pedal several times to dissipate the vacuum from the servo unit.

**6** Check that all pipes and hoses are secure,

unions tight and bleed screws closed. Remove the dust caps (where applicable), and clean any dirt from around the bleed screws.

**7** Unscrew the master cylinder reservoir cap, and top-up the master cylinder reservoir with the specified fluid to the "Maximum" level (see *"Weekly Checks"*). *Remember to maintain the fluid level at least above the "Minimum" level line throughout the procedure, otherwise there is a risk of further air entering the system.*

**8** There are a number of one-man, do-it-yourself brake bleeding kits currently available from motor accessory shops. It is recommended that one of these kits is used whenever possible, as they greatly simplify the bleeding operation, and also reduce the risk of expelled air and fluid being drawn back into the system. If such a kit is not available, the basic (two-man) method must be used, which is described in detail below.

**9** If a kit is to be used, prepare the vehicle as described previously, and follow the kit manufacturer's instructions, as the procedure may vary slightly according to the type being used; generally, they are as outlined below in the relevant sub-section.

**10** Whichever method is used, the same sequence must be followed (paragraphs 11 and 12) to ensure the removal of all air from the system.

### Bleeding sequence

**11** If the system has been only partially disconnected, and suitable precautions were taken to minimise fluid loss, it should be necessary to bleed only that part of the system (ie the primary or secondary circuit).

**12** If the complete system is to be bled, then it is suggested that you work in the following sequence:

a) *Left-hand front wheel.*
b) *Right-hand rear wheel.*
c) *Right-hand front wheel.*
d) *Left-hand rear wheel.*

### Bleeding - basic (two-man) method

**13** Collect a clean glass jar, a suitable length of plastic or rubber tubing which is a tight fit over the bleed screw, and a ring spanner to fit the screw. The help of an assistant will also be required.

**14** Remove the dust cap from the first screw in the sequence (if not already done). Fit a suitable spanner and tube to the screw, place the other end of the tube in the jar, and pour in sufficient fluid to cover the end of the tube.

**15** Ensure that the master cylinder reservoir fluid level is maintained at least above the "Minimum" level throughout the procedure.

**16** Have the assistant fully depress the brake pedal several times to build up pressure, then maintain it down on the final downstroke.

**17** While pedal pressure is maintained, unscrew the bleed screw (approximately one turn) and allow the compressed fluid and air to flow into the jar. The assistant should maintain

pedal pressure, following the pedal down to the floor if necessary, and should not release the pedal until instructed to do so. When the flow stops, tighten the bleed screw again. Have the assistant release the pedal slowly, and recheck the reservoir fluid level.

**18** Repeat the steps given in paragraphs 16 and 17 until the fluid emerging from the bleed screw is free from air bubbles. If the master cylinder has been drained and refilled, and air is being bled from the first screw in the sequence, allow at least five seconds between cycles for the master cylinder passages to refill.

**19** When no more air bubbles appear, tighten the bleed screw securely, remove the tube and spanner, and refit the dust cap (where applicable). Do not overtighten the bleed screw.

**20** Repeat the procedure on the remaining screws in the sequence, until all air is removed from the system and the brake pedal feels firm again.

### Bleeding - using a one-way valve kit

**21** As their name implies, these kits consist of a length of tubing with a one-way valve fitted, to prevent expelled air and fluid being drawn back into the system; some kits include a translucent container, which can be positioned so that the air bubbles can be more easily seen flowing from the end of the tube.

**22** The kit is connected to the bleed screw, which is then opened **(see illustration)**. The user returns to the driver's seat, depresses the brake pedal with a smooth, steady stroke, and slowly releases it; this is repeated until the expelled fluid is clear of air bubbles.

**23** Note that these kits simplify work so much that it is easy to forget the master cylinder reservoir fluid level; ensure that this is maintained at least above the "Minimum" level at all times.

### Bleeding - using a pressure-bleeding kit

**24** These kits are usually operated by the reservoir of pressurised air contained in the spare tyre. However, note that it will probably be necessary to reduce the pressure to a

**16.22 Bleeding a front brake using a one-way valve kit**

lower level than normal; refer to the instructions supplied with the kit.

**25** By connecting a pressurised, fluid-filled container to the master cylinder reservoir, bleeding can be carried out simply by opening each screw in turn (in the specified sequence), and allowing the fluid to flow out until no more air bubbles can be seen in the expelled fluid.

**26** This method has the advantage that the large reservoir of fluid provides an additional safeguard against air being drawn into the system during bleeding.

**27** Pressure-bleeding is particularly effective when bleeding "difficult" systems, or when bleeding the complete system at the time of routine fluid renewal.

### All methods

**28** When bleeding is complete, and firm pedal feel is restored, wash off any spilt fluid, tighten the bleed screws securely, and refit their dust caps.

**29** Check the hydraulic fluid level in the master cylinder reservoir, and top-up if necessary.

**30** Discard any hydraulic fluid that has been bled from the system; it will not be fit for re-use.

**31** Check the feel of the brake pedal. If it feels at all spongy, air must still be present in the system, and further bleeding is required. Failure to bleed satisfactorily after a reasonable repetition of the bleeding procedure may be due to worn master cylinder seals.

## 17 Vacuum servo unit - testing, removal and refitting

### Testing

**1** To test the operation of the servo, depress the footbrake four or five times to exhaust the vacuum, then start the engine while keeping the footbrake depressed. As the engine starts, there should be a noticeable "give" in the brake pedal as vacuum builds up. Allow the engine to run for at least two minutes, and then switch it off. If the brake pedal is depressed again, it should be possible to detect a hiss from the servo when the pedal is depressed. After about four or five applications, no further hissing will be heard, and the pedal will feel considerably firmer.

**2** Before assuming that a problem exists in the servo itself, check the non-return valve as described in the next Section.

### Removal

**3** Refer to Section 12 and remove the master cylinder.

**4** Disconnect the vacuum hose at the servo non-return valve by pulling it free. If it is reluctant to move, assist it by prising it free using a screwdriver with its blade inserted under the elbow flange.

**9**

**18.2 Detaching the vacuum hose from the servo unit**

5 Working inside the vehicle, move the front passenger seat fully rearwards, then peel back the footwell trim from the inner bulkhead on that side, to gain access to the two servo bracket retaining nuts. Unscrew and remove the nuts.

6 Unscrew and remove the four nuts securing the servo unit to the mounting bracket.

7 Withdraw the servo unit so that its studs are clear of the bracket and pivot the inner bracket to one side. Extract the clevis pin to release the actuating rod from its shaft, then remove the servo unit.

8 Note that the servo unit cannot be dismantled for repair or overhaul and, if faulty, must be renewed.

## Refitting

9 Refitting is a reversal of removal. Refer to Section 12 for details of refitting the master cylinder.

## 18 Vacuum servo unit vacuum hose and non-return valve - removal, testing and refitting

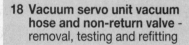

### Removal

1 Depress the brake pedal three or four times to exhaust any remaining vacuum from the servo unit.

2 Carefully pull free and detach the servo vacuum hose from the servo unit **(see illustration)**. If the hose is reluctant to move, prise it free with the aid of a screwdriver, inserting its blade under the flange of the elbow.

3 Detach the vacuum hose from its inlet manifold connection. Depending on the fixing **(see illustration)**, undo the union nut and withdraw the hose, or press the hose and its retaining collar inwards, then holding the collar in, withdraw the hose.

4 If the hose or the fixings are damaged or in poor condition, they must be renewed.

### Non-return valve testing

5 Examine the non-return valve for damage and signs of deterioration, and renew it if necessary. The valve may be tested by blowing through its connecting hoses in both directions. It should only be possible to blow from the servo end to the manifold end.

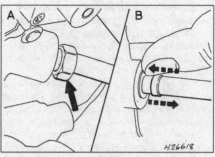

**18.3 Servo vacuum hose detachment from the manifold**

- *A  Hose secured by union nut*
- *B  Hose secured by retaining collar*

## Refitting

6 Refitting is a reversal of removal. If fitting a new non-return valve, ensure that it is fitted the correct way round.

## 19 Handbrake shoes (disc brake models) - renewal

**Note:** *Before starting work, refer to the warning at the beginning of Section 9 concerning the dangers of asbestos dust.*

1 Remove the rear brake disc as described in Section 11.

2 Note carefully the fitted positions of the springs, adjuster and handbrake shoes **(see illustration)**.

3 Release the handbrake cable from the relay lever, referring to Section 22 if necessary.

4 Remove the shoe steady springs by depressing and turning them through 90°. Remove the springs and pins.

5 Pull the lower ends of the shoes apart to release the adjuster, then disconnect the lower pull-off spring from both shoes **(see illustration)**.

6 Detach the upper ends of the shoes from the handbrake cable relay lever, then disconnect the upper pull-off spring and remove the two handbrake shoes.

7 Renew the handbrake shoes if they are significantly worn or in any way contaminated.

8 Clean the adjuster and its associated components.

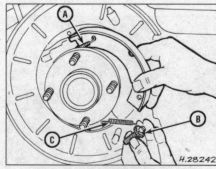

**19.5 Handbrake shoe upper pull-off spring (A), adjuster (B) and lower pull-off spring (C)**

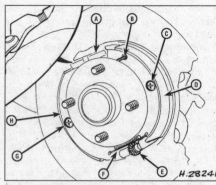

**19.2 Handbrake shoe components (rear disc brake models)**

| | |
|---|---|
| *A  Relay lever* | *E  Adjuster* |
| *B  Upper pull-off spring* | *F  Lower pull-off spring* |
| *C  Steady spring* | *G  Steady spring* |
| *D  Brake shoe* | *H  Brake shoe* |

9 Clean the backplate, then apply a little high-melting-point grease to the shoe contact points.

10 Refitting the handbrake shoes is a reversal of removal.

11 Repeat the procedure on the remaining rear brake.

12 On completion, adjust the handbrake as described in Chapter 1.

## 20 Handbrake lever - removal and refitting

### Removal

1 Chock the roadwheels to secure the vehicle.

2 Remove the front seats as described in Chapter 11.

3 Where applicable, remove the centre console as described in Chapter 11.

4 Peel back the carpet from the area around the handbrake lever to provide suitable access the lever and fittings. Release the handbrake.

5 Detach the handbrake warning light lead from the switch.

6 Prise free the retaining clip and remove the primary cable pin **(see illustration)**.

**20.6 Handbrake primary cable-to-lever pin and retaining clip (arrowed)**

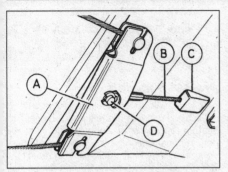

**21.4 Handbrake cable equaliser components**

A Equaliser
B Primary cable
C Cable guide
D Equaliser pin and spring clip

7 Undo the two retaining bolts, and remove the handbrake lever and spreader plate.

### Refitting

8 Refit in the reverse order of removal. Ensure that the retaining bolts are securely tightened. Check the handbrake adjustment as described in Chapter 1 to complete.

## 21 Handbrake primary cable - removal and refitting

### Removal

1 Release the primary cable from the handbrake lever, as described in the previous Section.
2 Chock the front wheels then jack up the rear of the car and support it on axle stands (see "Jacking and vehicle support").
3 Where applicable, detach the exhaust system and remove the heat shields from the underside floorpan to allow access to the primary cable connections underneath the vehicle (see Chapter 4E).
4 Release the spring clip securing the pin, and extract the equaliser/cable pin. Detach the equaliser from the primary cable (see illustration).
5 Detach the cable guide from the floorpan, then withdraw the cable rearwards from the vehicle.

**22.6a Compress the handbrake cable retaining lugs to release the cable from the brake backplate**

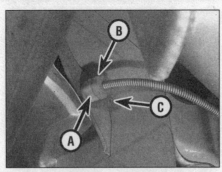

**22.4 Handbrake cable adjuster nut (A) locknut (B) and lockpin (C)**

### Refitting

6 Refit in the reverse order of removal. Ensure that the cable guide is secured in the floorpan, and lubricate the pivot pin with a liberal amount of high-melting-point grease.
7 Refit the exhaust system and heat shields with reference to Chapter 4E (where applicable).
8 Refer to Chapter 1 for details, and adjust the handbrake as required before lowering the vehicle to the ground.

## 22 Handbrake cable - removal and refitting

### Removal

1 Chock the front wheels then jack up the rear of the car and support it on axle stands (see "Jacking and vehicle support"). Fully release the handbrake lever and remove the rear roadwheels.
2 Refer to the previous Section for details, and disconnect the handbrake primary cable from the equaliser.
3 Disengage the right/left-hand cable(s) from the equaliser (as required).
4 Remove the lockpin from the adjuster, and the spring clip from the cable guides on the side concerned, then detach them from the underbody (see illustration).

### Drum brake models

5 Remove the rear brake drum(s) and shoes as described in Sections 5 and 6 respectively.
6 Compress the handbrake cable retainer

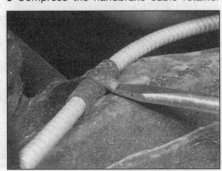

**22.6b Release the handbrake cable from its locating clips**

lugs and release the cable from the backplate, then pull the cable through. Release the cable from the underbody fixings, and remove it from the vehicle (see illustrations).

### Disc brake models

7 Detach the handbrake return spring, then disconnect the cable end from the handbrake shoe relay lever.
8 Extract the circlip securing the handbrake outer cable to the support bracket, and withdraw the cable.
9 Release the cable from the underbody fixings, and remove it from the vehicle.

### Refitting
### All models

10 Refitting is a reversal of the removal procedure. Where applicable, refer to the appropriate Sections for details on the refitting of the brake shoes and drums.
11 When the cable is fully refitted (but before lowering the vehicle rear wheels to the ground) check and adjust the handbrake as described in Chapter 1.

## 23 Brake pressure control valves - removal and refitting

**Note:** Before starting work, refer to the warning at the beginning of Section 16 concerning the dangers of hydraulic fluid.

### Removal

1 The pressure control valves are located in the engine compartment, fixed to the left-hand inner wing panel or screwed directly into the master cylinder fluid outlet ports (see illustration).
2 Minimise hydraulic fluid loss by removing the master cylinder reservoir cap, placing a piece of plastic film over the reservoir and sealing it with an elastic band. Detach the rigid brake pipes from the valves. As the pipes are disconnected, tape over the exposed ends, or fit plugs, to prevent the ingress of dirt and excessive fluid loss.
3 To remove the inner wing panel mounted assembly, unscrew and remove the valve support bracket retaining nut (under the wheel arch), and remove the valve assembly from

**23.1 Inner wing mounted brake pressure control valves**

9

the vehicle. To remove the valves from the bracket, slide free the retaining clips and detach the valve(s).

4 To remove the master cylinder mounted valves, unscrew them from the master cylinder body.

### Refitting

5 Refitting is a reversal of the removal procedure.

6 On completion, bleed the complete hydraulic system as described in Section 16.

### 24 Light-laden valve (Van models) - removal and refitting

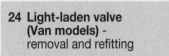

**Note:** *Before starting work, refer to the warning at the beginning of Section 16 concerning the dangers of hydraulic fluid.*

### Removal

1 For this operation, the vehicle must be raised for access underneath at the rear, but must still be resting on its wheels. Suitable ramps (or an inspection pit) will therefore be required. If positioning the vehicle on a pair of ramps, chock the front roadwheels.

2 Detach the brake pipes from the valve **(see illustration)**, and drain the fluid into a suitable container for disposal. Due to its location, care will be needed not to spill the fluid onto the hands - wear suitable protective gloves.

3 Detach the spring clip from the link rod at the axle end. Withdraw the washer and the valve link rod from the bracket on the axle, but take care not to dismantle the spacer tube from the link rod.

4 The axle bracket bush must be removed for renewal if it is worn or damaged.

5 Unscrew and remove the two retaining bolts, then withdraw the valve and the link rod from the mounting bracket.

### Refitting

6 Where applicable, fit the new bush into the axle bracket.

7 Relocate the valve on the mounting bracket, and fit the retaining bolts.

8 Check that the brake pipe connections are clean, then reconnect the pipes.

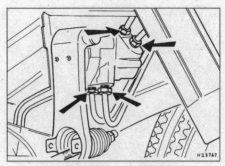

**24.2 Brake pipe connections to the light-laden valve**

9 Smear the axle bush end of the link rod with a small amount of general-purpose grease. Fit the link rod into the bush, refit the washer, and secure with the spring clip.

10 Bleed the brake hydraulic system as described in Section 16. If the original valve has been refitted, ensure that the valve is held fully open whilst bleeding. If a new valve has been fitted, the bleed clip must be left in position whilst the system is completely bled, then removed. The valve will need to be adjusted as described in the following Section.

### 25 Light-laden valve (Van models) - adjustment

1 For this operation, the vehicle must be raised for access underneath at the rear, but must be standing on its wheels. Suitable ramps (or an inspection pit) will therefore be required. If positioning the vehicle on a pair of ramps, chock the front roadwheels. The vehicle must be empty, and the fuel tank no more than half-full.

2 To adjust an original light-laden valve linkage, grip the flats on the end of the rod to prevent it from rotating, and turn the adjuster nut to position the end face of the rubber seal within the setting groove width **(see illustrations)**.

3 To adjust a new light-laden valve, rotate the spacer tube to position the end face of the rubber seal within the setting groove width, then crimp over the end of the spacer tube against the threaded rod flats (next to the knurled section) **(see illustration)**.

### 26 Anti-lock braking system (ABS) - general information

#### Pre-1996 models

A Teves Mk. IV anti-lock braking system is available on certain models in the range. The system operates in conjunction with the conventional braking system but additionally comprises a hydraulic unit, an ABS module, a wheel speed sensor on each front wheel hub, and a combined pedal position sensor and brake stop light switch assembly.

The hydraulic unit consists of a twin-circuit electric pump and a twin-channel valve block containing one inlet and one outlet solenoid valve for each hydraulic channel.

The ABS module is located in the engine compartment, and has four main functions: to control the ABS system; to monitor the rotational speed of the front wheels; to monitor the electric components in the system; and to provide "on-board" system fault diagnosis. The electrical functions of the ABS module are continuously monitored by two microprocessors, and these also periodically check the solenoid-operated valves by means of a test pulse during the operation of the system. The module checks the signals sent by the system sensors to provide a means of fault diagnosis. In the event of a fault occurring in the ABS system, a warning light on the instrument panel will come on and remain on until the ignition is switched off. A particular fault is represented by a two-digit code stored within the module memory. A fault code reader or similar system tester is required to read the codes, so in the event of a fault being indicated, the vehicle must be taken to a Ford garage for analysis.

The ABS system functions as follows. During normal braking, pressure from the brake pedal is applied to the master cylinder by the servo unit pushrod. The servo unit pushrod acts directly on the pressure piston in the master cylinder. The resulting increase in hydraulic pressure moves the intermediate piston in the cylinder, and the pressure which increases in front of the intermediate piston flows through the open inlet solenoid valves in the hydraulic unit valve block, to the brake calipers and wheel cylinders. The outlet

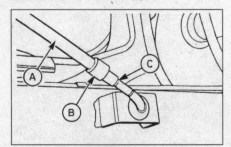

**25.2a Light-laden valve linkage adjustment**

*A Spacer tube    C Setting groove*
*B Rubber seal*

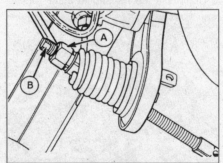

**25.2b Light-laden valve linkage adjustment on a used valve, showing adjuster nut (A) and flats on the end of the rod (B)**

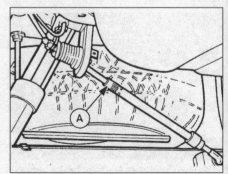

**25.3 Light-laden valve adjustment on a new valve showing the crimping point (A)**

solenoid valves in the valve block remain shut.

The wheel speed sensors continually monitor the speed of the front wheels by generating an electrical signal as the wheel is rotated. This information is passed to the ABS module which is then able to determine wheel speed, wheel acceleration and wheel deceleration. The module compares the signals received from each front wheel and if the onset of lock at either wheel is detected, a signal is sent to the hydraulic unit which regulates the brake pressure in the hydraulic circuit for the relevant wheel.

ABS hydraulic pressure regulation is carried out in three phases; pressure holding, pressure reduction and pressure build-up.

In the pressure holding phase, to prevent any further build-up of hydraulic pressure in the circuit being controlled, the inlet solenoid valve in the hydraulic unit is shut and the outlet solenoid valve remains shut. The pressure cannot now be increased in the controlled circuit by any further application of the brake pedal.

If the wheel speed sensor signals indicate that wheel rotation has now stabilised, the ABS module will instigate the pressure build-up phase, allowing braking to continue. If wheel lock is still detected after the pressure holding phase, the module instigates the pressure reduction phase.

A controlled braking operation can be instigated with a pressure reduction phase or it can follow a pressure holding phase. The inlet solenoid valve is, or remains shut and the outlet solenoid valve is opened. As long as the outlet solenoid valve is open, the brake fluid discharges back into the master cylinder reservoir.

If the brake pedal begins to creep down during a pressure reduction phase, a signal is sent to the ABS module from the combined pedal position sensor and brake stop light switch assembly mounted on the brake pedal bracket. When this signal is detected, the ABS module activates the electric pump on the hydraulic unit. Hydraulic fluid is pumped from the master cylinder reservoir back into the brake hydraulic circuit, forcing back the master cylinder piston (and the brake pedal). When the module detects that the pedal has returned to its initial position, the pump is switched off.

The pressure build-up phase is instigated after the wheel rotation has stabilised. The outlet solenoid valve is shut and the inlet solenoid valve is opened. The brake pressure from the master cylinder flows through the inlet solenoid valve to the relevant brake caliper/wheel cylinder allowing braking to continue.

The whole ABS control cycle takes place four to ten times per second for each affected wheel and this ensures maximum braking effect and control during ABS operation.

The rear wheels are not fitted with wheel speed sensors, but are prevented from locking up (under all braking conditions) by means of a load-apportioning valve incorporated in each rear circuit. These valves are housed in a common casting, and are actuated by an arm connected to the rear axle. The load-apportioning valve is checked for adjustment and set during the vehicle pre-delivery inspection using a special tool. Any further checks or adjustments required must therefore be entrusted to a Ford dealer.

### 1996 models onward

The Teves 20-I anti-lock braking system fitted to later models is a totally revised version of the original system, with a number of significant differences to the hydraulic unit and ABS module software. From 1998 onwards, the system may also optionally incorporate traction control.

As with the earlier system, Teves 20-I operates in conjunction with the conventional braking system but additionally comprises a hydraulic unit, an ABS module, and a wheel speed sensor on each wheel hub (four in total). The function of the ABS module is essentially the same as on the earlier system however, to reduce external electrical connections to a minimum and improve reliability, the module is now integral with the hydraulic unit.

The hydraulic unit consists of an electric motor operating a return pump with eccentric drive and twin radial pistons, inlet and outlet solenoid valves, pressure accumulators and pulsation dampers. The unit controls the hydraulic pressure applied to the brake for each individual front wheel and each individual rear wheel. The return pump is switched on when the ABS is activated and returns hydraulic fluid, drained off during the pressure reduction phase, back into the brake circuit.

The ABS system functions as follows. During normal braking, pressure from the brake pedal is applied to the master cylinder by the vacuum servo unit pushrod. The servo unit pushrod acts directly on the pressure piston in the master cylinder which pressurises the hydraulic fluid in the brake pipes to the hydraulic control unit. The inlet solenoid valve and outlet solenoid valve both remain in the 'at rest' position (inlet solenoid valve open and outlet solenoid valve closed). Hydraulic pressure is transmitted to each brake caliper or wheel cylinder, thus operating the brakes. When the brake pedal is released, a one-way valve opens allowing the hydraulic pressure in the circuit to rapidly decrease.

The ABS module continually monitors wheel speed from the signals provided by the wheel speed sensors. If the module detects the incidence of wheel lock on one or more wheels, ABS is automatically initiated in three phases: pressure holding, pressure reduction and pressure build-up. As the system operates individually on each wheel, any or all of the wheels could be in any one of the following phases at any particular moment.

In the pressure holding phase, to prevent any further build-up of hydraulic pressure in the circuit being controlled, the ABS module closes the inlet solenoid valve and allows the outlet solenoid valve to remain closed. The hydraulic fluid line from the master cylinder to the brake caliper or wheel cylinder is closed, and the hydraulic fluid in the controlled circuit is maintained at a constant pressure. The pressure cannot now be increased in that circuit by any further application of the brake pedal.

If the wheel speed sensor signals indicate that wheel rotation has now stabilised, the ABS module will instigate the pressure build-up phase, allowing braking to continue. If wheel lock is still detected after the pressure holding phase, the module instigates the pressure reduction phase.

In the pressure reduction phase, the inlet solenoid valve remains closed and the outlet solenoid valve is opened by means of a series of short activation pulses. The pressure in the controlled circuit decreases rapidly as the fluid flows from the brake caliper or wheel cylinder into the pressure accumulator. At the same time, the ABS module actuates the electric motor to operate the return pump. The hydraulic fluid is then pumped back into the pressure side of the master cylinder. This process creates a pulsation which can be felt in the brake pedal action, but which is softened by the pulsation damper.

The pressure build-up phase is instigated after the wheel rotation has stabilised. The inlet and outlet solenoid valves are returned to the at rest position (inlet solenoid valve open and exhaust solenoid valve closed) which re-opens the hydraulic fluid line from the master cylinder to the brake caliper or wheel cylinder. Hydraulic pressure is reinstated, thus re-introducing operation of the brake. After a brief period, a short pressure holding phase is re-introduced and the ABS module continually shifts between pressure build-up and pressure holding until the wheel has decelerated to a sufficient degree where pressure reduction is once more required.

The whole ABS control cycle takes place 4 to 10 times per second for each affected wheel and this ensures maximum braking effect and control during ABS operation.

Where the system incorporates traction control, essentially the reverse principle is applied. When the ABS module detects that one or more front wheels are rotating faster than the reference value, the brake is actually applied on the relevant wheel(s) to reduce the rotational speed.

To prevent rear wheel lock-up, the ABS module contains additional software for rear brake hydraulic fluid pressure regulation during normal (non-ABS regulated) braking. As the rear brake hydraulic pressure is controlled by the ABS module and hydraulic unit, the mechanical load-apportioning valves used in the earlier system are not required.

### 27 Anti-lock braking system (ABS) components - removal and refitting

**9**

#### Hydraulic unit
**Pre-1996 models**

1 Disconnect the battery negative (earth) lead (refer to Chapter 5A, Section 1).
2 Remove the filler cap from the master cylinder reservoir (noting that the filler cap must not be inverted). The reservoir should now be emptied by siphoning or drawing out the fluid with a pipette.
3 Identify each brake pipe and its connection

to the master cylinder, then unscrew the union nuts and disconnect them **(see illustration)**. When disconnecting the fluid return pipes from the reservoir, press the retaining boss into the reservoir, and pull free the fluid line. Plug the connections, and tape over the pipe ends, to prevent the entry of dust and dirt.

**4** Disconnect the wiring multi-plug adjacent to the hydraulic unit.

**5** Unscrew the union nuts, and disconnect the fluid pipes from the hydraulic unit at the rear. Plug the connections.

**6** Unscrew the retaining nut securing the multi-plug connector bracket, and the nut and bolt securing the hydraulic unit to the bracket **(see illustration)**. Withdraw the hydraulic unit from the bracket, and remove it from the vehicle.

**7** Prise free and detach the fluid return lines from the hydraulic unit **(see illustration)**. Plug the connections, and tape over the pipe ends, to prevent the entry of dust and dirt.

**8** Remove the plugs from the connections as the pipes and fluid return lines are refitted. Refit in the reverse order of removal, noting the torque settings for the unit-to-bracket nut and bolt. Ensure that all connections are clean and secure.

**9** On completion, bleed the system as described in Section 16. Inspect the hydraulic line connections at the master cylinder/hydraulic unit for any sign of leaks.

### 1996 models onward

**10** Disconnect the battery negative (earth) lead (refer to Chapter 5A, Section 1).

**11** Remove the filler cap from the master cylinder reservoir (noting that the filler cap must not be inverted). The reservoir should now be emptied by siphoning or drawing out the fluid with a pipette.

**12** Identify each brake pipe and its connection to the hydraulic unit, then unscrew the union nuts and disconnect them. Plug the connections, and tape over the pipe ends, to prevent the entry of dust and dirt.

**13** Disconnect the wiring multi-plug from the ABS module located on the side of the hydraulic unit.

**14** Undo the three bolts and remove the hydraulic unit from the engine compartment.

**15** Refit in the reverse order of removal, ensuring that all connections are clean and secure.

**16** On completion, bleed the system as described in Section 16. Inspect the hydraulic line connections at the hydraulic unit for any sign of leaks.

### ABS module

#### Pre-1996 models

**17** Disconnect the battery negative (earth) lead (refer to Chapter 5A, Section 1).

**18** The module is situated opposite the battery, at the rear of the engine compartment. Swing the retaining clip out of the way, and disconnect the wiring multi-plug from the module.

**19** Unscrew and remove the three retaining bolts, and withdraw the module from the vehicle **(see illustration)**.

**20** Refit in the reverse order of removal, but

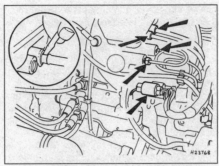

**27.3 Detach the hydraulic lines and the wiring multi-plug from the points indicated**

take particular care when reconnecting the multi-plug.

### 1996 models onward

**21** The ABS module on later models is an integral part of the hydraulic unit and cannot be separated.

### Front wheel speed sensor

**22** An ABS wheel speed sensor is fitted in the front spindle carrier on each side. To remove a sensor, apply the handbrake, then raise and support the front of the vehicle on axle stands so the front wheels are clear of the ground.

**23** Unclip and detach the sensor cable from the wiring loom. Unscrew the retaining bolt, and withdraw the sensor from its location in the spindle carrier. Remove the sensor and lead from the vehicle.

**24** If renewing the sensor, the replacement must have the correct lead length (on models fitted with an anti-roll bar, the lead is longer).

**25** Refit in the reverse order of removal. When inserting the sensor into position, ensure that the mating surfaces are clean, free from oil and grease. Feed the cable through the wheel arch, and ensure that it is clipped in position. Secure the cable with any ties provided. When the sensor is refitted, turn the steering from lock to lock, to ensure that the sensor lead does not foul on any steering or suspension components before lowering the vehicle to the ground.

### Rear wheel speed sensor

**26** Rear wheel speed sensors are only fitted to 1996 models onward, equipped with the Teves 20-I anti-lock braking system.

**27** The removal and refitting procedure is essentially the same as for the front wheel

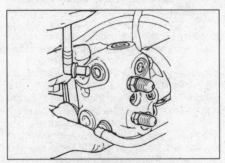

**27.7 Disconnect the fluid return lines from the ABS hydraulic unit**

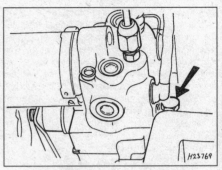

**27.6 ABS hydraulic unit-to-bracket retaining bolt location**

speed sensor except that the rear sensor is bolted to the brake backplate rather than the front spindle carrier.

### Front wheel speed sensor ring

**28** Referring to Chapter 10 for details, remove the spindle carrier, then remove the wheel hub from the spindle carrier.

**29** Where applicable, unscrew and remove the sensor ring-to-hub retaining bolts, then detach the sensor ring from the hub. In some instances, the sensor ring will be press-fitted on the hub, and will require a suitable withdrawal tool to remove it.

**30** Refitting is a reversal of the removal procedure. Ensure that the sensor and hub mating faces are clean. Refer to the appropriate Sections in Chapter 10 for details on refitting the hub and spindle carrier.

### Rear wheel speed sensor ring

**31** Remove the rear brake drum/hub assembly as described in Chapter 10, Section 10.

**32** Extract the sensor ring from the drum/hub assembly. The sensor ring is a press-fit on the hub, and will require a suitable withdrawal tool to remove it.

**33** Press the new sensor ring onto the hub, then refit the hub/drum assembly as described in Chapter 10, Section 10.

### Load-apportioning valve

**34** The removal of the load-apportioning valve on pre-1996 ABS-equipped models is not recommended, since a special resetting tool is required to adjust the valve when it is refitted. The removal and refitting of the load-apportioning valve is therefore a task to be entrusted to a suitably-equipped Ford dealer.

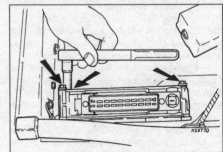

**27.19 Location of the ABS module retaining bolts**

# Chapter 10
# Suspension and steering

# Contents

# Degrees of difficulty

|  |  |  | | |
|---|---|---|---|---|
| **Easy,** suitable for novice with little experience | **Fairly easy,** suitable for beginner with some experience | **Fairly difficult,** suitable for competent DIY mechanic | **Difficult,** suitable for experienced DIY mechanic | **Very difficult,** suitable for expert DIY or professional |

# Specifications

### Wheel alignment and steering angles
Front wheel toe setting (all models):
  Tolerance allowed before resetting required . . . . . . . . . . . . . . . . . . 0.5 mm toe-out to 4.5 mm toe-in (0°05' toe-out to 0°45' toe-in)
  Adjustment setting (if required) . . . . . . . . . . . . . . . . . . . . . . . . . . . . 2.0 mm toe-in ± 1.0 mm (0°20' toe-in ± 0°10')

### Roadwheels
Wheel types and sizes (dependent on model):
  Steel . . . . . . . . . . . . . . . . . . . . . . . . . . . . . . . . . . . . . . . . . . . . . . 13 x 5 (Heavy Duty Van), 14 x 6 or 15 x 6
  Alloy . . . . . . . . . . . . . . . . . . . . . . . . . . . . . . . . . . . . . . . . . . . . . . . 13 x 5, 14 x 6 or 15 x 6

### Tyres
Tyre sizes (dependent on model) . . . . . . . . . . . . . . . . . . . . . . . . . . . 155R 13 78T, 165R 13-C, 165R 13-T, 165R13-REINF,
175/70R 13 82T, 175/70R 13 82H, 185/50R 14H/V, 185/60R 14 82H,
185/60R 14 V, 195/50R 15 V, 195/55R 15V
Tyre pressures . . . . . . . . . . . . . . . . . . . . . . . . . . . . . . . . . . . . . . . . . See "Weekly Checks"

## Torque wrench settings

| | Nm | lbf ft |
|---|---|---|
| **Front suspension** | | |
| Hub/driveshaft retaining nut: | | |
|   M20 x 1.5 (23-spline driveshaft) .............................. | 220 | 162 |
|   M22 x 1.5 (25-spline driveshaft) .............................. | 235 | 173 |
| Lower arm balljoint-to-spindle carrier clamp bolt ................... | 54 | 40 |
| Lower arm to subframe bolts (using torque-to-yield method with vehicle standing on its wheels): | | |
|   Stage 1 ........................................................ | 50 | 37 |
|   Stage 2 ........................................................ | Slacken completely | |
|   Stage 3 ........................................................ | 50 | 37 |
|   Stage 4 ........................................................ | Tighten through a further 90° | |
| Anti-roll bar link to suspension strut ............................. | 50 | 37 |
| Anti-roll bar link to anti-roll bar ............................... | 50 | 37 |
| Anti-roll bar-to-subframe clamp bolts ............................. | 24 | 18 |
| Subframe retaining bolts ......................................... | 85 | 63 |
| Suspension top mounting nut ...................................... | 46 | 34 |
| Suspension strut piston rod top spring seat nut .................. | 58 | 43 |
| Suspension strut-to-spindle carrier clamp bolt ................... | 85 | 63 |
| **Rear suspension (Hatchback, Saloon and Estate)** | | |
| Rear hub bearing nut ............................................. | 260 | 192 |
| Axle front mounting bracket bolts ................................ | 50 | 37 |
| Axle front bush/bracket pivot nuts/bolts* ........................ | 120 | 88 |
| Strut upper mounting nuts (Hatchback and Saloon) ................. | 35 | 25 |
| Strut lower mounting (Hatchback and Saloon) ...................... | 120 | 88 |
| Strut upper through-bolt (Hatchback and Saloon) .................. | 50 | 37 |
| Shock absorber upper mounting (Estate) ........................... | 50 | 37 |
| Shock absorber lower mounting (Estate) ........................... | 69 | 51 |
| *Torque to be measured from the bolt head (not the nut) | | |
| **Rear suspension (Van)** | | |
| Rear hub bearing nut ............................................. | 260 | 192 |
| Shock absorber upper mounting .................................... | 50 | 37 |
| Shock absorber lower mounting .................................... | 68 | 50 |
| Shock absorber mounting bracket to body .......................... | 35 | 25 |
| Axle/spring U-bolt nuts .......................................... | 41 | 30 |
| Front spring mounting bolt ....................................... | 84 | 62 |
| Rear shackle upper stud/nut ...................................... | 50 | 37 |
| Rear shackle lower mounting bolt ................................. | 84 | 62 |
| **Steering (manual)** | | |
| Steering wheel-to-column shaft bolt .............................. | 50 | 37 |
| Steering gear-to-subframe bolts .................................. | 84 | 62 |
| Steering column mounting nuts .................................... | 25 | 18 |
| Steering column-to-pinion shaft clamp bolt ....................... | 25 | 18 |
| Track rod end balljoint-to-spindle carrier arm .................. | 28 | 20 |
| Track rod end balljoint-to-track rod locknut .................... | 63 | 46 |
| Track rod to steering rack ....................................... | 79 | 58 |
| Adjustable steering through-bolt ................................. | 7 | 5 |
| **Steering (power-assisted)** | | |
| Steering wheel-to-column shaft bolt .............................. | 50 | 37 |
| Steering gear-to-subframe bolts: | | |
|   Stage 1 ........................................................ | 15 | 11 |
|   Stage 2 ........................................................ | Tighten through a further 90° | |
| Steering column mounting nuts .................................... | 25 | 18 |
| Steering column-to-pinion shaft clamp bolt ....................... | 25 | 18 |
| Track rod end balljoint-to-spindle carrier arm .................. | 28 | 20 |
| Track rod end balljoint-to-track rod locknut .................... | 63 | 46 |
| Track rod to steering rack ....................................... | 79 | 58 |
| Adjustable steering through-bolt ................................. | 7 | 5 |
| Steering pump bolts .............................................. | 25 | 18 |
| Steering pump pulley bolts ....................................... | 25 | 18 |
| Pressure hose to pump ............................................ | 28 | 20 |
| **Roadwheel nuts** | | |
| All models ....................................................... | 85 | 63 |

## 1 General information

The independent front suspension is of the MacPherson strut type, incorporating coil springs and integral telescopic shock absorbers. The struts are attached to spindle carriers at their lower ends, and the carriers are in turn attached to the lower suspension arm by balljoints. High-series models are fitted with an anti-roll bar, and this is attached to the subframe and lower suspension arms by link rods with rubber bushes.

On all except Van models, the semi-independent rear suspension is of trailing arm type, incorporating a twist type axle beam. This inverted V-section beam allows a limited torsional flexibility, giving each rear wheel a certain amount of independent movement whilst at the same time maintaining the track and wheel camber control for the rear axle. The axle is attached to the body by rubber void bushes, via brackets mounted on the underside of the body. Each bracket has a conical seating peg to ensure accurate alignment of the axle. It is important to note that the vehicle must never be jacked up at the rear under the axle beam. The axle beam itself is maintenance-free but where required, the pivot bushes of the trailing arm can be renewed.

The rear suspension struts on Hatchback and Saloon models are similar to those used for the front suspension, the combined coil spring and shock absorber being mounted between the suspension turret in the luggage area at the top and the trailing arm, inboard of the stub axle at the bottom. The Estate model differs in that the coil spring is separate from the shock absorber, and is enclosed between the underbody and the trailing suspension arm.

On Van models, the rear suspension comprises a transverse beam axle which is supported by a single leaf spring each side. Telescopic shock absorbers are used to control vertical movement.

A variable-ratio type rack-and-pinion steering gear is fitted, together with a conventional column and two-section shaft. The steering gear is bolted to the front subframe. A height adjustment mechanism is fitted to some models, and power-assisted steering is also available.

## 2 Front spindle carrier - removal and refitting

### Removal

**1** Remove the wheel trim on the relevant side for access to the driveshaft/hub nut. Using a suitable pin punch, peen back the locking tab securing the driveshaft/hub nut, then loosen off the nut.
**2** Chock the rear wheels then jack up the front of the car and support it on axle stands (see *"Jacking and vehicle support"*). Remove the appropriate front roadwheel.

**3** Unscrew the retaining nut, and detach the brake hose and its locating bracket from the suspension strut **(see illustration)**.
**4** Unscrew the brake caliper-to-carrier retaining bolts, then withdraw the caliper and suspend it from a suitable fixing in the inner wing to avoid straining the brake hose. Where applicable, detach the ABS sensor and its lead clip from the spindle carrier.
**5** Extract the split pin from the track rod end balljoint, then unscrew the nut and detach the rod from the spindle carrier using a conventional balljoint removal tool, but take care not to damage the balljoint seal.
**6** Note the direction of fitting, then unscrew and remove the lower arm balljoint-to-spindle carrier clamp bolt. Prise the joint open carefully using a large flat-bladed tool, and detach the balljoint from the spindle carrier **(see illustrations)**. Take care not to damage the balljoint seal during the separation procedures.
**7** Unscrew the brake disc retaining screw, and remove the brake disc from the hub.
**8** Unscrew and remove the driveshaft/hub nut and washer. Note that a new nut will be required for refitting.
**9** Note the direction of fitting, then unscrew and remove the suspension strut-to-spindle retaining bolt. Prise open the clamping slot using a suitable wedged tool, and release the spindle from the strut. If necessary, tap the spindle carrier downwards to separate the two components **(see illustrations)**.
**10** Connect up a universal puller to the spindle carrier, and withdraw it from the

**2.3 Disconnect the brake hose from the front suspension strut**

**2.6a Removing the lower arm-to-spindle clamp bolt and nut**

**2.6b Prise open the joint . . .**

**2.6c . . . and detach the lower arm balljoint from the spindle**

**2.9a Remove the suspension strut-to-spindle carrier clamp bolt . . .**

**2.9b . . . and separate the spindle carrier from the strut**

10

driveshaft. When the driveshaft is free of the spindle, suspend it from a suitable fixing point under the wheel arch. This will prevent it from hanging down and its joint being pivoted excessively.

### Refitting

**11** Refitting is a reversal of removal, but observe the following points:

a) *Ensure that all mating faces, particularly those of the disc and hub flange, are clean before refitting.*

b) *Lubricate the hub splines with molybdenum disulphide grease, and take care not to dislodge the hub bearings as the driveshaft is refitted through the hub.*

c) *Tighten all nuts and bolts to the specified torque. Fit a new split pin to the track rod end balljoint nut to secure it. When reconnecting the suspension lower arm balljoint to the spindle carrier, ensure that the clamp bolt is fully engaged in the locating groove, and prevent the bolt from turning as the nut is tightened.*

d) *With the (new) hub nut tightened to its specified torque setting, stake the nut flange into the groove in the end of the driveshaft.*

### 3  Front hub bearings (23-spline type) - renewal

**Note:** *The front hub bearings should only be removed from the spindle carrier if they are to be renewed. The removal procedure renders the bearings unserviceable, and they must not be re-used. Prior to dismantling, it should be noted that a hub/bearing puller and an assortment of metal tubes of various diameters (and preferably, a press) will be required. Unless these tools are available, the renewal of the spindle carrier/hub bearings will have to be entrusted to a Ford garage. Under no circumstances attempt to tap the hub bearings into position, as this will render them unserviceable. On ABS-equipped models, care must be taken during the bearing removal and refitting procedures not to damage the ABS wheel sensor ring.*

### Removal

**1** Remove the spindle carrier from the vehicle as described in Section 2.
**2** The hub must now be removed from the bearing inner races. It is preferable to use a press to do this, but it is possible to drive out the hub using a length of metal tube of suitable diameter.
**3** Part of the inner race will remain on the hub, and this should be removed using a puller.
**4** Using a suitable punch, tap the outer bearing race at diametrically-opposed points and remove it from the spindle carrier **(see illustration)**. Do not allow the bearing to tilt during its withdrawal from the housing, or it

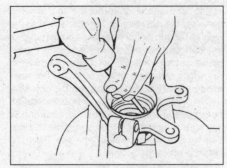

**3.4  Using a punch to remove the hub bearing outer race from the spindle carrier**

will jam and possibly damage the surface of the bore. Any burrs left in a bearing bore will prevent the new bearing from seating correctly.
**5** Thoroughly clean the bearing bore and hub before reassembly begins.

### Refitting

**6** Press the new outer bearing assembly into the spindle carrier using a length of metal tube of diameter slightly less than the outer race. Do not apply any pressure to the inner race. Alternatively, a long threaded rod or bolt, a nut and large flat washers may be used to draw the bearing into position **(see illustration)**. Fit the new inner bearing assembly in the same way.
**7** Support the inner race on a length of metal tube, then press the hub fully into the bearing.
**8** Check that the hub spins freely in the bearings, then refit the spindle carrier as described in Section 2.

### 4  Front hub bearings (25-spline type) - renewal

**Note:** *The front hub bearings should only be removed from the spindle carrier if they are to be renewed. The removal procedure renders the bearings unserviceable, and they must not be re-used. Prior to dismantling, it should be noted that a hub/bearing puller and an assortment of metal tubes of various diameters (and preferably, a press) will be required. Unless these tools are available, the renewal of the spindle carrier/hub bearings will have to be entrusted to a Ford garage. Under no circumstances attempt to tap the hub bearings into position, as this will render them unserviceable. On ABS-equipped models, care must be taken during the bearing removal and refitting procedures not to damage the ABS wheel sensor ring.*

### Removal

**1** Remove the spindle carrier from the vehicle as described in Section 2.
**2** The hub must now be removed from the bearing inner races. It is preferable to use a press to do this, but it is possible to drive out

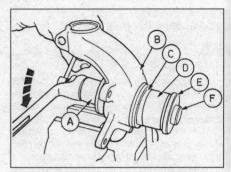

**3.6  Using home-made tools to fit the outer bearing assembly to the spindle carrier**

| A | Steel tube | D | Steel tube |
| B | Spindle carrier | E | Flat washer |
| C | Bearing | F | Threaded bolt |

the hub using a length of metal tube of suitable diameter.
**3** Part of the inner race will remain on the hub, and this should be removed using a puller.
**4** Extract the bearing retaining circlip using circlip pliers, then drive the bearing outer race from the spindle carrier. Do not allow the bearing to tilt during its withdrawal from the housing, or it will jam and possibly damage the surface of the bore. Any burrs left in a bearing bore will prevent the new bearing from seating correctly. If necessary, insert the old inner race to facilitate removal of the bearing.
**5** Thoroughly clean the bearing bore and hub before reassembly begins.

### Refitting

**6** Press the new outer bearing assembly into the spindle carrier, using a length of metal tube of diameter slightly less than the outer race. Do not apply any pressure to the inner race. Alternatively, a long threaded rod or bolt, a nut and large flat washers may be used to draw the bearing into position **(see illustration 3.6)**.
**7** Secure the bearing in the spindle carrier using the circlip.
**8** Support the inner race on a length of metal tube, then press the hub fully into the bearing.
**9** Check that the hub spins freely in the bearings, then refit the spindle carrier as described in Section 2.

### 5  Front suspension strut - removal and refitting

### Removal

**1** Chock the rear wheels then jack up the front of the car and support it on axle stands (see *"Jacking and vehicle support"*). Remove the appropriate front roadwheel.
**2** Open and support the bonnet. Prise free the protective cap from the strut upper retaining nut, then loosen off, *but do not remove,* the central retaining nut. As the nut is

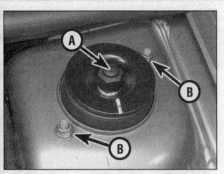

**5.2a Front suspension strut upper mounting showing the protective cap over retaining nut (A) and the strut-to-body mounting nuts (B)**

**5.2b Method to use when loosening off the strut upper mounting**

loosened off, hold the strut piston rod with an Allen key to prevent the rod from turning as the nut is loosened (see illustrations).

**3** Detach the front brake hose from the support bracket on the strut.

**4** Where applicable, unbolt and detach the anti-roll bar link rod from the suspension strut.

**5** Unscrew and remove the strut-to-spindle carrier clamp bolt.

**6** Note the direction of fitting, then unscrew and remove the lower arm balljoint-to-spindle carrier clamp bolt. Prise the joint open using a large flat-bladed tool, and detach the balljoint from the spindle carrier. Take care not to damage the balljoint seal during the separation procedures.

**7** Prise open the spindle carrier-to-strut joint, and separate the carrier from the strut. Tap the carrier downwards using a soft-faced hammer to release it from the strut if necessary.

**8** Support the weight of the strut underneath, and unscrew the two nuts securing it to the turret at the top. Lower the strut and remove it from the vehicle.

### Refitting

**9** Refitting is a reversal of removal. Tighten all the retaining bolts to the specified torque. When reconnecting the suspension lower arm balljoint to the spindle carrier, ensure that the clamp bolt is fully engaged in the locating groove, and prevent the bolt from turning as the nut is tightened.

## 6 Front suspension strut - dismantling, examination and reassembly

⚠️ *Warning: Before attempting to dismantle the suspension strut, a suitable tool to hold the coil spring in compression must be obtained. Adjustable coil spring compressors which can be positively secured to the spring coils are readily available, and are recommended for this operation. Any attempt to dismantle the strut without such a tool is likely to result in damage or personal injury.*

### Dismantling

**1** With the strut removed from the vehicle, clean away all external dirt, then mount it upright in a vice.

**2** Fit the spring compressor tool (ensuring that it is fully engaged) and compress the coil spring until all tension is relieved from the upper mounting (see illustration).

**3** Hold the strut piston with an Allen key, and unscrew the nut with a ring spanner.

**4** Withdraw the cup, retainer (top mounting), the bearing and upper spring seat, followed by the gaiter and the bump stop (see illustration).

**5** The suspension strut and coil spring can now be separated. If a new coil spring or strut is to be fitted, the original coil spring must be released from the compressor. If it is to be re-used, the coil spring can be left in compression.

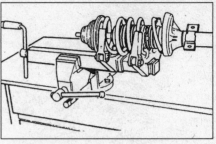

**6.2 Ford special tool in use to compress the front suspension strut coil spring**

### Examination

**6** With the strut assembly now completely dismantled, examine all the components for wear, damage or deformation, and check the bearing for smoothness of operation. Renew any of the components as necessary.

**7** Examine the strut for signs of fluid leakage. Check the strut piston for pitting along its length, and check the strut body for signs of damage or elongation of the mounting bolt holes. Test the operation of the strut, holding it in an upright position, by moving the piston through a full stroke, and then through short strokes of 50 to 100 mm. In both cases, the resistance felt should be smooth and continuous. If the resistance is jerky, or uneven, or if there is any visible sign of wear or damage to the strut, renewal is necessary.

### Reassembly

**8** Reassembly is a reversal of dismantling, but make sure that the spring ends are correctly

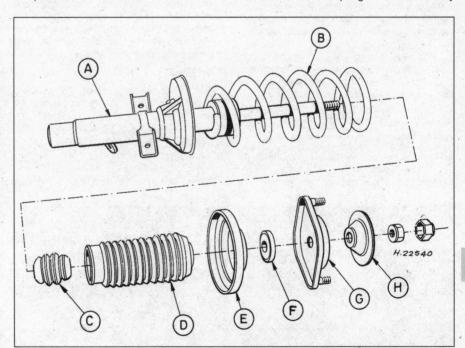

**6.4 Front suspension strut components**

| | | |
|---|---|---|
| A  Strut | C  Bump stop | E  Upper spring seat | G  Top retainer |
| B  Spring | D  Gaiter | F  Bearing | H  Top mounting cup |

**10**

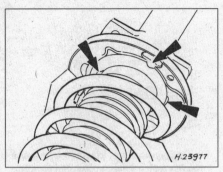

**6.8a Spring location in the lower seat**

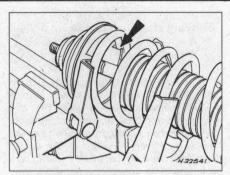

**6.8b Spring end location in the upper seat**

located in the upper and lower seats **(see illustrations)**. Check that the bearing is correctly fitted to the piston rod seat. Tighten the upper nut to the specified torque.

## 7 Front suspension anti-roll bar - removal and refitting

### Removal

1 Remove the front subframe as described in Section 9. If only the anti-roll bar bushes are to be renewed, this can be done without removing the subframe or anti-roll bar (see paragraph 3).
2 Unscrew the retaining nuts or bolts, and remove the anti-roll bar mounting brackets from the subframe each side, then withdraw the anti-roll bar from the subframe.
3 Check the bar for damage, and the rubber bushes for wear and deterioration. Renewing the bushes can be achieved without removing the bar - the bushes are split. If the bar-to-subframe mountings are disconnected, the bushes can be opened up and prised off the bar, and new ones fitted **(see illustration)**. Lubricate the new bushes with rubber grease, prior to fitting. If the link rod bushes need renewal, new link rods must be fitted.

### Refitting

4 Refitting is a reversal of the removal procedure. Tighten the retaining nuts/bolts to the specified torque setting.

## 8 Front suspension lower arm - removal and refitting

### Removal

1 Chock the rear wheels then jack up the front of the car and support it on axle stands (see "Jacking and vehicle support"). Remove the appropriate front roadwheel.
2 Note the direction of fitting, then unscrew and remove the lower arm balljoint-to-spindle carrier clamp bolt. Prise the joint open using a large flat-bladed tool, and detach the balljoint from the spindle carrier. Take care not to damage the balljoint seal during the separation procedures.
3 Unscrew and remove the inboard retaining bolts on the subframe, and withdraw the suspension arm from it **(see illustration)**.
4 If the balljoint and/or the inboard mounting bushes are found to be in poor condition, the complete suspension arm must be renewed. The suspension arm must also be renewed if it has suffered structural damage.

### Refitting

5 Refitting is a reversal of the removal procedure, but note the following special points:
a) When reconnecting the arm to the subframe, the bolts must be fitted from underneath, and hand-tightened until the vehicle is resting on its wheels.
b) When reconnecting the suspension lower

arm balljoint to the spindle carrier, ensure that the clamp bolt is fully engaged in the locating groove, and prevent the bolt from turning as the nut is tightened.
c) Fully tighten the suspension arm-to-subframe bolts when the vehicle is lowered and is standing on its wheels. These bolts must then be tightened in the sequence specified.

## 9 Subframe - removal and refitting

### Removal

1 Chock the rear wheels then jack up the front of the car and support it on axle stands (see "Jacking and vehicle support"). Remove the front roadwheels.
2 Disconnect the battery negative (earth) lead (refer to Chapter 5A, Section 1).
3 Fit an engine support bar (or a sling and hoist) to support the combined weights of the engine and transmission when the subframe is detached (as during engine/transmission removal and refitting).
4 Centralise the steering so that it is in the straight-ahead position, then working within the vehicle, unscrew and remove the steering column-to-pinion shaft clamp bolt.
5 Undo the engine/transmission mounting bracket bolts at the subframe connection **(see illustration)**.
6 Where applicable, disconnect the oxygen sensor wiring multi-plug, then undo the retaining nuts and detach the exhaust downpipe (see Chapter 4E). Remove the exhaust heat shields as necessary for access to the gear linkage.
7 Disconnect the gear linkage at the transmission (see Chapter 7A or 7B).
8 Extract the split pin and unscrew the track rod end balljoint nut on each side, then using a conventional separator tool, detach each joint from its spindle carrier connection.
9 Note the direction of fitting, then unscrew and remove the lower arm balljoint-to-spindle carrier clamp bolt. Prise the joint open using a large flat-bladed tool, and detach the balljoint from the spindle carrier. Take care not to

**7.3 Anti-roll bar-to-subframe mounting**

**8.3 Suspension arm-to-subframe retaining bolts (arrowed)**

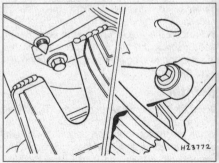

**9.5 Engine/transmission mounting bracket securing bolt locations on the subframe**

**9.12a Link rod-to-strut connection**

**9.12b Link rod-to-bar connection**

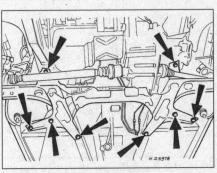

**9.14 Subframe securing bolt locations (arrowed)**

damage the balljoint seal during the separation procedure.

**10** Unscrew the retaining bolt, and detach the right-hand engine support bar from the subframe.

**11** Unscrew and remove the second engine/transmission mounting bolt.

**12** Where applicable, unscrew the retaining nuts and detach the anti-roll bar link rods from the suspension strut and anti-roll bar, each side **(see illustrations)**.

**13** Where applicable, detach the power-assisted steering hydraulic lines from the steering gear (refer to Section 24 for details).

**14** Locate suitable support jacks or blocks under the subframe to support it, then unscrew and remove the eight subframe fixing bolts from the positions shown **(see illustration)**. Lower the support jacks or blocks and withdraw the subframe. As it is lowered, disengage the steering pinion shaft from the column.

**15** When the subframe is lowered from the vehicle, the steering gear, the suspension arms and the anti-roll bar (where applicable) can be unbolted and removed from it as necessary.

**16** If the subframe and/or its associated components have suffered damage or are in poor condition, they must be renewed.

### Refitting

**17** Refitting is a reversal of removal, but observe the following points:

a) Ensure that all mating faces are clean before refitting.

b) When raising the subframe into position, ensure that the location dowels engage in the guide bores in the floorpan, and

carefully engage the steering pinion shaft with the column shaft. Check that the various fixing bolt holes are in alignment, then loosely insert all of the retaining bolts before tightening them to the specified torque setting.

c) When reconnecting the suspension lower arm balljoint to the spindle carrier, ensure that the clamp bolt is fully engaged in the locating groove, and prevent the bolt from turning as the nut is tightened.

d) Tighten all nuts and bolts to the specified torque. Fit a new split pin to the track rod end balljoint nut to secure it.

e) On completion, have the front wheel toe setting checked (see Section 28).

## 10 Rear hub bearings - renewal

### Drum brake models

**1** Chock the front wheels then jack up the rear of the car and support it on axle stands (see "Jacking and vehicle support"). Remove the appropriate rear roadwheel.

**2** On pre-1996 models, release the handbrake. On 1996 on models, unclip the handbrake lever gaiter to gain access to the adjuster nut on the side of the lever and slacken the cable right off. If the drum is stuck on the shoes, remove the rubber blanking plug from the inside face of the brake backplate, reach through with a suitable screwdriver, and release the automatic brake adjuster by levering the catch from the pawl.

**3** On certain models, the brake drum may be removed independently of the hub if desired. Remove the drum retaining screw (if fitted), and withdraw the drum off the wheel hub.

**4** Prise free the outer grease cap from the centre of the hub **(see illustration)**. The cap will be deformed during its removal, and will need to be renewed when the hub is refitted.

**5** Unscrew and remove the hub nut, but note that the hub nut threads on pre-1996 models are "handed" according to side - right-hand to right, left-hand to left **(see illustration)**. A left-hand thread unscrews in a **clockwise** direction. The hub nuts fitted to models from 1996 onwards are both right-hand thread.

**6** Withdraw the brake drum/hub from the spindle of the rear stub axle **(see illustration)**.

### Disc brake models

**7** Chock the front wheels then jack up the rear of the car and support it on axle stands (see "Jacking and vehicle support"). Remove the appropriate rear roadwheel.

**8** Refer to Chapter 9, and remove the rear brake pads.

**9** Referring to Chapter 9, undo the two rear brake caliper retaining bolts, and slide the caliper off the brake disc. Tie up the caliper using string or wire, but take care not to stretch the flexible brake hose.

**10** Undo the brake disc retaining screw, and withdraw the disc off the handbrake shoes and wheel hub.

**11** Prise free the outer grease cap from the centre of the hub. The cap will be deformed during its removal, and will need to be renewed when the hub is refitted.

**10.4 Remove the outer grease cap from the centre of the rear hub . . .**

**10.5 . . . unscrew the hub nut . . .**

**10.6 . . . and remove the brake drum**

**10.16 Use a suitable punch to drive out the bearing cups from the rear hub**

**11.3 Rear strut lower mounting on Hatchback and Saloon models**

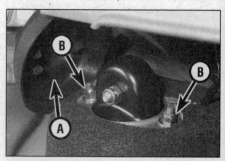

**11.4 Rear strut upper mounting on Hatchback and Saloon models showing the protective cap (A) and the mounting nuts (B)**

**12** Unscrew and remove the hub nut, but note that the hub nut threads on pre-1996 models are "handed" according to side - right-hand to right, left-hand to left **(see illustration)**. *A left-hand thread unscrews in a* **clockwise** *direction.* The hub nuts fitted to models from 1996 onwards are both right-hand thread.

**13** Withdraw the wheel hub from the spindle of the rear stub axle.

## All models

**14** Use a screwdriver or suitable lever to prise free the grease retainer (seal) from the hub bore, but take care not to damage the bore surface.

**15** Remove the inner and outer bearing cones from the bore of the hub.

**16** To remove the bearing cups from the hub, drive them out using a suitable punch. Drive each cup from its respective end by tapping it alternately at diametrically-opposed points **(see illustration)**. Do not allow the cups to tilt in the bore, or the surfaces may become burred and prevent the new bearings from seating correctly as they are fitted.

**17** Clean the bore and spindle thoroughly before reassembly.

**18** To reassemble, tap the new bearing cups into position in the hub, using a piece of tubing slightly smaller in its outside diameter than that of the bearing cup. Ensure that the cups are squarely inserted and abut their respective shoulders in the hub.

**19** Pack the inner bearing cone with grease, and insert it into its cup in the hub.

**20** To fit the grease retainer (seal), first lubricate its inner lip to ease installation, then lightly tap the seal into position using a block of wood. Ensure that the seal is correctly orientated.

**21** Pack the outer bearing cone with grease, and fit it into position in its cup.

**22** The brake drum/hub or separate wheel hub (according to model) can now be refitted to the axle spindle. Before fitting into position, first check that the brake surface area in the drum is free of grease and oil. Locate the drum/hub into position, then fit a new retaining nut. Tighten it to the specified torque wrench setting whilst simultaneously rotating the assembly to ensure that the bearings are correctly seated.

**23** Carefully tap the new hub grease cap into

position in a progressive manner around its outer edge until it is fully fitted.

**24** On models with disc brakes or separate brake drums, refit the disc or drum, and secure with the retaining screw (where fitted).

**25** On models with disc brakes, refit the brake caliper and tighten the retaining bolts to the specified torque. Refer to Chapter 9 and refit the rear brake pads.

### Pre 1996 models

**26** Refit the rubber blanking plug to the brake backplate, and firmly apply the footbrake a few times to take up the brake adjustment. Check that the rear brakes do not bind when the brakes are released. Refit the roadwheel, lower the vehicle and then tighten the retaining nuts to the specified torque setting.

### 1996 on models

**27** Refit the rubber blanking plug to the brake backplate. Adjust the handbrake cable, as described in Chapter 1, and firmly apply the footbrake a few times to take up the brake adjustment. Check that the rear brakes do not bind when the brakes are released. Refit the roadwheel, lower the vehicle and then tighten the retaining nuts to the specified torque setting.

## 11 Rear strut (Hatchback and Saloon models) - removal and refitting

### Removal

**1** Chock the front wheels then jack up the rear of the car and support it on axle stands (see *"Jacking and vehicle support"*). Remove the inner wheel arch trim.

**2** On ABS-equipped models, unscrew the retaining nut and detach the load-apportioning valve connecting link (where fitted) from the axle beam.

**3** Unscrew and remove the securing bolt from the strut-to-axle mounting **(see illustration)**.

**4** Prise free the protective cap from the top of the shock absorber mounting, located in the luggage compartment **(see illustration)**.

**5** Unscrew and remove the two retaining nuts to detach the strut from its upper mounting. Do not unscrew the central upper mounting bolt.

**6** Withdraw the suspension strut from the vehicle.

### Refitting

**7** Refitting is a reversal of the removal procedure, but note the following points:

a) With the suspension strut located to its upper mounting, tighten the retaining nuts to the specified torque wrench setting.

b) When reconnecting the suspension strut to the lower mounting, hand-tighten the retaining bolt, then lower the vehicle so that it is standing on its wheels before fully tightening the bolt to its specified torque.

## 12 Rear strut (Hatchback and Saloon models) - dismantling, examination and reassembly

⚠️ **Warning: Before attempting to dismantle the suspension strut, a suitable tool to hold the coil spring in compression must be obtained. Adjustable coil spring compressors which can be positively secured to the spring coils are readily available, and are recommended for this operation. Any attempt to dismantle the strut without such a tool is likely to result in damage or personal injury.**

### Dismantling

**1** With the strut removed from the vehicle, clean away all external dirt, then secure it in a vice.

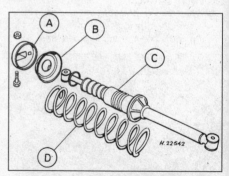

**12.3 Rear strut components as fitted to Hatchback and Saloon models**

A Upper mounting cup
B Spring seat
C Suspension strut
D Spring

**2** Fit the spring compressor tool (ensuring that it is fully engaged) and compress the coil spring until all tension is relieved from the upper mounting.

**3** Unscrew and remove the upper mounting through-bolt and nut **(see illustration)**.

**4** Withdraw the upper mounting cup and the spring seat.

**5** The suspension strut and coil spring can now be separated. If the coil spring or strut is to be renewed, the original coil spring must be released from the compressor. If it is to be re-used, the coil spring can be left in compression.

### Examination

**6** With the strut assembly now completely dismantled, examine all components for wear, damage or deformation. Renew any of the components as necessary.

**7** Examine the strut for signs of fluid leakage. Check the strut piston for signs of pitting along its entire length, and check the strut body for signs of damage or elongation of the mounting bolt holes. Test the operation of the strut, holding it in an upright position, by moving the piston through a full stroke, and then through short strokes of 50 to 100 mm. In both cases, the resistance felt should be smooth and continuous. If the resistance is jerky, or uneven, or if there is any visible sign of wear or damage to the strut, renewal is necessary.

### Reassembly

**8** Reassembly is a reversal of the dismantling procedure but note the following points:

a) *When the spring is located over the suspension strut, the spring seat, cup and through-bolt fitted, tighten the retaining bolt to the specified torque setting.*

b) *When reassembled, check that the upper and lower spring tails are correctly engaged with their spring seats before removing the spring compressor.*

## 13 Rear axle (Hatchback, Saloon and Estate models) - removal and refitting

### Removal

**1** Chock the front wheels then jack up the rear of the car and support it on axle stands (see *"Jacking and vehicle support"*). Remove the rear roadwheels.

**2** Refer to Chapter 9 for details, and disconnect the handbrake cable equaliser from the primary cable. Detach the non-adjustable cable circlip and the cable from the underbody fastenings.

**3** Disconnect the rear brake flexible hydraulic brake hoses from their rigid line connections. Clamp the hoses before disconnecting them, to minimise the fluid loss and air entry into the hydraulic system (see Chapter 9 for details).

**4** On ABS-equipped models, undo the retaining nut and detach the ABS load-apportioning valve (where fitted) from the axle beam. Do not remove the load-apportioning valve (see Chapter 9).

### Hatchback and Saloon models

**5** Locate suitable jacks or axle stands under the axle beam to support its weight (not to lift it), then unscrew the mounting bracket bolts each side **(see illustration)**.

**6** Unscrew and remove the strut-to-axle mounting bolt each side.

**7** Check that all associated fittings are clear, then lower the axle and remove it from under the vehicle.

**8** If the twist beam axle has been damaged, it must be renewed. Refer to Chapter 9 for details on removing the rear brakes from the axle. To remove the front mounting/pivot brackets from the axle, unscrew the pivot bolt.

### Estate models

**9** Position a jack under the coil spring area of the suspension arm (not under the axle beam) each side, and raise them so that they just take the weight of the trailing arms.

**10** Unscrew and remove the shock absorber retaining bolt from the lower attachment point to the rear axle each side.

**11** Slowly lower the jack under the suspension arm each side, and allow the trailing arms to drop and the compression in the coil springs to be released.

**12** With the coil springs fully relaxed, withdraw them from their mounting locations between the body and the suspension arms. As they are removed, mark each for its direction of fitting and side so that they are refitted to their original locations.

**13** Reposition the jacks, or place axle stands under the axle beam to support its weight (not to lift it), then unscrew the mounting bracket bolts each side.

**14** Check that all associated fittings are clear, then lower the axle and remove it from under the vehicle.

**15** If the twist beam axle has been damaged, it must be renewed. Refer to Chapter 9 for details on removing the rear brakes from the axle. To remove the front mounting/pivot brackets from the axle, unscrew the pivot bolt.

### Refitting

**16** Refitting is a reversal of the removal procedure, but note the following:

a) *Reconnect the axle at the front floor mountings first, and tighten the retaining bolts to the specified torque setting.*

b) *On Hatchback and Saloon models, reconnect the axle to the suspension struts, but do not fully retighten the securing bolts until after the vehicle is lowered to the ground and is standing on its wheels.*

c) *On Estate models, when relocating the coil springs between the body and the suspension arm each side, ensure that they are correctly orientated, and that their tails abut against the stops. When the coil springs are correctly located, raise the jacks under the suspension*

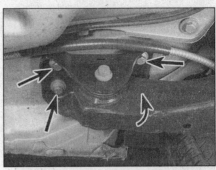

**13.5 Rear axle forward mounting bolts (arrowed)**

*arms, and reconnect the shock absorber each side.*

d) *Ensure that all brake fluid line connections are clean before reconnecting them. Refer to the appropriate Sections in Chapter 9 for specific details on reconnecting the brake lines, bleeding the brake hydraulic system, and for reconnecting the handbrake cable and its adjustment.*

e) *When the vehicle is lowered and is standing on its wheels, tighten the suspension fastenings to the specified torque wrench settings.*

## 14 Rear axle pivot bushes (Hatchback, Saloon and Estate models) - renewal

**1** Chock the front wheels then jack up the rear of the car and support it on axle stands (see *"Jacking and vehicle support"*).

**2** Position a suitable support (preferably adjustable) under the axle twist beam so that it is capable of carrying the weight of the axle (not the weight of the vehicle).

**3** Unscrew the nuts and pivot bolts, then lower the rear axle so that the bushes are clear of their mounting brackets. Take care not to allow the brake pipes to become distorted and stretched - if necessary, disconnect the hydraulic lines (see Chapter 9 for details).

**4** Using a steel tube of suitable diameter, various flat washers and a long bolt and nut, draw the bush out of its location in the axle arm.

**5** Clean the bush eye in the axle arm; lubricate it, and the new bush, with a soapy solution (washing-up liquid, for example) prior to installation.

**6** Locate the new bush in position, together with the steel tube, washers, bolt and nut as used for removal. Ensure that the bush flange is positioned on the outside, then draw the bush fully into position so that its lip is engaged.

**7** Raise the axle to reposition the bush pin bores in line with the bolt holes in the mounting brackets, then insert the pivot bolts. Screw the retaining nuts into position on the pivot bolts, but do not fully tighten them at this stage.

**10**

8 If necessary, reconnect the brake lines, then bleed the braking system as described in Chapter 9.

9 Lower the vehicle to the ground, then tighten the rear axle pivot bolts nuts to the specified torque wrench setting.

## 15 Rear shock absorber (Estate and Van models) - removal, testing and refitting

### Removal

1 Chock the front wheels then jack up the rear of the car and support it on axle stands (see "*Jacking and vehicle support*"). Remove the appropriate roadwheel.

2 On Estate models, position a jack under the coil spring area of the suspension arm (not under the axle beam), and raise it to just take the weight of the suspension.

3 Unscrew and remove the shock absorber retaining bolt from the lower mounting **(see illustration)**.

4 On Estate models, unscrew the retaining nuts securing the shock absorber top mounting on the underside of the body (from underneath) and withdraw the shock absorber **(see illustration)**.

5 On Van models, unscrew and remove the four shock absorber upper mounting bracket-to-body retaining bolts **(see illustration)**. Remove the shock absorber and its upper mounting bracket from the vehicle. To disconnect the shock absorber from the mounting bracket, unscrew the retaining nut,

**15.3 Rear shock absorber-to-axle mounting (Estate models)**

**15.4 Rear shock absorber upper mounting (Estate models)**

withdraw the through-bolt and remove the shock absorber from the bracket.

### Testing

6 Mount the shock absorber in a vice, gripping it by the lower mounting. Check the mounting rubbers for damage and deterioration. Examine the shock absorber for signs of fluid leakage. Extend the shock absorber, then check the piston for signs of pitting along its entire length. Check the body for signs of damage or elongation of the mounting bolt holes. Test the operation of the shock absorber, by moving the piston through a full stroke, and then through short strokes of 50 to 100 mm. In both cases, the resistance felt should be smooth and continuous. If the resistance is jerky, or uneven, or if there is any visible sign of wear or damage to the strut, renewal of the complete is necessary.

### Refitting

7 Refitting is a reversal of removal procedure. Tighten the retaining nuts and bolts to the specified torque wrench settings (where given), then lower the vehicle to the ground.

## 16 Rear coil springs (Estate models) - removal and refitting

### Removal

1 Chock the front wheels then jack up the rear of the car and support it on axle stands (see "*Jacking and vehicle support*"). Remove the rear roadwheels.

2 Position a jack under the coil spring area of the suspension arm (not under the axle beam) each side, and raise them so that they just take the weight of the trailing arms.

3 Unscrew and remove the shock absorber retaining bolt from the lower attachment point to the rear axle each side.

4 Slowly lower the jack under the suspension arm each side, and allow the trailing arms to drop and the compression in the coil springs to be released. Check that no excessive strain is imposed on the handbrake cables and/or the hydraulic hoses to the rear brakes. Disconnect them as described in Chapter 9 if necessary.

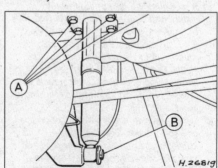
**15.5 Shock absorber upper (A) and lower (B) mountings on Van models**

5 With the coil springs fully relaxed, withdraw them from their mounting locations between the body and the suspension arms. As they are removed, mark each for its direction of fitting and side, so that they are refitted to their original locations (where applicable).

### Refitting

6 Refitting is a reversal of the removal procedure but note the following points:

a) *When relocating the coil springs between the body and the suspension arm each side, ensure that they are correctly orientated, and that their tails abut against the stops.*

b) *When the coil springs are correctly located, raise the jacks under the suspension arms, and reconnect the shock absorber each side.*

c) *Tighten the retaining bolts to the specified torque setting.*

d) *If the brake cables and/or the hydraulic hoses were detached, refer to Chapter 9 for the reconnecting details, and to bleed the hydraulic system.*

## 17 Rear leaf spring, shackle and bushes (Van models) - removal, inspection and refitting

### Removal

1 Chock the front wheels then jack up the rear of the car and support it on axle stands (see "*Jacking and vehicle support*"). Remove the appropriate rear roadwheel.

2 Position a jack under the rear axle, then raise the jack to support the weight of the axle, and to take the loading from the front and rear spring mountings.

3 Unscrew and remove the shock absorber lower mounting bolt, and detach the shock absorber from its mounting bracket.

4 Unscrew and remove the spring-to-axle U-bolt retaining nuts, and remove the U-bolts. Remove the counterplate and the bump stop from the top of the spring.

5 Unscrew and remove the mounting bolt and nut from the rear spring shackle **(see illustration)**.

6 Unscrew and remove the retaining nut or

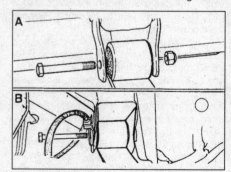
**17.5 Leaf spring rear (A) and front (B) locations and securing bolts**

bolt (as applicable) from the front mounting. Withdraw the mounting bolt (noting the flat washer fitted under the bolt head), then lower the jack under the axle just enough to allow the spring to be removed. Carefully withdraw the spring from the vehicle.

### Inspection

**7** If the spring mounting (shackle) bolts are noticeably worn, they must be renewed. If the spring eye bushes are worn and in need of replacement, they can be withdrawn using a suitable drawbolt and spacer. New bushes can be pressed into position in the spring eye using a vice (or press).

**8** If required, the rear spring shackle can be removed by unscrewing the retaining nut, removing the inboard shackle plate and withdrawing the outboard shackle plate complete with the upper shackle stud. The upper split type bushes must be renewed if they are worn.

### Refitting

**9** Refit the rear shackle, and initially hand-tighten the shackle bolt and nut.

**10** Relocate the spring over the axle, align the front spring eye with the mounting, and insert the bolt. Loosely secure the bolt (and where applicable, the nut) at this stage.

**11** Align the rear spring eye with the shackle at the rear, and loosely fit the mounting bolt and nut.

**12** Locate the counterplate and bump stop on the top of the spring over the axle, then refit the U-bolts and fit the retaining nuts. The jack under the axle may need to be raised to enable the U-bolt assemblies to be relocated.

**13** Reconnect the shock absorber to the rear axle, then tighten the various fixings to their specified torque wrench settings.

**14** Refit the roadwheel, and lower the vehicle to the ground.

### 18 Rear axle (Van models) - removal and refitting

### Removal

**1** Chock the front wheels then jack up the rear of the car and support it on axle stands (see "Jacking and vehicle support"). Remove the rear roadwheels.

**2** Position a single jack centrally (or preferably, two jacks each side of centre) under the axle beam, and raise to just take the weight of the axle - do not lift the vehicle.

**3** Clamp the hydraulic hoses of the light-laden valve, to prevent excessive fluid loss and the ingress of air and dirt into the hydraulic system, then disconnect the hydraulic lines to the light-laden valve and remove the clips.

**4** Refer to Chapter 9 for details, and remove the brake drum/hubs and then the backplate from the rear axle on each side. The backplates may be left attached to the axle, but it will still be necessary to detach the wheel cylinder brake line, and also to disconnect and withdraw the handbrake cable from each rear brake backplate. As each assembly is removed, keep them separated, and mark them to identify the right- and left-hand assemblies. Note that they are "handed", and must not be confused or they could be incorrectly refitted later.

**5** Unscrew and remove the shock absorber lower fixing bolts, and detach them from the rear axle.

**6** Unscrew and remove the axle-to-leaf spring U-bolt retaining nuts, remove the U-bolts, then carefully lower the axle and remove it from under the vehicle.

### Refitting

**7** Refitting is a reversal of the removal procedure, but note the following:

a) Reconnect the axle to the spring, reconnect the U-bolts and the shock absorbers to the axle on each side, and then tighten the retaining bolts to the specified torque wrench settings.

b) Refer to the appropriate Sections in Chapter 9 to refit the brake backplate and brake assemblies, and ensure that they are correctly located according to side.

c) Ensure that all brake fluid line connections are clean before reconnecting them. Refer to the appropriate Sections in Chapter 9 for specific details on reconnecting the

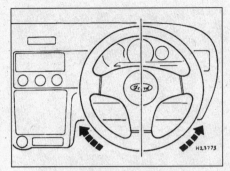

**19.2 Steering wheel alignment - centralised within a tolerance of 30° each side of vertical**

brake lines, bleeding the brake hydraulic system, and reconnecting the handbrake cable. Details of handbrake adjustment will be found in Chapter 1.

### 19 Steering wheel - removal and refitting

### Removal

#### Models without air bag

**1** Disconnect the battery negative (earth) lead (refer to Chapter 5A, Section 1).

**2** Turn the ignition key to release the steering lock, then set the front roadwheels in the straight-ahead position. With the steering centralised, the steering wheel should be positioned as shown (see illustration). Move the ignition key to the OFF position.

**3** Prise free the outer pad from the centre of the steering wheel (see illustration).

**4** Prise free the inner horn pad (see illustration), then note the connections and detach the horn wiring at the spade connectors (these differ in size to ensure correct refitting). Once the wiring is free, withdraw the inner horn pad. As it is withdrawn, note that it has a directional arrow mark which points up when the steering wheel is in the straight-ahead position.

**5** Unscrew the retaining bolt from the centre of the steering wheel, then gripping the wheel

**19.3 Remove the outer horn pad from the centre of the steering wheel**

**19.4 Prise free the inner horn pad and detach the wires**

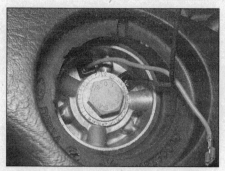

19.5a ... unscrew the retaining bolt ...

19.5b ... and withdraw the steering wheel

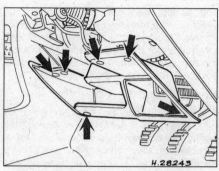

19.12 Undo the screws (arrowed) and withdraw the detachable lower facia panel from beneath the steering column

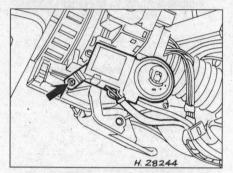

19.13 Undo the screw (arrowed) and withdraw the Passive Anti-Theft System (PATS) transceiver from the ignition switch/steering lock barrel

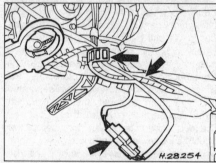

19.14 Release the steering column wiring harness and multi-plug as indicated

each side, pull and withdraw it from the column shaft (see illustrations).

 **HAYNES HiNT** *If the wheel is tight, tap it up near the centre, using the palm of your hand, or twist it from side to side, whilst pulling upwards to release it from the shaft splines.*

## Models with air bag

⚠️ *Warning: Handle the air bag with extreme care as a precaution against personal injury, and always hold it with the cover facing away from your body. If in doubt concerning any proposed work involving the air bag or its control circuitry, consult a Ford dealer or other qualified specialist.*

**6** Disconnect the battery negative (earth) lead (refer to Chapter 5A, Section 1).

⚠️ *Warning: Before proceeding, wait a minimum of 15 minutes, as a precaution against accidental firing of the air bag. This period ensures that any stored energy in the back-up capacitor is dissipated.*

**7** Undo the two screws, and remove the steering column upper shroud.

**8** Turn the steering wheel as necessary so that one of the air bag retaining bolts becomes accessible from the rear of the steering wheel. Undo the bolt, then turn the steering wheel again until the second bolt is accessible. Undo this bolt also.

**9** Withdraw the air bag from the steering wheel far enough to access the wiring multi-plug. Some force may be needed to free the air bag from the additional steering wheel spoke retainers.

**10** Disconnect the multi-plug from the rear of the air bag, and remove the air bag from the vehicle.

⚠️ *Warning: Position the air bag module in a safe place, with the mechanism facing downwards as a precaution against accidental operation.*

**11** Undo the four screws, and remove the steering column lower shroud.

**12** Undo the screws and withdraw the detachable lower facia panel from beneath the steering column (see illustration).

**13** Where applicable, undo the single screw and withdraw the Passive Anti-Theft System (PATS) transceiver from the ignition switch/steering lock barrel (see illustration).

**14** Release the steering column wiring harness from the retaining clips, and

disconnect the air bag control module wiring harness multi-plug (see illustration).

**15** Turn the steering wheel so the roadwheels are in the straight-ahead position, then remove the ignition key to lock the steering.

**16** Unscrew the retaining bolt from the centre of the steering wheel, then insert the ignition key and turn it to position "I". Grip the steering wheel each side, then pull and withdraw it from the column shaft.

## Refitting

### All models

**17** Refit in the reverse order of removal. Ensure that the indicator stalk is set in its central (off) position, to avoid damaging it with the tag of the wheel as it is pushed down the shaft. Make sure the wheel is centralised, as noted on removal. Turn the ignition key to position "I" (steering unlocked). Tighten the retaining bolt to the specified torque.

## 20 Steering column - removal and refitting

## Removal

**1** Disconnect the battery negative (earth) lead (refer to Chapter 5A, Section 1).

**2** Remove the steering wheel as described in the previous Section.

**3** Remove the screws and withdraw the steering column upper and lower shrouds (see illustrations).

20.3a Remove the upper ...

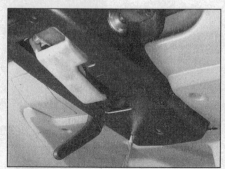

20.3b ... and lower column shrouds

**20.6 Detach the bonnet release cable from the lever**

**21.3 Releasing the steering lock**

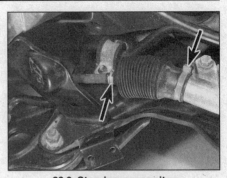

**22.2 Steering gear gaiter and retaining clips (arrowed)**

**4** Remove the multi-function switch assembly from the column, referring to Chapter 12.
**5** Disconnect the ignition switch multi-plug, and release the wiring from the wiring loom guide.
**6** Detach the bonnet release cable from the lever, then remove the lever from the column **(see illustration)**.
**7** Unscrew and remove the clamp bolt securing the steering column to the pinion shaft.
**8** Loosen off the column lower retaining nuts, then unscrew and remove the upper retaining nuts. Remove the steering column from the vehicle.

### Refitting

**9** Refitting is a reversal of the removal procedure, but note the following:
a) *Tighten the respective retaining bolts to their specified torque settings.*
b) *Check that the steering is centralised with the wheels in the straight-ahead position before refitting the steering wheel as described in Section 19.*
c) *Refit the steering wheel before securing the steering column coupling to the pinion shaft with the clamp bolt.*
d) *Ensure that the wiring connections are securely made. On completion, check for satisfactory operation of the steering, the column switches and the horn.*

## 21 Steering column -
dismantling and reassembly

### Dismantling

**1** Remove the steering column as described in the previous Section, then securely locate it in a vice fitted with protective jaws.
**2** Remove the upper thrust bearing tolerance ring from the column, then withdraw the column shaft from the column tube.
**3** Insert the ignition key into the lock/switch, and turn it to the "I" position. Now use a small screwdriver or a suitable rod to depress the plunger in the side of the barrel, and simultaneously pull on the key to withdraw the lock/switch from the column **(see illustration)**.
**4** Withdraw the spring from the column shaft.

**5** Prise free the lower and upper thrust bearings from the column tube and the lock/switch body.
**6** To remove the steering column height adjuster (where fitted) unscrew the through-bolt and locknut, remove the handle and lockplates, then remove the adjuster from the column.
**7** If any part of the steering column (and in particular, the universal joints) is found to be excessively worn, or if any part of the column assembly has been damaged, it must be renewed; no repairs are possible.

### Reassembly

**8** Reassembly is a reversal of the dismantling procedure, but note the following points:
a) *When refitting the height adjuster, coat the threads of the through-bolt with Loctite, and locate the handle in the locked position. Tighten the retaining bolt and nut to the specified torque setting.*
b) *Take care when fitting the lower thrust bearing into the column tube and the upper bearing to the steering lock/ignition switch body.*
c) *When fitting the steering column lock/ ignition switch, ensure that the key is in the "I" position. As the switch/lock is fitted into its barrel, it may be necessary to move the key clockwise and anti-clockwise slightly, to enable the housing drive to align with the barrel and fully engage.*
d) *When assembling the column shaft to the tube, ensure that the upper thrust bearing tolerance ring is fitted with its tapered face towards the bearing.*

**23.3a Steering gear bolt (arrowed) to the subframe on the right-hand side**

## 22 Steering gear
rubber gaiters - renewal

**1** Remove the track rod end balljoint and its locknut from the track rod (see Section 27).
**2** Release the clip(s), and slide the gaiter off the rack-and-pinion housing and track rod **(see illustration)**.
**3** Scrape off all grease from the old gaiter, and apply to the track rod inner joint. Wipe clean the seating areas on the rack-and-pinion housing and track rod.
**4** Slide the new gaiter onto the housing and track rod, and tighten the clip(s).
**5** Refit the track rod end balljoint as described in Section 27.

## 23 Steering gear
(manual steering) -
removal and refitting

### Removal

**1** Disconnect the battery negative (earth) lead (refer to Chapter 5A, Section 1).
**2** Refer to Section 9 for details, and remove the subframe from the vehicle as described. Note that complete removal of the subframe may not be necessary if it is carefully lowered to allow access to the steering gear for its separation and withdrawal.
**3** Unscrew and remove the two steering gear-to-subframe retaining bolts, then withdraw the assembly from the vehicle **(see illustrations)**.

**10**

**23.3b Steering gear bolt (arrowed) to the subframe on the left-hand side**

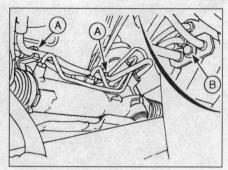

**24.4 Power steering gear and hydraulic pipe connections**

A  Hydraulic pipe locating clips
B  Valve clamp plate bolt

## Refitting

4 Refit the steering gear to the subframe in the reverse order of removal, and tighten the retaining bolts to the specified torque setting.
5 Refer to Section 9 for the relevant details on refitting the subframe assembly to the vehicle.

## 24 Steering gear (power-assisted steering) - removal and refitting

## Removal

1 Disconnect the battery negative (earth) lead (refer to Chapter 5A, Section 1).
2 Refer to Section 9 and proceed as described in paragraphs 1 to 12 inclusive, then proceed as follows.
3 Undo the retaining screws, and detach the clips securing the power steering hydraulic pressure pipes to the steering gear.
4 Position a suitable container under the hydraulic pipe connections to the steering gear. Unscrew the bolt securing the hydraulic valve clamp plate to the valve body on the steering rack, then detach the pipes from the valve body. Withdraw the pipes from the steering gear, and drain the hydraulic fluid into the container **(see illustration)**.
5 Plug the exposed ends of the hydraulic line connections, to prevent the ingress of dirt and further fluid loss. Note that new O-ring seals will be needed for the pressure and return hose connections when reconnecting.
6 Locate suitable jacks or blocks under the subframe to support it, then unscrew and remove the eight subframe fixing bolts **(see illustration 9.14).** Lower the support jacks or blocks, and withdraw the subframe. As it is lowered, disengage the steering gear shaft from the column. Note that complete removal of the subframe from the vehicle may not be necessary if it is carefully lowered to allow access to the steering gear for its separation and withdrawal.
7 Unscrew and remove the two steering gear-to-subframe retaining bolts, then withdraw the from the vehicle.

## Refitting

8 Refit the steering gear to the subframe in the reverse order of removal, and tighten the retaining bolts to the specified torque setting.
9 Refer to Section 9 for the relevant details, and refit the subframe assembly to the vehicle. When the subframe is loosely in position, remove the temporary plugs from the hydraulic fluid lines, and check that the connections are clean. Fit new O-ring seals to the pressure and return hoses, then reconnect the hydraulic lines to the steering gear. Check that the hydraulic lines and fixings are secure, then continue refitting the steering gear and subframe as described in Section 9.
10 On completion, top-up the power steering fluid reservoir and bleed the system as described in Section 26. Check for any signs of fluid leakage from the system hoses and connections. Finally, have the front wheel toe setting checked (see Section 28).

## 25 Power-assisted steering pump - removal and refitting

## Removal

1 Disconnect the battery negative (earth) lead (refer to Chapter 5A, Section 1).
2 Where fitted, undo the two bolts and remove the drivebelt upper guard from the top of the pump **(see illustration)**.
3 Apply the handbrake, then raise and support the front of the vehicle on axle stands.
4 Undo the retaining screws, and remove the drivebelt lower guard from the underbody.
5 Loosen off the drivebelt tension by turning the tension adjustment bolt in a clockwise direction. Noting the routing of the belt around the pulleys, disengage the drivebelt from the power steering pump pulley.
6 Position a suitable container beneath the power steering pump, then unscrew and detach the fluid pressure and return hoses from the pump **(see illustration)**. As they are detached from the pump, allow the fluid to drain from the hoses (and the pump) into the container. Plug the exposed ends of the hydraulic hoses and the pump connections,

**25.2 Where fitted, remove the drivebelt upper guard from the top of the power steering pump**

to prevent the ingress of dirt and excessive fluid loss.
7 Insert a 9 mm Allen key into the centre of the pump drive spindle to prevent it from turning, then unscrew and remove the three pump pulley retaining bolts. Withdraw the pulley from the pump.
8 Unscrew the four retaining bolts shown **(see illustration)** and withdraw the pump from the vehicle.

## Refitting

9 Refitting is a reversal of removal, but tighten all nuts and bolts to the specified torque. Remove the plugs from the pipes, and ensure that the pipes are located correctly so that they do not foul any surrounding components.
10 Refit the drivebelt, referring to Chapter 1.
11 On completion, fill the power steering system with the specified fluid up to the maximum level mark, and bleed the system as described in Section 26. Check for any signs of fluid leakage from the system hoses and connections.

## 26 Power-assisted steering system - bleeding

1 This will normally only be required if any part of the hydraulic system has been disconnected.
2 Referring to "Weekly Checks", remove the fluid reservoir filler cap, and top-up with the specified fluid to the maximum level mark.

**25.6 Power steering pump and hose connections on the CVH engine**

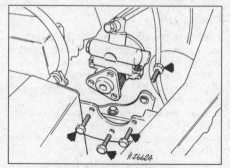

**25.8 Power steering pump and securing bolts**

3 Start the engine and allow it to idle, slowly moving the steering from lock-to-lock four times to purge out the air, then top-up the level in the fluid reservoir. Add the fluid slowly, to prevent the possibility of aeration of the fluid in the circuit.

4 Switch the engine off, then recheck the fluid level in the reservoir, and further top-up if necessary. Finally check the system hoses and connections for any signs of fluid leaks, which if found, must be rectified.

## 27 Track rod end balljoint - removal and refitting

### Removal

1 Apply the handbrake, then jack up the front of the vehicle and support it on axle stands. Remove the appropriate front roadwheel.

2 Using a suitable spanner, slacken the track rod end balljoint locknut on the track rod by a quarter of a turn (see illustration). Hold the balljoint stationary with another spanner engaged with the flats at its inner end to prevent it from turning.

3 Extract the split pin, then loosen off the retaining nut. If the balljoint is to be renewed, the nut can be fully removed. If the existing balljoint is to be reconnected, the nut should be slackened off a couple of turns only at first, and left in position to protect the joint threads as the joint is separated from the spindle carrier. To release the tapered shank of the joint from the spindle carrier, use a balljoint separator tool as shown (see illustration). If the joint is to be re-used, take care not to damage the rubber dust cover when using a separator tool.

4 Count the number of exposed threads visible on the inner section of the track rod, and record this figure.

5 Unscrew the balljoint from the track rod, counting the number of turns necessary to remove it.

### Refitting

6 Screw the balljoint into the track rod the number of turns noted during removal until the

balljoint just contacts the locknut. Now tighten the locknut while holding the balljoint.

7 Engage the shank of the balljoint with the spindle carrier arm, and refit the locknut. Tighten the locknut to the specified torque.

> **HAYNES HiNT** *If the balljoint shank turns while the locknut is being tightened, lever down on the top of the balljoint with a stout bar. The tapered fit of the shank will lock it and prevent rotation as the nut is tightened.*

8 Refit the roadwheel, and lower the vehicle to the ground.

9 Finally, have the front wheel toe setting checked (see Section 28).

## 28 Wheel alignment and steering angles - general information

### General

1 A car's steering and suspension geometry is defined in four basic settings - all angles are expressed in degrees (toe settings are also expressed as a measurement); the relevant settings are camber, castor, steering axis inclination, and toe-setting. With the exception of front wheel toe-setting, none of these settings are adjustable.

### Front wheel toe setting - checking and adjustment

2 Due to the special measuring equipment necessary to accurately check the wheel alignment, and the skill required to use it properly, checking and adjustment is best left to a Ford dealer or similar expert. Note that most tyre-fitting shops now possess sophisticated checking equipment. The following is provided as a guide, should the owner decide to carry out a DIY check.

3 The front wheel toe setting is checked by measuring the distance between the front and rear inside edges of the roadwheel rims. Proprietary toe measurement gauges are

available from motor accessory shops. Adjustment is made by screwing the track rods in or out of their track rod end balljoints, to alter the effective length of the track rod assemblies.

4 For **accurate** checking, the vehicle **must** be at the kerb weight, ie unladen and with a full tank of fuel.

5 Before starting work, check the tyre pressures and tread wear, the condition of the hub bearings, the steering wheel free play, and the condition of the front suspension components (see Chapter 1). Correct any faults found.

6 Park the vehicle on level ground, check that the front roadwheels are in the straight-ahead position, then rock the rear and front ends to settle the suspension. Release the handbrake, and roll the vehicle backwards 1 metre, then forwards again, to relieve any stresses in the steering and suspension components.

7 Measure the distance between the front edges of the wheel rims and the rear edges of the rims. Subtract the smallest measurement from the largest, and check that the result is within the specified range.

8 If adjustment is necessary, apply the handbrake, then jack up the front of the vehicle and support it securely on axle stands (see "Jacking and vehicle support"). Turn the steering wheel onto full-left lock, and record the number of exposed threads on the right-hand track rod. Now turn the steering onto full-right lock, and record the number of threads on the left-hand side. If there are the same number of threads visible on both sides, then subsequent adjustment should be made equally on both sides. If there are more threads visible on one side than the other, it will be necessary to compensate for this during adjustment. **Note:** *It is most important that after adjustment, the same number of threads are visible on each track rod end.*

9 First clean the track rod end threads; if they are corroded, apply penetrating fluid before starting adjustment. Release the rubber gaiter outboard clips (where necessary), and peel back the gaiter; apply a smear of grease to the inside of the gaiter, so that both are free, and will not be twisted or strained as their respective track rods are rotated.

10 Use a straight-edge and a scriber or similar to mark the relationship of each track rod to its track rod end balljoint, then, holding each track rod in turn, unscrew its locknut fully.

11 Alter the length of the track rods, bearing in mind the note made in paragraph 8. Screw them into or out of the track rod end balljoints, rotating the track rods using a self-grip wrench. Shortening the track rods (screwing them into their track rod end balljoints) will reduce toe-in/increase toe-out.

12 When the setting is correct, hold the track rods and securely tighten the track rod end balljoint locknuts. Count the exposed threads to check the length of both track rods. If they are not the same, then the adjustment has not

**10**

**27.2 Track rod end balljoint showing the locknut (A) retaining flats (B) and the balljoint-to-spindle carrier arm retaining nut and split pin (C)**

**27.3 Balljoint separator tool in position. Note that the nut should be left loosely in position when the thread of the joint is to be protected for re-use**

been made equally, and problems will be encountered with tyre scrubbing in turns; also, the steering wheel spokes will no longer be horizontal when the wheels are in the straight-ahead position.

**13** If the track rod lengths are the same, lower the vehicle to the ground and re-check the toe setting; re-adjust if necessary. When the setting is correct, tighten the track rod end balljoint locknuts to the specified torque setting. Ensure that the rubber gaiters are seated correctly, and are not twisted or strained, and secure them in position with new retaining clips (where necessary).

# Chapter 11
# Bodywork and fittings

## Contents

## Degrees of difficulty

| | | | | |
|---|---|---|---|---|
| **Easy,** suitable for novice with little experience  | **Fairly easy,** suitable for beginner with some experience  | **Fairly difficult,** suitable for competent DIY mechanic  | **Difficult,** suitable for experienced DIY mechanic | **Very difficult,** suitable for expert DIY or professional  |

## Specifications

### Powered hood - Cabriolet models

Power hood hydraulic system fluid type ..................... ESSO UNIVIS J26

### Torque wrench settings

| | Nm | lbf ft |
|---|---|---|
| Front seat slide to floor | 25 | 18 |
| Seat belt anchor bolts | 38 | 28 |
| Seat belt lower anchorage rail securing bolt | 38 | 28 |
| Front seat belt height adjuster bolt | 35 | 26 |
| Front seat slide to frame nuts | 25 | 18 |
| Bonnet hinge bolts | 10 | 7 |
| Bonnet latch bolts | 10 | 7 |
| Tailgate hinge bolts | 24 | 18 |
| Tailgate striker screws | 10 | 7 |
| Tailgate lock screws | 10 | 7 |
| Boot lid hinge bolts | 24 | 18 |
| Boot lid striker screws | 10 | 7 |
| Boot lid latch screws | 10 | 7 |

**11**

## 1 General information

The bodyshell and underframe on all models is of all-steel welded construction, incorporating progressive progressive crumple zones at the front and rear, and a rigid centre safety cell. The body style range is comprehensive, and includes the 3- and 5-door Hatchback, the 4-door Saloon, the 5-door Estate, the 2-door Cabriolet, and the Van.

A multi-stage anti-corrosion process is applied to all new vehicles. This includes zinc phosphating on some panels, the injection of wax into boxed sections, and a wax and PVC coating applied to the underbody for its protection.

Inertia reel seat belts are fitted to all models, and from the 1994 model year onwards, the front seat belt stalks are mounted on automatic mechanical tensioners (also known as "grabbers"). In the event of a serious front impact, a spring mass sensor releases a coil spring which pulls the stalk buckle downwards and tensions the seat belt. It is not possible to reset the tensioner once fired, and it must therefore be renewed. Later models may alternatively be fitted with pyrotechnic front seat belt tensioners. These units are activated by the air bag control module and tension the front seat belts by means of a contained explosive charge which operates within the seat belt mechanism.

Central locking is a standard or optional fitment on all models. Where double-locking is also fitted, the lock mechanism is disconnected (when the system is in use) from the interior door handles, making it impossible to open any of the doors or the tailgate/bootlid from inside the vehicle. This means that, even if a thief should break a side window, it will not be possible to open the door using the interior handle.

## 2 Maintenance - bodywork and underframe

The general condition of a vehicle's bodywork is the one thing that significantly affects its value. Maintenance is easy, but needs to be regular. Neglect, particularly after minor damage, can lead quickly to further deterioration and costly repair bills. It is important also to keep watch on those parts of the vehicle not immediately visible, for instance the underside, inside all the wheel arches, and the lower part of the engine compartment.

The basic maintenance routine for the bodywork is washing - preferably with a lot of water, from a hose. This will remove all the loose solids which may have stuck to the vehicle. It is important to flush these off in such a way as to prevent grit from scratching the finish. The wheel arches and underframe need washing in the same way, to remove any accumulated mud, which will retain moisture and tend to encourage rust. Oddly enough, the best time to clean the underframe and wheel arches is in wet weather, when the mud is thoroughly wet and soft. In very wet weather, the underframe is usually cleaned of large accumulations automatically, and this is a good time for inspection.

Periodically, except on vehicles with a wax-based underbody protective coating, it is a good idea to have the whole of the underframe of the vehicle steam-cleaned, engine compartment included, so that a thorough inspection can be carried out to see what minor repairs and renovations are necessary. Steam-cleaning is available at many garages, and is necessary for the removal of the accumulation of oily grime, which sometimes is allowed to become thick in certain areas. If steam-cleaning facilities are not available, there are some excellent grease solvents available which can be brush-applied; the dirt can then be simply hosed off. Note that these methods should not be used on vehicles with wax-based underbody protective coating, or the coating will be removed. Such vehicles should be inspected annually, preferably just prior to Winter, when the underbody should be washed down, and any damage to the wax coating repaired. Ideally, a completely fresh coat should be applied. It would also be worth considering the use of such wax-based protection for injection into door panels, sills, box sections, etc, as an additional safeguard against rust damage, where such protection is not provided by the vehicle manufacturer.

After washing paintwork, wipe off with a chamois leather to give an unspotted clear finish. A coat of clear protective wax polish will give added protection against chemical pollutants in the air. If the paintwork sheen has dulled or oxidised, use a cleaner/polisher combination to restore the brilliance of the shine. This requires a little effort, but such dulling is usually caused because regular washing has been neglected. Care needs to be taken with metallic paintwork, as special non-abrasive cleaner/polisher is required to avoid damage to the finish. Always check that the door and ventilator opening drain holes and pipes are completely clear, so that water can be drained out. Brightwork should be treated in the same way as paintwork. Windscreens and windows can be kept clear of the smeary film which often appears, by the use of proprietary glass cleaner. Never use any form of wax or other body or chromium polish on glass.

## 3 Maintenance - upholstery and carpets

Mats and carpets should be brushed or vacuum-cleaned regularly, to keep them free of grit. If they are badly stained, remove them from the vehicle for scrubbing or sponging, and make quite sure they are dry before refitting. Seats and interior trim panels can be kept clean by wiping with a damp cloth. If they do become stained (which can be more apparent on light-coloured upholstery), use a little liquid detergent and a soft nail brush to scour the grime out of the grain of the material. Do not forget to keep the headlining clean in the same way as the upholstery. When using liquid cleaners inside the vehicle, do not over-wet the surfaces being cleaned. Excessive damp could get into the seams and padded interior, causing stains, offensive odours or even rot.

**Note:** *If the inside of the vehicle gets wet accidentally, it is worthwhile taking some trouble to dry it out properly, particularly where carpets are involved.*

⚠️ **Warning: Do not leave oil or electric heaters inside the vehicle.**

## 4 Minor body damage - repair

### Repairs of minor scratches in bodywork

If the scratch is very superficial, and does not penetrate to the metal of the bodywork, repair is very simple. Lightly rub the area of the scratch with a paintwork renovator, or a very fine cutting paste, to remove loose paint from the scratch, and to clear the surrounding bodywork of wax polish. Rinse the area with clean water.

Apply touch-up paint to the scratch using a fine paint brush; continue to apply fine layers of paint until the surface of the paint in the scratch is level with the surrounding paintwork. Allow the new paint at least two weeks to harden, then blend it into the surrounding paintwork by rubbing the scratch area with a paintwork renovator or a very fine cutting paste. Finally, apply wax polish.

Where the scratch has penetrated right through to the metal of the bodywork, causing the metal to rust, a different repair technique is required. Remove any loose rust from the bottom of the scratch with a penknife, then apply rust-inhibiting paint to prevent the formation of rust in the future. Using a rubber or nylon applicator, fill the scratch with bodystopper paste. If required, this paste can be mixed with cellulose thinners to provide a very thin paste which is ideal for filling narrow scratches. Before the stopper-paste in the scratch hardens, wrap a piece of smooth cotton rag around the top of a finger. Dip the finger in cellulose thinners, and quickly sweep it across the surface of the stopper-paste in the scratch; this will ensure that the surface of the stopper-paste is slightly hollowed. The scratch can now be painted over as described earlier in this Section.

## Repairs of dents in bodywork

When deep denting of the vehicle's bodywork has taken place, the first task is to pull the dent out, until the affected bodywork almost attains its original shape. There is little point in trying to restore the original shape completely, as the metal in the damaged area will have stretched on impact, and cannot be reshaped fully to its original contour. It is better to bring the level of the dent up to a point which is about 3 mm below the level of the surrounding bodywork. In cases where the dent is very shallow anyway, it is not worth trying to pull it out at all. If the underside of the dent is accessible, it can be hammered out gently from behind, using a mallet with a wooden or plastic head. Whilst doing this, hold a suitable block of wood firmly against the outside of the panel, to absorb the impact from the hammer blows and thus prevent a large area of the bodywork from being "belled-out".

Should the dent be in a section of the bodywork which has a double skin, or some other factor making it inaccessible from behind, a different technique is called for. Drill several small holes through the metal inside the area - particularly in the deeper section. Then screw long self-tapping screws into the holes, just sufficiently for them to gain a good purchase in the metal. Now the dent can be pulled out by pulling on the protruding heads of the screws with a pair of pliers.

The next stage of the repair is the removal of the paint from the damaged area, and from an inch or so of the surrounding "sound" bodywork. This is accomplished most easily by using a wire brush or abrasive pad on a power drill, although it can be done just as effectively by hand, using sheets of abrasive paper. To complete the preparation for filling, score the surface of the bare metal with a screwdriver or the tang of a file, or alternatively, drill small holes in the affected area. This will provide a really good "key" for the filler paste.

To complete the repair, see the Section on filling and respraying.

## Repairs of rust holes or gashes in bodywork

Remove all paint from the affected area, and from an inch or so of the surrounding "sound" bodywork, using an abrasive pad or a wire brush on a power drill. If these are not available, a few sheets of abrasive paper will do the job most effectively. With the paint removed, you will be able to judge the severity of the corrosion, and therefore decide whether to renew the whole panel (if this is possible) or to repair the affected area. New body panels are not as expensive as most people think, and it is often quicker and more satisfactory to fit a new panel than to attempt to repair large areas of corrosion.

Remove all fittings from the affected area, except those which will act as a guide to the original shape of the damaged bodywork (eg headlight shells etc). Then, using tin snips or a hacksaw blade, remove all loose metal and any other metal badly affected by corrosion. Hammer the edges of the hole inwards, in order to create a slight depression for the filler paste.

Wire-brush the affected area to remove the powdery rust from the surface of the remaining metal. Paint the affected area with rust-inhibiting paint, if the back of the rusted area is accessible, treat this also.

Before filling can take place, it will be necessary to block the hole in some way. This can be achieved by the use of aluminium or plastic mesh, or aluminium tape.

Aluminium or plastic mesh, or glass-fibre matting, is probably the best material to use for a large hole. Cut a piece to the approximate size and shape of the hole to be filled, then position it in the hole so that its edges are below the level of the surrounding bodywork. It can be retained in position by several blobs of filler paste around its periphery.

Aluminium tape should be used for small or very narrow holes. Pull a piece off the roll, trim it to the approximate size and shape required, then pull off the backing paper (if used) and stick the tape over the hole; it can be overlapped if the thickness of one piece is insufficient. Burnish down the edges of the tape with the handle of a screwdriver or similar, to ensure that the tape is securely attached to the metal underneath.

## Bodywork repairs - filling and respraying

Before using this Section, see the Sections on dent, deep scratch, rust holes and gash repairs.

Many types of bodyfiller are available, but generally speaking, those proprietary kits which contain a tin of filler paste and a tube of resin hardener are best for this type of repair. A wide, flexible plastic or nylon applicator will be found invaluable for imparting a smooth and well-contoured finish to the surface of the filler.

Mix up a little filler on a clean piece of card or board - measure the hardener carefully (follow the maker's instructions on the pack), otherwise the filler will set too rapidly or too slowly. Using the applicator, apply the filler paste to the prepared area; draw the applicator across the surface of the filler to achieve the correct contour and to level the surface. As soon as a contour that approximates to the correct one is achieved, stop working the paste - if you carry on too long, the paste will become sticky and begin to "pick-up" on the applicator. Continue to add thin layers of filler paste at 20-minute intervals, until the level of the filler is just proud of the surrounding bodywork.

Once the filler has hardened, the excess can be removed using a metal plane or file. From then on, progressively-finer grades of abrasive paper should be used, starting with a 40-grade production paper, and finishing with a 400-grade wet-and-dry paper. Always wrap the abrasive paper around a flat rubber, cork, or wooden block - otherwise the surface of the filler will not be completely flat. During the smoothing of the filler surface, the wet-and-dry paper should be periodically rinsed in water. This will ensure that a very smooth finish is imparted to the filler at the final stage.

At this stage, the "dent" should be surrounded by a ring of bare metal, which in turn should be encircled by the finely "feathered" edge of the good paintwork. Rinse the repair area with clean water, until all of the dust produced by the rubbing-down operation has gone.

Spray the whole area with a light coat of primer - this will show up any imperfections in the surface of the filler. Repair these imperfections with fresh filler paste or bodystopper, and once more smooth the surface with abrasive paper. Repeat this spray-and-repair procedure until you are satisfied that the surface of the filler, and the feathered edge of the paintwork, are perfect. Clean the repair area with clean water, and allow to dry fully.

The repair area is now ready for final spraying. Paint spraying must be carried out in a warm, dry, windless and dust-free atmosphere. This condition can be created artificially if you have access to a large indoor working area, but if you are forced to work in the open, you will have to pick your day very carefully. If you are working indoors, dousing the floor in the work area with water will help to settle the dust which would otherwise be in the atmosphere. If the repair area is confined to one body panel, mask off the surrounding panels; this will help to minimise the effects of a slight mis-match in paint colours. Bodywork fittings (eg chrome strips, door handles etc) will also need to be masked off. Use genuine masking tape, and several thicknesses of newspaper, for the masking operations.

Before commencing to spray, agitate the aerosol can thoroughly, then spray a test area (an old tin, or similar) until the technique is mastered. Cover the repair area with a thick coat of primer; the thickness should be built up using several thin layers of paint, rather than one thick one. Using 400-grade wet-and-dry paper, rub down the surface of the primer until it is really smooth. While doing this, the work area should be thoroughly doused with water, and the wet-and-dry paper periodically rinsed in water. Allow to dry before spraying on more paint.

Spray on the top coat, again building up the thickness by using several thin layers of paint. Start spraying at one edge of the repair area, and then, using a side-to-side motion, work until the whole repair area and about 2 inches of the surrounding original paintwork is covered. Remove all masking material 10 to 15 minutes after spraying on the final coat of paint.

**11**

Allow the new paint at least two weeks to harden, then, using a paintwork renovator, or a very fine cutting paste, blend the edges of the paint into the existing paintwork. Finally, apply wax polish.

### Plastic components

With the use of more and more plastic body components by the vehicle manufacturers (eg bumpers. spoilers, and in some cases major body panels), rectification of more serious damage to such items has become a matter of either entrusting repair work to a specialist in this field, or renewing complete components. Repair of such damage by the DIY owner is not really feasible, owing to the cost of the equipment and materials required for effecting such repairs. The basic technique involves making a groove along the line of the crack in the plastic, using a rotary burr in a power drill. The damaged part is then welded back together, using a hot-air gun to heat up and fuse a plastic filler rod into the groove. Any excess plastic is then removed, and the area rubbed down to a smooth finish. It is important that a filler rod of the correct plastic is used, as body components can be made of a variety of different types (eg polycarbonate, ABS, polypropylene).

Damage of a less serious nature (abrasions, minor cracks etc) can be repaired by the DIY owner using a two-part epoxy filler repair material. Once mixed in equal proportions, this is used in similar fashion to the bodywork filler used on metal panels. The filler is usually cured in twenty to thirty minutes, ready for sanding and painting.

If the owner is renewing a complete component himself, or if he has repaired it with epoxy filler, he will be left with the problem of finding a suitable paint for finishing which is compatible with the type of plastic used. At one time, the use of a universal paint was not possible, owing to the complex range of plastics encountered in body component applications. Standard paints, generally speaking, will not bond to plastic or rubber satisfactorily. However, it is now possible to obtain a plastic body parts finishing kit which consists of a pre-primer treatment, a primer and coloured top coat. Full instructions are normally supplied with a kit, but basically, the

method of use is to first apply the pre-primer to the component concerned, and allow it to dry for up to 30 minutes. Then the primer is applied, and left to dry for about an hour before finally applying the special-coloured top coat. The result is a correctly-coloured component, where the paint will flex with the plastic or rubber, a property that standard paint does not normally possess.

### 5  Major body damage - repair

Where serious damage has occurred, or large areas need renewal due to neglect, it means that complete new panels will need welding-in, and this is best left to professionals. If the damage is due to impact, it will also be necessary to check completely the alignment of the bodyshell, and this can only be carried out accurately by a Ford dealer, using special jigs. If the body is left misaligned, it is primarily dangerous, as the car will not handle properly; secondly, uneven stresses will be imposed on the steering, suspension and possibly transmission, causing abnormal wear, or complete failure, particularly to such items as the tyres.

### 6  Bumpers - removal and refitting

#### Removal

##### Front bumper (pre-1996 models)

1 Remove the radiator grille as described in Section 38.
2 Chock the rear wheels then jack up the front of the car and support it on axle stands (see "Jacking and vehicle support").
3 Release the six fasteners and two clips, and remove the splash shield from the underside of the vehicle at the front. The six fasteners will either be clip types or plastic screws, in which case they can be prised free or unscrewed, or pop-rivets, which will need to be drilled through.

4 Undo the two bumper-to-wing retaining screws at the rear edge of the bumper each side (see illustration).
5 Unscrew and remove the four bumper retaining nuts (two each side) securing the bumper to the front end of the vehicle (see illustration).
6 Disconnect the wiring from the bumper mounted lights or indicators, where fitted.
7 Enlist the aid of an assistant, and carefully withdraw the bumper forwards from the vehicle.

##### Front bumper (1996 models onward)

8 Remove the radiator grille as described in Section 38.
9 Tie the radiator to the front body panel to secure it in place during subsequent operations.
10 Chock the rear wheels then jack up the front of the car and support it on axle stands (see "Jacking and vehicle support").
11 Undo the five screws each side and remove the left-hand and right-hand wheel arch liner extensions.
12 Release the hose from the right-hand radiator support.
13 Undo the two bolts each side and remove the left-hand and right-hand radiator support.
14 Undo the two screws each side securing the edge of the bumper to the wheel arch.
15 Where applicable, disconnect the wiring multiplugs to the bumper mounted light assemblies.
16 Undo the four bumper retaining nuts (two each side) securing the bumper to the front end of the vehicle.
17 Enlist the aid of an assistant, and carefully withdraw the bumper forwards from the vehicle.

##### Rear (single-piece) bumper

18 Prise free the number plate light from the bumper, then detach the wiring connectors and remove the light.
19 Undo the two retaining screws securing the forward ends of the bumper to the trailing end of the wheel arch each side (see illustration).
20 Where applicable, remove the rear trim panel in the rear luggage compartment to gain access to the bumper securing nuts.

6.4  Front bumper retaining screws

6.5  Front bumper retaining nuts

6.19  Rear bumper retaining screws

**6.21a Rear bumper retaining nuts (Hatchback and Saloon models)**

**6.21b Rear (upper) bumper retaining nut (Estate models)**

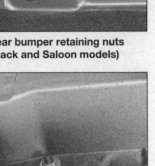

**6.21c Rear (lower) bumper retaining nut (Estate models)**

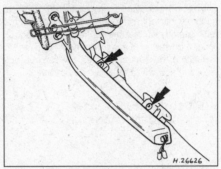

**6.23 Rear quarter bumper retaining screw locations (arrowed)**

*Refitting and adjustment*

**7** Refitting is a reversal of removal. Position the bonnet hinges within the outline marks made during removal, but alter its position as necessary to provide a uniform gap all round. Adjust the rear height of the bonnet by repositioning it on the hinges. Tighten the hinge retaining bolts to the specified torque. Adjust the front height by repositioning the lock with reference to Section 9, and turn the rubber buffers on the engine compartment front crosspanel up or down to support the bonnet.
**8** Ensure that the washer, wiring and earth lead connections are cleanly and securely made. Check the windscreen washer for satisfactory operation on completion.

**8 Bonnet release cable -** removal and refitting

*Removal*

**1** With the bonnet open, disconnect the cable from the locating slot in the lock frame, then release the inner cable nipple from the lock **(see illustration)**.
**2** Working inside the vehicle, undo the four retaining screws, and lower the bottom shroud from the steering column.
**3** Detach the inner cable nipple from the release lever, then withdraw the cable through the bulkhead (noting its routing) and remove it from the engine compartment side **(see illustration)**.

*Refitting*

**4** Refitting is a reversal of removal. On completion, check that the bonnet catch and release operate in a satisfactory manner.

**9 Bonnet lock -** removal and refitting

*Removal*

**1** With the bonnet open, disconnect the cable from the locating slot in the lock frame, then release the inner cable nipple from the lock.

**21** Unscrew and remove the bumper retaining nuts from the rear panel each side **(see illustrations)**. On some models, access to the nuts is from underneath the vehicle; on others, it is from within the luggage compartment after removal of the appropriate rear trim panel. Enlist the aid of an assistant, to help in pulling the bumper outwards to clear the body each side, and withdraw it rearwards from the vehicle.

**Rear quarter bumper**

**22** Reach behind the bumper, compress the rear number plate light retaining clips, and extract the light from the bumper. Disconnect the wiring connectors and remove the light.
**23** Working from above, between the bumper and the vehicle rear panel, undo the two Torx-type retaining screws and then remove the quarter bumper **(see illustration)**.

*Refitting*

**24** Refitting is a reversal of the removal procedure. Check the bumper for alignment before fully tightening the retaining nuts/screws. On rear bumpers, check the operation of the rear number plate light on completion.

**7 Bonnet -** removal, refitting and adjustment

*Removal*

**1** Open the bonnet, and support it in the open position using the stay.

**2** Release the fasteners and remove the insulation panel from the underside of the bonnet.
**3** Disconnect the windscreen washer hose from its connection to the washer jet, and from the locating clips on the bonnet and hinge.
**4** Undo the retaining screw, and detach the earth lead from the bonnet near the left-hand hinge. Also, where applicable, disconnect the heated washer multi-plug and wiring from the bonnet.
**5** To assist in correctly realigning the bonnet when refitting it, mark the outline of the hinges with a soft pencil, then loosen the two hinge retaining bolts each side.
**6** With the help of an assistant, remove the stay, unscrew the four bolts and lift the bonnet from the vehicle.

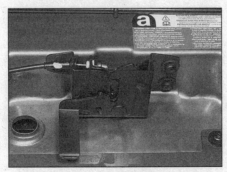

**8.1 Bonnet release cable and lock**

**8.3 Detach the cable from the bonnet release lever on the steering column**

**10.1a  Release the regulator retaining clip as shown . . .**

**10.1b  . . . and withdraw the manual window regulator handle**

2 Unscrew the three retaining screws, and remove the lock from the vehicle.

### Refitting

3 Refitting is a reversal of removal, but adjust the lock height so that the bonnet line is flush with the front wings, and so that it shuts securely without force. If necessary, adjust the lock laterally so that the striker enters the lock recess correctly; it may also be necessary to reposition the striker. Tighten the bonnet lock retaining screws to the specified torque.

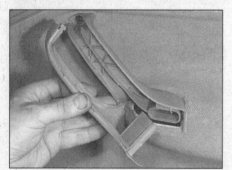

**10.2a  Remove the door handle trim capping . . .**

## 10  Door inner trim panel - removal and refitting

### Removal

#### Pre-1996 models

1 On models fitted with manual window regulators, fully shut the window, note the position of the regulator handle, then release the spring clip and withdraw the handle. The clip can be released by inserting a clean cloth between the handle and the door trim, and pulling the cloth back against the open ends of the clip to release its tension whilst simultaneously pulling the handle from the regulator shaft splines **(see illustrations)**.

2 Prise free the trim capping from the door handle, taking care not to break the single retaining clip, then undo the retaining screws and remove the handle **(see illustrations)**.

3 Undo the retaining screw from the inner door handle bezel, then slide free and remove the bezel **(see illustrations)**.

4 Unscrew and remove the door trim panel retaining screws **(see illustration)**, lift the panel to disengage it from the top edge clips (along the window edge), then remove the panel.

5 If required (and where fitted), the door pocket can be detached from the trim panel by unscrewing the three retaining screws, one of which is fitted from the inside-out. If an ashtray is fitted to the trim, it can be removed by carefully prising it free. If the door lock inner release or other internal components of the door are to be inspected or removed, first withdraw the bezel from the inner door release, then remove the insulation sheet from the door as follows.

6 Access to the inner door can be made by carefully extracting the insulator from the inner release, then peeling back the insulation sheet. In order not to damage and distort the insulation sheet, use a suitable knife to cut through the peripheral adhesive strip whilst the sheet is progressively peeled back and away from the door. Avoid touching the strip with the hands, as skin oils will adversely affect its adhesive properties **(see illustrations)**.

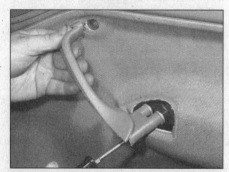

**10.2b  . . . and undo the retaining screws**

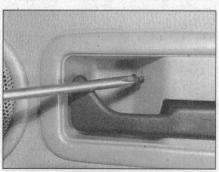

**10.3a  Undo the retaining screw . . .**

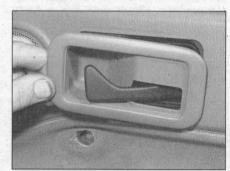

**10.3b  . . . and remove the bezel**

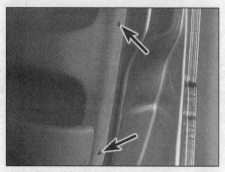

**10.4  Door trim retaining screws (arrowed)**

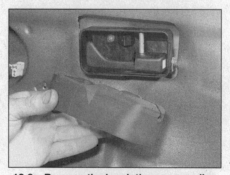

**10.6a  Remove the insulation surrounding the inner release handle**

**10.6b  Cut through the adhesive to remove the door insulation sheet**

**11.3 Undo the glass-to-regulator screws through apertures shown**

**11.4 Removing a door window glass**

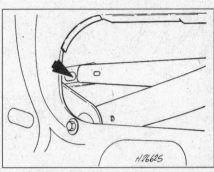

**11.9 Location of small slider bolt (arrowed) in front door of Cabriolet models**

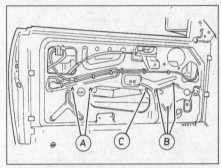

**11.10 Door window regulator bolts on the front doors of Cabriolet models**

A  *Large slider bolts*
B  *Regulator retaining bolts*
C  *Small slider bolt*

### 1996 models onward

7 Prise free the trim capping from the recess in the door pull, then undo the retaining screw behind.
8 On models fitted with manual window regulators, fully shut the window, note the position of the regulator handle, then release the spring clip and withdraw the handle. The clip can be released by inserting a clean cloth between the handle and the door trim, and pulling the cloth back against the open ends of the clip to release its tension whilst simultaneously pulling the handle from the regulator shaft splines.
9 Prise free the trim capping from the inner door handle bezel, undo the retaining screw then slide free and remove the bezel.
10 Prise free the trim cappings, where applicable and undo the eight screws securing the trim panel to the door.
11 Lift the panel to disengage it from the top edge, then remove the panel.
12 Access to the inner door can be made by carefully extracting the insulator from the inner release, then peeling back the insulation sheet. In order not to damage and distort the insulation sheet, use a suitable knife to cut through the peripheral adhesive strip whilst the sheet is progressively peeled back and away from the door. Avoid touching the strip with the hands, as skin oils will adversely affect its adhesive properties.

### *Refitting*

13 Refitting is a reversal of removal, but where necessary, apply suitable mastic to the door panel before fitting the insulation sheet. When the door trim panel is refitted, check the operation of the door catch release and the window regulator (where applicable).

### 11 Door window glass - removal and refitting

#### *Removal*

##### *Front door window glass (Hatchback, Saloon, Estate and Van models)*

1 Remove the inner trim panel and the insulation sheet from the door (Section 10).
2 Prise free the inner and outer weatherstrips

from the bottom of the window aperture in the door.
3 Wind the window up to close it, then have an assistant hold the window firmly in this position whilst you unscrew the window-to-regulator retaining screws through the aperture in the inner door **(see illustration)**.
4 Lower the window regulator, then tilting the window as required, withdraw it outwards from the door **(see illustration)**.

##### Front door window glass (Cabriolet models)

5 Remove the inner trim panel and the insulation sheet from the door (see Section 10).
6 Wind down the window in the door, then prise free the inner and outer weatherstrips from the bottom of the window aperture in the door.
7 Undo the three retaining screws, partially withdraw the door-mounted speaker so that its wiring connections can be detached, then remove the speaker.
8 Undo the door mirror trim screw, remove the trim panel and then detach the mirror adjuster multi-plug.
9 Lower the window in the door, then unscrew the small slider bolt **(see illustration)**.
10 Raise the door glass, undo the large slider bolts, support the window regulator, and unscrew the three regulator retaining bolts **(see illustration)**.
11 Lower the regulator and detach the regulator wiring multi-plug.
12 Move the glass rearwards to disengage it from the front guide channel, then move it carefully towards the outer panel. Carefully pull the glass upwards to disengage it from the large slider and simultaneously away from the door mirror, and remove the glass from the door.

##### Rear door window glass (Hatchback, Saloon and Estate)

13 Remove the inner trim panel and insulation sheet (see Section 10).
14 Remove the window aperture exterior trim.
15 Wind down the window and remove the inner and outer weatherstrips from the bottom of the window aperture.
16 Move the window winder mechanism so that the pivot between the slider at the bottom of the window and the mechanism is accessible through the opening in the bottom of the door panel. Detach the window winder mechanism from the slider at the bottom of the window.

17 Remove the three upper retaining screws from the window slider.
18 Remove the lower retaining screw from the window slider.
19 Tip the glass to disengage it and remove the glass from outside the door.

### *Refitting*

20 Refitting is a reversal of removal, but note then following:
 a) *When the glass is lowered into position in the door on Cabriolet models, loosely fit the retaining bolts, then close the window to ensure that the glass fits correctly before tightening the slider bolts to secure.*
 b) *Where applicable, ensure that the wiring looms in the door are clear of the window and its regulating mechanism, and that the connections are secure.*
 c) *On refitting the window glass, check that it operates fully and freely before refitting the insulation sheet and the door trim panel.*

### 12 Rear quarter window glass (Cabriolet models) - removal and refitting

#### *Removal*

1 Open the roof, and lift the rear seat cushion.
2 Refer to Section 34 for details, and remove the rear side quarter trim panel.

**11**

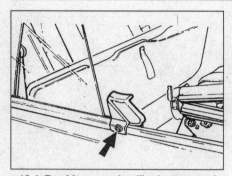

**12.4  Roof frame main pillar bottom seal screw (arrowed) on Cabriolet models**

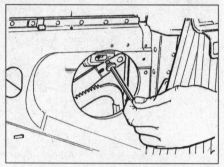

**12.8  Unscrewing the shouldered bolt securing the regulator arm to the support channel on Cabriolet models**

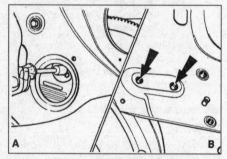

**12.9  Quarter window adjustment bolts on Cabriolet models**
*A  Height adjustment     B  Lateral adjustment*

3  Where applicable, undo the speaker retaining screws, partially withdraw the speaker to detach the wiring connections, and then remove the speaker.
4  Undo the screw, remove the cup washer, and detach the roof frame main pillar bottom seal **(see illustration)**.
5  Remove the outer and inner weather strips.
6  Carefully peel back and remove the insulation sheet. In order not to damage and distort the insulation sheet, use a suitable knife to cut through the peripheral adhesive strip as the sheet is peeled progressively back and away from the door. Avoid touching the strip with the hands, as skin oils will adversely affect its adhesive properties.
7  Reconnect the window regulator (handle or switch, as applicable) and with the window fully lowered, prise free and detach the window regulator arm from the channel.

8  Raise the window, then unscrew the shouldered bolt securing the regulator arm to the support channel **(see illustration)**. Tilt and lift the glass from the car.

### Refitting

9  Refitting is a reversal of removal, but note then following:
  a) *When the glass is lowered into position, and the regulator arm-to-support bolt is fitted, adjust the position of the glass by loosening the adjuster bolts as required. Tighten them once the necessary adjustment has been made (see illustration).*
  b) *Where applicable, ensure that the wiring looms are clear of the window and its regulating mechanism, and that the connections are secure.*
  c) *On refitting the window glass, check that it operates fully and freely before refitting the insulation sheet and the quarter trim panel.*

## 13  Rear quarter window regulator (Cabriolet models) - removal and refitting

### Removal

1  Remove the rear quarter window as described in the previous Section.
2  On models fitted with electric windows, detach the wiring multi-plug from the regulator motor.
3  Unscrew and remove the regulator arm retaining bolts.
4  Unscrew and remove the three regulator retaining bolts (to the right of the arm bolts), then withdraw the regulator from the side panel lower aperture.

### Refitting

5  Refitting is a reversal of removal. Ensure that the wiring connections are securely made, and check the operation of the regulator before refitting the window. Refer to Section 12 for details on refitting the window.

## 14  Door window regulator - removal and refitting

### Removal

1  Remove the door trim and the insulation sheet as described in Section 10.
2  Locate the glass in the door so that the guide channel can be detached from the regulator. Disconnect the ball and socket(s) (two per front door, one per rear door), then lower the glass to the base of the door.
3  The regulator is secured by seven pop-rivets (front door) or four pop-rivets (rear door). Drill through the centre of each rivet, detach the regulator from the door, and

**14.3  Drilling out the door window regulator rivets**

withdraw it from the lower aperture **(see illustration)**.

### Refitting

4  Refitting is a reversal of removal. Obtain the correct number of rivets to fit the regulator to the door. Check that the operation of the window regulator is satisfactory before refitting the door trim.

## 15  Door lock, lock cylinder and handles - removal and refitting

### Removal

1  Remove the door inner trim panel and the insulation sheet as described in Section 10. Proceed as described below in the appropriate sub-Section. On 1993-on Cabriolet models, it will be necessary to remove the door window glass, as described in Section 11, for access to the door lock components.

#### Door lock barrel

2  Where fitted, undo the two screws and remove the door lock barrel shield. Slide free the barrel retaining clip, detach the connecting rod and remove the lock barrel **(see illustrations)**.

#### Door lock

3  Remove the lock barrel as described above.
4  On models with central locking, detach the wiring multi-plugs from the lock motor (attached to and removed with the lock).

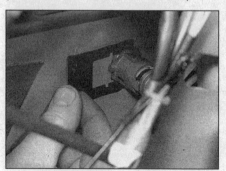

**15.2a  Remove the inner retaining clip . . .**

15.2b . . . and withdraw the lock barrel from the door

15.6 Door lock retaining screws

15.8a Remove the door release . . .

15.8b . . . and the door lock with cable

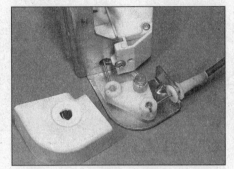

15.8c Remove cover to detach the cable from the lock

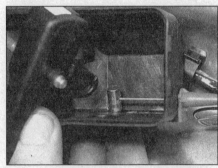

15.10a Detach the inner release handle . . .

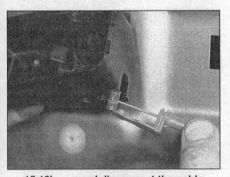

15.10b . . . and disconnect the cable from the casing

15.11a Exterior handle retaining screws

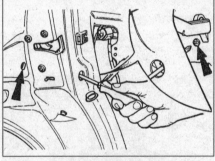

15.11b Exterior handle retaining screw access point in rear door

5 Unscrew and remove the inner door release retaining screw.

6 Unscrew and remove the three (four on 1993-on Cabriolet models) door lock retaining screws (see illustration).

7 Remove the window rear guide (rear doors only).

8 Slide free the inner release from the door, then withdraw the lock together with the remote control inner release and cable. If required, the connecting cable to the inner release handle can be detached from the lock by removing the cover, sliding the outer cable from its locating slot in the lock, and then withdrawing the inner cable from the actuating pivot on the lock (see illustrations).

9 On models with central locking, undo the two retaining screws to detach the lock from the actuating motor.

### Inner release handle

10 Slide free the inner release and detach it from the door, then disconnect the release operating cable from the release handle case (see illustrations).

### Exterior release handle

11 Undo the two retaining screws, detach the link rod from the release arm of the exterior handle, and remove the handle from the door (see illustration). Note that on the rear doors it will be necessary to remove the blanking plug in the edge of the door to gain access to one of the handle securing screws (see illustration).

### Refitting

12 Refitting is a reversal of removal. Check for satisfactory operation of the lock and its

associated components before refitting the door trim. Check that the striker enters the lock centrally when the door is closed. If necessary, loosen it with a Torx key, re-position and re-tighten it.

## 16 Door - removal and refitting

### Removal

1 Fully open the door, then untwist and detach the wiring multi-plug connector (see illustration).

2 Disconnect the door check strap by unscrewing the Torx screw on the door pillar (see illustration).

**11**

**16.1 Disconnect the wiring multi-plug connector**

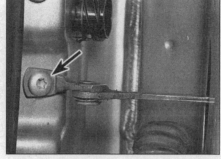

**16.2 Door check strap screw (arrowed)**

**16.4 Door hinge pin bolt (arrowed)**

**3** Support the door on blocks of wood.

**4** Unscrew the door hinge pin retaining bolt from each hinge (see illustration), then lift the door clear of the hinges.

### Refitting

**5** Refitting is a reversal of removal. Check that the striker enters the lock centrally when the door is closed. If necessary, loosen it with a Torx key, re-position and re-tighten it.

## 17 Exterior mirror and glass - removal and refitting

### Removal

**1** If the mirror glass is to removed, insert a thin flat-bladed tool between the glass and the housing, and carefully prise it free. Where applicable, disconnect the wiring from the connectors on the rear face of the mirror (see illustrations).

**2** To remove the mirror, first remove the door trim as described in Section 10.

**3** Undo the door mirror trim retaining screw, and remove the trim (see illustration).

**4** Carefully prise free the control unit from the trim, and where applicable, detach the wiring connector from the adjuster.

**5** Support the mirror, undo the three retaining screws, and remove the mirror from the door.

**6** The motor can be removed if required by undoing the three retaining screws (see illustration).

### Refitting

**7** Refit in the reverse order of removal. Check that the operation of the mirror adjuster is satisfactory.

**17.1a Prise free the door mirror glass . . .**

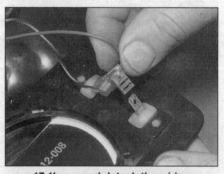

**17.1b . . . and detach the wiring connectors, where applicable**

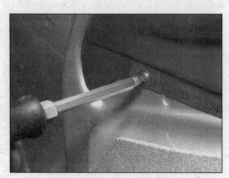

**17.3 Undo the screw and remove the mirror trim**

**17.6 Mirror motor and retaining screws (arrowed)**

## 18 Interior mirror - removal and refitting

### Removal

**1** Using a length of strong thin cord or fishing line, break the adhesive bond between the base of the mirror and the glass. Have an assistant support and remove the mirror as it is released.

**2** If the original mirror is to be refitted, thoroughly clean its base with methylated spirit and a lint-free cloth. Allow a period of one minute for the spirit to evaporate. Clean the windscreen black patch in a similar manner.

### Refitting

**3** During the installation of the mirror, it is important that the mirror base, windscreen black patch and the adhesive patch are not touched or contaminated in any way - poor adhesion will result.

**4** Prior to fitting the mirror, the temperature inside the vehicle should ideally be around 20°C. While this isn't critical, it's worth ensuring that the inside of the vehicle is as warm and dry as possible.

**5** With the contact surfaces thoroughly cleaned, remove the protective tape from one side of the adhesive patch, and press it firmly into contact with the mirror base.

**6** If fitting the mirror to a new windscreen, the protective tape must first be removed from the windscreen black patch.

**7** Warm the mirror base and the adhesive patch for about 30 seconds to a temperature of 50 to 70°C. Peel back the protective tape from the other side of the adhesive patch on the mirror base, then align the mirror base and the windscreen patch, and press the mirror firmly into position. Hold the base of the mirror firmly against the windscreen for a minimum period of two minutes to ensure full adhesion.

**8** Wait at least thirty minutes before adjusting the mirror position.

## 19 Boot lid - removal, refitting and adjustment

### Removal

**1** Open the boot lid, and mark the position of the hinges with a pencil.

**2** Where applicable, disconnect the wiring multi-plug and the earth lead for the central locking motor from the boot lid (**see illustration**). Attach a suitable length of strong cord to the end of the wire, then withdraw the lead from the bootlid. Detach the cord and leave it in position in the boot. This will then act as an aid to guiding the wiring through the lid when it is refitted.

**3** Place cloth rags beneath each corner of the boot lid to prevent damage to the paintwork.

**4** With the help of an assistant, unscrew the mounting bolts and lift the boot lid from the car.

### Refitting and adjustment

**5** Refitting is a reversal of removal. Check that the boot lid is correctly aligned with the surrounding bodywork, with an equal clearance around its edge. Adjustment is made by loosening the hinge bolts and moving the boot lid within the elongated mounting holes. Tighten the hinge bolts to the specified torque setting. Check that the lock enters the striker centrally when the boot lid is closed, and if necessary adjust the striker's position within the elongated holes.

## 20 Boot lid lock components - removal and refitting

### Removal

#### Lock barrel

**1** Open the boot and undo the screw securing the barrel retaining clip, then remove the clip.

**2** Detach the barrel from the link rod, and withdraw the lock from the boot lid.

#### Lock

**3** Open the boot lid and remove the lock barrel (see above for details).

**4** Undo the three retaining screws, then withdraw the lock from the boot lid.

#### Lock striker and remote release

**5** Open the boot, undo the two retaining screws, and remove the trim from the rear face of the luggage compartment.

**6** Using a soft pencil, mark an outline around the striker and the release unit, to act as a guide for repositioning on refitting. Undo the two Torx-type screws, and remove the lock striker and the release unit. Detach the operating cable from the release unit to remove it.

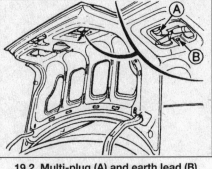

**19.2 Multi-plug (A) and earth lead (B) connection points in the boot lid**

#### Release cable

**7** Remove the striker and release unit as described above, then detach the release cable from it.

**8** Detach and remove the kick panel trim beneath the front and rear doors on the driver's side. Fold back the carpet from around the bootlid lock release handle.

**9** Withdraw the outer cable from the slot in the lever mounting plate, then detach the inner cable from the lever.

**10** Remove the appropriate side trim panels from the rear of the vehicle on the side concerned, to expose the cable routing.

> **HAYNES HINT** *Where the cable has to pass through cavities in the body, tie a suitable length of cord to the cable end before pulling the cable through and removing it. The cord can be untied from the cable, and left in situ in the vehicle. It will then act as a "puller-guide" when the cable is being refitted.*

#### Refitting

**11** Refitting is a reversal of removal. When refitting the lock, check that the striker enters the lock centrally when the boot lid is closed, and if necessary re-position the striker by loosening the mounting screws. Tighten the lock and striker mounting screws to the specified torque setting.

## 21 Tailgate - removal, refitting and adjustment

### Removal

**1** Open the tailgate, then undo the seven retaining screws and remove the trim panel from the tailgate.

**2** Using a soft pencil, mark the fitted position outline around the tailgate hinges to act as a guide for repositioning when refitting.

**3** Prise free and remove the plug for access to the washer jet, then detach the hose from the jet. Attach a suitable length of strong cord to the end of the hose to assist in guiding the hose back through the aperture of the tailgate

**21.4 Detach the wiring connector from the tailgate**

when it is being refitted. Now prise free the flexible grommet on the left-hand side, and withdraw the washer jet hose from the tailgate. Undo the cord from the hose, and leave it in position in the tailgate.

**4** Where applicable, detach the central locking lead multi-connector and earth lead from the tailgate (**see illustration**). Attach a suitable length of strong cord to the end of the wire, to assist in guiding the wiring back through the aperture of the tailgate when it is being refitted. Now prise free the flexible grommet on the right-hand side, and withdraw the central locking wires from the tailgate. Undo the cord from the wire, and leave it in position in the tailgate.

**5** Have an assistant support the tailgate in the open position, then prise open the support strut balljoint securing clip, and detach the strut each side from the tailgate.

**6** Unscrew and remove the hinge bolts, then lift the tailgate clear of the vehicle (**see illustration**).

### Refitting and adjustment

**7** Refitting is a reversal of removal, but check that the tailgate is correctly aligned with the surrounding bodywork, with an equal clearance around its edge. Adjustment is made by loosening the hinge bolts and moving the tailgate within the elongated mounting holes. Tighten the hinge bolts to the specified torque setting. Adjust the rear height by turning the rubber bump stop each side in the desired direction. Check that the striker enters the lock centrally when the tailgate is closed, and if necessary adjust the position of the striker within the elongated holes.

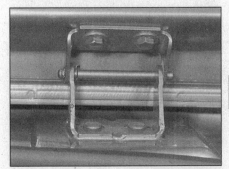

**21.6 Tailgate hinge and retaining bolts**

**11**

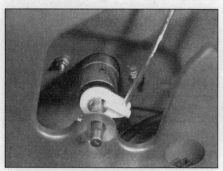

**23.2 Tailgate lock barrel, operating rod and retaining nuts**

**23.5 Undo the three tailgate lock retaining screws**

**23.6 Tailgate lock striker and release unit retaining screws**

## 22 Tailgate support strut - removal and refitting

### Removal

**1** Support the tailgate in its open position. If both struts are to be removed, the tailgate will need to be supported by an alternative means.
**2** Disconnect each end of the support strut by prising out the spring clip retainers with a small screwdriver and pulling the strut from the ball mountings.

### Refitting

**3** Refitting is a reversal of removal, but note that the piston end of the strut faces downwards.

## 23 Tailgate lock components - removal and refitting

### Removal

#### Lock barrel

**1** Open the tailgate, then remove the seven screws and remove the inner trim panel from the rear of the luggage area.
**2** Depending on type, unscrew and remove the lock barrel clip retaining screw, then remove the clip or undo the two retaining nuts **(see illustration)**.
**3** Disengage the operating rod and remove the barrel.

#### Lock

**4** Open the tailgate and remove the lock barrel as described above.
**5** Undo the three Torx-type retaining screws and remove the lock. Where applicable, detach the wiring in-line connector from the lock **(see illustration)**.

#### Striker and release unit

**6** Using a soft pencil, mark an outline around the striker and the release unit to act as a guide for repositioning on refitting. Undo the two Torx-type screws (and where applicable, the earth lead screw), then remove the lock striker and release unit. Detach the operating

cable from the release unit to remove it **(see illustration)**.

#### Release cable

**7** Remove the striker and release unit as described above, then detach the release cable from it.
**8** Detach and remove the kick panel trim beneath the front and rear doors on the driver's side. Fold back the carpet from around the tailgate release handle.
**9** Withdraw the outer cable from the slot in the lever mounting plate, then detach the inner cable from the lever.
**10** Remove the appropriate side trim panels from the rear of the vehicle on the side concerned, to expose the cable routing.

> **HAYNES HINT** *Where the cable has to pass through cavities in the body, tie a suitable length of cord to the cable end before pulling the cable through and removing it. The cord can be untied from the cable, and left in situ in the vehicle. It will then act as a "puller-guide" when the cable is being refitted.*

### Refitting

**11** Refitting is a reversal of removal. When refitting the lock, check that the striker enters the lock centrally when the tailgate is closed, and if necessary re-position the striker by loosening the mounting screws. Tighten the lock and striker mounting screws to the specified torque setting.

**24.3 Central locking system control module location**

## 24 Central locking system control module - removal and refitting

### Removal

**1** Disconnect the battery negative (earth) lead (refer to Chapter 5A, Section 1).
**2** Remove the front footwell side cowl trim panel from the driver's side, as described in Section 34.
**3** Withdraw the central locking module from its location bracket, and detach the multi-plug wiring connections from it **(see illustration)**.

### Refitting

**4** Refit in the reverse order of removal. Check the operation of the system to complete.

## 25 Windscreen and fixed windows - removal and refitting

### Removal

#### Windscreen and rear quarter and rear window/tailgate glass

**1** The windscreen, rear quarter and rear window/tailgate glass are bonded in place with special mastic. Special tools are required to cut free the old glass and fit replacements, together with cleaning solutions and primers. It is therefore recommended that this work is entrusted to a Ford dealer or windscreen replacement specialist.

#### Rear window(s) - Van models

**2** Working from the inner face of the door concerned, use a blunt-ended instrument to push the inner lip of the weatherseal beneath the window frame, starting at the top. Get an assistant to support the window on the outside during this operation.
**3** With the weatherseal free, withdraw the window from the door.

#### Rear window - Cabriolet models

**4** Detach the heated rear window lead, and withdraw the lead from the weatherstrip.
**5** Arrange for an assistant to support the

glass from the outside, then wearing protective gloves, press the window outwards and remove it from its frame. Take care not to apply undue strain to the hood material or the hood frame as the window is pressed out.

6 Remove the weatherstrip from the glass.

## Refitting

7 Clean the window and aperture in the body/frame. Petrol or spirit-based solvents must not be used for this purpose, as they are harmful to the weatherstrip.

8 Fit the weatherseal on the window, then insert a cord in the weatherseal groove so that the ends project from the bottom of the window and are overlapped by approximately 150 mm.

9 Locate the window on its location aperture, and pass the ends of the cord inside the vehicle. Have an assistant hold the window in position.

10 Slowly pull one end of the cord (at right-angles to the window frame, towards the centre of the glass) so that the lip of the weatherseal goes over the aperture. At the same time, have the assistant press firmly on the outside of the window. When the cord reaches the middle top of the window, pull the remaining length of cord to position the other half of the weatherseal.

11 Reconnect the heated rear window lead, and press it under the weatherstrip (Cabriolet models).

## 26 Door and tailgate weatherstrips - removal and refitting

## Removal

1 To remove a weatherstrip seal from its aperture flange, grip the strip at its joint end, and progressively pull it free, working around the aperture to the other end of the strip.

## Refitting

2 First check that the contact surfaces of the weatherstrip and the aperture flange are clean. Check around the aperture flange for any signs of distortion, and rectify as necessary.

3 To refit the weatherstrip, start by roughly locating its ends midway along the base of the aperture concerned, but do not press them into position over the flange at this stage. Proceed as follows, according to type.

## Door weatherstrip

4 In the case of a door weatherstrip, press the strip into position at the corners to initially locate it. Check that the distances between each contact point are such that the strip will fit smoothly around the aperture (without distortion), then firmly press the strip fully into position, starting at the top edge and working down each side to finish at the bottom joint. Check that the seal is correctly located, then apply a suitable sealant to the joint, to prevent

the possibility of water leakage through it caused by capillary action.

5 Shut the door, and check it for fit. Adjust if required by resetting the position of the striker plate to suit.

## Tailgate weatherstrip

6 Position the ends of the weatherstrip so that they are centralised within 300 mm of the tailgate striker plate. A new weatherstrip will need to be measured and cut to length. Progressively fit the weatherstrip around the aperture flange, squeezing it closed over the flange by hand to secure. When fitted, check that it is not distorted, then close the tailgate and check it for fit. Adjustment of the striker plate and the tailgate bump stops may be necessary to obtain a satisfactory fit and seal.

## 27 Body side-trim mouldings and adhesive emblems - removal and refitting

## Removal

1 Insert a length of strong cord (fishing line is ideal), between the moulding or emblem concerned, and break the adhesive bond between the moulding (or emblem) and the panel.

2 Thoroughly clean all traces of adhesive from the panel using methylated spirit, and allow the moulding/emblem location to dry.

## Refitting

3 Peel back the protective paper from the rear face of the new moulding/emblem, and then fit it into position on the panel concerned, taking care not to touch the adhesive. When in position, apply a hand pressure to the moulding/emblem for a short period to ensure maximum adhesion to the panel.

## 28 Roof moulding (Van models) - removal and refitting

## Removal

1 Prise free and lift the moulding up from the roof at the front end, then pull the moulding from its location channel in the roof.

2 Clean the contact faces of the moulding and the roof channel before refitting.

## Refitting

3 Locate the moulding into position over the channel, check that it is correctly realigned, then progressively press it into place using the palm of the hand.

## 29 Sunroof - checking and adjustment

1 The sunroof should operate freely, without

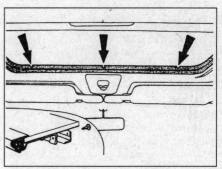

**29.2 Sunroof lower frame-to-glass panel retaining screws (arrowed)**

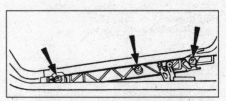

**29.3 Loosen off these screws (arrowed) to adjust the sunroof glass panel**

sticking or binding, as it is opened and closed. When in the closed position, check that the panel is flush with the surrounding roof panel, the maximum allowable gap at the front edge being 1.0 mm.

2 If adjustment is required, open the sun blind, then undo and remove the three lower frame-to-glass panel retaining screws **(see illustration)**. Slide the lower frame back into the roof.

3 Loosen off the central and front securing screws, adjust the glass roof panel so that it is flush at its front edge with the roof panel, then retighten the securing screws **(see illustration)**.

4 Pull the lower frame forwards, insert and tighten its retaining screws to complete.

## 30 Sunroof panel - removal and refitting

## Removal

1 Open the sun blind, unscrew and remove the three screws securing the lower frame, and slide the frame back into the roof.

2 Undo the three roof panel-to-sliding gear screws, then push the panel up and out to remove it from the vehicle. Have an assistant lift the panel free from above as it is raised, to avoid the possibility of the panel and/or the surrounding roof from being damaged.

## Refitting

3 Refit in the reverse order of removal. When the panel is in position, adjust it as described in the previous Section.

**11**

## 31 Sunroof weatherstrip - removal and refitting

### Removal

1 Wind the sunroof panel into the tilted open position, then grip the ends of the weatherstrip and pull it free from the flanged periphery of the roof panel.
2 Clean the contact faces of the panel and the weatherstrip (where the original strip is to be used) before refitting.

### Refitting

3 Refit in the reverse order of removal. Ensure that the weatherstrip joint is located in the middle of the rear face of the panel.

## 32 Seats - removal and refitting

### Removal

#### Front seat

⚠️ **Warning: On vehicles fitted with mechanical seat belt pre-tensioning stalks, be careful when handling the seat, as the tensioning device ("grabber") contains a powerful spring, which could cause injury if released** in an uncontrolled fashion. The tensioning mechanism should be immobilised by inserting a safety "transit clip" available from Ford parts stockists (see illustration 32.2). You are strongly advised to seek the advice of a Ford dealer as to the correct use of the "transit clip" and the safety implications before proceeding.

⚠️ *Warning: On vehicles fitted with pyrotechnic seat belt pre-tensioners, disconnect the battery negative (earth) lead (refer to Chapter 5A, Section 1), then wait a minimum of two minutes before proceeding.*

1 On later models, pull off the trim cover from the base of the seat, adjacent to the door aperture.
2 On vehicles fitted with mechanical seat belt pre-tensioning stalks, fit the safety "transit clip" **(see illustration)**. On vehicles fitted with pyrotechnic seat belt pre-tensioners, disconnect the wiring multi-plug located behind the previously removed trim cover.
3 Slide the seat forwards to the full extent of its travel, then unscrew and remove the rear mounting bolts (one on the outer slide and two on the inner) **(see illustrations)**. On some models it will be necessary to prise open and remove the trim cover for access to the mounting bolts
4 Now slide the seat fully to the rear, then unscrew the front securing bolt each side **(see illustration)**. Lift the seat and remove it from the vehicle.

### Rear seat cushion

5 Prise free the blanking plugs, then unscrew and remove the cushion hinge retaining screw each side **(see illustration)**. Remove the cushion from the vehicle.

### Rear seat backrest (Hatchback, Saloon and Estate models)

6 Pivot the rear seat cushion forwards, then fold the backrest down. Undo the two screws retaining the hinge to the backrest each side, and remove the backrest from the vehicle **(see illustration)**.

### Rear seat backrest (Cabriolet models)

7 Raise the seat cushion, then unscrew and remove the seat belt lower reel anchor bolts.
8 Unscrew and remove the screws (one each side) securing the backrest upper section.
9 Pivot the seat backrest down (release knob in boot), pull back the backrest cover, then unscrew and remove the two screws each side retaining the top section.
10 Detach the seat belt guide from the top of the backrest, then lift the backrest and feed the belt reel lower anchor plate through the backrest to allow the backrest to be removed from the car.
11 Unscrew the bolts securing the lower backrest to the hinges on each side, and remove the backrest lower section.

### Refitting

12 Refitting is a reversal of the removal procedure. Where applicable, tighten the seat belt anchor bolts to the specified torque.

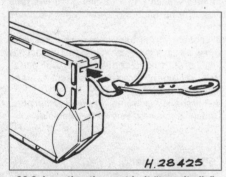

H.28425

**32.2 Inserting the seat belt "transit clip" (early type shown) to immobilise the mechanical seat belt pre-tensioner**

**32.3a Front seat/runner rear outboard retaining bolt**

**32.3b Front seat/runner rear inboard retaining bolts**

**32.4 Front seat/runner forward mounting bolt**

**32.5 Rear seat cushion retaining screw (Saloon)**

**32.6 Rear seat backrest-to-cushion hinge screws**

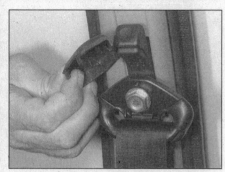

33.5 Remove the cover for access to the seat belt upper anchor bolt

33.9 Inertia reel unit and retaining bolt

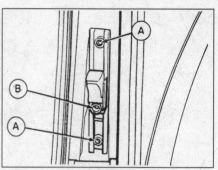

33.12 Front seat belt height adjuster retaining bolts (A) and anchor plate bolt (B)

## 33 Seat belts - removal and refitting

### Removal

**Note:** *Seat belts and associated components which have been subject to impact loads must be renewed.*

#### Front seat belt (3-door Hatchback and Cabriolet models)

**1** Prise free the upper cover, then unscrew and remove the front seat belt upper anchor plate retaining bolt. Remove the plate and spacer.

**2** Undo the lower anchor rail retaining bolt, pivot the rail towards the centre of the vehicle, pull it free from its mounting and then slide the belt from the rail.

**3** Remove the rear quarter trim panel, then on Cabriolet models, undo the two retaining screws and remove the belt guide.

**4** Unscrew the bolt retaining the inertia reel unit, then remove the reel and the belt.

#### Front seat belt (5-door Hatchback, Saloon, Estate and Van models)

**5** Prise free the cover, then unscrew and remove the front seat belt upper anchor plate retaining bolt. Remove the plate and spacer **(see illustration)**.

**6** Unscrew and remove the lower anchor plate retaining bolt.

**7** Remove the trim from the centre "B" pillar by pulling free the weatherstrip, unscrewing the two retaining screws, withdrawing the trim from the panel and detaching the securing pegs (where applicable).

**8** Undo the six screws retaining the scuff plate in position, extract the belt from the slotted hole, and remove the scuff plate.

**9** Undo the retaining bolt, and detach the inertia reel unit from the central pillar **(see illustration)**.

#### Front seat belt height adjuster

**10** Prise free the upper cover, then unscrew and remove the front seat belt upper anchor plate retaining bolt. Remove the plate and spacer.

**11** Remove the trim from the centre "B" pillar

by pulling free the weatherstrip, unscrewing the two retaining screws, withdrawing the trim from the panel and detaching the securing pegs (where applicable).

**12** Unscrew the retaining bolts and remove the height adjuster **(see illustration)**.

#### Front seat belt stalk

⚠️ *Warning: On vehicles fitted with mechanical or pyrotechnic seat belt pre-tensioners, any work on the seat belt stalk should be entrusted to a Ford dealer. The following procedure is therefore only applicable to models with conventional seat belt stalks which DO NOT incorporate any form of pre-tensioning device.*

**13** Remove the relevant front seat as described in Section 32.

**14** Undo the single retaining bolt and remove the stalk from the side of the seat.

#### Rear seat belts (3-door Hatchback models)

**15** Prise free the upper cover, then unscrew and remove the front seat belt upper anchor plate retaining bolt. Remove the plate and spacer.

**16** Undo the lower anchor rail retaining bolt, pivot the rail towards the centre of the vehicle, pull it free from its mounting and then slide the belt from the rail.

**17** Lift the rear seat cushion for access, then unscrew the bolt and remove the centre buckle/belt anchor plate **(see illustration)**.

**18** Unscrew the lower reel belt anchor plate bolt.

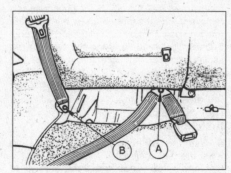

33.17 Rear seat belt anchor plates for the central buckle/belt (A) and the reel belt (B)

**19** Unscrew and remove the upper anchor plate bolt, and detach the plate and spacer from the rear "C" pillar.

**20** Pivot the rear seat backrest down, and undo the two Torx screws securing the backrest.

**21** Remove the trim from the centre "B" pillar by pulling free the weatherstrip, unscrewing the two retaining screws, withdrawing the trim from the panel and detaching the securing pegs (where applicable).

**22** Remove the rear quarter trim panel (Section 34).

**23** Remove the trim panel from the "C" pillar as described in Section 34.

**24** Undo the three Torx bolts, and detach the rear seat backrest catch bracket.

**25** Unscrew the inertia reel retaining bolt, and withdraw the inertia reel unit and belt.

#### Rear seat belts (5-door Hatchback models)

**26** Lift the rear seat cushion for access, then unscrew the retaining bolt and remove the centre buckle/belt anchor plate.

**27** Unscrew the lower reel belt anchor plate bolt.

**28** Detach the cover for access, then unscrew and remove the anchor plate and spacer from the "C" pillar **(see illustration)**.

**29** Pivot the rear seat backrest down, and undo the two Torx screws securing the backrest catch.

**30** Remove the trim panel from the "C" pillar as described in Section 34.

**31** Undo the three Torx bolts, and detach the rear seat backrest catch bracket.

33.28 Rear seat belt upper anchor bolt

**11**

**33.46  Rear seat backrest catch mounting (Estate models)**

**33.47  Rear seat inertia reel unit (Estate models)**

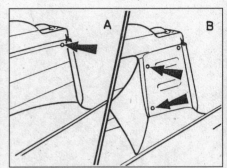

**33.51  Rear seat backrest upper section screw locations on Cabriolet models**

**32** Unscrew the inertia reel retaining bolt, and withdraw the inertia reel unit and belt.

### Rear seat belts (Saloon models)

**33** Lift the rear seat cushion for access, then unscrew the retaining bolt and remove the centre buckle/belt anchor plate.

**34** Unscrew the lower reel belt anchor plate bolt.

**35** Detach the cover for access, then unscrew and remove the anchor plate and spacer from the "C" pillar.

**36** Pivot the rear seat backrest down, and remove the trim panel from the "C" pillar as described in Section 34.

**37** Unscrew the retaining nut, and remove the rear seat backrest catch pull knob from its bracket in the boot. Pull the cable from the clip on the underside of the boot.

**38** Undo the two Torx screws, and release the seat back catch from the mounting bracket.

**39** Undo the three Torx bolts, and detach the rear seat backrest catch bracket.

**40** Unscrew the inertia reel retaining bolt, and withdraw the inertia reel unit and belt.

### Rear seat belts (Estate models)

**41** Lift the rear seat cushion for access, unscrew the retaining bolt and remove the centre buckle/belt anchor plate.

**42** Unscrew the lower reel belt anchor plate bolt.

**43** Detach the cover for access, then unscrew and remove the anchor plate and spacer from the "C" pillar.

**44** Pivot the rear seat backrest down, undo the two Torx screws and remove the backrest catch.

**45** Detach and remove the "C" and "D" pillar trim panels, followed by the rear luggage area trim panel, as described in Section 34.

**46** Undo the three Torx screws, and detach the backrest catch mounting **(see illustration)**.

**47** Unscrew the retaining bolt, and remove the inertia reel/belt unit **(see illustration)**.

### Rear seat belts (Cabriolet models)

**48** Lift the rear seat cushion for access, then unscrew the retaining bolt and remove the centre buckle/belt anchor plate.

**49** Unscrew the lower anchor plate bolt. To remove the centre lap belt, remove the lower belt buckle and twin buckle assemblies.

**50** Unscrew and remove the lower reel belt anchor plate bolt.

**51** Release the catch in the boot, and fold down the rear seat backrest. Pull free the cover from the rear face of the backrest for access to its upper section. Undo the two retaining screws on each side **(see illustration)**. Remove the belt guide from the top of the backrest.

**52** Raise the backrest, feed the belt anchor plate through and then remove the backrest.

**53** Unscrew the retaining bolt and remove the inertia reel/belt.

### Refitting

**54** On all models, refitting of the front and rear seat belts is a reversal of the removal procedure. Tighten all fastenings to the specified torque, and check for satisfactory operation.

---

## 34 Interior trim panels - removal and refitting

### Removal

#### Windscreen "A" pillar trim

**1** Pull free the weatherstrip from the flange on the "A" pillar. Undo the retaining screw, release the retaining clips and withdraw the trim from the pillar.

#### Centre "B" pillar

**2** Pull free the weatherstrip from the pillar flange. Prise free the cover, then unscrew and remove the front seat belt upper anchor plate retaining bolt. Remove the plate and spacer.

**3** On 5-door models, undo the two screws securing the centre pillar trim.

**4** Carefully prise free and detach the trim from the central pillar (to which it is attached by plastic pegs).

#### Rear "C" pillar trim (Hatchback models)

**5** Hinge the rear seat cushion forwards, and lower the seat backrest.

**6** Where fitted, undo the three screws to withdraw the speaker, and detach the speaker wire. Do not remove the speaker itself.

**7** Undo the two Torx-type retaining screws, and remove the backrest catch. Also prise free and remove the rear suspension top mounting cover (just to the rear of the catch).

**8** Unscrew and remove the rear seat belt lower anchor plate bolt.

**9** Prise free the seat belt upper anchor plate cover, then unscrew the retaining bolt and detach the upper anchor plate and spacer.

**10** Prise free the door weatherstrip from the pillar flange.

**11** On 3-door models, remove the rear quarter trim as described later in this Section.

**12** Undo the retaining screws and withdraw the trim panel from the pillar, feeding the seat belt and anchor through the trim. Note that it is necessary to remove a cover for access to the rear retaining screw.

#### Rear "C" pillar trim (Saloon models)

**13** Hinge the rear seat cushion forwards, and lower the seat backrest.

**14** Detach and remove the rear parcel shelf (see paragraphs 22 to 24).

**15** Unscrew and remove the rear seat belt lower anchor plate bolt.

**16** Prise free the seat belt upper anchor plate cover, then unscrew the retaining bolt and detach the upper anchor plate and spacer.

**17** Undo the two "C" pillar retaining screws. Prise free the door weatherstrip from the "C" pillar flange, then carefully prise free the trim panel from the pillar, feeding the seat belt through it as it is withdrawn.

#### "C" pillar trim (Estate models)

**18** Hinge the rear seat cushion forwards, and lower the seat backrest.

**19** Prise free the seat belt upper anchor plate cover, then unscrew the retaining bolt and detach the upper anchor plate and spacer.

**20** Carefully prise free and remove the trim panel from the "C" pillar.

#### "D" pillar trim (Estate models)

**21** Prise free the trim panel from the "D" pillar to release it from the retaining clips, and remove the trim.

#### Rear parcel shelf (Saloon models)

**22** Hinge down the rear seat backrest. Where fitted, detach and remove the rear speakers from the parcel shelf.

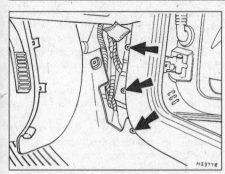

34.30 Location of front footwell side cowl trim panel retaining tabs (arrowed)

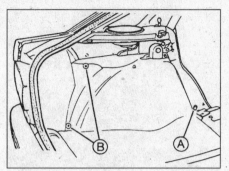

34.36a Luggage area trim retaining clip (A) and screws (B) - Hatchback models

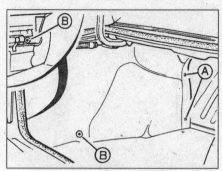

34.36b Luggage area trim retaining clips (A) and screws (B) - Saloon models

**23** Undo the retaining screw, and remove the seat belt guide trim panel each side.
**24** Unscrew and remove the three parcel shelf retaining screws, then lift the panel at the front edge to detach it from the four plastic retaining clips, and withdraw the panel from the car.

### Rear quarter trim panel

**25** Detach the front seat belt at its upper and lower anchor points, as described in Section 33.
**26** Detach and remove the centre "B" pillar trim as described previously in this Section.
**27** Undo the two scuff plate retaining screws, and ease the plate away from the quarter panel.
**28** Hinge forward the rear seat cushion and backrest, then detach the belt trim guide bezel from the quarter panel.
**29** Unscrew and remove the retaining screws at the rear of the panel. Prise free the quarter panel from the "B" pillar, and withdraw the panel. As it is withdrawn, disengage the seat belt and anchors through the panel slots.

### Front footwell side cowl trim panel

**30** Rotate the plastic retaining clip at the front of the panel through 90° to release the panel at the forward fixing, then ease the panel away from the three tab fasteners at the rear edge (see illustration).

### Scuff plate

**31** Remove the front footwell side cowl trim panel as described above.
**32** Prise free the door weatherstrip from the door sill flange.
**33** On 5-door Hatchback, Saloon, Estate and Van models, unscrew and remove the screw at the lower end of the "B" pillar trim (just above the seat belt slot in the scuff plate).
**34** Unscrew and remove the six scuff plate retaining screws, then feeding the seat belt through it (where applicable), withdraw the scuff plate.

### Luggage area trim (Hatchback and Saloon models)

**35** Hinge down the rear seat backrest(s), and on Hatchback models, prise free and remove the trim cap from the rear suspension top mounting.

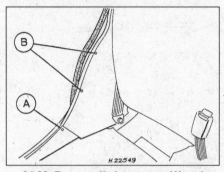

34.38 Rear scuff plate screw (A) and luggage area trim forward screws (B) (Estate models)

**36** Prise free the trim panel clips using a suitable flat-bladed tool (see illustrations).
**37** Unscrew and remove the two trim retaining screws together with their large washers, then withdraw the trim panel.

### Luggage area trim (Estate models)

**38** Lift the rear seat cushion and unscrew the scuff plate screw at the rear, then unscrew and remove the two luggage area trim screws (see illustration).
**39** Hinge down the rear seat backrest, then prise free the upper cover and remove the rear seat belt upper anchor plate retaining bolt. Remove the plate and spacer.
**40** Undo the two Torx screws, and remove the rear seat backrest catch.
**41** Prise the trim panel from the "C" pillar, and remove it.
**42** Similarly, prise the trim panel from the "D" pillar, and remove it.
**43** Undo the screw attaching the trim panel to the "C" pillar, then the screws securing the luggage area trim panel to the "D" pillar (see illustration).
**44** Undo the three luggage area trim panel-to-floor screws, and the single screw securing the panel to the rear crossmember.
**45** Lift the trim panel to release it from the inner side panel, then withdraw it.

### Partition panel (Van models)

**46** Working from the front of the panel, unscrew and remove the three panel-to-crossmember bolts on its lower edge.
**47** Working from the rear of the panel, unscrew and remove the two bolts securing

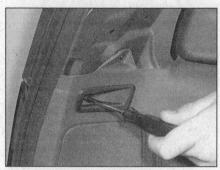

34.43 Luggage area side trim retaining screws removal (Estate)

the panel to the rear face of the "B" pillar each side, then withdraw the partition panel.

### Sun visor

**48** Release the visor from the retaining clip, undo the two retaining screws at its hinge mounting, and remove the visor. To remove the retaining clip, prise open the cover flap to expose the retaining screw, then undo the screw and remove the clip.

### Passenger grab handle

**49** Prise back the trim flaps at each end of the grab handle to expose the screws. Undo the screws and remove the handle.

### *Refitting*

**50** Refitting is a reversal of the removal procedure. Ensure any wiring connections are securely made. Tighten the seat belt fixings to the specified torque and check the seat belt(s) for satisfactory operation on completion.

## 35 Facia - removal and refitting

*Warning: On vehicles fitted with a passenger's air bag, seek the advice of a Ford dealer concerning safety implications when removing the facia assembly.*

### *Removal*

#### Pre-1996 models

**1** Disconnect the battery negative (earth) lead.

**11**

**35.5 Side vent panel removal on the driver's side**

**35.8a Pull free the weatherstrip for access to the outboard facia screws**

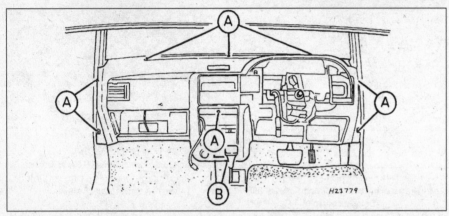

**35.8b Facia retaining screw locations "A" (screw only) and "B" (screw and washers)**

**2** Refer to Chapter 10 for details, and remove the steering wheel.

**3** Undo the two upper and four lower retaining screws, and remove the upper and lower steering column shrouds.

**4** Refer to the appropriate Chapters concerned for details, and remove the following facia-associated items:

  a) *Steering column multi-function switch (Chapter 12).*
  b) *Instrument panel (Chapter 12).*
  c) *Choke cable, where applicable (Chapter 4A).*
  d) *Heating/ventilation controls and control panel (Chapter 3).*
  e) *Cigar lighter and ashtray (Chapter 12).*
  f) *Radio/cassette player (Chapter 12).*
  g) *Clock (Chapter 12).*

**5** Undo the two retaining screws, and remove the side vent panel from the facia on the driver's side. As it is withdrawn, disconnect any wiring connections from the panel-mounted switches **(see illustration)**.

**6** Undo the two hinge/retaining screws securing the glovebox lid, and remove it. Undo the two catch screws, and remove the lock/catch. As the catch is withdrawn, disconnect the bulbholder/switch wiring connector.

**7** Where fitted, detach and remove the footwell lights from the driver and passenger side lower facia.

**8** Pull free the weatherstrip from the leading edge of the door aperture each side to gain access to the outboard mounting screws. Unscrew and remove the retaining screws from the points indicated **(see illustrations)**.

**9** With the help of an assistant, withdraw the facia from its mounting. As it is withdrawn, note the routing of the cables attached to the facia, then detach the cable-ties and remove the facia from the vehicle.

**10** The associated components of the facia can (if required) be detached by undoing the appropriate retaining screws.

**1996 models onward**

**11** Disconnect the battery negative (earth) lead (refer to Chapter 5A, Section 1).

**12** Refer to Chapter 10 for details, and remove the steering wheel.

**13** Undo the single retaining screw, and withdraw the steering column multi-function switch upwards from the column. Detach the wiring connector and cable-tie clips from the switch.

**14** Detach the three multiplugs located at the rear of the detachable lower facia panel then disconnect them.

**15** Detach and remove the footwell lights from the driver and passenger side lower facia.

**16** Refer to Chapter 12 and remove the radio/cassette player.

**17** Remove the footwell side cowl trim panel on the driver's side by rotating the retaining clip at the front of the panel through 90°, then ease the panel away from the three tab fasteners at the rear edge.

**18** Pull free the weatherstrip from the leading edge of the door aperture each side. Undo the two screws and release the upper portion of the scuff plate from the area below the facia. Undo the retaining screw and remove the "A" pillar trim on each side.

**19** Undo the lower bolt and detach the earth lead from the cowl panel beneath the facia on the driver's side.

**20** Unclip and withdraw the fusebox from its location below the facia. Disconnect the three multi-plugs from the relay panel on top of the fusebox.

**21** Disconnect the two multi-plugs adjacent to the driver's side cowl panel.

**22** Detach the right-hand and left-hand heater control cables from the heater assembly.

**23** Remove the centre console as described in Section 36.

**24** Carefully prise up the trim covers over the three retaining screws along the upper edge of the facia, adjacent to the windscreen. Undo and remove the three screws now exposed.

**25** Carefully prise out the blanking plug from the upper edge of the radio aperture below the heater controls. Undo and remove the retaining screw now exposed.

**26** Undo the remaining retaining screws at each side of the facia and at the base below the ashtray housing.

**27** Detach the speedometer cable from the retaining clip on the bulkhead in the engine compartment.

**28** Move the gear lever to the rear and ease the facia from its location. When sufficient clearance exists, disconnect the speedometer cable from the instrument panel and the multi-plug from the air bag control module.

**29** With the aid of an assistant, manoeuvre the facia clear of the steering column and out from the driver's side of the car.

### Refitting

**30** Refitting is a reversal of the removal procedure. Ensure that all wiring and cables are correctly routed and securely reconnected. Refer to the appropriate Chapters for details on refitting the associated fittings to the facia panel.

**31** When the facia panel is completely refitted, reconnect the battery then test the various facia and steering column switches to ensure that they operate in a satisfactory manner.

## 36 Centre console - removal and refitting

### Removal

**Short console (manual transmission) - pre-1996 models**

**1** Unscrew and remove the knob from the gear lever, then prise free the lever gaiter and

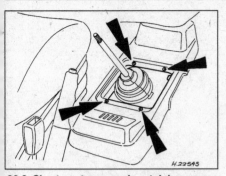

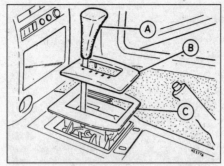

**36.2 Short centre console retaining screw locations (arrowed)**

**36.5 Automatic transmission selector lever knob (A), lever indicator panel (B) and panel bezel (C)**

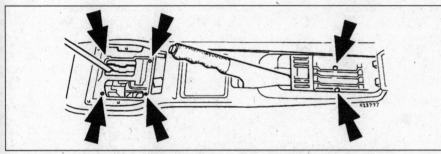

**36.7 Long centre console retaining nut and screw locations (arrowed) - automatic transmission console shown**

bezel. Slide the gaiter and bezel up the lever, and lift them off.
**2** Unscrew the four retaining screws, and remove the console **(see illustration)**.

**Long console (manual and automatic transmission) - pre-1996 models**

**3** Disconnect the battery negative (earth) lead (refer to Chapter 5A, Section 1).
**4** On manual transmission models, remove the knob from the gear lever, then prise free the lever gaiter and bezel. Slide the gaiter and bezel up the lever, and lift them off.
**5** On automatic transmission models, select "P" (Park). Unscrew and remove the knob from the lever, then prise free the lever indicator panel, followed by the bezel **(see illustration)**.
**6** On vehicles with electric windows or an electrically-operated luggage compartment lock, carefully prise out the switch panel or switch, and disconnect the wiring connectors.
**7** Undo the four console retaining nuts and two screws **(see illustration)**.
**8** Pull up the handbrake lever as far as possible, and manipulate the console over the handbrake lever and gear lever. If insufficient clearance exists, slacken the handbrake adjuster as described in Chapter 1.

**Long console (manual and automatic transmission) - 1996 models onward**

**9** Disconnect the battery negative (earth) lead (refer to Chapter 5A, Section 1).
**10** On manual transmission models, remove the knob from the gear lever, then prise free the lever gaiter and bezel. Slide the gaiter and bezel up the lever, and lift them off.

**11** On automatic transmission models, select "P" (Park). Unscrew and remove the knob from the lever, then prise free the lever indicator panel, followed by the bezel.
**12** Push the switch assembly (where fitted) out from the underside of the console, disconnect the multi-plugs and remove the assembly.
**13** Release the handbrake lever surround from the console and slide the surround and gaiter off the lever.
**14** Undo the four nuts and remove the gear lever floor gaiter and retaining plate. Recover the O-ring.
**15** Open the stowage box lid at the rear of the console and undo the screw in the stowage box floor. On models without a stowage box, prise off the trim cap and undo the screw now exposed.
**16** Pull up the handbrake lever as far as possible, lift the console up at the rear and

slide it rearwards to release it from the facia at the front. If insufficient clearance exists between the console and handbrake lever, slacken the handbrake adjuster as described in Chapter 1.
**17** Lift the console over the handbrake and gear lever and remove it from the car.

**Refitting**

**18** Refitting is a reversal of removal. Where it was necessary to slacken the handbrake adjustment for removal of the console, re-check the adjustment as described in Chapter 1.

## 37 Wheel arch liners - removal and refitting

**Removal**

**1** Apply the handbrake, then loosen off the front roadwheel nuts on the side concerned. Raise the vehicle at the front end, and support it on axle stands (see *"Jacking and vehicle support"*). Remove the roadwheel.
**2** Unscrew and remove the seven Torx-type retaining screws **(see illustration)**.
**3** Press the liner inwards at the top to disengage it from the locating tang, then withdraw it from the vehicle.

**Refitting**

**4** Refit in the reverse order of the removal procedure. Tighten the roadwheel nuts to the specified torque wrench setting.

## 38 Radiator grille - removal and refitting

**Removal**

**Pre-1993 models**

**1** Raise and support the bonnet. Unscrew and remove the four retaining screws along the top edge of the grille, then carefully lift the grille free, and disengage it from the locating socket each side at the bottom **(see illustration)**.

**1993 to 1996 models**

**2** Raise and support the bonnet. Undo the

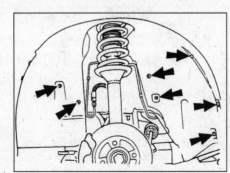

**37.2 Wheel arch liner retaining screw locations (arrowed)**

**38.1 Radiator (front) grille panel retaining screw removal - pre-1993 models**

**11**

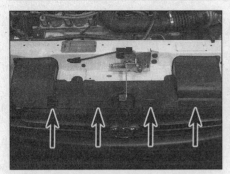

38.3 Air deflector top edge retaining screws (arrowed) - 1996 models onward

38.4 Radiator grille side retaining screw (arrowed) - 1996 models onward

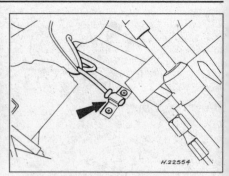

39.4 Cabriolet powered hood spring wire rod retainers

three nuts securing the grille to the inside of the bonnet, and lift off the grille.

### 1996 models onward

3 Raise and support the bonnet. Unscrew and remove the screws on the top face, release the upper and edge retaining studs and remove the air deflector (see illustration).
4 Undo the two screws (one each side) and remove the grille (see illustration).

### Refitting

5 Refit in the reverse order of removal.

### 39 Powered hood (Cabriolet models) - removal and refitting

Note: The following instructions detail the removal and refitting of the hood cover only. The removal, repair and refitting of the hood frame, insulation and headlining are specialised tasks, and must be entrusted to a Ford garage or an automotive upholstery specialist.

### Removal

1 Open the roof, then remove the rear seat cushion by prising free the blanking plugs and unscrewing the seat hinge screw each side.
2 Remove the rear quarter trim panel as described in Section 34.
3 Raise the roof just enough the allow access to the rear parcel shelf.
4 Disconnect the spring wire rod from the retainer on each side (see illustration).
5 Unscrew and remove the spring wire securing screw on each side.
6 Disconnect the spring wire from the housing at the other end on each side.
7 Detach the wiring from the heated rear window connectors.
8 Unscrew and remove the two hinge damper bolts on each side (see illustration), then fully open the roof.
9 Prise free the hydraulic rod securing clip, then unscrew and remove the three retaining bolts from the brackets (see illustration).
10 Enlist the aid of an assistant to help in removing the roof assembly from the car. Grip the roof and pull it towards the front to release it at the rear end, then carefully lift clear of the car.

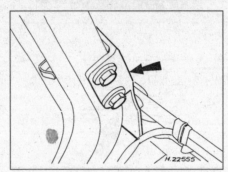

39.8 Cabriolet powered hood hinge damper (arrowed)

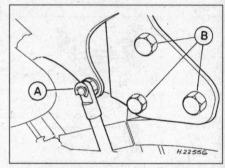

39.9 Cabriolet powered hood hydraulic rod
A Securing clip     B Retaining bolts

### Refitting

11 Refitting is a reversal of the removal procedure. When the roof assembly is fully reconnected, check that it operates in a satisfactory manner before refitting the rear quarter panel and seat cushion.

### 40 Powered hood system (Cabriolet) - hose removal, refitting and system bleeding

### Hose removal

1 Open the boot lid and lower the hood. Remove the appropriate trim panels to gain access to the pump (in the left-hand side of the luggage area) and the hydraulic ram

(located behind the rear quarter panel) on the side concerned.
2 Where more than one hose is to be detached from the pump, the respective hoses and their connections to the pump should be labelled and marked for correct identification, to avoid the possibility of confusion when reconnecting them (see illustrations).
3 Loosen off the fluid filler plug on the pump to depressurise the system.
4 Disconnect the hose(s) from the location tangs to the body, and the tape securing it to the ram and other hoses. Loosen off the hose-to-pump union(s), and detach the hose(s). Note that it may well be necessary to detach and partially remove the pump as described in Section 42 to enable a hose on the left-hand

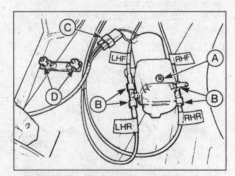

40.2a Hydraulic hose connections to the powered hood pump unit

A  Filler plug          C  Pump multi-plug
B  Hose unions and     D  Pump mounting
   markings

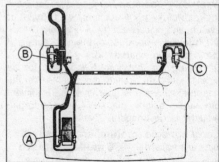

40.2b Cabriolet powered hood operating components and hydraulic hose routings

A  Hydraulic pump
B  Hydraulic ram (left-hand side)
C  Hydraulic ram (right-hand side)

side of the pump to be disconnected. Catch any spillage of hydraulic fluid in a suitable container, and plug the hose(s)/connection(s) to prevent the ingress of dirt. Note that the hood must not be raised whilst the hydraulic lines are disconnected, or hydraulic fluid remaining in the system will be ejected

### Hose refitting

**5** Refitting is a reversal of the removal procedure. When the hoses are reconnected, top-up and bleed the hydraulic system as follows.

### System bleeding

**6** Remove the fluid filler plug from the pump. Top-up the fluid level with the specified fluid type (see *Specifications*) to the "MAX" mark, then loosely retighten the plug. Unscrew and open the by-pass tap 90 to 180° (maximum), then manually raise and lower the hood once. Recheck the fluid level in the pump, top-up the level if required, tighten the by-pass tap and refit the filler plug **(see illustration)**.
**7** Turn the ignition switch to position "I" (accessory), then close and open the roof five times using the roof operating switch. At the end of this cycle, the roof should operate smoothly in each direction, and the pump motor should have a constant operating sound.
**8** With the roof in the open position, recheck the hydraulic fluid level in the pump, and top-up if required.

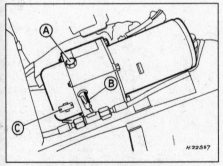

**40.6 Cabriolet powered hood hydraulic pump**

A  Filler plug    C  Fluid level
B  By-pass tap       MAX mark

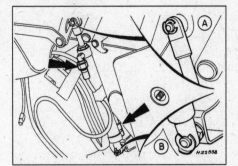

**41.4 Cabriolet powered hood hydraulic ram hose connections, showing the upper (A) and lower (B) mounting circlips**

### 41 Powered hood damper/ hydraulic ram (Cabriolet) - removal and refitting

#### Removal

**1** Lower the hood, then detach and remove the left-hand trim panel in the luggage area to gain access to the hydraulic pump.
**2** Depressurise the hydraulic system by loosening off the pump hydraulic fluid filler plug.
**3** Remove the rear quarter trim panel from the side concerned, as described in Section 34.
**4** Label the hoses and their connections to the hydraulic ram, to identify them for refitting **(see illustration)**.
**5** Release the circlips securing the ram at each end to its attachment points to the vehicle. Note that the lower securing point has the larger of the circlips.
**6** Loosen off the hydraulic hose union connectors to the ram, withdraw the ram from its mounting points, and hold it and the hydraulic connections over a suitable container. Detach the hydraulic hoses, and drain all of the fluid into the container before removing the ram. Use plugs to seal off the hoses and the hydraulic connections to the ram, so preventing the ingress of dirt and any further fluid leakage. Note that the hood must not be raised whilst the hydraulic lines are disconnected, or hydraulic fluid remaining in the system will be ejected.

#### Refitting

**7** Refitting is a reversal of the removal procedure. When the ram is refitted to its mountings and the hoses are reconnected to

it, top-up and bleed the hydraulic system as described in the previous Section, before refitting the quarter trim panel (Section 34) and the pump cover/side trim in the luggage area.

### 42 Powered hood motor and pump (Cabriolet) - removal and refitting

#### Removal

**1** Disconnect the battery negative (earth) lead (refer to Chapter 5A, Section 1).
**2** Open the boot lid, then detach and remove the left-hand side trim in the luggage area for access to the pump/motor.
**3** Unscrew the by-pass tap 90 to 180° **(see illustration 40.6)**.
**4** Lower the roof manually, then allow any residual pressure in the system to escape by loosening off the filler plug on the top of the pump.
**5** Retighten the filler plug and tap. Detach the wiring connector to the pump motor.
**6** Label the respective hoses and their connections to the pump for correct identification prior to detaching them, to avoid any possibility of confusion when reconnecting them **(see illustration 40.2a)**.
**7** Undo the pump retaining nuts, then partially withdraw the pump. Locate a suitable container (or some rags) beneath it, then unscrew the hydraulic hose unions and detach the hoses from the pump. Plug the exposed ends of the pump and hoses, to prevent the ingress of dirt and further fluid leakage. Remove the pump. Note that the hood must not be raised whilst the hydraulic lines and pump are disconnected, or hydraulic fluid remaining in the system will be ejected.

#### Refitting

**8** Ensure that the hose connections are clean, then reconnect the hoses to the pump, hand-tightening them at this stage.
**9** Reconnect the pump motor wiring connection, relocate the pump into position, and tighten its retaining nuts. Check that the hoses are not distorted or under undue tension, then fully tighten their unions.
**10** Top-up the pump with the specified hydraulic fluid, and bleed the system as described in Section 40.
**11** Reconnect the battery earth lead.

# Chapter 12
# Body electrical systems

## Contents

## Degrees of difficulty

| Easy, suitable for novice with little experience  | Fairly easy, suitable for beginner with some experience  | Fairly difficult, suitable for competent DIY mechanic ⚒ | Difficult, suitable for experienced DIY mechanic ⚒ | Very difficult, suitable for expert DIY or professional ⚒ |
|---|---|---|---|---|

## Specifications

### Fuses (in vehicle fusebox) - pre-1996 models

**Note:** *Fuse ratings and circuits may change from year to year. Consult the vehicle handbook or consult a Ford dealer for specific information.*

| No | Rating (amps) | Circuit(s) protected |
|---|---|---|
| 1 | 25 | Heated rear window, adjustable door mirrors |
| 2 | 30 | Anti-lock braking system |
| 3 | 10 | Oxygen sensor |
| 4 | 15 | Right-hand main beam, right-hand auxiliary light |
| 5 | 20 | Fuel pump |
| 6 | 10 | Right-hand sidelight |
| 7 | 10 | Left-hand sidelight |
| 8 | 10 | Rear foglight |
| 9 | 30 | Radiator cooling fan |
| 10 | 10 | Left-hand dip beam |
| 11 | 15 | Front foglights |
| 12 | 10 | Direction indicator, reversing lights |
| 13 | 20 | Wiper motor, washer pump |
| 14 | 20 | Heater blower |
| 15 | 30 | Anti-lock braking system |
| 16 | 3 | Heated windscreen |
| 17 | - | - |
| 18 | 15 | Left-hand main beam, left-hand auxiliary light |
| 19* | 20 | Central locking system, anti- theft alarm, electric door mirrors |
| 19** | 3 | ABS module |
| 20 | 15 | Horn |
| 21 | 15 | Interior lights, clock, radio, cigar lighter |
| 22 | 30 | Electric windows |
| 23 | 30 | Headlight washer system |
| 24 | 10 | Right-hand dip beam |
| 25 | 3 | EEC IV engine management system |
| 26 | 5 | Heated front seats |
| 27 | 10 | Brake stop-lights |
| 28 | 10 | Air conditioning system |
| 29** | 20 | Central locking system, anti-theft alarm |

*\* Early models*
*\*\* Later models*

**12**

## Fuses (in vehicle fusebox) - 1996 and 1997 models

**Note:** *Fuse ratings and circuits may change from year to year. Consult the vehicle handbook or consult a Ford dealer for specific information.*

| No | Rating (amps) | Circuit(s) protected |
|----|----|----|
| 1 | 10 | Rear foglights |
| 2 | - | - |
| 3 | 10 | Right-hand sidelights |
| 4 | - | - |
| 5 | 15 | Left-hand main beam |
| 6 | 10 | Right-hand main beam, right-hand auxiliary light |
| 7 | 3 | EEC IV engine management system |
| 8 | 10 | Left-hand sidelights |
| 9 | 30 | Anti-lock braking system |
| 10 | 30 | Headlight washer system |
| 11 | 10 | Illumination and warning lights |
| 12 | 7.5 | Air bag |
| 13 | 20 | Cold start valve, engine management system, fuel shut off |
| 14 | 10 | Oxygen sensor |
| 15 | 10 | Left-hand dip beam |
| 16 | 20 | Ignition coil |
| 17 | 10 | Right-hand dip beam |
| 18 | 30 | Electric windows and sunroof |
| 19 | - | - |
| 20 | 25 | Heater blower |
| 21 | 3 | ABS module |
| 22 | 30 | Radiator cooling fan |
| 23 | 15 | Heated front seats |
| 24 | 20 | Wiper motor, washer pump |
| 25 | 30 | Anti-lock braking system |
| 26 | 10 | Direction indicator, reversing lights |
| 27 | 25 | Heated rear window, adjustable door mirrors |
| 28 | 15 | Horn, hazard flasher |
| 29 | 15 | Interior lights, clock, radio, cigar lighter |
| 30 | 20 | Central locking system, electrically adjustable seats |
| 31 | 15 | Front fog lights |
| 32 | 15 | Air conditioning system |
| 33 | 20 | Fuel pump |
| 34 | 15 | Heated washer jets, brake stop lights |

## Fuses (in vehicle fusebox) - 1998 models onward

**Note:** *Fuse ratings and circuits may change from year to year. Consult the vehicle handbook or consult a Ford dealer for specific information.*

| No | Rating (amps) | Circuit(s) protected |
|----|----|----|
| 1 | 30 | Starter solenoid |
| 2 | 25 | Heater blower, air conditioning compressor clutch |
| 3 | 15 | Headlight switch |
| 4 | 10 | Right-hand sidelights |
| 5 | 15 | Left-hand main beam |
| 6 | 15 | Right-hand main beam |
| 7 | 10 | Left-hand sidelights, auxiliary driving light |
| 8 | 7.5 | EEC IV/V engine management system |
| 9 | 20 | Anti-lock braking system |
| 10 | 30 | Headlight washer system |
| 11 | 7.5 | Air bag |
| 12 | 10 | Illumination and warning lights, main beam switch |
| 13 | - | - |
| 14 | 15 | Fuel pump |
| 15 | 10 | Oxygen sensor |
| 16 | 20 | Cold start valve, engine management system |
| 17 | 15 | Heated front seats |
| 18 | 15 | Supplemtary audio equipment |
| 19 | 30 | Electric front windows, sunroof |
| 20 | 30 | Radiator/air conditioning cooling fan |
| 21 | 7.5 | ABS module |
| 22 | 20 | Ignition coil |
| 23 | 25 | Electric rear windows |
| 24 | 30 | Anti-lock braking system |
| 25 | 20 | Wiper motor, washer pump |
| 26 | 10 | Direction indicator, reversing lights |
| 27 | 25 | Heated rear window, electric door mirrors |
| 28 | 15 | Horn, hazard flasher |

| No | Rating | | Circuit |
|----|--------|---|---------|
| 29 | 15 | .......................................... | Interior lights, clock, radio, cigar lighter |
| 30 | 10 | .......................................... | Left-hand dip beam |
| 31 | 10 | .......................................... | Right-hand dip beam |
| 32 | 15 | .......................................... | Front fog lights |
| 33 | 20 | .......................................... | Electrically operated seats |
| 34 | 15 | .......................................... | Heated washer jets, brake stop lights |
| 35* | 20 | .......................................... | Central locking |

*Auxiliary fuse located on the outside of the fusebox.

## Additional fuses (in engine compartment) - all models

**Note:** Fuse ratings and circuits may change from year to year. Consult the vehicle handbook or consult a Ford dealer for specific information.

| No | Rating (amps) | | Circuit(s) protected |
|----|--------------|---|---------------------|
| A | 80 | .......................................... | Supply cables to main fuse block |
| B | 60 | .......................................... | Supply cables to main fuse block |
| C | 60 | .......................................... | Supply cables to main fuse block |
| D | 40/50 | .......................................... | Radiator/air conditioning cooling fan relay |
| E | 50 | .......................................... | Heated windscreen/rear window relay |

## Relays (pre-1996 models)

| No | Colour | | Circuit |
|----|--------|---|---------|
| R1 | Grey | .......................................... | Heated windscreen |
| R2 | Red | .......................................... | Windscreen wiper intermittent control |
| R3 | Grey | .......................................... | Heated rear windscreen |
| R4 | Dark green | .......................................... | Anti-lock braking (system) |
| R5 | Violet | .......................................... | Anti-lock braking (pump) |
| R6 | White/Yellow | .......................................... | Main beam |
| R7 | Orange | .......................................... | Rear wiper intermittent control |
| R8 | Green/Red/Yellow | .......................................... | CFi delay relay or EFi supply relay or EEC IV supply relay |
| R9 | Brown | .......................................... | Fuel pump |
| 10 | Brown | .......................................... | Magnetic clutch (air conditioning system) |
| 11 | Green | .......................................... | Air conditioning system |
| 12 | Brown | .......................................... | Engine running |
| 13 | - | | |
| 14 | - | | |
| 15 | - | | |
| 16* | - | | |
| 16** | Violet | .......................................... | Fuel pump |
| 17 | Yellow | .......................................... | Interior light delay |
| 18 | Green | .......................................... | Electric windows |
| 19 | Grey | .......................................... | Rear foglight (module) |
| 20 | Spare | | |
| 21 | - / White | .......................................... | Busbar/front foglights (module) |
| 22 | Blue | .......................................... | Headlight washer system |
| 23 | White | .......................................... | Dip beam |
| 24 | - / Red or Yellow | .......................................... | Busbar/automatic transmission/alarm |
| 25 | White | .......................................... | Front foglights |
| 26 | Black | .......................................... | Steering lock/starter switch |
| 27 | - | | |

* Early models
** Later models

## Relays (1996 and 1997 models)

| No | Colour | | Circuit |
|----|--------|---|---------|
| R1 | Black | .......................................... | Ignition lock |
| R2 | Brown | .......................................... | Fuel injection, engine management |
| R3 | Brown | .......................................... | Fuel pump |
| R4 | Brown | .......................................... | Magnetic clutch (air conditioning system) |
| R5 | Grey | .......................................... | Heated mirrors/rear window timer |
| R6 | Red | .......................................... | Windscreen wiper intermittent control |
| R7 | Orange | .......................................... | Rear wiper intermittent control |
| R8 | Brown | .......................................... | Dip beam |
| R9 | Brown | .......................................... | Main beam |
| R10 | Brown | .......................................... | Main beam (right-hand drive only) |
| R11 | Yellow | .......................................... | Interior light delay |
| R12 | Grey | .......................................... | Rear foglights |
| R13 | Yellow | .......................................... | Starter inhibitor |
| R14 | White | .......................................... | Front foglight control |

**12**

## Relays (1996 and 1997 models) (continued)

| No | Colour | Circuit |
|----|--------|---------|
| R15 | Brown | Front foglight supply |
| R16 | Blue | Headlight washer system |
| R17 | Blue | Air conditioning system |
| R18 | - | |
| R19 | - | |
| R20 | - | |
| R21 | Violet | Anti-lock braking system |
| R22 | Dark green | Anti-lock braking system |

## Relays (1998 models onward)

| No | Colour | Circuit |
|----|--------|---------|
| R1 | Black | Ignition lock |
| R2 | Brown | Fuel injection, engine management |
| R3 | Brown | Fuel pump |
| R4 | Brown | Magnetic clutch (air conditioning system) |
| R5 | Grey | Heated mirrors/rear window timer |
| R6 | Red | Windscreen wiper intermittent control |
| R7 | Orange | Rear wiper intermittent control |
| R8 | Brown | Dip beam |
| R9 | Brown | Main beam |
| R10 | - | |
| R11 | Yellow | Interior light delay |
| R12 | - | |
| R13 | Green | Starter inhibitor |
| R14 | White | 'Lights-on' audible warning |
| R15 | Brown | Front foglights |
| R16 | Blue | Headlight washer system |
| R17 | Blue/brown | Air conditioning system |
| R18 | - | |
| R19 | Brown | Rear foglights |
| R20 | - | |
| R21 | - | |
| R22 | White | Anti-theft alarm system |

## Bulbs

| | Wattage |
|---|---------|
| Headlights (halogen H4) | 60/55 |
| Sidelights | 5 |
| Front indicator lights | 21 |
| Side indicator repeater lights | 5 |
| Tail lights (Hatchback/Saloon) | 5 |
| Brake stop lights (Hatchback/Saloon) | 21 |
| Brake stop/tail lights (Estate/Van) | 21/5 |
| High-level stop light | 5 |
| Reversing lights | 21 |
| Rear direction indicators | 21 |
| Rear foglights | 21 |
| Rear number plate light (Hatchback/Saloon/Estate) | 10 |
| Rear number plate light (Van) | 5 |
| Instrument panel warning lights | 1.3 |
| Hazard warning light switch bulb | 1.3 |
| Instrument panel illumination bulb | 2.6 |
| Clock illumination bulb | 1.2 |
| Cigar lighter illumination bulb | 1.4 |
| Glovebox illumination light bulb | 10 |
| Luggage area illumination bulb | 10 |
| Courtesy light | 10 |

## Torque wrench settings

| | Nm | lbf ft |
|---|----|--------|
| Wiper motor (original) to mounting bracket | 10 | 7 |
| Wiper motor (new) to mounting bracket | 12 | 9 |
| Wiper motor bracket to bulkhead (or tailgate) | 7 | 5 |
| Wiper motor arm-to-spindle nut | 24 | 18 |
| Wiper arm nut | 20 | 15 |
| Horn-to-body retaining nuts | 30 | 22 |

## 1  General information and precautions

### General information

The electrical system is of 12-volt negative earth type. Power for the lights and all electrical accessories is supplied by a lead/acid battery, which is charged by the engine-driven alternator.

This Chapter covers repair and service procedures for the various electrical components not associated with the engine. Information on the battery, ignition system, alternator, and starter motor can be found in Chapter 5, Parts A and B.

It should be noted that, prior to working on any component in the electrical system, the battery negative lead should first be disconnected, to prevent the possibility of electrical short-circuits and/or fires. If a radio/cassette player with anti-theft security code is fitted, refer to the information given in the reference sections of this manual before disconnecting the battery.

### Precautions

 *Warning: Before carrying out any work on the electrical system, read through the precautions given in "Safety first!" at the beginning of this manual and in Chapter 5A, Section 1.*

 *Warning: Later models are equipped with an air bag system. When working on the electrical system, refer to the precautions given in Section 29, to avoid the possibility of personal injury.*

## 2  Electrical fault-finding - general information

**Note:** *Refer to the precautions given in "Safety first!" and in Section 1 of this Chapter before starting work. The following tests relate to testing of the main electrical circuits, and should not be used to test delicate electronic circuits (such as engine management systems, anti-lock braking systems, etc), particularly where an electronic control unit is used.*

### General

1  A typical electrical circuit consists of an electrical component, any switches, relays, motors, fuses, fusible links or circuit breakers related to that component, and the wiring and connectors which link the component to both the battery and the chassis. To help to pinpoint a problem in an electrical circuit, wiring diagrams are included at the end of this manual.
2  Before attempting to diagnose an electrical fault, first study the appropriate wiring diagram, to obtain a more complete understanding of the components included in the particular circuit concerned. The possible sources of a fault can be narrowed down by noting whether other components related to the circuit are operating properly. If several components or circuits fail at one time, the problem is likely to be related to a shared fuse or earth connection.
3  Electrical problems usually stem from simple causes, such as loose or corroded connections, a faulty earth connection, a blown fuse, a melted fusible link, or a faulty relay. Visually inspect the condition of all fuses, wires and connections in a problem circuit before testing the components. Use the wiring diagrams to determine which terminal connections will need to be checked, in order to pinpoint the trouble-spot.
4  The basic tools required for electrical fault-finding include a circuit tester or voltmeter (a 12-volt bulb with a set of test leads can also be used for certain tests); a self-powered test light (sometimes known as a continuity tester); an ohmmeter (to measure resistance); a battery and set of test leads; and a jumper wire, preferably with a circuit breaker or fuse incorporated, which can be used to bypass suspect wires or electrical components. Before attempting to locate a problem with test instruments, use the wiring diagram to determine where to make the connections.
5  To find the source of an intermittent wiring fault (usually due to a poor or dirty connection, or damaged wiring insulation), a "wiggle" test can be performed on the wiring. This involves wiggling the wiring by hand, to see if the fault occurs as the wiring is moved. It should be possible to narrow down the source of the fault to a particular section of wiring. This method of testing can be used in conjunction with any of the tests described in the following sub-Sections.
6  Apart from problems due to poor connections, two basic types of fault can occur in an electrical circuit - open-circuit, or short-circuit.
7  Open-circuit faults are caused by a break somewhere in the circuit, which prevents current from flowing. An open-circuit fault will prevent a component from working, but will not cause the relevant circuit fuse to blow.
8  Short-circuit faults are normally caused by a breakdown in wiring insulation, which allows a feed wire to touch either another wire, or an earthed component such as the bodyshell. This allows the current flowing in the circuit to "escape" along an alternative route, usually to earth. As the circuit does not now follow its original complete path, it is known as a "short" circuit. A short-circuit fault will normally cause the relevant circuit fuse to blow.

### Finding an open-circuit

9  To check for an open-circuit, connect one lead of a circuit tester or voltmeter to either the negative battery terminal or a known good earth.
10  Connect the other lead to a connector in the circuit being tested, preferably nearest to the battery or fuse.
11  Switch on the circuit, bearing in mind that some circuits are live only when the ignition switch is moved to a particular position.
12  If voltage is present (indicated either by the tester bulb lighting or a voltmeter reading, as applicable), this means that the section of the circuit between the relevant connector and the battery is problem-free.
13  Continue to check the remainder of the circuit in the same fashion.
14  When a point is reached at which no voltage is present, the problem must lie between that point and the previous test point with voltage. Most problems can be traced to a broken, corroded or loose connection.

### Finding a short-circuit

15  To check for a short-circuit, first disconnect the load(s) from the circuit (loads are the components which draw current from a circuit, such as bulbs, motors, heating elements, etc).
16  Remove the relevant fuse from the circuit, and connect a circuit tester or voltmeter to the fuse connections.
17  Switch on the circuit, bearing in mind that some circuits are live only when the ignition switch is moved to a particular position.
18  If voltage is present (indicated either by the tester bulb lighting or a voltmeter reading, as applicable), this means that there is a short-circuit.
19  If no voltage is present, but the fuse still blows with the load(s) connected, this indicates an internal fault in the load(s).

### Finding an earth fault

20  The battery negative terminal is connected to "earth" - the metal of the engine/transmission and the car body - and most systems are wired so that they only receive a positive feed, the current returning via the metal of the car body. This means that the component mounting and the body form part of that circuit. Loose or corroded mountings can therefore cause a range of electrical faults, ranging from total failure of a circuit, to a puzzling partial fault. In particular, lights may shine dimly (especially when another circuit sharing the same earth point is in operation), motors (eg wiper motors or the radiator cooling fan motor) may run slowly, and the operation of one circuit may have an apparently-unrelated effect on another. Note that earth straps are used between certain components, such as the engine/transmission and the body, usually where there is no metal-to-metal contact between components, due to flexible rubber mountings, etc.
21  To check whether a component is properly earthed, disconnect the battery, and connect one lead of an ohmmeter to a known good earth point. Connect the other lead to the wire or earth connection being tested. The resistance reading should be zero; if not, check the connection as follows.
22  If an earth connection is thought to be faulty, dismantle the connection, and clean back to bare metal both the bodyshell and the wire terminal or the component earth

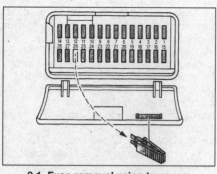

**3.1 Fuse removal using tweezers**

**3.4 Additional "main" fuses at the front of the battery**

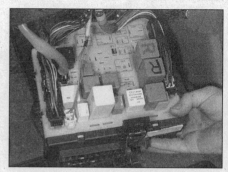

**3.6 Relay locations on the underside of the fuse board**

connection mating surface. Be careful to remove all traces of dirt and corrosion, then use a knife to trim away any paint, so that a clean metal-to-metal joint is made. On reassembly, tighten the joint fasteners securely; if a wire terminal is being refitted, use serrated washers between the terminal and the bodyshell, to ensure a clean and secure connection. When the connection is remade, prevent the onset of corrosion in the future by applying a coat of petroleum jelly or silicone-based grease, or by spraying on (at regular intervals) a proprietary ignition sealer or water-dispersant lubricant.

## 3 Fuses and relays - general information

**Note:** *It is important to note that the ignition switch and the appropriate electrical circuit must always be switched off before any of the fuses (or relays) are removed and renewed. In the event of the fuse/relay having to be removed, the vehicle anti-theft system must be de-activated and the battery earth lead detached. When disconnecting the battery, refer to Chapter 5A, Section 1.*

1 The main fuse and relay block is located below the facia panel on the driver's side within the vehicle. The fuses can be inspected and if necessary renewed, by unclipping and removing the access cover. Each fuse location is numbered - refer to the fuse chart in the *Specifications* at the start of this Chapter to check which circuits are protected by each fuse. Plastic tweezers are attached to the inside face of the cover to remove and fit the fuses **(see illustration)**.

2 To remove a fuse, use the tweezers provided to pull it out of the holder. Slide the fuse sideways from the tweezers. The wire within the fuse is clearly visible, and it will be broken if the fuse is blown.

3 Always renew a fuse with one of an identical rating. Never renew a fuse more than once without tracing the source of the trouble. The fuse rating is stamped on top of the fuse.

4 Additional "main" fuses are located separately in a box positioned in front of the battery and these are accessible for inspection by first raising and supporting the bonnet, then unclipping and hinging back the cover from the

fusebox **(see illustration)**. Each of these fuses is lettered for identification - refer to the *Specifications* at the start of this Chapter to check which circuits they protect. To remove fuses A, B and C, it is first necessary to remove the fusebox. Fuses D and E can be removed from their locations by carefully pulling them free from the location socket in the box. In the event of one of these fuses blowing, it is essential that the circuits concerned are checked and any faults rectified before renewing the faulty fuse. If necessary, entrust this task to a Ford dealer or a competent automotive electrician.

5 With the exception of the indicator flasher relay and where applicable, the Cabriolet powered roof relays, the remainder of the relays are fitted to the reverse side of the "in-vehicle" fuse board. To inspect a relay mounted on the main fuse board, disconnect the battery, remove the fusebox cover and unclip the fusebox. Unscrew the six securing screws to detach and remove the lower facia panel on the driver's side. Carefully withdraw the fuse/relay block.

6 The various relays can be removed from their respective locations on the fuse board by carefully pulling them from the sockets **(see illustration)**.

7 The direction indicator flasher relay is attached to the base of the multi-function switch unit. Access to the relay is made by undoing the retaining screws and removing the steering column lower shroud. The relay can then be withdrawn from the base of the switch **(see illustration)**.

8 The Cabriolet powered roof system has four relays. Relays I and II (and a thermal cut-out) are located behind the A-pillar on the driver's side,

relays III and IV (together with a 15 amp fuse) are located in the left-hand side of the luggage area, next to the powered roof hydraulic pump. Removal of the appropriate trim panel and where applicable, the associated components, gives access to the relay(s) for inspection and renewal (refer to Chapter 11).

9 If a system controlled by a relay becomes inoperative and the relay is suspect, listen to the relay as the circuit is operated. If the relay is functioning, it should be possible to hear it click as it is energised. If the relay proves satisfactory, the fault lies with the components or wiring of the system. If the relay is not being energised, then it is not receiving a main supply voltage or a switching voltage, or the relay is faulty.

## 4 Switches - removal and refitting

### Ignition switch

1 Disconnect the battery negative (earth) lead (refer to Chapter 5A, Section 1).

2 Undo the two upper and four lower retaining screws, and remove the upper and lower shrouds from the steering column.

3 Where applicable, undo the single screw and withdraw the Passive Anti-Theft System (PATS) transceiver from the ignition switch/steering lock barrel.

4 Insert the key and turn the ignition switch to position "I". Depress the two ignition switch-to-lock securing tabs, and withdraw the switch from the lock **(see illustrations)**.

**3.7 Direction indicator flasher relay removal**

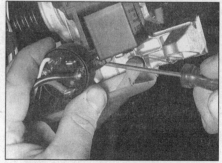

**4.4a Depress the lock tabs . . .**

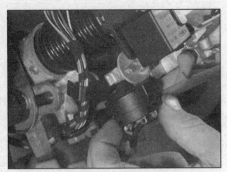
4.4b . . . and remove the ignition switch

4.9a Undo the retaining screw . . .

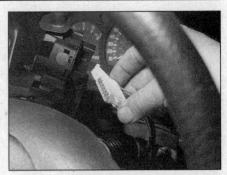
4.9b . . . lift the switch clear and detach the wiring connector

**5** Undo the six retaining screws, and remove the lower facia panel on the driver's side. Unclip the fusebox panel, then detach the ignition switch wiring multi-plug connector from the fusebox. Release the switch wire from the tie clips and remove the switch.

**6** Refitting is a reversal of the removal procedure. When relocating the switch to the steering lock, the barrel driveshaft must align with the switch shaft as it is pushed into position. Check the switch for satisfactory operation on completion.

### Steering column multi-function switch

**7** Remove the steering wheel as described in Chapter 10.

**8** Undo the two upper and four lower retaining screws, and remove the upper and lower steering column shrouds.

**9** Undo the single retaining screw, and withdraw the switch upwards from the steering column. Detach the wiring connector and cable-tie clips from the switch **(see illustrations)**.

**10** Separate the indicator/hazard warning relay and switch from the indicator switch unit.

**11** Refit in the reverse order of removal. Refer to Chapter 10 for information required when refitting the steering wheel.

### Facia switches

**12** Disconnect the battery negative (earth) lead (refer to Chapter 5A, Section 1).

**13** The facia and associated panel-mounted switches are secured in position by integral plastic or metal retaining clips. In some

instances, it is possible to release the switch from the panel using a suitable small screwdriver inserted between the switch and the facia to lever the switch from its aperture, but take care not to apply too much force when trying this method.

> **HAYNES HiNT**
> *Where a switch is reluctant to be released, remove the section of the facia panel or the adjoining panel or component to allow access to the rear side of the switch and compress the retaining clips to enable the switch to be withdrawn.*

**14** Once the switch is released and partially withdrawn from the panel, detach the wiring connector and remove the switch **(see illustration)**.

**15** Refitting is a reversal of removal.

### Courtesy light switches

**16** Disconnect the battery negative (earth) lead (refer to Chapter 5A, Section 1).

**17** With the door open, undo the retaining screw and withdraw the switch from the door pillar. Pull out the wiring slightly, and tie a piece of string to it, so that it can be retrieved if it drops down into the door pillar.

**18** Disconnect the wiring from the switch.

**19** Refitting is a reversal of removal.

### Luggage area contact plate

**20** Disconnect the battery negative (earth) lead (refer to Chapter 5A, Section 1).

**21** Open the tailgate, undo the two securing screws and remove the rear trim panel to gain access to the rear side of the plate.

**22** Release the side retaining clips using a thin-bladed screwdriver, and push the contact plate from its location in the body **(see illustration)**.

**23** Disconnect the wiring connectors and remove the plate.

**24** Refit in the reverse order of removal.

### Luggage area contact switch

**25** Disconnect the battery negative (earth) lead (refer to Chapter 5A, Section 1).

**26** Open the tailgate and remove its inner trim panel.

**27** Working through the access aperture in the tailgate, use a thin-bladed screwdriver to depress the switch retaining clips and extract the switch from the panel **(see illustration)**.

**28** Disconnect the wiring connectors and remove the switch.

**29** Refit in the reverse order of removal. Make sure that the pins and their contacts are clean. On completion, check the operation of the rear wipers, courtesy light, heated rear window and the tailgate release/central locking system.

### Handbrake warning light switch (pre-1996 models)

**30** Disconnect the battery negative (earth) lead (refer to Chapter 5A, Section 1).

**31** Refer to Chapter 11 for details, and remove the front passenger (left-hand) seat and the centre console.

4.14 Facia switch removal

4.22 Luggage area contact plate removal from the rear panel

4.27 Contact switch unit in the tailgate

4.32 Handbrake warning light switch

4.39 Brake stop-light switch location

**32** Detach the wiring connector from the handbrake warning light switch, then undo the two retaining screws and remove the switch **(see illustration)**.
**33** Refit in the reverse order of removal. Check that the switch operates in a satisfactory manner before refitting the console and seat.

### Handbrake warning light switch (1996 models onward)

**34** Disconnect the battery negative (earth) lead (refer to Chapter 5A, Section 1).
**35** Carefully prise up the gaiter and trim surround from the handbrake lever.
**36** Disconnect the multi-plug, undo the screw and remove the switch from the lever.
**37** Refit in the reverse order of removal.

### Brake stop-light switch

**38** Disconnect the battery negative (earth) lead (refer to Chapter 5A, Section 1).
**39** The brake stop-light switch is attached to the brake pedal mounting bracket **(see illustration)**.
**40** Detach the wiring connector from the switch, then twist the switch through a quarter of a turn (90°) and withdraw it from the bracket **(see illustration)**.
**41** Insert the switch into its locating slot in the pedal bracket.
**42** Support the brake pedal in the "at rest" position and push the switch down until the switch plunger is fully in.
**43** Turn the switch through 40° to back it off 1.0 mm and lock it in position.
**44** Reconnect the wiring and the battery and test the switch operation.

4.40 Brake stop-light switch removal

### Heater/blower motor switch (pre-1996 models)

**45** Disconnect the battery negative (earth) lead (refer to Chapter 5A, Section 1).
**46** Carefully prise free the three heater/fresh air and blower/air conditioning switch control knobs.
**47** Unscrew and remove the two instrument bezel retaining screws, and remove the bezel.
**48** Undo the four screws, and remove the heater panel facia. Detach the wiring connector to the heater panel illumination bulb.
**49** Compress the switch tabs to pull free the switch, then detach the wiring multi-plug from the switch **(see illustration)**.
**50** Refit in the reverse order of removal.

### Heater/blower motor switch (1996 models onward)

**51** Disconnect the battery negative (earth) lead (refer to Chapter 5A, Section 1).
**52** Undo the two retaining screws, and remove the upper steering column shroud.
**53** Similarly, undo the four screws and remove the lower steering column shroud.
**54** Refer to Chapter 10 and remove the steering wheel.
**55** Carefully prise free the three heater/fresh air and blower/air conditioning switch control knobs.
**56** Undo the two retaining screws from the underside top edge of the instrument panel bezel and withdraw the bezel. Disconnect the wiring multi-plugs and remove the bezel.
**57** Compress the switch tabs to pull free the

4.49 Heater blower motor switch removal - pre-1996 models

switch, then detach the wiring multi-plug from the switch.
**58** Refit in the reverse order of removal.

### Electric window switches

**59** Disconnect the battery negative (earth) lead (refer to Chapter 5A, Section 1).
**60** On pre-1996 models, insert a thin-bladed screwdriver between the switch and the console, then carefully prise free the switch from its location. If the switch is reluctant to release, do not apply excessive force; remove the centre console (see Chapter 11 for details) and release the switch from the underside.
**61** On 1996 models, carefully prise up the gaiter and trim surround from the base of the gear lever.
**62** Detach the wire connector from the switch, and remove it.
**63** Refit in the reverse order of removal, then check the switch for satisfactory operation.

### Electric door mirror switch

**64** Disconnect the battery negative (earth) lead (refer to Chapter 5A, Section 1).
**65** Carefully prise free the switch using a thin-bladed screwdriver as a lever, but insert a suitable protective pad between the screwdriver and the housing to avoid damage.
**66** Detach the wiring multi-plug connector and remove the switch.
**67** Refit in the reverse order of removal, then adjust the mirror and check that the operation of the switch is satisfactory.

### Headlight beam adjuster switch

**68** Refer to Section 9.

### Powered roof switch (Cabriolet)

**69** This switch is removed in the same manner as that described for the electric window switches in paragraphs 59 to 63 above.

### Starter inhibitor switch (automatic transmission)

**70** Disconnect the battery negative (earth) lead (refer to Chapter 5A, Section 1).
**71** The starter inhibitor switch is located on the transmission housing, and prevents the engine from being started with the selector lever in any position except "P" or "N". Access to the switch is gained after raising and supporting the vehicle at the front end on axle stands (see *"Jacking and vehicle support"*).
**72** Detach the switch multi-plug, then unscrew and remove the switch from the transmission, together with its O-ring. As the switch is removed, catch any fluid spillage in a suitable container, and plug the switch aperture in the transmission to prevent any further loss.
**73** Refitting is a reversal of the removal procedure. Use a new O-ring, and tighten the switch securely. Ensure that the wiring connection is securely made. On completion, check that the engine only starts when the selector is in the "P" or "N" position.

**5.1 On 1996 models onward, remove the cover from the rear of the headlight**

**5.2a Headlight bulb wiring connector on pre-1996 models . . .**

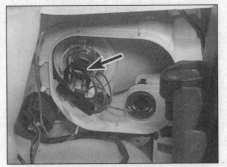

**5.2b . . . and on 1996 models onward (arrowed)**

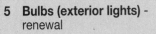

## 5 Bulbs (exterior lights) - renewal

**Note:** *Ensure all exterior lights are switched off before disconnecting the wiring connectors to any exterior light bulbs. The headlight and front sidelight bulbs are removable from within the engine compartment with the bonnet raised. Note that if a bulb fails, and has just been in use, it will still be extremely hot, particularly in the case of a headlight bulb.*

**5.2c Remove the rubber protector cap on pre-1996 models**

**5.3 . . . compress the clips . . .**

### *Headlight*

**1** On 1996 models onward, release the spring clip and remove the cover from the rear of the headlight unit **(see illustration)**.
**2** Pull free the wiring connector from the rear of the headlight on the side concerned. On pre-1996 models, prise free the protector cap from the rear of the headlight unit **(see illustrations)**.
**3** Compress the bulb retaining wire clips and pivot them out of the way **(see illustration)**.
*Caution: Take care not to touch the bulb glass with your fingers - if accidentally touched, clean the bulb with methylated spirit.*
**4** Withdraw the bulb from its location in the headlight **(see illustration)**.
**5** Fit the new bulb using a reversal of the removal procedure. Make sure that the tabs

on the bulb support are correctly located in the lens assembly.
**6** Check the headlight beam alignment as described in Section 8.

### *Front sidelight*

#### All models except XR3i

**7** On 1996 models onward, release the spring clip and remove the cover from the rear of the headlight unit.
**8** On pre-1996 models, compress the wire retaining clip, and detach the wiring connector from the sidelight **(see illustration)**.
**9** Pull free the sidelight bulbholder from its location in the rear of the headlight **(see illustration)**.
**10** Remove the bulb from the bulbholder.
**11** Fit the new bulb using a reversal of the removal procedure. Check for satisfactory operation on completion.

#### XR3i models

**12** Unhook the retaining spring from the rear of the sidelight, and move the sidelight forwards in order to release it.
**13** Turn the bulbholder and pull it free from the sidelight (do not pull on the wire).
**14** Depress and twist the bulb to remove it from the bulbholder.
**15** Fit the new bulb using a reversal of the removal procedure. As the light is fitted into position, engage its tags in the slots of the headlight unit. Check for satisfactory operation on completion.

### *Front direction indicator*

#### Pre-1996 models except XR3i

**16** Unhook the retaining spring from the rear of the direction indicator, and move the

**5.4 . . . and withdraw the headlight bulb**

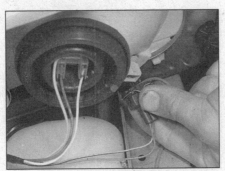

**5.8 Detach the wiring connector from the sidelight bulb on pre-1996 models**

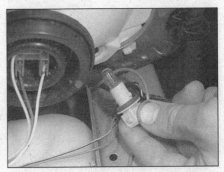

**5.9 Removing the sidelight bulbholder**

**12**

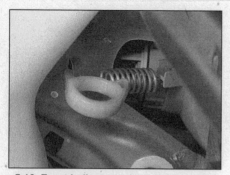

5.16 Front indicator unit retaining spring

5.18 Front indicator bulb renewal on pre-1996 models

5.19 Engage the tags in their locating slots when refitting the front indicator unit

direction indicator forwards in order to release it (see illustration).

17 Turn the direction indicator bulbholder and pull it free from the indicator (do not pull on the wire).

18 Depress and twist the bulb to remove it from the bulbholder (see illustration).

19 Fit the new bulb using a reversal of the removal procedure. As the light is fitted into position, engage its tags in the slots of the headlight (see illustration). Check for satisfactory operation on completion.

### 1996 models onward

20 Turn the direction indicator bulbholder anticlockwise and withdraw it from the rear of the headlight unit.

21 Depress and twist the bulb to remove it from the bulbholder.

22 Fit the new bulb and bulbholder using a reversal of the removal procedure. Check for satisfactory operation on completion.

### XR3i models

23 Insert a small screwdriver between the top edge of the direction indicator light and the bumper, and lift up the retaining clip (see illustration).

24 Carefully withdraw the light unit from the bumper.

25 Turn the bulbholder and release it from the rear of the light unit.

26 Withdraw the old bulb and fit the new.

27 Guide the indicator back into the bumper until the retaining clip engages.

28 Check for satisfactory operation.

## Front direction indicator side repeater

29 Turn the light in a clockwise direction to release it from the front wing.

30 Pull out the bulbholder and wiring, then remove the bulb (see illustration).

31 Fit the new bulb using a reversal of the

removal procedure, and check for satisfactory operation.

## Front foglight

### 1996 models onward

32 Working under the front bumper, remove the protective cap from the rear of the foglight unit.

33 Push the retaining clip outward and remove the bulb assembly.

34 Disconnect the wiring at the in-line connector and remove the bulb.

35 Fit the new bulb using a reversal of the removal procedure, and check for satisfactory operation.

### XR3i models

36 Withdraw the front direction indicator as described previously.

37 Swing back the direction indicator spring clip then ease the foglight out on the spring clip side, and pull it forward (see illustration).

38 Detach the bulbholder and remove the bulb.

39 Refitting is a reversal of removal. Check that the operation of the foglight is satisfactory on completion.

## Rear light cluster

### Hatchback and Saloon models

40 On pre-1993 model year vehicles, working in the luggage area, press the lock tabs (recessed in the rear face of the bulbholder on the side concerned) in towards the centre, and pull free the bulbholder. On 1993 to 1995 models, release the two clips and remove the light cluster trim. Disconnect the wiring multi-plug, press the bulbholder retainer upwards, and pull free the bulbholder (see illustrations).

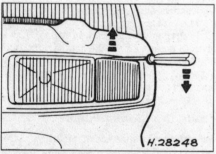

5.23 Using a screwdriver to release the direction indicator light unit - XR3i models

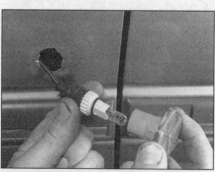

5.30 Side repeater light assembly

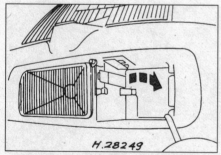

5.37 On XR3i models, swing back the indicator unit retaining spring clip, then ease the foglight out on the spring clip side

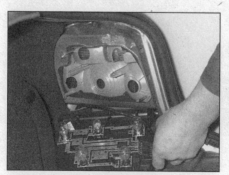

5.40a Rear bulbholder removal on pre-1993 Saloon and Hatchback models

5.40b On 1993 to 1995 models, press the bulbholder retainer (arrowed) upwards and pull free the bulbholder

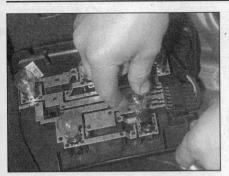

**5.41 Removing a bulb from the bulbholder**

**5.43 Rear light cluster removal on Estate models**

**5.49 Number plate light removal from the bumper on Estate models**

On 1996 models onward, press the lock tabs in the rear face of the bulbholder in towards the centre, and pull free the bulbholder.

**41** Depress and twist the bulb concerned to remove it from the holder **(see illustration)**.

**42** Fit the new bulb using a reversal of the removal procedure. Relocate the holder by pressing it in until the retainers engage. Refit the multi-plug, where applicable. Check the operation of the rear lights on completion.

### Estate models

**43** Prise back the rear trim cover on the side concerned to gain access to the light from within the luggage area. Press the lock tab down, lift the holder a fraction and withdraw it **(see illustration)**.

**44** Depress and twist free the bulb concerned from the holder.

**45** Fit the new bulb using a reversal of the removal procedure. Relocate the holder by sliding the lower end into position first, then press the upper end into position so that it clicks into place. Check the operation of the rear lights on completion.

### Van models

**46** Working from within the rear of the vehicle on the side concerned, turn the appropriate bulbholder in an anti-clockwise direction and withdraw the holder.

**47** Depress and untwist the bulb to release it from its holder.

**48** Fit the new bulb using a reversal of the removal procedure. Check the rear lights for satisfactory operation on completion.

### *Number plate lights*

**49** Prise the number plate light from the rear bumper using a screwdriver **(see illustration)**.

**50** Disconnect the wiring plug and earth lead from the light.

**51** On Hatchback, Saloon and Estate models, prise open the plastic retaining clip to withdraw the bulbholder from the light unit, then depress and untwist the bulb to remove it from the holder **(see illustrations)**.

**52** To remove the bulb on Van models, twist the bulbholder anti-clockwise and withdraw it, then pull free the bulb.

**53** Fit the new bulb using a reversal of the removal procedure. Check the operation of the lights on completion.

### *Rear foglight (1993 models onward)*

**54** With the tailgate open, release the cover from the inner trim panel to access the bulbholder.

**55** Twist the bulbholder anti-clockwise and withdraw it, then pull free the bulb.

**56** Fit the new bulb using a reversal of the removal procedure. Check the operation of the light on completion.

### *High-level stop light*

#### All models except Cabriolet

**57** Open the tailgate on Hatchback and Estate models, or enter the rear passenger compartment on Saloon models.

**58** Undo the two retaining screws and withdraw the light unit from its location.

**59** Spread the edges of the light unit outward to release the bulbholder and reflector. Release the four locating tags and separate the reflector from the bulbholder.

**60** Pull free the relevant bulb(s) from the bulbholder.

**61** Fit the new bulb(s) and the light unit using a reversal of the removal procedure. Check the operation of the light on completion.

#### Cabriolet models

**62** From within the luggage compartment, release the fastenings and withdraw the light unit from its location.

**63** Twist the relevant bulbholder anti-clockwise and withdraw it, then pull free the bulb.

**64** Fit the new bulb and the light unit using a reversal of the removal procedure. Check the operation of the light on completion.

| 6 | **Bulbs (interior lights) -** renewal |

### *Courtesy lights*

**1** Prise out the light using a small flat-bladed screwdriver **(see illustration)**.

**2** Release the festoon-type bulb from the spring contacts.

**3** Fit the new bulb using a reversal of the removal procedure. Check the tension of the spring contacts, and if necessary bend them so that they firmly contact the bulb end caps.

**5.51a Prise open the clip . . .**

**5.51b . . . and separate the number plate light unit and bulbholder**

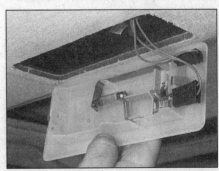

**6.1 Roof-mounted courtesy light removal**

**12**

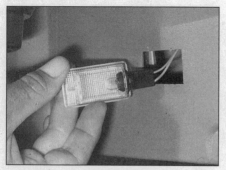

**6.4 Luggage area light removed for bulb replacement**

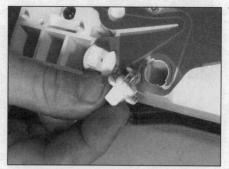

**6.8 Bulbholder removal from the instrument panel**

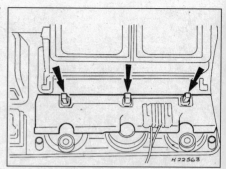

**6.11 Heater control panel illumination bulb locations (arrowed)**

### Luggage area light

**4** Prise free and withdraw the light **(see illustration)**. On later models, turn the bulbholder anticlockwise and remove it from the light unit.

**5** Pull free the bulb from its holder and remove it.

**6** Fit the new bulb and refit the light using a reversal of the removal procedure.

### Instrument panel illumination and warning lights

**7** Remove the instrument panel as described in Section 10.

**8** Turn the bulbholder a quarter-turn to align the shoulders with the slots, then remove it and pull the capless bulb from the bulbholder **(see illustration)**.

**9** Fit the new bulb in reverse order.

### Heater control panel illumination

#### Pre-1996 models

**10** Undo the two retaining screws from its upper edge, and withdraw the instrument panel surround.

**11** Carefully prise free the three heater/fresh air and blower/air conditioning switch control knobs, then undo the heater control panel retaining screws. Withdraw the panel from the facia just enough to gain access to the bulbs on its rear face **(see illustration)**.

**12** Twist the bulbs anti-clockwise to remove them.

**13** Refit in the reverse order of removal, and check for satisfactory operation on completion.

#### 1996 models onward

**14** Disconnect the battery negative (earth) lead (refer to Chapter 5A, Section 1).

**15** Undo the two retaining screws, and remove the upper steering column shroud.

**16** Similarly, undo the four retaining screws and remove the lower steering column shroud.

**17** Refer to Chapter 10 and remove the steering wheel.

**18** Carefully prise free the three heater/fresh air and blower/air conditioning switch control knobs.

**19** Undo the two retaining screws from the underside top edge of the instrument panel bezel. Release the bezel from the retaining clips (two at the top, four along the bottom, and one at the side furthest away from the steering wheel). Use a screwdriver with protective pad or cloth to prevent damage to the bezel and facia when releasing the clips. Withdraw the bezel and disconnect the wiring multi-plugs.

**20** Twist the bulbs anti-clockwise to remove them.

**21** Refit in the reverse order of removal, and check for satisfactory operation on completion.

### Automatic transmission selector illumination

**22** Prise out the lever quadrant cover (taking care not to scratch the console), then pull the bulbholder from under the selector lever position indicator, untwist and remove the bulb from the holder.

**23** Fit the new bulb in the reverse order of removal.

### Glovebox light

**24** Open the glovebox, then undo the two retaining screws and withdraw the light/switch unit.

**25** Prise free the switch/bulbholder, then untwist and remove the bulb from the holder **(see illustration)**.

**26** Fit the new bulb using a reversal of the removal procedure.

### Hazard warning light tell-tale

**27** Pull free the cover from the switch, then pull free the bulb from the switch/holder.

**28** Refit in the reverse order of removal, and check for satisfactory operation.

### Clock illumination

#### Pre-1996 models

**29** Engage the hooked ends of a pair of circlip pliers in the two holes in the underside of the clock bezel as shown, and carefully pull free the clock from its aperture in the facia. The bulbholder can then be untwisted and withdrawn from the rear face of the clock and the bulb renewed **(see illustration)**.

**30** Refit in the reverse order of removal.

#### 1996 models onward

**31** Remove the instrument panel bezel as described in paragraphs 14 to 19 above.

**32** Twist the relevant bulbholder anti-clockwise to remove, then remove the bulb from the holder.

**33** Refit in the reverse order of removal, and check for satisfactory operation on completion.

### Cigar lighter illumination

**34** Remove the lighter as described in Section 13.

**35** On pre-1996 models, withdraw the illumination ring from the facia. Remove the bulb from the illumination ring.

**36** On 1996 models onward, remove the bulbholder from the lighter housing and remove the bulb from the holder.

**37** Refit in the reverse order of removal. Check for satisfactory operation on completion.

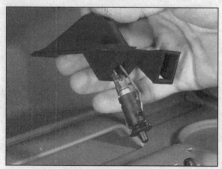

**6.25 Glovebox light switch/bulbholder removal**

**6.29 Bulbholder attachment at the rear of the clock**

## 7  Exterior light units - removal and refitting

1 Disconnect the battery negative (earth) lead (refer to Chapter 5A, Section 1), before removing any of the light units.

### Headlight

#### Pre-1996 models

2 Open and support the bonnet, then on pre-1993 models, undo the four screws along the top edge of the grille panel, and lift the panel clear. On 1993-on XR3i models, undo the four screws, release the two clips and remove the plastic support bracket above the radiator.
3 Remove the front direction indicator as described later in this Section.
4 Detach the wiring connections from the headlight and sidelight in the rear of the appropriate headlight unit.
5 Working through the cut-out of the direction indicator, unscrew the headlight lower retaining screw, then undo the two upper securing screws from the points indicated (see illustration). On later models, there is an additional upper retaining screw. Withdraw the headlight forwards from the vehicle.
6 If a new headlight is to be fitted, remove the headlight and sidelight bulbs/holders, and transfer them to the new light unit as described in Section 5. The individual parts of the headlight are not otherwise renewable.
7 Refitting is a reversal of the removal procedure. When fitting the headlight into position, ensure that the location pin sits in its recess, and note the arrangement of the insulating washers on the retaining screws (see illustrations). Loosely locate the headlight, and temporarily fit the indicator to check that the gap between the headlight and the indicator is even. Fully tighten the upper retaining screws, then remove the indicator to tighten the lower headlight screw.
8 When the headlight and indicator units are fitted and their wiring connectors attached, check the lights for satisfactory operation before fitting the front grille panel.
9 Finally, check the headlight beam alignment as described in Section 8.

#### 1996 models onward

10 Remove the radiator grille and the front bumper as described in Chapter 11.
11 Undo the three screws securing the headlight unit to the body panel.
12 Pull the locating spigots out of the retaining plate.
13 Disconnect the wiring connectors at the rear and remove the headlight unit.
14 Refitting is a reversal of the removal procedure. Check the lights for operation and check the headlight beam alignment as described in Section 8 on completion.

7.5  Headlight unit retaining screws (arrowed)

### Front direction indicator

#### Pre-1996 models except XR3i

15 Unhook the retaining spring from the rear of the direction indicator (see illustration 5.16).
16 Move the direction indicator forwards in order to release it.
17 Turn the bulbholder and release it from the rear of the direction indicator.
18 Remove the direction indicator from the vehicle.
19 Refitting is a reversal of removal. Check that the operation of the indicator is satisfactory on completion.

#### XR3i models

20 Insert a small screwdriver between the top edge of the light and the bumper, and lift up the retaining clip.
21 Carefully withdraw the indicator assembly from the bumper.
22 Turn the bulbholder and release it from the rear of the direction indicator.
23 Refitting is a reversal of removal. Check that the operation of the indicator is satisfactory on completion.

#### 1996 models onward

24 On 1996 onwards models, the direction indicator is an integral part of the headlight unit. Refer to paragraphs 10 to 14.

### Front sidelight (XR3i models)

25 Unhook the retaining spring from the rear of the sidelight unit.

7.7a  Headlight engagement pin

26 Move the sidelight forwards to release it.
27 Turn the bulbholder and release it from the rear of the sidelight.
28 Remove the sidelight from the vehicle.
29 Refitting is a reversal of removal. Check that the operation of the sidelight is satisfactory on completion.

### Front foglight (XR3i models)

30 Insert a small screwdriver between the top edge of the direction indicator light and the bumper, and lift up the retaining clip.
31 Carefully withdraw the direction indicator from the bumper.
32 Turn the bulbholder and release it from the rear of the direction indicator.
33 Swing back the direction indicator retaining spring clip then ease the foglight out, on the spring clip side, and pull it forward.
34 Detach the bulbholder and remove the unit.
35 Refitting is a reversal of removal. Check that the operation of the foglight is satisfactory on completion.

### Direction indicator side repeater

36 Raise and support the bonnet. Detach the indicator wiring multi-plug at the bulkhead, and attach a length of string to the connector end of the wire going to the side repeater. This will act as a guide to feed the wire back through the body channels when refitting the repeater unit.
37 Rotate the light in a clockwise direction to release it from the body panel, and withdraw it from the vehicle. When the wiring connector and string are drawn through, they can be separated and the string left in position.
38 Refitting is a reversal of removal. Attach the wire to the string and draw it through the body panels, then disconnect the string and reconnect the light multi-plug at the bulkhead. When the light is refitted, check for satisfactory operation.

### Rear light cluster

39 Working in the luggage area, release the rear bulbholder (according to type) from the side concerned as described in Section 5.
40 Unscrew the mounting nuts and withdraw

7.7b  Headlight retaining screw showing washer arrangement

12

**7.40 Rear light lens showing the retaining nuts**

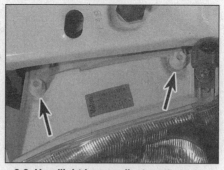

**8.2 Headlight beam adjustment screws (arrowed)**

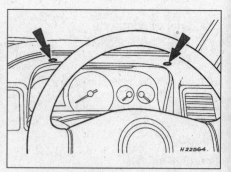

**10.3 Instrument panel bezel retaining screw locations (arrowed)**

the rear light lens from the rear of the vehicle **(see illustration)**.

41 Renew the seal gasket if it is in poor condition. Refit in the reverse order to removal, and check for satisfactory operation of the rear lights on completion.

### Number plate lights

42 Prise the number plate light from the rear bumper using a small screwdriver, then disconnect the wiring plug.

43 Refitting is a reversal of removal.

### Rear foglight (1993 model year onwards)

44 With the tailgate open, undo the ten retaining screws and withdraw the tailgate inner trim panel.

45 Disconnect the bulbholder multi-plug, then undo the retaining nut and remove the foglight.

46 Refitting is a reversal of removal.

### High-level stop light

47 Removal and refitting is described as part of the bulb renewal procedure in Section 5.

## 8 Headlight beam alignment - general information

1 Accurate adjustment of the headlight beam is only possible using optical beam-setting equipment, and this work should therefore be carried out by a Ford dealer or service station with the necessary facilities.

2 For reference, the headlight adjustment screws are located on the top of the headlight unit. The outer adjuster alters the horizontal height of the beam and the inner adjuster alters the vertical beam height **(see illustration)**.

3 Later models may be equipped with a variable-position electrical beam adjuster unit - this can be used to adjust the vertical position of the headlight beam, to compensate for the relevant load which the vehicle is carrying. An adjuster switch is provided on the facia. The adjuster switch should be positioned as follows, according to the load being carried in the vehicle. Note that higher switch positions may be necessary if the vehicle is towing a trailer.

### Hatchback, Saloon and Estate models

| | |
|---|---|
| **Position 0** | Front seat(s) occupied, luggage compartment empty |
| **Position 1.5** | Front seat(s) occupied, luggage compartment loaded up to 100 kg |
| **Position 1.5** | Front and rear seat(s) occupied, luggage compartment loaded up to 30 kg |
| **Position 2.5** | Front and rear seats fully occupied, luggage compartment fully loaded |
| **Position 3.5** | Driver's seat only occupied, luggage compartment fully loaded |

### Van models

| | |
|---|---|
| **Position 0** | Front seat(s) occupied, luggage compartment empty or loaded up to 100 kg |
| **Position 3.5** | Driver's seat only occupied, luggage compartment fully loaded |

## 9 Headlight beam adjustment components - removal and refitting

### General

1 Refer to Section 8.

### Adjuster switch

#### Removal

2 Remove the instrument panel bezel as described in Section 10.

3 Depress the retaining tabs on the side of the switch body and push the switch out from its location.

#### Refitting

4 Refitting is a reversal of removal.

### Adjuster motor

#### Removal

5 Remove the relevant headlight unit as described in Section 7.

6 Disconnect the wiring connector from the adjuster motor.

7 Rotate the adjuster motor body to release it from the headlight unit. Withdraw the motor and detach the motor balljoint from the adjuster lever. Take care, as the adjuster lever is easily broken.

8 Remove the motor.

#### Refitting

9 Engage the motor balljoint with the headlight adjuster lever until it is heard to click into place. Refit the motor body to the headlight unit, and rotate the motor to lock it in position.

10 Refit the headlight as described in Section 7.

## 10 Instrument panel - removal and refitting

### Removal

#### Pre-1996 models

1 Disconnect the battery negative (earth) lead (refer to Chapter 5A, Section 1).

2 Although not strictly necessary, in order to withdraw the instrument panel, the removal of the steering wheel will provide much improved access, particularly when detaching (and subsequently reconnecting) the speedometer cable and wiring multi-plugs from the rear of the unit. Refer to Chapter 10 for steering wheel removal and refitting procedures.

3 Undo the two retaining screws from the underside top edge of the instrument panel bezel and withdraw the bezel, releasing it from the location clips each side and underneath **(see illustration)**.

4 Unscrew and remove the four instrument panel screws, and carefully withdraw the panel to the point where the wiring multi-plugs and the speedometer cable can be detached from the rear **(see illustrations)**. Note that it may be necessary to push the speedometer cable through the from the engine compartment side to allow the instrument panel to be sufficiently withdrawn. Take care when handling the instrument panel whilst it is removed, and position it in a safe place where it will not get knocked or damaged. If a tachometer is fitted, do not lay the panel on its

**10.4a  Instrument cluster retaining screws on pre-1996 models**

**10.4b  Detach the wiring multi-plugs from the instrument panel**

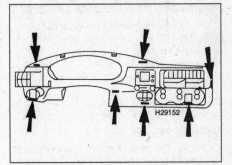

**10.10a  On 1996 models onward, release the instrument panel bezel retaining clips (arrowed) . . .**

face for extended periods, as the silicone fluid in the tachometer may well be released.

### 1996 models onward

**5** Disconnect the battery negative (earth) lead (refer to Chapter 5A, Section 1).
**6** Undo the two retaining screws, and remove the upper steering column shroud.
**7** Similarly, undo the four retaining screws and remove the lower steering column shroud.
**8** Refer to Chapter 10 and remove the steering wheel.
**9** Carefully prise free the three heater/fresh air and blower/air conditioning switch control knobs.
**10** Undo the two retaining screws from the underside top edge of the instrument panel bezel. Release the bezel from the retaining clips using a screwdriver with protective pad or cloth to prevent damage to the bezel and facia **(see illustrations)**. Withdraw the bezel and disconnect the wiring multi-plugs.
**11** Unscrew and remove the four instrument panel retaining screws, and carefully withdraw the panel to the point where the wiring multi-plugs and the speedometer cable can be detached from the rear. Note that it may be necessary to push the speedometer cable through from the engine compartment side to allow the instrument panel to be sufficiently withdrawn. Take care when handling the instrument panel whilst it is removed, and position it in a safe place where it will not get knocked or damaged. If a tachometer is fitted,

do not lay the panel on its face for extended periods, as the silicone fluid in the tachometer may well be released.

### Refitting

**12** Refitting is a reversal of removal. On completion check the function of all electrical components.

---

### 11  Instrument panel components - removal and refitting

### Removal (pre-1996 models)

**1** Remove the instrument panel as described in Section 10. As mentioned, take particular care when handling the panel.

### Printed circuit

**2** Untwist and remove all of the illumination light bulbs/holders from the rear of the instrument panel **(see illustration)**.
**3** Carefully release and remove the wiring multi-plug connector from the rear face of the panel. Pull free the printed circuit, releasing it from the securing pins and the air-cored gauge terminals on the rear face of the panel.

### Speedometer

**4** Remove the odometer reset knob, then release the four securing clips and remove the two bulbs and the panel surround from the panel. Withdraw the speedometer **(see illustration)**.

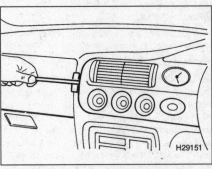

**10.10b  . . . using a screwdriver and protective pad**

### Tachometer

**5** Remove the odometer reset knob, release the securing clips, remove the two bulbs and the panel surround from the panel.
**6** Applying great care, detach the printed circuit from the air-cored gauge terminals, and remove the tachometer from the panel. Do not lay the gauge on its face for extended periods, as the silicone fluid in the tachometer may well be released.

### Fuel/temperature gauge

**7** Remove the odometer reset knob, release the securing clips, remove the two bulbs and the panel surround from the panel.
**8** Applying great care, detach the printed circuit from the air-cored gauge terminals. Undo the two retaining screws, and remove the fuel/temperature gauge from the panel **(see illustration)**.

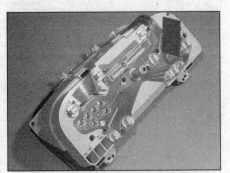

**11.2  Rear face of the instrument panel**

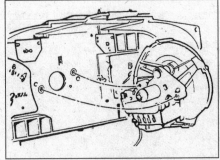

**11.4  Speedometer removal from the instrument cluster**

**11.8  Air-cored fuel/temperature gauge removal from the instrument cluster**

## Removal (1996 models onward)

9 Remove the instrument panel as described in Section 10. As mentioned, take particular care when handling the panel.
10 Untwist and remove the two illumination light bulbs/holders from the top of the instrument panel.
11 Release the four retaining lugs and remove the instrument panel glass.

### Tachometer

12 Undo the two retaining screws and carefully lift out the tachometer.

### Fuel/temperature gauge

13 Undo the two screws and carefully lift out the combined fuel/temperature gauge.

### Speedometer

14 Release the retainers and withdraw the speedometer from the panel.

### Printed circuit

15 Untwist and remove all of the illumination/warning light bulbs/holders from the rear of the instrument panel.
16 Carefully release and remove the two wiring multi-plug connectors from the rear face of the panel. Release all the pin contacts from the instrument panel body then carefully pull free the printed circuit. If necessary, the pin contacts can be removed from the printed circuit after the circuit is removed.

## Refitting

17 Refitting is a reversal of removal.

## 12 Speedometer cable - removal and refitting

### Removal

1 Remove the instrument panel (Section 10).
2 Unscrew the speedometer cable from the pinion/speed sensor on the transmission.
3 Release the cable-ties and retaining clips in the engine compartment, and withdraw the cable grommet from the bulkhead.
4 Note the cable routing for use when refitting. Pull the speedometer cable through into the engine compartment, and remove it from the car.

### Refitting

5 Refitting is the reversal of removal. Ensure that the cable is routed as noted before removal, secured with the relevant clips and cable-ties, and that the grommet is properly located in the bulkhead.

## 13 Cigar lighter - removal and refitting

### Removal (pre-1996 models)

1 Disconnect the battery negative (earth) lead (refer to Chapter 5A, Section 1).

2 Undo the two screws and remove the stowage compartment above the cigar lighter.
3 Reaching through the stowage compartment aperture, disconnect the wiring from the cigar lighter.
4 Extract the lighter element then reach through with a thin-bladed screwdriver and remove the bulbholder housing from the lighter body.
5 Push the lighter body from the rear to free it from the illumination ring.
6 If required, the lighter illumination ring can be pulled free and withdrawn from the facia.

### Removal (1996 models onward)

7 Disconnect the battery negative (earth) lead (refer to Chapter 5A, Section 1).
8 Remove the stowage compartment above the cigar lighter by simply pulling it out of the aperture in the facia.
9 Reaching through the stowage compartment aperture, disconnect the wiring from the cigar lighter.
10 Extract the lighter element, press the ashtray in at the sides to release the retaining lugs and remove the ashtray and cigar lighter assembly from the facia.
11 Remove the bulbholder housing from the lighter body then push the lighter body from the rear to free it from the ashtray.
12 Release the catches at the side and withdraw the lighter body from the illumination ring.

### Refitting

13 Refitting is a reversal of removal. On pre-1996 models, engage the bulbholder housing with the illumination ring before fitting the ring.

## 14 Clock - removal and refitting

### Removal

1 Disconnect the battery negative (earth) lead (refer to Chapter 5A, Section 1).
2 On pre-1996 models, proceed as described in Section 6, paragraph 29, and carefully prise the clock from the facia. Disconnect the wiring plug from the rear face of the clock.
3 On 1996 models onward, remove the

16.2 Windscreen wiper arm retaining nut

instrument panel bezel as described in Section 6, paragraphs 14 to 19. Undo the three screws and remove the clock from the instrument panel bezel.

### Refitting

4 Refitting is a reversal of removal. Reset the clock on completion.

## 15 Horn - removal and refitting

### Removal

1 The horn(s) are located on the body front valance, behind the front bumper. To remove a horn, first apply the handbrake, then jack up the front of the vehicle and support it on axle stands (see "Jacking and vehicle support").
2 Disconnect the horn wiring plug(s).
3 Unscrew the nut securing the horn(s) to the mounting bracket, and remove the horn(s) from the vehicle.

### Refitting

4 Refitting is a reversal of removal. Tighten the retaining nut to the specified torque.

## 16 Wiper arms - removal and refitting

### Removal

1 With the wiper(s) "parked" (ie in the normal at-rest position), mark the positions of the blade(s) on the screen, using a wax crayon or strips of masking tape.
2 Lift up the plastic cap from the bottom of the wiper arm, and loosen the nut one or two turns (see illustration).
3 Lift the wiper arm, and release it from the taper on the spindle by moving it from side to side.
4 Completely remove the nut and washer, then withdraw the wiper arm from the spindle.

### Refitting

5 Refitting is a reversal of the removal procedure. Make sure that the arm is fitted in the previously-noted position. Tighten the wiper arm nut to the specified torque.

## 17 Windscreen wiper motor and linkage - removal and refitting

### Removal

#### Wiper motor

1 Operate the wiper motor, then switch it off so that it returns to its rest position.
2 Disconnect the battery negative (earth) lead (refer to Chapter 5A, Section 1).

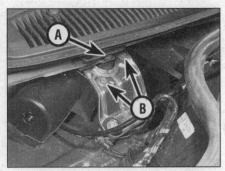

**17.3 Windscreen wiper motor showing link arm-to-spindle connection (A) and two of the wiper motor-to-mounting bolts (B)**

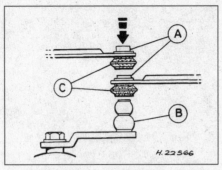

**17.7a Windscreen wiper linkage to motor balljoint connection**

A  *Pivot bush*     C  *Rubber seal*
B  *Wiper motor arm*

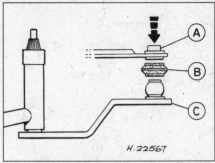

**17.7b Windscreen wiper linkage-to-pivot shaft connection**

A  *Pivot bush*     C  *Pivot shaft*
B  *Rubber seal*

**3** Unscrew and remove the link arm-to-motor spindle retaining nut **(see illustration)**. Disengage the arm from the spindle.
**4** Undo the three wiper motor retaining bolts, then move the wiper motor sideways from its mounting bracket.
**5** Detach the wiper motor wiring multi-plug, withdraw the wiper motor and remove its insulating cover.

### Linkage

**6** Remove the windscreen wiper arms (and blades) from the pivots as described in Section 16.
**7** Disconnect the battery negative (earth) lead (refer to Chapter 5A, Section 1). Move the wiper linkage to the required position for access to the linkage balljoints, then carefully prise free the linkages from their ball pins using a suitable open-ended spanner as a lever **(see illustrations)**.
**8** Remove the rubber seal from the pivot bushes. Where the surfaces of the ball pins are damaged, the pivot shaft and/or motor must be renewed. The rubber seals which are located over the edge of the pivot bushes must be renewed during refitting.

### *Refitting*

**9** Refitting is a reversal of removal. Lubricate the pivot bushes and the rubber seals during reassembly. When reconnecting the link arm on the motor spindle, ensure that the arm lug engages in the slot in the taper of the motor spindle. Tighten all fastenings to the specified torque settings (where given). Check for satisfactory operation on completion.

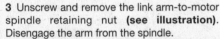

**18 Windscreen wiper pivot shaft** - removal and refitting

### Removal

**1** Operate the wiper motor, then switch it off so that it returns to its rest position.
**2** Disconnect the battery negative (earth) lead (refer to Chapter 5A, Section 1).

**3** Remove the windscreen wiper arms as described in Section 16.
**4** Detach and remove the cowl grille. This is secured by six plastic screws and two cross-head screws located under plastic caps **(see illustration)**.
**5** Unscrew and remove the four wiper motor bracket retaining bolts, then remove the wiper motor bracket assembly **(see illustration)**. Disconnect the wiring multi-plug as the motor bracket assembly is withdrawn.
**6** Prise free the wiper linkage from the pivot shaft using a suitable open-ended spanner.
**7** On pre-1996 models, pull free the pivot shaft cap from the housing, release the circlip, withdraw the two special washers and remove

the pivot shaft. The special washer and spring washer can then be removed from the shaft **(see illustration)**.
**8** On 1996 models onwards, release the circlip, withdraw the special washer and sealing ring, followed by a further two special washers and remove the pivot shaft. The spring washer can them be removed from the shaft **(see illustration)**.

### *Refitting*

**8** Refitting is a reversal of removal. Lubricate the pivot shaft, bushes and rubber seals during reassembly. When reconnecting the link arm on the motor spindle, ensure that the arm lug engages in the slot in the taper of the

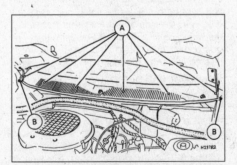

**18.4 Remove the plastic screws (A) and the cross-head screws (B) to remove the cowl grille**

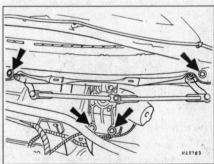

**18.5 Wiper motor bracket retaining bolt locations**

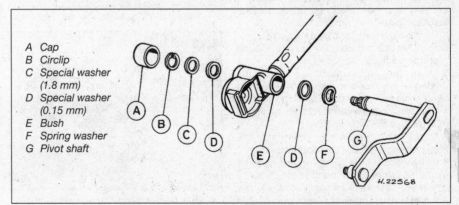

A  *Cap*
B  *Circlip*
C  *Special washer (1.8 mm)*
D  *Special washer (0.15 mm)*
E  *Bush*
F  *Spring washer*
G  *Pivot shaft*

**18.7 Wiper pivot shaft components (pre-1996 models)**

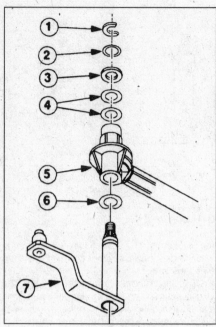

**18.8 Wiper pivot shaft components (1996 models onwards)**

| | |
|---|---|
| 1 Circlip | 4 Special washers |
| 2 Special washer | (0.15 mm) |
| (1.8 mm) | 5 Bush |
| 3 Sealing ring | 6 Spring washer |
| | 7 Pivot shaft |

motor spindle. Tighten all fastenings to the specified torque settings (where given).Check for satisfactory operation on completion.

## 19 Tailgate wiper motor assembly - removal and refitting

### Removal

**1** Operate the wiper, then switch it off so that it returns to its rest position. Note that the wiper motor will only operate with the tailgate shut, as the spring-tensioned connector pins must be in contact with the contact plates.
**2** Disconnect the battery negative (earth) lead (refer to Chapter 5A, Section 1).
**3** Remove the wiper arm (see Section 16).
**4** Unscrew the nut from the spindle housing protruding through the tailgate.
**5** Undo the eight plastic screws (early models), ten screws (later models) and remove the trim panel from inside the tailgate.
**6** Disconnect the earth lead and the wiring multi-plug to the wiper motor.
**7** Unbolt and remove the wiper assembly from inside the tailgate **(see illustrations)**.
**8** If necessary, the wiper motor can be detached from its mounting bracket by unscrewing the three retaining bolts. As they are detached, note the location of the washers and insulators.

**19.7a Tailgate wiper motor and mounting bolts (arrowed) on Hatchback models**

### Refitting

**9** Refitting is a reversal of removal. When the wiper arm is refitted, its park position should be set correctly. On Hatchback models, the distance from the point where the arm meets the centre of the wiper blade should be 90 ± 5 mm from the bottom of the rear window. On Estate models, this distance should be 75 ± 5 mm.

## 20 Washer system components - removal and refitting

### Removal

#### Washer pump

**1** To remove the pump from the reservoir, first syphon out any remaining fluid from the reservoir, then detach the washer hoses and the wiring multi-plug to the washer pump. The pump can now be pulled (or if required), levered free from the reservoir.

#### Reservoir and pump

**2** To remove the washer reservoir and pump, first unscrew and remove the reservoir retaining bolt in the engine compartment.
**3** Refer to Chapter 11 for details, and remove the wheel arch liner trim on the left-hand side.
**4** Detach the pump multi-plug, the washer low fluid level switch multi-plug (where fitted) and the pump hoses, and disconnect them from the reservoir. Drain any fluid remaining in the reservoir/pump into a suitable container.
**5** Unscrew and remove the two reservoir

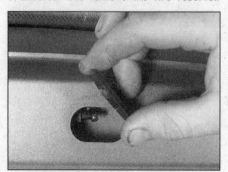

**20.9 Remove trim for access to the tailgate washer nozzle**

**19.7b Tailgate wiper motor and mounting bolts (arrowed) on Estate models**

retaining bolts from under the wheel arch, then remove the reservoir and pump from the vehicle.
**6** If required, pull or prise free the pump to remove it from the reservoir.

#### Hoses

**7** The hose system to the windscreen washers is in sections, with nylon connector pieces where required. This means that any section of hose can be renewed individually when required. Access to the hoses in the engine compartment is good, but it will be necessary to detach and remove the insulation panel from the underside of the bonnet to allow access to the hoses and connections to the washer nozzles.
**8** The front washer reservoir also supplies the rear tailgate washer by means of a tube running along the left-hand side within the body apertures.

#### Windscreen/tailgate washer nozzles

**9** These are secured to the body panels by retaining tabs which are an integral part of the washer nozzle stem. To remove a washer nozzle, first detach and remove the insulation from the underside of the bonnet, or the appropriate trim piece (according to type) for the tailgate washer **(see illustration)**.
**10** Using suitable needle-nosed pliers, squeeze together the nozzle retaining tabs, twist the nozzle a quarter of a turn, and withdraw it from its aperture in the body **(see illustration)**. Once withdrawn, the hose can be detached and the nozzle removed. Do not allow the hose to fall into the body whilst the

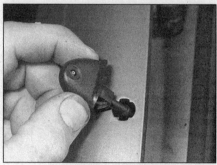

**20.10 Washer nozzle removal**

nozzle is detached - tape the hose to the body to prevent this.

### Headlight washer nozzles

**11** Unclip the cover from the nozzle assembly below the headlight.

**12** Withdraw the nozzle together with its mounting bracket out from under the front bumper and detach the washer hose.

### *Refitting*

**13** Refitting is a reversal of removal. Always renew the pump-to-reservoir seal washer, and ensure that all connections are securely made. When reconnecting the pump hoses, ensure that the hose marked with white tape is connected to the corresponding white connection on the pump.

**14** On completion, top-up the washer reservoir (*"see Weekly Checks"*) and check that the operation of the washers is satisfactory. If necessary, adjust the washer jets by inserting a pin into the centre of the jet and directing the flow at the top part of the windscreen/rear window.

---

## 21 Radio/cassette player -
### removal and refitting

### *Removal*

**1** Disconnect the battery negative (earth) lead (refer to Chapter 5A, Section 1).

**2** In order to release the radio retaining clips, two U-shaped rods must be inserted into the special holes on each side of the radio **(see illustration)**. If possible, it is preferable to obtain purpose-made rods from an audio specialist, as these have cut-outs which snap firmly into the clips so that the radio can be pulled out. Pull the unit squarely from its aperture, or it may jam. If the unit proves difficult to withdraw, remove the cassette tray (or where applicable, the CD player) from beneath the unit, then reach through the aperture and ease it out from behind. From 1993 model year onwards, on some audio units it will first be necessary to remove the two side bezels using a Ford tool, to gain access to the removal tool holes.

**3** With the radio/cassette sufficiently withdrawn, disconnect the feed, earth, aerial

**21.2 Radio/cassette removal**

and speaker leads. Where applicable, also detach and remove the plastic support bracket from the rear of the unit.

### *Refitting*

**4** Refitting is a reversal of removal. When the leads are reconnected to the rear of the unit, press it into position to the point where the retaining clips are felt to engage. Reactivate the unit in accordance with the code and the instructions given in the Ford Audio Operating Manual supplied with the vehicle.

---

## 22 Compact disc player -
### removal and refitting

The removal and refitting procedures for this (where fitted) are similar to those described for the radio/cassette player in the previous Section, but do not remove the bezel securing screws above the CD player.

---

## 23 Compact disc autochanger -
### removal and refitting

### *Removal*

**1** Remove the front passenger seat as described in Chapter 11.

**2** Undo the three screws each side securing the autochanger to the mounting brackets.

**3** Disconnect the wiring connector and remove the autochanger.

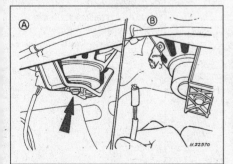

**24.4 Bolt (A) and wiring plug (B) of the shelf-mounted speaker on Saloon models**

**24.5 Rear parcel shelf-mounted speaker (Hatchback models)**

**24.1 Door-mounted speaker removal**

### *Refitting*

**4** Refitting is a reversal of removal.

---

## 24 Speakers -
### removal and refitting

### *Removal*
#### Door-mounted speaker

**1** Remove the trim panel from the door concerned as described in Chapter 11. Undo the speaker retaining screws, then withdraw the speaker from the door and disconnect the wiring **(see illustration)**. Note that the speaker must not be detached from its moulding.

#### Rear quarter panel-mounted speaker (Cabriolet models)

**2** Lower the hood. If the hood is manually-operated, lock it in the lowered position, then pull free the roof release lever knob.

**3** Remove the quarter window regulator or lift switches (according to type), and remove the rear quarter trim panel as described in Chapter 11. Undo the three retaining screws and withdraw the speaker. Disconnect the wiring from the speaker. Note that the speaker must not be detached from its moulding.

#### Rear parcel shelf-mounted speaker (Saloon models)

**4** Detach the wiring connector from the speaker, then loosen off the speaker retaining bolt sufficiently to allow the speaker to be withdrawn, leaving the bracket and bolt in position in the speaker recess **(see illustration)**.

#### Rear parcel tray-mounted speaker (Hatchback models)

**5** Unscrew the three retaining screws, lower the speaker from the parcel tray, then detach the wiring connections **(see illustration)**. Note that the speaker and its moulding must not be separated.

#### Luggage area trim-mounting speaker (Estate models)

**6** Remove the appropriate luggage area side trim panel as described in Chapter 11 for access to the speaker.

**7** Unscrew the three retaining screws, withdraw the speaker and detach the wiring

 **12**

**24.7 Luggage area-mounted speaker (Estate models)**

connections **(see illustration)**. Note that the speaker and its moulding must not be separated.

### *Refitting*

**8** Refitting is a reversal of removal.

## 25 Radio aerial - removal and refitting

### *Removal*

#### Manual aerial (Hatchback, Saloon and Estate models)

**1** Disconnect the battery negative (earth) lead (refer to Chapter 5A, Section 1).
**2** Remove the trim cover from the access aperture in the headlining beneath the aerial by carefully prising it free. On models equipped with a sunroof, remove the operating handle (manual type) then release the trim caps over the two roof console retaining screws. Undo the screws and slide the console rearward to release the retaining clips. Remove the roof console after disconnecting the wiring connectors (where applicable).
**3** Working through the aperture in the headlining, undo the single retaining screw, withdraw the aerial and detach the cable base from the roof.

#### Manual aerial (Cabriolet models)

**4** Open the boot lid, disconnect its support strut from the left-hand side panel, then undo the two retaining screws and remove the luggage area side trim panel.
**5** Unscrew and remove the aerial mast, then unscrew and remove the collar retaining nut to remove the spacer and upper seal washer.
**6** Working within the luggage area side of the quarter panel, unscrew the lead and remove the aerial.

#### Electric aerial (Cabriolet models)

**7** Open the boot lid, disconnect its support strut from the left-hand side panel, then undo the two retaining screws and remove the luggage area side trim panel.
**8** Unscrew the aerial upper retaining nut, then remove the bezel and the seal washer.
**9** Working from the luggage area side, unscrew and remove the self-tapping screw securing the aerial bottom bracket to the apron.
**10** Unscrew the knurled type nut to detach the aerial from the base of the unit, then detach the wiring and aerial lead at their connections, and withdraw the aerial from the vehicle.

### *Refitting*

**11** Refitting is a reversal of removal. Ensure that the contact surfaces of both the body panel and the aerial are clean before fitting the aerial into position.

## 26 Power amplifier - removal and refitting

### *Removal*

**1** This is fitted to models equipped with the Premium Sound System, and is located in the area between the glovebox and the bulkhead.
**2** To remove the amplifier, undo the retaining screw, lower the unit complete with its support bracket, and detach the wiring multi-plug connectors. If required, the bracket and the amplifier can be separated by unscrewing the four Torx screws.

### *Refitting*

**3** Refit in the reverse order of removal.

## 27 Anti-theft systems - general information

### *Anti-theft alarm system*

**1** This system provides an added form of vehicle security **(see illustration)**. When the

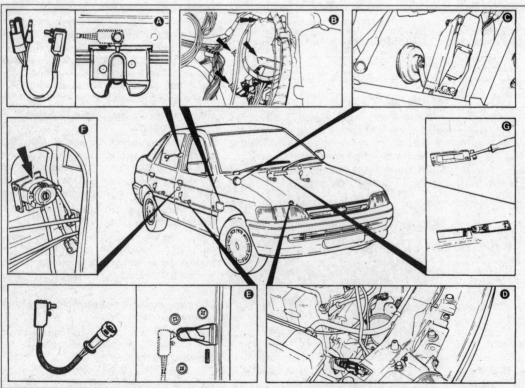

**27.1 Anti-theft alarm system components and their locations**

A  Trip switch (luggage compartment)
B  System module
C  Alarm horn
D  Alarm switch (bonnet)
E  Alarm switch (doors)
F  Activation switches
G  Clock

system is activated, the alarm will sound if the vehicle is broken into through any one of the doors, the bonnet, boot (or tailgate). The alarm will also be triggered if the ignition system is turned on or the radio/cassette disconnected whilst the system is activated.

**2** This system is activated/de-activated whenever one of the front doors is locked/unlocked by the key. The system operates on all doors, the bonnet and boot lid (or tailgate) whenever each door is individually locked (or, in the case of central locking, when the central locking is engaged). In addition, the ignition/starting system is also immobilised when the system is activated.

**3** A further security feature included is that even though the battery may be disconnected whilst the system is activated, the alarm activation continues as soon as the battery is reconnected. Because of this feature, it is important to ensure that the system is de-activated before disconnecting the battery at any time, such as when working on the vehicle.

**4** The system incorporates a diagnostic mode to enable Ford technicians to quickly identify any faults in the system.

### Passive Anti-Theft System (PATS)

**5** From the 1994 model year onwards, a Passive Anti-Theft System (PATS) is fitted. This system, (which works independently of the standard alarm system) is a vehicle immobiliser which prevents the engine from being started unless a specific code, programmed into the ignition key, is recognised by the PATS transceiver.

**6** The PATS transceiver, fitted around the ignition switch, decodes a signal from the ignition key as the key is turned from position "O" to position "II". If the coded signal matches that stored in the memory of the PATS module, the engine will start. If the signal is not recognised, the engine will crank on the starter but will not fire.

### 28 Anti-theft system components - removal and refitting

#### Removal

**1** Before disconnecting any components of the anti-theft alarm system, first check that the system is de-activated, then disconnect the battery negative (earth) lead (refer to Chapter 5A, Section 1).

#### Door lock switch

**2** Remove the trim panel and the insulation sheet from the door, as described in Chapter 11. On later models, undo the two screws and remove the door lock assembly shield.

**3** Detach the wiring multi-plug connector from the alarm switch in the door **(see illustration)**.

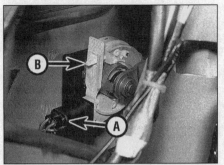
**28.3 Door lock switch wiring connector (A) and retaining catch (B)**

**4** Release the snap-lock catch, withdraw the switch from the door lock cylinder, and remove it from the door.

#### Door lock ajar switch

**5** Remove the trim panel and the insulation sheet from the door - see Chapter 11.
**6** Detach the wiring multi-plug from the door lock ajar switch.
**7** Remove the door lock as described in Chapter 11.
**8** Release the retaining clip, and detach the door ajar switch from the door lock. It is probable that the retaining clip will break when releasing the switch, in which case it will need to be renewed.

#### Bootlid/tailgate ajar switch

**9** Undo the retaining screws, and remove the trim panel from the bootlid or tailgate (as applicable).
**10** Detach the wiring loom multi-plug, then referring to Chapter 11 for details, remove the lock from the bootlid/tailgate.
**11** Release the retaining clip and detach the ajar switch from the lock unit. It is probable that the retaining clip will break when releasing the switch, in which case it will need to be renewed.

#### Bonnet alarm switch

**12** Grip the switch flange, and pull the switch up and clear of its aperture in the front cross-panel (see illustration).
**13** Disconnect the wiring connector and remove the switch.

#### Alarm horn (pre-1994 models)

**14** Where the vehicle is fitted with ABS, detach and remove the ABS module as described in Chapter 9.
**15** Detach the wiring from the horn, undo the horn bracket retaining bolts, and remove the horn together with its retaining bracket.

#### Alarm horn (1994 models onward)

**16** Remove the C-pillar interior trim and the luggage area trim on the left-hand side.
**17** Undo the horn retaining bolt and lift the unit off the two retaining hooks.
**18** Disconnect the wiring and remove the horn.

#### Alarm system module

**19** Detach and remove the cowl side trim

**28.12 Bonnet alarm switch removal (anti-theft alarm system)**

kick panel from the driver's side front footwell.
**20** Detach the wiring multi-plug from the module, then release the module from the four retaining clips and remove it.

#### PATS transceiver

**21** Undo the two upper and four lower retaining screws, and remove the steering column upper and lower shrouds.
**22** Undo the five screws and withdraw the detachable lower facia panel from beneath the steering column.
**23** Undo the single screw, and withdraw the PATS transceiver from the ignition switch/steering lock barrel **(see illustration)**.
**24** Release the wiring harness from the clips on the steering column, trace the harness under the facia, and disconnect the wiring multi-plug. Remove the transceiver from the car.

#### PATS module

**25** Refer to Chapter 11 and remove the facia.
**26** Disconnect the wiring multi-plug from the PATS module, located on the bulkhead on the passenger's side.
**27** Pull the module downwards to remove it from the mounting bracket.

#### Refitting

**28** The refitting of the respective components is a reversal of the removal procedure. Ensure that all component retaining clips are secure, that the wiring looms are correctly routed, and that the wiring connections are secure. Check for satisfactory operation of the systems to complete.

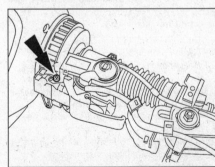
**28.23 Undo the screw (arrowed) and withdraw the PATS transceiver from the ignition switch/steering lock barrel**

**12**

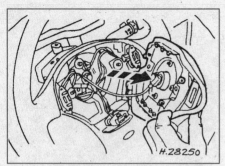

**30.4  Withdrawing the air bag from the steering wheel**

## 29 Air bag system - general information, precautions and system de-activation

### General information

All models from 1994 onwards are fitted with a driver's air bag, which is designed to prevent serious chest and head injuries to the driver during an accident. A similar bag for the front seat passenger is also available. The combined sensor and electronics for the air bag(s) is located next to the steering column inside the vehicle, and contains a back-up capacitor, crash sensor, decelerometer, safety sensor, integrated circuit and microprocessor. The air bags are inflated by gas generators, which force the bags out from their locations in the centre of the steering wheel, and the passenger's side facia, where applicable. A "clock spring" ensures that a good electrical connection is maintained with the driver's air bag at all times - as the steering wheel is turned in each direction, the spring winds and unwinds.

### Precautions

 *Warning:  The  following precautions must be observed when  working  on  vehicles equipped  with  an  air  bag system, to prevent the possibility of personal injury.*

#### General precautions

The following precautions **must** be observed when carrying out work on a vehicle equipped with an air bag.

a) Do not disconnect the battery with the engine running.
b) Before carrying out any work in the vicinity of the air bag, removal of any of the air bag components, or any welding work on the vehicle, de-activate the system as described in the following sub-Section.
c) Do not attempt to test any of the air bag system circuits using test meters or any other test equipment.
d) If the air bag warning light comes on, or any fault in the system is suspected, consult a Ford dealer without delay. **Do**

*not attempt to carry out fault diagnosis, or any dismantling of the components.*

### Precautions to be taken when handling an air bag

a) Transport the air bag by itself, bag upward.
b) Do not put your arms around the air bag.
c) Carry the air bag close to the body, bag outward.
d) Do not drop the air bag or expose it to impacts.
e) Do not attempt to dismantle the air bag unit.
f) Do not connect any form of electrical equipment to any part of the air bag circuit.

### Precautions to be taken when storing an air bag unit

a) Store the unit in a cupboard with the air bag upward.
b) Do not expose the air bag to temperatures above 80°C.
c) Do not expose the air bag to flames.
d) Do not attempt to dispose of the air bag - consult a Ford dealer.
e) Never refit an air bag which is known to be faulty or damaged.

### De-activation of air bag system

The system must be de-activated as follows, before carrying out any work on the air bag components or surrounding area.

a) Switch off the ignition.
b) Remove the ignition key.
c) Switch off all electrical equipment.
d) Disconnect the battery negative lead.
e) Insulate the end of the battery negative lead and the battery negative terminal to prevent any possibility of contact.
f) Wait for at least fifteen minutes before carrying out any further work.

## 30 Air bag system components - removal and refitting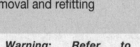

 *Warning:  Refer  to  the precautions given in Section 29 before attempting to carry out work on the air bag components.*

### Driver's side air bag unit

#### Removal

**1** De-activate the air bag system as described in Section 29.
**2** Undo the two screws, and remove the steering column upper shroud.
**3** Turn the steering wheel as necessary so that one of the air bag retaining bolts becomes accessible from the rear of the steering wheel. Undo the bolt, then turn the steering wheel again until the second bolt is accessible. Undo this bolt also.
**4** Withdraw the air bag from the steering wheel far enough to access the wiring multi-

plug **(see illustration)**. Some force may be needed to free the unit from the additional steering wheel spoke retainers.
**5** Disconnect the multi-plug from the rear of the unit, and remove it from the vehicle.

#### Refitting

**6** Refitting is a reversal of the removal procedure.

### Passenger's side air bag unit
#### Removal (pre-1996 models)

**7** De-activate the air bag system as described in Section 29.
**8** Open the glovebox and undo the three screws at the top of the glovebox aperture.
**9** Remove the centre and left-hand (passenger's side) face level air vents as described in Chapter 3.
**10** Working through the air vent apertures, undo the air bag surround retaining nuts, and withdraw the surround and air bag unit from the facia.
**11** Disconnect the two wiring connectors from the rear of the air bag unit, and unclip the wiring harness from the mounting bracket.
**12** Undo the two bolts each side and the two bolts in the centre and remove the mounting brackets from the air bag surround.
**13** Withdraw the air bag unit from the surround.

#### Refitting

**14** Refitting is a reversal of the removal procedure, ensuring that the wiring is correctly routed.

#### Removal (1996 models onward)

**15** De-activate the air bag system as described in Section 29.
**16** Remove the facia as described in Chapter 11.
**17** Open the glovebox and undo the two air bag surround retaining screws at the top of the glovebox aperture.
**18** Undo the four nuts securing the air bag mounting brackets to the facia.
**19** Undo the two retaining screws and carefully withdraw the air bag surround and air bag unit from the facia. Disconnect the two wiring connectors from the rear of the air bag unit and remove the assembly from the facia. Note that on later models there is only one air bag wiring connector.
**20** Undo the two screws and remove the face level air vent from the air bag surround.
**21** Undo the two screws each side and remove the left-hand and right-hand mounting brackets from the air bag unit and the surround.
**22** Undo the remaining two retaining screws and slide the air bag unit out of the surround.

#### Refitting

**23** Refitting is a reversal of the removal procedure, ensuring that the wiring is correctly routed.

### Air bag control module
#### Removal

**24** De-activate the air bag system as described in Section 29.

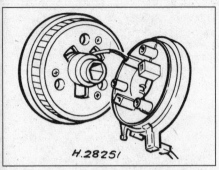

**30.33 Removing the air bag clock spring assembly from the steering wheel**

**25** Undo the six screws and withdraw the detachable lower facia panel from beneath the steering column.
**26** Remove the instrument panel as described in Section 9.
**27** Support the module and undo the mounting bolts.
**28** Disconnect the multi-plug from the module, by pressing the locking tab upwards and swivelling the retaining strap. Remove the module from the car.

### Refitting

**29** Refitting is a reversal of the removal procedure.

## Air bag clock spring

### Removal

**30** De-activate the air bag system as described in Section 29.
**31** Remove the steering wheel as described in Chapter 10.
**32** Disconnect the wires at the two horn terminals in the centre of the steering wheel.
**33** Undo the three retaining screws, and remove the clock spring/horn slip ring from the steering wheel (see illustration). As the unit is withdrawn, note which aperture in the steering wheel the air bag wiring passes through, as an aid to reassembly.

### Refitting

**34** Apply a smear of molybdenum disulphide grease to the horn slip rings.
**35** Position the clock spring/horn slip ring on the steering wheel, and secure with the retaining screws.
**36** Reconnect the two horn wires to their terminals.
**37** The clock spring must now be centred as follows.
**38** Depress the locking pin, and rotate the clock spring outer rotor fully anti-clockwise until it is tight (see illustration).
**39** Now turn the outer rotor approximately

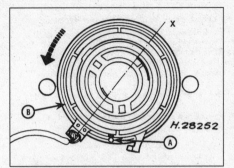

**30.38 Centring the air bag clock spring. Depress locking pin (A) and rotate outer rotor (B) anti-clockwise ("X" is the relative position of the direction indicator cancelling cam to the cable connector - see text)**

3.75 turns clockwise, then release the locking pin. Ensure that the locking pin engages when it is released.
**40** Check that the relative position of the direction indicator cancelling cam to the cable connector on the clock spring assembly is as shown (see illustration 30.38).
**41** Refit the steering wheel as described in Chapter 10.

**31 Auxiliary warning system -** general information and component renewal

### General information

**1** An auxiliary warning system is available as an option on certain models. On pre-1996 models, the system has three functions - low fuel warning, low washer fluid level warning, and an "ignition off, lights on, driver's door open" warning. On 1996 models onward the system has only two functions - "ignition off, lights on, driver's door open" warning, and door ajar warning (when an anti-theft alarm system is fitted).
**2** The low fuel and washer fluid level warnings are provided by warning lights in the instrument panel and the "ignition off, lights on, driver's door open" warning is provided by an audible alarm tone.
**3** The warning lights are activated by floats which monitor the fuel and fluid levels. The float for the low fuel level is an integral part of the fuel gauge sender, and activates the warning light when the fuel level in the tank drops to below 10 litres (2.2 gallons). The float for the washer fluid level is contained in the fluid reservoir, and consists of a magnet

which operates a reed switch inserted in the side of the reservoir. When the fluid level falls to the level of the reed switch, the magnet on the float activates the switch to illuminate the warning light.
**4** The alarm tone for the "ignition off, lights on, driver's door open" warning is activated by the driver's door courtesy light switch if the door is opened with the ignition switched off and the lights left on. On pre-1996 models, the operation of the system is controlled by a control module assembly located under the facia above the fusebox. This module also emits the alarm tone for the "ignition off, lights on, driver's door open" warning. On 1996 models onward, the alarm tone is emitted by a relay buzzer located under the facia either above the fusebox or mounted on the main fuse board. The door ajar warning light is operated by the anti-theft alarm system module.

### Component renewal

#### Warning lights

**5** The procedure for warning light bulb renewal is contained in Section 6.

#### Low fuel level float (pre-1996 models)

**6** The low fuel level float is part of the fuel gauge sender - removal and refitting procedures are contained in Chapter 4.

#### Low washer fluid level reed switch (pre-1996 models)

**7** Remove the windscreen washer reservoir as described in Section 20.
**8** Withdraw the switch from the side of the reservoir by levering against the switch body.
**9** Ensure that the sealing grommet is correctly fitted in the reservoir, then push the switch fully into the grommet to refit.
**10** Refit the washer reservoir (see Section 20).

#### Control module assembly/relay buzzer

**11** Disconnect the battery negative (earth) lead (refer to Chapter 5A, Section 1).
**12** Undo the six screws and withdraw the detachable lower facia panel from beneath the steering column. On later models, detach the courtesy light assembly and and any additional wiring clipped to the panel.
**13** On pre-1998 models, unclip the control module, and disconnect the multi-plug. On 1998 models onward, remove the relay buzzer from the relay board (refer to the *Specifications*, and Section 3 for additional information).
**14** Refitting is a reversal of removal.

**12**

1. All diagrams are divided into numbered circuits depending on function e.g. Diagram 10 : Typical Interior lighting.
2. Items are arranged in relation to a plan view of the vehicle.
3. Items may appear on more than one diagram so are found using a grid reference e.g. 2/A1 denotes an item on diagram 2 grid location A1.
4. Complex items appear on the diagrams as blocks and are expanded on the internal connections page.
5. Feed wires are coloured red (black when switched) and all earth wires are coloured brown.
6. Brackets show how the circuit may be connected in more than one way.
7. Not all items are fitted to all models.

## CENTRAL ELECTRIC BOX

| FUSE | RATING | CIRCUIT |
|---|---|---|
| 1 | 30A | Heated Rear Window And Electric Mirrors |
| 2 | 30A | Anti-lock Braking System |
| 3 | 10A | Lambda Sensor |
| 4 | 15A | Main Beam RH |
| 5 | 20A | Fuel Pump |
| 6 | 10A | Side Light LH, Instrument Illumination |
| 7 | 10A | Side Light RH |
| 8 | 10A | Foglight Rear |
| 9 | 30A | Cooling Fan |
| 10 | 10A | Dip Beam LH |
| 11 | 15A | Foglight Front |
| 12 | 10A | Direction Indicator, Reversing Lights |
| 13 | 20A | Wiper Motor, Washer Pump |
| 14 | 20A | Heater Blower |
| 15 | 30A | Anti-lock Braking System |
| 16 | 3A | Windscreen De-ice |
| 17 | 3A | Windscreen De-ice Relay |
| 18 | 15A | Main Beam LH |
| 19 | 20A | Central Door Locking/Anti-thieft Alarm |
| 20 | 15A | Horn, Hazard Flashers |
| 21 | 15A | Interior Lights, Cigar Lighter, Radio, Clock |
| 22 | 30A | Electric Windows |
| 24 | 10A | Dip Beam RH |
| 25 | 3A | EEC IV Module |
| 27 | 10A | Stop Lights, Heated Washer Jets |

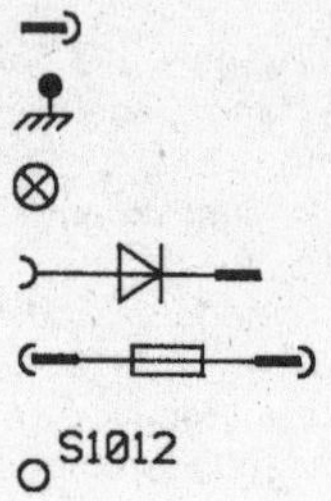

## MAXI-FUSEBOX

| FUSE | RATING | CIRCUIT |
|---|---|---|
| A | 80A | Central Electric Box |
| B | 60A | Central Electric Box |
| C | 60A | Central Electric Box |
| D | 50A | Cooling Fan Motor |
| E | 50A | Heated Windscreen |
| F | 50A | Glow Plug Relay (Diesel) |

## INTERNAL CONNECTION DETAILS

a = Alternator Warning Light
b = Handbrake Warning Light
c = Main Beam Warning Light
d = Instrument Illumination
e = Fuel Gauge
f = Temperature Gauge
g = Oil Pressure Light
h = Tachometer
i = Voltage Stabilizer
j = ABS Warning Light
k = Choke Warning Light
l = Flasher Warning Light LH
m = Flasher Warning Light RH

KEY TO INSTRUMENT CLUSTER
   (ITEM 98)

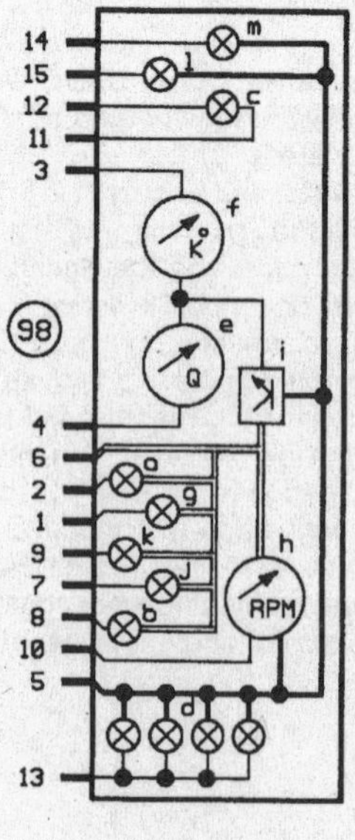

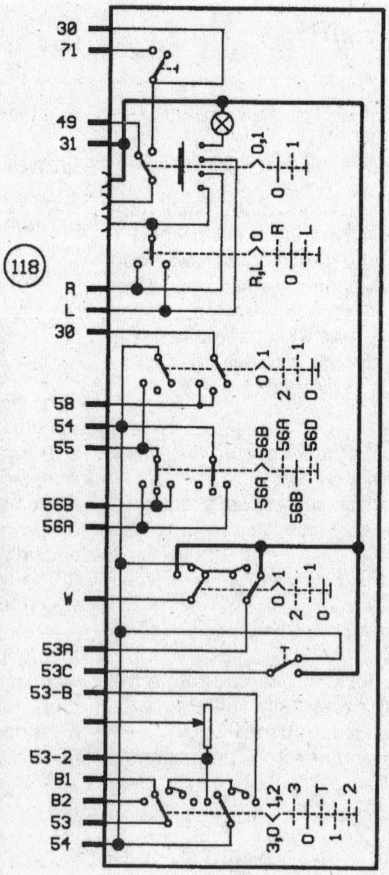

## KEY TO SYMBOLS

PLUG-IN CONNECTOR

EARTH

BULB

DIODE

FUSE

SOLDERED JOINT    S1012

**Information for wiring diagrams - pre-1995 models**

H24880

T.M.MARKE

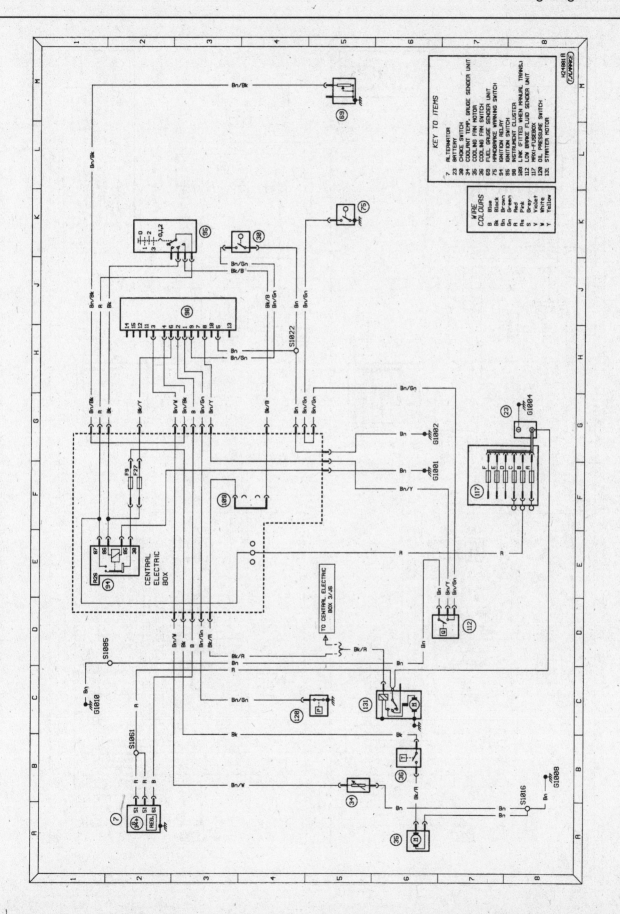

Diagram 1: Typical starting, charging, cooling fan, warning lights and gauges - pre-1995 models

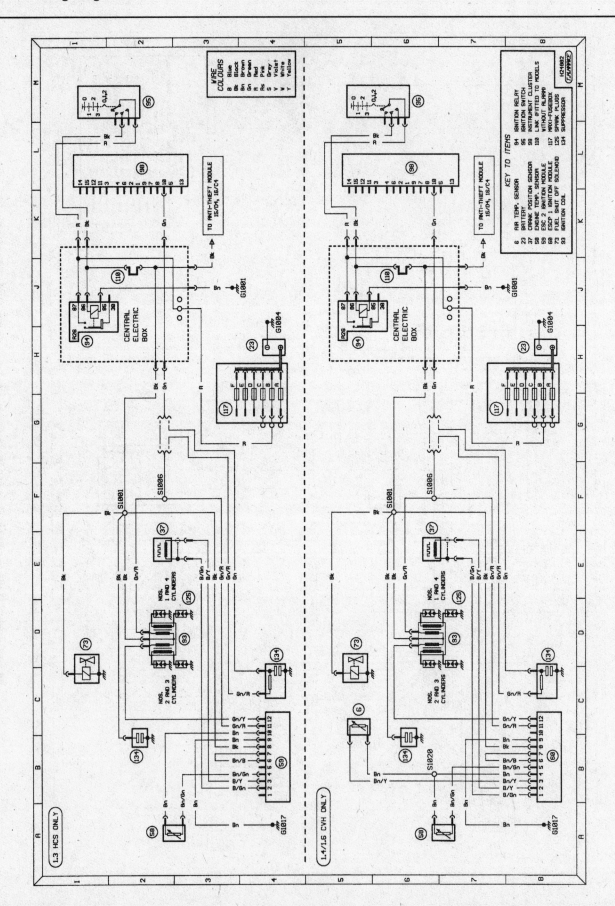

Diagram 2: Typical ignition variation (all carburettor models - manual transmission only) - pre-1995 models

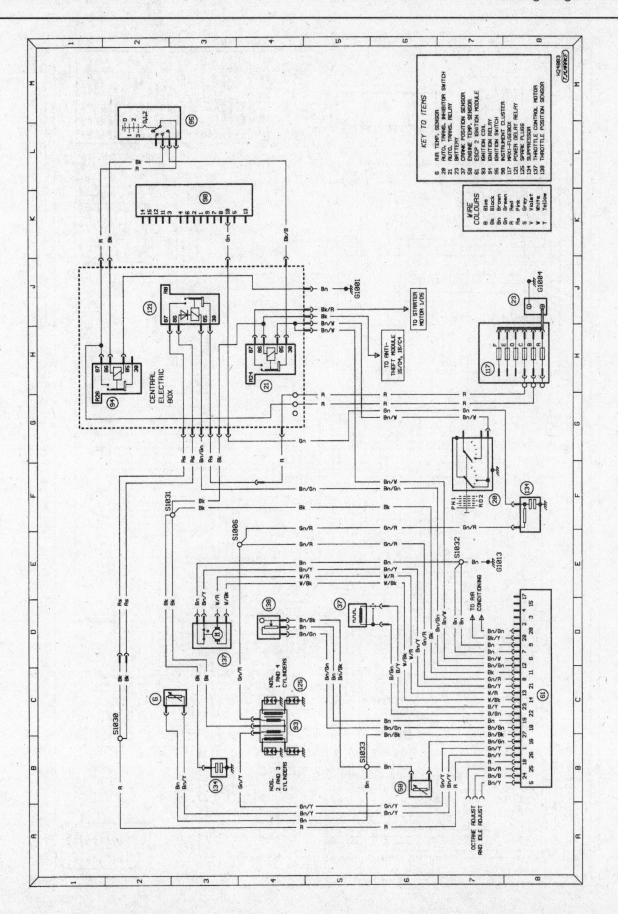

Diagram 3: Typical ignition variation (1.6 CVH automatic) - pre-1995 models

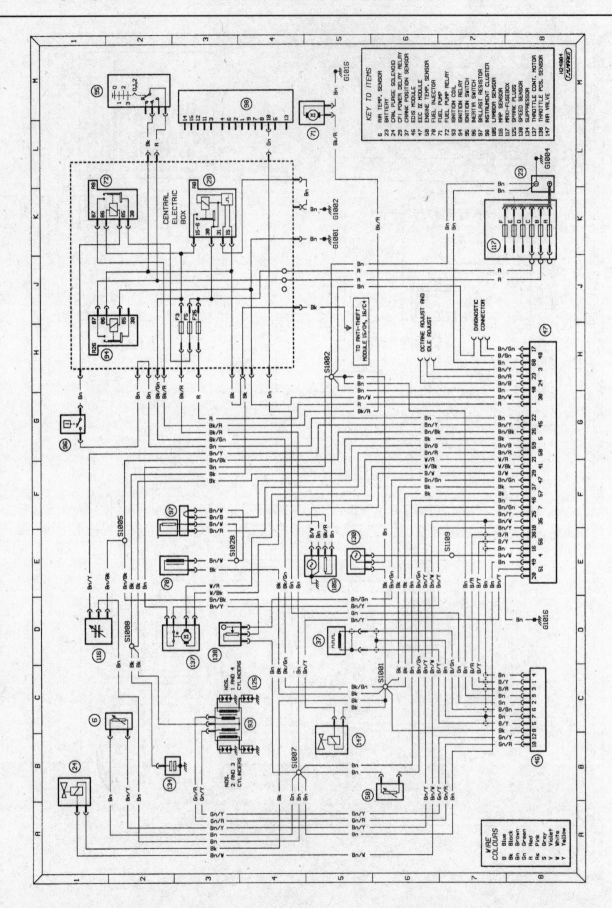

**Diagram 4: Typical 1.3 CFi fuel injection and ignition – pre-1995 models**

KEY TO ITEMS

| | |
|---|---|
| 6 | AIR TEMP. SENSOR |
| 23 | BATTERY |
| 24 | CRNL PURGE SOLENOID |
| 29 | CFI POWER DELAY RELAY |
| 37 | CRNK POSITION SENSOR |
| 46 | EDIS MODULE |
| 47 | ECU IDLE |
| 58 | ENGINE TEMP. SENSOR |
| 70 | FUEL INJECTOR |
| 71 | FUEL PUMP |
| 72 | FUEL PUMP RELAY |
| 93 | IGNITION COIL |
| 94 | IGNITION RELAY |
| 95 | IGNITION SWITCH |
| 96 | INERTIA SWITCH |
| 97 | INSTRUMENT CLUSTER |
| 98 | BRLLAST RESISTOR |
| 116 | LAMBDA SENSOR |
| 117 | MAXI-FUSEBOX |
| 125 | MAP SENSOR |
| 130 | SPARK PLUGS |
| 134 | SPEED SENSOR |
| 137 | SUPPRESSOR |
| 138 | THROTTLE CONT. MOTOR |
| 147 | THROTTLE POS. SENSOR |
| | AIR VALVE |

WIRE COLOURS

| | |
|---|---|
| B | Blue |
| Bk | Black |
| Bn | Brown |
| Gn | Green |
| R | Red |
| Rs | Pink |
| S | Grey |
| V | Violet |
| W | White |
| Y | Yellow |

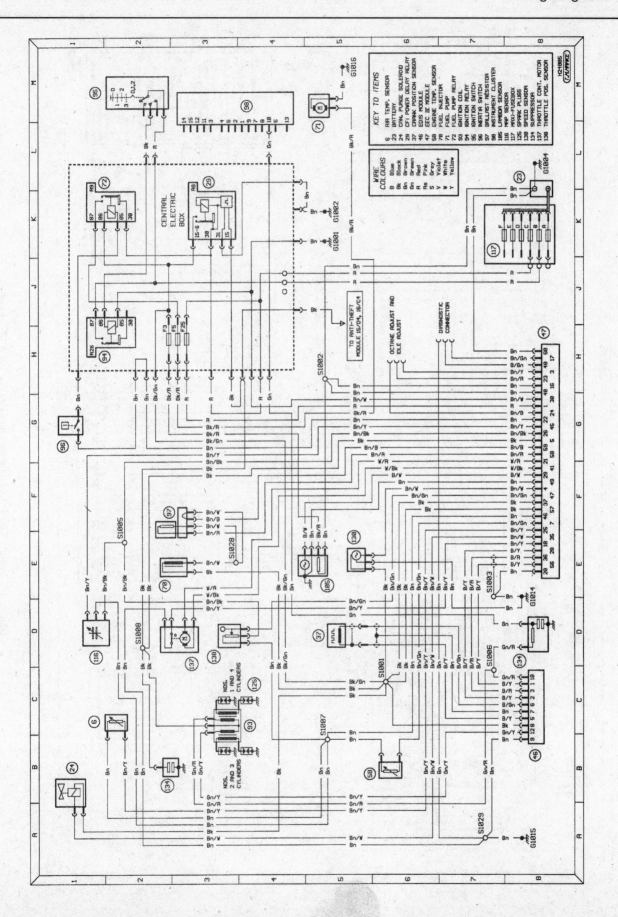

Diagram 5: Typical 1.4 CFi fuel injection and ignition - pre-1995 models

**12**

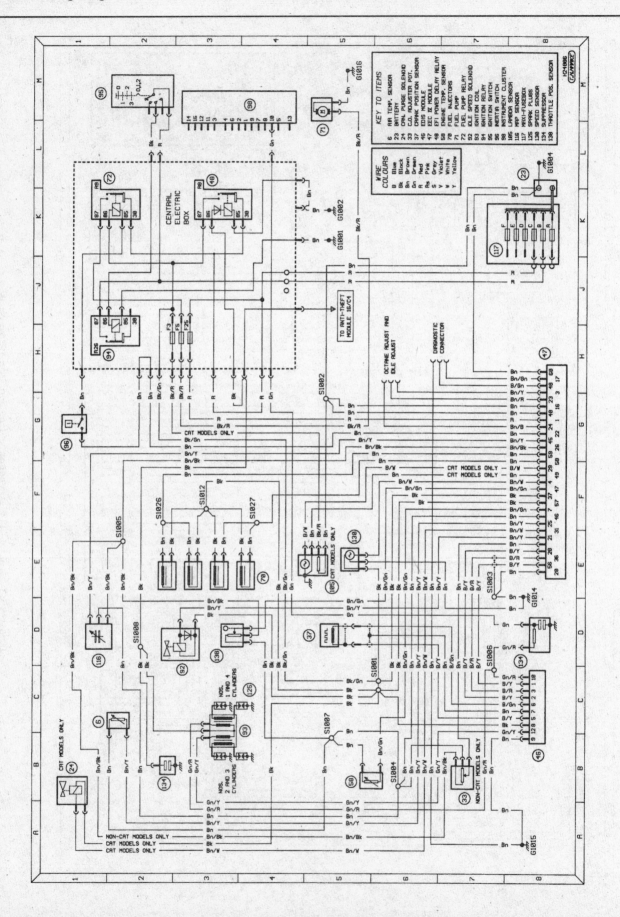

Diagram 6: Typical 1.6 EFi fuel injection and ignition - pre 1995 models

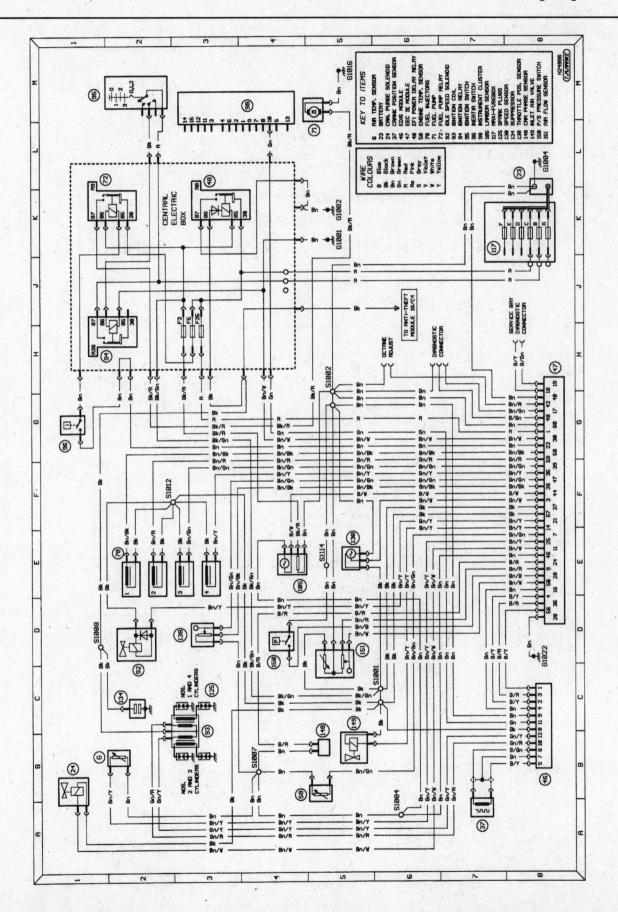

Diagram 7: Typical Zetec (16V) fuel injection and ignition - pre-1995 models

**KEY TO ITEMS**

6    AIR TEMP. SENSOR
23   BATTERY
24   OVAL PURGE SOLENOID
37   CRANK POSITION SENSOR
46   EDIS MODULE
47   EEC IV MODULE
48   EFI POWER DELAY RELAY
58   ENGINE TEMP. SENSOR
59   EFI INJECTORS
70   FUEL INJECTORS
71   FUEL PUMP
72   FUEL PUMP RELAY
92   FUEL PUMP RELAY
93   IDLE IGN COIL
94   MAIN IGN SOLENOID
95   IGNITION RELAY
96   IGNITION SWITCH
98   INERTIA SWITCH
105  INSTRUMENT CLUSTER
117  MAXI-FUSEBOX
125  LAMBDA SENSOR
130  SPARK PLUGS
131  SPEED SENSOR
134  SUPPRESSOR
138  THROTTLE POS. SENSOR
148  CRM PHASE SENSOR
149  INLET AIR VALVE
150  P/S PRESSURE SWITCH
151  AIR FLOW SENSOR

**WIRE COLOURS**

B    Blue
Bk   Black
Bn   Brown
Gn   Green
P    Pink
Rs   Pink
R    Red
S    Grey
V    Violet
W    White
Y    Yellow

**12**

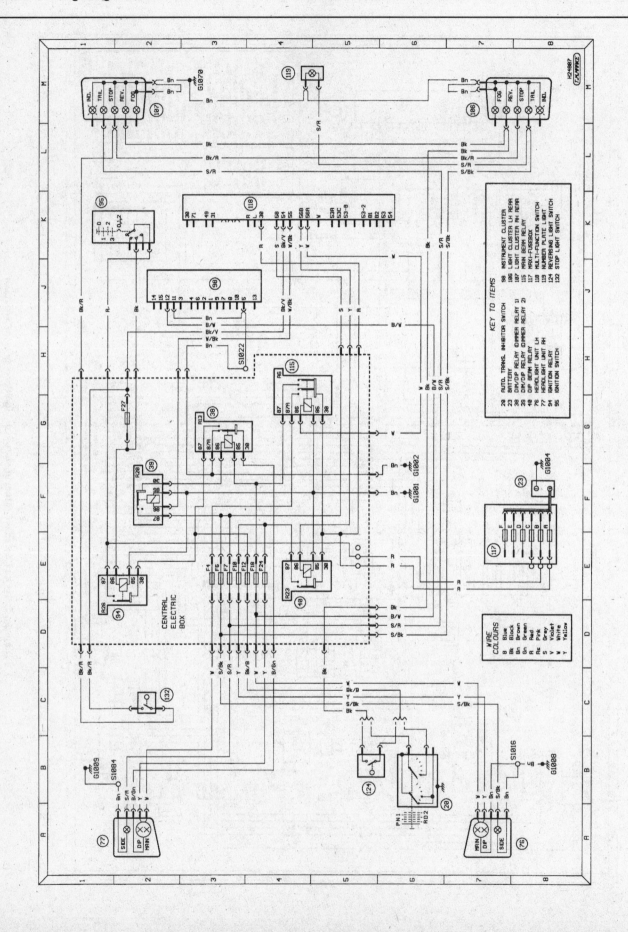

Diagram 8: Typical exterior lighting - headlight/sidelight, stop and reversing lights - pre-1995 models

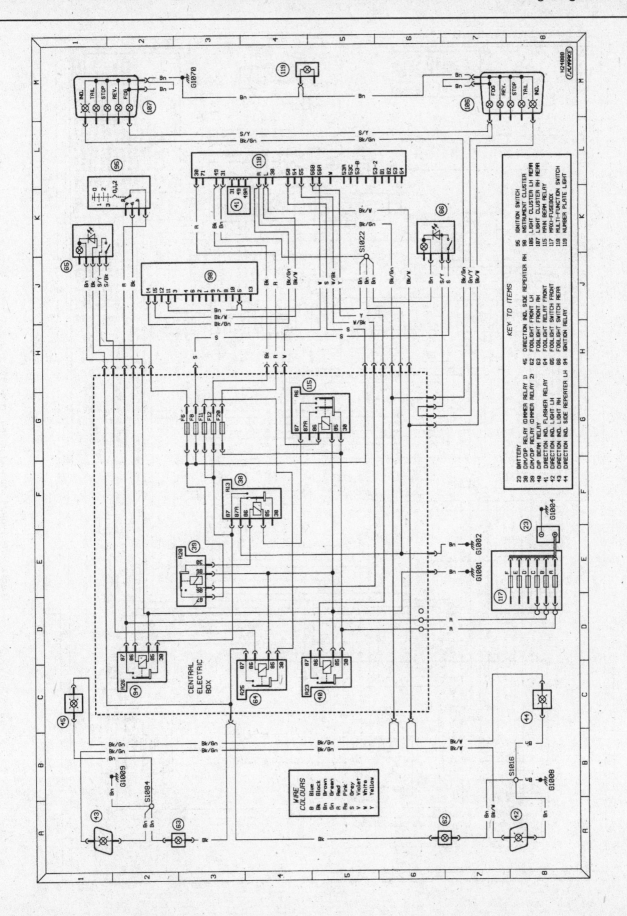

Diagram 9: Typical exterior lighting - fog and direction indicator lights - pre-1995 models

**KEY TO ITEMS**

| | | | |
|---|---|---|---|
| 23 | BATTERY | 45 | DIRECTION IND. SIDE REPEATER RH |
| 38 | DIM/DIP RELAY (DIMMER RELAY 1) | 62 | FOGLIGHT FRONT LH |
| 39 | DIM/DIP RELAY (DIMMER RELAY 2) | 63 | FOGLIGHT FRONT RH |
| 40 | DIP BEAM RELAY | 64 | FOGLIGHT RELAY FRONT |
| 41 | DIRECTION IND. FLASHER RELAY | 65 | FOGLIGHT SWITCH FRONT |
| 42 | DIRECTION IND. LIGHT LH | 66 | FOGLIGHT SWITCH REAR |
| 43 | DIRECTION IND. LIGHT RH | 94 | IGNITION RELAY |
| 44 | DIRECTION IND. SIDE REPEATER LH | | |

| | |
|---|---|
| 95 | IGNITION SWITCH |
| 98 | INSTRUMENT CLUSTER |
| 106 | LIGHT CLUSTER LH REAR |
| 107 | LIGHT CLUSTER RH REAR |
| 115 | MAIN BEAM RELAY |
| 117 | MAXI-FUSEBOX |
| 118 | MULTI-FUNCTION SWITCH |
| 119 | NUMBER PLATE LIGHT |

**WIRE COLOURS**

| | |
|---|---|
| B | Blue |
| Bk | Black |
| Bn | Brown |
| Gn | Green |
| R | Red |
| Rs | Pink |
| S | Grey |
| V | Violet |
| W | White |
| Y | Yellow |

CENTRAL ELECTRIC BOX

12

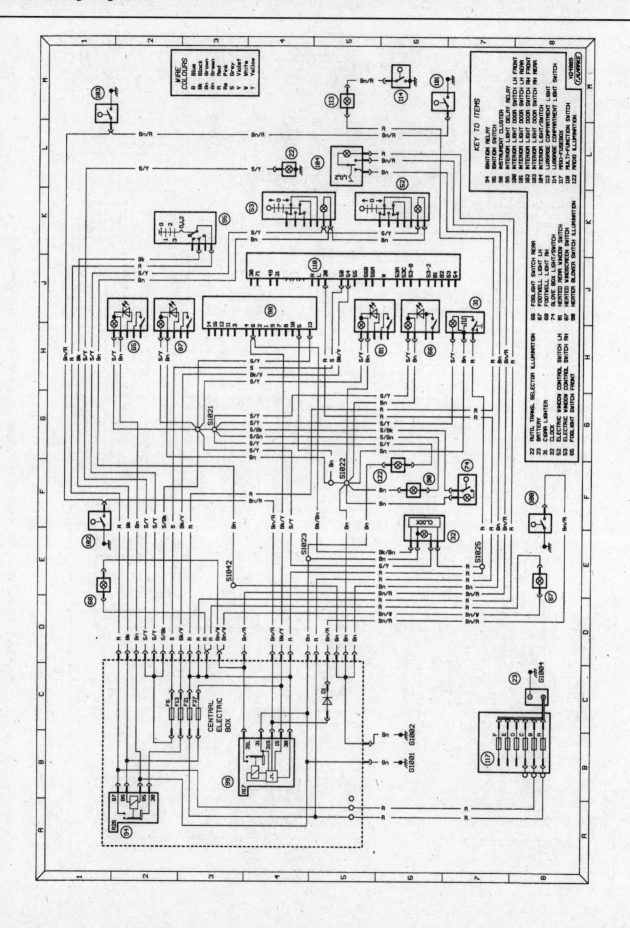

Diagram 10: Typical interior lighting - pre-1995 models

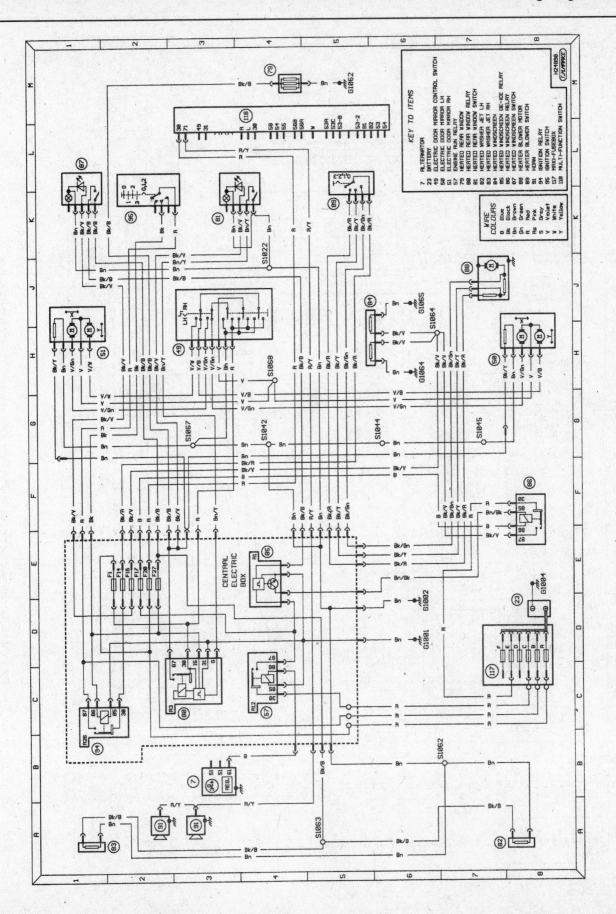

Diagram 11: Typical horn, heater blower, heated mirrors and screens - pre-1995 models

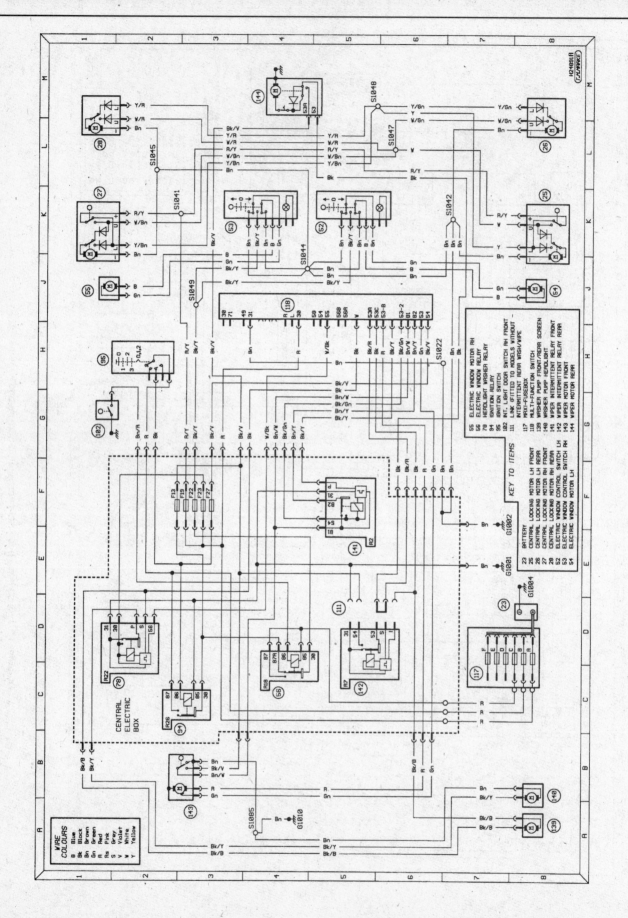

Diagram 12: Typical wash/wipe, central locking and electric windows - pre-1995 models

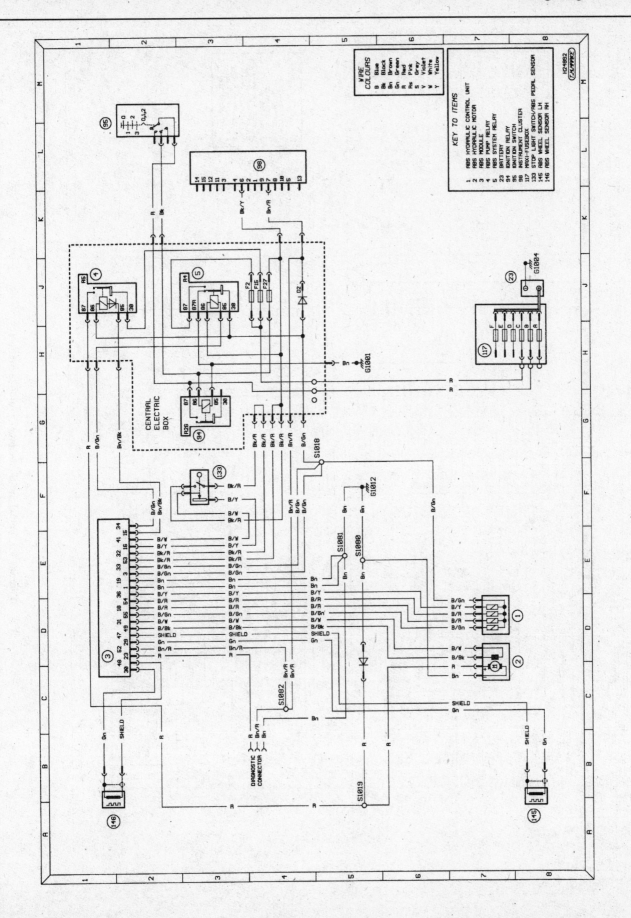

Diagram 13: Typical anti-lock brakes - pre-1995 models

WIRE COLOURS

| B | Blue |
|---|---|
| Bk | Black |
| Bn | Brown |
| Gn | Green |
| Rs | Pink |
| R | Red |
| S | Grey |
| V | Violet |
| W | White |
| Y | Yellow |

KEY TO ITEMS

1  ABS HYDRAULIC CONTROL UNIT
2  ABS HYDRAULIC MOTOR
3  ABS MODULE
4  ABS PUMP RELAY
5  ABS SYSTEM RELAY
23 BATTERY
94 IGNITION RELAY
95 IGNITION SWITCH
98 INSTRUMENT CLUSTER
117 MAXI-FUSEBOX
132 STOP LIGHT SWITCH/ABS PEDAL SENSOR
145 ABS WHEEL SENSOR LH
146 ABS WHEEL SENSOR RH

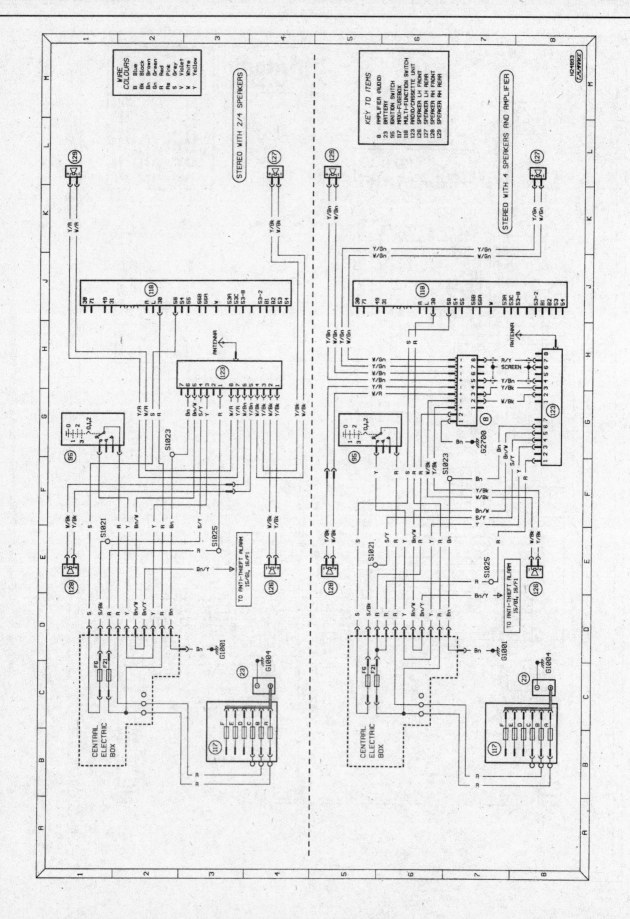

**Diagram 14: Typical radio/cassette - pre-1995 models**

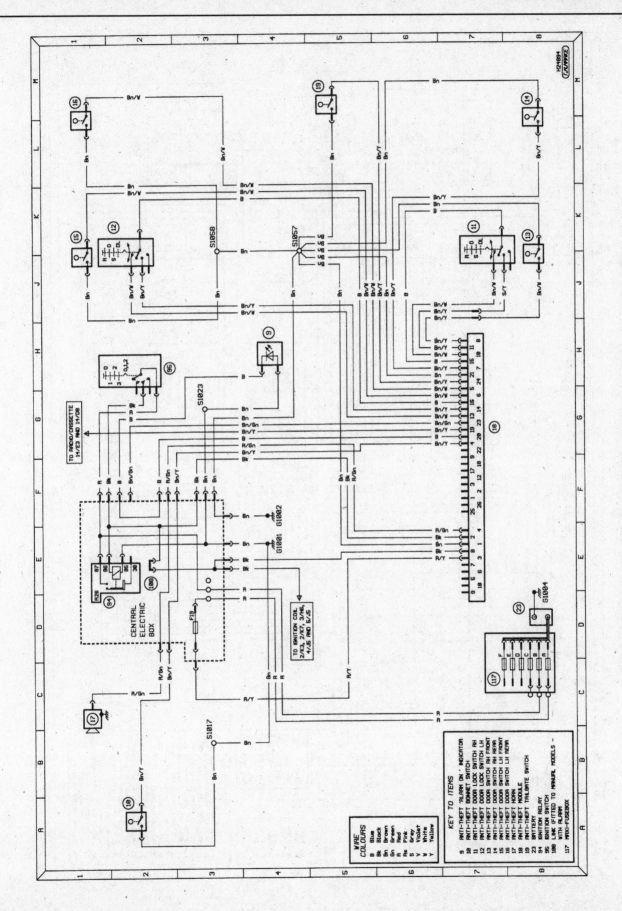

Diagram 15: Typical anti-theft alarm (models without central locking) - pre-1995 models

**KEY TO ITEMS**

9  ANTI-THEFT 'ALARM ON' INDICATOR
10  ANTI-THEFT BONNET SWITCH
11  ANTI-THEFT DOOR LOCK SWITCH RH
12  ANTI-THEFT DOOR LOCK SWITCH LH
13  ANTI-THEFT DOOR SWITCH RH FRONT
14  ANTI-THEFT DOOR SWITCH RH REAR
15  ANTI-THEFT DOOR SWITCH LH FRONT
16  ANTI-THEFT DOOR SWITCH LH REAR
17  ANTI-THEFT HORN
18  ANTI-THEFT MODULE
19  ANTI-THEFT TAILGATE SWITCH
23  BATTERY
94  IGNITION RELAY
95  IGNITION SWITCH
108  LINK (FITTED TO MANUAL MODELS - WITH ALARM
117  MAXI-FUSEBOX

**WIRE COLOURS**

B  Blue
Bk  Black
Bn  Brown
Gn  Green
R  Red
Rs  Pink
S  Grey
V  Violet
W  White
Y  Yellow

CENTRAL ELECTRIC BOX

TO RADIO/CASSETTE 14/E3 AND 14/D8

TO IGNITION COIL 2/K3, 2/K7, 3/H6, 4/J5 AND 6/J5

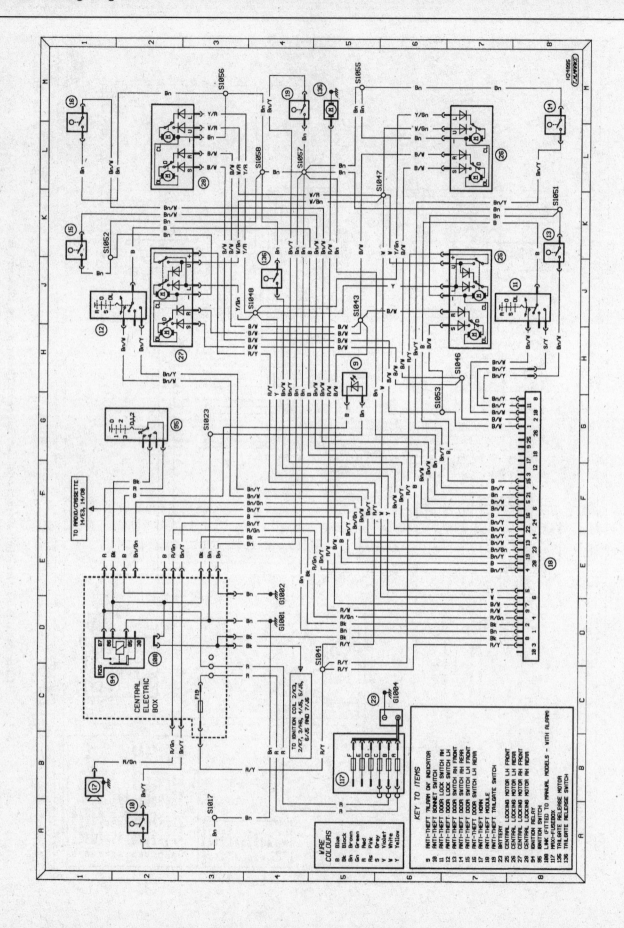

Diagram 16: Typical anti-theft alarm (models with central locking) - pre-1995 models

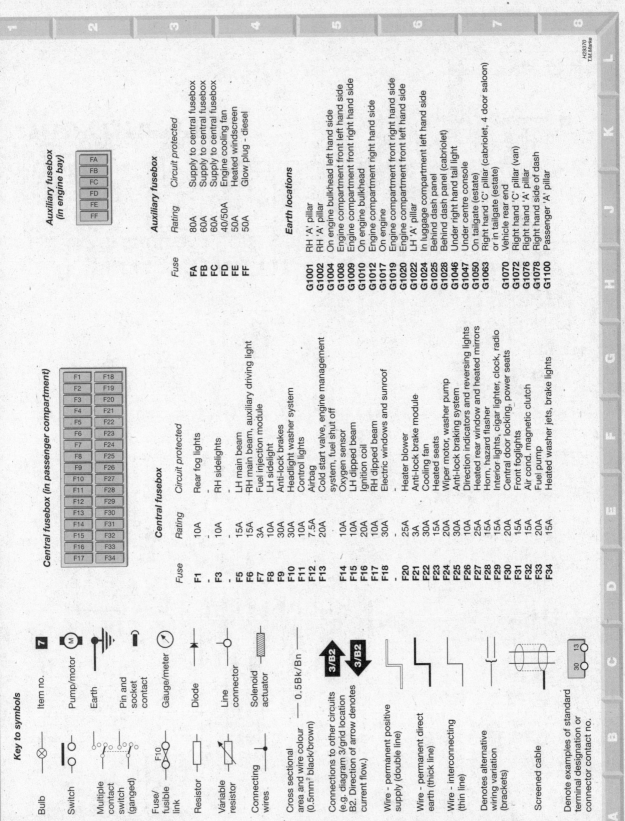

## Key to symbols

|  |  |
|---|---|
| Bulb | Bulb |
| Switch | Switch |
| Multiple contact switch (ganged) | Multiple contact switch |
| Fuse/ fusible link | Fuse/fusible link |
| Resistor | Resistor |
| Variable resistor | Variable resistor |
| Connecting wires | Connecting wires |
| Cross sectional area and wire colour | 0.5Bk/Bn (0.5mm² black/brown) |

Item no.

Pump/motor

Earth

Pin and socket contact

Gauge/meter

Diode

Line connector

Solenoid actuator

Connections to other circuits (e.g. diagram 3/grid location B2. Direction of arrow denotes current flow.)

Wire - permanent positive supply (double line)

Wire - permanent direct earth (thick line)

Wire - interconnecting (thin line)

Denotes alternative wiring variation (brackets)

Screened cable

Denote examples of standard terminal designation or connector contact no.

### Auxiliary fusebox (in engine bay)

FA
FB
FC
FD
FE
FF

### Auxiliary fusebox

| Fuse | Rating | Circuit protected |
|---|---|---|
| FA | 80A | Supply to central fusebox |
| FB | 60A | Supply to central fusebox |
| FC | 60A | Supply to central fusebox |
| FD | 40/50A | Engine cooling fan |
| FE | 50A | Heated windscreen |
| FF | 50A | Glow plug - diesel |

### Earth locations

| | |
|---|---|
| G1001 | RH 'A' pillar |
| G1002 | RH 'A' pillar |
| G1004 | On engine bulkhead left hand side |
| G1008 | Engine compartment front left hand side |
| G1009 | Engine compartment front right hand side |
| G1010 | On engine bulkhead |
| G1012 | Engine compartment right hand side |
| G1017 | On engine |
| G1019 | Engine compartment front right hand side |
| G1020 | Engine compartment front left hand side |
| G1022 | LH 'A' pillar |
| G1024 | In luggage compartment left hand side |
| G1025 | Behind dash panel |
| G1028 | Behind dash panel (cabriolet) |
| G1046 | Under right hand tail light |
| G1047 | Under centre console |
| G1050 | On tailgate (estate) |
| G1063 | Right hand 'C' pillar (cabriolet, 4 door saloon) or in tailgate (estate) |
| G1070 | Vehicle rear end |
| G1072 | Right hand 'C' pillar (van) |
| G1076 | Right hand 'A' pillar |
| G1078 | Right hand side of dash |
| G1100 | Passenger 'A' pillar |

### Central fusebox (in passenger compartment)

F1 F18
F2 F19
F3 F20
F4 F21
F5 F22
F6 F23
F7 F24
F8 F25
F9 F26
F10 F27
F11 F28
F12 F29
F13 F30
F14 F31
F15 F32
F16 F33
F17 F34

### Central fusebox

| Fuse | Rating | Circuit protected |
|---|---|---|
| F1 | 10A | Rear fog lights |
| F3 | 10A | RH sidelights |
| F5 | 15A | LH main beam |
| F6 | 15A | RH main beam, auxiliary driving light |
| F7 | 3A | Fuel injection module |
| F8 | 10A | LH sidelight |
| F9 | 30A | Anti-lock brakes |
| F10 | 10A | Headlight washer system |
| F11 | 7.5A | Control lights |
| F12 | 20A | Airbag |
| F13 | | Cold start valve, engine management system, fuel shut off |
| F14 | 10A | Oxygen sensor |
| F15 | 10A | LH dipped beam |
| F16 | 10A | Ignition coil |
| F17 | 30A | RH dipped beam |
| F18 | | Electric windows and sunroof |
| F20 | 25A | Heater blower |
| F21 | 3A | Anti-lock brake module |
| F22 | 30A | Cooling fan |
| F23 | 15A | Heated seats |
| F24 | 20A | Wiper motor, washer pump |
| F25 | 30A | Anti-lock braking system |
| F26 | 10A | Direction indicators and reversing lights |
| F27 | 25A | Heated rear window and heated mirrors |
| F28 | 15A | Horn, hazard flasher |
| F29 | 15A | Interior lights, cigar lighter, clock, radio |
| F30 | 20A | Central door locking, power seats |
| F31 | 15A | Front foglights |
| F32 | 15A | Air cond. magnetic clutch |
| F33 | 20A | Fuel pump |
| F34 | 15A | Heated washer jets, brake lights |

**Diagram 1 : Information for wiring diagrams - post 1995 models**

H29370
T.M.Marke

12

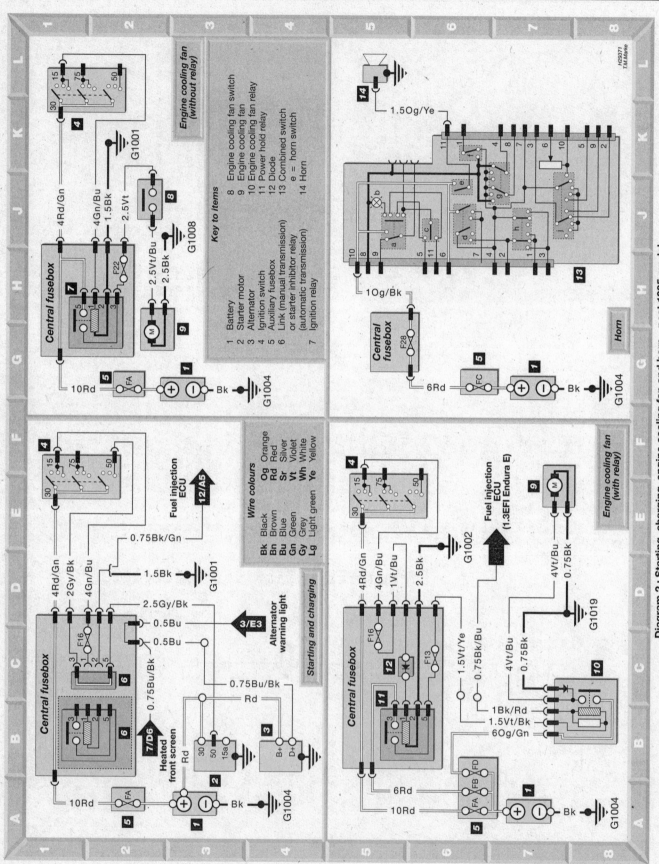

Diagram 2 : Starting, charging, engine cooling fan and horn - post 1995 models

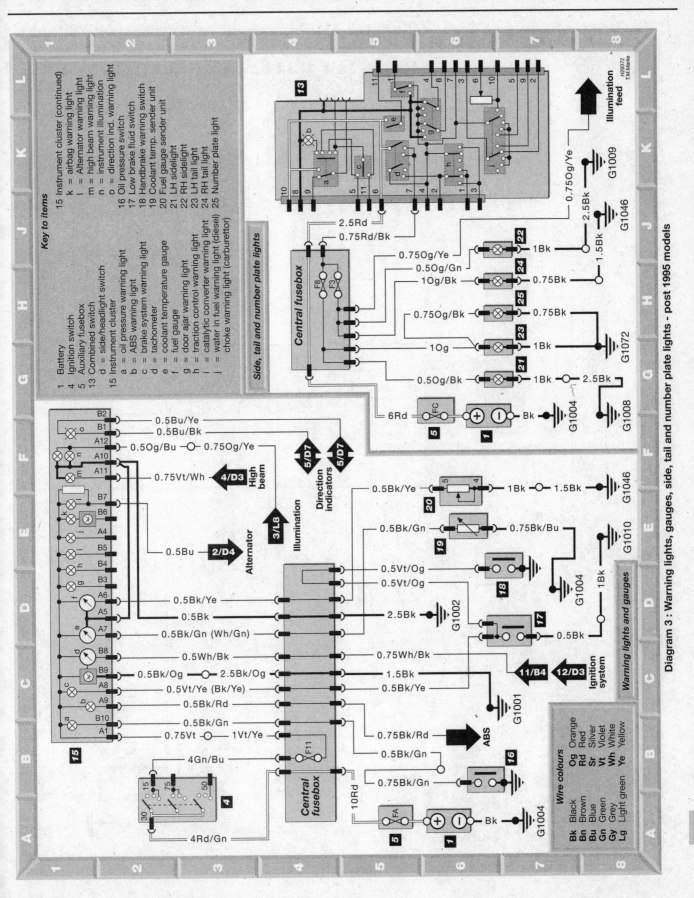

**Key to items**

15 Instrument cluster (continued)
  k = airbag warning light
  l = Alternator warning light
  m = high beam warning light
  n = instrument illumination
  o = direction ind. warning light
16 Oil pressure switch
17 Low brake fluid switch
18 Handbrake warning switch
19 Coolant temp. sender unit
20 Fuel gauge sender unit
21 LH sidelight
22 RH sidelight
23 LH tail light
24 RH tail light
25 Number plate light

1 Battery
4 Ignition switch
5 Auxiliary fusebox
13 Combined switch
  d = side/headlight switch
15 Instrument cluster
  a = oil pressure warning light
  b = ABS warning light
  c = brake system warning light
  d = tachometer
  e = coolant temperature gauge
  f = fuel gauge
  g = door ajar warning light
  h = traction control warning light
  i = catalytic converter warning light
  j = water in fuel warning light (diesel)
      choke warning light (carburettor)

Side, tail and number plate lights

Central fusebox

Illumination feed

Warning lights and gauges

Central fusebox

Direction indicators

Illumination

Alternator

High beam

Ignition system

ABS

**Wire colours**
Bk  Black
Bn  Brown
Bu  Blue
Gn  Green
Gy  Grey
Lg  Light green
Og  Orange
Rd  Red
Sr  Silver
Vt  Violet
Wh  White
Ye  Yellow

Diagram 3 : Warning lights, gauges, side, tail and number plate lights - post 1995 models

12

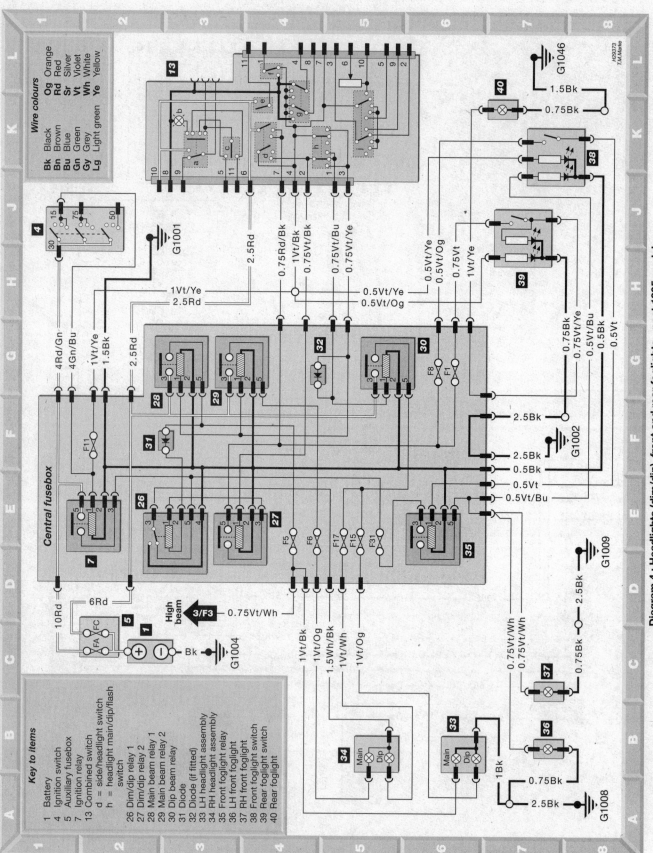

Diagram 4 : Headlights (dim/dip), front and rear foglights - post 1995 models

**Wire colours**

| | |
|---|---|
| Bk | Black |
| Bn | Brown |
| Bu | Blue |
| Gn | Green |
| Gy | Grey |
| Lg | Light green |

| | |
|---|---|
| Og | Orange |
| Rd | Red |
| Sr | Silver |
| Vt | Violet |
| Wh | White |
| Ye | Yellow |

**Key to items**

1 Battery
2 Ignition switch
4 Auxiliary fusebox
5 Ignition relay
13 Combined switch
  d = side/headlight switch
  h = headlight main/dip/flash switch
26 Dim/dip relay 1
27 Dim/dip relay 2
28 Main beam relay 1
29 Main beam relay 2
30 Dip beam relay
31 Diode
32 Diode (if fitted)
33 LH headlight assembly
34 RH headlight assembly
35 Front foglight relay
36 LH front foglight
37 RH front foglight
38 Front foglight switch
39 Rear foglight switch
40 Rear foglight

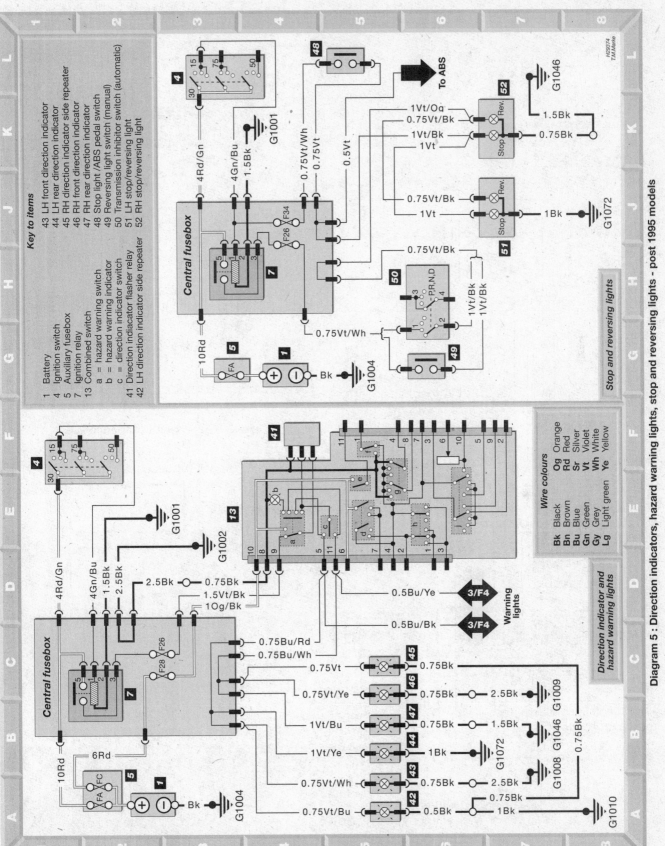

**Key to items**

1   Battery
4   Ignition switch
5   Auxiliary fusebox
7   Ignition relay
13  Combined switch
    a = hazard warning switch
    b = hazard warning indicator
    c = direction indicator switch
41  Direction indicacator flasher relay
42  LH direction indicator side repeater

43  LH front direction indicator
44  LH rear direction indicator
45  RH direction indicator side repeater
46  RH front direction indicator
47  RH rear direction indicator
48  Stop light/ABS pedal switch
49  Reversing light switch (manual)
50  Transmission inhibitor switch (automatic)
51  LH stop/reversing light
52  RH stop/reversing light

To ABS

Central fusebox

**Stop and reversing lights**

**Wire colours**

| Bk | Black | Og | Orange |
|---|---|---|---|
| Bn | Brown | Rd | Red |
| Bu | Blue | Sr | Silver |
| Gn | Green | Vt | Violet |
| Gy | Grey | Wh | White |
| Lg | Light green | Ye | Yellow |

Warning lights

**Direction indicator and hazard warning lights**

Diagram 5 : Direction indicators, hazard warning lights, stop and reversing lights - post 1995 models

**12**

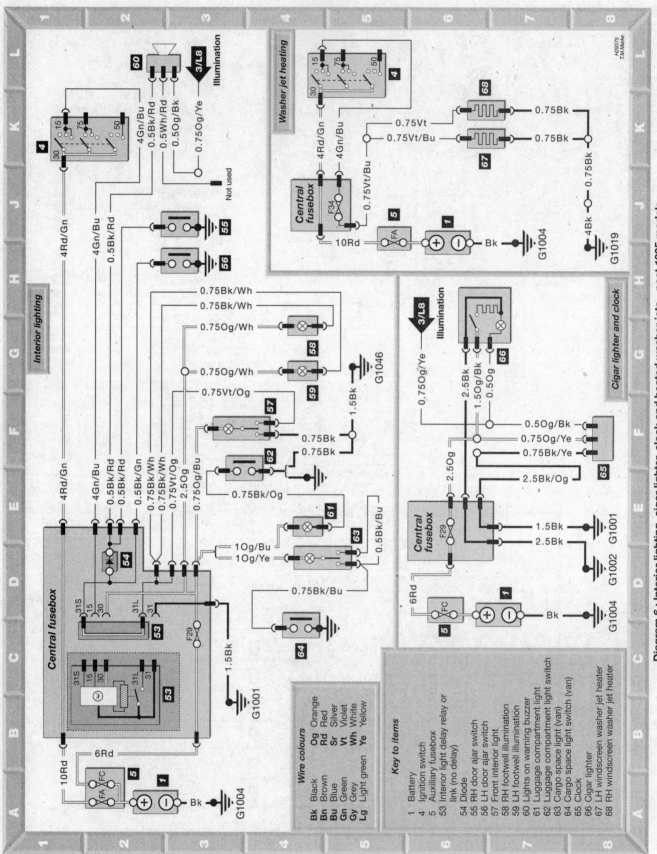

Diagram 6 : Interior lighting, cigar lighter, clock and heated washer jets – post 1995 models

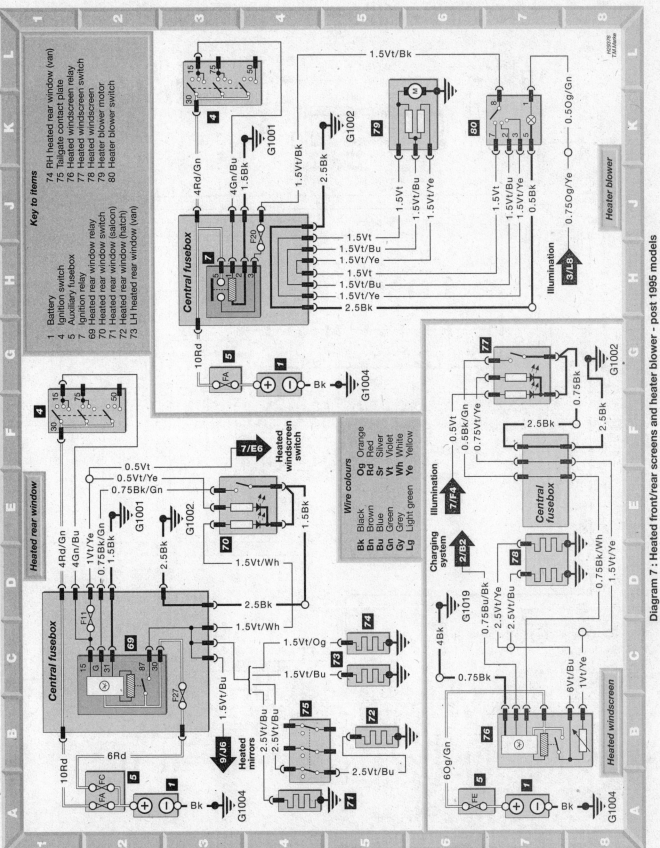

**Key to items**

1  Battery
4  Ignition switch
5  Auxiliary fusebox
7  Ignition relay
69  Heated rear window relay
70  Heated rear window switch
71  Heated rear window (saloon)
72  Heated rear window (hatch)
73  LH heated rear window (van)
74  RH heated rear window (van)
75  Tailgate contact plate
76  Heated windscreen relay
77  Heated windscreen switch
78  Heated windscreen
79  Heater blower motor
80  Heater blower switch

**Wire colours**

| Bk | Black | Og | Orange |
| Bn | Brown | Rd | Red |
| Bu | Blue | Sr | Silver |
| Gn | Green | Vt | Violet |
| Gy | Grey | Wh | White |
| Lg | Light green | Ye | Yellow |

Diagram 7 : Heated front/rear screens and heater blower - post 1995 models

**12**

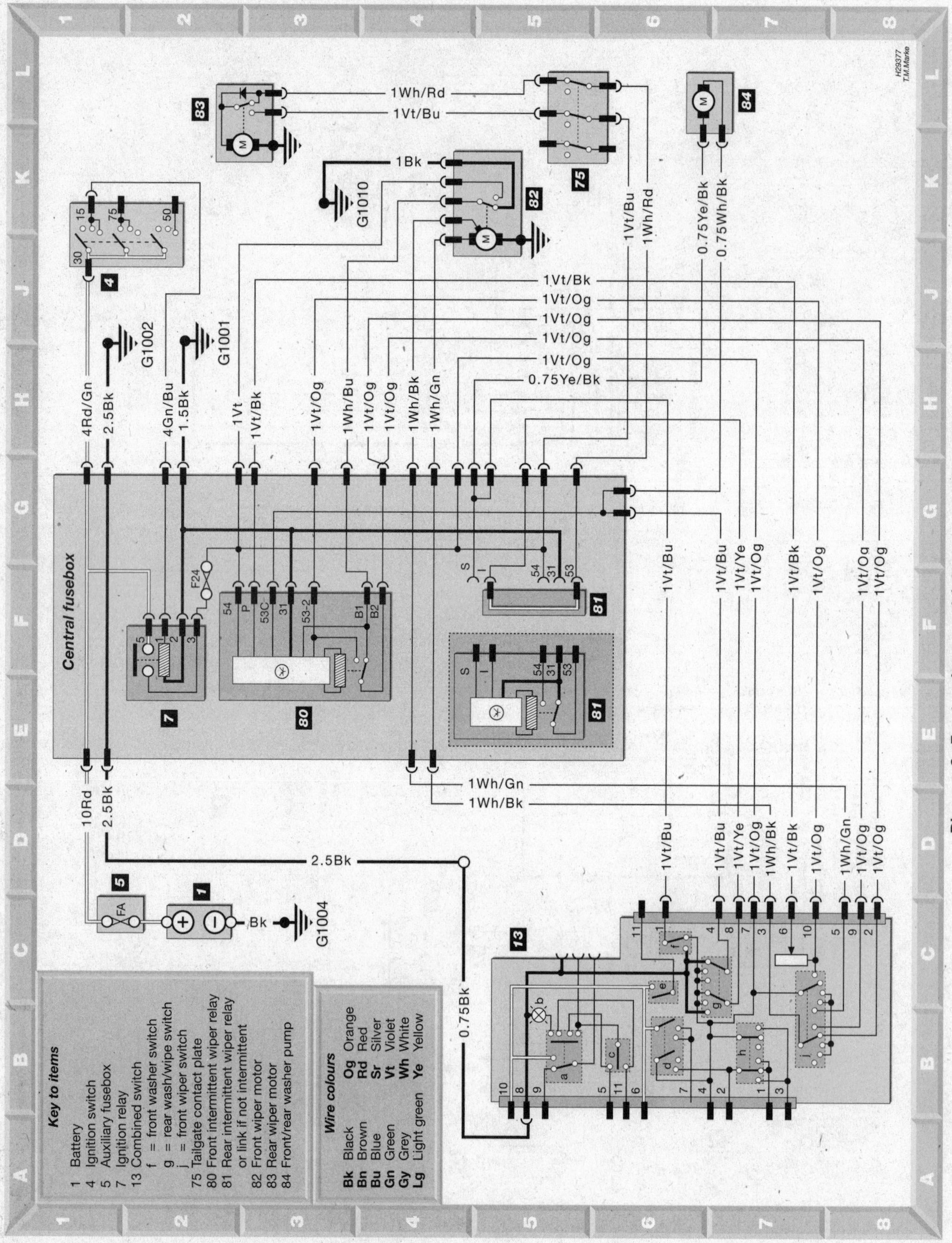

**Key to items**

1  Battery
4  Ignition switch
5  Auxiliary fusebox
7  Ignition relay
13  Combined switch
    f = front washer switch
    g = rear wash/wipe switch
    j = front wiper switch
75  Tailgate contact plate
80  Front intermittent wiper relay
81  Rear intermittent wiper relay
    or link if not intermittent
82  Front wiper motor
83  Rear wiper motor
84  Front/rear washer pump

**Wire colours**

| | | | |
|---|---|---|---|
| Bk | Black | Og | Orange |
| Bn | Brown | Rd | Red |
| Bu | Blue | Sr | Silver |
| Gn | Green | Vt | Violet |
| Gy | Grey | Wh | White |
| Lg | Light green | Ye | Yellow |

Diagram 8 : Front and rear wash/wipe – post 1995 models

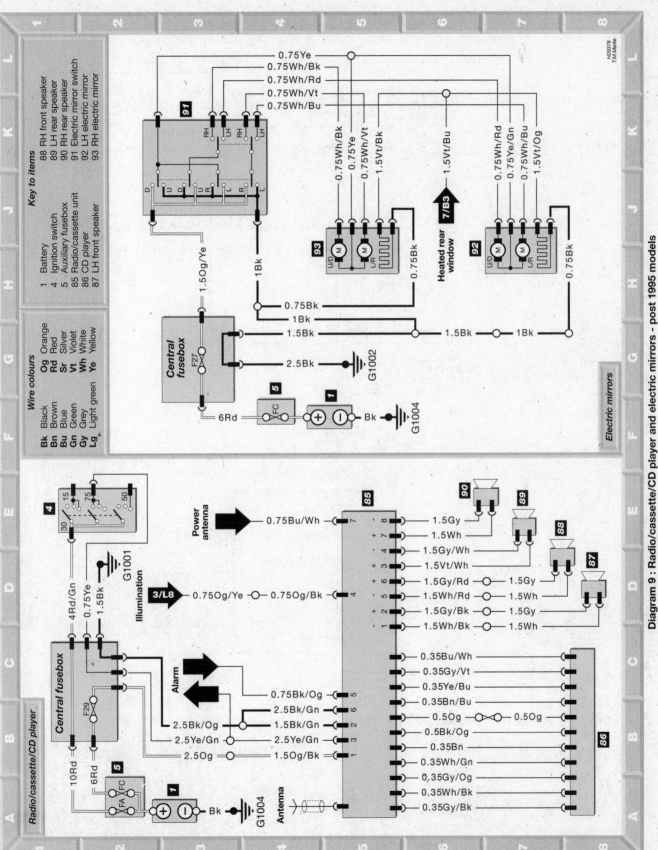

Diagram 9 : Radio/cassette/CD player and electric mirrors - post 1995 models

**Key to items**

1   Battery
4   Ignition switch
5   Auxiliary fusebox
85  Radio/cassette unit
86  CD player
87  LH front speaker
88  RH front speaker
89  LH rear speaker
90  RH rear speaker
91  Electric mirror switch
92  LH electric mirror
93  RH electric mirror

**Wire colours**

| | | | |
|---|---|---|---|
| Bk | Black | Og | Orange |
| Bn | Brown | Rd | Red |
| Bu | Blue | Sr | Silver |
| Gn | Green | Vt | Violet |
| Gy | Grey | Wh | White |
| Lg | Light green | Ye | Yellow |

*Electric mirrors*

*Radio/cassette/CD player*

**12**

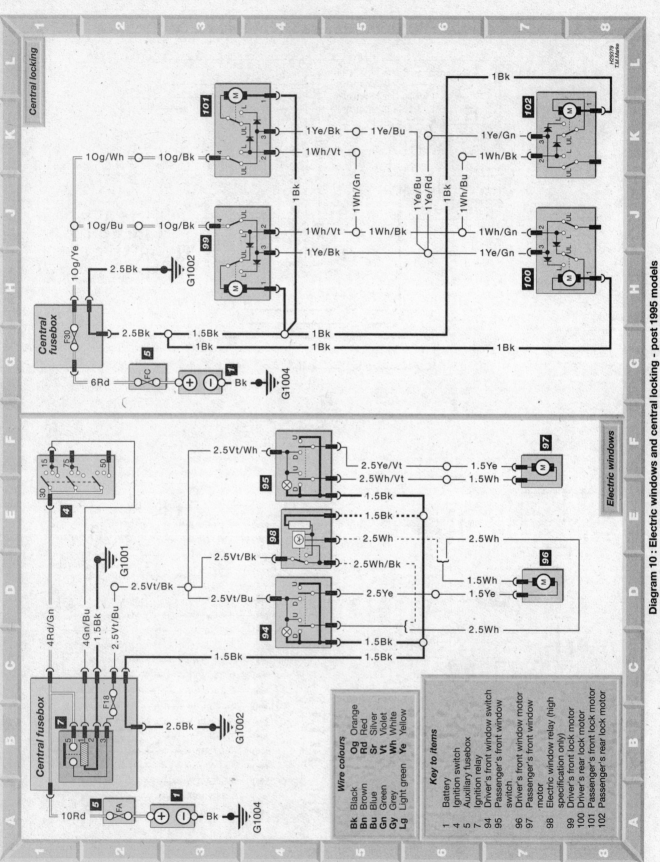

**Diagram 10 : Electric windows and central locking - post 1995 models**

| Wire colours | | |
|---|---|---|
| **Bk** Black | **Og** Orange | |
| **Bn** Brown | **Rd** Red | |
| **Bu** Blue | **Sr** Silver | |
| **Gn** Green | **Vt** Violet | |
| **Gy** Grey | **Wh** White | |
| **Lg** Light green | **Ye** Yellow | |

**Key to items**

| | |
|---|---|
| 1 | Battery |
| 4 | Ignition switch |
| 5 | Auxiliary fusebox |
| 7 | Ignition relay |
| 94 | Driver's front window switch |
| 95 | Passenger's front window switch |
| 96 | Driver's front window motor |
| 97 | Passenger's front window motor |
| 98 | Electric window relay (high specification only) |
| 99 | Driver's front lock motor |
| 100 | Driver's rear lock motor |
| 101 | Passenger's front lock motor |
| 102 | Passenger's rear lock motor |

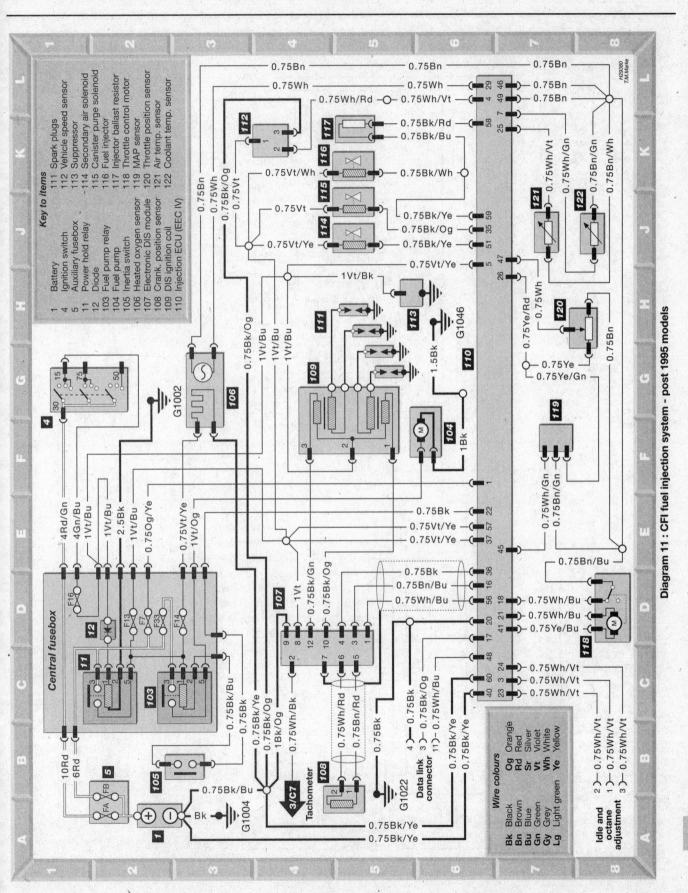

**Key to items**

| | | | |
|---|---|---|---|
| 1 | Battery | 111 | Spark plugs |
| 4 | Ignition switch | 112 | Vehicle speed sensor |
| 5 | Auxiliary fusebox | 113 | Suppressor |
| 11 | Power hold relay | 114 | Secondary air solenoid |
| 12 | Diode | 115 | Canister purge solenoid |
| 103 | Fuel pump relay | 116 | Fuel injector |
| 104 | Fuel pump | 117 | Injector ballast resistor |
| 105 | Inertia switch | 118 | Throttle control motor |
| 106 | Heated oxygen sensor | 119 | MAP sensor |
| 107 | Electronic DIS module | 120 | Throttle position sensor |
| 108 | Crank. position sensor | 121 | Air temp. sensor |
| 109 | DIS ignition coil | 122 | Coolant temp. sensor |
| 110 | Injection ECU (EEC IV) | | |

**Wire colours**

| | | | |
|---|---|---|---|
| Bk | Black | Og | Orange |
| Bn | Brown | Rd | Red |
| Bu | Blue | Sr | Silver |
| Gn | Green | Vt | Violet |
| Gy | Grey | Wh | White |
| Lg | Light green | Ye | Yellow |

**Diagram 11 : CFI fuel injection system - post 1995 models**

**Central fusebox**

**Data link connector**

**Tachometer**

**Idle and octane adjustment**

12

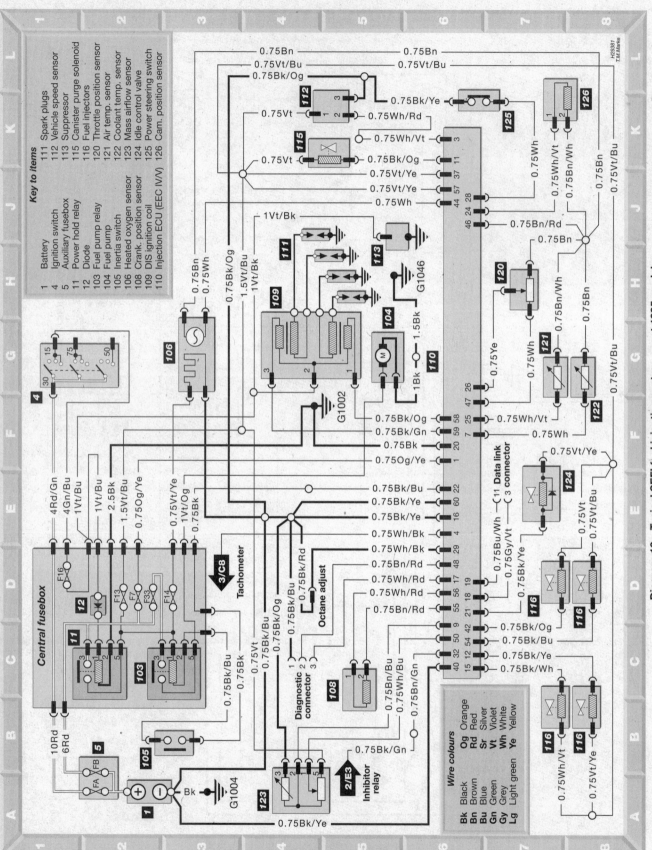

Diagram 12 : Typical SEFI fuel injection system - post 1995 models

**Key to items**

1 Battery
4 Ignition switch
5 Auxiliary fusebox
11 Power hold relay
12 Diode
103 Fuel pump relay
104 Fuel pump
105 Inertia switch
106 Heated oxygen sensor
108 Crank. position sensor
109 DIS ignition coil
110 Injection ECU (EEC IV/V)
111 Spark plugs
112 Vehicle speed sensor
113 Suppressor
115 Canister purge solenoid
116 Fuel injectors
120 Throttle position sensor
121 Air temp. sensor
122 Coolant temp. sensor
123 Mass airflow sensor
124 Idle control valve
125 Power steering switch
126 Cam. position sensor

**Wire colours**

| Bk | Black | Og | Orange |
|----|-------|----|--------|
| Bn | Brown | Rd | Red |
| Bu | Blue | Sr | Silver |
| Gn | Green | Vt | Violet |
| Gy | Grey | Wh | White |
| Lg | Light green | Ye | Yellow |

# Dimensions and weights

**Note:** *All figures are approximate, and may vary according to model.  Refer to manufacturer's data for exact figures.*

## Dimensions

Overall length:
  Escort Hatchback/Cabriolet . . . . . . . . . . . . . . . . . . .4036 mm
  Escort Estate . . . . . . . . . . . . . . . . . . . . . . . . . . . . . .4268 mm
  Escort Van . . . . . . . . . . . . . . . . . . . . . . . . . . . . . . . .4256 mm
  Escort/Orion Saloon . . . . . . . . . . . . . . . . . . . . . . . .4229 mm
Overall width - including mirrors . . . . . . . . . . . . . . . . . .1875 mm
Overall height (unladen):
  Escort Hatchback/Cabriolet . . . . . . . . . . . . . . . . . . .1395 mm
  Escort Estate . . . . . . . . . . . . . . . . . . . . . . . . . . . . . .1409 mm
  Escort Van . . . . . . . . . . . . . . . . . . . . . . . . . . . . . . . .1625 mm
  Escort/Orion Saloon . . . . . . . . . . . . . . . . . . . . . . . .1395 mm
Wheelbase:
  All models except Escort Van . . . . . . . . . . . . . . . . .2525 mm
  Escort Van . . . . . . . . . . . . . . . . . . . . . . . . . . . . . . . .2598 mm
Front track . . . . . . . . . . . . . . . . . . . . . . . . . . . . . . . . . .1440 mm
Rear track:
  All models except Escort Van . . . . . . . . . . . . . .1439 to 1462 mm*
  Escort Van . . . . . . . . . . . . . . . . . . . . . . . . . . . . . . . .1436 mm

*Dependent on rear brake type/specification.*

## Weights

Kerb weight*:
  Escort 3-door Hatchback . . . . . . . . . . . . . . . . . . . .901 to 1006 kg
  Escort 5-door Hatchback . . . . . . . . . . . . . . . . . . . .921 to 1026 kg
  Escort Cabriolet . . . . . . . . . . . . . . . . . . . . . . . . . . . . . . . .1117 kg
  Escort Estate . . . . . . . . . . . . . . . . . . . . . . . . . . . .976 to 1041 kg
  Escort/Orion 4-door Saloon . . . . . . . . . . . . . . . .1006 to 1021 kg
  Escort Van . . . . . . . . . . . . . . . . . . . . . . . . . . . . . .975 to 1010 kg
Maximum gross vehicle weight:
  Escort 3-door Hatchback . . . . . . . . . . . . . . . . . .1350 to 1450 kg
  Escort 5-door Hatchback . . . . . . . . . . . . . . . . . .1375 to 1475 kg
  Escort Cabriolet . . . . . . . . . . . . . . . . . . . . . . . . . . . . . . .1525 kg
  Escort Estate . . . . . . . . . . . . . . . . . . . . . . . . . .1425 to 1525 kg
  Escort/Orion 4-door Saloon . . . . . . . . . . . . . . . .1425 to 1500 kg
  Escort Van . . . . . . . . . . . . . . . . . . . . . . . . . . . . . .575 to 1800 kg
Maximum roof rack load . . . . . . . . . . . . . . . . . . . . . . . . . . .75 kg
Maximum towing weight . . . . . .Refer to your Ford dealer for weights
                    and legal requirements concerning
                    anticipated gradients and altitudes.

*Exact kerb weight varies depending on model - refer to VIN plate.*

## Length (distance)

| | | | | | |
|---|---|---|---|---|---|
| Inches (in) | x 25.4 | = Millimetres (mm) | x 0.0394 | = | Inches (in) |
| Feet (ft) | x 0.305 | = Metres (m) | x 3.281 | = | Feet (ft) |
| Miles | x 1.609 | = Kilometres (km) | x 0.621 | = | Miles |

## Volume (capacity)

| | | | | | |
|---|---|---|---|---|---|
| Cubic inches (cu in; in³) | x 16.387 | = Cubic centimetres (cc; cm³) | x 0.061 | = | Cubic inches (cu in; in³) |
| Imperial pints (Imp pt) | x 0.568 | = Litres (l) | x 1.76 | = | Imperial pints (Imp pt) |
| Imperial quarts (Imp qt) | x 1.137 | = Litres (l) | x 0.88 | = | Imperial quarts (Imp qt) |
| Imperial quarts (Imp qt) | x 1.201 | = US quarts (US qt) | x 0.833 | = | Imperial quarts (Imp qt) |
| US quarts (US qt) | x 0.946 | = Litres (l) | x 1.057 | = | US quarts (US qt) |
| Imperial gallons (Imp gal) | x 4.546 | = Litres (l) | x 0.22 | = | Imperial gallons (Imp gal) |
| Imperial gallons (Imp gal) | x 1.201 | = US gallons (US gal) | x 0.833 | = | Imperial gallons (Imp gal) |
| US gallons (US gal) | x 3.785 | = Litres (l) | x 0.264 | = | US gallons (US gal) |

## Mass (weight)

| | | | | | |
|---|---|---|---|---|---|
| Ounces (oz) | x 28.35 | = Grams (g) | x 0.035 | = | Ounces (oz) |
| Pounds (lb) | x 0.454 | = Kilograms (kg) | x 2.205 | = | Pounds (lb) |

## Force

| | | | | | |
|---|---|---|---|---|---|
| Ounces-force (ozf; oz) | x 0.278 | = Newtons (N) | x 3.6 | = | Ounces-force (ozf; oz) |
| Pounds-force (lbf; lb) | x 4.448 | = Newtons (N) | x 0.225 | = | Pounds-force (lbf; lb) |
| Newtons (N) | x 0.1 | = Kilograms-force (kgf; kg) | x 9.81 | = | Newtons (N) |

## Pressure

| | | | | | |
|---|---|---|---|---|---|
| Pounds-force per square inch (psi; lbf/in²; lb/in²) | x 0.070 | = Kilograms-force per square centimetre (kgf/cm²; kg/cm²) | x 14.223 | = | Pounds-force per square inch (psi; lbf/in²; lb/in²) |
| Pounds-force per square inch (psi; lbf/in²; lb/in²) | x 0.068 | = Atmospheres (atm) | x 14.696 | = | Pounds-force per square inch (psi; lbf/in²; lb/in²) |
| Pounds-force per square inch (psi; lbf/in²; lb/in²) | x 0.069 | = Bars | x 14.5 | = | Pounds-force per square inch (psi; lbf/in²; lb/in²) |
| Pounds-force per square inch (psi; lbf/in²; lb/in²) | x 6.895 | = Kilopascals (kPa) | x 0.145 | = | Pounds-force per square inch (psi; lbf/in²; lb/in²) |
| Kilopascals (kPa) | x 0.01 | = Kilograms-force per square centimetre (kgf/cm²; kg/cm²) | x 98.1 | = | Kilopascals (kPa) |
| Millibar (mbar) | x 100 | = Pascals (Pa) | x 0.01 | = | Millibar (mbar) |
| Millibar (mbar) | x 0.0145 | = Pounds-force per square inch (psi; lbf/in²; lb/in²) | x 68.947 | = | Millibar (mbar) |
| Millibar (mbar) | x 0.75 | = Millimetres of mercury (mmHg) | x 1.333 | = | Millibar (mbar) |
| Millibar (mbar) | x 0.401 | = Inches of water (inH₂O) | x 2.491 | = | Millibar (mbar) |
| Millimetres of mercury (mmHg) | x 0.535 | = Inches of water (inH₂O) | x 1.868 | = | Millimetres of mercury (mmHg) |
| Inches of water (inH₂O) | x 0.036 | = Pounds-force per square inch (psi; lbf/in²; lb/in²) | x 27.68 | = | Inches of water (inH₂O) |

## Torque (moment of force)

| | | | | | |
|---|---|---|---|---|---|
| Pounds-force inches (lbf in; lb in) | x 1.152 | = Kilograms-force centimetre (kgf cm; kg cm) | x 0.868 | = | Pounds-force inches (lbf in; lb in) |
| Pounds-force inches (lbf in; lb in) | x 0.113 | = Newton metres (Nm) | x 8.85 | = | Pounds-force inches (lbf in; lb in) |
| Pounds-force inches (lbf in; lb in) | x 0.083 | = Pounds-force feet (lbf ft; lb ft) | x 12 | = | Pounds-force inches (lbf in; lb in) |
| Pounds-force feet (lbf ft; lb ft) | x 0.138 | = Kilograms-force metres (kgf m; kg m) | x 7.233 | = | Pounds-force feet (lbf ft; lb ft) |
| Pounds-force feet (lbf ft; lb ft) | x 1.356 | = Newton metres (Nm) | x 0.738 | = | Pounds-force feet (lbf ft; lb ft) |
| Newton metres (Nm) | x 0.102 | = Kilograms-force metres (kgf m; kg m) | x 9.804 | = | Newton metres (Nm) |

## Power

| | | | | | |
|---|---|---|---|---|---|
| Horsepower (hp) | x 745.7 | = Watts (W) | x 0.0013 | = | Horsepower (hp) |

## Velocity (speed)

| | | | | | |
|---|---|---|---|---|---|
| Miles per hour (miles/hr; mph) | x 1.609 | = Kilometres per hour (km/hr; kph) | x 0.621 | = | Miles per hour (miles/hr; mph) |

## Fuel consumption*

| | | | | | |
|---|---|---|---|---|---|
| Miles per gallon (mpg) | x 0.354 | = Kilometres per litre (km/l) | x 2.825 | = | Miles per gallon (mpg) |

## Temperature

Degrees Fahrenheit = (°C x 1.8) + 32

Degrees Celsius (Degrees Centigrade; °C) = (°F - 32) x 0.56

*It is common practice to convert from miles per gallon (mpg) to litres/100 kilometres (l/100km), where mpg x l/100 km = 282*

Spare parts are available from many sources, including maker's appointed garages, accessory shops, and motor factors. To be sure of obtaining the correct parts, it will sometimes be necessary to quote the vehicle identification number (see *"Vehicle identification"* on page REF•5). If possible, it can also be useful to take the old parts along for positive identification. Items such as starter motors and alternators may be available under a service exchange scheme - any parts returned should always be clean.

Our advice regarding spare part sources is as follows.

## Officially-appointed garages

This is the best source of parts which are peculiar to your car, and which are not otherwise generally available (eg badges, interior trim, certain body panels, etc). It is also the only place at which you should buy parts if the vehicle is still under warranty.

## Accessory shops

These are very good places to buy materials and components needed for the maintenance of your car (oil, air and fuel filters, spark plugs, light bulbs, drivebelts, oils and greases, brake pads, touch-up paint, etc). Components of this nature sold by a reputable shop are of the same standard as those used by the car manufacturer.

Besides components, these shops also sell tools and general accessories, usually have convenient opening hours, charge lower prices, and can often be found not far from home. Some accessory shops have parts counters where the components needed for almost any repair job can be purchased or ordered.

## Motor factors

Good factors will stock all the more important components which wear out comparatively quickly, and can sometimes supply individual components needed for the overhaul of a larger assembly (eg brake seals and hydraulic parts, bearing shells, pistons, valves, alternator brushes). They may also handle work such as cylinder block reboring, crankshaft regrinding and balancing, etc.

## Tyre and exhaust specialists

These outlets may be independent, or members of a local or national chain. They frequently offer competitive prices when compared with a main dealer or local garage, but it will pay to obtain several quotes before making a decision. When researching prices, also ask what "extras" may be added - for instance, fitting a new valve and balancing the wheel are both commonly charged on top of the price of a new tyre.

## Other sources

Beware of parts or materials obtained from market stalls, car boot sales or similar outlets. Such items are not invariably sub-standard, but there is little chance of compensation if they do prove unsatisfactory. In the case of safety-critical components such as brake pads, there is the risk not only of financial loss but also of an accident causing injury or death.

Second-hand components or assemblies obtained from a car breaker can be a good buy in some circumstances, but this sort of purchase is best made by the experienced DIY mechanic.

# Jacking and vehicle support

The jack supplied with the vehicle tool kit should only be used for changing the roadwheels - see *"Wheel changing"* at the front of this manual. When jacking up the vehicle to carry out repair or maintenance tasks, a pillar or trolley type jack of suitable lifting capacity must be used, supplemented with axle stands positioned only beneath the appropriate points under the vehicle **(see illustrations)**. Note that the vehicle must never be jacked up at the rear under the axle beam.

*The maximum kerb weight of the vehicle must not be exceeded when jacking and supporting the vehicle. Do not under any circumstances jack up the rear of the vehicle under the rear axle.* **Never** *work under, around or near a raised vehicle unless it is supported in at least two places with axle stands.*

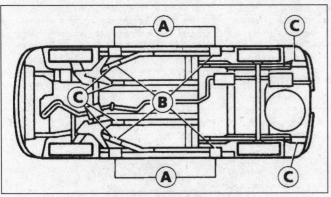

**Jacking point locations on vehicle underbody - all models except Van**

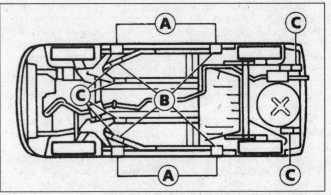

**Jacking point locations on vehicle underbody - Van models**

A  *Jacking points for emergency jack supplied with vehicle*
B  *Jacking points for workshop jack*
C  *Support points for axle stands or workshop jack  - jack to be used under points B and C only*

A  *Jacking points for emergency jack supplied with vehicle*
B  *Jacking points for workshop jack*
C  *Support points for axle stands or workshop jack  - jack to be used under points B and C only*

Whenever servicing, repair or overhaul work is carried out on the car or its components, observe the following procedures and instructions. This will assist in carrying out the operation efficiently and to a professional standard of workmanship.

## Joint mating faces and gaskets

When separating components at their mating faces, never insert screwdrivers or similar implements into the joint between the faces in order to prise them apart. This can cause severe damage which results in oil leaks, coolant leaks, etc upon reassembly. Separation is usually achieved by tapping along the joint with a soft-faced hammer in order to break the seal. However, note that this method may not be suitable where dowels are used for component location.

Where a gasket is used between the mating faces of two components, a new one must be fitted on reassembly; fit it dry unless otherwise stated in the repair procedure. Make sure that the mating faces are clean and dry, with all traces of old gasket removed. When cleaning a joint face, use a tool which is unlikely to score or damage the face, and remove any burrs or nicks with an oilstone or fine file.

Make sure that tapped holes are cleaned with a pipe cleaner, and keep them free of jointing compound, if this is being used, unless specifically instructed otherwise.

Ensure that all orifices, channels or pipes are clear, and blow through them, preferably using compressed air.

## Oil seals

Oil seals can be removed by levering them out with a wide flat-bladed screwdriver or similar implement. Alternatively, a number of self-tapping screws may be screwed into the seal, and these used as a purchase for pliers or some similar device in order to pull the seal free.

Whenever an oil seal is removed from its working location, either individually or as part of an assembly, it should be renewed.

The very fine sealing lip of the seal is easily damaged, and will not seal if the surface it contacts is not completely clean and free from scratches, nicks or grooves. If the original sealing surface of the component cannot be restored, and the manufacturer has not made provision for slight relocation of the seal relative to the sealing surface, the component should be renewed.

Protect the lips of the seal from any surface which may damage them in the course of fitting. Use tape or a conical sleeve where possible. Lubricate the seal lips with oil before fitting and, on dual-lipped seals, fill the space between the lips with grease.

Unless otherwise stated, oil seals must be fitted with their sealing lips toward the lubricant to be sealed.

Use a tubular drift or block of wood of the appropriate size to install the seal and, if the seal housing is shouldered, drive the seal down to the shoulder. If the seal housing is unshouldered, the seal should be fitted with its face flush with the housing top face (unless otherwise instructed).

## Screw threads and fastenings

Seized nuts, bolts and screws are quite a common occurrence where corrosion has set in, and the use of penetrating oil or releasing fluid will often overcome this problem if the offending item is soaked for a while before attempting to release it. The use of an impact driver may also provide a means of releasing such stubborn fastening devices, when used in conjunction with the appropriate screwdriver bit or socket. If none of these methods works, it may be necessary to resort to the careful application of heat, or the use of a hacksaw or nut splitter device.

Studs are usually removed by locking two nuts together on the threaded part, and then using a spanner on the lower nut to unscrew the stud. Studs or bolts which have broken off below the surface of the component in which they are mounted can sometimes be removed using a stud extractor. Always ensure that a blind tapped hole is completely free from oil, grease, water or other fluid before installing the bolt or stud. Failure to do this could cause the housing to crack due to the hydraulic action of the bolt or stud as it is screwed in.

When tightening a castellated nut to accept a split pin, tighten the nut to the specified torque, where applicable, and then tighten further to the next split pin hole. Never slacken the nut to align the split pin hole, unless stated in the repair procedure.

When checking or retightening a nut or bolt to a specified torque setting, slacken the nut or bolt by a quarter of a turn, and then retighten to the specified setting. However, this should not be attempted where angular tightening has been used.

For some screw fastenings, notably cylinder head bolts or nuts, torque wrench settings are no longer specified for the latter stages of tightening, "angle-tightening" being called up instead. Typically, a fairly low torque wrench setting will be applied to the bolts/nuts in the correct sequence, followed by one or more stages of tightening through specified angles.

## Locknuts, locktabs and washers

Any fastening which will rotate against a component or housing during tightening should always have a washer between it and the relevant component or housing.

Spring or split-washers should always be renewed when they are used to lock a critical component such as a big-end bearing retaining bolt or nut. Locktabs which are folded over to retain a nut or bolt should always be renewed.

Self-locking nuts can be re-used in non-critical areas, providing resistance can be felt when the locking portion passes over the bolt or stud thread. However, it should be noted that self-locking stiffnuts tend to lose their effectiveness after long periods of use, and should then be renewed as a matter of course.

Split pins must always be replaced with new ones of the correct size for the hole.

When thread-locking compound is found on the threads of a fastener which is to be re-used, it should be cleaned off with a wire brush and solvent, and fresh compound applied on reassembly.

## Special tools

Some repair procedures in this manual entail the use of special tools such as a press, two or three-legged pullers, spring compressors, etc. Wherever possible, suitable readily-available alternatives to the manufacturer's special tools are described, and are shown in use. In some instances, where no alternative is possible, it has been necessary to resort to the use of a manufacturer's tool, and this has been done for reasons of safety as well as the efficient completion of the repair operation. Unless you are highly-skilled and have a thorough understanding of the procedures described, never attempt to bypass the use of any special tool when the procedure described specifies its use. Not only is there a very great risk of personal injury, but expensive damage could be caused to the components involved.

## Environmental considerations

When disposing of used engine oil, brake fluid, antifreeze, etc, give due consideration to any detrimental environmental effects. Do not, for instance, pour any of the above liquids down drains into the general sewage system, or onto the ground to soak away. Many local council refuse tips provide a facility for waste oil disposal, as do some garages. If none of these facilities are available, consult your local Environmental Health Department, or the National Rivers Authority, for further advice.

With the universal tightening-up of legislation regarding the emission of environmentally-harmful substances from motor vehicles, most vehicles have tamperproof devices fitted to the main adjustment points of the fuel system. These devices are primarily designed to prevent unqualified persons from adjusting the fuel/air mixture, with the chance of a consequent increase in toxic emissions. If such devices are found during servicing or overhaul, they should, wherever possible, be renewed or refitted in accordance with the manufacturer's requirements or current legislation.

*Note: It is antisocial and illegal to dump oil down the drain. To find the location of your local oil recycling bank, call this number free.*

Modifications are a continuing and unpublicised process in vehicle manufacture, quite apart from major model changes. Spare parts manuals and lists are compiled upon a numerical basis, the individual vehicle identification numbers being essential to correct identification of the component concerned.

When ordering spare parts, always give as much information as possible. Quote the vehicle model, year of manufacture, body and engine numbers as appropriate.

The *vehicle identification plate* is located on the top of the front crossmember in the engine compartment **(see illustration)**. In addition to many other details, it carries the Vehicle Identification Number (VIN), maximum vehicle weight information, and codes for interior trim and body colours.

The *Vehicle Identification Number (VIN)* is given on the vehicle identification plate. It is also located in a recess in the floor to the right-hand side of the driver's seat, access being gained after lifting the aperture cover **(see illustration)**. On later models, the number is also stamped on a metal tag fixed to the right-hand side of the facia, which can be read through the windscreen.

The *body number and paint code numbers* are located on the vehicle identification plate.

The *engine number* location is dependent on the engine type. On the HCS and Endura-E engines, it is stamped on the front left-hand side of the cylinder block towards the transmission (facing the radiator) **(see illustration)**. On the CVH and PTE engines, the location of the engine number is dependent on the equipment fitted, but is on the exhaust side of the engine, facing either towards the timing belt end or the transmission end **(see illustration)**. On the Zetec and Zetec-E engines, the number can be found on the forward-facing side of the cylinder block, level with the starter motor, or on the cylinder head just above the thermostat housing **(see illustrations)**.

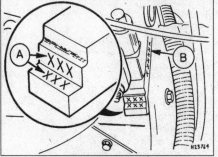

**Vehicle identification plate**

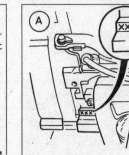

**Chassis number etched into the floor to the right of the driver's seat**

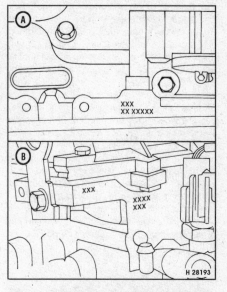

**Zetec and Zetec-E engine identification number on forward-facing side of cylinder block level with the starter motor (A), or on cylinder head just above thermostat (B)**

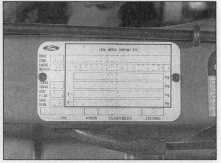

**HCS and Endura-E engine identification numbers location**
*A Engine code (side or upper face)*
*B Serial number*

**CVH and PTE engine identification number location is on (A) the right-hand side or (B) the left-hand side, according to model and equipment**

# Radio/cassette unit anti-theft system - precaution

The radio/cassette unit fitted as standard or optional equipment may be equipped with a built-in security code, to deter thieves. If the power source to the unit is cut, the anti-theft system will activate. Even if the power source is immediately reconnected, the radio/cassette unit will not function until the correct security code has been entered. Therefore, if you do not know the correct security code for the radio/cassette unit **do not** disconnect either of the battery terminals, or remove the radio/cassette unit from the vehicle.

To enter the correct security code, follow the instructions provided with the radio/cassette player or vehicle handbook.

If an incorrect code is entered, the unit will become locked, and cannot be operated.

If this happens, or if the security code is lost or forgotten, seek the advice of your Ford dealer.

Tools and working facilities

## Introduction

A selection of good tools is a fundamental requirement for anyone contemplating the maintenance and repair of a motor vehicle. For the owner who does not possess any, their purchase will prove a considerable expense, offsetting some of the savings made by doing-it-yourself. However, provided that the tools purchased meet the relevant national safety standards and are of good quality, they will last for many years and prove an extremely worthwhile investment.

To help the average owner to decide which tools are needed to carry out the various tasks detailed in this manual, we have compiled three lists of tools under the following headings: *Maintenance and minor repair*, *Repair and overhaul*, and *Special*. Newcomers to practical mechanics should start off with the *Maintenance and minor repair* tool kit, and confine themselves to the simpler jobs around the vehicle. Then, as confidence and experience grow, more difficult tasks can be undertaken, with extra tools being purchased as, and when, they are needed. In this way, a *Maintenance and minor repair* tool kit can be built up into a *Repair and overhaul* tool kit over a considerable period of time, without any major cash outlays. The experienced do-it-yourselfer will have a tool kit good enough for most repair and overhaul procedures, and will add tools from the *Special* category when it is felt that the expense is justified by the amount of use to which these tools will be put.

## Maintenance and minor repair tool kit

The tools given in this list should be considered as a minimum requirement if routine maintenance, servicing and minor repair operations are to be undertaken. We recommend the purchase of combination spanners (ring one end, open-ended the other); although more expensive than open-ended ones, they do give the advantages of both types of spanner.

☐ *Combination spanners:*
*Metric - 8 to 19 mm inclusive*
☐ *Adjustable spanner - 35 mm jaw (approx.)*
☐ *Spark plug spanner (with rubber insert) - petrol models*
☐ *Spark plug gap adjustment tool - petrol models*
☐ *Set of feeler gauges*
☐ *Brake bleed nipple spanner*
☐ *Screwdrivers:*
*Flat blade - 100 mm long x 6 mm dia*
*Cross blade - 100 mm long x 6 mm dia*
*Torx - various sizes (not all vehicles)*
☐ *Combination pliers*
☐ *Hacksaw (junior)*
☐ *Tyre pump*
☐ *Tyre pressure gauge*
☐ *Oil can*
☐ *Oil filter removal tool*
☐ *Fine emery cloth*
☐ *Wire brush (small)*
☐ *Funnel (medium size)*
☐ *Sump drain plug key (not all vehicles)*

## Repair and overhaul tool kit

These tools are virtually essential for anyone undertaking any major repairs to a motor vehicle, and are additional to those given in the *Maintenance and minor repair* list. Included in this list is a comprehensive set of sockets. Although these are expensive, they will be found invaluable as they are so versatile - particularly if various drives are included in the set. We recommend the half-inch square-drive type, as this can be used with most proprietary torque wrenches.

The tools in this list will sometimes need to be supplemented by tools from the *Special* list:

☐ *Sockets (or box spanners) to cover range in previous list (including Torx sockets)*
☐ *Reversible ratchet drive (for use with sockets)*
☐ *Extension piece, 250 mm (for use with sockets)*
☐ *Universal joint (for use with sockets)*
☐ *Flexible handle or sliding T "breaker bar" (for use with sockets)*
☐ *Torque wrench (for use with sockets)*
☐ *Self-locking grips*
☐ *Ball pein hammer*
☐ *Soft-faced mallet (plastic or rubber)*
☐ *Screwdrivers:*
*Flat blade - long & sturdy, short (chubby), and narrow (electrician's) types*
*Cross blade – long & sturdy, and short (chubby) types*
☐ *Pliers:*
*Long-nosed*
*Side cutters (electrician's)*
*Circlip (internal and external)*
☐ *Cold chisel - 25 mm*
☐ *Scriber*
☐ *Scraper*
☐ *Centre-punch*
☐ *Pin punch*
☐ *Hacksaw*
☐ *Brake hose clamp*
☐ *Brake/clutch bleeding kit*
☐ *Selection of twist drills*
☐ *Steel rule/straight-edge*
☐ *Allen keys (inc. splined/Torx type)*
☐ *Selection of files*
☐ *Wire brush*
☐ *Axle stands*
☐ *Jack (strong trolley or hydraulic type)*
☐ *Light with extension lead*
☐ *Universal electrical multi-meter*

Sockets and reversible ratchet drive

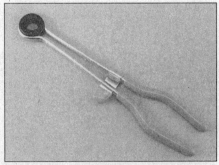

Brake bleeding kit

Torx key, socket and bit

Hose clamp

Angular-tightening gauge

## Special tools

The tools in this list are those which are not used regularly, are expensive to buy, or which need to be used in accordance with their manufacturers' instructions. Unless relatively difficult mechanical jobs are undertaken frequently, it will not be economic to buy many of these tools. Where this is the case, you could consider clubbing together with friends (or joining a motorists' club) to make a joint purchase, or borrowing the tools against a deposit from a local garage or tool hire specialist. It is worth noting that many of the larger DIY superstores now carry a large range of special tools for hire at modest rates.

The following list contains only those tools and instruments freely available to the public, and not those special tools produced by the vehicle manufacturer specifically for its dealer network. You will find occasional references to these manufacturers' special tools in the text of this manual. Generally, an alternative method of doing the job without the vehicle manufacturers' special tool is given. However, sometimes there is no alternative to using them. Where this is the case and the relevant tool cannot be bought or borrowed, you will have to entrust the work to a dealer.

- [ ] Angular-tightening gauge
- [ ] Valve spring compressor
- [ ] Valve grinding tool
- [ ] Piston ring compressor
- [ ] Piston ring removal/installation tool
- [ ] Cylinder bore hone
- [ ] Balljoint separator
- [ ] Coil spring compressors (where applicable)
- [ ] Two/three-legged hub and bearing puller
- [ ] Impact screwdriver
- [ ] Micrometer and/or vernier calipers
- [ ] Dial gauge
- [ ] Stroboscopic timing light
- [ ] Dwell angle meter/tachometer
- [ ] Fault code reader
- [ ] Cylinder compression gauge
- [ ] Hand-operated vacuum pump and gauge
- [ ] Clutch plate alignment set
- [ ] Brake shoe steady spring cup removal tool
- [ ] Bush and bearing removal/installation set
- [ ] Stud extractors
- [ ] Tap and die set
- [ ] Lifting tackle
- [ ] Trolley jack

## Buying tools

Reputable motor accessory shops and superstores often offer excellent quality tools at discount prices, so it pays to shop around.

Remember, you don't have to buy the most expensive items on the shelf, but it is always advisable to steer clear of the very cheap tools. Beware of 'bargains' offered on market stalls or at car boot sales. There are plenty of good tools around at reasonable prices, but always aim to purchase items which meet the relevant national safety standards. If in doubt, ask the proprietor or manager of the shop for advice before making a purchase.

## Care and maintenance of tools

Having purchased a reasonable tool kit, it is necessary to keep the tools in a clean and serviceable condition. After use, always wipe off any dirt, grease and metal particles using a clean, dry cloth, before putting the tools away. Never leave them lying around after they have been used. A simple tool rack on the garage or workshop wall for items such as screwdrivers and pliers is a good idea. Store all normal spanners and sockets in a metal box. Any measuring instruments, gauges, meters, etc, must be carefully stored where they cannot be damaged or become rusty.

Take a little care when tools are used. Hammer heads inevitably become marked, and screwdrivers lose the keen edge on their blades from time to time. A little timely attention with emery cloth or a file will soon restore items like this to a good finish.

## Working facilities

Not to be forgotten when discussing tools is the workshop itself. If anything more than routine maintenance is to be carried out, a suitable working area becomes essential.

It is appreciated that many an owner-mechanic is forced by circumstances to remove an engine or similar item without the benefit of a garage or workshop. Having done this, any repairs should always be done under the cover of a roof.

Wherever possible, any dismantling should be done on a clean, flat workbench or table at a suitable working height.

Any workbench needs a vice; one with a jaw opening of 100 mm is suitable for most jobs. As mentioned previously, some clean dry storage space is also required for tools, as well as for any lubricants, cleaning fluids, touch-up paints etc, which become necessary.

Another item which may be required, and which has a much more general usage, is an electric drill with a chuck capacity of at least 8 mm. This, together with a good range of twist drills, is virtually essential for fitting accessories.

Last, but not least, always keep a supply of old newspapers and clean, lint-free rags available, and try to keep any working area as clean as possible.

**Micrometers**

**Dial test indicator ("dial gauge")**

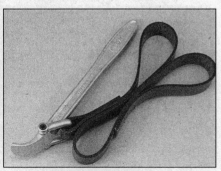

**Strap wrench**

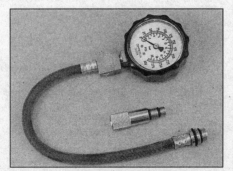

**Compression tester**

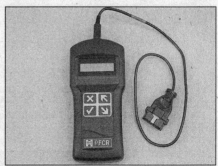

**Fault code reader**

This is a guide to getting your vehicle through the MOT test. Obviously it will not be possible to examine the vehicle to the same standard as the professional MOT tester. However, working through the following checks will enable you to identify any problem areas before submitting the vehicle for the test.

Where a testable component is in borderline condition, the tester has discretion in deciding whether to pass or fail it. The basis of such discretion is whether the tester would be happy for a close relative or friend to use the vehicle with the component in that condition. If the vehicle presented is clean and evidently well cared for, the tester may be more inclined to pass a borderline component than if the vehicle is scruffy and apparently neglected.

It has only been possible to summarise the test requirements here, based on the regulations in force at the time of printing. Test standards are becoming increasingly stringent, although there are some exemptions for older vehicles.

An assistant will be needed to help carry out some of these checks.

*The checks have been sub-divided into four categories, as follows:*

**1** Checks carried out **FROM THE DRIVER'S SEAT**

**2** Checks carried out **WITH THE VEHICLE ON THE GROUND**

**3** Checks carried out **WITH THE VEHICLE RAISED AND THE WHEELS FREE TO TURN**

**4** Checks carried out on **YOUR VEHICLE'S EXHAUST EMISSION SYSTEM**

---

**1** Checks carried out **FROM THE DRIVER'S SEAT**

### Handbrake

☐ Test the operation of the handbrake. Excessive travel (too many clicks) indicates incorrect brake or cable adjustment.

☐ Check that the handbrake cannot be released by tapping the lever sideways. Check the security of the lever mountings.

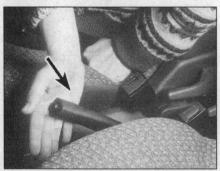

### Footbrake

☐ Depress the brake pedal and check that it does not creep down to the floor, indicating a master cylinder fault. Release the pedal, wait a few seconds, then depress it again. If the pedal travels nearly to the floor before firm resistance is felt, brake adjustment or repair is necessary. If the pedal feels spongy, there is air in the hydraulic system which must be removed by bleeding.

☐ Check that the brake pedal is secure and in good condition. Check also for signs of fluid leaks on the pedal, floor or carpets, which would indicate failed seals in the brake master cylinder.

☐ Check the servo unit (when applicable) by operating the brake pedal several times, then keeping the pedal depressed and starting the engine. As the engine starts, the pedal will move down slightly. If not, the vacuum hose or the servo itself may be faulty.

### Steering wheel and column

☐ Examine the steering wheel for fractures or looseness of the hub, spokes or rim.

☐ Move the steering wheel from side to side and then up and down. Check that the steering wheel is not loose on the column, indicating wear or a loose retaining nut. Continue moving the steering wheel as before, but also turn it slightly from left to right.

☐ Check that the steering wheel is not loose on the column, and that there is no abnormal

movement of the steering wheel, indicating wear in the column support bearings or couplings.

### Windscreen, mirrors and sunvisor

☐ The windscreen must be free of cracks or other significant damage within the driver's field of view. (Small stone chips are acceptable.) Rear view mirrors must be secure, intact, and capable of being adjusted.

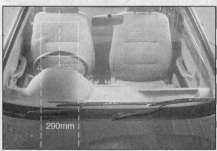

290mm

☐ The driver's sunvisor must be capable of being stored in the "up" position.

## Seat belts and seats

**Note:** *The following checks are applicable to all seat belts, front and rear.*

☐ Examine the webbing of all the belts (including rear belts if fitted) for cuts, serious fraying or deterioration. Fasten and unfasten each belt to check the buckles. If applicable, check the retracting mechanism. Check the security of all seat belt mountings accessible from inside the vehicle.

☐ Seat belts with pre-tensioners, once activated, have a "flag" or similar showing on the seat belt stalk. This, in itself, is not a reason for test failure.

☐ The front seats themselves must be securely attached and the backrests must lock in the upright position.

## Doors

☐ Both front doors must be able to be opened and closed from outside and inside, and must latch securely when closed.

## 2 Checks carried out WITH THE VEHICLE ON THE GROUND

## Vehicle identification

☐ Number plates must be in good condition, secure and legible, with letters and numbers correctly spaced – spacing at (A) should be at least twice that at (B).

☐ The VIN plate and/or homologation plate must be legible.

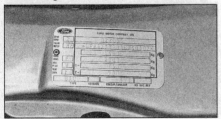

## Electrical equipment

☐ Switch on the ignition and check the operation of the horn.

☐ Check the windscreen washers and wipers, examining the wiper blades; renew damaged or perished blades. Also check the operation of the stop-lights.

☐ Check the operation of the sidelights and number plate lights. The lenses and reflectors must be secure, clean and undamaged.

☐ Check the operation and alignment of the headlights. The headlight reflectors must not be tarnished and the lenses must be undamaged.

☐ Switch on the ignition and check the operation of the direction indicators (including the instrument panel tell-tale) and the hazard warning lights. Operation of the sidelights and stop-lights must not affect the indicators - if it does, the cause is usually a bad earth at the rear light cluster.

☐ Check the operation of the rear foglight(s), including the warning light on the instrument panel or in the switch.

☐ The ABS warning light must illuminate in accordance with the manufacturers' design. For most vehicles, the ABS warning light should illuminate when the ignition is switched on, and (if the system is operating properly) extinguish after a few seconds. Refer to the owner's handbook.

## Footbrake

☐ Examine the master cylinder, brake pipes and servo unit for leaks, loose mountings, corrosion or other damage.

☐ The fluid reservoir must be secure and the fluid level must be between the upper (A) and lower (B) markings.

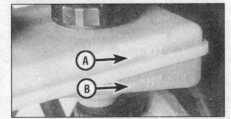

☐ Inspect both front brake flexible hoses for cracks or deterioration of the rubber. Turn the steering from lock to lock, and ensure that the hoses do not contact the wheel, tyre, or any part of the steering or suspension mechanism. With the brake pedal firmly depressed, check the hoses for bulges or leaks under pressure.

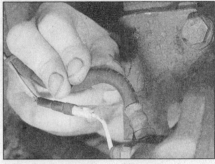

## Steering and suspension

☐ Have your assistant turn the steering wheel from side to side slightly, up to the point where the steering gear just begins to transmit this movement to the roadwheels. Check for excessive free play between the steering wheel and the steering gear, indicating wear or insecurity of the steering column joints, the column-to-steering gear coupling, or the steering gear itself.

☐ Have your assistant turn the steering wheel more vigorously in each direction, so that the roadwheels just begin to turn. As this is done, examine all the steering joints, linkages, fittings and attachments. Renew any component that shows signs of wear or damage. On vehicles with power steering, check the security and condition of the steering pump, drivebelt and hoses.

☐ Check that the vehicle is standing level, and at approximately the correct ride height.

## Shock absorbers

☐ Depress each corner of the vehicle in turn, then release it. The vehicle should rise and then settle in its normal position. If the vehicle continues to rise and fall, the shock absorber is defective. A shock absorber which has seized will also cause the vehicle to fail.

## Exhaust system

☐ Start the engine. With your assistant holding a rag over the tailpipe, check the entire system for leaks. Repair or renew leaking sections.

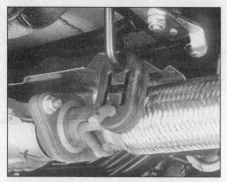

**3** Checks carried out
**WITH THE VEHICLE RAISED AND THE WHEELS FREE TO TURN**

*Jack up the front and rear of the vehicle, and securely support it on axle stands. Position the stands clear of the suspension assemblies. Ensure that the wheels are clear of the ground and that the steering can be turned from lock to lock.*

## Steering mechanism

☐ Have your assistant turn the steering from lock to lock. Check that the steering turns smoothly, and that no part of the steering mechanism, including a wheel or tyre, fouls any brake hose or pipe or any part of the body structure.

☐ Examine the steering rack rubber gaiters for damage or insecurity of the retaining clips. If power steering is fitted, check for signs of damage or leakage of the fluid hoses, pipes or connections. Also check for excessive stiffness or binding of the steering, a missing split pin or locking device, or severe corrosion of the body structure within 30 cm of any steering component attachment point.

## Front and rear suspension and wheel bearings

☐ Starting at the front right-hand side, grasp the roadwheel at the 3 o'clock and 9 o'clock positions and rock gently but firmly. Check for free play or insecurity at the wheel bearings, suspension balljoints, or suspension mountings, pivots and attachments.

☐ Now grasp the wheel at the 12 o'clock and 6 o'clock positions and repeat the previous inspection. Spin the wheel, and check for roughness or tightness of the front wheel bearing.

☐ If excess free play is suspected at a component pivot point, this can be confirmed by using a large screwdriver or similar tool and levering between the mounting and the component attachment. This will confirm whether the wear is in the pivot bush, its retaining bolt, or in the mounting itself (the bolt holes can often become elongated).

☐ Carry out all the above checks at the other front wheel, and then at both rear wheels.

## Springs and shock absorbers

☐ Examine the suspension struts (when applicable) for serious fluid leakage, corrosion, or damage to the casing. Also check the security of the mounting points.

☐ If coil springs are fitted, check that the spring ends locate in their seats, and that the spring is not corroded, cracked or broken.

☐ If leaf springs are fitted, check that all leaves are intact, that the axle is securely attached to each spring, and that there is no deterioration of the spring eye mountings, bushes, and shackles.

☐ The same general checks apply to vehicles fitted with other suspension types, such as torsion bars, hydraulic displacer units, etc. Ensure that all mountings and attachments are secure, that there are no signs of excessive wear, corrosion or damage, and (on hydraulic types) that there are no fluid leaks or damaged pipes.

☐ Inspect the shock absorbers for signs of serious fluid leakage. Check for wear of the mounting bushes or attachments, or damage to the body of the unit.

## Driveshafts (fwd vehicles only)

☐ Rotate each front wheel in turn and inspect the constant velocity joint gaiters for splits or damage. Also check that each driveshaft is straight and undamaged.

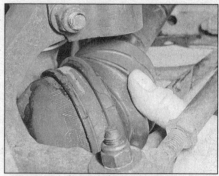

## Braking system

☐ If possible without dismantling, check brake pad wear and disc condition. Ensure that the friction lining material has not worn excessively, (A) and that the discs are not fractured, pitted, scored or badly worn (B).

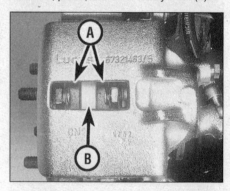

☐ Examine all the rigid brake pipes underneath the vehicle, and the flexible hose(s) at the rear. Look for corrosion, chafing or insecurity of the pipes, and for signs of bulging under pressure, chafing, splits or deterioration of the flexible hoses.

☐ Look for signs of fluid leaks at the brake calipers or on the brake backplates. Repair or renew leaking components.

☐ Slowly spin each wheel, while your assistant depresses and releases the footbrake. Ensure that each brake is operating and does not bind when the pedal is released.

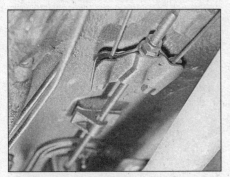

☐ Examine the handbrake mechanism, checking for frayed or broken cables, excessive corrosion, or wear or insecurity of the linkage. Check that the mechanism works on each relevant wheel, and releases fully, without binding.

☐ It is not possible to test brake efficiency without special equipment, but a road test can be carried out later to check that the vehicle pulls up in a straight line.

## Fuel and exhaust systems

☐ Inspect the fuel tank (including the filler cap), fuel pipes, hoses and unions. All components must be secure and free from leaks.

☐ Examine the exhaust system over its entire length, checking for any damaged, broken or missing mountings, security of the retaining clamps and rust or corrosion.

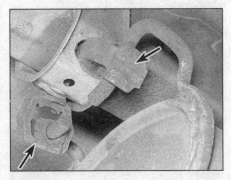

## Wheels and tyres

☐ Examine the sidewalls and tread area of each tyre in turn. Check for cuts, tears, lumps, bulges, separation of the tread, and exposure of the ply or cord due to wear or damage. Check that the tyre bead is correctly seated on the wheel rim, that the valve is sound and properly seated, and that the wheel is not distorted or damaged.

☐ Check that the tyres are of the correct size for the vehicle, that they are of the same size and type on each axle, and that the pressures are correct.

☐ Check the tyre tread depth. The legal minimum at the time of writing is 1.6 mm over at least three-quarters of the tread width. Abnormal tread wear may indicate incorrect front wheel alignment.

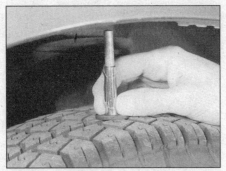

## Body corrosion

☐ Check the condition of the entire vehicle structure for signs of corrosion in load-bearing areas. (These include chassis box sections, side sills, cross-members, pillars, and all suspension, steering, braking system and seat belt mountings and anchorages.) Any corrosion which has seriously reduced the thickness of a load-bearing area is likely to cause the vehicle to fail. In this case professional repairs are likely to be needed.

☐ Damage or corrosion which causes sharp or otherwise dangerous edges to be exposed will also cause the vehicle to fail.

## 4 Checks carried out on YOUR VEHICLE'S EXHAUST EMISSION SYSTEM

## Petrol models

☐ Have the engine at normal operating temperature, and make sure that it is in good tune (ignition system in good order, air filter element clean, etc).

☐ Before any measurements are carried out, raise the engine speed to around 2500 rpm, and hold it at this speed for 20 seconds. Allow the engine speed to return to idle, and watch for smoke emissions from the exhaust tailpipe. If the idle speed is obviously much too high, or if dense blue or clearly-visible black smoke comes from the tailpipe for more than 5 seconds, the vehicle will fail. As a rule of thumb, blue smoke signifies oil being burnt (engine wear) while black smoke signifies unburnt fuel (dirty air cleaner element, or other carburettor or fuel system fault).

☐ An exhaust gas analyser capable of measuring carbon monoxide (CO) and hydrocarbons (HC) is now needed. If such an instrument cannot be hired or borrowed, a local garage may agree to perform the check for a small fee.

## CO emissions (mixture)

☐ At the time of writing, for vehicles first used between 1st August 1975 and 31st July 1986 (P to C registration), the CO level must not exceed 4.5% by volume. For vehicles first used between 1st August 1986 and 31st July 1992 (D to J registration), the CO level must not exceed 3.5% by volume. Vehicles first

used after 1st August 1992 (K registration) must conform to the manufacturer's specification. The MOT tester has access to a DOT database or emissions handbook, which lists the CO and HC limits for each make and model of vehicle. The CO level is measured with the engine at idle speed, and at "fast idle". The following limits are given as a general guide:

*At idle speed -*
CO level no more than 0.5%
*At "fast idle" (2500 to 3000 rpm) -*
CO level no more than 0.3%
(Minimum oil temperature 60°C)

☐ If the CO level cannot be reduced far enough to pass the test (and the fuel and ignition systems are otherwise in good condition) then the carburettor is badly worn, or there is some problem in the fuel injection system or catalytic converter (as applicable).

## HC emissions

☐ With the CO within limits, HC emissions for vehicles first used between 1st August 1975 and 31st July 1992 (P to J registration) must not exceed 1200 ppm. Vehicles first used after 1st August 1992 (K registration) must conform to the manufacturer's specification. The MOT tester has access to a DOT database or emissions handbook, which lists the CO and HC limits for each make and model of vehicle. The HC level is measured with the engine at "fast idle". The following is given as a general guide:

*At "fast idle" (2500 to 3000 rpm) -*
HC level no more than 200 ppm
(Minimum oil temperature 60°C)

☐ Excessive HC emissions are caused by incomplete combustion, the causes of which can include oil being burnt, mechanical wear and ignition/fuel system malfunction.

## Diesel models

☐ The only emission test applicable to Diesel engines is the measuring of exhaust smoke density. The test involves accelerating the engine several times to its maximum unloaded speed.

**Note:** *It is of the utmost importance that the engine timing belt is in good condition before the test is carried out.*

☐ The limits for Diesel engine exhaust smoke, introduced in September 1995 are:
*Vehicles first used before 1st August 1979:*
Exempt from metered smoke testing, but must not emit "dense blue or clearly visible black smoke for a period of more than 5 seconds at idle" or "dense blue or clearly visible black smoke during acceleration which would obscure the view of other road users".
*Non-turbocharged vehicles first used after 1st August 1979:* 2.5m⁻¹
*Turbocharged vehicles first used after 1st August 1979:* 3.0m⁻¹

☐ Excessive smoke can be caused by a dirty air cleaner element. Otherwise, professional advice may be needed to find the cause.

## Engine . . . . . . . . . . . . . . . . . . . . . . . . . . . . .1

☐ Engine backfires
☐ Engine difficult to start when cold
☐ Engine difficult to start when hot
☐ Engine fails to rotate when attempting to start
☐ Engine hesitates on acceleration
☐ Engine idles erratically
☐ Engine lacks power
☐ Engine misfires at idle speed
☐ Engine misfires throughout the driving speed range
☐ Engine noises
☐ Engine rotates, but will not start
☐ Engine runs-on after switching off
☐ Engine stalls
☐ Engine starts, but stops immediately
☐ Oil pressure warning light illuminated with engine running
☐ Starter motor noisy or excessively-rough in engagement

## Cooling system . . . . . . . . . . . . . . . . . . . . . .2

☐ Corrosion
☐ External coolant leakage
☐ Internal coolant leakage
☐ Overcooling
☐ Overheating

## Fuel and exhaust systems . . . . . . . . . . . . . . .3

☐ Excessive fuel consumption
☐ Excessive noise or fumes from exhaust system
☐ Fuel leakage and/or fuel odour

## Clutch . . . . . . . . . . . . . . . . . . . . . . . . . . . . . .4

☐ Clutch fails to disengage (unable to select gears)
☐ Clutch slips (engine speed increases, with no increase in vehicle speed)
☐ Judder as clutch is engaged
☐ Noise when depressing or releasing clutch pedal
☐ Pedal travels to floor - no pressure or very little resistance

## Manual transmission . . . . . . . . . . . . . . . . . . .5

☐ Jumps out of gear
☐ Lubricant leaks
☐ Noisy in neutral with engine running
☐ Noisy in one particular gear
☐ Vibration

## Automatic transmission . . . . . . . . . . . . . . . . .6

☐ Engine will not start in any gear, or starts in gears other than Park or Neutral
☐ Fluid leakage
☐ General gear selection problems
☐ Transmission fluid brown, or has burned smell
☐ Transmission slips, shifts roughly, is noisy, or has no drive in forward or reverse gears
☐ Transmission will not downshift (kickdown) with accelerator fully depressed

## Driveshafts . . . . . . . . . . . . . . . . . . . . . . . . . .7

☐ Clicking or knocking noise on turns (at slow speed on full-lock)
☐ Vibration when accelerating or decelerating

## Braking system . . . . . . . . . . . . . . . . . . . . . . .8

☐ Brake pedal feels spongy when depressed
☐ Brakes binding
☐ Excessive brake pedal effort required to stop vehicle
☐ Excessive brake pedal travel
☐ Judder felt through brake pedal or steering wheel when braking
☐ Noise (grinding or high-pitched squeal) when brakes applied
☐ Rear wheels locking under normal braking
☐ Vehicle pulls to one side under braking

## Suspension and steering systems . . . . . . . . . .9

☐ Excessive pitching and/or rolling around corners, or during braking
☐ Excessive play in steering
☐ Excessively-stiff steering
☐ Lack of power assistance
☐ Tyre wear excessive
☐ Vehicle pulls to one side
☐ Wandering or general instability
☐ Wheel wobble and vibration

## Electrical system . . . . . . . . . . . . . . . . . . . . .10

☐ Battery will only hold a charge for a few days
☐ Central locking system
☐ Electric windows
☐ Horn inoperative, or unsatisfactory in operation
☐ Ignition warning light fails to come on
☐ Ignition warning light remains illuminated with engine running
☐ Instrument readings inaccurate or erratic
☐ Lights inoperative
☐ Windscreen/tailgate washers
☐ Windscreen/tailgate wipers

# Introduction

The vehicle owner who does his or her own maintenance according to the recommended service schedules should not have to use this section of the manual very often. Modern component reliability is such that, provided those items subject to wear or deterioration are inspected or renewed at the specified intervals, sudden failure is comparatively rare. Faults do not usually just happen as a result of sudden failure, but develop over a period of time. Major mechanical failures in particular are usually preceded by characteristic symptoms over hundreds or even thousands of miles. Those components which do occasionally fail without warning are often small and easily carried in the vehicle.

With any fault-finding, the first step is to decide where to begin investigations. Sometimes this is obvious, but on other occasions, a little detective work will be necessary. The owner who makes half a dozen haphazard adjustments or replacements may be successful in curing a fault (or its symptoms), but will be none the wiser if the fault recurs, and ultimately may have spent more time and money than was necessary. A calm and logical approach will be found to be more satisfactory in the long run. Always take into account any warning signs or abnormalities that may have been noticed in the period preceding the fault - power loss, high or low gauge readings, unusual smells, etc - and remember that failure of components such as fuses or spark plugs may only be pointers to some underlying fault.

The pages which follow provide an easy reference guide to the more common problems which may occur during the operation of the vehicle. These problems and their possible causes are grouped under headings denoting various components or systems, such as Engine, Cooling system, etc. The Chapter and/or Section which deals with the problem is also shown in brackets. Whatever the fault, certain basic principles apply. These are as follows:

*Verify the fault.* This is simply a matter of being sure that you know what the symptoms are before starting work. This is particularly important if you are investigating a fault for someone else, who may not have described it very accurately.

*Don't overlook the obvious.* For example, if the vehicle won't start, is there petrol in the tank? (Don't take anyone else's word on this particular point, and don't trust the fuel gauge either!) If an electrical fault is indicated, look for loose or broken wires before using the test gear.

*Cure the disease, not the symptom.* Substituting a flat battery with a fully-charged one will get you off the hard shoulder, but if the underlying cause is not attended to, the new battery will go the same way. Similarly, changing oil-fouled spark plugs for a new set will get you moving again, but remember that the reason for the fouling (if it wasn't simply an incorrect grade of plug) will have to be established and corrected.

*Don't take anything for granted.* Particularly, don't forget that a "new" component may itself be defective (especially if it's been rattling around in the boot for months), and don't leave components out of a fault diagnosis sequence just because they are new or recently fitted. When you do finally diagnose a difficult fault, you'll probably realise that all the evidence was there from the start.

# 1 Engine

## Engine fails to rotate when attempting to start

☐ Battery terminal connections loose or corroded (*"Weekly Checks"*).
☐ Battery discharged or faulty (Chapter 5A).
☐ Broken, loose or disconnected wiring in the starting circuit (Chapter 5A).
☐ Defective starter solenoid or switch (Chapter 5A).
☐ Defective starter motor (Chapter 5A).
☐ Flywheel ring gear or starter pinion teeth loose or broken (Chapters 2A, 2B, 2C or 5A).
☐ Engine earth strap broken or disconnected (Chapter 5A).
☐ Automatic transmission not in Park/Neutral position, or selector lever position sensor faulty (Chapter 7B).

## Engine rotates, but will not start

☐ Fuel tank empty.
☐ Battery discharged (engine rotates slowly) (Chapter 5A).
☐ Battery terminal connections loose or corroded (*"Weekly Checks"*).
☐ Ignition components damp or damaged (Chapters 1 and 5B).
☐ Broken, loose or disconnected wiring in the ignition circuit (Chapters 1 and 5B).
☐ Worn, faulty or incorrectly-gapped spark plugs (Chapter 1).
☐ Major mechanical failure (eg camshaft drive) (Chapters 2A, 2B or 2C).

## Engine difficult to start when cold

☐ Battery discharged (Chapter 5A).
☐ Battery terminal connections loose or corroded (*"Weekly Checks"*).
☐ Worn, faulty or incorrectly-gapped spark plugs (Chapter 1).
☐ Other ignition system fault (Chapters 1 and 5B).
☐ Engine management system fault (Chapters 1, 4 or 5B).
☐ Low cylinder compressions (Chapters 2A, 2B or 2C).

## Engine difficult to start when hot

☐ Air filter element dirty or clogged (Chapter 1).
☐ Engine management system fault (Chapters 1, 4 or 5B).
☐ Low cylinder compressions (Chapters 2A, 2B or 2C).
☐ Faulty hydraulic tappet(s) (Chapters 2B or 2C).

## Starter motor noisy or excessively-rough in engagement

☐ Flywheel ring gear or starter pinion teeth loose or broken (Chapters 2A, 2B, 2C or 5A).
☐ Starter motor mounting bolts loose or missing (Chapter 5A).
☐ Starter motor internal components worn or damaged (Chapter 5A).

## Engine starts but stops immediately

☐ Loose or faulty electrical connections in the ignition circuit (Chapters 1 and 5B).
☐ Engine management system fault (Chapters 1, 4 or 5B).
☐ Vacuum leak at the inlet manifold (Chapters 1 or 4).

## Engine idles erratically

☐ Engine management system fault (Chapters 1, 4 or 5B).
☐ Air filter element clogged (Chapter 1).
☐ Vacuum leak at the inlet manifold or associated hoses (Chapters 1 or 4).
☐ Worn, faulty or incorrectly-gapped spark plugs (Chapter 1).
☐ Incorrect valve clearances (Chapter 2A).
☐ Faulty hydraulic tappet(s) (Chapters 2B or 2C).
☐ Uneven or low cylinder compressions (Chapters 2A, 2B or 2C).
☐ Camshaft lobes worn (Chapters 2A, 2B or 2C).
☐ Timing chain and sprockets worn (Chapter 2A).
☐ Timing belt incorrectly-tensioned (Chapters 2B or 2C).

## Engine misfires at idle speed

☐ Worn, faulty or incorrectly-gapped spark plugs (Chapter 1).
☐ Faulty spark plug HT leads (Chapter 1).
☐ Engine management system fault (Chapters 1, 4 or 5B).
☐ Vacuum leak at the inlet manifold or associated hoses (Chapters 1 or 4).
☐ Incorrect valve clearances (Chapter 2A).
☐ Faulty hydraulic tappet(s) (Chapters 2B or 2C).
☐ Uneven or low cylinder compressions (Chapters 2A, 2B and 2C).
☐ Disconnected, leaking or perished crankcase ventilation hoses (Chapters 1 and 4E).

## Engine misfires throughout the driving speed range

☐ Fuel filter choked (Chapter 1).
☐ Fuel pump faulty or delivery pressure low (Chapter 4).
☐ Fuel tank vent blocked or fuel pipes restricted (Chapter 4).
☐ Vacuum leak at the inlet manifold or associated hoses (Chapters 1 or 4).
☐ Worn, faulty or incorrectly-gapped spark plugs (Chapter 1).
☐ Faulty spark plug HT leads (Chapter 1).
☐ Faulty ignition coil (Chapter 5B).
☐ Engine management system fault (Chapters 1, 4 or 5B).
☐ Uneven or low cylinder compressions (Chapters 2A, 2B or 2C).

## Engine hesitates on acceleration

☐ Worn, faulty or incorrectly-gapped spark plugs (Chapter 1).
☐ Engine management system fault (Chapters 1, 4 or 5B).
☐ Vacuum leak at the inlet manifold or associated hoses (Chapters 1, 4 and 6).

## Engine stalls

☐ Engine management system fault (Chapters 1, 4, 5 and 6).
☐ Vacuum leak at the inlet manifold or associated hoses (Chapters 1 or 4).
☐ Fuel filter choked (Chapter 1).
☐ Fuel pump faulty or delivery pressure low (Chapter 4).
☐ Fuel tank vent blocked or fuel pipes restricted (Chapter 4).

# 1 Engine (continued)

## Engine lacks power

- [ ] Engine management system fault (Chapters 1, 4 or 5B).
- [ ] Timing chain or belt incorrectly fitted or incorrectly tensioned (Chapters 2A, 2B or 2C).
- [ ] Fuel filter choked (Chapter 1).
- [ ] Fuel pump faulty or delivery pressure low (Chapter 4).
- [ ] Uneven or low cylinder compressions (Chapters 2A, 2B or 2C).
- [ ] Worn, faulty or incorrectly-gapped spark plugs (Chapter 1).
- [ ] Vacuum leak at the inlet manifold or associated hoses (Chapters 1 or 4).
- [ ] Brakes binding (Chapters 1 and 9).
- [ ] Clutch slipping (Chapter 6).
- [ ] Automatic transmission fluid level incorrect (Chapter 1).

## Engine backfires

- [ ] Engine management system fault (Chapters 1, 4 or 5B).
- [ ] Timing chain or belt incorrectly fitted or incorrectly tensioned (Chapters 2A, 2B or 2C).
- [ ] Vacuum leak at the inlet manifold or associated hoses (Chapters 1 or 4).

## Oil pressure warning light illuminated with engine running

- [ ] Low oil level or incorrect oil grade ("Weekly Checks").
- [ ] Faulty oil pressure warning light switch (Chapters 2A, 2B or 2C).
- [ ] Worn engine bearings and/or oil pump (Chapters 2A, 2B or 2C).
- [ ] High engine operating temperature (Chapter 3).
- [ ] Oil pressure relief valve defective (Chapters 2A, 2B or 2C).
- [ ] Oil pick-up strainer clogged (Chapters 2A, 2B or 2C).

## Engine runs-on after switching off

- [ ] Idle speed excessively high (Chapter 4).
- [ ] Engine management system fault (Chapters 1, 4 or 5B).

- [ ] Excessive carbon build-up in engine (Chapters 2A, 2B or 2C).
- [ ] High engine operating temperature (Chapter 3).

## Engine noises

### Pre-ignition (pinking) or knocking during acceleration or under load

- [ ] Incorrect grade of fuel (Chapter 4).
- [ ] Vacuum leak at the inlet manifold or associated hoses (Chapters 1 or 4).
- [ ] Excessive carbon build-up in engine (Chapters 2A, 2B or 2C).

### Whistling or wheezing noises

- [ ] Leaking inlet manifold gasket (Chapter 4).
- [ ] Leaking exhaust manifold gasket or downpipe-to-manifold joint (Chapter 4E).
- [ ] Leaking vacuum hose (Chapters 1, 4 or 9).
- [ ] Blowing cylinder head gasket (Chapters 2A, 2B or 2C).

### Tapping or rattling noises

- [ ] Incorrect valve clearance adjustment (Chapter 2A).
- [ ] Faulty hydraulic tappet(s) (Chapters 2B or 2C).
- [ ] Worn valve gear or camshaft (Chapters 2A, 2B, 2C or 2D).
- [ ] Worn timing chain, belt or tensioner (Chapters 2A, 2B or 2C).
- [ ] Ancillary component fault (water pump, alternator, etc) (Chapters 3 and 5A).

### Knocking or thumping noises

- [ ] Worn big-end bearings (regular heavy knocking, perhaps less under load) Chapter 2D).
- [ ] Worn main bearings (rumbling and knocking, perhaps worsening under load) Chapter 2D).
- [ ] Piston slap (most noticeable when cold) (Chapter 2D).
- [ ] Ancillary component fault (water pump, alternator, etc) (Chapters 3 and 5A).

# 2 Cooling system

## Overheating

- [ ] Insufficient coolant in system ("Weekly Checks").
- [ ] Thermostat faulty (Chapter 3).
- [ ] Radiator core blocked or grille restricted (Chapter 3).
- [ ] Radiator electric cooling fan(s) or coolant temperature sensor faulty (Chapter 3).
- [ ] Engine management system fault (Chapters 1, 4 or 5B).
- [ ] Pressure cap faulty (Chapter 3).
- [ ] Auxiliary drivebelt worn or slipping (Chapter 1).
- [ ] Inaccurate coolant temperature gauge sender (Chapter 3).
- [ ] Airlock in cooling system (Chapter 1).

## Overcooling

- [ ] Thermostat faulty (Chapter 3).
- [ ] Inaccurate coolant temperature gauge sender (Chapter 3).

## External coolant leakage

- [ ] Deteriorated or damaged hoses or hose clips (Chapter 1).
- [ ] Radiator core or heater matrix leaking (Chapter 3).
- [ ] Pressure cap faulty (Chapter 3).
- [ ] Water pump seal leaking (Chapter 3).
- [ ] Boiling due to overheating (Chapter 3).
- [ ] Core plug leaking (Chapter 2D).

## Internal coolant leakage

- [ ] Leaking cylinder head gasket (Chapters 2A, 2B or 2C).
- [ ] Cracked cylinder head or cylinder bore (Chapter 2D).

## Corrosion

- [ ] Infrequent draining and flushing (Chapter 1).
- [ ] Incorrect antifreeze mixture, or inappropriate antifreeze type ("Weekly Checks" and Chapter 1).

# 3 Fuel and exhaust systems

### Excessive fuel consumption

☐ Unsympathetic driving style, or adverse conditions.
☐ Air filter element dirty or clogged (Chapter 1).
☐ Engine management system fault (Chapters 1, 4 or 5B).
☐ Tyres under-inflated ("Weekly Checks").

### Fuel leakage and/or fuel odour

☐ Damaged or corroded fuel tank, pipes or connections (Chapter 1).
☐ Charcoal canister and/or connecting pipes leaking (Chapter 4E).

### Excessive noise or fumes from exhaust system

☐ Leaking exhaust system or manifold joints (Chapters 1 or 4E).
☐ Leaking, corroded or damaged silencers or pipe (Chapters 1 or 4E).
☐ Broken mountings, causing body or suspension contact (Chapters 1 or 4E).

# 4 Clutch

### Pedal travels to floor - no pressure or very little resistance

☐ Broken clutch cable (Chapter 6).
☐ Faulty clutch automatic adjuster (Chapter 6).
☐ Incorrect clutch pedal free play adjustment (Chapter 1).
☐ Broken clutch release bearing or fork (Chapter 6).
☐ Broken diaphragm spring in clutch pressure plate (Chapter 6).

### Clutch fails to disengage (unable to select gears)

☐ Faulty clutch automatic adjuster (Chapter 6).
☐ Incorrect clutch pedal free play adjustment (Chapter 1).
☐ Clutch disc sticking on transmission input shaft splines (Chapter 6).
☐ Clutch disc sticking to flywheel or pressure plate (Chapter 6).
☐ Faulty pressure plate assembly (Chapter 6).
☐ Clutch release mechanism worn or incorrectly assembled (Chapter 6).

### Clutch slips (engine speed increases, with no increase in vehicle speed)

☐ Faulty clutch automatic adjuster (Chapter 6).

☐ Incorrect clutch pedal free play adjustment (Chapter 1).
☐ Clutch disc linings excessively worn (Chapter 6).
☐ Clutch disc linings contaminated with oil or grease (Chapter 6).
☐ Faulty pressure plate or weak diaphragm spring (Chapter 6).

### Judder as clutch is engaged

☐ Clutch disc linings contaminated with oil or grease (Chapter 6).
☐ Clutch disc linings excessively worn (Chapter 6).
☐ Clutch cable sticking or frayed (Chapter 6).
☐ Faulty or distorted pressure plate or diaphragm spring (Chapter 6).
☐ Worn or loose engine/transmission mountings (Chapters 2A, 2B or 2C).
☐ Clutch disc hub or transmission input shaft splines worn (Chapter 6).

### Noise when depressing or releasing clutch pedal

☐ Worn clutch release bearing (Chapter 6).
☐ Worn or dry clutch pedal bushes (Chapter 6).
☐ Faulty pressure plate assembly (Chapter 6).
☐ Pressure plate diaphragm spring broken (Chapter 6).
☐ Broken clutch disc cushioning springs (Chapter 6).

# 5 Manual transmission

### Noisy in neutral with engine running

☐ Input shaft bearings worn (noise apparent with clutch pedal released, but not when depressed) (Chapter 7A).*
☐ Clutch release bearing worn (noise apparent with clutch pedal depressed, possibly less when released) (Chapter 6).

### Noisy in one particular gear

☐ Worn, damaged or chipped gear teeth (Chapter 7A).*

### Difficulty engaging gears

☐ Clutch fault (Chapter 6).
☐ Worn or damaged gear linkage (Chapter 7A).
☐ Incorrectly-adjusted gear linkage (Chapter 7A).
☐ Worn synchroniser assemblies (Chapter 7A).*

### Jumps out of gear

☐ Worn or damaged gear linkage (Chapter 7A).
☐ Incorrectly-adjusted gear linkage (Chapter 7A).

☐ Worn synchroniser assemblies (Chapter 7A).*
☐ Worn selector forks (Chapter 7A).*

### Vibration

☐ Lack of oil (Chapter 1).
☐ Worn bearings (Chapter 7A).*

### Lubricant leaks

☐ Leaking differential side gear oil seal (Chapter 7A).
☐ Leaking housing joint (Chapter 7A).*
☐ Leaking input shaft oil seal (Chapter 7A).*
☐ Leaking selector shaft oil seal (Chapter 7A).
☐ Leaking speedometer drive pinion O-ring (Chapter 7A).

* Although the corrective action necessary to remedy the symptoms described is beyond the scope of the home mechanic, the above information should be helpful in isolating the cause of the condition, so that the owner can communicate clearly with a professional mechanic.

# 6 Automatic transmission

**Note:** *Due to the complexity of the automatic transmission, it is difficult for the home mechanic to properly diagnose and service this unit. For problems other than the following, the vehicle should be taken to a dealer service department or automatic transmission specialist.*

## Fluid leakage

☐ Automatic transmission fluid is usually deep red in colour. Fluid leaks should not be confused with engine oil, which can easily be blown onto the transmission by airflow.

☐ To determine the source of a leak, first remove all built-up dirt and grime from the transmission housing and surrounding areas, using a degreasing agent, or by steam-cleaning. Drive the vehicle at low speed, so airflow will not blow the leak far from its source. Raise and support the vehicle, and determine where the leak is coming from. The following are common areas of leakage:

a) Transmission fluid sump (Chapters 1 and 7B).
b) Dipstick tube (Chapters 1 and 7B).
c) Transmission-to-fluid cooler pipes/unions (Chapter 7B).
d) Speedometer drive pinion O-ring.
e) Differential output fluid seals (Chapter 7B).

## Transmission fluid brown, or has burned smell

☐ Transmission fluid level low, or fluid in need of renewal (Chapter 1).

## General gear selection problems

☐ Chapter 7B deals with checking and adjusting the selector cable on automatic transmissions. The following are common problems which may be caused by a poorly-adjusted cable:

a) Engine starting in gears other than Park or Neutral.
b) Indicator on gear selector lever pointing to a gear other than the one actually being used.
c) Vehicle moves when in Park or Neutral.
d) Poor gear shift quality or erratic gear changes.
    Refer to Chapter 7B for the selector cable adjustment procedure.

## Transmission will not downshift (kickdown) with accelerator pedal fully depressed

☐ Low transmission fluid level (Chapter 1).
☐ Incorrect selector cable adjustment (Chapter 7B).
☐ Engine management system fault (Chapters 1, 4 or 5B).

## Engine will not start in any gear, or starts in gears other than Park or Neutral

☐ Incorrect selector lever position sensor adjustment (Chapter 7B).
☐ Incorrect selector cable adjustment (Chapter 7B).

## Transmission slips, is noisy, or has no drive in forward or reverse gears

☐ There are many probable causes for the above problems, but the home mechanic should be concerned with only one possibility - fluid level. Before taking the vehicle to a dealer or transmission specialist, check the fluid level and condition of the fluid as described in Chapter 1. Correct the fluid level as necessary, or change the fluid if needed. If the problem persists, professional help will be necessary.

# 7 Driveshafts

## Clicking or knocking noise on turns (at slow speed on full-lock)

☐ Lack of constant velocity joint lubricant (Chapter 8).
☐ Worn outer constant velocity joint (Chapter 8).

## Vibration when accelerating or decelerating

☐ Worn inner constant velocity joint (Chapter 8).
☐ Bent or distorted driveshaft (Chapter 8).

# 8 Braking system

**Note:** *Before assuming that a brake problem exists, make sure that the tyres are in good condition and correctly inflated, that the front wheel alignment is correct, and that the vehicle is not loaded with weight in an unequal manner. Apart from checking the condition of all pipe and hose connections, any faults occurring on the Anti-lock Braking System (ABS) should be referred to a Ford dealer for diagnosis.*

## Vehicle pulls to one side under braking

☐ Worn, defective, damaged or contaminated front or rear brake pads/shoes on one side (Chapter 1).
☐ Seized or partially-seized front or rear brake caliper/wheel cylinder piston (Chapter 9).
☐ A mixture of brake pad/shoe lining materials fitted between sides (Chapter 1).
☐ Brake caliper mounting bolts loose (Chapter 9).
☐ Rear brake backplate mounting bolts loose (Chapter 9).
☐ Worn or damaged steering or suspension components (Chapter 10).

## Noise (grinding or high-pitched squeal) when brakes applied

☐ Brake pad or shoe friction lining material worn down to metal backing Chapter 1).
☐ Excessive corrosion of brake disc or drum (may be apparent after the vehicle has been standing for some time) (Chapter 1).

## Excessive brake pedal travel

☐ Inoperative rear brake self-adjust mechanism (Chapter 9).
☐ Faulty master cylinder (Chapter 9).
☐ Air in hydraulic system (Chapter 9).

## Brake pedal feels spongy when depressed

☐ Air in hydraulic system (Chapter 9).
☐ Deteriorated flexible rubber brake hoses (Chapter 9).
☐ Master cylinder mounting nuts loose (Chapter 9).
☐ Faulty master cylinder (Chapter 9).

# 8 Braking system (continued)

### Excessive brake pedal effort required to stop vehicle

☐ Faulty vacuum servo unit (Chapter 9).
☐ Disconnected, damaged or insecure brake servo vacuum hose (Chapter 9).
☐ Primary or secondary hydraulic circuit failure (Chapter 9).
☐ Seized brake caliper or wheel cylinder piston(s) (Chapter 9).
☐ Brake pads or brake shoes incorrectly fitted (Chapter 9).
☐ Incorrect grade of brake pads or brake shoes fitted (Chapter 1).
☐ Brake pads or brake shoe linings contaminated (Chapter 1).

### Judder felt through brake pedal or steering wheel when braking

☐ Excessive run-out or distortion of front discs or rear discs/drums (Chapter 9).

☐ Brake pad or brake shoe linings worn (Chapter 1).
☐ Brake caliper or rear brake backplate mounting bolts loose (Chapter 9).
☐ Wear in suspension or steering components or mountings (Chapter 10).

### Brakes binding

☐ Seized brake caliper or wheel cylinder piston(s) (Chapter 9).
☐ Faulty handbrake mechanism (Chapter 9).
☐ Faulty master cylinder (Chapter 9).

### Rear wheels locking under normal braking

☐ Rear brake pad/shoe linings contaminated (Chapter 1).
☐ Faulty brake pressure regulator (Chapter 9).

# 9 Suspension and steering systems

**Note:** *Before diagnosing suspension or steering faults, be sure that the trouble is not due to incorrect tyre pressures, mixtures of tyre types, or binding brakes.*

### Vehicle pulls to one side

☐ Defective tyre (Chapter 1).
☐ Excessive wear in suspension or steering components (Chapter 10).
☐ Incorrect front wheel alignment (Chapter 10).
☐ Accident damage to steering or suspension components (Chapter 10).

### Wheel wobble and vibration

☐ Front roadwheels out of balance (vibration felt mainly through the steering wheel) (Chapter 1).
☐ Rear roadwheels out of balance (vibration felt throughout the vehicle) Chapter 1).
☐ Roadwheels damaged or distorted (Chapter 1).
☐ Faulty or damaged tyre (*"Weekly Checks"*).
☐ Worn steering or suspension joints, bushes or components (Chapter 10).
☐ Roadwheel nuts loose (Chapter 1).
☐ Wear in driveshaft joint, or loose driveshaft nut (vibration worst when under load) (Chapter 8).

### Excessive pitching and/or rolling around corners, or during braking

☐ Defective shock absorbers (Chapter 10).
☐ Broken or weak coil/leaf spring and/or suspension component (Chapter 10).
☐ Worn or damaged anti-roll bar or mountings (Chapter 10).

### Wandering or general instability

☐ Incorrect front wheel alignment (Chapter 10).
☐ Worn steering or suspension joints, bushes or components (Chapter 10).
☐ Tyres out of balance (*"Weekly Checks"*).
☐ Faulty or damaged tyre (*"Weekly Checks"*).
☐ Roadwheel nuts loose (Chapter 1).
☐ Defective shock absorbers (Chapter 10).

### Excessively-stiff steering

☐ Lack of steering gear lubricant (Chapter 10).
☐ Seized track-rod end balljoint or suspension balljoint (Chapter 10).

☐ Broken or slipping auxiliary drivebelt (Chapter 1).
☐ Incorrect front wheel alignment (Chapter 10).
☐ Steering rack or column bent or damaged (Chapter 10).

### Excessive play in steering

☐ Worn steering column universal joint(s) or flexible coupling (Chapter 10).
☐ Worn steering track-rod end balljoints (Chapter 10).
☐ Worn rack-and-pinion steering gear (Chapter 10).
☐ Worn steering or suspension joints, bushes or components (Chapter 10).

### Lack of power assistance

☐ Broken or slipping auxiliary drivebelt (Chapter 1).
☐ Incorrect power steering fluid level (Chapter 1).
☐ Restriction in power steering fluid hoses (Chapter 10).
☐ Faulty power steering pump (Chapter 10).
☐ Faulty rack-and-pinion steering gear (Chapter 10).

### Tyre wear excessive

#### Tyres worn on inside or outside edges

☐ Tyres under-inflated (wear on both edges) (*"Weekly Checks"*).
☐ Incorrect camber or castor angles (wear on one edge only) (Chapter 10).
☐ Worn steering or suspension joints, bushes or components (Chapter 10).
☐ Excessively-hard cornering.
☐ Accident damage.

#### Tyre treads exhibit feathered edges

☐ Incorrect toe setting (Chapter 10).

#### Tyres worn in centre of tread

☐ Tyres over-inflated (*"Weekly Checks"*).

#### Tyres worn on inside and outside edges

☐ Tyres under-inflated (*"Weekly Checks"*).

#### Tyres worn unevenly

☐ Tyres out of balance (*"Weekly Checks"*).
☐ Excessive wheel or tyre run-out (Chapter 1).
☐ Worn shock absorbers (Chapter 10).
☐ Faulty tyre (*"Weekly Checks"*).

# 10 Electrical system

**Note:** *For problems associated with the starting system, refer to the faults listed under "Engine" earlier in this Section.*

## Battery will only hold a charge for a few days

- ☐ Battery defective internally (Chapter 5A).
- ☐ Battery electrolyte level low (Chapter 1).
- ☐ Battery terminal connections loose or corroded (*"Weekly Checks"*).
- ☐ Auxiliary drivebelt worn or incorrectly-adjusted (Chapter 1).
- ☐ Alternator not charging at correct output (Chapter 5A).
- ☐ Alternator or voltage regulator faulty (Chapter 5A).
- ☐ Short-circuit causing continual battery drain (Chapters 5A and 12).

## Ignition (no-charge) warning light remains illuminated with engine running

- ☐ Auxiliary drivebelt broken, worn, or incorrectly-adjusted (Chapter 1).
- ☐ Alternator brushes worn, sticking, or dirty (Chapter 5A).
- ☐ Alternator brush springs weak or broken (Chapter 5A).
- ☐ Internal fault in alternator or voltage regulator (Chapter 5A).
- ☐ Disconnected or loose wiring in charging circuit (Chapter 5A).

## Ignition (no-charge) warning light fails to come on

- ☐ Warning light bulb blown (Chapter 12).
- ☐ Broken, disconnected, or loose wiring in warning light circuit (Chapters 5A and 12).
- ☐ Alternator faulty (Chapter 5A).

## Lights inoperative

- ☐ Bulb blown (Chapter 12).
- ☐ Corrosion of bulb or bulbholder contacts (Chapter 12).
- ☐ Blown fuse (Chapter 12).
- ☐ Faulty relay (Chapter 12).
- ☐ Broken, loose, or disconnected wiring (Chapter 12).
- ☐ Faulty switch (Chapter 12).

## Instrument readings inaccurate or erratic

### Instrument readings increase with engine speed

- ☐ Faulty voltage regulator (Chapter 12).

### Gauges give no reading

- ☐ Faulty gauge sender unit (Chapters 3 or 4A, 4B, 4C, or 4D).
- ☐ Wiring open-circuit (Chapter 12).
- ☐ Faulty gauge (Chapter 12).

### Gauges give continuous maximum reading

- ☐ Faulty gauge sender unit (Chapters 3 or 4A, 4B, 4C, or 4D).
- ☐ Wiring short-circuit (Chapter 12).
- ☐ Faulty gauge (Chapter 12).

## Horn inoperative, or unsatisfactory in operation

### Horn fails to operate

- ☐ Blown fuse (Chapter 12).
- ☐ Cable or cable connections loose or disconnected (Chapter 12).
- ☐ Faulty horn (Chapter 12).

### Horn emits intermittent or unsatisfactory sound

- ☐ Cable connections loose (Chapter 12).
- ☐ Horn mountings loose (Chapter 12).
- ☐ Faulty horn (Chapter 12).

### Horn operates all the time

- ☐ Horn push either earthed or stuck down (Chapter 12).
- ☐ Horn cable to horn push earthed (Chapter 12).

## Windscreen/tailgate wipers

### Wipers fail to operate, or operate very slowly

- ☐ Wiper blades stuck to screen, or linkage seized (Chapter 12).
- ☐ Blown fuse (Chapter 12).
- ☐ Cable or cable connections loose or disconnected (Chapter 12).
- ☐ Faulty relay (Chapter 12).
- ☐ Faulty wiper motor (Chapter 12).

### Wiper blades sweep over the wrong area of glass

- ☐ Wiper arms incorrectly-positioned on spindles (Chapter 1).
- ☐ Excessive wear of wiper linkage (Chapter 1).
- ☐ Wiper motor or linkage mountings loose or insecure (Chapter 12).

### Wiper blades fail to clean the glass effectively

- ☐ Wiper blade rubbers worn or perished (*"Weekly Checks"*).
- ☐ Wiper arm tension springs broken, or arm pivots seized (Chapter 1).
- ☐ Insufficient windscreen washer additive to adequately remove road film (*"Weekly Checks"*).

## Windscreen/tailgate washers

### One or more washer jets inoperative

- ☐ Blocked washer jet (*"Weekly Checks"* or Chapter 1).
- ☐ Disconnected, kinked or restricted fluid hose (Chapter 1).
- ☐ Insufficient fluid in washer reservoir (*"Weekly Checks"*).

### Washer pump fails to operate

- ☐ Broken or disconnected wiring or connections (Chapter 12).
- ☐ Blown fuse (Chapter 12).
- ☐ Faulty washer switch (Chapter 12).
- ☐ Faulty washer pump (Chapter 12).

### Washer pump runs for some time before fluid is emitted from jets

- ☐ Faulty one-way valve in fluid supply hose (Chapter 12).

## Electric windows

### Window glass will only move in one direction

- ☐ Faulty switch (Chapter 12).

### Window glass slow to move

- ☐ Incorrectly-adjusted door glass guide channels (Chapter 11).
- ☐ Regulator seized or damaged, or lack of lubrication (Chapter 11).
- ☐ Door internal components or trim fouling regulator (Chapter 11).
- ☐ Faulty motor (Chapter 12).

### Window glass fails to move

- ☐ Incorrectly-adjusted door glass guide channels (Chapter 11).
- ☐ Blown fuse (Chapter 12).
- ☐ Faulty relay (Chapter 12).
- ☐ Broken or disconnected wiring or connections (Chapter 12).
- ☐ Faulty motor (Chapter 12).

## Central locking system

### Complete system failure

- ☐ Blown fuse (Chapter 12).
- ☐ Faulty relay (Chapter 12).
- ☐ Broken or disconnected wiring or connections (Chapter 12).

### Latch locks but will not unlock, or unlocks but will not lock

- ☐ Faulty master switch (Chapter 11).
- ☐ Broken or disconnected latch operating rods or levers (Chapter 11).
- ☐ Faulty relay (Chapter 12).

### One lock motor fails to operate

- ☐ Broken or disconnected wiring or connections (Chapter 12).
- ☐ Faulty lock motor (Chapter 11).
- ☐ Broken, binding or disconnected latch operating rods or levers (Chapter 11).
- ☐ Fault in door latch (Chapter 11).

## A

**ABS (Anti-lock brake system)** A system, usually electronically controlled, that senses incipient wheel lockup during braking and relieves hydraulic pressure at wheels that are about to skid.

**Air bag** An inflatable bag hidden in the steering wheel (driver's side) or the dash or glovebox (passenger side). In a head-on collision, the bags inflate, preventing the driver and front passenger from being thrown forward into the steering wheel or windscreen.

**Air cleaner** A metal or plastic housing, containing a filter element, which removes dust and dirt from the air being drawn into the engine.

**Air filter element** The actual filter in an air cleaner system, usually manufactured from pleated paper and requiring renewal at regular intervals.

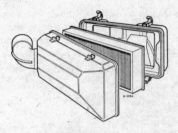

*Air filter*

**Allen key** A hexagonal wrench which fits into a recessed hexagonal hole.

**Alligator clip** A long-nosed spring-loaded metal clip with meshing teeth. Used to make temporary electrical connections.

**Alternator** A component in the electrical system which converts mechanical energy from a drivebelt into electrical energy to charge the battery and to operate the starting system, ignition system and electrical accessories.

**Ampere (amp)** A unit of measurement for the flow of electric current. One amp is the amount of current produced by one volt acting through a resistance of one ohm.

**Anaerobic sealer** A substance used to prevent bolts and screws from loosening. Anaerobic means that it does not require oxygen for activation. The Loctite brand is widely used.

**Antifreeze** A substance (usually ethylene glycol) mixed with water, and added to a vehicle's cooling system, to prevent freezing of the coolant in winter. Antifreeze also contains chemicals to inhibit corrosion and the formation of rust and other deposits that would tend to clog the radiator and coolant passages and reduce cooling efficiency.

**Anti-seize compound** A coating that reduces the risk of seizing on fasteners that are subjected to high temperatures, such as exhaust manifold bolts and nuts.

**Asbestos** A natural fibrous mineral with great heat resistance, commonly used in the composition of brake friction materials. Asbestos is a health hazard and the dust created by brake systems should never be inhaled or ingested.

**Axle** A shaft on which a wheel revolves, or which revolves with a wheel. Also, a solid beam that connects the two wheels at one end of the vehicle. An axle which also transmits power to the wheels is known as a live axle.

**Axleshaft** A single rotating shaft, on either side of the differential, which delivers power from the final drive assembly to the drive wheels. Also called a driveshaft or a halfshaft.

## B

**Ball bearing** An anti-friction bearing consisting of a hardened inner and outer race with hardened steel balls between two races.

**Bearing** The curved surface on a shaft or in a bore, or the part assembled into either, that permits relative motion between them with minimum wear and friction.

*Bearing*

**Big-end bearing** The bearing in the end of the connecting rod that's attached to the crankshaft.

**Bleed nipple** A valve on a brake wheel cylinder, caliper or other hydraulic component that is opened to purge the hydraulic system of air. Also called a bleed screw.

**Brake bleeding** Procedure for removing air from lines of a hydraulic brake system.

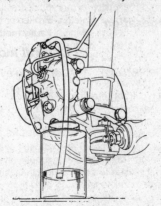

*Brake bleeding*

**Brake disc** The component of a disc brake that rotates with the wheels.

**Brake drum** The component of a drum brake that rotates with the wheels.

**Brake linings** The friction material which contacts the brake disc or drum to retard the vehicle's speed. The linings are bonded or riveted to the brake pads or shoes.

**Brake pads** The replaceable friction pads that pinch the brake disc when the brakes are applied. Brake pads consist of a friction material bonded or riveted to a rigid backing plate.

**Brake shoe** The crescent-shaped carrier to which the brake linings are mounted and which forces the lining against the rotating drum during braking.

**Braking systems** For more information on braking systems, consult the *Haynes Automotive Brake Manual*.

**Breaker bar** A long socket wrench handle providing greater leverage.

**Bulkhead** The insulated partition between the engine and the passenger compartment.

## C

**Caliper** The non-rotating part of a disc-brake assembly that straddles the disc and carries the brake pads. The caliper also contains the hydraulic components that cause the pads to pinch the disc when the brakes are applied. A caliper is also a measuring tool that can be set to measure inside or outside dimensions of an object.

**Camshaft** A rotating shaft on which a series of cam lobes operate the valve mechanisms. The camshaft may be driven by gears, by sprockets and chain or by sprockets and a belt.

**Canister** A container in an evaporative emission control system; contains activated charcoal granules to trap vapours from the fuel system.

*Canister*

**Carburettor** A device which mixes fuel with air in the proper proportions to provide a desired power output from a spark ignition internal combustion engine.

**Castellated** Resembling the parapets along the top of a castle wall. For example, a castellated balljoint stud nut.

**Castor** In wheel alignment, the backward or forward tilt of the steering axis. Castor is positive when the steering axis is inclined rearward at the top.

**Catalytic converter** A silencer-like device in the exhaust system which converts certain pollutants in the exhaust gases into less harmful substances.

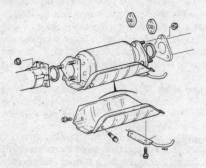

*Catalytic converter*

**Circlip** A ring-shaped clip used to prevent endwise movement of cylindrical parts and shafts. An internal circlip is installed in a groove in a housing; an external circlip fits into a groove on the outside of a cylindrical piece such as a shaft.

**Clearance** The amount of space between two parts. For example, between a piston and a cylinder, between a bearing and a journal, etc.

**Coil spring** A spiral of elastic steel found in various sizes throughout a vehicle, for example as a springing medium in the suspension and in the valve train.

**Compression** Reduction in volume, and increase in pressure and temperature, of a gas, caused by squeezing it into a smaller space.

**Compression ratio** The relationship between cylinder volume when the piston is at top dead centre and cylinder volume when the piston is at bottom dead centre.

**Constant velocity (CV) joint** A type of universal joint that cancels out vibrations caused by driving power being transmitted through an angle.

**Core plug** A disc or cup-shaped metal device inserted in a hole in a casting through which core was removed when the casting was formed. Also known as a freeze plug or expansion plug.

**Crankcase** The lower part of the engine block in which the crankshaft rotates.

**Crankshaft** The main rotating member, or shaft, running the length of the crankcase, with offset "throws" to which the connecting rods are attached.

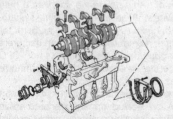

*Crankshaft assembly*

**Crocodile clip** See Alligator clip

## D

**Diagnostic code** Code numbers obtained by accessing the diagnostic mode of an engine management computer. This code can be used to determine the area in the system where a malfunction may be located.

**Disc brake** A brake design incorporating a rotating disc onto which brake pads are squeezed. The resulting friction converts the energy of a moving vehicle into heat.

**Double-overhead cam (DOHC)** An engine that uses two overhead camshafts, usually one for the intake valves and one for the exhaust valves.

**Drivebelt(s)** The belt(s) used to drive accessories such as the alternator, water pump, power steering pump, air conditioning compressor, etc. off the crankshaft pulley.

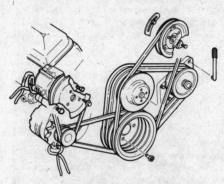

*Accessory drivebelts*

**Driveshaft** Any shaft used to transmit motion. Commonly used when referring to the axleshafts on a front wheel drive vehicle.

**Drum brake** A type of brake using a drum-shaped metal cylinder attached to the inner surface of the wheel. When the brake pedal is pressed, curved brake shoes with friction linings press against the inside of the drum to slow or stop the vehicle.

## E

**EGR valve** A valve used to introduce exhaust gases into the intake air stream.

**Electronic control unit (ECU)** A computer which controls (for instance) ignition and fuel injection systems, or an anti-lock braking system. For more information refer to the *Haynes Automotive Electrical and Electronic Systems Manual*.

**Electronic Fuel Injection (EFI)** A computer controlled fuel system that distributes fuel through an injector located in each intake port of the engine.

**Emergency brake** A braking system, independent of the main hydraulic system, that can be used to slow or stop the vehicle if the primary brakes fail, or to hold the vehicle stationary even though the brake pedal isn't depressed. It usually consists of a hand lever that actuates either front or rear brakes mechanically through a series of cables and linkages. Also known as a handbrake or parking brake.

**Endfloat** The amount of lengthwise movement between two parts. As applied to a crankshaft, the distance that the crankshaft can move forward and back in the cylinder block.

**Engine management system (EMS)** A computer controlled system which manages the fuel injection and the ignition systems in an integrated fashion.

**Exhaust manifold** A part with several passages through which exhaust gases leave the engine combustion chambers and enter the exhaust pipe.

## F

**Fan clutch** A viscous (fluid) drive coupling device which permits variable engine fan speeds in relation to engine speeds.

**Feeler blade** A thin strip or blade of hardened steel, ground to an exact thickness, used to check or measure clearances between parts.

*Feeler blade*

**Firing order** The order in which the engine cylinders fire, or deliver their power strokes, beginning with the number one cylinder.

**Flywheel** A heavy spinning wheel in which energy is absorbed and stored by means of momentum. On cars, the flywheel is attached to the crankshaft to smooth out firing impulses.

**Free play** The amount of travel before any action takes place. The "looseness" in a linkage, or an assembly of parts, between the initial application of force and actual movement. For example, the distance the brake pedal moves before the pistons in the master cylinder are actuated.

**Fuse** An electrical device which protects a circuit against accidental overload. The typical fuse contains a soft piece of metal which is calibrated to melt at a predetermined current flow (expressed as amps) and break the circuit.

**Fusible link** A circuit protection device consisting of a conductor surrounded by heat-resistant insulation. The conductor is smaller than the wire it protects, so it acts as the weakest link in the circuit. Unlike a blown fuse, a failed fusible link must frequently be cut from the wire for replacement.

## G

**Gap** The distance the spark must travel in jumping from the centre electrode to the side electrode in a spark plug. Also refers to the spacing between the points in a contact breaker assembly in a conventional points-type ignition, or to the distance between the reluctor or rotor and the pickup coil in an electronic ignition.

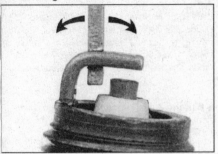

*Adjusting spark plug gap*

**Gasket** Any thin, soft material - usually cork, cardboard, asbestos or soft metal - installed between two metal surfaces to ensure a good seal. For instance, the cylinder head gasket seals the joint between the block and the cylinder head.

*Gasket*

**Gauge** An instrument panel display used to monitor engine conditions. A gauge with a movable pointer on a dial or a fixed scale is an analogue gauge. A gauge with a numerical readout is called a digital gauge.

## H

**Halfshaft** A rotating shaft that transmits power from the final drive unit to a drive wheel, usually when referring to a live rear axle.

**Harmonic balancer** A device designed to reduce torsion or twisting vibration in the crankshaft. May be incorporated in the crankshaft pulley. Also known as a vibration damper.

**Hone** An abrasive tool for correcting small irregularities or differences in diameter in an engine cylinder, brake cylinder, etc.

**Hydraulic tappet** A tappet that utilises hydraulic pressure from the engine's lubrication system to maintain zero clearance (constant contact with both camshaft and valve stem). Automatically adjusts to variation in valve stem length. Hydraulic tappets also reduce valve noise.

## I

**Ignition timing** The moment at which the spark plug fires, usually expressed in the number of crankshaft degrees before the piston reaches the top of its stroke.

**Inlet manifold** A tube or housing with passages through which flows the air-fuel mixture (carburettor vehicles and vehicles with throttle body injection) or air only (port fuel-injected vehicles) to the port openings in the cylinder head.

## J

**Jump start** Starting the engine of a vehicle with a discharged or weak battery by attaching jump leads from the weak battery to a charged or helper battery.

## L

**Load Sensing Proportioning Valve (LSPV)** A brake hydraulic system control valve that works like a proportioning valve, but also takes into consideration the amount of weight carried by the rear axle.

**Locknut** A nut used to lock an adjustment nut, or other threaded component, in place. For example, a locknut is employed to keep the adjusting nut on the rocker arm in position.

**Lockwasher** A form of washer designed to prevent an attaching nut from working loose.

## M

**MacPherson strut** A type of front suspension system devised by Earle MacPherson at Ford of England. In its original form, a simple lateral link with the anti-roll bar creates the lower control arm. A long strut - an integral coil spring and shock absorber - is mounted between the body and the steering knuckle. Many modern so-called MacPherson strut systems use a conventional lower A-arm and don't rely on the anti-roll bar for location.

**Multimeter** An electrical test instrument with the capability to measure voltage, current and resistance.

## N

**NOx** Oxides of Nitrogen. A common toxic pollutant emitted by petrol and diesel engines at higher temperatures.

## O

**Ohm** The unit of electrical resistance. One volt applied to a resistance of one ohm will produce a current of one amp.

**Ohmmeter** An instrument for measuring electrical resistance.

**O-ring** A type of sealing ring made of a special rubber-like material; in use, the O-ring is compressed into a groove to provide the sealing action.

**Overhead cam (ohc) engine** An engine with the camshaft(s) located on top of the cylinder head(s).

**Overhead valve (ohv) engine** An engine with the valves located in the cylinder head, but with the camshaft located in the engine block.

**Oxygen sensor** A device installed in the engine exhaust manifold, which senses the oxygen content in the exhaust and converts this information into an electric current. Also called a Lambda sensor.

## P

**Phillips screw** A type of screw head having a cross instead of a slot for a corresponding type of screwdriver.

**Plastigage** A thin strip of plastic thread, available in different sizes, used for measuring clearances. For example, a strip of Plastigage is laid across a bearing journal. The parts are assembled and dismantled; the width of the crushed strip indicates the clearance between journal and bearing.

*Plastigage*

**Propeller shaft** The long hollow tube with universal joints at both ends that carries power from the transmission to the differential on front-engined rear wheel drive vehicles.

**Proportioning valve** A hydraulic control valve which limits the amount of pressure to the rear brakes during panic stops to prevent wheel lock-up.

## R

**Rack-and-pinion steering** A steering system with a pinion gear on the end of the steering shaft that mates with a rack (think of a geared wheel opened up and laid flat). When the steering wheel is turned, the pinion turns, moving the rack to the left or right. This movement is transmitted through the track rods to the steering arms at the wheels.

**Radiator** A liquid-to-air heat transfer device designed to reduce the temperature of the coolant in an internal combustion engine cooling system.

**Refrigerant** Any substance used as a heat transfer agent in an air-conditioning system. R-12 has been the principle refrigerant for many years; recently, however, manufacturers have begun using R-134a, a non-CFC substance that is considered less harmful to the ozone in the upper atmosphere.

**Rocker arm** A lever arm that rocks on a shaft or pivots on a stud. In an overhead valve engine, the rocker arm converts the upward movement of the pushrod into a downward movement to open a valve.

**Rotor** In a distributor, the rotating device inside the cap that connects the centre electrode and the outer terminals as it turns, distributing the high voltage from the coil secondary winding to the proper spark plug. Also, that part of an alternator which rotates inside the stator. Also, the rotating assembly of a turbocharger, including the compressor wheel, shaft and turbine wheel.

**Runout** The amount of wobble (in-and-out movement) of a gear or wheel as it's rotated. The amount a shaft rotates "out-of-true." The out-of-round condition of a rotating part.

# S

**Sealant** A liquid or paste used to prevent leakage at a joint. Sometimes used in conjunction with a gasket.

**Sealed beam lamp** An older headlight design which integrates the reflector, lens and filaments into a hermetically-sealed one-piece unit. When a filament burns out or the lens cracks, the entire unit is simply replaced.

**Serpentine drivebelt** A single, long, wide accessory drivebelt that's used on some newer vehicles to drive all the accessories, instead of a series of smaller, shorter belts. Serpentine drivebelts are usually tensioned by an automatic tensioner.

*Serpentine drivebelt*

**Shim** Thin spacer, commonly used to adjust the clearance or relative positions between two parts. For example, shims inserted into or under bucket tappets control valve clearances. Clearance is adjusted by changing the thickness of the shim.

**Slide hammer** A special puller that screws into or hooks onto a component such as a shaft or bearing; a heavy sliding handle on the shaft bottoms against the end of the shaft to knock the component free.

**Sprocket** A tooth or projection on the periphery of a wheel, shaped to engage with a chain or drivebelt. Commonly used to refer to the sprocket wheel itself.

**Starter inhibitor switch** On vehicles with an automatic transmission, a switch that prevents starting if the vehicle is not in Neutral or Park.

**Strut** See MacPherson strut.

# T

**Tappet** A cylindrical component which transmits motion from the cam to the valve stem, either directly or via a pushrod and rocker arm. Also called a cam follower.

**Thermostat** A heat-controlled valve that regulates the flow of coolant between the cylinder block and the radiator, so maintaining optimum engine operating temperature. A thermostat is also used in some air cleaners in which the temperature is regulated.

**Thrust bearing** The bearing in the clutch assembly that is moved in to the release levers by clutch pedal action to disengage the clutch. Also referred to as a release bearing.

**Timing belt** A toothed belt which drives the camshaft. Serious engine damage may result if it breaks in service.

**Timing chain** A chain which drives the camshaft.

**Toe-in** The amount the front wheels are closer together at the front than at the rear. On rear wheel drive vehicles, a slight amount of toe-in is usually specified to keep the front wheels running parallel on the road by offsetting other forces that tend to spread the wheels apart.

**Toe-out** The amount the front wheels are closer together at the rear than at the front. On front wheel drive vehicles, a slight amount of toe-out is usually specified.

**Tools** For full information on choosing and using tools, refer to the *Haynes Automotive Tools Manual*.

**Tracer** A stripe of a second colour applied to a wire insulator to distinguish that wire from another one with the same colour insulator.

**Tune-up** A process of accurate and careful adjustments and parts replacement to obtain the best possible engine performance.

**Turbocharger** A centrifugal device, driven by exhaust gases, that pressurises the intake air. Normally used to increase the power output from a given engine displacement, but can also be used primarily to reduce exhaust emissions (as on VW's "Umwelt" Diesel engine).

# U

**Universal joint or U-joint** A double-pivoted connection for transmitting power from a driving to a driven shaft through an angle. A U-joint consists of two Y-shaped yokes and a cross-shaped member called the spider.

# V

**Valve** A device through which the flow of liquid, gas, vacuum, or loose material in bulk may be started, stopped, or regulated by a movable part that opens, shuts, or partially obstructs one or more ports or passageways. A valve is also the movable part of such a device.

**Valve clearance** The clearance between the valve tip (the end of the valve stem) and the rocker arm or tappet. The valve clearance is measured when the valve is closed.

**Vernier caliper** A precision measuring instrument that measures inside and outside dimensions. Not quite as accurate as a micrometer, but more convenient.

**Viscosity** The thickness of a liquid or its resistance to flow.

**Volt** A unit for expressing electrical "pressure" in a circuit. One volt that will produce a current of one ampere through a resistance of one ohm.

# W

**Welding** Various processes used to join metal items by heating the areas to be joined to a molten state and fusing them together. For more information refer to the *Haynes Automotive Welding Manual*.

**Wiring diagram** A drawing portraying the components and wires in a vehicle's electrical system, using standardised symbols. For more information refer to the *Haynes Automotive Electrical and Electronic Systems Manual*.

**Note:** *References throughout this index are in the form - "Chapter number" • "page number"*

# Haynes Manuals – The Complete List

| Title | Book No. |
|---|---|
| **ALFA ROMEO** | |
| Alfa Romeo Alfasud/Sprint (74 - 88) up to F | 0292 |
| Alfa Romeo Alfetta (73 - 87) up to E | 0531 |
| **AUDI** | |
| Audi 80 (72 - Feb 79) up to T | 0207 |
| Audi 80, 90 (79 - Oct 86) up to D & Coupe (81 - Nov 88) up to F | 0605 |
| Audi 80, 90 (Oct 86 - 90) D to H & Coupe (Nov 88 - 90) F to H | 1491 |
| Audi 100 (Oct 82 - 90) up to H & 200 (Feb 84 - Oct 89) A to G | 0907 |
| Audi 100 & A6 Petrol & Diesel (May 91 - May 97) H to P | 3504 |
| Audi A4 (95 - Feb 00) M to V | 3575 |
| **AUSTIN** | |
| Austin A35 & A40 (56 - 67) * | 0118 |
| Austin Allegro 1100, 1300, 1.0, 1.1 & 1.3 (73 - 82)* | 0164 |
| Austin Healey 100/6 & 3000 (56 - 68) * | 0049 |
| Austin/MG/Rover Maestro 1.3 & 1.6 (83 - May 95) up to M | 0922 |
| Austin/MG Metro (80 - May 90) up to G | 0718 |
| Austin/Rover Montego 1.3 & 1.6 (84 - 94) A to L | 1066 |
| Austin/MG/Rover Montego 2.0 (84 - 95) A to M | 1067 |
| Mini (59 - 69) up to H | 0527 |
| Mini (69 - Oct 96) up to P | 0646 |
| Austin/Rover 2.0 litre Diesel Engine (86 - 93) C to L | 1857 |
| **BEDFORD** | |
| Bedford CF (69 - 87) up to E | 0163 |
| Bedford/Vauxhall Rascal & Suzuki Supercarry (86 - Oct 94) C to M | 3015 |
| **BMW** | |
| BMW 1500, 1502, 1600, 1602, 2000 & 2002 (59 - 77)* | 0240 |
| BMW 316, 320 & 320i (4-cyl) (75 - Feb 83) up to Y | 0276 |
| BMW 320, 320i, 323i & 325i (6-cyl) (Oct 77 - Sept 87) up to E | 0815 |
| BMW 3-Series (Apr 91 - 96) H to N | 3210 |
| BMW 3- & 5-Series (sohc) (81 - 91) up to J | 1948 |
| BMW 520i & 525e (Oct 81 - June 88) up to E | 1560 |
| BMW 525, 528 & 528i (73 - Sept 81) up to X | 0632 |
| **CITROËN** | |
| Citroën 2CV, Ami & Dyane (67 - 90) up to H | 0196 |
| Citroën AX Petrol & Diesel (87 - 97) D to P | 3014 |
| Citroën BX (83 - 94) A to L | 0908 |
| Citroën C15 Van Petrol & Diesel (89 - Oct 98) F to S | 3509 |
| Citroën CX (75 - 88) up to F | 0528 |
| Citroën Saxo Petrol & Diesel (96 - 01) N to X | 3506 |
| Citroën Visa (79 - 88) up to F | 0620 |
| Citroën Xantia Petrol & Diesel (93 - 98) K to S | 3082 |
| Citroën XM Petrol & Diesel (89 - 00) G to X | 3451 |
| Citroën Xsara Petrol & Diesel (97 - Sept 00) R to W | 3751 |
| Citroën ZX Diesel (91 - 98) J to S | 1922 |
| Citroën ZX Petrol (91 - 98) H to S | 1881 |
| Citroën 1.7 & 1.9 litre Diesel Engine (84 - 96) A to N | 1379 |
| **FIAT** | |
| Fiat 126 (73 - 87) * | 0305 |
| Fiat 500 (57 - 73) up to M | 0090 |
| Fiat Bravo & Brava (95 - 00) N to W | 3572 |
| Fiat Cinquecento (93 - 98) K to R | 3501 |
| Fiat Panda (81 - 95) up to M | 0793 |
| Fiat Punto Petrol & Diesel (94 - Oct 99) L to V | 3251 |
| Fiat Regata (84 - 88) A to F | 1167 |
| Fiat Tipo (88 - 91) E to J | 1625 |
| Fiat Uno (83 - 95) up to M | 0923 |
| Fiat X1/9 (74 - 89) up to G | 0273 |
| **FORD** | |
| Ford Anglia (59 - 68) * | 0001 |
| Ford Capri II (& III) 1.6 & 2.0 (74 - 87) up to E | 0283 |

| Title | Book No. |
|---|---|
| Ford Capri II (& III) 2.8 & 3.0 (74 - 87) up to E | 1309 |
| Ford Cortina Mk III 1300 & 1600 (70 - 76) * | 0070 |
| Ford Cortina Mk IV (& V) 1.6 & 2.0 (76 - 83) * | 0343 |
| Ford Cortina Mk IV (& V) 2.3 V6 (77 - 83) * | 0426 |
| Ford Escort Mk I 1100 & 1300 (68 - 74) * | 0171 |
| Ford Escort Mk I Mexico, RS 1600 & RS 2000 (70 - 74)* | 0139 |
| Ford Escort Mk II Mexico, RS 1800 & RS 2000 (75 - 80)* | 0735 |
| Ford Escort (75 - Aug 80) * | 0280 |
| Ford Escort (Sept 80 - Sept 90) up to H | 0686 |
| Ford Escort & Orion (Sept 90 - 00) H to X | 1737 |
| Ford Fiesta (76 - Aug 83) up to Y | 0334 |
| Ford Fiesta (Aug 83 - Feb 89) A to F | 1030 |
| Ford Fiesta (Feb 89 - Oct 95) F to N | 1595 |
| Ford Fiesta (Oct 95 - 01) N-reg. onwards | 3397 |
| Ford Focus (98 - 01) S to Y | 3759 |
| Ford Granada (Sept 77 - Feb 85) up to B | 0481 |
| Ford Granada & Scorpio (Mar 85 - 94) B to M | 1245 |
| Ford Ka (96 - 02) P-reg. onwards | 3570 |
| Ford Mondeo Petrol (93 - 99) K to T | 1923 |
| Ford Mondeo Diesel (93 - 96) L to N | 3465 |
| Ford Orion (83 - Sept 90) up to H | 1009 |
| Ford Sierra 4 cyl. (82 - 93) up to K | 0903 |
| Ford Sierra V6 (82 - 91) up to J | 0904 |
| Ford Transit Petrol (Mk 2) (78 - Jan 86) up to C | 0719 |
| Ford Transit Petrol (Mk 3) (Feb 86 - 89) C to G | 1468 |
| Ford Transit Diesel (Feb 86 - 99) C to T | 3019 |
| Ford 1.6 & 1.8 litre Diesel Engine (84 - 96) A to N | 1172 |
| Ford 2.1, 2.3 & 2.5 litre Diesel Engine (77 - 90) up to H | 1606 |
| **FREIGHT ROVER** | |
| Freight Rover Sherpa (74 - 87) up to E | 0463 |
| **HILLMAN** | |
| Hillman Avenger (70 - 82) up to Y | 0037 |
| Hillman Imp (63 - 76) * | 0022 |
| **HONDA** | |
| Honda Accord (76 - Feb 84) up to A | 0351 |
| Honda Civic (Feb 84 - Oct 87) A to E | 1226 |
| Honda Civic (Nov 91 - 96) J to N | 3199 |
| **HYUNDAI** | |
| Hyundai Pony (85 - 94) C to M | 3398 |
| **JAGUAR** | |
| Jaguar E Type (61 - 72) up to L | 0140 |
| Jaguar MkI & II, 240 & 340 (55 - 69) * | 0098 |
| Jaguar XJ6, XJ & Sovereign; Daimler Sovereign (68 - Oct 86) up to D | 0242 |
| Jaguar XJ6 & Sovereign (Oct 86 - Sept 94) D to M | 3261 |
| Jaguar XJ12, XJS & Sovereign; Daimler Double Six (72 - 88) up to F | 0478 |
| **JEEP** | |
| Jeep Cherokee Petrol (93 - 96) K to N | 1943 |
| **LADA** | |
| Lada 1200, 1300, 1500 & 1600 (74 - 91) up to J | 0413 |
| Lada Samara (87 - 91) D to J | 1610 |
| **LAND ROVER** | |
| Land Rover 90, 110 & Defender Diesel (83 - 95) up to N | 3017 |
| Land Rover Discovery Petrol & Diesel (89 - 98) G to S | 3016 |
| Land Rover Series IIA & III Diesel (58 - 85) up to C | 0529 |
| Land Rover Series II, IIA & III Petrol (58 - 85) up to C | 0314 |
| **MAZDA** | |
| Mazda 323 (Mar 81 - Oct 89) up to G | 1608 |
| Mazda 323 (Oct 89 - 98) G to R | 3455 |
| Mazda 626 (May 83 - Sept 87) up to E | 0929 |
| Mazda B-1600, B-1800 & B-2000 Pick-up (72 - 88) up to F | 0267 |
| Mazda RX-7 (79 - 85) * | 0460 |

| Title | Book No. |
|---|---|
| **MERCEDES-BENZ** | |
| Mercedes-Benz 190, 190E & 190D Petrol & Diesel (83 - 93) A to L | 3450 |
| Mercedes-Benz 200, 240, 300 Diesel (Oct 76 - 85) up to C | 1114 |
| Mercedes-Benz 250 & 280 (68 - 72) up to L | 0346 |
| Mercedes-Benz 250 & 280 (123 Series) (Oct 76 - 84) up to B | 0677 |
| Mercedes-Benz 124 Series (85 - Aug 93) C to K | 3253 |
| Mercedes-Benz C-Class Petrol & Diesel (93 - Aug 00) L to W | 3511 |
| **MG** | |
| MGA (55 - 62) * | 0475 |
| MGB (62 - 80) up to W | 0111 |
| MG Midget & AH Sprite (58 - 80) up to W | 0265 |
| **MITSUBISHI** | |
| Mitsubishi Shogun & L200 Pick-Ups (83 - 94) up to M | 1944 |
| **MORRIS** | |
| Morris Ital 1.3 (80 - 84) up to B | 0705 |
| Morris Minor 1000 (56 - 71) up to K | 0024 |
| **NISSAN** | |
| Nissan Bluebird (May 84 - Mar 86) A to C | 1223 |
| Nissan Bluebird (Mar 86 - 90) C to H | 1473 |
| Nissan Cherry (Sept 82 - 86) up to D | 1031 |
| Nissan Micra (83 - Jan 93) up to K | 0931 |
| Nissan Micra (93 - 99) K to T | 3254 |
| Nissan Primera (90 - Aug 99) H to T | 1851 |
| Nissan Stanza (82 - 86) up to D | 0824 |
| Nissan Sunny (May 82 - Oct 86) up to D | 0895 |
| Nissan Sunny (Oct 86 - Mar 91) D to H | 1378 |
| Nissan Sunny (Apr 91 - 95) H to N | 3219 |
| **OPEL** | |
| Opel Ascona & Manta (B Series) (Sept 75 - 88) up to F | 0316 |
| Opel Ascona (81 - 88) *(Not available in UK see Vauxhall Cavalier 0812)* | 3215 |
| Opel Astra (Oct 91 - Feb 98) *(Not available in UK see Vauxhall Astra 1832)* | 3156 |
| Opel Astra & Zafira Diesel (Feb 98 - Sept 00) *(See Astra & Zafira Diesel Book No. 3797)* | |
| Opel Astra & Zafira Petrol (Feb 98 - Sept 00) *(See Vauxhall/Opel Astra & Zafira Petrol Book No. 3758)* | |
| Opel Calibra (90 - 98) *(See Vauxhall/Opel Calibra Book No. 3502)* | |
| Opel Corsa (83 - Mar 93) *(Not available in UK see Vauxhall Nova 0909)* | 3160 |
| Opel Corsa (Mar 93 - 97) *(Not available in UK see Vauxhall Corsa 1985)* | 3159 |
| Opel Frontera Petrol & Diesel (91 - 98) *(See Vauxhall/Opel Frontera Book No. 3454)* | |
| Opel Kadett (Nov 79 - Oct 84) up to B | 0634 |
| Opel Kadett (Oct 84 - Oct 91) *(Not available in UK see Vauxhall Astra & Belmont 1136)* | 3196 |
| Opel Omega & Senator (86 - 94) *(Not available in UK see Vauxhall Carlton & Senator 1469)* | 3157 |
| Opel Omega (94 - 99) *(See Vauxhall/Opel Omega Book No. 3510)* | |
| Opel Rekord (Feb 78 - Oct 86) up to D | 0543 |
| Opel Vectra (Oct 88 - Oct 95) *(Not available in UK see Vauxhall Cavalier 1570)* | 3158 |
| Opel Vectra Petrol & Diesel (95 - 98) *(Not available in UK see Vauxhall Vectra 3396)* | 3523 |
| **PEUGEOT** | |
| Peugeot 106 Petrol & Diesel (91 - 01) J to X | 1882 |
| Peugeot 205 Petrol (83 - 97) A to P | 0932 |
| Peugeot 206 Petrol and Diesel (98 - 01) S to X | 3757 |
| Peugeot 305 (78 - 89) up to G | 0538 |

\* Classic reprint

| Title | Book No. |
|---|---|
| Peugeot 306 Petrol & Diesel (93 - 99) K to T | 3073 |
| Peugeot 309 (86 - 93) C to K | 1266 |
| Peugeot 405 Petrol (88 - 97) E to P | 1559 |
| Peugeot 405 Diesel (88 - 97) E to P | 3198 |
| Peugeot 405 Petrol & Diesel (96 - 97) N to R | 3394 |
| Peugeot 505 (79 - 89) up to G | 0762 |
| Peugeot 1.7/1.8 & 1.9 litre Diesel Engine (82 - 96) up to N | 0950 |
| Peugeot 2.0, 2.1, 2.3 & 2.5 litre Diesel Engines (74 - 90) up to H | 1607 |
| **PORSCHE** | |
| Porsche 911 (65 - 85) up to C | 0264 |
| Porsche 924 & 924 Turbo (76 - 85) up to C | 0397 |
| **PROTON** | |
| Proton (89 - 97) F to P | 3255 |
| **RANGE ROVER** | |
| Range Rover V8 (70 - Oct 92) up to K | 0606 |
| **RELIANT** | |
| Reliant Robin & Kitten (73 - 83) up to A | 0436 |
| **RENAULT** | |
| Renault 4 (61 - 86) * | 0072 |
| Renault 5 (Feb 85 - 96) B to N | 1219 |
| Renault 9 & 11 (82 - 89) up to F | 0822 |
| Renault 18 (79 - 86) up to D | 0598 |
| Renault 19 Petrol (89 - 94) F to M | 1646 |
| Renault 19 Diesel (89 - 96) F to N | 1946 |
| Renault 21 (86 - 94) C to M | 1397 |
| Renault 25 (84 - 92) B to K | 1228 |
| Renault Clio Petrol (91 - May 98) H to R | 1853 |
| Renault Clio Diesel (91 - June 96) H to N | 3031 |
| Renault Clio Petrol & Diesel (May 98 - May 01) R to Y | 3906 |
| Renault Espace Petrol & Diesel (85 - 96) C to N | 3197 |
| Renault Fuego (80 - 86) * | 0764 |
| Renault Laguna Petrol & Diesel (94 - 00) L to W | 3252 |
| Renault Mégane & Scénic Petrol & Diesel (96 - 98) N to R | 3395 |
| Renault Mégane & Scénic (Apr 99 - 02) T-reg onwards | 3916 |
| **ROVER** | |
| Rover 213 & 216 (84 - 89) A to G | 1116 |
| Rover 214 & 414 (89 - 96) G to N | 1689 |
| Rover 216 & 416 (89 - 96) G to N | 1830 |
| Rover 211, 214, 216, 218 & 220 Petrol & Diesel (Dec 95 - 98) N to R | 3399 |
| Rover 414, 416 & 420 Petrol & Diesel (May 95 - 98) M to R | 3453 |
| Rover 618, 620 & 623 (93 - 97) K to P | 3257 |
| Rover 820, 825 & 827 (86 - 95) D to N | 1380 |
| Rover 3500 (76 - 87) up to E | 0365 |
| Rover Metro, 111 & 114 (May 90 - 98) G to S | 1711 |
| **SAAB** | |
| Saab 90, 99 & 900 (79 - Oct 93) up to L | 0765 |
| Saab 95 & 96 (66 - 76) * | 0198 |
| Saab 99 (69 - 79) * | 0247 |
| Saab 900 (Oct 93 - 98) L to R | 3512 |
| Saab 9000 (4-cyl) (85 - 98) C to S | 1686 |
| **SEAT** | |
| Seat Ibiza & Cordoba Petrol & Diesel (Oct 93 - Oct 99) L to V | 3571 |
| Seat Ibiza & Malaga (85 - 92) B to K | 1609 |
| **SKODA** | |
| Skoda Estelle (77 - 89) up to G | 0604 |
| Skoda Favorit (89 - 96) F to N | 1801 |
| Skoda Felicia Petrol & Diesel (95 - 01) M to X | 3505 |

| Title | Book No. |
|---|---|
| **SUBARU** | |
| Subaru 1600 & 1800 (Nov 79 - 90) up to H | 0995 |
| **SUNBEAM** | |
| Sunbeam Alpine, Rapier & H120 (67 - 76) * | 0051 |
| **SUZUKI** | |
| Suzuki SJ Series, Samurai & Vitara (4-cyl) (82 - 97) up to P | 1942 |
| Suzuki Supercarry & Bedford/Vauxhall Rascal (86 - Oct 94) C to M | 3015 |
| **TALBOT** | |
| Talbot Alpine, Solara, Minx & Rapier (75 - 86) up to D | 0337 |
| Talbot Horizon (78 - 86) up to D | 0473 |
| Talbot Samba (82 - 86) up to D | 0823 |
| **TOYOTA** | |
| Toyota Carina E (May 92 - 97) J to P | 3256 |
| Toyota Corolla (Sept 83 - Sept 87) A to E | 1024 |
| Toyota Corolla (80 - 85) up to C | 0683 |
| Toyota Corolla (Sept 87 - Aug 92) E to K | 1683 |
| Toyota Corolla (Aug 92 - 97) K to P | 3259 |
| Toyota Hi-Ace & Hi-Lux (69 - Oct 83) up to A | 0304 |
| **TRIUMPH** | |
| Triumph Acclaim (81 - 84) * | 0792 |
| Triumph GT6 & Vitesse (62 - 74) * | 0112 |
| Triumph Herald (59 - 71) * | 0010 |
| Triumph Spitfire (62 - 81) up to X | 0113 |
| Triumph Stag (70 - 78) up to T | 0441 |
| Triumph TR2, TR3, TR3A, TR4 & TR4A (52 - 67)* | 0028 |
| Triumph TR5 & 6 (67 - 75) * | 0031 |
| Triumph TR7 (75 - 82) * | 0322 |
| **VAUXHALL** | |
| Vauxhall Astra (80 - Oct 84) up to B | 0635 |
| Vauxhall Astra & Belmont (Oct 84 - Oct 91) B to J | 1136 |
| Vauxhall Astra (Oct 91 - Feb 98) J to R | 1832 |
| Vauxhall/Opel Astra & Zafira Diesel (Feb 98 - Sept 00) R to W | 3797 |
| Vauxhall/Opel Astra & Zafira Petrol (Feb 98 - Sept 00) R to W | 3758 |
| Vauxhall/Opel Calibra (90 - 98) G to S | 3502 |
| Vauxhall Carlton (Oct 78 - Oct 86) up to D | 0480 |
| Vauxhall Carlton & Senator (Nov 86 - 94) D to L | 1469 |
| Vauxhall Cavalier 1300 (77 - July 81) * | 0461 |
| Vauxhall Cavalier 1600, 1900 & 2000 (75 - July 81) up to W | 0315 |
| Vauxhall Cavalier (81 - Oct 88) up to F | 0812 |
| Vauxhall Cavalier (Oct 88 - 95) F to N | 1570 |
| Vauxhall Chevette (75 - 84) up to B | 0285 |
| Vauxhall Corsa (Mar 93 - 97) K to R | 1985 |
| Vauxhall/Opel Corsa (Apr 97 - Oct 00) P to X | 3921 |
| Vauxhall/Opel Frontera Petrol & Diesel (91 - Sept 98) J to S | 3454 |
| Vauxhall Nova (83 - 93) up to K | 0909 |
| Vauxhall/Opel Omega (94 - 99) L to T | 3510 |
| Vauxhall Vectra Petrol & Diesel (95 - 98) N to R | 3396 |
| Vauxhall/Opel 1.5, 1.6 & 1.7 litre Diesel Engine (82 - 96) up to N | 1222 |
| **VOLKSWAGEN** | |
| Volkswagen 411 & 412 (68 - 75) * | 0091 |
| Volkswagen Beetle 1200 (54 - 77) up to S | 0036 |
| Volkswagen Beetle 1300 & 1500 (65 - 75) up to P | 0039 |
| Volkswagen Beetle 1302 & 1302S (70 - 72) up to L | 0110 |
| Volkswagen Beetle 1303, 1303S & GT (72 - 75) up to P | 0159 |
| Volkswagen Beetle Petrol & Diesel (Apr 99 - 01) T reg onwards | 3798 |
| Volkswagen Golf & Bora Petrol & Diesel (April 98 - 00) R to X | 3727 |

| Title | Book No. |
|---|---|
| Volkswagen Golf & Jetta Mk 1 1.1 & 1.3 (74 - 84) up to A | 0716 |
| Volkswagen Golf, Jetta & Scirocco Mk 1 1.5, 1.6 & 1.8 (74 - 84) up to A | 0726 |
| Volkswagen Golf & Jetta Mk 1 Diesel (78 - 84) up to A | 0451 |
| Volkswagen Golf & Jetta Mk 2 (Mar 84 - Feb 92) A to J | 1081 |
| Volkswagen Golf & Vento Petrol & Diesel (Feb 92 - 96) J to N | 3097 |
| Volkswagen LT vans & light trucks (76 - 87) up to E | 0637 |
| Volkswagen Passat & Santana (Sept 81 - May 88) up to E | 0814 |
| Volkswagen Passat Petrol & Diesel (May 88 - 96) E to P | 3498 |
| Volkswagen Passat 4-cyl Petrol & Diesel (Dec 96 - Nov 00) P to X | 3917 |
| Volkswagen Polo & Derby (76 - Jan 82) up to X | 0335 |
| Volkswagen Polo (82 - Oct 90) up to H | 0813 |
| Volkswagen Polo (Nov 90 - Aug 94) H to L | 3245 |
| Volkswagen Polo Hatchback Petrol & Diesel (94 - 99) M to S | 3500 |
| Volkswagen Scirocco (82 - 90) up to H | 1224 |
| Volkswagen Transporter 1600 (68 - 79) up to V | 0082 |
| Volkswagen Transporter 1700, 1800 & 2000 (72 - 79) up to V | 0226 |
| Volkswagen Transporter (air-cooled) (79 - 82) up to Y | 0638 |
| Volkswagen Transporter (water-cooled) (82 - 90) up to H | 3452 |
| Volkswagen Type 3 (63 - 73) * | 0084 |
| **VOLVO** | |
| Volvo 120 & 130 Series (& P1800) (61 - 73) * | 0203 |
| Volvo 142, 144 & 145 (66 - 74) up to N | 0129 |
| Volvo 240 Series (74 - 93) up to K | 0270 |
| Volvo 262, 264 & 260/265 (75 - 85) * | 0400 |
| Volvo 340, 343, 345 & 360 (76 - 91) up to J | 0715 |
| Volvo 440, 460 & 480 (87 - 97) D to P | 1691 |
| Volvo 740 & 760 (82 - 91) up to J | 1258 |
| Volvo 850 (92 - 96) J to P | 3260 |
| Volvo 940 (90 - 96) H to N | 3249 |
| Volvo S40 & V40 (96 - 99) N to V | 3569 |
| Volvo S70, V70 & C70 (96 - 99) P to V | 3573 |
| **AUTOMOTIVE TECHBOOKS** | |
| Automotive Air Conditioning Systems | 3740 |
| Automotive Brake Manual | 3050 |
| Automotive Carburettor Manual | 3288 |
| Automotive Diagnostic Fault Codes Manual | 3472 |
| Automotive Diesel Engine Service Guide | 3286 |
| Automotive Electrical and Electronic Systems Manual | 3049 |
| Automotive Engine Management and Fuel Injection Systems Manual | 3344 |
| Automotive Gearbox Overhaul Manual | 3473 |
| Automotive Service Summaries Manual | 3475 |
| Automotive Timing Belts Manual – Austin/Rover | 3549 |
| Automotive Timing Belts Manual – Ford | 3474 |
| Automotive Timing Belts Manual – Peugeot/Citroën | 3568 |
| Automotive Timing Belts Manual – Vauxhall/Opel | 3577 |
| Automotive Welding Manual | 3053 |
| In-Car Entertainment Manual (3rd Edition) | 3363 |

* Classic reprint

CL13.4/02

# Preserving Our Motoring Heritage

< The Model J Duesenberg Derham Tourster. Only eight of these magnificent cars were ever built – this is the only example to be found outside the United States of America

Almost every car you've ever loved, loathed or desired is gathered under one roof at the Haynes Motor Museum. Over 300 immaculately presented cars and motorbikes represent every aspect of our motoring heritage, from elegant reminders of bygone days, such as the superb Model J Duesenberg to curiosities like the bug-eyed BMW Isetta. There are also many old friends and flames. Perhaps you remember the 1959 Ford Popular that you did your courting in? The magnificent 'Red Collection' is a spectacle of classic sports cars including AC, Alfa Romeo, Austin Healey, Ferrari, Lamborghini, Maserati, MG, Riley, Porsche and Triumph.

## A Perfect Day Out

Each and every vehicle at the Haynes Motor Museum has played its part in the history and culture of Motoring. Today, they make a wonderful spectacle and a great day out for all the family. Bring the kids, bring Mum and Dad, but above all bring your camera to capture those golden memories for ever. You will also find an impressive array of motoring memorabilia, a comfortable 70 seat video cinema and one of the most extensive transport book shops in Britain. The Pit Stop Cafe serves everything from a cup of tea to wholesome, home-made meals or, if you prefer, you can enjoy the large picnic area nestled in the beautiful rural surroundings of Somerset.

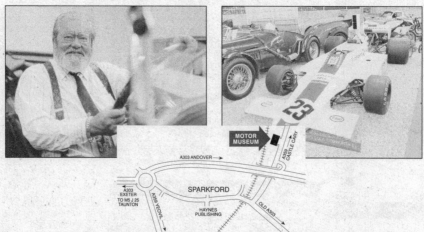

> John Haynes O.B.E., Founder and Chairman of the museum at the wheel of a Haynes Light 12.

< Graham Hill's Lola Cosworth Formula 1 car next to a 1934 Riley Sports.

The Museum is situated on the A359 Yeovil to Frome road at Sparkford, just off the A303 in Somerset. It is about 40 miles south of Bristol, and 25 minutes drive from the M5 intersection at Taunton.

Open 9.30am - 5.30pm (10.00am - 4.00pm Winter) 7 days a week, *except Christmas Day, Boxing Day and New Years Day*

Special rates available for schools, coach parties and outings Charitable Trust No. 292048